Major
Problems
in
American
Foreign
Policy

Major Problems in American Foreign Policy

DOCUMENTS AND ESSAYS

VOLUME II: SINCE 1914

Edited by
Thomas G. Paterson
University of Connecticut

D. C. HEATH AND COMPANY Lexington, Massachusetts   Toronto

For Rebecca Virginia Paterson

Cartography by Russell H. Lenz

Cover photograph: courtesy of Brown Brothers

Printed in the United States of America.

International Standard Book Number: 0-669-00476-6

Library of Congress Catalog Card Number: 77-79496

Preface

The goal of this volume is to provide students and instructors with the most distinguished writing in American diplomatic history. Each chapter addresses a major theme or question on which contemporary statesmen and later scholars have conspicuously differed. The primary documents in each chapter help to identify the problem, outline the issues, and reveal the flavor of the times. The essays, or secondary accounts, have been selected for their differing points of view, their provocative and intelligent reasoning, and their recognized high quality as scholarship. Studies by past masters, which have been applauded by their colleagues as being significant, are combined with the recent works of scholars and publicists who also speak with authority. The introductions and headnotes set the readings in historical and interpretive perspective; the maps supply a valuable dimension; and the Further Reading sections suggest additional books and articles for continued research on the topics at hand.

I am grateful to Melvyn Leffler, Paul A. Varg, J. Garry Clifford, Jean-Donald Miller, and Kenneth J. Hagan for their helpful comments on the choice of selections. Their sense of proportion was precise and their standards were high. Don Miller was especially helpful, and I thank him as a friend and colleague in the history of American foreign policy. Holly Izard Paterson, as always, helped in countless ways. The dedication is to my daughter Becki, whose good humor and independent mind make a father proud—and alert.

THOMAS G. PATERSON
University of Connecticut

Contents

Maps

1

The Characteristics
of Modern American
Foreign Policy

Scholars have identified several key characteristics of recent American foreign policy. Whether called motives or roots, these characteristics are fundamental and enduring. Which are most important in generating American foreign policy is a question of much debate. Some students of history stress an American ideological quest for democratic political principles and equal opportunity as well as a humanitarian, reformist sense of mission fueled by an unbounded American optimism. Others point to national security, economic needs, capitalism, or an anti-revolutionary penchant for order. Words like "democracy," "moralism," "national security," "capitalism," "economic expansion," and "open door" have frequently been used to describe the roots of American behavior in international relations. A study of these various factors helps to explain why the United States became an interventionist, global power in the twentieth century. In short, what is the mainspring of American foreign policy?

ESSAYS

The first essay, written by Dexter Perkins, one of the deans of diplomatic history and an author of major books on the Monroe Doctrine, reflects a viewpoint that has often been called "nationalist." Indeed, Perkins is seldom critical of American foreign policy; rather, he strongly commends the American record, finding it characterized by a sincere attempt to implant abroad the best of America—its democratic principles.

   The second essay, by George F. Kennan, is critical of such an interpretation and of the characteristic itself. As an historian and career diplomat who helped to articulate the containment doctrine in the late 1940s, Kennan has consistently argued in his many position papers and publications, especially in *American Diplomacy, 1900–1950,* that a streak of "moral-legalism" has characterized United States foreign policy, making it abruptly changeable whenever fickle public opinion shifted.

The final essay, by William Appleman Williams of Oregon State University, who is a major influence in the development of a critical interpretation of United States foreign policy, argues that American diplomacy has amounted to a "tragedy," because the American people, driven by an "open door" economic expansionism that has meant coercion abroad, have violated their best ideals.

Democracy

DEXTER PERKINS

It is a truism, but one that needs to be constantly reiterated, that words are often used by men to arouse emotion and fortify prejudice, rather than to describe exactly or appeal to reason. The language of politics, national and international, is full of clichés which serve these convenient purposes. To many of those who lean towards the left, the partisans of the right are always "reactionaries"; while no other word than "radical" or "socialist" or perhaps "Communist" will satisfy some conservatives in describing the friends of moderate change. In international affairs, "honor" and "justice" and the "interests of humanity" are likely to be the exclusive concern of one nation, while sinister motives are unvaryingly ascribed to its rival, together with what is usually described since the days of Hitler as "warmongering." Among the convenient terms of abuse in the vocabulary of contemporary international politics is the term "imperialism." To the Soviet Union the peoples of the West and, particularly, the United States are imperialists. The cliché has wide influence; beyond question, along with many other Russian propaganda devices, it produces a certain degree of confusion in the minds of excellent people who are not free from a touch of masochism; and it reminds the newborn nations of the world of the "oppression" which preceded their liberation. It is well worth while, then, to examine what is termed American imperialism, to determine its character and its limitations, and to assess the strength of the imperialist motive in American foreign policy historically and in the present day.

At the outset of this analysis it is important to draw a clear distinction between expansion and imperialism. Expansion, in the view that will be taken in the following pages, is the process by which the political control of a given nation is extended over territory which then becomes assimilated and incorporated in the political and constitutional system of the expanding state. The cession of Louisiana by France to the United States in 1803, or even the acquisition of California by conquest from Mexico in 1848, are examples of expansion. The regions thus acquired became a part of the federal union, and whatever moral judgment we may wish to make with regard to these acquisitions, we shall nat-

---

Reprinted by permission of the author and publishers from *The American Approach to Foreign Policy,* Revised Edition, by Dexter Perkins, Cambridge, Mass.: Harvard University Press, Copyright © 1962 by the President and Fellows of Harvard College.

urally recognize the fact that today the regions so acquired present no special problem, so far as their political status is concerned, but constitute parts of a united nation.

The question of how to deal with territories acquired outside the continental area of the United States did not arise until the end of the nineteenth century. Not that there was no appetite for such territories. Americans had had their eyes on Cuba since the days of Jefferson; on at least two occasions the purchase of the island was seriously discussed, and once, in the case of the well-known Ostend Manifesto, its seizure, in the event that Spain refused to sell, was somewhat blatantly advocated. After the Mexican War there was a movement for the annexation of all of Mexico, and in 1848 President Polk proposed the occupation of Yucatan. Just after the Civil War Secretary Seward negotiated a treaty for the purchase of the Danish West Indies; and President Grant proposed the annexation of the Dominican Republic. But none of these projects came to fruition. Down to 1860 Northern antagonism to slavery put a damper on the acquisition of any territory which might increase the influence of the South; and in the twenty years after the Civil War the country was primarily concerned with the problems of reconstruction and with its own remarkable internal development. In the period of the Spanish-American War, however, as we have already seen, the United States acquired dominion over Puerto Rico, Guam, and the Philippines, and in 1899 it acquired title to a part of the Samoan islands. In 1903, taking advantage of the revolution which gave birth to the independent republic of Panama, the American government established a virtual protectorate over the new state and secured the Panama Canal Zone. In 1916 it bought the Virgin Islands. And in the twenty-year period between 1898 and 1918, it intervened in the affairs of Cuba for a brief period (1906–1909) and occupied for longer intervals the territory of three independent states, Nicaragua, Haiti, and the Dominican Republic. It would seem reasonable to describe this period as one of American imperialism, and it is well worth while to examine what this "imperialism" was like in practice.

There is one essential generalization with which we ought to begin. American rule over other peoples has always been rule with an uneasy conscience. Implicit in it at all times has been faith in the democratic process, the belief that it was the duty of an imperial power to prepare the way to self-government for the peoples over whom it exercised control. This is something that ought never to be forgotten in any discussion of the whole problem. Indeed, it means that "imperialism," as it is conceived by the Americans, can be only a passing phase. We can see this principle at work in the discussions at the end of the Spanish-American War. The very assumption of imperial rule over the territories acquired from Spain was bitterly contested in principle. The idea of such rule was regarded by substantial numbers of Americans—including some eminent members of the dominant Republican Party—as inconsistent with the Declaration of Independence and the Constitution. The treaty for the acquisition of these territories passed the Senate with a single vote to spare, after vigorous congressional and public debate and, although the imperialists won, the anti-imperialists, in a sense, called the tune. The establishment of a wide measure of self-government for the peoples brought under American sway was regarded as desirable by both parties and became the basis of American policy. Let us look at the record in this respect, first of all in the case of the Philippines.

After a brief period of military rule and the unsavory episode of American repression of a Filipino insurrection, a civil government was established in the islands in 1901, and the Filipinos were admitted to not a few administrative offices. By 1907 a Filipino Assembly had been created, with complete legislative power, a commissioner elected to the United States House of Representatives to watch over the interests of the islands, and a majority of Filipinos established on the Filipino Commission, which carried on the work of the administration under the direction of the governor and which also exercised legislative powers. In 1916 a two-chamber legislature was created and, though the right of veto existed in the governor, under the Wilson administration wide authority was given to the new body, and it was left free to formulate general policies with little interference. There was a reaction under the governorship of General Leonard Wood, who displayed a somewhat autocratic temper, but this was short-lived. Finally, in 1934, Congress provided for the calling of a constitutional convention and for the complete independence of the islands. There was to be an interim period during which the United States was represented in the islands by a high commissioner, with strictly limited powers; but this lasted for only ten years, and in 1946 the independent Filipino Republic came into being. While the United States, with the consent of the Filipino government, retains bases in the islands, it no longer exercises any direct political authority over the conduct of Filipino affairs.

Let us look next at Puerto Rico. For a short time the island remained under military government. But in 1900 there was set up a civil regime which provided for a legislature, the lower house of which was elected by the Puerto Ricans themselves, and which gave to the island a civil governor. This very moderate measure of popular control was enlarged by the Jones Act of 1917. By this legislation, both houses of the Puerto Rican legislature were to be chosen by the inhabitants of the island, a substantial number of the administrative posts were placed in their hands, a bill of rights was enacted, and a Puerto Rican commissioner was given a seat in the House of Representatives. Thus the way was provided for a greater degree of self-rule. In 1947, still another step was taken. The governor of the island, instead of being chosen by the President of the United States, was henceforth to be elected by the Puerto Ricans and was to hold office for a fixed term. Virtually the whole administrative machinery was placed in native hands, leaving only the judges of the supreme court to be chosen by the President of the United States. And while, in theory, the power of veto over Puerto Rican legislation exists, and can be exercised either by the President or through congressional enactment, in practice the inhabitants of the island enjoy a wide degree of self-government.

The other territories acquired by the United States are Samoa, Guam, and the Virgin Islands, all of them small ones, with populations in each case under 60,000. The first two have been under naval rule, but even here there has been some representation accorded to the native population, and Guam has been transferred to civil authority. The third enjoys today the status accorded to

Puerto Rico before the legislation of 1947. Even in these instances, then, the principle of self-government has been given expression.

In addition to controlling the territories mentioned, the United States exercised supervision and control over various Caribbean republics, setting up governments there which, in one form or another, were under the control of the American marines. Though a variety of motives explain these interventions (and we shall have more to say of this later), among them was the hope of bringing about orderly government based on a respect for constitutional and democratic processes. It may be instructive to see how much success was achieved. Indeed, by an analysis of the situation in these communities today, we may gain some insight into the fundamental question as to whether democratic institutions can be exported successfully and made to function efficiently.

The situation has varied in the five states under review (Panama, Cuba, Haiti, the Dominican Republic, and Nicaragua). In the Dominican Republic, for example, the departure of the Americans was soon followed by the establishment of a military dictatorship which was one of the most ruthless and cruel in the history of the Caribbean. Rafael Leonidas Trujillo, until his death in 1961, governed the state with a rod of iron for more than thirty years. He certainly brought peace to the Dominicans, but to speak of democracy is out of the question. A somewhat milder autocratic rule was that established by Anastasio Somoza in Nicaragua. In Haiti, there have been better and worse rulers since American evacuation in 1934, but hardly popular government. In Cuba, there have also been better and worse periods. Interspersed with administrations which observed, to a substantial extent, democratic forms, there have been the dictatorships of Gerardo Machado, Fulgencio Batista, and Fidel Castro. The hope for genuine democracy in Cuba has never seemed less bright than it does as these words are written. Furthermore, even in the better eras, the venality and corruption of Cuban politicians has been notorious. The most hopeful picture presented has been that of Panama. There popular processes have been reasonably democratic. Yet there were revolutions in Panama in 1949 and 1951, and rule by a virtual dictator from 1951 to 1955.

As we look at the record as a whole we shall find in it some reason for questioning the universal validity of the democratic idea. We may well ask whether popular institutions are adapted to peoples with a very different tradition and a very different social composition from our own. We may well ask whether something does not depend upon political habit, whether something does not depend upon the diffusion of knowledge, whether something does not depend upon the existence of a broadly based middle class which desires order and peace and which, from its very position, practices those arts of compromise which are of the essence of democratic rule. The story of American interventions demonstrates that the imposition of a brief period of tutelage by no means guarantees the solidity of popular government, as we understand it in this country.

Whether one accepts these conclusions or not, however, the experiment carried on in the second two decades of the century was short-lived. With relation to Latin America, there has been a strong current of feeling that conducts the

United States in a very different direction, and that was manifest even in the palmy days of the imperialist idea. In the period between 1910 and 1917, Mexico was in chronic disorder. The temptation to teach the Mexicans a lesson, to "clean up" a bad situation, was most certainly present. Yet neither the Taft nor the Wilson administration attempted to do anything of the kind. In the broad sense they let the Mexican peoples decide their own destinies. Wilson, it is true, found himself led by his prejudice against the Mexican dictator Victoriano Huerta to the occupation of Vera Cruz, a step which resulted in Huerta's overthrow, but he never desired full-scale intervention in Mexico. Even when the end of the war in Europe freed American hands from foreign complications, there was no attempt to police Mexico into good democratic behavior. The restraint shown by the United States was a remarkable example of the strength of the anti-imperialist impulse in American politics at a time when there was substantial pressure for another course of action. Policing little nations, rather than comparatively big ones, was as far as the United States was ready to go even in the imperialist decades.

Moreover, government by marines, inaugurated in Nicaragua in 1912, in the Dominican Republic in 1915, and in Haiti in 1916, did not long prove to be very popular with the American people. As early as the campaign of 1920, Senator Warren G. Harding, then a candidate for the presidency, actuated (it is fair to assume) by political motives rather than by profound knowledge of the situation in the Caribbean, sharply criticized the acts of the previous administration. And, with the advent of the Republican regime into power, the first steps were taken towards the liquidation of one of these military governments, that of the Dominican Republic, and the evacuation of Dominican territory was consummated in 1925. In the same year an attempt was made at withdrawal from Nicaragua and, though unsettled conditions again brought about American intervention, the way was soon prepared for a new withdrawal. In the meantime, important modifications were taking place in the view held by the United States with regard to the Roosevelt corollary of the Monroe Doctrine, which, as we have seen, formed a justification of interference in the affairs of other states. The State Department at this time (1928) drew up the famous Clark memorandum which, after analyzing the history of the Doctrine, came to the conclusion that it did not justify the use of force for the chastisement of unruly republics and the setting up of military rule. The next year the Senate of the United States, in ratifying the Kellogg-Briand Pact for the outlawry of war, adopted a kind of declaration or gloss on that instrument as to the limits to be placed on the principles of Monroe. At the time the Clark memorandum had not yet been published. Thus the Senate vote of 1929 was the first public repudiation by a body that was a part of the treaty-making power of the doctrine of intervention which had been practiced scarcely more than a decade before.

The change in American opinion was accelerated by the pressure of the Latin American republics themselves. At the Pan-American conference in Havana in 1928, the American delegation was made aware of the intensely critical attitude of most of our southern neighbors with regard to the whole problem of intervention. The administration, indeed, foreseeing what would be the tone of discussion there, had drawn Charles Evans Hughes from retirement to justify the position of the United States. But Hughes, though he was successful in postponing a vote on a resolution condemning all interventions, could not exorcise the essential hostility of the Latin American republics to the claims of the United States to exercise international police power. And the net result of the conference was probably to strengthen the movement away from imperialism.

It seems probable that the Great Depression also accentuated this tendency. The nation was in no mood, with the advent of the thirties, to use its physical power to protect American investors abroad. The hostility of the New Deal to the great financial interests made it relatively easy for the Roosevelt administration to forswear the habits of the past and place our relationship with Latin America on a new basis. At the Conference of Montevideo in 1933, Secretary Hull put his name to a protocol which bound the signatory states to abstain from all interference in the domestic concerns of any one of them. True, the Secretary boggled slightly at the proposed formula, and he even made a reservation intended to leave the door open for positive action for the protection of American interests. But the Senate of the United States, amazingly enough, ratified this protocol unanimously, and in 1936, when at Buenos Aires a new declaration was drawn up asserting the same principle in stronger terms, it was accepted without difficulty by the American delegation and ratified, like its predecessor, without a dissenting vote in the Senate.

In 1948 the United States went further. At the Conference of Bogota it put its name to a protocol which declared: "no state or *group of states* has the right to intervene, directly or indirectly, in the internal or external affairs of any other state. The foregoing principle prohibits not only armed force but also any other form of interference or attempted threat against the personality of the state or against its political or economic or cultural elements." It would hardly have been possible to make a more sweeping commitment of an anti-imperialistic character.

At no time since the signing of these three agreements has the American government intervened by force of arms at any place in the New World. In 1938 it bore tolerantly the expropriation of American oil interests in Mexico and in Bolivia. In 1940 it made no protest against the Cuban constitution, which dealt harshly in some respects with American interests. Only once has the pledge given in the Montevideo, Buenos Aires, and Bogota protocols, even by a broad construction, been violated: this was in 1961. At that time there had been established in Cuba a government under Fidel Castro which formed a close connection with Communist Russia and Communist China, and which was itself Communist or proto-Communist in character. In April 1961, the American government gave encouragement and some measure of actual military and economic support to an attempted invasion of the island by counterrevolutionaries. Its action failed; it met with considerable criticism at home; and the Kennedy administration, notwithstanding provocations of an extreme character, reiterated previous pledges that it would take no direct hostile action against the Castro regime. This episode might raise the question (which only the future will resolve) as to whether the United States is bound to stand by while American governments are subverted with the encouragement and open aid of its avowed antagonists. It can hardly serve to shake the thesis that in its relation with its Latin American neighbors the United States has demonstrated a restraint such as has only rarely been practiced by a nation possessed of great physical power. Moreover, it is one thing to abstain from interference with the freedom of action of the New World republics; it is another thing to permit the subversion of the free and independent states of the New World by international Communism.

A second aspect of United States relations with its "southern neighbors" should be mentioned. During the Second World War, by arrangement with other governments, notably Guatemala, Ecuador, Panama, and Brazil, its armed forces were stationed on the soil of these states. Today they are to be found in none of them. Even in the case of Panama, where an important security interest is plainly at stake, the American government, after long negotiations, withdrew its forces from Panamanian territory.

What was the record of the United States towards its conquered enemies at the end of the Second World War? What of Germany and Japan? In both cases the American government smiled upon the establishment of democratic regimes. In no way, once these regimes had been established, did it attempt to control them. True, American troops remain on German and Japanese soil. But they are there by agreement with the states concerned. They are there not as agents of control, but as symbols of the readiness of the American government to sustain the forces of popular rule. To speak of this as imperialism would be an absurdity.

One reservation must be made. In the islands of the Pacific conquered from Japan (of which Okinawa is the most important), the concern of our own military and naval men for security has resulted in the continuation of American administration. The treaty of peace with Japan, however, provided for the establishment of a United Nations trusteeship. As of the present writing, this provision has not been implemented. Yet the very willingness of the United States, in theory at least, to accept something less than unlimited sovereignty is a partial answer to its critics, and if the country follows precedents established, let us say, in the case of Guam, it will give a substantial voice to the inhabitants of these territories in the determination of their own affairs.

Up to this point we have been considering imperialism only in its political aspects. Now we must examine it on the economic side. Here, the questions that call for an answer are these: Where American political control or supervision has been extended, have the results been beneficial to the inhabitants of the area concerned, looking at the matter from the economic point of view? Second, have American business interests exercised—and do they exercise—a substantial and noxious control over the governments of other states in which they do business? And third, are the policies of the United States today, in America, in Europe, or in Asia, justly to be criticized as examples of "economic imperialism"?

To the first of these questions the answer seems clear. Such countries as Puerto Rico and the Philippines could almost certainly not have found the capital for their own development if they had operated as independent governments from 1898 thenceforward. They would have remained, as they then were, relatively backward communities. American rule gave to American capitalists the assurance of peace and order, and indeed of protection against arbitrary exaction, and thus contributed powerfully to encourage investment on a substantial scale. The case becomes still stronger when we are talking of regions in which chronic misgovernment existed before American control. You cannot expect foreign money to enter a country where disorder is virtually endemic. Whatever else American rule in the Dominican Republic may have done, to cite one example, it most certainly paved the way for a period of domestic tranquillity and opened the door to American entrepreneurs. The progress of the island since the American occupation has been remarkable, and it has had a far larger national income than before. Though the gain was less spectacular in Nicaragua or in Haiti, there, also, the net result of the American occupation was undoubtedly an economic advance.

It will be said that the profits from a situation of this kind go to a very few. That they are equitably distributed (assuming that we could agree upon what the word "equitably" implies), I should not for a moment attempt to assert. But that *some* benefit trickles down to a portion of the masses is certain. In the countries we have mentioned, American entrepreneurs usually pay higher wages than native employers and take better care of those who work for them. By their expanding activities, the number of workers is increased. The taxes which are levied upon them may go, if the government is honestly administered, or even if it is not, to serve the public interest and to make social progress possible without imposing an undue burden upon the less fortunate class in the community. There is, undeniably, a net economic gain which extends beyond the narrow circle of the entrepreneurs themselves.

Nor can we entirely neglect other contributions that are sometimes made by an occupying power which indirectly promote the welfare of those temporarily under its rule. The United States, in its brief period of control in Cuba, did much to set going a system of public instruction and to check the ravages of yellow fever. It did something for education in the Dominican Republic. It did much for the building of roads in both the Dominican Republic and Haiti. It reorganized the railroad system in Nicaragua. And it provided in every case a domestic tranquillity which could hardly fail to be of value to the mass of the population, for it certainly means something to relieve the average man of the plunder of revolutionary armies and the depredations of civil war. In addition to all this, the United States has often expended its own funds on a very substantial scale to assist the economies of such communities as the Virgin Islands, Puerto Rico, and the Philippines.

The second question which we posed concerned the influence of American business corporations in countries where they do business but where there is no political control by the United States itself. There are undeniably shoddy episodes in the American past in this regard. The most reprehensible have to do with the fomenting of revolution or with the giving of support to revolutionary factions, of course with the hope of return if these factions come into power. The revolution of 1910 in Nicaragua, to cite a case, was beyond much question instigated by American interests on the east coast of the republic, and there was a connection, though a tenuous one, between these interests and the State Department. In the course of the next year, the revolution which broke out in Honduras was financed from New Orleans, and those who promoted it naturally had interested objects in view. In the Mexican turmoil of the period 1910 to 1917, the oil companies at times maintained private armies which bid defiance to the authority of the state, and some of them heavily backed the so-called Constitutionalists, participating actively in what was virtually a civil war. Less reprehensible, no doubt, but still not to be defended, are the cases, not innumerous in the history of the Central American republics in the same and in an earlier period, when fantastic privileges were secured by foreign corporations from complacent or corrupt legislatures, and when corporate influence was often powerful enough to permit the circumvention or defiance of the law.

To judge from the surface evidence, this kind of thing is far less likely to occur today. In the first place, the standard of American business morals, while not so high as to please the exacting, has undeniably improved. In the second, since the Latin American states (in which most of these episodes have occurred) are now protected against intervention by the United States by the protocols of Montevideo and Buenos Aires, they can make a more effective resistance to the exactions of foreign capitalists. To state the matter in another way, the capital-receiving state can and does prescribe the terms under which the foreign entrepreneur operates. The American government has left and does leave to other countries wide latitude in the fixing of these terms. It has, invariably, contented itself with formal protests and demands for compensation, even in cases of expropriation. It is bound not to intervene by physical force. It rests, then, with the capital-receiving state to form its policies so that, on the one hand, by inordinate exactions it does not kill the goose that lays the golden eggs and, on the other hand, it appropriates for its own people a reasonable part of the profits that come from foreign enterprise.

It is entirely wrong to regard the export of American capital to other lands as in itself immoral or exploitative. On the contrary, it is of the very essence of economic progress that states with a surplus of fluid capital use it to develop the economies of those which do not, that those who have the best managerial skills and technological know-how use these skills and this knowledge to develop the resources of lands less fortunate in their capacity to act for themselves. Certainly, there must be some basis of understanding between the foreign entrepreneur and the state in which he operates. The entrepreneur must not be grasping; he must operate his business with some regard for the climate of opinion and for the social interests inevitably connected with his activities; the state must, on its part, not be oppressive in its policies and must recognize that those who invest their funds within its borders must not be prevented from making a fair profit on their investment. But with these things understood, the practice of capital export is beneficent, not maleficent—more, we repeat, it is indispensable to world progress. This fact should be self-evident. Unhappily it is not. The cliché "economic imperialism" is used to make odious what is normal and desirable. We need very emphatically to put this cliché in its place and to analyze very carefully the thought of those who put it forward.

This brings us to the third question asked at the beginning of our discussion:

are American public policies today on the economic side rightly subject to criticism as imperialistic?

In the course of the last few years, the export of private capital has been supplemented—or supplanted—by the export of *public* capital. Should such capital export fall under moral condemnation? Was the Marshall Plan reprehensible, as our enemies asserted? I do not see how this question can be answered in the affirmative. True, the American grants of aid to European states implied some concession to American opinion on the part of the receiving states. But how could aid be given on any other terms? Is it not reasonable to ask assurances that it be used for the ends for which it is granted, and in a way that will assist the purposes we have in view? When and by what government would aid be given on any other basis? Is there any evidence that majority opinion in the countries aided, fully and freely expressed, regarded the conditions as unduly onerous? Was the national independence of the states concerned seriously curtailed? Was there any great national revolt against the acceptance of our support? Or is it not more likely that Europeans would say of the Marshall Plan, as Churchill did of Lend-Lease, that it was one of the most unsordid acts in history? It is a distortion of terms to apply the word "imperialism" to such an expedient of European recovery as the Marshall Plan.

What applies to the Marshall Plan applies no less to the military and economic grants made by the American government in various parts of the world. It is elementary that these grants should be something more than mere handouts; their beneficiaries can hardly object to provisions which guard against misuse and ensure the attainment of the purpose the United States has in view. It would indeed be a verbal topsy-turvydom in which arrangements freely entered into for the defense or economic stimulation of other states were represented as "imperialism." The fact that some confused minds accept such a definition proves nothing, except the melancholy ability of some of us to accept the illogical.

There is, finally, the vague term "moral imperialism." It is difficult to invest this phrase with exact content. Perhaps the nearest we can come to it is to deal with the problem of recognition. Historically, the American government has sometimes abstained from recognition of regimes whose moral origins it did not approve. The Central American treaties of 1907, negotiated with the encouragement of the State Department, called for the withholding of recognition of Revolutionary regimes until free elections had taken place. Woodrow Wilson declined to recognize the Mexican ruler, Victoriano Huerta, because his rise to power was stained by the murder of his enemies. The Roosevelt administration refused to deal in 1944 with an Argentine government it did not believe representative of the Argentine people. The Soviet regime was recognized by the United States only in 1933, nearly sixteen years after its establishment. Other examples might be cited, including the consistent refusal of Washington to acknowledge the Chinese government at Peiping. Such pressure, it may be conceded, has in most instances been rather futile. Indeed, the practice of withholding recognition on moral grounds has been very largely abandoned. Only in the case of Communist China, which is still technically at war with the United States and which has violated many of the terms entered into for a truce in Korea, has the American government steadily refused to enter into formal relations with a regime of which it disapproves. Whatever one may think of the practice, the record of experience does not suggest that this type of moral imperialism constitutes a serious danger to the integrity or the continuance or the effective international action of the state against which it is directed.

In this review of American policy, it is not pretended that the record is above reproach. In the Philippines sharp hostilities preceded the establishment of American rule. In Haiti, Santo Domingo, and Nicaragua there was substantial local resistance to American authority. Our relations with Cuba are not without blemish. But, nonetheless, by the comparative standard, the United States has no reason to apologize for its record.

One other aspect of the problem of imperialism may be mentioned. What has been the attitude of the United States towards the imperialism of others? Has it been the stalwart defender of rule imposed from above, or has it been the champion of wider freedom? On the whole, it has been the latter. It favored the independence of India and of Indonesia. It has not been unfriendly to the establishment of the new and independent states of Africa. Its influence was exerted to encourage British withdrawal from Egypt. On occasion, caught between the interests of its European allies and its sympathy with self-determination, it has not always spoken so clearly. Yet its own example pleads strongly in its behalf. Its own imperialist impulse came late and, as we have seen, was soon exhausted. It does not lie with the Soviet Union to direct reproaches against it.

Powerful nations, by the ineluctable necessities of international politics, almost inevitably make their power felt. The question is, how do they exert it? Do they exert it with utter ruthlessness, as did Hitlerian Germany? Do they assert the universal validity of the principles on which their own governments are founded, as the Russian government does today? Do they intrigue to subvert regimes which they do not find attractive? Or are they led towards tolerance, as the United States has clearly been in accepting the doctrine of non-intervention in Latin America, and as it has shown in its attitude towards other forms of government in various parts of the world, until some issue of national security was involved? Have they used their economic power harshly, or towards good ends? The answer to those questions suggests that, in the moderation that ought to go with strength, the United States on the whole has played and is playing a creditable role.

Moralism-Legalism

GEORGE F. KENNAN

After many years of official duty in the Foreign Service of the United States, it fell to me to bear a share of the responsibility for forming the foreign policy of the United States in the difficult years following World War II. The Policy Planning Staff—it was my duty to set up this office and direct it through the

George F. Kennan, *American Diplomacy, 1900–1950* (Chicago: University of Chicago Press, 1951), pp. v–vi, 65–66, 95–101. Copyright © 1951 by The University of Chicago Press.

first years of its existence—was the first regular office of the Department of State to be charged in our time with looking at problems from the standpoint of the totality of American national interest, as distinct from a single portion of it. People working in this institutional framework soon became conscious of the lack of any general agreement, both within and without our government, on the basic concepts underlying the conduct of the external relations of the United States.

It was this realization of the lack of an adequately stated and widely accepted theoretical foundation to underpin the conduct of our external relations which aroused my curiosity about the concepts by which our statesmen had been guided in recent decades. After all, the novel and grave problems with which we were forced to deal seemed in large measure to be the products of the outcome of these past two world wars. The rhythm of international events is such that the turn of the century seemed a suitable starting point for an examination of American diplomacy and its relation to these two great cycles of violence. One and a half decades elapsed between the conclusion of the war with Spain and the dispatch of the first "Open Door" notes, on the one hand, and the outbreak of World War I, on the other. Measured against what we know of the relationships between cause and effect in the great matters of international life, this is a respectable period of time and one in which the influence of a country as powerful as the United States of that day could, if exerted consistently and with determination, have affected perceptibly the course of world affairs. The same was plainly true of the interval between the two world wars. By 1900 we were generally aware that our power had world-wide significance and that we could be affected by events far afield; from that time on our interests were constantly involved in important ways with such events.

By what concepts were our statesmen animated in their efforts to meet these new problems? What assumptions had they made concerning the basic purposes of this country in the field of foreign policy? What was it they felt they were trying to achieve? And were these concepts, in the light of retrospect, appropriate and effective ones? Did they reflect some deeper understanding of the relationship of American democracy to its world environment—something which we, perhaps, had forgotten but ought to resurrect and place again at the foundation of our conduct? Or had they been inadequate and superficial all along? . . .

It is surely a curious characteristic of democracy: this amazing ability to shift gears overnight in one's ideological attitudes, depending on whether one considers one's self at war or at peace. Day before yesterday, let us say, the issues at stake between ourselves and another power were not worth the life of a single American boy. Today, nothing else counts at all; our cause is holy; the cost is no consideration; violence must know no limitations short of unconditional surrender.

Now I know the answer to this one. A democracy is peace-loving. It does not like to go to war. It is slow to rise to provocation. When it has once been provoked to the point where it must grasp the sword, it does not easily forgive its adversary for having produced this situation. The fact of the provocation then becomes itself the issue. Democracy fights in anger—it fights for the very reason that it was forced to go to war. It fights to punish the power that was rash enough and hostile enough to provoke it—to teach that power a lesson it will not forget, to prevent the thing from happening again. Such a war must be carried to the bitter end.

This is true enough, and, if nations could afford to operate in the moral climate of individual ethics, it would be understandable and acceptable. But I sometimes wonder whether in this respect a democracy is not uncomfortably similar to one of those prehistoric monsters with a body as long as this room and a brain the size of a pin: he lies there in his comfortable primeval mud and pays little attention to his environment; he is slow to wrath—in fact, you practically have to whack his tail off to make him aware that his interests are being disturbed; but, once he grasps this, he lays about him with such blind determination that he not only destroys his adversary but largely wrecks his native habitat. You wonder whether it would not have been wiser for him to have taken a little more interest in what was going on at an earlier date and to have seen whether he could not have prevented some of these situations from arising instead of proceeding from an undiscriminating indifference to a holy wrath equally undiscriminating. . . .

As you have no doubt surmised, I see the most serious fault of our past policy formulation to lie in something that I might call the legalistic-moralistic approach to international problems. This approach runs like a red skein through our foreign policy of the last fifty years. It has in it something of the old emphasis on arbitration treaties, something of the Hague Conferences and schemes for universal disarmament, something of the more ambitious American concepts of the role of international law, something of the League of Nations and the United Nations, something of the Kellogg Pact, something of the idea of a universal "Article 51" pact, something of the belief in World Law and World Government. But it is none of these, entirely. Let me try to describe it.

It is the belief that it should be possible to suppress the chaotic and dangerous aspirations of governments in the international field by the acceptance of some system of legal rules and restraints. This belief undoubtedly represents in part an attempt to transpose the Anglo-Saxon concept of individual law into the international field and to make it applicable to governments as it is applicable here at home to individuals. It must also stem in part from the memory of the origin of our own political system—from the recollection that we were able, through acceptance of a common institutional and juridical framework, to reduce to harmless dimensions the conflicts of interest and aspiration among the original thirteen colonies and to bring them all into an ordered and peaceful relationship with one another. Remembering this, people are unable to understand that what might have been possible for the thirteen colonies in a given set of circumstances might not be possible in the wider international field.

It is the essence of this belief that, instead of taking the awkward conflicts of national interest and dealing with them on their merits with a view to finding the solutions least unsettling to the stability of international life, it would be better to find some formal criteria of a juridical nature by which the permissible behavior of states could be defined. There would then be judicial entities competent to measure the actions of governments against these criteria and to decide when their behavior was acceptable and when unacceptable. Behind all this, of course, lies the American assumption that the things for which other peoples in this world are apt to contend are for the most part neither creditable nor important and might justly be expected to take second place behind the desirability of an orderly world, untroubled by international violence. To the American mind, it is implausible that people should have positive aspirations, and ones that they regard as legitimate, more important to them than the peacefulness and orderliness of international life. From this standpoint, it is not apparent why other peoples should not join us in accepting the rules of the game in international politics, just as we accept such rules in the competition of sport in order that the game may not become too cruel and too destructive and may not assume an importance we did not mean it to have.

If they were to do this, the reasoning runs, then the troublesome and chaotic manifestations of the national ego could be contained and rendered either unsubstantial or subject to easy disposal by some method familiar and comprehensible to our American usage. Departing from this background, the mind of American statesmanship, stemming as it does in so large a part from the legal profession in our country, gropes with unfailing persistence for some institutional framework which would be capable of fulfilling this function.

I cannot undertake in this short lecture to deal exhaustively with this thesis or to point out all the elements of unsoundness which I feel it contains. But some of its more outstanding weaknesses are worthy of mention.

In the first place, the idea of the subordination of a large number of states to an international juridical regime, limiting their possibilities for aggression and injury to other states, implies that these are all states like our own, reasonably content with their international borders and status, at least to the extent that they would be willing to refrain from pressing for change without international agreement. Actually, this has generally been true only of a portion of international society. We tend to underestimate the violence of national maladjustments and discontents elsewhere in the world if we think that they would always appear to other people as less important than the preservation of the juridical tidiness of international life.

Second, while this concept is often associated with a revolt against nationalism, it is a curious thing that it actually tends to confer upon the concept of nationality and national sovereignty an absolute value it did not have before. The very principle of "one government, one vote," regardless of physical or political differences between states, glorifies the concept of national sovereignty and makes it the exclusive form of participation in international life. It envisages a world composed exclusively of sovereign national states with a full equality of status. In doing this, it ignores the tremendous variations in the firmness and soundness of national divisions: the fact that the origins of state borders and national personalities were in many instances fortuitous or at least poorly related to realities. It also ignores the law of change. The national state pattern is not, should not be, and cannot be a fixed and static thing. By nature, it is an unstable phenomenon in a constant state of change and flux. History has shown that the will and the capacity of individual peoples to contribute to their world environment is constantly changing. It is only logical that the organizational forms (and what else are such things as borders and governments?) should change with them. The function of a system of international relationships is not to inhibit this process of change by imposing a legal strait jacket upon it but rather to facilitate it: to ease its transitions, to temper the asperities to which it often leads, to isolate and moderate the conflicts to which it gives rise, and to see that these conflicts do not assume forms too unsettling for international life in general. But this is a task for diplomacy, in the most old-fashioned sense of the term. For this, law is too abstract, too inflexible, too hard to adjust to the demands of the unpredictable and the unexpected.

By the same token, the American concept of world law ignores those means of international offense—those means of the projection of power and coercion over other peoples—which by-pass institutional forms entirely or even exploit them against themselves: such things as ideological attack, intimidation, penetration, and disguised seizure of the institutional paraphernalia of national sovereignty. It ignores, in other words, the device of the puppet state and the set of techniques by which states can be converted into puppets with no formal violation of, or challenge to, the outward attributes of their sovereignty and their independence.

This is one of the things that have caused the peoples of the satellite countries of eastern Europe to look with a certain tinge of bitterness on the United Nations. The organization failed so completely to save them from domination by a great neighboring country, a domination no less invidious by virtue of the fact that it came into being by processes we could not call "aggression." And there is indeed some justification for their feeling, because the legalistic approach to international affairs ignores in general the international significance of political problems and the deeper sources of international instability. It assumes that civil wars will remain civil and not grow into international wars. It assumes the ability of each people to solve its own internal political problems in a manner not provocative of its international environment. It assumes that each nation will always be able to construct a government qualified to speak for it and cast its vote in the international arena and that this government will be acceptable to the rest of the international community in this capacity. It assumes, in other words, that domestic issues will not become international issues and that the world community will not be put in the position of having to make choices between rival claimants for power within the confines of the individual state.

Finally, this legalistic approach to international relations is faulty in its assumptions concerning the possibility of sanctions against offenses and violations. In general, it looks to collective action to provide such sanction against the bad behavior of states. In doing so, it forgets the limitations on the effectiveness of military coalition. It forgets that, as a circle of military associates widens in any conceivable political-military venture, the theoretical total of available military strength may increase, but only at the cost of compactness and ease of control. And the wider a coalition becomes, the more difficult it becomes to retain political unity and general agreement on the purposes and effects of what is being done. As we are seeing in the case of Korea, joint military operations against an aggressor have a different meaning for each participant and raise specific political issues for each one which are extraneous to the action in question and affect many other facets of international life. The wider the circle of military associates, the more cumbersome the problem of political control over their actions, and the more circumscribed the least common denominator of agreement. This law of diminishing returns lies so heavily on the possibilities for multilateral military action that it makes it doubtful whether the participation of smaller states can really add very much to the ability of the great powers to assure stability of international life. And this is tremendously important, for it brings us back to the realization that even under a system of world law the sanction against destructive international behavior might continue to rest basically, as it has in the past, on the alliances and relationships among the great powers themselves. There might be a state, or perhaps more than one state, which all the rest of the world community together could not successfully coerce into following a line of action to which it was violently averse. And if this is true, where are we? It seems to me that we are right back in the realm of the forgotten art of diplomacy from which we have spent fifty years trying to escape.

These, then, are some of the theoretical deficiencies that appear to me to be inherent in the legalistic approach to international affairs. But there is a greater deficiency still that I should like to mention before I close. That is the inevitable association of legalistic ideas with moralistic ones: the carrying-over into the affairs of states of the concepts of right and wrong, the assumption that state behavior is a fit subject for moral judgment. Whoever says there is a law must of course be indignant against the lawbreaker and feel a moral superiority to him. And when such indignation spills over into military contest, it knows no bounds short of the reduction of the law-breaker to the point of complete submissiveness—namely, unconditional surrender. It is a curious thing, but it is true, that the legalistic approach to world affairs, rooted as it unquestionably is in a desire to do away with war and violence, makes violence more enduring, more terrible, and more destructive to political stability than did the older motives of national interest. A war fought in the name of high moral principle finds no early end short of some form of total domination.

The Open Door Policy

WILLIAM APPLEMAN WILLIAMS

A re-examination of the history of twentieth-century American foreign relations (and the relationship between foreign policy and the domestic economy) offers the most promising approach to . . . a reconsideration of our assumptions. First,

Specified excerpts from pp. 9–11, 49–50, 53–58, 303–308, with footnotes deleted, from *The Tragedy of American Diplomacy* by William Appleman Williams. Copyright © 1959 by William Appleman Williams. Reprinted by permission of Thomas Y. Crowell Company, Inc.

we thereby confront directly what happened. We learn the ideas and the actions of the men who made or influenced policy, and the consequences of those events at home and abroad. Second, at the end of such a review of the past, we return to the present better informed. Finally, that increased knowledge and understanding may help us to muster the nerve to act in ways that can transform the tragedy into a new beginning.

For history is a way of learning, of getting closer to the truth. It is only by abandoning the clichés that we can even define the tragedy. When we have done that, we will no longer be merely acquiescing in the deadly inertia of the past. We will have taken the first and vital step in making history. Such a re-examination of history must be based upon a searching review of the way America has defined its own problems and objectives, and its relationship with the rest of the world. The reason for this is simple: realism goes nowhere unless it starts at home. Combined with a fresh look at Soviet behavior, such an understanding of American policy should help in the effort to outline new programs and policies designed to bring America's ideals and practical objectives closer to realization.

In the realm of ideas and ideals, American policy is guided by three conceptions. One is the warm, generous, humanitarian impulse to help other people solve their problems. A second is the principle of self-determination applied at the international level, which asserts the right of every society to establish its own goals or objectives, and to realize them internally through the means it decides are appropriate. These two ideas can be reconciled; indeed, they complement each other to an extensive degree. But the third idea entertained by many Americans is one which insists that other people cannot *really* solve their problems and improve their lives unless they go about it in the same way as the United States.

This feeling is not peculiar to Americans, for all other peoples reveal some degree of the same attitude toward the rest of the world. But the full scope and intensity of the American version is clearly revealed in the blunt remark of former Secretary of State Dean G. Acheson. He phrased it this way in explaining and defending the American program of foreign aid as it was being evolved shortly after the end of World War II: "We are willing to help people who believe the way we do, to continue to live the way they want to live."

This insistence that other people ought to copy America contradicts the humanitarian urge to help them and the idea that they have the right to make such key decisions for themselves. In some cases, the American way of doing things simply does not work for the other people. In another instance it may be satisfactory, but the other society may prefer to do it in a different way that produces equally good results—perhaps even better ones. But even if the American way were the *only* effective approach, the act of forcing it upon the other society—and economic and political pressure are forms of force— violates the idea of self-determination. It also angers the other society and makes it even less apt to accept the American suggestion on its own merits. Hence it is neither very effective nor very idealistic to try to help other people by insisting from the outset that they follow closely the lead and the example of the United States on all central and vital matters.

The same kind of difficulty arises in connection with the economic side of American foreign policy. The United States needs raw materials and other goods and services from foreign countries, just as it needs to sell some of its own goods and services to them. It might be able literally to isolate itself and survive, but that is not the issue. Not even the isolationists of the late 1920's and early 1930's advocated that kind of foreign policy. The vital question concerns instead the way in which America gets what it needs and exports what it wants to sell.

Most Americans consider that trade supplies the answer to this problem. But trade is defined as the exchange of goods and services between producers dealing with each other in as open a market as it is possible to create, and doing this without one of them being so beholden to the other that he cannot bargain in a meaningful and effective way. Trade is not defined by the transfer of goods and services under conditions established and controlled largely by one of the parties.

Here is a primary source of America's troubles in its economic relations with the rest of the world. For in expanding its own economic system throughout much of the world, America has made it very difficult for other nations to retain any economic independence. This is particularly true in connection with raw materials. Saudi Arabia, for example, is not an independent oil producer. Its oil fields are an integrated and controlled part of the American oil industry. But a very similar, if often less dramatic, kind of relationship also develops in manufacturing industries. This is the case in countries where established economic systems are outmoded or lethargic, as well as in the new, poor nations that are just beginning to industrialize. American corporations exercise very extensive authority, and even commanding power, in the political economy of such nations.

Unfortunately, there is an even more troublesome factor in the economic aspect of American foreign policy. That is the firm conviction, even dogmatic belief, that America's *domestic* well-being depends upon such sustained, ever-increasing overseas economic expansion. Here is a convergence of economic practice with intellectual analysis and emotional involvement that creates a very powerful and dangerous propensity to define the essentials of American welfare in terms of activities outside the United States.

It is dangerous for two reasons. First, it leads to an indifference toward, or a neglect of, internal developments which are nevertheless of primary importance. And second, this strong tendency to externalize the sources or causes of good things leads naturally enough to an even greater inclination to explain the lack of the good life by blaming it on foreign individuals, groups, and nations. This kind of externalizing evil serves not only to antagonize the outsiders, but further intensifies the American determination to make them over in the proper manner or simply push them out of the way.

The over-all result of these considerations is that America's humanitarian urge to assist other peoples is undercut—even subverted—by the way it goes about helping them. Other societies come to feel that American policy causes them to lose their economic, political, and even psychological independence. . . .

In summation, the true nature and full significance of the Open Door Policy can only be grasped when its four essential features are fully understood.

First: it was neither a military strategy nor a traditional balance-of-power policy. *It was conceived and designed to win the victories without the wars.* In a truly perceptive and even noble sense, the makers of the Open Door Policy understood that war represented the failure of policy. Hence it is irrelevant to criticize the Open Door Policy for not emphasizing, or not producing, extensive military readiness.

Second: it was derived from the proposition that America's overwhelming economic power would cast the economy and the politics of the poorer, weaker, underdeveloped countries in a pro-American mold. American leaders assumed the opposition of one or many industrialized rivals. Over a period of two generations the policy failed because some of those competitors, among them Japan and Germany, chose to resort to force when they concluded (on solid grounds) that the Open Door Policy was working only too well; and because various groups inside the weaker countries such as China and Cuba decided that America's extensive influence in and upon their societies was harmful to their specific and general welfare.

Third (and clearly related to the second point): the policy was neither legalistic nor moralistic in the sense that those criticisms are usually offered. It was extremely hard-headed and practical. In some respects, at any rate, it was the most impressive intellectual achievement in the area of public policy since the generation of the Founding Fathers.

Fourth: unless and until it, and its underlying *Weltanschauung,* were modified to deal with its own consequences, the policy was certain to produce foreign policy crises that would become increasingly severe.

Once these factors are understood, it becomes useful to explore the way that ideological and moralistic elements became integrated with the fundamentally secular and economic nature of the Open Door Policy. The addition of those ingredients served to create a kind of expansionism that aimed at the marketplace of the mind and the polls as well as of the pocketbook.

Taken up by President Theodore Roosevelt and his successors, the philosophy and practice of secular empire that was embodied in the Open Door Notes became the central feature of American foreign policy in the twentieth century. American economic power gushed into some underdeveloped areas within a decade and into many others within a generation. It also seeped, then trickled, and finally flooded into the more developed nations and their colonies until, by 1939, America's economic expansion encompassed the globe. And by that time the regions where America's position was not extensively developed were precisely the areas in which the United States manifested a determination to retain and expand its exploratory operations—or to enter in force for the first time.

Throughout these same years, the rise of a new crusading spirit in American diplomacy contributed an outward thrust of its own and reinforced the secular expansion. This righteous enthusiasm was both secular, emphasizing political and social ideology, and religious, stressing the virtues (and necessities) of Protestant Christianity. In essence, this twentieth-century Manifest Destiny was identical with the earlier phenomenon of the same name.

Americans assumed a posture of moral and ideological superiority at an early date. Despite the persistence of the Puritan tradition, however, this assertiveness took predominantly secular forms. Supernatural authority was invoked to explain and account for the steady enlargement of the United States, but the justifications for expansion were generally based on standards derived from this world. The phrase "Manifest Destiny," for example, symbolized the assertion that God was on America's side rather than the more modest claim that the country had joined the legions of the Lord. As that logic implied, the argument was that America was the "most progressive" society whose citizens made "proper use of the soil." For these and similar reasons, it was added, the laws of "political gravitation" would bring many minor peoples into the American system.

Though it had appeared as early as the eve of the American Revolution, the assertion that the expansion of the United States "extended the area of free-dom" gained general currency after the War of 1812. President Andrew Jackson seems to have coined the phrase, with his wildcatting intellectual sup-porters making many variations. One of the more persuasive and popular, which won many converts during and after the war with Mexico, stressed America's responsibility to extend its authority over "semi-barbarous people." By thus taking up the duty of "regeneration and civilization," America could perform the noble work of teaching inferiors to appreciate the blessings they already enjoyed but were inclined to overlook. In turn, this would prepare them for the better days to follow under America's benevolent leadership.

Near the end of the century, American missionaries and domestic religious leaders began to impart a more theological tone to this crusading fervor. This resulted in part from the effort by the clergy to marry traditional Christianity with the new doctrine of evolution and in that way adjust their theology to the latest revelations, and also to sustain their influence in the age of science. Josiah Strong was an innovator of that kind. As a Congregationalist minister in whom the frontier experience and outlook exercised an important influence, Strong concluded that the theory of evolution only substantiated the doctrine of predestination. America had been hand-picked by the Lord to lead the Anglo-Saxons in transforming the world. "It would seem," he explained with reference to the American Indians and other benighted peoples, "as if these inferior tribes were only precursors of a superior race, voices in the wilderness crying: Prepare ye the way of the Lord."

Ever since New England ministers had accepted the challenge of saving the heathens of Hawaii, a crusade that began in the eighteenth century, American missionaries had been noticeably concerned about Asia—and in particular China. As the Reverend Hudson Taylor explained in 1894, there was "a great Niagara of souls passing into the dark in China." Though they never lost faith, a growing number of missionaries did get discouraged enough to question whether hell-fire sermons on the dangers of damnation were an approach sufficient unto the need. Some thought fondly of the sword of righteousness, and toyed with the idea of a "Society for the Diffusion of Cannon Balls." That kind of crusade was never organized, but the missionaries did begin in the 1890's to demand formal support and protection from the American Government.

This request, while never acted upon with the same vigor as those from business groups, did receive sympathetic and favorable consideration. For one thing, the religious stake in China was significant: America had over 500 missionaries in that country, and their schools claimed a total student body of nearly 17,000 Chinese. Many churches had also supported intervention in Cuba. But the most important factor was the way that the missionary movement began to evolve an approach that offered direct support to secular expansion.

Missionaries had always tended to operate on an assumption quite similar to the frontier thesis. "Missionaries are an absolute necessity," explained the Reverend Henry Van Dyke of Princeton in 1896, "not only for the conversion of the heathen, but also, and much more, for the preservation of the Church. Christianity is a religion that will not keep." Religious leaders began to link the missionary movement with economic expansion in what the Reverend Francis E. Clark of the Christian Endeavor organization called "the widening of our empire." The Board of Foreign Missions also welcomed such expansion as "an ally."

Then, beginning in the mid-1890's, the missionaries began to change their basic strategy in a way that greatly encouraged such liaison with secular expansionists. Shifting from an emphasis on the horrors of hell to a concern with practical reform as the lever of conversion, they increasingly stressed the need to remake the underdeveloped societies. Naturally enough, they were to be reformed in the image of the United States. Such changes would lead to regeneration identified with Christianity and witnesses for the Lord would accordingly increase.

Not only did this program mesh with the idea of American secular influence (how else were the reforms to be initiated?), but it was very similar to the argument that American expansion was justified because it created more progressive societies. Missionaries came to sound more and more like political leaders, who were themselves submerging their domestic ideological differences at the water's edge in a general agreement on expansion as a reform movement.

The domestic reformer La Follette offers an excellent example of this convergence of economic and ideological expansion that took place across political lines. He approved taking the Philippines because it would enable America "to conquer [its] rightful share of that great market now opening [in China] for the world's commerce." Expansion was also justified because the United States had a "bounden *duty* to establish and *maintain* stable government" in the islands. Pointing out that from the beginning "the policy of this government has been to expand," La Follette justified it on the grounds that "it has *made men free*." Thus, he concluded, "we can legally and morally reserve unto ourselves perpetual commercial advantages of priceless value to our foreign trade for all time to come" by taking the Philippines.

Theodore Roosevelt's outlook reveals an even more significant aspect of this progressive integration of secular and ideological expansionism. His concern for economic expansion was complemented by an urge to extend Anglo-Saxon ideas, practices, and virtues throughout the world. Just as his Square Deal program centered on the idea of responsible leaders using the national government to regulate and moderate industrial society at home, so did his international outlook revolve around the idea of American supremacy being used to define and promote the interests of "collective civilization."

Thus it was necessary, he warned in his Presidential Message of December 1901, to exercise restraint in dealing with the large corporations. "Business concerns which have the largest means at their disposal . . . take the lead in the strife for commercial supremacy among the nations of the world. America has only just begun to assume the commanding position in the international business world which we believe will more and more be hers. It is of the utmost importance that this position be not jeopardized, especially at a time when the overflowing abundance of our own natural resources and the skill, business energy, and mechanical aptitude of our people make foreign markets essential."

Roosevelt integrated that kind of expansion with ideological considerations and imperatives to create an all-inclusive logic and set of responsibilities which made peace itself the consequence of empire. In his mind, at any rate, it was America's "duty toward the people living in barbarism to see that they are freed from their chains, and we can free them only by destroying barbarism itself." Thus, he concluded, "peace cannot be had until the civilized nations have expanded in some shape over the barbarous nations."

The inherent requirements of economic expansion coincided with such religious, racist, and reformist drives to remake the world. The reason for this is not difficult to perceive. As they existed, the underdeveloped countries were poor, particularistic, and bound by traditions which handicapped business enterprise. They were not organized to link up with the modern industrial system in a practical and efficient manner. It was economically necessary to change them *in certain ways and to a limited degree* if the fruits of expansion were to be harvested. As with the missionaries, therefore, the economic and political leaders of the country decided that what was good for Americans was also good for foreigners. Humanitarian concern was thus reinforced by hard-headed economic requirements.

The administrations of Theodore Roosevelt understood this relationship between economic expansion and overseas reform, and explicitly integrated it into the strategy of the Open Door Policy. It was often commented upon in dispatches and policy statements concerning China and Latin America. In his famous Corollary to the Monroe Doctrine, for example, Roosevelt (who thought of the Open Door Policy as the Monroe Doctrine for Asia) stressed the need for reforms and asserted the right and the obligation of the United States to see that they were made—and honored. . . .

America can neither take its place in nor make its contribution to the world community until it believes and demonstrates that it can sustain prosperity and democracy without recourse to open-door imperial expansion. The central issue of the mid-twentieth century is how to sustain democracy and prosperity without imperial expansion and the conflicts it engenders. The reason is obvious: the sparks from those collisions now fall into a nuclear tinderbox. It is all very well to converse bravely, seriously, and learnedly about surviving such a holocaust, but that is like sitting around the evening fire talking about what to do in the morning after the horse has been stolen instead of discussing ways and means of barring the barn door that night.

It is true that there are no completely foolproof locks, but it does not follow from that quite mundane observation that the risks of using the ones we have are greater than the risks and costs of getting along without the horse—or of buying another one. Yet this is precisely what we are doing when we give up on disarmament on the grounds that it cannot be 100 per cent guaranteed in advance, and turn instead to discussions of how to intimidate the Soviets with superweapons, or of how to rebuild the United States after a nuclear war.

One of the most disturbing features of international affairs between 1952 and 1962 was the extent to which it was the Russians, rather than the Americans, who sensed and appreciated this essential aspect of reality. For this is the real meaning of the Soviet doctrine of coexistence. They are proposing that the existing political and military balance be accepted as the foundation of world politics for an indefinite period. It is ironic, but in a deadly way, that it has been the United States and China which have refused to agree to this proposition.

The American nonrecognition of Mao Tse-tung's government has served in this sense to mask an unspoken entente between them on this crucial point of policy. There is not even any conscious thought—let alone any conspiracy—involved on the American side of this agreement. For that matter, American policy-makers seem wholly deaf and unconscious to the point despite the very broad hints that have been shouted from the Kremlin. As far as Washington is concerned, it could in this respect be called the best-kept secret treaty in the nation's entire history. The only way that the United States can break free of this entangling alliance with the Red Chinese is by accepting the Soviet doctrine of coexistence.

Americans must do this, not only to make it possible to slow down the dangerous momentum of the cold war toward thermonuclear war, not only to strengthen the advocates of coexistence in China, but even more in order that Americans themselves can apply their intelligence and humanitarianism to the very real and serious problems in the United States. This proposal has nothing to do with reviving and embracing either the theory or the practice of isolationism. There is no longer any question of whether or not we shall have relations with the rest of the world; there is the far more significant one of the kind of relations we shall have. That problem cannot be discussed intelligently to any relevant conclusions so long as it is defined in the narrow terms of the existing approach. We need to ask questions about the very *nature* of the traditional foreign policy of the United States, not questions concerning merely the *means* of putting it into operation. The right kind of questions are admittedly those that make us squirm. But isn't it time to find out whether we can still take that kind of question?

Isn't it time to stop defining trade as the control of markets for our surplus products and control of raw materials for our factories? Isn't it time to stop depending so narrowly—in our thinking as well as in our practice—upon an informal empire for our well-being and welfare?

Isn't it time to ask ourselves if we are really so unimaginative that we have to have a frontier in the form of an informal empire in order to have democracy and prosperity at home? Isn't it time to say that we can make American society function even better on the basis of equitable relationships with other people?

Isn't it time to stop defining trade as a weapon against other people with whom we have disagreements? Isn't it time to start thinking of trade as a means to moderate and alleviate those tensions—and to improve the life of the other people?

Isn't it time to stop trying to expand our exports on the grounds that such a campaign will make foreigners foot the bill for our military security? Isn't it time instead to concern ourselves with a concerted effort to halt and then cancel the armaments race?

Isn't it time to stop saying that all the evil in the world resides in the Soviet Union and other communist countries? Isn't it time to admit that there is good as well as evil in those societies, and set about to help increase the amount of good?

Isn't it time to admit that our own intelligence reports mean that the Russians have been following a defensive policy in nuclear weapons? Isn't it time to take advantage of that attitude on their part, break out of our neurosis about a Pearl Harbor attack, and go on to negotiate an arms control measure?

Isn't it time to admit, in short, that we can avoid living with communist countries only by embarking upon a program that will kill millions of human beings? Isn't it time, therefore, to evolve and adopt a program that will encourage and enable the communist countries to move in the direction of their own utopian vision of the good society as we endeavor to move in accordance with our own ideals?

For beyond acceptance of coexistence, the United States must embark upon a patient and concerted effort to establish and maintain by continued negotiation and development a *modus vivendi* with the Soviet Union, the People's Republic of China, and their allies. To this effort, economic agreements, involving normal credits and loans and a continuing increase of trade in consumer items and goods needed for general economic development, are basic. Such an approach will facilitate two processes essential to continued peace. First, it will open the way for continued reform within communist countries. That will make it easier, secondly, for the United States to allocate its aid and assistance to other nations through the appropriate agencies of the United Nations. Future requests to the United States for aid should be referred to such committees of the United Nations for mutual discussion and decision. If approved, such grants should be administered by the United Nations. For if America's objective is the improvement of life throughout the world, then there is no better way to speed that process. Such a policy would also strengthen America's own position. For it is true, as Thucydides is reputed to have remarked, that the greatest exercise of power lies in its restraint.

Once freed from its myopic concentration on the cold war, the United States could come to grips with the central problem of reordering its own society so that it functions through such a balanced relationship with the rest of the world, and so that the labor and leisure of its own citizens are invested with creative meaning and purpose. A new debate over the first principles and practices of government and economics is long overdue, and a statement of a twentieth-century political economy comparable to *The Federalist* papers would do more to enhance America's role in the world than any number of rockets and satellites. The configuration of the world of outer space will be decided on the cool green hills of earth long before the first colonizing spaceships blast free of the atmosphere.

Having structured a creative response to the issue of democracy and prosperity at home, the United States could again devote a greater share of its attention and energy to the world scene. Its revamped foreign policy would be geared to helping other peoples achieve their own aspirations in their own way. The essence of such a foreign policy would be an open door for revolutions. Having come to terms with themselves—having achieved maturity—Americans could exhibit the self-discipline necessary to let other peoples come to terms with themselves. Having realized that "self-righteousness is the hallmark of inner guilt," Americans would no longer find it necessary to embark upon crusades to save others.

In this fashion, and through a policy of an open door for revolutions, Americans would be able to cope with the many as yet unknown revolutions that are dependent upon peace for their conception and maturation. Only in this way can either the general or the specific tragedy of American diplomacy be transcended in a creative, peaceful manner. Otherwise the next Cuba may very well be the last. For unless the existing attitudes and policies are changed, another Cuba will clearly be dealt with through military intervention involving American troops. And that—even without direct Soviet or Chinese retaliation in kind—could insure the final catastrophe.

Of course, such an American intervention would have profound and reactionary consequences in Russia and China, and hence upon the relationship between them. The result would be a further acceleration of the already very serious momentum toward thermonuclear war. It would very probably, and whatever the outcome of the specific intervention by the United States, produce an increasing loss of control on both sides.

The way to transcend tragedy is to reconcile the contrasting truths which define the tragedy. Left instead to run out the string of their own logic, as they were and did in Cuba, the clashing truths will sooner rather than later kindle a global nuclear fire. To transcend tragedy requires the nerve to fail. But a positive effort to transcend the cold war would very probably carry the United States and the world on into an era of peace and creative human endeavor.

For the nerve to fail has nothing at all to do with blustering and self-righteous crusades up to or past the edge of violence. It is instead the kind of quiet confidence that comes with and from accepting limits, and a concurrent understanding that accepting limits does not mean the end of existence itself or of the possibility of a creative life. For Americans, the nerve to fail is in a real sense the nerve to say—and mean—that we no longer need what Turner called "the gate of escape" provided by the frontier. It is only in adolescence or senility that human beings manifest a compulsive drive to play to win. The one does not yet know, and the other has forgotten, that what counts is how the game is played. It would actually be pathetic rather than tragic if the United States jumped from childhood to old age without ever having matured. Yet that is precisely what it will do unless it sloughs off the ideology of the Open Door Policy and steps forth to open the door to the revolutions that can transform the material world and the quality of human relationships.

Perhaps it is by now apparent to the reader that there is a basic irony involved in this conception and interpretation of American foreign policy as tragedy. This irony arises from, and is in that sense caused by, the truth that this essay is in two respects written from a radical point of view.

First, it is radical in that it seeks to uncover, describe, and analyze the character and logic of American foreign policy since the 1890's. It is therefore critical in the intellectual sense of not being content with rhetoric and other appearances, and of seeking instead to establish by research and analysis a fuller, more accurate picture of reality.

Second, it is radical in that it concludes from the research and reflection, that American foreign policy must be changed fundamentally in order to sustain the wealth and welfare of the United States on into the future. This essay recommends that the frontier-expansionist explanation of American democracy and prosperity, and the strategy of the Open Door Policy, be abandoned on the grounds that neither any longer bears any significant relation to reality.

FURTHER READING

Richard J. Barnet, *Roots of War* (1972)

William P. Bundy, ed., *Two Hundred Years of American Foreign Policy* (1977)

Arthur A. Ekirch, Jr., *Ideas, Ideals, and American Diplomacy* (1966)

Lloyd C. Gardner, *Imperial America* (1976)

Norman A. Graebner, *Ideas and Diplomacy* (1964)

Jonathan Knight, "George Frost Kennan and the Study of American Foreign Policy: Some Critical Comments," *Western Political Quarterly*, 20 (1967), 149–160

Gabriel Kolko, *The Roots of American Foreign Policy* (1969)

Walter Lippmann, *U. S. Foreign Policy: Shield of the Republic* (1943)

Frank Merli and Theodore A. Wilson, eds., *Makers of American Diplomacy* (1974)

Hans J. Morgenthau, *In Defense of the National Interest* (1951)

Charles E. Neu, "The Changing Interpretive Structure of American Foreign Policy," in John Braeman et al., eds., *Twentieth-Century American Foreign Policy* (1971)

Robert E. Osgood, *Ideals and Self-Interest in America's Foreign Relations* (1953)

Thomas G. Paterson, J. Garry Clifford, and Kenneth J. Hagan, *American Foreign Policy: A History* (1977)
Dexter Perkins, *The Evolution of American Foreign Policy* (1948)
David Potter, *People of Plenty* (1954)
Arthur M. Schlesinger, Jr., *The Imperial Presidency* (1973)
Franz Schurmann, *Logic of World Power* (1974)
Robert Tucker, *The Radical Left and American Foreign Policy* (1971)

2

United States Entry into World War I

In August 1914 Europe became engulfed in war. Because the United States was a world power and a major trader on the high seas, it was drawn into the catastrophic event. Until early 1917, the Wilson administration struggled to define a policy that would end the bloodshed in Europe, protect America's interests and ideals, and keep the United States out of the conflagration. But in April of that year, President Woodrow Wilson chose war.

Why did Wilson decide to enter the conflict? Most historians point to the German U-boat as the catalyst, but disagree on why the President reacted to submarine warfare the way he did. Did the United States enter the war to ensure its national security? Or its economic well-being? That is, did realism characterize American diplomacy? Or did idealism, a defense of principles and honor, govern Wilson's decision for war? And was American entry inevitable or could Wilson have compromised and followed alternative policies? Finally, how "neutral" was American diplomacy?

DOCUMENTS

The first document, a memorandum of a conversation between Secretary of State Robert Lansing and Count Johann-Heinrich Bernstorff, the German Ambassador to the United States, held on April 20, 1916, illustrates the centrality of the submarine issue. The meeting took place less than a month after the torpedoing of the *Sussex,* and the conversation helped to produce a German pledge not to attack merchant vessels and liners without warning.

But in late January 1917, the German government announced an unrestricted submarine campaign. On February 4 the United States broke diplomatic relations with Berlin, and on April 2, after the sinking of several vessels, Wilson asked Congress for a declaration of war. The vote for war—82 to 6 in the Senate and 373 to 50 in the House—came four days later. One of the "nay" votes was that of noted reformer Senator Robert LaFollette of Wisconsin. Like many of his countrymen, he questioned the necessity of American intervention and warned against the dire consequences to the nation if it should go to war. Portions of a LaFollette speech on April 4 are reprinted here.

Lansing and Bernstorff Discuss Submarine Warfare, 1916

L. Good morning.

B. Good morning, Sir. You handed me a copy of the note yesterday, and in the present state of affairs of course my chief object is to find a way how this break can be avoided, because I hope it can be avoided. My idea is to find a way out of it, but of course I had to telegraph my Government that this Government seemed to offer little opportunity for settlement. If it means the entire stopping of the use of submarines, I am afraid that it cannot be arranged.

L. You will recall that we said in the first *Lusitania* note that we thought it was impossible to use submarines in a really humane way and that later, in our note of July 21, we said that the way submarine warfare had been conducted for the past two months showed that it was possible and therefore we hoped that course would be pursued. Then we had the sinking of the *Arabic* right on top of that, which was another great disaster. Our position is that, if submarine warfare had been conducted in that way, that possibly there would have been no further question raised. But it has not. It has been conducted in the most indiscriminate way and we cannot help but believe that it is ruthless. In those conditions submarine warfare should stop against commercial vessels, unless visit and search is observed.

B. That, of course, is impossible. Germany cannot abandon submarine warfare. No government could come out and say—"We give up the use of submarines." They would have to resign.

L. What possible methods in the use of submarines, that are effective from a belligerent standpoint, can be suggested which will comply with the law?

B. I had always supposed that warning was to be given.

L. We do not consider that the people on board—the non-combatants on board the vessels—are in a place of safety when put into an open boat a hundred miles from land. It might be calm there, but in the two days it would take them to reach land there might be a severe storm. That is one of the grounds of complaint.

B. That, of course, speaking of neutral vessels—

L. The fact that we do not have Americans on these vessels does not remove the menace to American lives. The sinking of neutral vessels shows that

Americans cannot travel with safety on neutral vessels even. That is the serious part of it and I do not know how your Government can modify submarine warfare and make it effective and at the same time obey the law and the dictates of humanity.

B. Humanity. Of course war is never humane.

L. "Humanity" is a relative expression when used with "war" but the whole tendency in the growth of international law in regard to warfare in the past 125 years has been to relieve non-combatants of needless suffering.

B. Of course I think it would be an ideal state of affairs, but our enemies violate all the rules and you insist on their being applied to Germany.

L. One deals with life; the other with property.

B. Yes.

L. The German method seems reckless to me. It is as if a man who has a very dim vision should go out on the street with a revolver in search of an enemy and should see the outline of a figure and should immediately fire on him and injure him seriously and then go up and apologize and say he made a mistake. I do not think that would excuse him. That seems to be the course pursued by your submarine commanders—they fire first and inquire afterwards.

B. I myself cannot at all explain how it comes that so many neutral vessels have been attacked. I have not the slightest evidence. I do not know anything about it from our communications.

L. Of course we are gradually collecting the evidence. We have not in all the cases but we have in certain ones. The *Tubantia,* for example, seems to have been torpedoed by a German torpedo—a Schwartz kopf.

B. She was at anchor.

L. No. I do not think she had let her anchor down but she was preparing to anchor. She was at rest.

B. Yes, I know. And then there was a Spanish vessel which—

L. Of course there is this, Mr. Ambassador, that any discussion of the submarine and its present method of attack cannot go on indefinitely.

B. What was your idea to prevent the break—that we should for the time being stop?

L. I think the only way is to declare an abandonment and then if the German Government desires to discuss a method of renewal—

B. An absolute abandonment, to my mind, is impossible. It might be possible to announce stopping for a time for discussion and giving the reason plainly for the purpose of quieting our public opinion, that might be possible.

L. I understand you are speaking entirely without instructions.

B. I am not at all instructed. I am speaking to you purely from my desire to prevent a break.

L. In view of our note I would not want to say that that would be satisfactory, but if it was made—

B. I am only trying to see what can be done because a declaration to my Government to absolutely abandon submarine warfare would make a break absolutely necessary. To abandon it would mean the overthrow of the Chancellor.

L. Probably you would get a more radical man. I realize that.

B. So the question is what we can do.

L. There would have to be a complete abandonment first and then if the German Government desires to discuss the matter—

B. I want to do what I can, because I am perfectly convinced they do not want to break; quite apart from the sentimental side I think they do not want a break. A break would prolong the war. It would last for years.

L. We do not any of us want to prolong the war.

B. That is exactly why I want to get out of this present difficulty. From the present state of affairs it looks as if the end is coming and if now there was a break and the United States was brought into the war it would prolong it. It would cause new complications.

L. New complications?

B. New economic difficulties.

L. I think that would be Germany's problem. The only possible course is an abandonment of submarine warfare, whether limited or not would depend on the terms. I would want to see an abandonment first and then possibly a discussion could follow as to how submarine warfare can be conducted within the rules of international law and entire safety of non-combatants, because, of course, in my viewpoint that is the chief question of international law in regard to attacks by belligerents on enemy's commerce.

B. Then I am to understand that you do not recognize the law of retaliation?

L. We do not recognize retaliation when it affects the rights of neutrals.

B. The British retaliate by stopping all commerce to Germany.

L. It is a very different thing. The right to life is an inherent right, which man has from birth; the right of property is a purely legal right.

B. Only in this case, England's methods affect the lives of non-combatants of Germany.

L. Not neutrals.

B. No, but it affects non-combatants.

L. Does it affect their lives? I thought from the statements which have been made that Germany was not suffering from want of food.

B. But they are trying to starve them. You do not stop England but insist we must stop our retaliation.

L. But you must appreciate that we care more for the lives of our people than we do for the property.

B. We have the same difficulty—our people are getting to care more for lives. That is the whole difficulty—we are dealing with a warlike population.

L. I realize that. I appreciate that you have great difficulty with your public.

B. If you and I were to have the say in settling the case it would be an easy matter, because one can discuss the matter without heat.

L. I realize that. It makes it very difficult, but I do not think there is any other course. That certainly may be an impossible course for your Government to pursue, yet I see no other way, and I think I am as anxious to preserve peace as anyone.

B. I wanted to find out what I could do, because I do not see how they can do it though they might do it temporarily. I am sure that in the first place they would say they believed in the submarine entirely and that secondly the rules of international law must be modified by conditions. Your idea is that the submarine cannot be used if it does comply with the rules.

L. That is true. My view is that certain instruments of war are not proper to use under certain conditions, and that is the viewpoint that has largely been held in regard to the submarine as a commerce destroyer. You can not and do not know the nationality of the boat attacking. It attacks without being seen and so avoids responsibility. It gives every opportunity to kill indiscriminately and recklessly.

B. I perfectly agree with you that sinking without warning would have to stop entirely, sinking without warning is an international offense, and that is why I thought possibly my Government might give up the retaliation, but I do not think it would be possible to say we would give up submarine warfare. I do not think we would do it.

L. And if they should now sink another vessel it would be very serious—that is the way I look at the situation.

B. And if they continue the submarine warfare and an instance should happen directly after the break of diplomatic relations, if that should come, it would be still more serious.

L. That is logical.

B. That is why I look at it so seriously.

L. I do not feel that breaking off of diplomatic relations necessarily means war.

B. I do not say it myself but I do not see how it can be avoided. If we refuse it will be because we are to continue submarine warfare and then something might happen which would mean war. I came to see if something could not be done.

L. I am very much obliged to you for coming in, sir.

B. Good bye, Mr. Secretary.

L. Good bye.

Woodrow Wilson's War Message, 1917

I have called the Congress into extraordinary session because there are serious, very serious, choices of policy to be made, and made immediately, which it was neither right nor constitutionally permissible that I should assume the responsibility of making.

On the third of February last I officially laid before you the extraordinary announcement of the Imperial German Government that on and after the first day of February it was its purpose to put aside all restraints of law or of humanity and use its submarines to sink every vessel that sought to approach either the ports of Great Britain and Ireland or the western coasts of Europe or any of the ports controlled by the enemies of Germany within the Mediterranean. That had seemed to be the object of the German submarine warfare earlier in the war, but since April of last year the Imperial Government had somewhat restrained the commanders of its undersea craft in conformity with its promise then given to us that passenger boats should not be sunk and that due warning would be given to all other vessels which its submarines might seek to destroy, when no resistance was offered or escape attempted, and care taken that their crews were given at least a fair chance to save their lives in their open boats. The precautions taken were meagre and haphazard enough, as was proved in distressing instance after instance in the progress of the cruel and unmanly business, but a certain degree of restraint was observed. The new policy has swept every restriction aside. Vessels of every kind, whatever their flag, their character, their cargo, their destination, their errand, have been ruthlessly sent to the bottom without warning and without thought of help or mercy for those on board, the vessels of friendly neutrals along with those of belligerents. Even hospital ships and ships carrying relief to the sorely bereaved and stricken people of Belgium, though the latter were provided with safe conduct through the proscribed areas by the German Government itself and were distinguished by unmistakable marks of identity, have been sunk with the same reckless lack of compassion or of principle.

I was for a little while unable to believe that such things would in fact be done by any government that had hitherto subscribed to the humane practices of civilized nations. International law had its origin in the attempt to set up some law which would be respected and observed upon the seas, where no nation had right of dominion and where lay the free highways of the world. By painful stage after stage has that law been built up, with meagre enough results, indeed, after all was accomplished that could be accomplished, but always with a clear view, at least, of what the heart and conscience of mankind demanded. This minimum of right the German Government has swept aside under the plea of retaliation and necessity and because it had no weapons which it could use at sea except these which it is impossible to employ as it is employing them without throwing to the winds all scruples of humanity or of respect for the understandings that were supposed to underlie the intercourse of the world. I am not now thinking of the loss of property involved, immense and serious as that is, but only of the wanton and wholesale destruction of the lives of noncombatants, men, women, and children, engaged in pursuits which have always, even in the darkest periods of modern history, been deemed innocent and legitimate. Property can be paid for; the lives of peaceful and innocent people cannot be. The present German submarine warfare against commerce is a warfare against mankind.

It is a war against all nations. American ships have been sunk, American lives taken, in ways which it has stirred us very deeply to learn of, but the ships and people of other neutral and friendly nations have been sunk and overwhelmed in the waters in the same way. There has been no discrimination. The challenge is to all mankind. Each nation must decide for itself how it will meet it. The choice we make for ourselves must be made with a moderation of counsel and a temperateness of judgment benefitting our character and our motives as a nation. We must put excited feeling away. Our motive will not be revenge or the victorious assertion of the physical might of the nation, but only the vindication of right, of human right, of which we are only a single champion.

When I addressed the Congress on the twenty-sixth of February last I thought that it would suffice to assert our neutral rights with arms, our right to use the seas against unlawful interference, our right to keep our people safe against unlawful violence. But armed neutrality, it now appears, is impracticable. Because submarines are in effect outlaws when used as the German submarines have been used against merchant shipping, it is impossible to defend ships against their attacks as the law of nations has assumed that merchantmen would defend themselves against privateers or cruisers, visible craft giving chase upon the open sea. It is common prudence in such circumstances, grim necessity indeed, to endeavour to destroy them before they have shown their own intention. They must be dealt with upon sight, if dealt with at all. The German Government denies the right of neutrals to use arms at all within the areas of the sea which it has proscribed, even in the defense of rights which no modern publicist has ever before questioned their right to defend. The intimation is conveyed that the armed guards which we have placed on our merchant ships will be treated as beyond the pale of law and subject to be dealt with as pirates would be. Armed neutrality is ineffectual enough at best; in such circumstances and in the face of such pretensions it is worse than ineffectual: it is likely only to produce what it was meant to prevent; it is practically certain to draw us into the war without either the rights or the effectiveness of belligerents. There is one choice we cannot make, we are incapable of making: we will not choose the path of submission and suffer the most sacred rights of our nation and our people to be ignored or violated. The wrongs against which we now array ourselves are no common wrongs; they cut to the very roots of human life.

With a profound sense of the solemn and even tragical character of the step I am taking and of the grave responsibilities which it involves, but in unhesitating obedience to what I deem my constitutional duty, I advise that the Congress declare the recent course of the Imperial German Government to be in fact nothing less than war against the government and people of the United States; that it formally accept the status of belligerent which has thus been thrust upon it; and that it take immediate steps not only to put the country in a more thorough state of defense but also to exert all its power and employ all its resources to bring the Government of the German Empire to terms and end the war. . . .

While we do these things, these deeply momentous things, let us be very clear, and make very clear to all the world what our motives and our objects are. My own thought has not been driven from its habitual and normal course by the unhappy events of the last two months, and I do not believe that the thought of the nation has been altered or clouded by them. . . . Our object now, as then, is to vindicate the principles of peace and justice in the life of the world as against selfish and autocratic power and to set up amongst the really free and self-governed peoples of the world such a concert of purpose and of action as will henceforth ensure the observance of those principles. Neutrality is no longer feasible or desirable where the peace of the world is involved and the freedom of its peoples, and the menace to that peace and freedom lies in the existence of autocratic governments backed by organized force which is controlled wholly by their will, not by the will of their people. We have seen the last of neutrality in such circumstances. We are at the beginning of an age in which it will be insisted that the same standards of conduct and of responsibility for wrong done shall be observed among nations and their governments that are observed among the individual citizens of civilized states.

We have no quarrel with the German people. We have no feeling towards them but one of sympathy and friendship. It was not upon their impulse that their government acted in entering this war. It was not with their previous knowledge or approval. It was a war determined upon as wars used to be determined upon in the old, unhappy days when peoples were nowhere consulted by their rulers and wars were provoked and waged in the interest of dynasties or of little groups of ambitious men who were accustomed to use their fellow men as pawns and tools. Self-governed nations do not fill their neighbour states with spies or set the course of intrigue to bring about some critical posture of affairs which will give them an opportunity to strike and make conquest. Such designs can be successfully worked out only under cover and where no one has the right to ask questions. Cunningly contrived plans of deception or aggression, carried, it may be, from generation to generation, can be worked out and kept from the light only within the privacy of courts or behind the carefully guarded confidences of a narrow and privileged class. They are happily impossible where public opinion commands and insists upon full information concerning all the nation's affairs.

A steadfast concert for peace can never be maintained except by a partnership of democratic nations. No autocratic government could be trusted to keep faith within it or observe its convenants. It must be a league of honour, a partnership of opinion. . . .

Does not every American feel that assurance has been added to our hope for the future peace of the world by the wonderful and heartening things that have been happening within the last few weeks in Russia? Russia was known by those who knew it best to have been always in fact democratic at heart, in all the vital habits of her thought, in all the intimate relationships of her people that spoke their natural instinct, their habitual attitude towards life. The autocracy that crowned the summit of her political structure, long as it had stood and terrible as was the reality of its power, was not in fact Russian in origin, character, or purpose; and now it has been shaken off and the great, generous Russian people have been added in all their naive majesty and might to the forces that are fighting for freedom in the world, for justice, and for peace. Here is a fit partner for a League of Honour.

One of the things that has served to convince us that the Prussian autocracy was not and could never be our friend is that from the very outset of the present war it has filled our unsuspecting communities and even our offices of government with spies and set criminal intrigues everywhere afoot against our national unity of counsel, our peace within and without, our industries and our commerce. . . . That it means to stir up enemies against us at our very doors the intercepted note to the German Minister at Mexico City is eloquent evidence.

We are accepting this challenge of hostile purpose because we know that in such a government, following such methods, we can never have a friend; and that in the presence of its organized power, always lying in wait to accomplish we know not what purpose, there can be no assured security for the democratic governments of the world. We are now about to accept gauge of battle with this natural foe to liberty and shall, if necessary, spend the whole force of the nation to check and nullify its pretensions and its power. We are glad, now that we see the facts with no veil of false pretense about them, to fight thus for the ultimate peace of the world and for the liberation of its peoples, the German peoples included: for the rights of nations great and small and the privilege of men everywhere to choose their way of life and of obedience. The world must be made safe for democracy. . . .

It is a distressing and oppressive duty, Gentlemen of the Congress, which I have performed in thus addressing you. There are, it may be, many months of fiery trial and sacrifice ahead of us. It is a fearful thing to lead this great peaceful people into war, into the most terrible and disastrous of all wars, civilization itself seeming to be in the balance. But the right is more precious than peace, and we shall fight for the things which we have always carried nearest our hearts,— for democracy, for the right of those who submit to authority to have a voice in their own governments, for the rights and liberties of small nations, for a universal dominion of right by such a concert of free peoples as shall bring peace and safety to all nations and make the world itself at last free. To such a task we can dedicate our lives and our fortunes, everything that we are and everything that we have, with the pride of those who know that the day has come when America is privileged to spend her blood and her might for the principles that gave her birth and happiness and the peace which she has treasured. God helping her, she can do no other.

Robert M. LaFollette Dissents, 1917

The poor, sir, who are the ones called upon to rot in the trenches, have no organized power, have no press to voice their will upon this question of peace or war; but, oh, Mr. President, at some time they will be heard. I hope and I believe they will be heard in an orderly and a peaceful way. I think they may be heard from before long. I think, sir, if we take this step, when the people to-day who are staggering under the burden of supporting families at the present prices of the necessaries of life find those prices multiplied, when they are raised a hundred per cent, or 200 per cent, as they will be quickly, aye, sir, when beyond that those who pay taxes come to have their taxes doubled and again doubled to pay the interest on the nontaxable bonds held by Morgan and his combinations, which have been issued to meet this war, there will come an awakening; they will have their day and they will be heard. It will be as certain and as inevitable as the return of the tides, and as resistless, too. . . .

Just a word of comment more upon one of the points in the President's address. He says that this is a war "for the things which we have always carried nearest to our hearts—for democracy, for the right of those who submit to authority to have a voice in their own government." In many places throughout the address is this exalted sentiment given expression.

It is a sentiment peculiarly calculated to appeal to American hearts and, when accompanied by acts consistent with it, is certain to receive our support; but in this same connection, and strangely enough, the President says that we have become convinced that the German Government as it now exists— "Prussian autocracy" he calls it—can never again maintain friendly relations with us. His expression is that "Prussian autocracy was not and could never be our friend," and repeatedly throughout the address the suggestion is made that if the German people would overturn their Government it would probably be the way to peace. So true is this that the dispatches from London all hailed the message of the President as sounding the death knell of Germany's Government.

But the President proposes alliance with Great Britain, which, however liberty-loving its people, is a hereditary monarchy, with a hereditary ruler, with a hereditary House of Lords, with a hereditary landed system, with a limited and restricted suffrage for one class and a multiplied suffrage power for another, and with grinding industrial conditions for all the wageworkers. The President has not suggested that we make our support of Great Britain conditional to her granting home rule to Ireland, or Egypt, or India. We rejoice in the establishment of a democracy in Russia, but it will hardly be contended that if Russia was still an autocratic Government, we would not be asked to enter this alliance with her just the same. Italy and the lesser powers of Europe, Japan in the Orient; in fact, all of the countries with whom we are to enter into alliance, except France and newly revolutionized Russia, are still of the old order—and it will be generally conceded that no one of them has done as much for its people in the solution of municipal problems and in securing social and industrial reforms as Germany.

Is it not a remarkable democracy which leagues itself with allies already far overmatching in strength the German nation and holds out to such beleaguered nation the hope of peace only at the price of giving up their Government? I am not talking now of the merits or demerits of any government, but I am speaking of a profession of democracy that is linked in action with the most brutal and domineering use of autocratic power. Are the people of this country being so well represented in this war movement that we need to go abroad to give other people control of their governments? Will the President and the supporters of this war bill submit it to a vote of the people before the declaration of war goes into effect? Until we are willing to do that, it illy becomes us to offer as an excuse for our entry into the war the unsupported claim that this war was forced upon the German people by their Government "without their previous knowledge or approval."

Who has registered the knowledge or approval of the American people of the course this Congress is called upon to take in declaring war upon Germany? Submit the question to the people, you who support it. You who support it dare not do it, for you know that by a vote of more than ten to one the American people as a body would register their declaration against it.

In the sense that this war is being forced upon our people without their knowing why and without their approval, and that wars are usually forced upon all peoples in the same way, there is some truth in the statement; but I venture to say that the response which the German people have made to the demands of this war shows that it has a degree of popular support which the war upon which we are entering has not and never will have among our people. The espionage bills, the conscription bills, and other forcible military measures which we understand are being ground out of the war machine in this country is the complete proof that those responsible for this war fear that it has no popular support and that armies sufficient to satisfy the demand of the entente allies can not be recruited by voluntary enlistments.

ESSAYS

In the first essay, Daniel M. Smith argues that the United States went to war to preserve its security; Germany constituted a serious danger and Woodrow Wilson grasped that reality. Ross Gregory of Central Michigan University questions this emphasis on "realism" and suggests instead that Wilson took the nation to war to preserve American principles. Finally, Otis L. Graham, Jr., of the University of California at Santa Barbara does not think the United States should have entered the war, is skeptical about Wilson's "realism," and suggests that the best way to have ensured American security was not war abroad, but an intensification of the progressive reform movement at home. He discusses some alternative policies that he suggests might have prevented American entry into World War I.

Realism and National Security

DANIEL M. SMITH

In recent years historians have examined closely the role of national self-interest in propelling the United States into World War I. For two decades after that war ended, the scholarly debate was centered on the question of whether the country had been genuinely neutral in 1914–1917, with the defenders of the Wilson administration contending that hostilities had resulted only because of German submarine attacks on American rights and lives on the high seas, while critics ("revisionists") attributed involvement to the administration's allegedly unneutral policies favoring the Allied cause. The coming of World War II, when the Axis powers posed a manifest threat to American security and national values, suggested the need for a reevaluation of the causes of the earlier strug-

Daniel M. Smith, *The Great Departure: The United States and World War I, 1914–1920* (New York: John Wiley & Sons, 1965), pp. 9–15, 18–21, 24–27, 80–82. Copyright © 1965 by John Wiley & Sons, Inc. Reprinted by permission of John Wiley & Sons, Inc.

gle. Wartime books, like Walter Lippmann's *U. S. Foreign Policy: Shield of the Republic,* reinterpreted the decision for war in 1917 as necessitated by the German challenge to Anglo-American control of the north Atlantic and to the security of the United States in the Western Hemisphere. A decisive German victory would have supplanted British with German naval power and would have constituted a real and immediate danger to North America. Since 1945 a number of scholars have reexamined President Wilson's foreign policies and have inquired into the role of considerations of the national economic and security interests in the decision for war. The answers reveal that realistic concepts of the national interests were held by Wilson and his principal advisers and were involved to a degree in the formulation of basic neutrality policies and the ultimate transition to belligerency.

In the years after the Spanish-American War, a number of influential Americans began to view Germany as a dynamic and imperialistic power potentially dangerous to the United States. Both countries were relatively new to the ranks of great world powers, and were rapidly industrializing and seeking overseas markets and coaling stations. A measure of rivalry was virtually inescapable. During the war with Spain, the German government had indicated a definite interest in acquiring a share of the Philippine Islands in case the United States relinquished them, and the conduct of the German naval squadron observing American military operations in Manila Bay gave rise to a legend of a hostile plot to intervene in Spain's behalf. After the brief war, some American naval and army officers were convinced that German economic and territorial ambitions constituted a threat to the nation's security and its hegemony in Latin America. The Navy General Board in 1901 emphasized the imperative necessity of controlling the Caribbean Sea and the approaches to the Panama Canal, and opposed acquisition of territory in the area by any foreign power as a menace to American security. The Board recommended purchase of the Danish West Indies, since "In view of the isthmian canal and the German settlements in South America, every additional acquisition by the United States in the West Indies is of value." Rumors of alleged German attempts to acquire naval bases in the Galapagos Islands and in Haiti brought repeated objections by the military departments to the State Department in 1910–1912. The vital Panama Canal, nearing completion, would be endangered by such foreign lodgments.

During these years, naval planners contended that Germany and Japan offered the most serious potential danger to American interests. The navy, therefore, should be sufficiently enlarged to cope with all eventualities. The Navy League of the United States, founded by civilian enthusiasts in 1902 with Navy Department approval and patterned after European organizations, clamored for a larger navy to cope with threats to the Monroe Doctrine. Germany was viewed as the principal challenger of that sacred national policy and the press releases of the Navy League pointed out the ominous portents of American naval inferiority to the Kaiser's fleets. Although its efforts were only moderately successful, a recurrent theme of the League's publications prior to 1914 was the possible German menace to American security. The Navy General Board concurred and a confidential estimate in 1910 depicted Germany as thwarted in its expansionist drives both in the Pacific and in Latin America: "it is seen that there are latent causes that render a break with Germany more probable than with either of the other two great maritime powers. . . ." The War Department shared these views and drafted plans for repelling a German attack on North America. A War College paper in 1909–1910 described Germany as surpassing the United States in many areas of economic competition in Latin America and the Far East and as colonizing extensively in Brazil in an apparently well-planned move. Because France and Great Britain had preempted most of Africa and the United States had blocked expansion in the Far East and Latin America, the author of the paper concluded that "while war may never result between the United States and Germany yet the student of history must recognize the existence of causes [economic] which tend to produce it. . . ."

Apprehension of Germany existed outside military circles. A. T. Mahan, advocate of naval expansion, published books and articles on America's interest in seapower and in the world balance of power. Theodore Roosevelt and members of his circle were greatly influenced by Mahan's realistic appraisals of world politics and his emphasis on an Anglo-American community of interest. Roosevelt wrote his friend Henry Cabot Lodge in 1901 that only Germany might be "a menace to us in anything like the immediate future," whereas "we are closer to her [England] than to any other nation; and . . . probably her interest and ours will run on rather parallel lines in the future." His friends Henry and Brooks Adams concurred that Anglo-American interests coincided, with the United States probably destined eventually to assume the leadership as British power slowly deteriorated.

Other informed citizens also began to view Germany as a potential enemy, while envisioning Great Britain with its sea power as fulfilling a benevolent and protective role. The editors of the *New York Times,* after 1898, advocated closer ties with England as the one great power that shared a community of interests with America, and they called for at least naval parity with Germany. American periodicals from time to time carried articles expressing great distrust of German ambitions as they affected the Western Hemisphere. Comparisons of the German and American navies were occasionally made. *Munsey's Magazine* in 1901 recommended increased naval construction and cooperation with Great Britain to meet the German challenge to the new world.

Articles from English journals on the same themes were reprinted in American periodicals. One of the most prophetic essays was written by an Indiana University professor of political science, Amos S. Hershey, in 1909 for *The Independent.* Professor Hershey depicted Germany as endangering both world peace and American economic and security interests, and he urged that the menace be countered by the formation of an Anglo-American alliance. If an Anglo-German war should occur, he predicted that America could hardly remain neutral if Germany seemed about to triumph and to wrest naval supremacy from Great Britain: "A blockade of the British Isles by German cruisers and submarine mines, or the loss involved in the dangers to contraband trade would be severely felt in this country." Writing in the same year, the well-known English commentator Sydney Brooks noted that a growing number of Americans were aware that isolationism was no longer feasible and that Germany was as much an American as a British problem. In a war between England and

Germany, he concluded that the United States would be benevolently neutral toward the British cause and might enter the struggle if Germany threatened to halt the export of American foodstuffs to the British Isles. On the eve of the great war, the American career diplomat Lewis Einstein joined this small group of writers in emphasizing the importance to the United States of a friendly British naval power and the dangers that would ensue if Germany achieved naval supremacy. In an article entitled "The United States and Anglo-German Rivalry," published anonymously in Britain in 1913, Einstein examined the probable results of a German victory, which he believed would affect adversely American economic and political interests in the Caribbean and the Far East. He predicted that the United States might find it necessary to intervene in order to prevent a British defeat and the consequent creation of an unfavorable balance of power.

The outbreak of war in 1914 enhanced the belief of a number of citizens that the national interest required an Allied victory. Editorials and letters in the *New York Times,* and several articles by historians George Louis Beer, George Burton Adams, and Albert Bushnell Hart, contended that security and maintenance of the Monroe Doctrine required the preservation of British naval supremacy. To Beer, "German ambitions in South America have been dormant only because the British fleet was an insuperable barrier. . . . Similar dangers threaten our economic interests in the Far East." Hart pointed out the nation's stake in the existing world equipoise, which affected the country's ability to defend the Monroe Doctrine: "Peace can be maintained only by convincing Germany and Japan, which are the two Powers most likely to be moved by an ambition to possess American territory." To Adams, apart from valid idealistic and ideological factors, "political and military expediency" justified intervention to preclude a German triumph over the Allies. A sweeping German success would leave no power in Europe able to restrain its ambitions; the United States at the minimum would have to exist in a hostile world as a result and probably would face direct Teutonic challenges. Other well-known scholars and commentators, such as Walter Lippmann of the *New Republic,* presented papers on these themes at the 1916 assembly of the American Academy of Political and Social Science. Books and articles by H. H. Powers, Roland G. Usher, and Hudson Maxim also warned of the dangers of a German victory.

The great majority of Americans, however, were not accustomed to the contemplation of foreign policy based on realistic appraisals of economic and political interests. Instead, popular reactions in 1914–1917 largely reflected traditional isolationist attitudes, modified by some emotional and ideological sympathy with the Allies. It is clear, nevertheless, that for over a decade a minority of informed citizens had been exposed to repeated warnings that an aggressive Germany potentially endangered an Anglo-American community of interests. They had come to view Great Britain as the bulwark standing between the Western Hemisphere and Europe, whose removal would expose the United States to great peril. Such views were particularly prevalent in the eastern part of the United States, and were held by people with considerable influence in the molding of public opinion. Existence of these attitudes and convictions made it inestimably easier to condemn Germany on moral and idealistic grounds and probably facilitated the ultimate entry into war.

The most influential advisers of President Wilson shared a "realistic" appraisal of the significance of the European war for the United States. Robert Lansing, counselor of the State Department and its second in command, presidential adviser Edward M. House, and ambassadors Walter Hines Page in London and James W. Gerard in Berlin, together with several cabinet members, fused pro-Ally sentiments and ideological considerations with apprehensions that a German victory would affect adversely American economic and political interests. . . .

A descendant of a distinguished New York family and trained in international law, Lansing had traveled extensively abroad and by 1914 had participated in more international arbitrations than probably any other living American. As a result of training and experience, he was eminently practical and "hard-headed" in his approach to world affairs and questions of foreign policy. Although he shared the American faith in the efficacy and future of democracy and as a devout Presbyterian believed in the moral imperative, Lansing recognized that amoral physical power was the underlying reality in international relations. Moral law did and should govern domestic society, but unfortunately relations between states were characterized by materialistic and selfish motives and conflicts usually were resolved by violence. In essence a nation dealt with other nations in a savage manner, regardless of how enlightened the conduct of its domestic affairs might be. To assume otherwise, to believe that foreign policy should be founded solely on altruistic motives, was fallacious and a grave error. Idealism had an important place in American foreign policy but it needed to be harmonized with common sense.

The initial response of Lansing to the war was one of relief that his country was spared the waste and sufferings of the conflict. Yet he was pro-Ally from the first, in part because of emotional and cultural attachments to Great Britain, and in part because of his conviction that the Allies represented the democratic impulse against the aggressive autocracy of the Central powers. He assumed, as many others, that the war would soon end in an Allied triumph, and at first he concentrated on perfecting American neutrality. By early 1915, however, he perceived that the war would be a long and bitter one seriously affecting the economic and political interests of the United States. Submarine warfare, a novel and rude challenge to trade and past international practices, seemed to Lansing to portend a possible German victory. The destruction of British passenger liners with American travelers aboard removed all doubt from his mind and underscored America's interest in the outcome of the war. Germany, he believed, was a very real danger to American ideals and to its economic interests and security.

On July 11, 1915, a few days after he had succeeded Bryan as secretary of state, Lansing recorded in his private notebook his views on policy:

I have come to the conclusion that the German Government is utterly hostile to all nations with democratic institutions because those who compose it see in democracy a menace to absolutism and the defeat of the German ambition for world domination. Everywhere German agents are plotting and intriguing to accomplish the supreme purpose of their Government. . . . Germany must not be permitted to win this war and to break even, though to prevent it this country is forced to take an active part. This ultimate necessity must be constantly in our minds in all our controversies with the belligerents. . . .

If Germany should win, the United States would be confronted with a hostile naval power threatening its interests in the Caribbean, in Latin America generally, and perhaps in the Far East as well. The United States had already experienced sharp controversies with an expansionist Japan, frequently rumored to be on the verge of deserting the Allies and realigning with the Central powers. Lansing could envision, therefore, the possibility of a future grand alliance between the three autocratic empires of Germany, Russia, and Japan, which would isolate the United States in a menacing world.

The new secretary was also imbued with the American faith in democracy and its eventual universal triumph. Democratic states were inherently peace-loving, he believed, because the ordinary citizen presumably never desires war and its costly sacrifices, which fall heaviest on the average man, whereas autocratic states with dynastic rivalries were basically aggressive and militaristic. From the point of view of Lansing and others similarly inclined, imperial Germany, the leading representative of a militaristic and statist philosophy, could be said to be a triple threat to the United States: ideologically it menaced democratic institutions and values, militarily it endangered the nation's security, and it was the most serious rival of the United States for economic and political influence in Latin America. To cope with these dangers, Lansing resolved to endeavor to watch carefully German activity in Latin America, especially in turbulent Mexico and the Caribbean area, to take steps to forestall possible German acquisition of bases by American purchase of the Danish West Indies (done in 1916–1917), to keep the submarine issue clearly defined, and to enter the war if it became necessary to avert a Teutonic victory.

Although ideological factors figured prominently in Lansing's thought, at least as important were considerations of the country's economic and security needs. In his private memoranda he repeatedly recorded the conviction that a German conquest in Europe would dangerously expose the United States. On the eve of America's entry into the war, he wrote: "The Allies must *not* be beaten. It would mean the triumph of Autocracy over Democracy; the shattering of all our moral standards; and a real, though it may seem remote, peril to our independence and institutions." In 1915–1916, however, he appreciated the fact that public opinion was divided, with pacifist and isolationist traditions still strong, and that the president was most reluctant to contemplate actual hostilities. Insofar as he was able, therefore, he tried to shape the American course so that dangerous disputes with the Allies would be avoided, while the submarine issue was clearly delineated and the American people were slowly prepared by events for the great leap into belligerency. Lansing usually did not speak to Wilson directly of his belief that the nation's vital self-interests required preparation for war, but with an understanding of the presidential psychology he instead used moralistic and legalistic arguments

to justify what he viewed as the correct policy. Often working in close cooperation with the similarly inclined Colonel House, Lansing was able to achieve
a large measure of influence on Wilsonian foreign policy.

Other officials within the State Department and the foreign service held
comparable views on the meaning of the war. James Brown Scott, William
Phillips, and Frank L. Polk (later undersecretary) were also pro-Ally in
sympathies and were persuaded that a German triumph would endanger
America. Chandler P. Anderson, a legal adviser on problems of neutrality,
remarked after a discussion with Lansing of a recent German note that it was
surly in tone and "a good example of the sort of lecturing and regulating that
all nations might expect if Germany succeeded in its ambition to rule the
world." From London, Ambassador Walter Hines Page sought to convince
Wilson and top administration figures that Britain's fight against Germany
was in the best interests of the United States. Only if the Allies won, he wrote,
would a favorable power balance be preserved in the Far East and in the
Atlantic. Ambassador James W. Gerard in Berlin had similar apprehensions
and predicted that if the Central powers emerged victorious "we are next on
their list." . . .

President Wilson entered office surprisingly uninformed about foreign
affairs. What was striking about this was not its novelty, since most presidents
after the Civil War had been similarly ill-equipped, but was, as Arthur Link
has pointed out, that it should have been true of Wilson, a professional historian and political scientist, author of a number of books and former president
of Princeton University. Yet his publications indicated little interest in foreign
affairs, and prior to 1898 he had written of diplomatic problems and machinery
as almost a minor aspect of government. After the "passing" of the frontier
and the Spanish-American War, he like others was made aware that the isolation of the nineteenth century was no longer possible and that the nation would
perforce play an ever larger role in world affairs. Nothing indicated, however,
that his knowledge and interest in international relations was more than per-
functory and superficial. In an oft-quoted remark, on the eve of his presidential inauguration, Wilson confessed to a friend that his primary interests
were in domestic reform and that it would be "the irony of fate" if he should
be compelled to concentrate on foreign affairs.

Wilson has been described by many scholars as primarily an idealist unresponsive to practical considerations in foreign relations and as unusually
independent of his pro-Ally advisers in shaping America's course during the
great war. Later studies have substantially modified such estimates. He was
deeply moralistic in his approach, the result of being steeped in Calvinistic piety
and training during his youth. Idealism usually meant for him, however, not
the ignoring of practical considerations but the exalting of noble purposes
and goals. He has been aptly described [by Arthur S. Link] as a "romantic
moralist, who . . . raised every issue and conflict to a high stage. . . ." He was
capable of sometimes being blinded to reality by his faith and goals, as was
painfully clear after the 1919 peace conference, but in the neutrality period
his moralistic impulses usually were reenforced rather than contradicted by
practical considerations of the national interest. Recent historians have re-

vealed also that Wilson was by no means impervious to the counsel of his close advisers and that he shared to a degree their analyses of the meaning of the war to America's economic, security, and ideological interests.

When the war began, Wilson's first reactions were based on emotional sympathy for England and its allies, and he tended to attribute to Germany primary responsibility for beginning the struggle. Within a few months, however, he had recovered emotional balance and had come to realize that the causes of the war were complex and that guilt was more evenly distributed than he had at first suspected. Yet he remained sympathetic toward the Allies, especially Great Britain and its leaders in whom he had much trust and whom he long believed were pursuing more reasonable goals than were the other belligerents. He also came to appreciate the view that a decisive German victory would pose some danger for the United States. He indicated agreement with House that "if Germany won it would change the course of our civilization and make the United States a military nation." Later in the fall of 1914, he told his private secretary Joseph Tumulty, that he would not pressure England to a dangerous point on the issue of neutral rights because Britain was fighting for the life of the world. During the *Arabic* crisis in mid-1915, he surprised House by stating that he had never been certain that America would not have to intervene in order to prevent a German victory. In 1916, in an effort to promote greater defensive military preparedness, Wilson repeatedly revealed in his public addresses serious concern for the national security and the long-range safety of Latin America. In these speeches he justified heavier expenditures on the army and navy as necessitated in part to protect American trade on the high seas and to avert possible dangers to the Western Hemisphere. Thus at Pittsburgh he asked rhetorically:

> What is it that we want to defend? . . . We want to defend the life of this Nation against any sort of interference. We want to maintain the equal right of this Nation as against the action of all other nations, and we wish to maintain the peace and unity of the Western Hemisphere.

Again, at Cleveland, he warned his audience that the United States "must play her part in keeping this conflagration from spreading to the people of the United States; she must also keep this conflagration from spreading on this side of the sea. These are matters in which our very life and our whole pride are embedded. . . ."

It must be emphasized, however, that in general Wilson did not believe that a German victory, undesirable though it would be, would pose an immediate threat to the United States. Like most of his fellow citizens, he was confident of an eventual Allied triumph. But if the opposite should result, he thought that Germany probably would be too weakened by the European war to offer more than a future menace to the security of the Western Hemisphere. He remarked to a sceptical Colonel House, in late 1914, that Germany would need at least several years for recuperation before it could undertake a direct challenge to the United States. He adopted policies, therefore, which protected those national interests that were immediately affected by the war (commerce, legal rights, and prestige), and relied upon such measures as purchase of the Danish West Indies and increased military preparations to ward off future dangers to the national security and to the Monroe Doctrine. He was long convinced, in fact, that neutrality was the wisest course for America and that peace without victory for either belligerent side would alone make possible a just and stable postwar world. The mission of the United States, therefore, was to stand as a bastion of liberty and peace, and to serve all mankind by helping to mediate this terrible struggle whenever events proved favorable. Not until early 1917, after the failure of his two peace overtures and the renewal of submarine warfare, did he accept the necessity for intervention in the war. . . .

American involvement in World War I, as in most other wars, defies simplistic explanations. In the 1930's the historical debate was polarized into the "submarine school," best represented by Charles Seymour, and the "revisionists," with Charles C. Tansill as the most effective spokesman. Seymour dismissed political and economic factors as at most peripheral causes of the war entry and instead emphasized the submarine challenge to American rights and lives. Tansill overlooked security aspects of the war and emphasized American unneutrality, the economic and sentimental ties to the Allies, as pulling the United States into conflict. Neither approach suffices to explain so complex an event. Seymour probably was right in the contention that there would have been no war without the submarine issue, for otherwise Germany and America would not have had a direct clash of interests and power. But the U-boat challenge alone does not explain why the United States adopted the strict accountability policy, since other alternatives were at least theoretically possible. As for the revisionist charges of unneutrality, it seems clear that American neutrality in fact was benevolent toward the Allies and grudgingly technical toward Germany. This did not result from deliberate planning, however, but rather from previous emotional and cultural affinities and from wartime economic connections with the Allies. In any case, Germany did not launch unrestricted submarine warfare merely from anger at the United States or just to cut off the arms trade. Although a different American posture perhaps could have influenced German policy along a more moderate course, the final decision for full underseas warfare was undertaken as the best remaining hope for decisive victory over the Allies through starving Britain into submission.

Just as clearly the hypothesis that the United States went to war in 1917 primarily to protect an endangered security against an immediate threat is not satisfactory. Although Lansing and House, and occasionally Wilson, thought of Germany as a menace to American security and stability, it was primarily as a future danger rather than an imminent peril. Yet Wilson was indeed far more practical in his policies and thinking than many scholars formerly believed, and he sought to promote the national interests as he envisioned them. Aided by his advisers, who exerted considerable influence on him, Wilson adopted policies that embodied economic and prestige interests, as well as moral considerations. The tacit acquiescence in the war trade and the permission of credits and loans to the belligerents reflected primarily economic interests; whereas the strict accountability policy toward U-boat warfare combined economic and moralistic factors with a desire to uphold the nation's prestige and honor as essential to any worthwhile diplomatic endeavors in the future including mediation of the war. Thus policies toward the Allies were favorable or benevolent because America's basic interests were essentially compatible with British control of the seas and Allied utilization of the American market. The course adopted toward Germany, on the other hand, was firmly nonacquiescent. Submarine warfare endangered American economic connections with Europe and as well violated moral sensibilities and affronted the national honor.

Among high administration officials, Lansing appears to have held the clearest conviction that American security would be endangered by a German triumph and that intervention in the struggle might be necessary—by late 1916 he believed it *was* necessary—to prevent that possibility. Although he sometimes indicated complete concurrence with Lansing's views, Colonel House believed that the most desirable culmination of the war would be enough of an Allied victory to check German ambitions but with Germany left sufficiently strong to play its proper role in the balance of power and to check Russian expansionism. A desire to preserve the balance of power, in the sense of ending the war short of victory for either side, was a factor behind the mediation plans of House and Wilson in 1915 and 1916.

Why did the reluctant president finally decide that belligerency was the only possible answer to unrestricted U-boat warfare? Why did he not rest content with the diplomatic rupture, or with armed neutrality or a limited naval war? The answer seems to have been that the prestige and honor of the nation were so committed as the result of previous policies that nothing less than a diplomatic break and a forceful defense of American interests were possible. By 1917 the evidence suggests that Wilson feared that a German victory was probable and that it would disturb the world balance, and although he was not apprehensive about an immediate threat to the United States, he did believe that such a result would endanger his idealistic hopes for a just peace and the founding of a new and stable world order. He referred to Germany as a madman who must be restrained. He finally accepted the necessity for actively entering the war, it would appear, with the submarine as the precipitant, only because he believed that larger reasons of national prestige, economic interests, and future security so demanded, and above all because of his commitment to the cause of an enduring world peace.

In Defense of Rights and Honor

ROSS GREGORY

In light of the controversy which later surrounded America's entry into the First World War, and the momentous effect that war had on the future of the world, it seems appropriate here to offer some final observations about

Reprinted from *The Origins of American Intervention in the First World War* by Ross Gregory. By permission of W. W. Norton & Company, Inc. Copyright © 1971 by W. W. Norton & Company, Inc.

Wilsonian diplomacy and the factors responsible for intervention. Wilson asked Congress to declare war in 1917 because he felt Germany had driven him to it. He could find no way, short of an unthinkable abandonment of rights and interests, to avoid intervention. He briefly had tried armed neutrality, and as he said in the war message, that tactic had not done the job. Germany was making war on the United States, and Wilson had no reasonable alternative to a declaration of hostilities. Hence submarine warfare must bear the immediate responsibility for provoking the decision for war. It nonetheless is not enough to say that the United States went to war simply because of the submarines, or that the events of January–March 1917 alone determined the fate of the United States, for a number of factors helped bring the nation to that point where it seemed impossible to do anything else. During the period of neutrality the American government made certain decisions, avoided others, found itself pulled one way or another by national sentiment and need and by the behavior of the belligerent nations.

Any account of American intervention would go amiss without some reference to the pro-Ally nature of American neutrality. American money and supplies allowed the Allies to sustain the war effort. While Wilson did not act openly partial to the Allies, he did promote American economic enterprise and declined to interfere—indeed showed no signs of dismay—when the enterprise developed in ways that were beneficial to Britain and France. Although Wilson did experience a considerable hardening of attitude toward the Allies in 1916 (his major advisers did not), he could not bring himself to limit the provisioning of Britain and France; and it was this traffic that brought on submarine warfare. Without American assistance to the Allies, Germany would have had no reason to adopt policy injurious to the interests of the United States.

There were several reasons why American policy functioned in a manner which favored the Allies. The first was a matter of circumstances: Britain controlled the sea, and the Allies were in desperate need of American products —conditions which assured that most American trade would go to Britain and France. The second factor was an assumption by much of the American population, most members of the administration, and the president that the political and material well-being of the United States was associated with preservation of Britain and France as strong, independent states. Germany unintentionally confirmed the assumption with the invasion of Belgium, use of submarines, and war tactics in general. While pro-Ally feeling was tempered by a popular desire to stay out of the conflict and by the president's wish to remain fair and formally neutral, it was sufficiently strong to discourage any policy that would weaken the Allied war effort. House, Lansing, and Page were so partial to the Allies that they acted disloyally to the president. Wilson frequently complained about Britain's intolerable course; he sent notes of protest and threatened to do more. He grumbled about Page's bias for the British and questioned the usefulness of his ambassador in Britain. Yet he did nothing to halt Britain's restrictions on trade with continental Europe, and Page stayed on in London until the end of the war. Wilson declined to press the British because he feared that such action would increase Germany's chances of winning and lead to drastic economic repercussions in the United States. Favoritism for the Allies did not cause the United States to go to war with Germany. It did help create those conditions of 1917 in which war seemed the only choice.

The United States (or much of the population) preferred that Britain and France not collapse, and the nation was equally anxious that Germany not succeed, at least not to the extent of dominating Europe. A prewar suspicion of German militarism and autocratic government, and accounts, during the war, of "uncivilized" German warfare influenced Wilson and a majority of the American people to believe that the United States faced an evil world force, that in going to war with Germany the nation would be striking a blow for liberty and democracy. This general American attitude toward the war of 1914–18 probably influenced Wilson's decision to resist submarine warfare, and thus affected his neutrality policies. More important, it made the decision to intervene seem all the more noble and did much to determine the way the United States, once it became belligerent, prosecuted the war. It was not, however, the major reason for accepting intervention. For all the popular indignation over the invasion of Belgium and other allegedly atrocious German warfare, there still did not develop in the United States a large movement for intervention. Even in 1917 Wilson showed the utmost reluctance to bring the nation into the war. Americans evidently were willing to endure German brutality, although they did not like it, as long as it did not affect their interests; and one must wonder what the American response—and the response of the president—would have been had no Americans been aboard the *Lusitania*. Wilson's vilification on April 2 of the German political system was more a means of sanctifying the cause than a reason for undertaking it. He was a curious crusader. Before April 1917 he would not admit that there was a need for America to take up the sword of righteousness. Against his will he was driven to the barricades, but once he was in the streets he became the most thorough and enthusiastic of street fighters.

The most important influence on the fate of the United States 1914–17 was the nation's world position. National need and interests were such that it was nearly impossible to avoid the problems which led the nation into war. Even if the administration had maintained a rigidly neutral position and forced Britain to respect all maritime rights of the United States, it is doubtful that the result would have been different. Grey testified that Britain would have yielded rather than have serious trouble with the United States, which means that, faced with American pressure, Britain would have allowed a larger amount of American trade through to Germany. This was the most the Germans could have expected from the United States, and it would not have affected the contraband trade with the Allies. Germany used submarines not because of the need to obtain American supplies, but from a desire to prevent the Allies from getting them.

The course that would have guaranteed peace for the United States was unacceptable to the American people and the Wilson administration. Only by severing all its European ties could the nation obtain such a guarantee. In

1914 that act would have placed serious strain on an economy that already showed signs of instability; by 1916 it would have been economically disastrous. At any time it would have been of doubtful political feasibility, even if one were to premise American popular disinterest in who won the war. The British understood this fact and reacted accordingly. If such thoughts suggest that the United States was influenced by the needs of an expanding capitalist economy, so let it be. It is by no means certain that another economic structure would have made much difference.

One might argue that measures short of a total embargo, a different arrangement of neutral practices—for instance, stoppage of the munitions traffic, and/or a ban on American travel on belligerent ships—would have allowed a profitable, humane, yet nonprovocative trade with Europe. Though a reply to that contention can offer no stronger claim to truth than the contention itself, one can offer these points: Wilson argued that yielding one concession on the seas ultimately would lead to pressure to abandon all rights. The pragmatic behavior of belligerents, especially the Germans, makes that assessment seem fair. Lest the German chancellor appear a hero to opponents of American intervention, it is well to remember that Bethmann's views on submarine warfare were not fashioned by love of the United States, or by the agony of knowing his submarines were sending innocent victims to their death. He was guided by simple national interest and the desire to use submarines as fully as circumstances allowed. It also is worth noting that Germany, when it reopened submarine warfare in 1917, was interested not merely in sinking munitions ships, but wanted to prevent all products going to Britain and was especially anxious to halt shipments of food. Had the United States wished to consider Bryan's proposals, keeping people and property out of the danger zone, it would have been easier early in the war, perhaps in February 1915, than after the sinkings began, and above all after the *Lusitania* went down. Yielding in the midst of the *Lusitania* crisis involved nothing short of national humiliation. If Bryan's proposals would have eliminated the sort of incident that provoked intervention, they also would have required a huge sacrifice— too great, as it turned out, for Wilson to accept. The United States would have faced economic loss, loss of national prestige, and probably the eventual prospect of a Europe dominated by Hindenburg, Ludendorff, and Wilhelm II.

No less than the nation as a whole, Wilson found himself accountable for the world standing of the United States. He felt a need and an obligation to promote economic interests abroad. When dealing with Germany he usually spoke in terms of principle; in relations with the Allies he showed awareness of practical considerations. In the hectic days of August 1914, he took steps to get American merchant ships back to sea. In the summer of 1915, advisers alerted him to the financial strain Britain had come to experience, the weakening of the pound sterling and the need to borrow funds in the United States. The secretary of the treasury recommended approval of foreign loans. "To maintain our prosperity we must finance it," he said. Lansing, who believed similarly, wrote the president: "If the European countries cannot find the means to pay for the excess of goods sold them over those purchased from them, they will have to stop buying and our present export trade will shrink proportionately. The result will be restriction of output, industrial depression, idle capital, idle labor, numerous failures, financial demoralization, and general unrest and suffering among the laboring masses." Shortly afterward the administration acquiesced as the House of Morgan floated loans of $500 million for the British and French governments. War traffic with the Allies prompted the German attempt to stop it with submarines. Submarine warfare led to destruction of property and loss of American lives. What had started as efforts to promote prosperity and neutral rights developed into questions of national honor and prestige. Wilson faced not merely the possibility of abandoning economic rights but the humiliating prospect of allowing the Germans to force him to it. The more hazardous it became to exercise American rights, the more difficult it was to yield them.

Wilson's definition of right and honor was itself conditioned by the fact that he was president of the United States and not some less powerful nation. His estimate of what rights belonged to the United States, what was for belligerents fair and humane warfare, rested not simply on a statement of principle, but on the power of the United States to compel observance of these principles. He could not send demands to the German government without some reason for believing the Germans would obey. Interpretation of national honor varies with national economic and military strength. The more powerful the nation, the more the world expects of it and the more the nation expects of itself. Such small seafaring states as Denmark and the Netherlands suffered extensive losses from submarine warfare, and yet these governments did not feel themselves honor bound to declare war. Wilson credited his right to act as a mediator to his position as leader of the most powerful neutral state. Indeed, he sometimes felt obligated to express moral principle. He could not, and would not, have acted these ways had he been, let us say, president of the Dominican Republic. It is thus possible to say that despite Wilson's commanding personality, his heavy-handedness in foreign policy and flair for self-righteousness, American diplomacy in final analysis was less a case of the man guiding affairs of the nation than the nation, and belligerent nations, guiding the affairs of the man.

It is tempting to conclude that inasmuch as the United States was destined to enter the conflict, it might as well have accepted that fact and reacted accordingly. Presumably this response would have involved an earlier declaration of war, certainly a large and rapid rearmament program. In recent years some "realist" scholars, notably George F. Kennan, have considered that this course would have been practical. However wise that policy might have been, it did not fit conditions of the period of neutrality. Wilson opposed entering the war earlier, and had he thought differently, popular and congressional support were highly questionable. People did not know in 1914 that commercial relations would lead them into the World War; most of them believed during the entire period that they could have trade and peace at the same time. The body of the United States was going one way during the period of neutrality, its heart and mind another. For a declaration of war there needed to be a merging of courses.

Then, too, it was not absolutely certain that the United States had to enter the conflict, for the nation after all did avoid intervention for over two and one-half years, two-thirds of the war's fighting time. That same strength which eventually brought the nation into the war for a while helped it avoid intervention. From this perspective the campaign for mediation might have represented some of Wilson's soundest thinking. German officials never were certain about American strength, and the longer they had to endure a costly, indecisive conflict, the more they were willing to consider the type of gamble taken in 1917. American intervention was all but certain unless the United States made a drastic change in policy—which, as we have seen, it was unwilling to do— or unless someone beforehand brought the war to an end. It incidentally also seems fair to say that an indecisive settlement, a "peace without victory," would have better served the interests of the United States, not to mention the interests of the world, than the vindictive treaty drawn up in 1919. These thoughts, of course, are hindsight, but it is ironic that Wilson made the same observations weeks before the United States entered the war. . . .

One of the most provocative features of Wilsonian diplomacy was the president's apparent obsession with moral principle and international law. To critics this tendency suggested blindness to realistic goals, ignorance of the way nations deal with one another, if not a profession of personal superiority. In some ways the critics were right. Wilson was dedicated to principle. He thought the old system of interstate relations was unsatisfactory and looked to a time when nations would find rules to govern relations among themselves no less effective than laws within individual states. He wished to have a large part in making those rules. His propensity to quibble about shipments of cargo and techniques of approaching ships at sea seemed a ridiculous and remote abstraction at a time when the fate of nations hung in balance. It was naïve to expect nations to respect legal principles when they had so much at stake. If they obeyed Wilson's command, their obedience was due less to principle than to his nation's ability to retaliate. At the same time international law was to Wilson more than an ideal; it was a manifestation of neutral intent and a device for defining American neutrality. Unless the United States decided to declare war or to stay out of the mess entirely, it would have to deal with complicated questions of neutral rights. International law was not merely convenient, it was the only device available. There fortunately was no conflict between Wilsonian principle and American rights and needs—the principle could be used to uphold the need. That the United States found an attraction for international law is not surprising: the restraints the law placed on belligerents would benefit any nation wishing to engage in neutral wartime commerce. International law looked to an orderly international society, and the United States, a satisfied nation, would profit from order. The chaos of 1914–17 strengthened feeling in the United States that American interests coincided with world interests, or, put another way, that what was good for the United States was good for the world.

Even so, it is not adequate to say that Wilson was a realist who clothed practical considerations with moral rhetoric. He was both practical and idealistic, at least during the period of American neutrality. If he believed that upholding principle would advance American interests, he also hoped that promoting American interests would serve the cause of international morality. By demonstrating that the United States would not condone brutality, disorder, and lawlessness, he hoped to set a standard for other nations to follow. Wilson wanted to help reform the world, but he would have settled for protecting the interests of the United States and keeping the nation at peace.

Evidence from various quarters supports these final conclusions: there is no indication that Wilson went to war to protect American loans to the Allies and large business interests, although these interests, and economic factors in general, helped bring the United States to a point where war seemed unavoidable. There is no evidence that Wilson asked for war to prevent the defeat of Britain and France. It could well have been, as several scholars have written, that preservation of Britain and France was vital to the interests of the United States. American neutrality, incidentally or by design, functioned to sustain that thesis. Even so, Wilson did not intervene to prevent these nations' collapse; the Allies, while not winning, were not on the verge of losing in the spring of 1917. Nor did Wilson go to war to preserve American security. This is not to say that he was not concerned with security; he simply did not see it in jeopardy. The president did ask his countrymen for war as a means of protecting American honor, rights, and general interest—for both moral and practical reasons. He saw no contradiction between the two. But Wilson's idea of right and interest grew out of what the nation was at the time, and the First World War made clear what had been true for some years: the United States was in all respects a part of the world, destined to profit from its riches and suffer from its woes.

Wilson's Wrong Choices

OTIS L. GRAHAM, JR.

This desire to end the emotional and political division of the country was prominent among the factors leading Wilson to ask for war. Now, with the step taken, the war required unity for its prosecution. The wave of relief and enthusiasm that greeted his war message could not be expected to last beyond a few days. The articulate people who had never believed that the issues between Europeans were worth one American life would surely not be silenced by the Declaration of War by Congress. And their arguments might have a certain effect: we were not under attack, no official person had declared that our national security was in jeopardy, we would have to travel thousands of miles even to become involved in the war, and the war was sure to have its unpleasant

Otis L. Graham, Jr., *The Great Campaigns: Reform and War in America, 1900–1928,* © 1971, pp. 85–96. Reprinted by permission of Prentice-Hall, Inc., Englewood Cliffs, New Jersey.

costs, particularly in lives and money. To preserve a workable majority against such divisive thoughts would require that the war have a powerful, simple, emotionally appealing, and durable justification. Wilson may have asked for war, as a leading historian has said, because he had no other choice, but it would not do to attempt to prepare the nation for its exertions with such flimsy stuff. In April, 1917, and for the months ahead, the entry of the nation into the European war must have an explanation to enlist the energies and loyalties of a democratic people—simple, emotional, a tiny bit skeptical, deeply romantic. For this task it is impossible to imagine a more appropriate citizen than Woodrow Wilson. At calling men to sacrifice, at simplifying the complex, at extracting principle from secular confusion, no man of that generation was his equal. He understood from the start the need for public education of the most dramatic effectiveness (although he had some doubts of its side effects), and made his April 2 address the most impressive justification for American belligerency ever offered.

Wilson's war message . . . repays close reading. His first and presumably chief reason for calling America to arms was to defend the rights of all mankind, now imperiled by German submarine warfare. The human rights under attack were broader than the right to travel safely on the seas even during a world war; they were the rights to peace and justice, of which the present German government had shown itself to be an implacable foe. The United States fought also for ends that were closely related to American self-interest and security, although Wilson did not state the matter quite in those terms—to defend the American form of government against authoritarianism (the Russian Revolution of March made this construction possible), to avoid those naval humiliations that would have eliminated the nation's status as a great power, and to construct a postwar "concert of free peoples as shall bring peace and safety to all nations."

When Wilson left the joint session to a deafening applause, when his old enemy Senator Lodge gripped his hand and thanked him for expressing the "loftiest . . . sentiments of the American people," he must have known that the message was a superb success. He had provided the vocabulary for, and started in motion, that avalanche of "moist and numerous language," to borrow Mr. Dooley's phrase, which informed the American people why they must now become involved in a war that three years, and in some cases even days earlier, they had regarded with disgust. Editorial writers, preachers, stump speakers, teachers, and professors would see to it in the days ahead that the reasons we fought—simple, noble, overwhelming—were communicated throughout the country. The average draftee who was not a close reader of the *New York Times* or the *Congressional Record* now could be expected to understand why we were in the World War, and not to bother himself very much about it. But Wilson's success at framing convincing and communicable goals did as much as anything else to defeat those goals for which he had contended since foreign affairs began to claim so much of his attention in 1914.

It is hard in retrospect to approve either Wilson's timing or his reasoning in the fateful, difficult foreign policy decisions forced on him by the Great War in Europe. He argued that the United States could no longer tolerate non-belligerency because to submit to humiliations would be to permit the destruction of human rights and national prestige. If the national prestige was involved at all it was because he willed it so; neither law, economic necessity, nor tradition required a guarantee of rights of travel on armed belligerent vessels. As for the notion that human rights were somehow in jeopardy if Americans died on the high seas, the less said about that mystical idea the better for Wilson's reputation as an incisive thinker. Yet intelligent men have found reason to defend Wilson's decision to ask for intervention, not as the best of poor alternatives, but as a wise and proper step. In the view of the Realists, armed intervention was justified by a rational calculation of the national interest. America could not tolerate the domination of Europe by an undemocratic, expansionist Germany, and her vital interests now required armed intervention in a European war to secure the balance of power and construct an unprecedented union of nations for collective security. This view of international affairs was held as early as 1914 by men like Lewis Einstein and Walter Lippmann and has been adopted by most scholars since the 1940s. Some feel that Wilson stumbled accidentally onto the right course, others that despite his abstract language about principles, he intuitively understood that a German victory constituted a threat to American security and so conducted American foreign policy as to refuse to permit it. If he did not use phrases like "balance of power" and "American vital interests," it was because he faced a public of implacable naïveté and uninformed idealism, one which could only be motivated to the necessary sacrifices through the thrilling language of Protestant evangelism. But his drive to put himself and his country in a commanding position to mediate was strong from the beginning; it was one of the reasons he finally decided to intervene, and the sort of peace he wished to mediate did bear a close resemblance to the balance-of-power compromise the Realists approve.

Respected scholars have repeatedly made this argument for Wilson's intuitive realism, even though it requires some redefinition of his terminology and some careful scrutiny of the spaces between the lines. But if the president saw that our security was involved in the contest going on in Europe, as a few of his private remarks suggest, he made no effort to explain the matter to the American public. This may be credited to his own uncertainty rather than to political timidity. Wilson proved in the Brandeis appointment and later in the League fight that he was not afraid of political risks. But whether he was a slightly confused half-realist or a secret realist with exaggerated fears of the political risks involved in candor, Wilson spent the years from 1914 to 1917 talking about ideals, rights, and proper naval behavior. When he wrote state papers with his unrivaled eloquence, they were usually for the purpose of educating the Germans in their human and Christian responsibilities, not in educating his countrymen in the hard realities of modern geopolitics. When he asked for military preparedness, a logical step for one who wished his country to be in a position to influence events, he shaped a program of naval rearmament and left the army still puny—exactly what one would do who was in fact concerned with maritime rights rather than with European power dispositions. When he finally asked for intervention, he came across as a pure idealist on a mission of rescue for high, unassailable, but somehow precious ideals.

Guided by their president's words, which were repeated many times by pulpit and press, the boys went to beat the hell out of Germany for sinking our ships and for not being peace loving and democratic. Apparently the thrashing would be educational for the Germans, would produce great moral improvement among them, and would not only restore threatened human rights to their rightful place but would vindicate them forever. The attractiveness of this high enterprise, along with a general boredom, a habit of obedience, and perhaps above all an unrealistic expectation of what war would be like (Wilson himself thought the war would be over in six months and that our part in it would be primarily naval, and he was not alone) was enough to call the nation to arms.

Of course, it is almost certain that he could not have persuaded the country to enter the war for realistic reasons. He could never have convinced an isolationist and parochial society to participate in history's most horrible war for such uninspiring goals as the restoration of the balance of power and the defense of England's security on the novel grounds that both had a close relation to our own *vital* interests. The number of Americans who thought in such terms was so small that the entire group could easily be locked into a White House bathroom. Many wished to declare war, but merely wishing a declaration of war on Germany did not make one a Realist. Even those around the president who favored war did not know until after April that the Allies were in grave danger of losing. They, too, in the days before April 2, had talked of principles and human rights. Wilson himself might have tried over the months from August, 1914, to create a realistic public understanding of the American stake in the war, but no sensible person argues that this would have been enough. Twenty years later another persuasive president tried, and never convinced a majority of his countrymen. But if an effort to achieve limited but attainable goals was ruled out by American tradition and the state of popular education, by what logic does one take the nation into war for goals that are unattainable and in fact hardly coherent, and whose only virtue has not to do with their connection to reality but their ability to move public opinion behind belligerency? Wilson got the country to act, but for the wrong reasons at the wrong time.

There were men, like Theodore Roosevelt, who thought that war had no costs of any consequence, that fighting was in some way a beneficial experience for men and nations. But Wilson was wiser than that. There is an apocryphal story, told by the journalist Frank Cobb, in which Wilson on the eve of the war message predicted that going into the war would cost the country most of the New Freedom gains and much of its internal tolerance and sanity. Although Cobb's story has recently been challenged, we know that Wilson reckoned the costs of war much more realistically than most contemporaries, especially the domestic costs. In addition, he knew that the language and ideas he must employ to create a large, enthusiastic majority out of the refractory isolationists and temporary pacifists who surrounded him would create a type of fervor that would probably make his goals unattainable. For Wilson, whatever his talk of moral absolutes and "force without stint or limit," went to Europe basically to effect a compromise. He remained more interested in diplomacy than in victory, and while he led the nation against the forces of darkness he was sure the guilt in Europe was not all on one side and insisted that the United States be designated an "associated power," not an ally. Three times in his war message he spoke of restraint, of the necessity to fight without passion or vindictiveness. But Americans listened to the Wilson they preferred: the moralist, not the conciliator. To get the nation into the war he had proclaimed war aims that made restrained action and limited involvement impossible and made reaction inevitable among a people who had not been dealt with candidly.

The disappointments he feared—but did not fear enough—came in full measure. Germany was beaten, but she did not learn the moral lessons Wilson intended. If human rights were better off for American entry, no man has yet found a way to measure the improvement. Nor did the American influence at Versailles create a lasting peace. Because we were there, the settlement was a bastard compromise, "fairer" than the one the Germans would have dictated if the United States had not entered, but by no means more conducive to the stability of Europe and the avoidance of the horrors of 1939–45. The democracies won the war, but their victory did not stem the slide of Western civilization into dictatorship and philosophic malaise.

These disappointments came to Wilson's international aspirations, and there is no evidence that he foresaw the possibility of such defeats, although a number of hardened cynics were predicting them. Domestically, the costs of American involvement were far, far beyond even Wilson's relatively astute premonitions: 130,000 American lives lost in combat, 35,000 permanently disabled, approximately 500,000 influenza deaths in the U.S. in the winter of 1918–19 from a virus imported from the battlefields; an expenditure of $33.5 billion by 1919, to which may be added at least the $13 billion spent as of 1931 (according to economist John M. Clark) on veterans' pensions and interest on the war debt; 20 million person-years of labor diverted to war, or six months' work by every American; the 25 race riots of 1919; the stimulus to private indulgence and social irresponsibility; the decimation of the liberal center and the hobbling of the Left.

Such a brief sketch of the high costs and low yields of American participation in the war suggest an error in judgment. While Wilson had nothing like the influence over events that either he or his critics assumed, many doors of history hinged on his decisions. If it is too much to ask of any mortal political leader that, given the circumstances of spring, 1917, he choose division and national humiliation over unity and pride, it is not too much to ask for a different line of diplomacy reaching back to 1914, one that would not allow such restricted and self-defeating alternatives to hem him in.

It might be objected that a concentration on Wilson's decisions from 1914 forward ignores the historic trend toward a more active world role for the United States that commenced in the 1890s, and that this short-sighted perspective exaggerates his freedom. True, the United States in the twenty years before Wilson's Presidency had acquired an empire, intervened militarily in four countries where affairs had not gone to our liking and exerted diplomatic pressure in countless others, had built a modern navy, and had steadily expanded her international commercial contacts. But while this trend meant the inexorable approach of world power and involvement, it did not imply intervention in World War I. Our early military interventions had been limited in scope, had occurred in Latin America and the Far East, and had not been wildly popular.

Another argument with which I am not sympathetic holds that progressivism had an affinity for war. Progressives were activists, moralists, and had a strong sense of mission. They were therefore especially prone to foreign crusades, so the indictment runs. Those advancing this argument point to the fact that wars followed hard upon the reform eras of the 1890s, the Wilson years, the New Deal, the Fair Deal, the New Frontier. Further, they point to progressive Theodore Roosevelt's activist role in Panama and elsewhere, to Wilson's bellicose Mexican policy and his strong internationalism after World War I was over. A progressive President, a progressive country in 1914–1917—war was inevitable! But as plausible as these associations may appear, the case fails to convince. Close studies of progressive attitudes toward foreign policy consistently fail to detect a "progressive" position, whether activist, isolationist, or any other. Progressive T.R. wanted to intervene early, progressive Wilson tried for three years to stay out, and progressives LaFollette and Bryan fought intervention before 1917 and disapproved of it later. Reformers were of diverse minds on American foreign policy, and while some were quite jingoistic, the most opposition to the war came from the Left, liberal as well as radical.

Nonetheless, there is a tendency among modern students of Wilson to be so impressed with the long-term trend toward international involvement, and the supposed predisposition of the reform mind to crusades, not to mention the President's political and diplomatic difficulties, that Wilson's policies are presented as virtually inevitable. Sympathetic scholars point out that Wilson presided over often uncontrollable tides of passion and group interest and that he was forced many times to drift and wait, passive before forces he knew to be beyond his Constitutional and personal powers to shape. But he also acted decisively many times, channeling events within a reasonably wide belt of possibility. Where he had no alternatives or no reasonable ones, we cannot be revisionists. Where he had them we must make judgments, so long as they are tempered with a respect for historic forces which always dwarf men, and with sympathy for this brilliant, patriotic Christian who inherited such baffling dilemmas.

Perhaps no other president would have seen the importance of the early decisions regarding the British blockade and the Declaration of London. The way was politically clear for the administration to insist on the declaration, but most men would have weakened and let it go. No one expected a long war. But many of the decisions of the spring of 1915 bore Wilson's personal stamp. Demands on the belligerents could have been linked, and Germany could have been held to the same postwar accounting reserved for the Allies. Bryan requested a passenger ban at that time, and Wilson was not on principle opposed. Yet he declined to suggest one, insuring that the idea would come from Congress and require his opposition.

The loan decision is an interesting case. Charles Beard showed some years ago that Bryan himself flinched before the bankers' arguments. The country was in an economic recession in 1914, a recession that produced "the largest number of business failures in our country's history," according to *Bradstreet's Journal,* and that brought Andrew Carnegie to write Wilson on 23 November, 1914: "The present financial and industrial situations are very distressing. I have never known such conditions, such pressing calls upon debtors to pay. . . ." No one, from the Harvard Economics Department through the entire range of federal agencies, had any idea how to cope with it beyond maintaining a happy investment climate for the men who hired other men. We now know that recovery could have been achieved by having the government borrow funds from New York banks and reemploy people by a program of spending—on ships and tanks if it wished, but preferably on schools, hospitals, and housing. But this was advocated only by a few unbelievable socialists. The bankers showed Wilson a golden opportunity to put idle funds to work by simply *allowing* Europeans to borrow in New York and spend the money in this country. The pressure was enormous, and there were no real counterpressures and no constructive countersuggestions. Here was an apparently painless cure for America's economic troubles, and the enthusiasm for Allied loans and trade would certainly have broken Wilson politically had he blocked it only with arguments drawn from moral repugnance. *The New York Times* editorialized in early 1915:

> We have oversupplied ourselves with forces of production and they are idle in unusual proportion. . . . The Promise of the new year is that we shall accomplish a peaceful penetration of the world's markets to an extent we have never dreamed of. What others have shed blood to obtain through politics and force we shall obtain while bestowing our benevolence. . . . It is a new translation of the old beatitude, revised: blessed are the keepers of the peace for prosperity shall be within their homes and palaces.

Well might British ambassador Spring-Rice write to Grey in October: "When it became apparent that a loan was necessary, many secret forces began to act in its favour." It may now seem incredible that to achieve recovery the United States must ship to Europe both money and goods and call it a sharp bargain. But it made sense in a capitalistic order with only a rudimentary economic science, and there was literally no other plausible way in 1915 to get idle funds to work. The loan decision, while not inevitable, must be seen sympathetically in this light. Keynes' *General Theory* was twenty-one years away.

But if Wilson could hardly have been expected to maintain the ban against loans to good customers abroad, he might have eliminated munitions from the resulting trade. The Hitchcock bill of December, 1914, would have accomplished that, and there was ample precedent and political support for it. Embargoes on munitions were imposed by Denmark, Sweden, Italy, the Netherlands, Spain, and Norway. The United States itself had embargoed munitions to Mexico in 1913. A passenger ban might have easily been added in the spring of 1916, if not earlier. When the liner *Persia* was sunk on January 3, the principal Congressional reaction was anger that *American citizens had been aboard.* That month Wilson left for a speaking tour to gain support for preparedness and learned that the Congress accurately reflected the country's mood. A passenger ban was his for the asking; and while this would not have diminished the Allied trade, there would be no loss of American life to inflame the issue if Germany eventually resorted to unrestricted submarine warfare despite a ban on munitions, as she well might.

These two changes in policy taken together would have vastly altered the equation of forces. There were no other good alternatives of comparable importance, although Wilson passed up some minor opportunities for a more neutral course. The Lansing modus vivendi on armed ships could have been put into effect, but probably would not have made cruiser warfare the rule. Britain had been sending few armed ships to America anyway, and with Q-ships operating in British waters the submarines were still in danger on the surface. Yet the move would have been helpful. As for Wilson's mediation efforts, it is hard to fault his intentions or his persistence, except to wish that his general appeal had been issued earlier, and from a position of greater neutrality. But there was never much interest in a negotiated peace. Some small things he might have done. He might have fired Page and secured an ambassador to London who would not weaken protests against the blockade. He might, as some progressives urged, have dampened some enthusiasm in important quarters by declaring that, in the event of war, he would draft capital as well as men.

But the passenger ban and the munitions embargo were probably enough, and they were politically possible. Naval troubles with Germany would have arisen, but would have been manageable. With Wilson's rhetorical power and discipline of mind, the road to neutrality was diplomatically and politically passable.

Had Wilson acted along these lines the result would almost certainly have been a German victory, either in the form of a negotiated or a dictated peace. Hohenzollern Germany would dominate the continent—a nation adept in the industrial arts, astonishingly vigorous, nominally Christian, capitalistic, racially arrogant, militaristic, deep in its own internal struggle between the socialists and the entrenched and unimaginative conservatives of land and industry. At least the last years of the war and perhaps more, with their relentless butchery and crippling moral and political consequences, would have been averted. One is permitted to doubt the November, 1917 success of Lenin. Speculation could go on. It should also be noted that the education the American people supposedly received in their new international responsibilities would not have taken place, or at least not in the same way. In view of American foreign policy attitudes from 1919 through 1941, one contemplates the loss of this schooling with relative calm.

The allure of a different American diplomacy springs not from a blind aversion to warfare but from a reasoned conception of the nature of American security. Wilson was sure that our security lay in a respect for law, in the spread of parliamentary governments, in the prestige that comes to nations that do not tolerate the infringement of their rights, in a defeated Germany, in a just peace, and in a postwar league of nations. Much of this is silly, but some of it represents the deepest insight into modern international relations. His mistake lay not in his instincts, a compound of the profound and the harmless, so much as in his judgment of the circumstances. Given the circumstances—the uncontrollable passions of Europe and the ignorance that gripped his own great democracy—there was only one *sure* way to pursue American security, a familiar way, without staggering risks, and without death. It was by an intensification of that surge of internal reform to which he had already become committed: the purification of our own democracy, the diversion of more resources to the education and physical well-being of our people, the broadening of the sway of equality, the conservation of our resources, the humanizing of our hours and conditions of work, the enhancement of the efficiency of our industry, the beautification and ordering of our cities, the narrowing of the gap between the classes. But a decision was reached to interrupt this work for a different approach to national unity, a different approach to economic prosperity, a different approach to the respect of nations.

Ernest May has guessed that Wilson would have chosen differently if he had foreseen the casualties of the Argonne and Chateau-Thierry. In the last speech before his stroke, delivered at Pueblo, Colorado, on 25 September 1919, Wilson said, his face streaked with tears, "What of our pledges to the men that lie dead in France . . . ? There seems to me to stand between us and the rejection or qualification of this treaty the serried ranks of those boys in khaki, not only those boys who came home, but those dear ghosts that still deploy upon the fields of France." We have seen much more of the twentieth century than Woodrow Wilson, and the doubts grow stronger.

FURTHER READING

Thomas A. Bailey and Paul B. Ryan, *The Lusitania Disaster* (1975)
Paul Birdsall, "Neutrality and Economic Pressure, 1914–1917," *Science and Society,* 3 (1939), 217–228
John M. Blum, *Woodrow Wilson and the Politics of Morality* (1956)
Edward H. Buehrig, ed., *Wilson's Foreign Policy in Perspective* (1957)
John Garry Clifford, *The Citizen Soldiers* (1972)
John M. Cooper, *The Vanity of Power* (1969)
Patrick Devlin, *Too Proud to Fight* (1975)
Ross Gregory, "To Do Good in the World: Woodrow Wilson and America's Mission," in Frank J. Merli and Theodore A. Wilson, eds., *Makers of American Diplomacy* (1974)
Ross Gregory, *Walter Hines Page* (1970)
Arthur S. Link, *Wilson,* 5 vols. (1947–1965)
Arthur S. Link, *Wilson the Diplomatist* (1963)
Ernest R. May, *The World War and American Isolation, 1914–1917* (1959)
Walter Millis, *Road to War* (1935)
Daniel M. Smith, "National Interest and American Intervention, 1917: An Historiographical Appraisal," *Journal of American History,* 52 (1965), 5–24
Daniel M. Smith, *Roger Lansing and American Neutrality, 1914–1917* (1958)
Charles C. Tansill, *America Goes to War* (1938)
Barbara Tuchman, *The Zimmermann Telegram* (1958)

3

Woodrow Wilson, Versailles, and the League

During the First World War, President Woodrow Wilson said he wanted a "peace without victory"—a lenient peace—and some historians have in fact suggested that Wilson asked for war in April 1917 to ensure himself a place at the peace table. In January 1918 he issued his peace program of Fourteen Points. To Wilson, the fourteenth point proposing a League of Nations was the most important. The war ended on November 11, 1918, a few days after the Republicans captured both Houses of Congress in the fall elections. In January of the following year, the President attended the Paris Peace Conference at Versailles and, over several months, made compromises in order to secure a peace treaty and his cherished Covenant of the League of Nations.

At home, however, many Americans began to question Wilson's handiwork and to offer amendments and reservations to protect United States sovereignty, which they claimed was threatened, especially by Article 10 of the Covenant prescribing collective security. The President battled back in a vigorous national debate, generally refused to compromise, and ultimately witnessed the defeat, in the United States Senate, of the treaty and American membership in the League in November 1919 and again in March 1920.

Historians disagree in their explanations for the rejection. Some concentrate on the personal feud between Wilson and Republican Senator Henry Cabot Lodge, whereas others stress the President's arrogance and stubbornness in the face of overwhelming political odds. Still others note that the debate centered on key questions about the national interest and that the final verdict was determined by American nationalists who were not willing to throw off their tradition of unilateralism in favor of collective security.

DOCUMENTS

Wilson issued his Fourteen Points in a speech on January 8, 1918. The League of Nations was created at Versailles and its Article 10, reprinted here, aroused heated controversy in the United States; Wilson considered the article the heart of the Covenant and the key to collective security. In a speech on September 17, 1919, in San Francisco, the President defended the League against mounting criticism. Led by Senator Henry Cabot Lodge of Massachusetts, critics offered a number of reservations to the Covenant and incorporated them in a Lodge resolution dated November 19, 1919.

The Fourteen Points, 1918

We entered this war because violations of right had occurred which touched us to the quick and made the life of our own people impossible unless they were corrected and the world secured once for all against their recurrence. What we demand in this war, therefore, is nothing peculiar to ourselves. It is that the world be made fit and safe to live in; and particularly that it be made safe for every peace-loving nation which, like our own, wishes to live its own life, determine its own institutions, be assured of justice and fair dealing by the other peoples of the world as against force and selfish aggression. All the peoples of the world are in effect partners in this interest, and for our own part we see very clearly that unless justice be done to others it will not be done to us. The programme of the world's peace, therefore, is our programme; and that programme, the only possible programme, as we see it, is this:

I. Open covenants of peace, openly arrived at, after which there shall be no private international understandings of any kind but diplomacy shall proceed always frankly and in the public view.

II. Absolute freedom of navigation upon the seas, outside territorial waters, alike in peace and in war, except as the seas may be closed in whole or in part by international action for the enforcement of international covenants.

III. The removal, so far as possible, of all economic barriers and the establishment of an equality of trade conditions among all the nations consenting to the peace and associating themselves for its maintenance.

IV. Adequate guarantees given and taken that national armaments will be reduced to the lowest point consistent with domestic safety.

V. A free, open-minded, and absolutely impartial adjustment of all colonial claims, based upon a strict observance of the principle that in determining all such questions of sovereignty the interests of the populations concerned must have equal weight with the equitable claims of the government whose title is to be determined.

VI. The evacuation of all Russian territory and such a settlement of all questions affecting Russia as will secure the best and freest cooperation of the other nations of the world in obtaining for her an unhampered and unembarrassed opportunity for the independent determination of her own political development and national policy and assure her of a sincere welcome into the society of free nations under institutions of her own choosing; and, more than a welcome, assistance also of every kind that she may need and may herself desire. The treatment accorded Russia by her sister nations in the months to come will be the acid test of their good will, of their comprehension of her needs as distinguished from their own interests, and of their intelligent and unselfish sympathy.

VII. Belgium, the whole world will agree, must be evacuated and restored, without any attempt to limit the sovereignty which she enjoys in common with all other free nations. No other single act will serve as this will serve to restore confidence among the nations in the laws which they have themselves set and determined for the government of their relations with one another. Without this healing act the whole structure and validity of international law is forever impaired.

VIII. All French territory should be freed and the invaded portions restored, and the wrong done to France by Prussia in 1871 in the matter of Alsace-Lorraine, which has unsettled the peace of the world for nearly fifty years, should be righted, in order that peace may once more be made secure in the interest of all.

IX. A readjustment of the frontiers of Italy should be effected along clearly recognizable lines of nationality.

X. The peoples of Austria-Hungary, whose place among the nations we wish to see safeguarded and assured, should be accorded the freest opportunity of autonomous development.

XI. Rumania, Serbia, and Montenegro should be evacuated; occupied territories restored; Serbia accorded free and secure access to the sea; and the relations of the several Balkan states to one another determined by friendly counsel along historically established lines of allegiance and nationality; and international guarantees of the political and economic independence and territorial integrity of the several Balkan states should be entered into.

XII. The Turkish portions of the present Ottoman Empire should be assured a secure sovereignty, but the other nationalities which are now under Turkish rule should be assured an undoubted security of life and an absolutely unmolested opportunity of autonomous development, and the Dardanelles should be permanently opened as a free passage to the ships and commerce of all nations under international guarantees.

XIII. An independent Polish state should be erected which should include the territories inhabited by indisputably Polish populations, which should be assured a free and secure access to the sea, and whose political and economic independence and territorial integrity should be guaranteed by international covenant.

XIV. A general association of nations must be formed under specific covenants for the purpose of affording mutual guarantees of political independence and territorial integrity to great and small states alike. . . .

We have spoken now, surely, in terms too concrete to admit of any further doubt or question. An evident principle runs through the whole programme I have outlined. It is the principle of justice to all peoples and nationalities, and their right to live on equal terms of liberty and safety with one another, whether they be strong or weak. Unless this principle be made its foundation no part of the structure of international justice can stand. The people of the United States could act upon no other principle; and to the vindication of this principle they are ready to devote their lives, their honor, and everything that they possess. The moral climax of this the culminating and final war for human liberty has come, and they are ready to put their own strength, their own highest purpose, their own integrity and devotion to the test.

Article 10 of the League Covenant, 1919

Article 10. The Members of the League undertake to respect and preserve as against external aggression the territorial integrity and existing political independence of all Members of the League. In case of any such aggression or in case of any threat or danger of such aggression the Council shall advise upon the means by which this obligation shall be fulfilled.

The Lodge Reservations, 1919

Resolved . . . That the Senate advise and consent to the ratification of the treaty of peace with Germany . . . subject to the following reservations and understandings . . . which ratification is not to take effect or bind the United States until the said reservations and understandings . . . have been accepted by . . . at least three of the four principal allied and associated powers. . . .

1. . . . in case of notice of withdrawal from the league of nations, as provided in said article [Article 1], the United States shall be the sole judge as to whether all its international obligations . . . have been fulfilled, and notice of withdrawal . . . may be given by a concurrent resolution of the Congress of the United States.

2. The United States assumes no obligation to preserve the territorial integrity or political independence of any other country . . . under the provisions of article 10, or to employ the military or naval forces of the United States under any article of the treaty for any purpose, unless in any particular case the Congress, which . . . has the sole power to declare war . . . shall . . . so provide.

3. No mandate shall be accepted by the United States under article 22 . . . except by action of the Congress of the United States.

4. The United States reserves to itself exclusively the right to decide what questions are within its domestic jurisdiction. . . .

5. The United States will not submit to arbitration or to inquiry by the assembly or by the council of the league of nations . . . any questions which in the judgment of the United States depend upon or relate to . . . the Monroe doctrine; said doctrine is to be interpreted by the United States alone and is . . . wholly outside the jurisdiction of said league of nations. . . .

6. The United States withholds its assent to articles 156, 157, and 158 [Shantung clauses]. . . .

7. The Congress of the United States will provide by law for the appointment of the representatives of the United States in the assembly and the council of the league of nations, and may in its discretion provide for the participation of the United States in any commission. . . . no person shall represent the United States under either said league of nations or the treaty of peace . . . except with the approval of the Senate of the United States. . . .

9. The United States shall not be obligated to contribute to any expenses of the league of nations . . . unless and until an appropriation of funds . . . shall have been made by the Congress of the United States.

10. If the United States shall at any time adopt any plan for the limitation of armaments proposed by the council of the league . . . it reserves the right to increase such armaments without the consent of the council whenever the United States is threatened with invasion or engaged in war. . . .

14. The United States assumes no obligation to be bound by any election, decision, report, or finding of the council or assembly in which any member of the league and its self-governing dominions, colonies, or parts of empire, in the aggregate have cast more than one vote.

Wilson Defends the League, 1919

It is my purpose, fellow citizens, to analyze the objections which are made to this great League, and I shall be very brief. In the first place, you know that one of the difficulties which have been experienced by those who are objecting to this League is that they do not think that there is a wide enough door open for us to get out. For my own part, I am not one of those who, when they go into a generous enterprise, think first of all how they are going to turn away from those with whom they are associated. I am not one of those who, when they go into a concert for the peace of the world, want to sit close to the door with their hand on the knob and constantly trying the door to be sure that it is not locked. If we want to go into this thing—and we do want to go into it—we will go in it with our whole hearts and settled purpose to stand by the great enterprise to the end. Nevertheless, you will remember—some of you, I dare say—that when I came home in March for an all too brief visit to this country, which seems to me the fairest and dearest in the world, I brought back with me the first draft of the Covenant of the League of Nations. I called into consultation the Committees on Foreign Affairs and on Foreign Relations of the House and Senate of the United States, and I laid the draft of the Covenant before them. One of the things that they proposed was that it should be explicitly stated that any member of the League should have the right to withdraw. I carried that suggestion back to Paris, and without the slightest hesitation it was accepted and acted upon; and every suggestion which was made in that conference at the White House was accepted by the conference of peace in Paris. There is not a feature of the Covenant, except one, now under debate upon which suggestions were not made at that time, and there is not one of those suggestions that was not adopted by the conference of peace.

The gentlemen say, "You have laid a limitation upon the right to withdraw. You have said that we can withdraw upon two years' notice, if at that time we shall have fulfilled all our international obligations and all our obligations under the Covenant." "Yes," I reply; "is it characteristic of the United States not to fulfill her international obligations? Is there any fear that we shall wish to withdraw dishonorably? Are gentlemen willing to stand up and say that they want to get out whether they have the moral right to get out or not?" I for one am too proud as an American to debate that subject on that basis. The United States has always fulfilled its international obligations, and, God helping her, she always will. There is nothing in the Covenant to prevent her acting upon her own judgment with regard to that matter. The only thing she has to fear, the only thing she has to regard, is the public opinion of mankind, and inasmuch as we have always scrupulously satisfied the public opinion of mankind with regard to justice and right, I for my part am not afraid at any time to go before that jury. It is a jury that might condemn us if we did wrong, but it is not a jury that could oblige us to stay in the League, so that there is absolutely no limitation upon our right to withdraw.

One of the other suggestions I carried to Paris was that the committees of the two Houses did not find the Monroe Doctrine safeguarded in the Covenant of the League of Nations. I suggested that to the conference in Paris, and they at once inserted the provision which is now there that nothing in the Covenant shall be construed as affecting the validity of the Monroe Doctrine. What is the validity of the Monroe Doctrine? The Monroe Doctrine means that if any outside power, any power outside this hemisphere, tries to impose its will upon any portion of the Western Hemisphere the United States is at liberty to act independently and alone in repelling the aggression; that it does not have to wait for the action of the League of Nations; that it does not have to wait for anything but the action of its own administration and its own Congress. This is the first time in the history of international diplomacy that any great government has acknowledged the validity of the Monroe Doctrine. Now for the first time all the great fighting powers of the world except Germany, which for the time being has ceased to be a great fighting power, acknowledge the validity of the Monroe Doctrine and acknowledge it as part of the international practice of the world.

They are nervous about domestic questions. They say, "It is intolerable to think that the League of Nations should interfere with domestic questions," and whenever they begin to specify they speak of the question of immigration, of the question of naturalization, of the question of the tariff. My fellow citizens, no competent or authoritative student of international law would dream of maintaining that these were anything but exclusively domestic questions, and the Covenant of the League expressly provides that the League can take no action whatever about matters which are in the practice of international law regarded as domestic questions. We did not undertake to enumerate samples of domestic questions for the very good reason, which will occur to any lawyer, that if you made a list it would be inferred that what you left out was not included. Nobody with a thoughtful knowledge of international practice has the least doubt as to what are domestic questions, and there is no obscurity whatever in this Covenant with regard to the safeguarding of the United States, along with other sovereign countries, in the control of domestic questions. I beg that you will not fancy, my fellow citizens, that the United States is the only country that is jealous of its sovereignty. Throughout these conferences it was necessary at every turn to safeguard the sovereign independence of the several governments who were taking part in the conference, and they were just as keen to protect themselves against outside intervention in domestic matters as we were. Therefore the whole heartiness of their concurrent opinion runs with this safeguarding of domestic questions.

It is objected that the British Empire has six votes and we have one. The answer to that is that it is most carefully arranged that our one vote equals the six votes of the British Empire. Anybody who will take the pains to read the Covenant of the League of Nations will find out that the assembly—and it is only in the assembly that the British Empire has six votes—is not a voting body. . . .

Not a single affirmative act or negative decision upon a matter of action taken by the League of Nations can be validated without the vote of the United States of America. We can dismiss from our dreams the six votes of the British Empire, for the real underlying conception of the assembly of the League of Nations is that it is the forum of opinion, not of action. It is the debating body; it is the body where the thought of the little nation along with the thought of the big nation is brought to bear upon those matters which affect the peace of the world, is brought to bear upon those matters which affect the good understanding between nations upon which the peace of the world depends; where this stifled voice of humanity is at last to be heard, where nations that have borne the unspeakable sufferings of the ages that must have seemed to them like æons will find voice and expression, where the moral judgment of mankind can sway the opinion of the world. That is the function of the assembly. The assembly is the voice of mankind. The council, where unanimous action is necessary, is the only means through which that voice can accomplish action.

You say, "We have heard a great deal about Article X." I just now said that the only substitute for the League of Nations which is offered by the opponents is a return to the old system. What was the old system? That the strong had all the rights and need pay no attention to the rights of the weak; that if a great powerful nation saw what it wanted, it had the right to go and take it; that the weak nations could cry out and cry out as they pleased and there would be no hearkening ear anywhere to their rights.

ESSAYS

Thomas A. Bailey has termed Wilson's uncompromising stance and the subsequent defeat of the League Covenant the "supreme infanticide." In short, an intransigent President killed his own offspring, because he refused to accept even moderate adjustments. Arthur S. Link, a scholar at Princeton University who has spent a lifetime sympathetically writing about Woodrow Wilson, agrees that the President was often uncompromising. But Link emphasizes that the American people were not yet ready for collective security—that Wilson was a prophet ahead of his time. That is why the President lost the vote and American membership in the League was defeated. Whatever the explanation, Woodrow Wilson was a powerful personality who commanded central attention on the world stage, as the work of Bailey, Link, and other historians makes quite evident.

The Supreme Infanticide

THOMAS A. BAILEY

Is it true that the invalid in the White House really strangled the treaty to death with his own enfeebled hands?

It is seldom that statesmen have a second chance—a second guess. They decide on a course of action, and the swift current of events beats them downstream from the starting point. Only rarely does the stream reverse itself and carry them back.

In November, Wilson had decided that he wanted deadlock, because he reasoned that deadlock would arouse public opinion and force the Senate to do his bidding. The tidal wave of public opinion did surge in, and Wilson got his second chance. But he threw it away, first by spurning compromise (except on his terms), and then by spurning the Lodge reservations.

There had been much more justification for Wilson's course in November than in March. In November [1919] he was sick, secluded, was fed censored news, and was convinced by Hitchcock that the strategy of deadlock was sound. In March, [1920] he was much improved in health, far less secluded, more in touch with the press and with the currents of opinion, though probably still not enough. He consulted even less with the Senate, presumably because he had

Reprinted with permission of Macmillan Publishing Co., Inc. from *Woodrow Wilson and the Great Betrayal* by Thomas A. Bailey. Copyright 1945 by Thomas A. Bailey, renewed 1973 by Thomas A. Bailey.

made up his mind in advance to oppose the Lodge reservations. In November, there was a fair possibility of reconsideration; in March, it was clear that the only possibility lay in making the League an issue in the coming campaign. Wilson, with his broad knowledge of government and politics, should have seen that this hope was largely if not completely illusory. Perhaps he would have seen it had he not been blinded by his feeling for Lodge.

The evidence is convincing that Wilson wanted this issue cast into the hurly-burly of politics. He could not accept Lodge's terms; Lodge would not accept his terms. The only possible chance of beating the senator—and this was slim indeed—was to win a resounding mandate in 1920.

Yet this strategy, as already noted, meant further delay. At Paris, the feeling at times had been, "Better a bad treaty today than a good treaty four months hence." Europe was still in chaos, and increasingly in need of America's helping hand. Well might the Europeans cry, "Better a treaty with the Lodge reservations today than a probable treaty without reservations after the election." Or as Dr. Frank Crane wrote in *Current Opinion,* "It is vastly more needful that some sort of League be formed, *any sort,* than that it be formed *perfectly.*" (Italics Crane's.)

Yet Wilson, for the reasons indicated, could not see all this clearly. Four days after the fatal vote he wrote Hitchcock, praising him for having done all in his power to protect the honor of the nation and the peace of the world against the Republican majority.

Mrs. Wilson, no doubt reflecting her husband's views, later wrote, "My conviction is that Mr. Lodge put the world back fifty years, and that at his door lies the wreckage of human hopes and the peril to human lives that afflict mankind today."

To the very end Wilson was a fighter. When the Scotch-Irish in him became aroused, he would nail his colors to the mast. He said in 1916 that he was "playing for the verdict of mankind." His conception of duty as he saw it was overpowering. He once remarked that if he were a judge, and it became his duty to sentence his own brother to the gallows, he would do so—and afterwards die of a broken heart.

It is well to have principles; it is well to have a noble conception of duty. But Wilson, as he became warmed up in a fight, tended to get things out of focus and to lose a proper sense of values.

The basic issue in 1920 was the Hitchcock reservations or the Lodge reservations. Wilson accepted those of Hitchcock while rejecting those of Lodge, which, he said, completely nullified the treaty and betrayed his promises to the Allies and to the American dead.

This, as we have seen, was a gross exaggeration. Minds no less acute than Wilson's, and less clouded with sickness and pride, denied that the Lodge reservations completely nullified the treaty. To the man in the street—in so far as he gave the dispute thought—there was little discernible difference between the two sets of reservations. How could one decry statements which merely reaffirmed the basic principles of the Constitution and of our foreign policy? To a vast number of Americans the Lodge reservations, far from nullifying the treaty, actually improved it. This was so apparent to even the most loyal Democrats in the Senate that Wilson could barely keep them in line.

In the final analysis the treaty was slain in the house of its friends rather than in the house of its enemies. In the final analysis it was not the two-thirds rule, or the "irreconcilables," or Lodge, or the "strong" and "mild reservationists," but Wilson and his docile following who delivered the fatal stab. If the President had been permitted to vote he would have sided with Borah, Brandegee, Johnson, and the other "bitter-enders"—though for entirely different reasons.

Wilson had said that the reservation to Article X was a knife thrust at the heart of the Covenant. Ironically, he parried this knife thrust, and stuck his own dagger, not into the heart of the Covenant, but into the entire treaty.

This was the supreme act of infanticide. With his own sickly hands Wilson slew his own brain child—or the one to which he had contributed so much.

This was the supreme paradox. He who had forced the Allies to write the League into the treaty, unwrote it; he who had done more than any other man to make the Covenant, unmade it—at least so far as America was concerned. And by his action, he contributed powerfully to the ultimate undoing of the League, and with it the high hopes of himself and mankind for an organization to prevent World War II.

The preceding dogmatic observations are of course qualified by the phrase, "in the last analysis."

Many elements enter into a log jam. Among them are the width of the stream, the depth of the stream, the swiftness of the current, the presence of boulders, the size of the logs, and the absence of enough lumberjacks. No one of these factors can be solely responsible for the pile-up.

Many elements entered into the legislative log jam of March, 1920. Among them were isolationism, partisanship, senatorial prerogative, confusion, apathy, personal pride, and private feuds. No one of them was solely responsible for the pile-up. *But as the pile-up finally developed, there was only one lumberjack who could break it, and that was Woodrow Wilson.* If at any time before the final vote he had told the Senate Democrats to support the treaty with the Lodge reservations, or even if he had merely told them that they were on their own, the pact would almost certainly have been approved. So "in the last analysis" the primary responsibility for the failure in March rested with Wilson.

What about Lodge? If the treaty would have passed by Wilson's surrendering, is it not equally true that it would have passed by Lodge's surrendering?

The answer is probably "Yes," but the important point is that Lodge had far less responsibility for getting the treaty through than Wilson. If Lodge had yielded, he probably would have created a schism within his ranks. His ultimate responsibility was to keep the party from breaking to pieces, and in this he succeeded. Wilson's ultimate responsibility was to get the treaty ratified, and in this he failed. With Lodge, as with any truly partisan leader, the party comes before country; with the President the country should come before party, though unhappily it often does not.

It is possible that Wilson saw all this—but not clearly enough. He might have been willing to compromise if his adversary had been any other than

Lodge. But so bitter was the feeling between the two men that Wilson, rather than give way, grasped at the straw of the election of 1920.

Lodge did not like Wilson either, but he made more of a show of compromising than the President. He actually supported and drove through amendments to his original reservations which were in line with Wilson's wishes, and he probably would have gone further had the "irreconcilables" not been on his back. He fought the crippling Irish reservation, as well as others supported by the "bitter-enders." Finally, he gave the Democrats a fair chance to reconsider their vote and get on the bandwagon, but they spurned it.

If Lodge's words mean anything, and if his actions were not those of a monstrous hypocrite, he actually tried to get the treaty through with his reservations. When he found that he could not, he washed his hands of the whole business in disgust.

The charge is frequently made that, if Wilson had yielded to his adversary, Lodge would have gleefully piled on more reservations until Wilson, further humiliated, would have had to throw out the whole thing.

The strongest evidence for this view is a circumstantial story which Secretary [of Agriculture] Houston relates. During a Cabinet meeting Wilson was called to the telephone, and agreed to make certain concessions agreeable to Lodge. Before adjournment the telephone rang again, and word came that Lodge would not adhere to his original proposal.

This story is highly improbable, because Wilson attended no Cabinet meetings between September 2, 1919, and April 13, 1920. By the latter date, all serious attempts at compromise had been dropped; by the earlier date the treaty was still before the Senate committee, and the Lodge reservations, though in an embryonic stage, were yet unborn. But, even if the story is true, it merely proves that Lodge veered about, as he frequently did under "irreconcilable" pressure.

In March, as in November, all Wilson had to do was to send over Postmaster General Burleson to the Senate a few minutes before the final vote with the quiet word that the Democrats were to vote "Yea." The treaty would then have passed with the Lodge reservations, and Lodge could hardly have dared incur for himself or his party the odium of moving to reconsider for the purpose of screwing on more reservations. Had he tried to do so, the "mild reservationists" almost certainly would have blocked him.

A few days after the disastrous final vote, Wilson's only comment to Tumulty was, "They have shamed us in the eyes of the world." If his previous words said what he really meant, he was hardly more shamed by the defeat of the treaty than by the addition of the Lodge reservations. In his eyes it all amounted to the same thing.

If the treaty had passed, would the President have been willing to go through with the exchange of ratifications? Would he not have pocketed it, as he threatened to do prior to the November vote?

Again, if Wilson's words may be taken at their face value, this is what he would have done. He had not backed down from his pre-November position. His Jackson Day message and his letter to Hitchcock made it unmistakably clear that he preferred the uncertainties of a political campaign to the certainties of ratification with the Lodge reservations. The addition of the indefensible Irish reservation provided even stronger justification for pocketing the entire pact.

It is probable that some of the loyal Democrats voted as they did partly because they were convinced that Wilson was going to pigeonhole the treaty anyhow. From their point of view it was better that the odium for defeat should seemingly rest on Lodge rather than on their President. It also seems clear that Wilson preferred, as in November, to have the blood of the treaty on the Senate doorstep rather than on his. As he wrote to Secretary [of State] Colby, on April 2, 1920, the slain pact lay heavily on the consciences of those who had stabbed it, and he was quite willing to have it lie there until those consciences were either awakened or crushed.

Yet it is one thing to say, just before Senate action, "I will pocket the treaty." It is another, after the pact is approved and sent to the White House, to assume this tremendous responsibility. The eyes of the world are upon the President; he is the only man keeping the nation out of the peace which it so urgently needs; he is the one man standing in the way of the rehabilitation which the world so desperately demands. Public pressure to ratify in such a case would be enormous—probably irresistible.

Some years later Senator Hitchcock said that in the event of senatorial approval Wilson would possibly have waited for the November election. If he had won, he would have worked for the removal of the Lodge reservations; if he had lost, then the compulsion to go through with ratification would have become overpowering. By November more than six months would have passed, and by that time Wilson might have developed a saner perspective.

But this is all speculation. Wilson gave orders that the treaty was to be killed in the Senate chamber. And there it died.

One other line of inquiry must be briefly pursued. Is it true, as some writers allege, that the thirty-odd Allied signatories of the original treaty would have rejected the Lodge reservations when officially presented? We recall that under the terms of the preamble these nations were privileged to acquiesce silently or file objections.

One will never know the answer to this question, because Wilson denied the other signatories a chance to act. But it seems proper to point to certain probabilities.

One or more of the Latin American nations might have objected to the reservation regarding the then hated Monroe Doctrine. Yet the Monroe Doctrine would have continued to exist anyhow; it was already in the Covenant; and these neighboring republics might well have swallowed their pride in the interest of world peace.

Italy probably would have acquiesced, and the evidence is strong that France would have done likewise. The Japanese could not completely overlook the Shantung reservation, but it was generally recognized in their press as meaningless, and for this reason it might have been tolerated, though not without some loss of face. It is noteworthy that the most important Japanese newspapers regretted the Senate stalemate as an encouragement to world instability, particularly in China.

Great Britain probably would have been the chief objector. The reservation on Ireland was highly offensive but completely innocuous, for the British lion had long endured Irish-American tail-twistings in pained but dignified silence. The reservation on six-to-one was a slap at the loyal and sacrificing Dominions, but it did not mean that their vote was to be taken away. Moreover, the contingency envisaged by this proviso was unlikely to arise very often, and in the long run would doubtless have proved inconsequential.

In sum, there were only two or three reservations to which the outside powers could seriously object. If they had objected, it is probable that a satisfactory adjustment could have been threshed out through diplomatic channels. For when it became clear that only a few phrases stood between the United States and peace, the dictates of common sense and the pressure of public opinion probably would have led to an acceptable compromise. If the Senate had refused to give ground in such a case, then the onus would have been clearly on it and not on Wilson.

The Fundamental Debate over Collective Security

ARTHUR S. LINK

The lines of battle over ratification of the Treaty of Versailles were first drawn, not after that treaty had been signed, but before Wilson went to Paris, as a consequence of three decisions that he made between October and December of 1918. The first was his decision to issue an appeal to the country on October 25 for the election of a Democratic Congress, and by so doing to make the forthcoming election a specific test of national confidence in his conduct of foreign affairs. The second was his decision to ignore the Senate and the Republican party in discussions of the possible terms of the settlement and in the appointment of the American delegation to the Paris conference, and to name only such men as he thought would be loyal to him and his ideals and subordinate to his direction. The third was Wilson's decision to go to Paris in person, as the head of the American commission.

The first two decisions were certainly egregious mistakes. On the other hand, Wilson was probably right in deciding that he had to go to Paris to take personal leadership in the fight for a liberal peace. However, the important point is not whether Wilson acted wisely or foolishly; it is the way in which his preparations for the peace conference predetermined the shape of the battle over the treaty that would be signed. By appealing for the election of a Democratic Congress on the ground that a Republican victory would imply a repudiation of his leadership in foreign affairs, and by appointing a peace commission composed with one unimportant exception of Democrats, Wilson made a partisan division on

Arthur S. Link, *Wilson the Diplomatist: A look at His Major Foreign Policies* (Baltimore: Johns Hopkins University Press, 1957), pp. 128–131, 132, 133–141, 148–150, 153–156. Copyright © 1957 by The Johns Hopkins University Press. Reprinted by permission of The Johns Hopkins University Press.

the issues of peace inevitabie. In other words, he made it certain that Republicans would oppose and Democrats would support whatever treaty he might help to write. Moreover, by first ignoring the Senate in his appointment of the commissioners, and then by going himself to Paris, Wilson made it inevitable that the treaty fight would renew in virulent form the old conflict between the president and the upper house for control of foreign policy.

While Wilson was in Paris there were unmistakable signs at home that he would encounter bitter opposition when he returned with his peace treaty. The most ominous of these was the so-called "Round Robin" resolution that Senator Lodge presented to the upper house on March 4, 1919. Signed by thirty-seven senators, it declared that the Covenant of the League of Nations, "in the form now proposed to the peace conference," was unacceptable. At the same time, frankly isolationist opponents of the League were beginning a furious rhetorical attack in the Senate chamber.

Although there were limits beyond which Wilson would not go in compromise, as he said in a New York address on the eve of his return to France after a brief visit to the United States in late February and early March of 1919, he yielded to the advice of friends who urged him to conciliate his critics. For example, he endeavored to assuage the signers of the "Round Robin" resolution by permitting Henry White, the Republican member of the American peace delegation, to attempt to ascertain from Lodge why the Covenant was unacceptable to them. Or again, after Lodge had refused to answer specifically, Wilson took the advice of former President William Howard Taft and other Republican supporters of the League and obtained amendments to meet certain American criticisms of the Covenant.

Undertaken reluctantly at best, these measures did little to conciliate the extreme opposition or to conceal Wilson's true feelings about his senatorial critics and his growing determination to defy them. The more he had to concede at Paris during the final months of the conference, the more this determination hardened. By the time he signed the Versailles Treaty, Wilson was obviously sick of making compromises and eager to return to a political arena in which he could fight hard again, without the necessity of giving ground to opponents who had as much power as he. "I have found one can never get anything in this life that is worth while without fighting for it," he told Colonel House, who had urged him to meet the Senate in a conciliatory spirit, on the day that he left Paris.

Arriving in Washington on July 8, the President made no effort to conceal his fighting mood. When a reporter asked him on July 10 whether the Versailles Treaty could be ratified if the Senate added certain reservations, Wilson shot back, "I do not think hypothetical questions are concerned. *The Senate is going to ratify the treaty.*" To cite another example, the French Ambassador, Jules Jusserand, went to the White House at about the same time with a plan that he thought would assure the Senate's approval of the treaty. Conceived by President Nicholas Murray Butler of Columbia University and approved by a large number of Republican senators, this plan envisaged the adoption of certain reservations to the treaty to protect American sovereignty and congressional control over the war-making power. If the President would only accept the reservations, Jusserand urged, there would be no doubt about the treaty's fate in the Senate. "Mr. Ambassador," Wilson replied, "I shall consent to nothing. The Senate must take its medicine." . . .

Many historians have been frankly puzzled by Wilson's refusal even to attempt to build support for the peace settlement in the Senate and the Republican party—among the very men who would have the power of life or death over the Treaty of Versailles. How could an authority on the American constitutional system have forgotten the Senate's jealous role in foreign affairs? How could an intelligent and astute political strategist have done the things best calculated to assure the defeat of plans upon which he thought depended the future happiness of mankind? The dilemma inherent in these hyperbolic questions is much more apparent than real. In fact, it is not too much to say that Wilson acted in the only way that it was possible for him to act, given his convictions concerning the President's control over foreign relations, his belief in party responsibility, his view of public opinion, and his own temperament. . . .

These are reasons enough to explain the President's methods and his posture of defiance at the beginning of the treaty fight. There was another reason that was more important than all the rest—Wilson's supreme confidence in his own creation and in the overwhelming support of the American people. He knew not only that he was right, but that the people would know that he was right and would crush any man who dared to obstruct the fulfillment of the age-old dream of peace. That was what he meant when he told reporters that of course the Senate would ratify the Versailles Treaty, or when in private he talked about the Senate, that is, the Republican Senate, having to take its medicine.

Actually, the situation was far less simple and reassuring than Wilson imagined at the beginning of the great debate. For one thing, powerful voices were already raised in outright and violent condemnation of the treaty on various grounds. There were the idealists who had thrilled at Wilson's vision of a new world and who now drew back in disgust because the treaty failed to establish a millennial order. There were the so-called hyphenate groups—the German-Americans, who believed that the treaty was a base betrayal of the Fatherland; the Italian-Americans, who were sulking over Wilson's opposition to Italy's demands; and, most important, the several million Irish-Americans, inflamed by the civil war then raging in Ireland, who were up in arms because Wilson had refused to press the cause of Irish independence at Paris and because the treaty allegedly benefited the hated English. There was the powerful chain of Hearst newspapers, marshaling and inciting all the hyphenate protests. There were the out-and-out isolationists, who believed that American membership in the League of Nations would mean entanglement in all of Europe's rivalries and wars. They had powerful advocates in a small group of so-called irreconcilables or bitter-enders in the Senate, led by Hiram Johnson of California, William E. Borah of Idaho, and James A. Reed of Missouri, who opposed the treaty for nationalistic reasons of their own divination.

These were the major groups who opposed ratification of the treaty. In the ensuing debate they were perhaps the loudest and busiest participants of all.

They were, however, a minority among the leaders of thought and political opinion, and they spoke for a minority of the people, at least before 1920 if not afterward. This is a simple point but a vital one, because in its important aspects the debate over the treaty was not a struggle between advocates of complete withdrawal on the one side and proponents of total international commitment on the other. It was, rather, a contest between the champions of a strong system of collective security and a group who favored a more limited commitment in international affairs. It was a choice between these alternatives, and not between complete isolation or complete internationalism, that the President, the Senate, and the American people eventually had to make. For this reason, therefore, I propose to let the arguments of the isolationists pass without analyzing them, and to concentrate my attention upon the two main and decisive courses of the debate.

Before we do this, it might be well to remind ourselves of the precise issues at stake. There were differences of opinion in the United States over the territorial and other provisions of the treaty, to be sure, but all of them were insignificant as compared to the differences evoked by the Covenant of the League and its provisions for universal collective security. Those provisions were clear and for the most part unequivocal. There was, of course, Article 10, which guaranteed the political independence and territorial integrity of every member nation throughout the world. There were, besides, Articles 11, 12, 13, 15, 16, and 17, which established the machinery of arbitration for all international disputes susceptible to that procedure and decreed that an act of war against one member nation should "*ipso facto* be deemed to . . . [be] an act of war against all the other Members" and should be followed automatically by an economic blockade against the aggressor and by the Council action to determine what military measures should be used to repel the aggression. These were almost ironclad guarantees of mutual security, meant to be effective and unencumbered by the right of any nation involved in a dispute to veto action by the League's Council. Whether such a world-wide system could work, and whether the American people were prepared at this stage of their development to support such a system even if it did—these were the two main issues of the great debate of 1919–1920.

The decisive opposition to the Versailles Treaty came from a group of men who to a varying degree gave negative answers to both these questions. This group included some of the most distinguished leaders in the Senate and out, men like Senator Frank B. Kellogg of Minnesota, Nicholas Murray Butler, former Secretary of State Elihu Root, Charles Evans Hughes, and Herbert Hoover. Most of them were Republicans, because few Democrats active in politics dared to incur the President's wrath by opposing him. They were not isolationists, but limited internationalists who in a varying degree believed that the United States should play an active role in preserving the peace of the world. Most of them favored, for example, arbitration, the establishment of something like a World Court to interpret and codify international law, and international agreements for disarmament, economic co-operation, and the like. Some of them even supported the idea of alliances with certain powers for specific purposes.

On the other hand, all the limited internationalists opposed any such approval of the treaty as would commit the United States unreservedly to such a system of collective security as the Covenant of the League had created. Their arguments might be summarized as follows:

First, a system of collective security that is world-wide in operation is not likely either to work or to endure the strains that will inevitably be put upon it, because in practice the great powers will not accept the limitations that the Covenant places upon their sovereignty, and no nation will go to war to vindicate Article 10 unless its vital interests compel it to do so. Such sweeping guarantees as the Covenant affords are, therefore, worse than no guarantees at all because they offer only an illusory hope of security.

Second, the Covenant's fundamental guarantee, embodied in Article 10, is impossible to maintain because its promise to perpetuate the *status quo* defies the very law of life. As Elihu Root put it:

> If perpetual, it would be an attempt to preserve for all time unchanged the distribution of power and territory made in accordance with the views and exigencies of the Allies in this present juncture of affairs. It would necessarily be futile. . . . It would not only be futile; it would be mischievous. Change and growth are the law of life, and no generation can impose its will in regard to the growth of nations and the distribution of power, upon succeeding generations.

Third, the American people are not ready to support the Covenant's sweeping commitments and in fact should not do so unless their vital interests are involved in a dispute. They would and should be ready to act to prevent the outbreak of any conflict that threatened to lead to a general war, but it is inconceivable that they would or should assume the risk of war to prevent a border dispute in the Balkans, or to help maintain Japanese control of the Shantung Province or British supremacy in Ireland and India. Unconditional ratification of the treaty by the United States would, therefore, be worse than outright rejection, for it would mean the making of promises that the American people could not possibly honor in the future.

Fourth, unqualified membership in the League will raise grave dangers to American interests and the American constitutional system. It will menace American control over immigration and tariff policies, imperil the Monroe Doctrine, increase the power of the president at the expense of Congress, and necessitate the maintenance of a large standing army for the fulfillment of obligations under the Covenant.

Fifth, and most important, full-fledged participation in such a system of collective security as the Covenant establishes will spell the end of American security in foreign affairs, because it will mean transferring the power of decision over questions of peace and war from the president and Congress to an international agency which the United States could not control.

Voicing these objections day in and out as the great debate reached its crescendo in the autumn of 1919, the limited internationalists made their purposes and program indelibly clear. They would accept most of the provisions of the treaty unrelated to the League and acquiesce in the ones that they did not like. They would also sanction American membership in the League of Nations.

But they would also insist upon reserving to the United States, and specifically to Congress, the power of decision concerning the degree of American participation in the League; and they would make no binding promise to enforce collective security anywhere in the future.

This was also the position of Senator Lodge, the man who devised and executed the Republican strategy in the upper house during the parliamentary phase of the treaty struggle. Personally, Lodge had little hope for the success of the League, a profound personal contempt for Wilson, and almost a sardonic scorn for the President's international ideals. The Massachusetts senator was an ardent nationalist, almost a jingoist, no isolationist, but a believer in a strong balance of power. His solution would have been harsh terms, including dismemberment, for Germany and the formation of an Anglo-Franco-American alliance as the best insurance for future peace. But as chairman of the Foreign Relations Committee and leader of his party in the Senate, it was his duty to sublimate his own strong feelings and to find a common ground upon which most Republicans could stand. That common ground, that program acceptable to an overwhelming majority of Republicans inside the Senate and out, was, in brief, to approve the treaty and accept membership in the League, subject to certain amendments and reservations that would achieve the objectives of the limited internationalists.

Debated all through the late summer of 1919, these amendments and reservations were embodied in the report that the Republican majority of the Foreign Relations Committee presented to the upper house on September 10. During the following weeks the Senate rejected the amendments and adopted most of them in the form of reservations, fourteen in all. Most of them were unimportant, but there was one that constituted a virtual rejection of the system of collective security that Wilson had constructed. It was Reservation 2, which declared that the United States assumed no obligations to preserve the territorial integrity or political independence of any other country, unless Congress should by act or joint resolution specifically assume such an obligation. In addition, the preamble to the reservations provided that American ratification of the treaty should not take effect until at least three of the four principal Allied powers had accepted the reservations in a formal exchange of notes.

This, then, was the program to which most of Wilson's opponents stood committed by the time that the Senate moved toward a formal vote on the Versailles Treaty. Whether Lodge himself was an irreconcilable who desired the defeat of the treaty, or whether he was merely a strong reservationist is an important question, but an irrelevant one at this point. The significant fact is that he had succeeded in uniting most Republicans and in committing them to a program that affirmed limited internationalism at the same time that it repudiated American support of collective security for virtually the entire world.

Meanwhile, despite his earlier show of intransigence, Wilson had been hard at work in preparation for the impending struggle. In an effort to split the Republican ranks, he held a series of conferences in late July with eleven moderate Republican senators who were called mild reservationists because they favored approval of the treaty after the adoption of a few interpretive reservations. On

August 19 the President met the Foreign Relations Committee at the White House for a three-hour grilling on all phases of the settlement. In spite of these overtures, there were unmistakable signs that Wilson had failed to win the support of any large number of Republican senators and that the strong reservationists and isolationists were rapidly gaining ground in the debate that was now proceeding in full fury throughout the country.

In response, Wilson made one of the most fateful decisions of his career. It was, as he put it, to go to the people and purify the wells of public opinion that had been poisoned by the isolationists and opponents of unreserved ratification. He was physically weakened by his labors at Paris, and his physician warned that a long speaking tour might endanger his life. Even so, he insisted upon making the effort to rally the people, the sources of authority, who had always sustained him in the past.

Leaving Washington on September 3, 1919, Wilson headed for the heartland of America, into Ohio, Indiana, Missouri, Iowa, Nebraska, Minnesota, and the Dakotas—into the region where isolationist sentiment was strongest. From there he campaigned through the Northwest and the major cities of the Pacific Coast. The final leg of his journey took him through Nevada, Utah, Wyoming, and Colorado, where the tour ended after Wilson's partial breakdown on September 25 and 26. In all he traveled 8,000 miles in twenty-two days and delivered thirty-two major addresses and eight minor ones. It was not only the greatest speaking effort of Wilson's career, but also one of the most notable forensic accomplishments in American history.

Everywhere that he went Wilson pleaded in good temper, not as a partisan, but as a leader who stood above party strife and advantage. He made his tour, he explained, first of all so that the people might know the truth about the Treaty of Versailles and no longer be confused by the misrepresentations of its enemies. . . .

There remained the greatest threat of all to the integrity of the Covenant, the challenge of the Lodge reservations to Article 10. This reservation, Wilson warned, would destroy the foundations of collective security, because it was a notice to the world that the American people would fulfill their obligations only when it suited their purposes to do so. "That," the President exclaimed at Salt Lake City, "is a rejection of the Covenant. That is an absolute refusal to carry any part of the same responsibility that the other members of the League carry." "In other words, my fellow citizens," he added at Cheyenne,

> what this proposes is this: That we should make no general promise, but leave the nations associated with us to guess in each instance what we were going to consider ourselves bound to do and what we were not going to consider ourselves bound to do. It is as if you said, "We will not join the League definitely, but we will join it occasionally. We will not promise anything, but from time to time we may coöperate. We will not assume any obligations." . . . This reservation proposes that we should not acknowledge any moral obligation in the matter; that we should stand off and say, "We will see, from time to time; consult us when you get into trouble, and then we will have a debate, and after two or three months we will tell you what we are going to do." The thing is un-

worthy and ridiculous, and I want to say distinctly that, as I read this, it would change the entire meaning of the treaty and exempt the United States from all responsibility for the preservation of peace. It means the rejection of the treaty, my fellow countrymen, nothing less. It means that the United States would take from under the structure its very foundations and support.

The irony of it all was, Wilson added, that the reservation was actually unnecessary, *if the objective of its framers was merely to reserve the final decision for war to the American government.* In the case of all disputes to which it was not a party, the United States would have an actual veto over the Council's decision for war, because that body could not advise member nations to go to war except by unanimous vote, exclusive of the parties to the dispute. Thus, the President explained, there was absolutely no chance that the United States could be forced into war against its will, unless it was itself guilty of aggression, in which case it would be at war anyway.

These were, Wilson admitted, legal technicalities, and, he added, he would not base his case for American participation in the League of Nations upon them. The issue was not who had the power to make decisions for war, but whether the American people were prepared to go wholeheartedly into the League, determined to support its collective system unreservedly, and willing to make the sacrifices that were necessary to preserve peace. Wilson summarized all his pleading with unrivaled feeling at the Mormon capital, as follows:

> Instead of wishing to ask to stand aside, get the benefits of the League, but share none of its burdens or responsibilities, I for my part want to go in and accept what is offered to us, the leadership of the world. A leadership of what sort, my fellow citizens? Not a leadership that leads men along the lines by which great nations can profit out of weak nations, not an exploiting power, but a liberating power, a power to show the world that when America was born it was indeed a finger pointed toward those lands into which men could deploy some of these days and live in happy freedom, look each other in the eyes as equals, see that no man was put upon, that no people were forced to accept authority which was not of their own choice, and that out of the general generous impulse of the human genius and the human spirit we were lifted along the levels of civilization to days when there should be wars no more, but men should govern themselves in peace and amity and quiet. That is the leadership we said we wanted, and now the world offers it to us. It is inconceivable that we should reject it.

We come now to the well-known tragic sequel. Following his address at Pueblo, Colorado, on September 25, 1919, the President showed such obvious signs of exhaustion that his physician canceled his remaining engagements and sped the presidential train to Washington. On October 2 Wilson suffered a severe stroke and paralysis of the left side of his face and body. For several days his life hung in the balance; then he gradually revived, and by the end of October he was clearly out of danger. But his recovery was only partial at best. His mind remained relatively clear; but he was physically enfeebled, and the disease had wrecked his emotional constitution and aggravated all his more unfortunate personal traits. . . .

Virtually all historians now agree that Wilson's refusal to permit his followers in the Senate to approve the treaty with the Lodge reservations was an error of tragic magnitude. Having built so grandly at Paris, having fought so magnificently at home for his creation, he then proceeded by his own hand to remove the cornerstone of his edifice of peace. Why? Were there inner demons of pride and arrogance driving him to what one historian has called "the supreme infanticide"? Did his illness and seclusion prevent him from obtaining a realistic view of the parliamentary situation, or so disarrange him emotionally that he became incompetent in the tasks of statesmanship? Or was he simply an idealist who would make no compromises on what he thought were fundamental principles?

The historian, who sees through a glass darkly when probing the recesses of the mind, is not able to give final answers to questions like these. Wilson, for all his high-mindedness and nobility of character, was headstrong and not much given to dealing graciously or to compromising with men whom he distrusted and disliked. Once before, in a violent dispute at Princeton over control of the graduate school, he had revealed these same traits and suffered defeat because he could not work with men whom he did not trust. The sympathetic biographer would like to believe that it was his illness, which aggravated his bitterness and his sense of self-righteousness, that drove Wilson to his fatal choice. Perhaps this is true. He had not always been incapable of compromise; perhaps he would have yielded in the end if disease had not dethroned his reason.

These attempts to extenuate ignore the fact that there were fundamental and vital issues at stake in the controversy over the treaty—whether the United States would take leadership in the League of Nations without hesitations and reservations, or whether it would join the League grudgingly and with no promises to help maintain universal collective security. To Wilson the difference between what he fought for and what Lodge and the Republicans would agree to was the difference between the success or failure and the life or death of man's best hope for peace. This he had said on his western tour, at a time when his health and reasoning faculties were unimpaired. This he believed with his heart and soul. It is, therefore, possible, even probable, that Wilson would have acted as he did even had he not suffered his breakdown, for it was not in his nature to compromise away the principles in which he believed.

If this is true, then in this, the last and greatest effort of his life, Wilson spurned the role of statesman for what he must have thought was the nobler role of prophet. The truth is that the American people were not prepared in 1920 to assume the world leadership that Wilson offered them, and that the powers of the world were not yet ready to enforce the world-wide, universal system of collective security that the President had created.

Collective security failed in the portentous tests of the 1930's, not because the League's machinery was defective, but because the people of the world, not merely the American people alone, were unwilling to confront aggressors with the threat of war. As a result a second and more terrible world conflict came, as Wilson prophesied it would, and at its end the United States helped to build a new and different league of nations and took the kind of international leadership that Wilson had called for. But events of the past decade have not fully justified Wilson's confidence in international organization; the only really promising systems of collective security, the regional ones like NATO, have been of a kind that Wilson fervently denounced; and only the future can reveal whether his dream of a universal system can ever be made a reality.

And so it was Wilson the prophet, demanding greater commitment, sacrifice, and idealism than the people could give, who was defeated in 1920. It is also Wilson the prophet who survives in history, in the hopes and aspirations of mankind and in whatever ideals of international service that the American people still cherish. One thing is certain, now that men have the power to sear virtually the entire face of the earth: The prophet of 1919 was right in his larger vision; the challenge that he raised then is today no less real and no less urgent than it was in his own time.

FURTHER READING

Thomas A. Bailey, *Woodrow Wilson and the Lost Peace* (1944)
Paul Birdsall, *Versailles Twenty Years After* (1941)
Denna F. Fleming, *The United States and the League of Nations, 1918–1920* (1942)
John A. Garraty, *Henry Cabot Lodge* (1953)
Lawrence E. Gelfand, *The Inquiry: American Preparations for Peace* (1963)
W. Stull Holt, *Treaties Defeated by the Senate* (1933)
Herbert Hoover, *The Ordeal of Woodrow Wilson* (1958)
Warren F. Kuehl, *Seeking World Order* (1969)
Keith Nelson, *Victors Divided* (1973)
Robert E. Osgood, *Ideals and Self-Interest in American Foreign Relations* (1953)
Ralph A. Stone, *The Irreconcilables* (1970)
Seth P. Tillman, *Anglo-American Relations at the Paris Peace Conference, 1919* (1961)

4

Allied Intervention in
Bolshevik Russia

*One of the topics that received considerable Allied attention at the conference
in Versailles was Bolshevik Russia. In March 1917 a successful revolution
struck czarist Russia, placing a Provisional Government in power. But in
November of the same year the government of Alexander Kerensky was top-
pled by V. I. Lenin's radical Bolsheviks, in part because the Provisional regime
tried to keep an exhausted Russia in the war against Germany. After the Brest-
Litovsk Treaty, Russia left the war; peace did not come, however, as a bloody
civil war brought further terror and devastation.*

*The Allies, alarmed by the outspoken radicalism of the Bolsheviks and by
the closing of the eastern front, decided to send troops to Russia. Reluctantly
President Woodrow Wilson agreed to join the expeditions. In June 1918 American servicemen joined other forces to occupy Northern Russia, and in July
Wilson authorized about 10,000 American soldiers to go to Siberia.*

*Why the Wilson administration, after arguing against military intervention,
reversed itself remains a controversial question. The answers vary: Wilson
sought to aid anti-German Czechs stranded in Russia, to deny Germany military
supplies, to thwart Japan (which sent a large force), or to contain Bolshevism.
Whatever the reasons, the venture, combined with other anti-Bolshevik actions,
soured initial American relations with Soviet Russia and left scars for the future.*

DOCUMENTS

The first document, an American note to Japan arguing against military intervention
in Siberia, was sent on March 5, 1918. Yet the Wilson administration changed
its mind: on July 17, 1918, Secretary of State Robert Lansing sent an *aide-mémoire*

to the Allied Ambassadors announcing the reasons why the United States would send American troops to Siberia. The third document, notes on a Big Four conversation at Versailles on January 16, 1919, reveals British and American concern that military intervention would not halt the "dangerous" Bolshevik movement and the hope that negotiations might limit it. About two months later, on March 28, adviser Herbert Hoover wrote a long memorandum to the President, stating that a relief program in Russia would help to stabilize politics and to deny the Bolsheviks some of their appeal. The concluding document, written by the State Department on September 9, 1919, summarizes Woodrow Wilson's critical comments on Bolshevik Russia.

The United States Advises Japan Against Intervention, 1918

At your earliest opportunity you will please read to the Japanese Government the following message but leave no copy unless they request you to do so:

The Government of the United States has been giving the most careful and anxious consideration to the conditions now prevailing in Siberia and their possible remedy. It realizes the extreme danger of anarchy to which the Siberian provinces are exposed and the imminent risk also of German invasion and domination. It shares with the governments of the Entente the view that, if intervention is deemed wise, the Government of Japan is in the best situation to undertake it and could accomplish it most efficiently. It has, moreover, the utmost confidence in the Japanese Government and would be entirely willing, so far as its own feelings towards that Government are concerned, to intrust the enterprise to it. But it is bound in frankness to say that the wisdom of intervention seems to it most questionable. If it were undertaken the Government of the United States assumes that the most explicit assurance would be given that it was undertaken by Japan as an ally of Russia, in Russia's interest, and with the sole view of holding it safe against Germany and at the absolute disposal of the final peace conference. Otherwise the Central powers could and would make it appear that Japan was doing in the East exactly what Germany is doing in the West and so seek to counter the condemnation which all the world must pronounce against Germany's invasion of Russia, which she attempts to justify on the pretext of restoring order. And it is the judgment of the Government of the United States, uttered with the utmost respect, that, even with such assurances given, they could in the same way be discredited by those whose interest it was to discredit them; that a hot resentment would be generated in Russia itself, and that the whole action might play into the hands of the enemies of Russia, and particularly of the enemies of the Russian revolution, for which the Government of the United States entertains the greatest sympathy, in spite of all the unhappiness and misfortune which has for the time being sprung out of it. The Government of the United States begs once more to express to the Government of Japan its warmest friendship and confidence and once more begs it to accept these expressions of judgment as uttered only in the frankness of friendship.

The American *Aide-Mémoire* for Intervention, 1918

The whole heart of the people of the United States is in the winning of this war. The controlling purpose of the Government of the United States is to do everything that is necessary and effective to win it. It wishes to cooperate in every practicable way with the Allied Governments, and to cooperate ungrudgingly; for it has no ends of its own to serve and believes that the war can be won only by common counsel and intimate concert of action. It has sought to study every proposed policy or action in which its cooperation has been asked in this spirit, and states the following conclusions in the confidence that, if it finds itself obliged to decline participation in any undertaking or course of action, it will be understood that it does so only because it deems itself precluded from participating by imperative considerations either of policy or of fact. . . .

It is the clear and fixed judgment of the Government of the United States, arrived at after repeated and very searching reconsiderations of the whole situation in Russia, that military intervention there would add to the present sad confusion in Russia rather than cure it, injure her rather than help her, and that it would be of no advantage in the prosecution of our main design, to win the war against Germany. It can not, therefore, take part in such intervention or sanction it in principle. Military intervention would, in its judgment, even supposing it to be efficacious in its immediate avowed object of delivering an attack upon Germany from the east, be merely a method of making use of Russia, not a method of serving her. Her people could not profit by it, if they profited by it at all, in time to save them from their present distresses, and their substance would be used to maintain foreign armies, not to reconstitute their own. Military action is admissible in Russia, as the Government of the United States sees the circumstances, only to help the CzechoSlovaks consolidate their forces and get into successful cooperation with their Slavic kinsmen and to steady any efforts at self-government or self-defense in which the Russians themselves may be willing to accept assistance. Whether from Vladivostok or from Murmansk and Archangel, the only legitimate object for which American or Allied troops can be employed, it submits, is to guard military stores which may subsequently be needed by Russian forces and to render such aid as may be acceptable to the Russians in the organization of their own self-defense. For helping the Czecho-Slovaks there is immediate necessity and sufficient justification. Recent developments have made it evident that it is in the interest of what the Russian people themselves desire, and the Government of the United States is glad to contribute the small force at its disposal for that purpose. It yields, also, to the judgment of the Supreme Command in the matter of establishing a small force at Murmansk, to guard the military stores at Kola, and to make it safe for Russian forces to come together in organized bodies in the north. But it owes it to frank counsel to say that it can go no further than these modest and experimental plans. It is not in a position, and has no expectation of being in a position, to take part in organized intervention in adequate force from either Vladivostok or Murmansk and Archangel. It feels that it ought to add, also, that it will feel at liberty to use the few troops it can spare only for the purposes here stated and shall feel obliged to withdraw those forces, in order to add them to the forces at the western front, if the plans in whose execution it is now intended that they should cooperate should develop into others inconsistent with the policy to which the Government of the United States feels constrained to restrict itself.

At the same time the Government of the United States wishes to say with the utmost cordiality and good will that none of the conclusions here stated is meant to wear the least color of criticism of what the other governments associated against Germany may think it wise to undertake. It wishes in no way to embarrass their choices of policy. All that is intended here is a perfectly frank and definite statement of the policy which the United States feels obliged to adopt for herself and in the use of her own military forces. The Government of the United States does not wish it to be understood that in so restricting its own activities it is seeking, even by implication, to set limits to the action or to define the policies of its associates.

It hopes to carry out the plans for safeguarding the rear of the Czecho-Slovaks operating from Vladivostok in a way that will place it and keep it in close cooperation with a small military force like its own from Japan, and if necessary from the other Allies, and that will assure it of the cordial accord of all the Allied powers; and it proposes to ask all associated in this course of action to unite in assuring the people of Russia in the most public and solemn manner that none of the governments uniting in action either in Siberia or in northern Russia contemplates any interference of any kind with the political sovereignty of Russia, any intervention in her internal affairs, or any impairment of her territorial integrity either now or hereafter, but that each of the associated powers has the single object of affording such aid as shall be acceptable, and only such aid as shall be acceptable, to the Russian people in their endeavor to regain control of their own affairs, their own territory, and their own destiny.

It is the hope and purpose of the Government of the United States to take advantage of the earliest opportunity to send to Siberia a commission of merchants, agricultural experts, labor advisers, Red Cross representatives, and agents of the Young Men's Christian Association accustomed to organizing the best methods of spreading useful information and rendering educational help of a modest sort, in order in some systematic manner to relieve the immediate economic necessities of the people there in every way for which opportunity may open. The execution of this plan will follow and will not be permitted to embarrass the military assistance rendered in the rear of the westward-moving forces of the Czecho-Slovaks.

The Big Four Discuss Bolshevik Russia at Versailles, 1919

Mr. Lloyd George commenced his statement setting forth the information in the possession of the British Government regarding the Russian situation, by referring to the matter which had been exposed recently in *L'Humanité*. He stated that he wished to point out that there had been a serious misconception on the part of the French Government as to the character of the proposal of the British Government. The British proposal did not contemplate in any sense whatsoever, a recognition of the Bolsheviki Government, nor a suggestion that Bolshevik delegates be invited to attend the Conference. The British proposal was to invite all of the different governments now at war within what used to be the Russian Empire, to a truce of God, to stop reprisals and outrages and to send men here to give, so to speak, an account of themselves. The Great Powers would then try to find a way to bring some order out of chaos. These men were not to be delegates to the Peace Conference, and he agreed with the French Government entirely that they should not be made members of the Conference.

Mr. Lloyd George then proceeded to set forth briefly the reasons which had led the British Government to make this proposal. They were as follows:

Firstly, the real facts are not known;

Secondly, if it is impossible to get the facts, the only way is to adjudicate the question; and

Thirdly, conditions in Russia are very bad; there is general misgovernment and starvation. It is not known who is obtaining the upper hand, but the hope that the Bolshevik Government would collapse has not been realized. In fact, there is one report that the Bolsheviki are stronger than ever, that their internal position is strong, and that their hold on the people is stronger. Take, for instance, the case of the Ukraine. Some adventurer raises a few men and overthrows the government. The government is incapable of overthrowing him. It is also reported that the peasants are becoming Bolsheviki. It is hardly the business of the Great Powers to intervene either in lending financial support to one side or the other, or in sending munitions to either side.

Mr. Lloyd George stated that there seemed to be three possible policies:

1. Military intervention. It is true that the Bolsheviki movement is as dangerous to civilization as German militarism, but as to putting it down by the sword, is there anyone who proposes it? It would mean holding a certain number of vast provinces in Russia. The Germans with one million men on their Eastern Front only held the fringe of this territory. If he now proposed to send a thousand British troops to Russia for that purpose, the armies would mutiny. The same applies to U.S. troops in Siberia; also to Canadians and French as well. The mere idea of crushing Bolshevism by a military force is

pure madness. Even admitting that it is done, who is to occupy Russia? No one can conceive or undertake to bring about order by force.

2. A cordon. The second suggestion is to besiege Bolshevik Russia. Mr. Lloyd George wondered if those present realized what this would mean. From the information furnished him Bolshevik Russia has no corn, but within this territory there are 150,000,000 men, women and children. There is now starvation in Petrograd and Moscow. This is not a health cordon; it is a death cordon. Moreover, as a matter of fact, the people who would die are just the people that the Allies desire to protect. It would not result in the starvation of the Bolsheviki; it would simply mean the death of our friends. The cordon policy is a policy which, as humane people, those present could not consider.

Mr. Lloyd George asked, who was there to overthrow the Bolsheviki? He had been told there were three men, Denikin, Kolchak and Knox. In considering the chances of these people to overthrow the Bolsheviki, he pointed out that he had received information that the Czecho-Slovaks now refused to fight; that the Russian Army was not to be trusted, and that while it was true that a Bolshevik Army had recently gone over to Kolchak it was never certain that just the reverse of this did not take place. If the Allies counted on any of these men, he believed they were building on quick-sand. He had heard a lot of talk about Denikin, but when he looked on the map he found that Denikin was occupying a little backyard near the Black Sea. Then he had been told that Denikin had recognized Kolchak, but when he looked on the map there was a great solid block of territory between Denikin and Kolchak. Moreover, from information received it would appear that Kolchak has been collecting members of the old regime around him, and would seem to be at heart a monarchist. It appeared that the Czecho-Slovaks were finding this out. The sympathies of the Czecho-Slovaks are very democratic, and they are not at all prepared to fight for the restoration of the old conditions in Russia.

Mr. Lloyd George stated that he was informed that at the present time two-thirds of Bolshevik Russia was starving.

Institutions of Bolsheviki are institutions of old Czarist regime. This is not what one would call creating a new world.

3. The third alternative was contained in the British proposal, which was to summon these people to Paris to appear before those present, somewhat in the way that the Roman Empire summoned chiefs of outlying tributary states to render an account of their actions.

Mr. Lloyd George pointed out the fact that the argument might be used that there were already here certain representatives of these Governments; but take, for instance, the case of Sassonoff, who claims to represent the Government of Omsk. As a matter of fact, Sassonoff cannot speak from personal observation. He is nothing but a partisan, like all the rest. He has never been in contact, and is not now in direct contact with the Government at Omsk.

It would be manifestly absurd for those who are responsible for bringing about the Peace Conference, to come to any agreement and leave Paris when one-half of Europe and one-half of Asia is still in flames. Those present must settle this question or make fools of themselves.

Mr. Lloyd George referred to the objection that had been raised to permitting Bolshevik delegates to come to Paris. It had been claimed that they would convert France and England to Bolshevism. If England becomes Bolshevist, it will not be because a single Bolshevist representative is permitted to enter England. On the other hand, if a military enterprise were started against the Bolsheviki, that would make England Bolshevist, and there would be Soviet in London. For his part, Mr. Lloyd George was not afraid of Bolshevism if the facts are known in England and the United States. The same applies to Germany. He was convinced that an educated democracy can be always trusted to turn down Bolshevism.

Under all the circumstances, Mr. Lloyd George saw no better way out than to follow the third alternative. Let the Great Powers impose their conditions and summon these people to Paris to give an account of themselves to the Great Powers, not to the Peace Conference.

M. Pichon suggested that it might be well to ask M. Noulens, the French Ambassador to Russia, who had just returned to France, to appear before the meeting tomorrow morning, and give those present his views on the Russian situation.

President Wilson stated that he did not see how it was possible to controvert the statement of Mr. Lloyd George. He thought that there was a force behind his discussion which was no doubt in his mind, but which it might be desirable to bring out a little more definitely. He did not believe that there would be sympathy anywhere with the brutal aspect of Bolshevism. If it were not for the fact of the domination of large vested interests in the political and economic world, while it might be true that this evil was in process of discussion and slow reform, it must be admitted, that the general body of men have grown impatient at the failure to bring about the necessary reform. He stated that there were many men who represented large vested interests in the United States who saw the necessity for these reforms and desired something which should be worked out at the Peace Conference, namely, the establishment of some machinery to provide for the opportunity of the individuals greater than the world has ever known. Capital and labor in the United States are not friends. Still they are not enemies in the sense that they are thinking of resorting to physical force to settle their differences. But they are distrustful, each of the other. Society cannot go on on that plane. On the one hand, there is a minority possessing capital and brains; on the other, a majority consisting of the great bodies of workers who are essential to the minority, but do not trust the minority, and feel that the minority will never render them their rights. A way must be found to put trust and cooperation between these two.

President Wilson pointed out that the whole world was disturbed by this question before the Bolsheviki came into power. Seeds need soil, and the Bolsheviki seeds found the soil already prepared for them.

President Wilson stated that he would not be surprised to find that the reason why British and United States troops would not be ready to enter Russia to fight the Bolsheviki was explained by the fact that the troops were not at all sure that if they put down Bolshevism they would not bring about a re-establishment of the ancient order. For example, in making a speech recently, to a well-dressed audience in New York City who were not to be expected to show such feeling, Mr. Wilson had referred casually to Russia, stating that the United States would do its utmost to aid her suppressed people. The audience exhibited the greatest enthusiasm, and this had remained in the President's mind as an index to where the sympathies of the New World are.

President Wilson believed that those present would be playing against the principle of free spirit of the world if they did not give Russia a chance to find herself along the lines of utter freedom. He concurred with Mr. Lloyd George's view and supported his recommendations that the third line of procedure be adopted.

President Wilson stated that he had also, like Mr. Lloyd George, received a memorandum from his experts which agreed substantially with the information which Mr. Lloyd George had received. There was one point which he thought particularly worthy of notice, and that was the report that the strength of the Bolshevik leaders lay in the argument that if they were not supported by the people of Russia, there would be foreign intervention, and the Bolsheviki were the only thing that stood between the Russians and foreign military control. It might well be that if the Bolsheviki were assured that they were safe from foreign aggression, they might lose support of their own movement.

President Wilson further stated that he understood that the danger of destruction of all hope in the Baltic provinces was immediate, and that it should be made very clear if the British proposal were adopted, that the Bolsheviki would have to withdraw entirely from Lithuania and Poland. If they would agree to this to refrain from reprisals and outrages, he, for his part, would be prepared to receive representatives from as many groups and centers of action, as chose to come, and endeavor to assist them to reach a solution of their problem.

He thought that the British proposal contained the only suggestions that led anywhere. It might lead nowhere. But this could at least be found out.

Herbert Hoover on the Bolshevik Danger, 1919

As the result of Bolshevik economic conceptions the people of Russia are dying of hunger and disease at the rate of some hundreds of thousands monthly in a country that formerly supplied food to a large part of the world.

I feel it is my duty to lay before you in just as few words as possible my views as to the American relation to Bolshevism and its manifestations. These views at least have the merit of being an analysis of information and thought gleaned from my own experience and the independent sources which I now have over the whole of Europe, through our widespread relief organization.

It simply cannot be denied that this swinging of the social pendulum from the tyranny of the extreme right to the tyranny of the extreme left is based on a foundation of real social grievance. The tyranny of the reactionaries in Eastern and Central Europe for generations before the war, and the suffering of their common people is but a commonplace to every social student. This situation was thrown into bold relief by the war and the breakdown of these reactionary tyrannies. After fighting actually stopped on the various fronts the famine which followed has further emphasized the gulf between the lower and upper classes. The poor were starved and driven mad in the presence of extravagance and waste.

It is to be noticed that the Bolshevik ascendancy or even their strong attempts so far are confined to areas of former reactionary tyranny. Their courses represent the not unnatural violence of a mass of ignorant humanity, who themselves have learned in grief of tyranny and violence over generations. Our people, who enjoy so great liberty and general comfort, cannot fail to sympathize to some degree with these blind gropings for better social condition. If former revolutions in ignorant masses are any guide, the pendulum will yet swing back to some moderate position when bitter experience has taught the economic and social follies of present obsessions. No greater fortune can come to the world than that these foolish ideas should have an opportunity somewhere of bankrupting themselves.

It is not necessary for any American to debate the utter foolishness of these economic tenets. We must all agree that our processes of production and distribution, the outgrowth of a hundred generations, in the stimulation to individual initiative, the large equality of opportunity and infinite development of mind and body, while not perfect, come about as near perfection as is possible from the mixture of avarice, ambition, altruism, intelligence, ignorance and education, of which the human animal is today composed. The Bolshevik's land of illusion is that he can perfect these human qualities by destroying the basic processes of production and distribution instead of devoting himself to securing a better application of the collective surplus.

Politically, the Bolsheviki most certainly represent a minority in every country where they are in control, and as such they constitute a tyranny that is the negation of democracy, for democracy as I see it must rest on the execution of the will of the majority expressed by free and unterrified suffrage. As a tyranny, the Bolshevik has resorted to terror, bloodshed and murder to a degree long since abandoned even amongst reactionary tyrannies.

He has even to a greater degree relied upon criminal instinct to support his doctrines than even autocracy did. By enveloping into his doctrines the cry of the helpless and the downtrodden, he has embraced a large degree of emotionalism and has thereby given an impulse to his propaganda comparable only to the impulse of large spiritual movements. This propaganda, however, in my view will stir other populations only in ratio to their proportions of the suffering and ignorant and criminal. I feel myself, therefore, that the political danger of spread of Bolshevism by propaganda is a direct factor of the social and political development of the population which they attempt to impregnate. Where the gulf between the middle classes and the lower classes is large, and where the lower classes have been kept in ignorance and distress, this propaganda will be fatal and do violence to normal democratic development. For these reasons, I have no fear of it in the United States, and my fears as to other countries would be gauged by the above criterion. It is possible that the Soviet type of government might take hold in some other countries as a primitive form of democracy, but its virulence will be tempered by their previous degree of political subversion.

There remains in my mind one more point to be examined, that is as to whether the Bolshevik centers now stirred by great emotional hopes will not undertake large military crusades in an attempt to impose their doctrines on other defenseless people. This is a point on which my mind is divided with the evidence at hand, and it seems to me that the whole treatment of the problem must revolve on the determination of this one question. If this spirit is inherent in their doctrine, it appears to me that we must disregard all other questions and be prepared to fight, for exactly the same reasons that we entered the European War against Germany. If this is not the case, then it appears to me that from an American point of view we should not involve ourselves in what may be a ten year military entanglement in Europe. The American people cannot say that we are going to insist that any given population must work out its internal social problems according to our particular conception of democracy. In any event, I have the most serious doubt that outside forces entering upon such an enterprise can do other than infinite harm, for any great wave of emotion must ferment and spread under repression. In the swing of the social pendulum from the extreme left back toward the right, it will find the point of stabilization based on racial instincts that could never be established by outside intervention.

I think we have also to contemplate what would actually happen if we undertook military intervention in, say, a case like Hungary. We should probably be involved in years of police duty, and our first act would probably in the nature of things make us a party of reestablishing the reactionary classes in their economic domination over the lower classes. This is against our fundamental national spirit, and I doubt whether our soldiers under these circumstances could resist infection with Bolshevik ideas. It also requires consideration as to whether or not our people at home, on gradual enlightenment as to the social wrongs of the lower classes in these countries, would stand for our providing power by which such reactionaries held their position, and we would perchance be thrown into an attempt as governors to work out some social reorganization of these countries. We thus become a mandatory with a vengeance. We become, in fact, one of four mandatories, each with a different political and social outlook, for it would necessarily be a joint Allied undertaking. Furthermore, in our present engagements with France, England and Italy, we become a junior in this partnership of four. It is therefore inevitable that in these matters where our views and principles are at variance with the European Allies we would find ourselves subordinated and even committed to policies against our convictions.

In all these lights, I have the following three suggestions:

First. We cannot even remotely recognize this murderous tyranny without stimulating actionist radicalism in every country in Europe and without transgressing on every National ideal of our own.

Second. That some Neutral of international reputation for probity and ability should be allowed to create a second Belgian Relief Commission for Russia. He should ask the Northern Neutrals who are especially interested both politically and financially in the restoration of better conditions in Russia, to give to him diplomatic, financial and transportation support; that he should open negotiations with the Allied governments on the ground of desire to enter upon the humane work of saving life, and ask the conditions upon which ships carrying food and other necessaries will be allowed to pass. He should be told that we will raise no obstructions and would even help in his humanitarian task if he gets assurances that the Bolsheviki will cease all militant action across certain defined boundaries and cease their subsidizing of disturbances abroad; under these conditions that he could raise money, ships and food, either from inside or outside Russia; that he must secure an agreement covering equitable distribution, and he might even demand that Germany help pay for this. This plan does not involve any recognition or relationship by the Allies of the Bolshevik murderers now in control any more than England recognized Germany in its deals with the Belgian Relief. It would appear to me that such a proposal would at least test out whether this is a militant force engrossed upon world domination. If such an arrangement could be accomplished it might at least give a period of rest along the frontiers of Europe and would give some hope of stabilization. Time can thus be taken to determine whether or not this whole system is a world danger, and whether the Russian people will not themselves swing back to moderation and themselves bankrupt these ideas. This plan, if successful, would save an immensity of helpless human life and would save our country from further entanglements which today threaten to pull us from our National ideals.

Third. I feel strongly the time has arrived for you again to reassert your spiritual leadership of democracy in the world as opposed to tyrannies of all kinds. Could you not take an early opportunity to analyze, as only you can, Bolshevism from its political, economic, humane and its criminal points of view, and, while yielding its aspirations, sympathetically to show its utter foolishness as a basis of economic development; show its true social ends; rap our own reactionaries for their destruction of social betterment and thereby their stimulation of Bolshevism; point, however, to the steady progress of real democracy in these roads of social betterment. I believe you would again align the hearts of the suffering for orderly progress against anarchy, not alone in Russia but in every Allied country.

If the militant features of Bolshevism were drawn in colors with their true parallel with Prussianism as an attempt at world domination that we do not stand for, it would check the fears that today haunt all men's minds.

Woodrow Wilson on Bolshevism, 1919

In a speech at Kansas City Saturday, September 6, urging the ratification of the Peace Treaty, the President made the following allusion to the situation in Russia and the character of the Bolshevik régime:

"My fellow citizens, it does not make any difference what kind of a minority governs you, if it is a minority. And the thing we must see to is that no minority anywhere masters the majority.

That is at the heart, my fellow citizens, of the tragical things that are happening in that great country which we long to help and can find no way that is effective to help—I mean the great realm of Russia. The men who now are measurably in control of the affairs of Russia represent nobody but themselves. They have again and again been challenged to call a constitutional convention. They have again and again been challenged to prove that they had some kind of a mandate, even from a single class of their fellow citizens. And they dared not attempt it; they have no mandate from anybody.

There are only thirty-four of them, I am told, and there were more than thirty-four men who used to control the destinies of Europe from Wilhelmstrasse. There is a closer monopoly of power in Petrograd and Moscow than there ever was in Berlin, and the thing that is intolerable is not that the Russian people are having their way but that another group of men more cruel than the Czar himself is controlling the destinies of that great people.

And I want to say here and now that I am against the control of any minority anywhere."

Following passage, same topic, from speech delivered at Des Moines also on September 6:

"What happened in Russia was not a sudden and accidental thing. The people of Russia were maddened with the suppression of Czarism. When at last the chance came to throw off those chains, they threw them off at first, with hearts full of confidence and hope and then they found out that they had been again deceived. There was no assembly chosen to frame a constitution for them, or rather there was an assembly chosen to choose a constitution for them and it was suppressed and dispersed, and a little group of men just as selfish, just as ruthless, just as pitiless as the Czar himself assumed control and exercised their power, by terror and not by right.

And in other parts of Europe the poison spread. The poison of disorder, the poison of revolt, the poison of chaos. And do you honestly think, my fellow citizens, that none of that poison has got in the veins of this free people? Do you know that the world is all now one single whispering gallery? These antennae of the wireless telegraph are the symbols of our age.

All the impulses of mankind are thrown out upon the air and reach to the ends of the earth. With the tongue of the wireless and the tongue of the telegraph all the suggestions of disorder are spread through the world. And money coming from nobody knows where is deposited in capitals like Stockholm to be used for the propaganda of disorder and discontent and dissolution throughout the world, and men look you calmly in the face in America and say that they are for that sort of revolution, when that sort of revolution means government by terror, government by force, not government by vote.

It is the negation of everything that is American, but it is spreading and so long as disorder continues, so long as the world is kept waiting for the answer of the kind of peace we are going to have and what kind of guarantees there are to be behind that peace, that poison will steadily spread, more and more rapidly until it may be that even this beloved land of ours will be distracted and distorted by it."

_____

ESSAYS

George F. Kennan, author of numerous studies on Soviet affairs, a self-professed conservative, and a career diplomat who served briefly in the 1950s as Ambassador to Russia, accepts the Wilson administration's official explanation as the essential reason why troops were dispatched: to aid the Czechs so that they could eventually fight the Germans. William Appleman Williams of Oregon State University stresses, on the other hand, that Wilson and other American leaders were strongly anti-Bolshevik, rejected the idea of any cooperation with the Communists, and took interventionist steps to cripple the young revolution. The "George Kennan" Williams mentions in his essay was the cousin of the grandfather of George F. Kennan.

_____

A War Decision Against Germany

GEORGE F. KENNAN

If we reflect today on the psychological background of the great conflict of outlook and aspiration between the United States and the ruling party of the Soviet Union, we see that whereas the bitterness of feeling among Americans relates mainly to things the Soviet government has done since the final phases of World War II, Soviet grievances against the United States have a longer historical background and include the behavior of the United States government around the time of the Russian Revolutions of 1917 and in the years immediately following those events. The Allied military intervention of the years 1918 to 1920, in particular, continues to occupy a prominent position in Soviet memory. It has recently been the subject of a number of works by Soviet historians. It has been repeatedly mentioned, just within the past year, in the statements of leading Soviet personalities. And the dominant theme of all this material has been one of bitter reproach to the United States, as having been a leading instigator and participant in the intervention and as having acted, throughout this episode, from motives which were unworthy in themselves and hostile to the interests of the Russian people.

A clear and authoritative view of the Soviet attitude toward the Allied

George F. Kennan, "American Troops in Russia: The True Record," *Atlantic Monthly,* 203 (1959), 36–42. Copyright © 1958, by The Atlantic Monthly Company, Boston, Mass. Reprinted with permission.

intervention was presented in the autumn of 1957 in the Theses published by the Central Committee of the Communist Party of the Soviet Union in connection with the forty-year anniversary of the Bolshevik Revolution. These Theses dwelt at length on the intervention and described it as consisting of "military campaigns against our country." Nothing was said to suggest that these expeditions might have been directed to any other purpose. The world war was not mentioned.

When the Bolsheviki assumed power in Petrograd in November, 1917, this event caused great concern in the Allied capitals. The leadership of the Bolshevik Party was known to consist of men who not only professed deepest disapproval and contempt for the ideals of the Western governments and peoples but who also publicly denounced the Allied cause in the war as an unworthy and imperialistic one, called for an immediate cessation of hostilities on terms that meant the abandonment of the stated Western war aims, and made it clear that they were resolved to make peace with the Germans. Within a month of their advent to power they moved to put this resolution into effect by entering into negotiations with the Germans. Coming as it did shortly after the military collapse on the Italian front, and with the German offensive of the following spring already looming ahead, the defection of Russia was a grievous and even heart-rending blow to the Allied cause.

One can have one's own view, in the light of history, as to the soundness of Allied war aims, and hence of Allied reasons for wishing to continue the war, in late 1917. But one cannot judge the people of the past by contemporary insights. It was idle to expect the Western governments and peoples to be anything other than deeply worried by the impending departure of Russia from the ranks of the Allied powers, with the prospects that some two million German soldiers might be transferred from the eastern to the western front and that the great physical resources of Russia might then become available to the German war machine.

In these circumstances, it was natural that Allied statesmen and military leaders should have thought of a possible Allied military action in Russia for the purpose of restoring an eastern front against Germany.

We must remember that the Allies did not regard themselves, in the winter of 1917–1918, as being under any obligation to respect the decision of the Soviet government to take Russia out of the war. They did not regard that government as representative of Russian public opinion. They were aware that it had not been elected to office. The Soviet authorities, furthermore, did not at that time control all the territory of the former Russian Empire; there were regions controlled by elements which still professed loyalty to the Allied cause.

In the winter of 1917–1918, the United States was not yet taking a prominent part in the war and was not participating in the military decisions that governed the Allied war effort. It was primarily the French and British military planners who were interested in the possibility of restoring an eastern front. But France and Britain could spare no troops for this purpose. Therefore they turned to America and to Japan for possible sources of manpower and supply for such a military effort.

In the case of Japan, this suggestion raised very delicate problems. Japan was formally a member of the Allied coalition, though it had taken little active part in the war. The political turmoil in European Russia had now thrown Siberia into a state of chaos and weakness. Japan could scarcely be expected to pass up so favorable an opportunity to improve its situation in Manchuria and Eastern Siberia at Russia's expense and thus to rectify the injustice it considered itself to have suffered in the outcome of the Russian-Japanese War.

So long as Russia had been an ally of the Western powers, the Western governments could not have encouraged any attempt by Japan to profit from Russia's weakness. But now that Russia was out of the war, now that the seats of power in Petrograd and Moscow had been seized by a political faction hostile to the Allied cause, now that the alternative to Japanese penetration of Russia seemed to many people to be German penetration, the question arose as to whether Japan should not be encouraged to enter Siberia, either in conjunction with other Allied forces or as a mandatory agent for the Allies as a whole. Perhaps—or so it seemed to the French and British military planners—perhaps Japanese forces might even be able to penetrate as far as European Russia and to make enough trouble for the Germans there to cause them to retain at least a substantial portion of their troops on the eastern front.

Throughout the winter of 1917–1918, while the Soviet and German negotiators haggled at Brest-Litovsk over the terms of the separate peace between Germany and Russia, the French and British repeatedly approached the United States government with suggestions along these lines. The American response was consistently negative. Neither President Wilson nor his Secretary of State, Robert Lansing, nor his intimate unofficial adviser, Colonel House, could see any merit in these proposals.

Secretary of State Lansing favored a policy of complete abstention from any interference in Russia. " 'Do nothing' should be our policy," he said to the President in December, 1917, "until the black period of terrorism comes to an end." "This government," he said in January, 1918, "must continue for the present a silent witness of the internal confusion which prevails in Russia."

Colonel House similarly warned the President against any action in Russia. To treat Russia as an enemy would, he said, be sure to throw it into the lap of Germany.

That Wilson shared these views of his advisers is clear beyond question. His position was reflected in a number of official statements of the United States government in the winter and spring of 1918, all of which had his official approval and some of which he drafted personally.

A fair example of these was a communication to the Japanese government, of January 20, 1918, which stated:

> The common interests of all the powers at war with Germany demand from them an attitude of sympathy with the Russian people . . . any movement looking towards the occupation of Russian territory would at once be construed as one hostile to Russia and would be likely to unite all factions in Russia against us.

The events of February and March, 1918—the reopening in February of hostilities against Russia by the Germans as a means of bringing pressure in the negotiations, the final signature of the Russian-German peace treaty on March 3, its ratification on March 16, and the opening of the great German offensive on the western front five days later—these events caused the heaviest sort of pressure to be brought on Wilson to change his stand and to sanction an intervention in Siberia by the Japanese. Since the Japanese themselves were not yet ready to take any action independently, and refused to act as mandatory for the Allies generally unless the United States joined in making the request, everything appeared to hang on Wilson's decision.

Despite these pressures, the President remained adamant throughout the winter and spring of the year. The wisdom of intervention, he said in a communication to the Allied governments on March 5, seemed to the United States government to be most questionable. If any action were to be taken by the Japanese, he assumed it would be accompanied by a declaration to the effect that they were acting "as an ally of Russia, in Russia's interest, and with the sole view of holding it safe against Germany." But even with such a declaration, he thought the action would be misinterpreted, that

> a hot resentment would be generated in Russia itself, and that the whole action might play into the hands of the enemies of Russia, and particularly of the enemies of the Russian Revolution, for which the Government of the United States entertains the greatest sympathy, in spite of all the unhappiness and misfortune which has for the time being sprung out of it.

In the absence of Wilson's approval the Japanese continued, for the moment, to abstain from action. In April, 1918, in the face of the new German offensive in the west, the French and British military planners conceived a somewhat more elaborate scheme for intervention in Russia. This scheme envisaged Allied landings both at Vladivostok and at the northern ports of European Russia. At Vladivostok it would be the Japanese who would bear the main burden; at Murmansk and Archangel a mixed Allied force, in which the Americans would play a prominent part. The expeditions at these widely separated points would combine with local anti-Bolshevik forces loyal to the Allied cause, would advance toward each other, and would eventually link up, thus creating a solid Allied front from Siberia to the upper Volga region and forcing the Germans to reconstitute their military position in the east.

This was a wholly impractical plan. There was, as American statesmen repeatedly pointed out, no reason at any time to believe that the Japanese were interested in any objectives further west than Irkutsk or that they could be prevailed upon to send their troops beyond the Trans-Baikal area. The anti-Bolshevik Russians with whom it was proposed to collaborate were far too weak to play anything resembling the role assigned to them in this scheme.

It was obvious at the time that Wilson would never have given his approval to such a plan, and the idea was apparently never made known to him in its entirety. Nevertheless, the French and British military planners did not wait for American approval before going ahead to implement the project to the extent they were able.

Insofar as Siberia was concerned, they could, for the moment, do no more than continue and intensify the pressure on Wilson to agree to a Japanese intervention, and this they did to the best of their ability throughout May and June. But with respect to the northern ports, they proceeded to take action at once. Allied warships had already been stationed at Murmansk for many months; the local Soviet there had adopted an attitude friendly to the Allies; and a few British marines had been landed in March with the full consent of the local authorities. Now, in May, the British sent to Murmansk such few soldiers as they were able to spare, under the command of a general who was supposed eventually to command the entire northern expedition. Since this force was wholly inadequate to the purpose in question, the British approached the United States government with the request that an American contingent also be made available for service at the North Russian ports.

Nothing was said to Wilson, on this occasion, about the plan for penetrating into the interior and linking up with the Siberian intervention. The plan was put to him as merely an arrangement for the defense of the northern ports, particularly Murmansk, against the Germans. He was told that there was danger of the Murmansk Railways being attacked by anti-Communist Finns who were supposed to be under German influence and that the Germans might seize Murmansk and develop the port as a submarine base if the Allies did not take preventative action.

We can see today that these fears were greatly exaggerated. But they were sincerely entertained, at the time, by both British and American representatives in Russia.

In addition, Wilson was given to understand that American troops were needed in the Russian North to protect great quantities of Allied war supplies, said to have accumulated in the ports of that region before the October Revolution. Actually, the overwhelming portion of the stores had already been seized and hauled off to the interior by the Bolsheviki, but neither the British government nor Wilson appears to have been aware of these facts.

Despite all the arguments in favor of intervention, Wilson remained at all times skeptical of the merits of this proposed expedition. But he observed, finally, to his Secretary of War that he felt obliged to do it anyhow because the British and French were pressing it on his attention so hard and he had refused so many of their requests that they were beginning to feel that he was not a good associate, much less a good ally. Opposition was made harder for him by the pro-Allied attitude of the local Soviet at Murmansk and by reports from Allied representatives in Russia that the Soviet government was not really so averse as it pretended to be to the idea of an Allied landing in the North.

Wilson therefore finally replied to the British government, in June, 1918, that while he had no enthusiasm for the scheme, he would abide in this instance by the opinion of Marshal Foch, the Allied commander in chief on the western front. If Foch really thought the requested American battalions would be of more use in Murmansk than in France, they would be sent. Foch, at British urging, confirmed to the President in writing that he approved the diversion of this force. The American units were therefore turned over to the British in England in July and placed under British command, to be used in the Russian North as the British might see fit. This was the origin of America's participation in the northern intervention.

Meanwhile, the situation in Siberia had been drastically altered by the outbreak at the end of May of the conflict between the Czechoslovak Corps and the Bolsheviki. This Czech force was made up largely of men who had been taken prisoner or had deserted from the Austro-Hungarian Army and who were desirous of fighting on the Allied side. In the spring of 1918, the Czech Corps was attempting to make its way from European Russia to the western front via Vladivostok. In April and May, it was strung out in trainloads along the Trans-Siberian Railway all the way from the Ukraine to Vladivostok. As a result of the breakdown of the old Russian Army, the Czech Corps was now probably the strongest single armed force in Russia.

On May 26, hostilities broke out between the Czechs and the Soviet authorities along the route. This uprising of the Czechs was not, as has been frequently alleged, the result of Allied instigation. It was a product of the frictions and misunderstandings occasioned by the effort of the Czechs to move across Siberia in the chaotic conditions then existing, and especially of the incidents which occurred when the Czechs encountered parties of Austrian or Hungarian war prisoners who were, after the conclusion of the Brest-Litovsk peace, due for repatriation and were trying to make their way along the railway in the opposite direction.

Not only were the French and British not responsible for the Czech uprising, but the uprising actually came as a setback to the Allied military planners, who had hoped to use a portion of the Czech Corps in the northern ports and had just made arrangements with the Soviet authorities to have this portion of the corps routed to the Russian North. The outbreak of the conflict between the Czechs and the Bolsheviki made this impossible, and the failure of the Czechs ever to arrive at Archangel had a good deal to do with the eventual failure of the northern expedition.

As a result of their uprising, the Czechs were successful in seizing, within a few days, most of the Trans-Siberian Railway from the Volga to Irkutsk. Another body of some eighteen thousand Czechs had by this time arrived at Vladivostok, but there were, at the time of the uprising, no Czech trains in the area between Vladivostok and Irkutsk. This territory thus remained initially in Soviet hands.

The Czechs in Vladivostok were now concerned to re-establish contact with their compatriots in Central and Western Siberia and to ensure the security of the passage of the main body of the corps to the Pacific. To this end, they seized Vladivostok at the end of June and mounted an operation westward to clear the railway toward Irkutsk. Finding themselves opposed by Communist forces in the neighborhood of Vladivostok, they appealed to the Allied governments, and particularly to the Japanese and United States governments, for military support. In doing so, they contrived to convey to official Washington the impression that the opposition with which they found themselves faced was provided not by Russian Communists but by German and Austrian prisoners of war who had been rearmed by the Bolsheviki and who now threatened to seize Siberia on behalf of the Central Powers.

Again, this was a very distorted impression. We know today that very few of the war prisoners in Siberia—two or three thousand at the most out of some eight hundred thousand—were armed by the Bolsheviki. These were all prisoners who had accepted the Communist orientation. They were mostly Hungarians. There were scarcely any Germans among them. Neither the German nor the Austrian government had had anything to do with the rearming of these men; both governments had in fact opposed it vigorously. But the myth of Siberia's being about to be seized by Germany through the agency of the war prisoners was diligently propagated by all those Allied officials, particularly the French, who wanted intervention; and the Czechs, who were now very anxious for American support, did not hesitate to avail themselves, sincerely or otherwise, of the same suggestion.

To Wilson, this apparent plight of the Czechs presented a wholly new situation. Here was an Allied force, apparently fighting to keep Siberia out of German hands, and it needed American support. Wilson had extremely friendly feelings for the Czechs, as he did for the other Slavic peoples of Eastern Europe. And he had, like many other Americans, a sentimental prejudice in favor of little countries. Little countries, he thought, were good; big countries (aside from his own) were bad. Thus the plight of the Czechs as he understood it appealed to him, and he thought he saw in it at long last a possibility for putting an end to the pressures of the British and French for action in Siberia without associating himself with their political schemes, of which he was deeply suspicious. He therefore arrived, on July 6, 1918, at his final decision. The text of it, as recorded in a confidential cabinet document, is now available. Wilson wrote every word of it himself.

In this memorandum, the President once again dismissed emphatically the whole idea of attempting to restore an eastern front against Germany by an action through Siberia. With this he would have nothing to do. But he did see justification for helping the Czechoslovaks at Vladivostok to establish contact with their compatriots further west. He was prepared, he said, to send seven thousand American soldiers, provided that the Japanese would put up a similar force, to guard the line of communication of the Vladivostok Czechs as they advanced westward along the Trans-Siberian Railway to make contact with their comrades at Irkutsk.

Wilson's decision has often been portrayed as part of a general Allied decision for intervention in Siberia. Actually, it was not this at all. It was in no way responsive to what the British and French had been urging on him, and he did not regard it as being so. He did not consider the action he was authorizing to be intervention against the Bolsheviki, and in communicating his decision to the other Allied governments he condemned the very idea of intervention in the roundest of terms. The British were furious with him over the whole affair; they regarded his decision as a unilateral one, not in any way responsive to their request, and in answer to it they proceeded to act on their own, with a view to realizing the plans they had conceived.

The Japanese, who were thrown into a great crisis of decision by Wilson's proposal, also proceeded after some hesitation to take what was virtually unilateral action, although they tried to present it as a response to Wilson's initiative. They sent to Siberia an expedition far greater than anything Wilson had proposed, and in conjunction with this they seized Northern Manchuria, an act which the United States government greatly deplored. At one moment, Wilson was inclined to withdraw from the entire undertaking, but it was too late. He realized that to withdraw would be to give the Japanese a free hand in Siberia and to forfeit all possibility of exercising any restraining influence on them by maintaining the semblance of Allied collaboration. The American force was therefore sent, as proposed.

So much for the origins of the American action in Russia. Now a word about the course it took. It is necessary to distinguish these two things quite sharply, for in both instances—North Russia and Siberia—the President's decision was taken against an inaccurate pattern of information, partly out of date, partly erroneous; and in neither case did the actual course of events resemble in any way what he had hoped would be the result of his decision.

The three battalions destined for service in the Russian North were turned over to the British in England in midsummer of 1918. Their fate was now in British hands. They were young recruits, mostly of Polish-American origin, from Michigan and Wisconsin. They had had very little training, no combat experience, and no political indoctrination whatsoever. I do not believe that one out of a hundred of them had the faintest idea why they were being sent to North Russia or against whom they were supposed to be acting. Equipped with British uniforms and Russian rifles, they were loaded onto troopships and dispatched northward at the end of August. The Spanish influenza broke out on board all three vessels. Medical supplies were not available. Both men and crews were decimated.

The British, meanwhile, without awaiting the arrival of the Americans, had landed at Archangel with a small, inadequate force, consisting mainly of some six hundred British and one French colonial battalion. The Archangel Soviet, in contrast to that of Murmansk, was not friendly to the Allies, and the bloodless entry of the Allied force was made possible only by a *putsch* carried out in the city by anti-Communist elements on the eve of the arrival of the Allied expedition. But the Bolsheviki mounted resistance on the outskirts of the city, and the British soon found themselves hard pressed even to maintain a perimeter some hundred kilometers from the center of the place. The American units, which were originally assigned to Murmansk, were therefore hastily rerouted to Archangel, where they arrived on September 4. Of those who were healthy, the majority were packed off the same evening for the front. By the next day, they found themselves deep in the swamps and forests of Northern Russia, under fire for the first time in their lives, and facing an adversary of whose identity they had no clear idea.

In the ensuing weeks and months, things developed in a highly unfavorable and unexpected way in the area held by the Allies around Archangel. The anti-Communist Russians within the Allied perimeter fell into two main categories: the Social Revolutionaries and the conservative former officers. These two factions loathed each other as violently as they did the Bolsheviki, and agreed on nothing. Their squabbles, superimposed on a complete lack of unity and of political understanding among the Allied representatives themselves, disgusted and antagonized the local population. It proved impossible to recruit any sizable and reliable Russian armed force. With the few foreign troops he had at his disposal, the British commander was able to do no more than to hold on to his perimeter around the city. The early descent of the arctic winter pinned the troops to their defensive positions, and any deep advance into the interior became out of the question.

In Siberia, things were no better. There, too, the Americans arrived in September. The junction of the Vladivostok Czechs with those on the western reaches of the Trans-Siberian Railway had, ironically enough, been effected on the day prior to the arrival of the main body of the Americans. The Czechs, furthermore, had decided, under Allied encouragement, not to try to make their way out of Russia through Vladivostok but rather to remain in Siberia and to fight the Bolsheviki in the area of the Urals. But the Japanese were now in Siberia, with ten times the number of troops Wilson had envisaged. No one wanted to leave the field entirely to them.

The Americans therefore settled down to guarding sections of the Amur Railway thousands of miles from any place where fighting was going on in the Russian civil war. It does not appear that any of these American forces ever fired a shot in regular combat against any unit of the Red Army during the year and a half of their stay in Siberia. There was one advance contingent of the Americans who, before the arrival of the American general, allowed themselves to be taken under Japanese command and were thus included, though not on the firing line, among the forces used in one small battle between the Japanese and the Czechs on the one hand and the Communists on the other. The American commander, General Graves, who arrived a few days later, put a stop to this use of his men. Graves was a fine soldier with an ironclad sense of duty. He took very seriously the President's injunction that he was not to get mixed up in Russian politics. He was extremely unpopular with the Allied representatives in Siberia, precisely for his firm refusal to participate in any action against the Bolsheviki or against any other Russian faction as such, and there were even charges from the British and French side that he was pro-Bolshevik.

Only a few weeks after the arrival of these American units in North Russia and Siberia World War I came to an end. This rendered unsubstantial the main military objectives for which the expeditions had been dispatched and raised the question of what should be done with them. In view of the fact that the situation in Russia was certain to be one of the first subjects for discussion among the senior Allied statesmen at the forthcoming Paris Peace Conference, no action was taken regarding the Allied forces in Russia in the initial weeks following the armistice.

At Paris, the whole question of Russia and the intervention was repeatedly discussed by the senior Allied figures. Wilson came to the conference convinced that the Allied intervention in Russia was a mistake and a failure. The Allied forces there, he said at one of the sessions of the Council of Ten in February, 1919, were doing no good. They did not know for whom or for what they were fighting. They were not assisting any promising common effort to establish order. They ought to be removed at once.

This remained his opinion throughout, and as soon as it became clear that the Peace Conference could find no useful action to take in the Russian problem as a whole, the British government was advised that the United States government desired that the American troops in North Russia should leave at the earliest opportunity. This could not be before late spring or early summer, owing to the ice conditions in the approaches to Archangel. Also, the United States government had no inclination to pull the troops out so abruptly as to cause military embarrassment to those Allied forces with whom they had been associated. They actually left Northern Russia in June and July, 1919, which was just about as soon as their departure could be decently arranged.

In the nine or ten months of their service on Russian soil, these Americans had taken no part in any actions other than ones of a defensive nature. Even this they had done under British command, and in the execution of a scheme which their President had never understood or sanctioned. They were a small force, three or four thousand men in all. Their withdrawal had nothing to do with any defeat in battle.

In Siberia, the situation of the American force was complicated by the fact that during the winter of 1919, before and during the Paris Peace Conference, the French and British succeeded in bringing about the establishment in Central and Western Siberia of an anti-Bolshevik authority under Admiral Kolchak. The Americans, who had nothing to do with this development, found themselves in effect guarding Kolchak's line of communication, or at least a small portion of it, far from the front. As the Peace Conference neared its end, reports were received in Paris that the Kolchak forces were doing well in their struggle against the Bolsheviki, and heavy pressure was brought to bear on Wilson, both by the British and by subordinates in his own American establishment, to give recognition and support to the Kolchak cause. Wilson authorized an investigation of Kolchak's situation, and pending the outcome of this investigation, he delayed the removal of the American force in Eastern Siberia. The investigation was not completed until late summer. It revealed that Kolchak was not doing well at all; he was doing so badly, in fact, that nothing short of a rescue expedition in the number of fifty thousand Allied troops could save him. Anything of this sort was out of the question.

By the time this report was received in Washington, Wilson was already embarked on his tragic speaking tour, trying to assure American ratification of the peace treaty and membership in the League of Nations. In the course of this tour he suffered a stroke, and he was never able fully to resume his control of American policy.

With Kolchak's defeat in the late autumn of 1919, it became clear that the American force could no longer be left in Siberia without danger of its becoming seriously embroiled in the Russian civil war. The decision to withdraw it was therefore taken, in the early winter of 1920, and the troops were removed as soon as this could be physically arranged, which was in April.

In 1933, when negotiations were undertaken between the United States and the Soviet Union looking toward a resumption of diplomatic relations, the Soviet negotiator, Litvinov, arrived in Washington prepared to advance a major claim against the United States government for damages allegedly done by the Americans in the course of the Siberian intervention. He was then permitted by the United States government to see certain of the materials in the American archives dealing with this subject. After examining these materials and communicating with his government, Litvinov addressed a letter to President Roosevelt formally renouncing, on behalf of the Soviet government, any claim for damages arising out of the American expedition in Siberia. The matter has never, to my knowledge, been officially raised since that time, though the Communist propaganda machine has worked the issue for all it was worth.

Viewed in their entirety, the American expeditions to North Russia and Siberia appear today as pathetic and ill-conceived ventures, to which Woodrow Wilson—poorly informed, harried with wartime burdens, and torn between his own instincts and his feeling of obligation to his Allies—was brought against his own better judgment. He did his best at all times to keep the American action from assuming the form of an interference in Russian internal affairs, and there is no suggestion more preposterous than that he was animated in these decisions by hostility toward the Russian people or by a desire to overthrow the Soviet regime with American forces. In both cases, his original decision was closely linked with America's wartime concerns. Had there been no great European war in progress, neither expedition would ever have been dispatched.

That the expeditions were regrettable—that it would have been better, from the standpoint of American interests, had they never been sent—seems hardly open to doubt. That they reflected imperialistic motives and constituted a serious injury to the Russian people is a figment of the imagination of Soviet propagandists, useful to their political purpose but not to the development of historical truth.

Anti-Bolshevism

WILLIAM APPLEMAN WILLIAMS

The vigorous reassertion in February 1918 of the fundamentally anti-Bolshevik attitudes of American leaders placed President Wilson under increasing pressure from the logic of his own outlook to intervene directly in Russia. His prob-

William A. Williams, "American Intervention in Russia, 1917–1920" (Part Two), *Studies on the Left*, 4 (1964), 39–57. Reprinted by permission of the author.

lem henceforward was to find a way to act against the Bolsheviks that would enable him to resolve or rationalize his moral dilemma, that would be effective against the revolutionary forces and that would offer a way of preventing Japan from exploiting intervention to weaken or even subvert the Open Door Policy in Asia.

It is not surprising, therefore, that Wilson and Lansing slapped aside a serious and dramatic French proposal to try collaboration with the Bolsheviks, or that they did so in an instantaneous and ruthless refusal. This striking reversal of earlier French policy, which favored military intervention, evolved in response to the clear indications that the Bolsheviks needed and wanted Allied assistance against the Germans. Renewed German operations in northern Russia prompted Trotsky to advise the coalition or revolutionaries in Murmansk on March 1 and 2, 1918, that it was "obliged to accept any help from the Allied Missions." Lenin supported that decision and later issued general orders to resist the Germans.

American and French representatives in Moscow knew of these decisions, and interpreted them as verification of their own estimates of Bolshevik policies. The American military advisors, who had been seeing Trotsky almost as often as Robins, filed strong recommendations in favor of supporting the Bolshevik effort against the Germans. Coupled with his continuing evaluation of the nature and meaning of the Revolution per se, this convergence of events led the French military attaché, Jacques Sadoul, to extend even further his own talents and energy in an effort to convince his superiors in Russia and Paris that cooperation was both the most rational and the most promising policy for France to follow.

Combining strong emotion and powerful logic with persuasive language, Sadoul's argument momentarily carried the day. The French Government reconsidered its heretofore militant anti-Bolshevism, supported Sadoul's negotiations with the Bolsheviks, and formally asked the United States if it would join in general collaboration with Lenin and Trotsky. American leaders considered the French proposal on February 19, conducting their talks in the context of a militantly anti-Bolshevik memorandum prepared by Miles.

The United States, Miles argued, defined democracy in terms of "the political freedom of its people." On the other hand, the Bolsheviks held that democracy was based on "equal economic freedom." His conclusion was unequivocal. "Fundamentally, these two conceptions are as different as black from white. It is idle to attempt to reconcile them as so many do. They are wholly different and cannot be reconciled." The Bolshevik view was "revolutionary in the deepest sense," and its advocates "have hitherto lived in the shadow." It is apparent, and should be made explicit, that American leaders were every bit as inflexible and deterministic as they accused the Bolsheviks of being; and, further, that it was the Bolsheviks who proved to be the more willing to diverge from the dictates of their theoretical and general opposition to collaboration with capitalist nations.

The decision on the French proposal was wholly in keeping with the logic and tone of the memorandum by Miles. He had not, of course, changed anybody's mind. But his analysis did reinforce the existing anti-Bolshevik consensus. Lansing personally took the French request to President Wilson. His brief pencilled notation documents their attitude: "This is out of the question. Submitted to Pres't who says the same thing." American leaders were of course interested in reestablishing resistance to the Germans on the eastern front, but they were not sufficiently anti-German to overcome their anti-Bolshevism.

Robins had no direct knowledge of this mid-February decision, and his efforts to arrange such cooperation with the Bolsheviks came to a climax between February 22, when the Bolshevik Central Committee voted to accept aid from the allies (with Lenin casting the crucial vote), and March 5, when Trotsky and Lenin gave Robins a written and specific inquiry designed to initiate a serious discussion concerning aid from the United States.

There is some evidence that a full copy of this document failed to reach Washington until after the Bolsheviks ratified the Brest-Litovsk treaty of peace with Germany. Even if this is true, and the evidence is not wholly convincing, the delay is far less significant than such writers as George Frost Kennan have made it appear. *Top American leaders already had explicit knowledge of the Bolshevik interest in obtaining assistance from the United States.* Furthermore, and as Washington was advised by several American military representatives in Russia, ratification of the treaty with Germany did not prevent the Germans from reopening their offensive—or the Bolsheviks from opposing that new attack as best they could. As late as March 26, for example, Francis told Lansing that the Red Army "is the only hope for saving European Russia from Germany." American policy-makers *could* have responded favorably to the overture from Lenin and Trotsky whenever it actually did arrive. For that matter, they could have offered such negotiations on their own initiative. They did neither.

Wilson's message to the Congress of Soviets of March 10 made it clear beyond any question that he had no intention even of exploring the possibilities of such cooperation. He bluntly told the Russian people that the United States, despite its great sympathy for their travail, was not going to help them through the Bolshevik Government. His words further carried the strong implication that the Bolsheviks were in league with the Germans. This document was prepared, moreover, in the course of continuing discussions designed to evolve a plan of intervention which would resolve the moral and practical dilemmas confronting Wilson and other American leaders. By February 26, for example, Lansing was referring in his conversations with Wilson to "our proposed policy." The resulting decision seems to have been produced by several convergent pressures, and was based upon a rather subtle strategy for controlling the variables involved in intervention.

After their proposal to collaborate with the Bolsheviks had been dismissed out of hand, the French returned to nagging Wilson for some kind of intervention in Siberia. The British supported this campaign to break down the President's resistance. And the Japanese, of course, continued their own push for permission to move onto the mainland of Asia. These pressures on the United States were powerful in and of themselves, and gained additional

strength from the political and psychological circumstances. Wilson was opposing other Allied suggestions, for example, and he seems to have felt that
he might gain some political ground by agreeing to some form of intervention.
The psychological factor involved the fatigue which was apparent in Wilson
and Lansing. They were tired men, and were no doubt particularly weary of
the Russian issue. The inclination to go on in and be done with it may have
become quite strong once they had turned their backs on the idea of working
with or through the Bolsheviks.

Even so, there was more than political higgling and ennui involved in Wilson's decision in February to approve Japanese intervention. For one thing,
Lansing and Wilson seem to have concluded that Japan might do something
regardless of American or allied approval. "My own belief," Lansing fretted
in a letter to the President on February 27, "is that Japan intends to go into
Siberia anyway." This raised the very difficult question of how to limit and
control the Japanese. Lansing first encouraged the Chinese to hold the line
in Manchuria. He told them that the United States wanted "the Chinese Government to take over and guard that part of the Trans-Siberian Railroad
system [i.e., the Chinese Eastern Railway] which passes through Manchuria."
And, since the Chinese already had troops near Harbin, and could send more,
this was not an empty gesture.

A second move was based on the old adage of publicly committing a suspect
to a self-denying pledge as a way of preventing the crime. Wilson and Lansing
had a perfect opportunity to do this: a Japanese spokesman had voluntarily
offered such assurances. It is not so often realized, however, that France and
the other allies were also concerned to check Japan. Perhaps the intensity of
the French desire to act has obscured this point. While it is true that neither
France nor England were as sensitive to Japanese operations in Manchuria,
or in North China, as the United States was, it is *not* true that they were indifferent to the implications of an unrestrained Japanese move into the mainland—particularly in view of Tokyo's seizure of Shantung Province, and its
Twenty One Demands of 1915. And, because it was a late-comer to the
scramble for concessions in Asia, and because it was rather self-conscious
about its lack of success prior to the war, Italy manifested an even stronger
resistance to unilateral, unchecked Japanese intervention.

Lansing had clear evidence of this concern before Wilson acted between
February 27 and March 1. The French were "very emphatic" and very explicit:
"A full understanding and agreement would have to be had with Japan by
all the other leading Allied powers, providing for the retirement of Japanese
troops from Russian soil after the war, in addition to certain other guarantees."
As if to make doubly sure that the meaning was understood, the French
"evinced a keen curiosity as to the reason for the United States Government's
opposing exclusive Japanese intervention."

France ideally preferred to bind Japan with a treaty, but Lansing demurred:
that approach would involve the Senate, and the ensuing debate would cause
jarring complications. A full, public discussion of policy toward Russia was
not desirable from the point of view of the Wilson administration. That would

open the way for Robins, Thompson, and other critics to force modifications in—or perhaps even a major change of—existing policy. The European powers acquiesced, and expressed themselves as being "quite satisfied with the way the matter is being handled by the President."

This support from England, Italy and France for the maneuver to control the Japanese encouraged Wilson and Lansing to feel, at least temporarily, and in conjunction with reports from Reinsch, Summers, and other American agents, that they could move in behind the Japanese and influence events in Russia along American lines through the use of economic power and diplomatic influence. Wilson's memorandum of the night of February 27 was a device to commit the Japanese to their own professions of moderation by announcing them publicly as the basis for American acquiescence in intervention. The United States, Wilson explained, "wishes to assure the Japanese Government that it has entire confidence that in putting an armed force into Siberia it is doing so as an ally of Russia, with no purpose but [to] save Siberia from the invasion of the armies and intrigues of Germany with entire willingness to leave the determination of all questions that may affect the permanent fortunes of Siberia to the Council of Peace."

This sly but all-inclusive caveat was intended to trap the Japanese. On the one hand, they dared not reject such a pleasant essay in praise of their integrity. On the other hand, it would do them no good to ignore it because in that contingency the United States could use it as an aide mémoire of an understanding based on earlier Japanese assurances. And, armed with the support of its European associates, America could feel confident of winning its point at the peace conference. In a real sense, Wilson was warning Japan to observe the conditions he specified or face united opposition.

Within 72 hours, however, Wilson withdrew even this support for Japanese intervention. The change, he told Polk, was "absolutely necessary." Several reasons account for the abrupt shift. The President was repeatedly and vigorously warned that the United States could not count on controlling Japan through the strategem of a self-denying pledge. These critics, such as Colonel House, argued that Wilson's approach risked creating an awful choice for the United States if the Japanese should decide to stay in Siberia, or turn their troops southward into China. If either of those conditions developed, the United States would have either to abandon the Open Door Policy or go to war against Japan. This analysis served to dramatize the second negative consideration, which was simply that Wilson was not ready to move immediately with a program of economic aid that would buttress American influence and also strengthen Russian and Chinese opposition to Japan.

In addition, the President also seems to have reconsidered the broad situation and, as a result, to have fallen back on the original strategy of December 1917, which was based on the axiom that direct intervention would provoke the Russians to support the Bolsheviks. Some Americans felt this would be particularly apt to occur if the Japanese went in alone; their reasoning being that racial antagonisms would be intensified by the memory of the Russian defeat in the Russo-Japanese War. And, finally, Wilson's central moral dilemma about intervention had been sharpened by reminders from men like Colonel House. They emphasized the loss of American influence if the principle of self-determination was so blatantly ignored.

All in all, the reversal of policy may well have been Wilson's finest moral hour. Torn by the conflict between his opposition to the Bolsheviks, which involved his entire political, economic, and social philosophy, and his deep involvement with the essential right of self-determination, the President chose to honor the moral axiom. Wilson's moral courage was no doubt reinforced by the fear that, given the existing circumstances, the Japanese outlook would triumph instead of his own. But that consideration should not be allowed to obscure either the intensity of Wilson's moral turmoil over intervention, or the central relationship between that agony and the change in policy. A man so essentially moralistic as Wilson could hardly be expected to view the Bolsheviks as anything but heretics, and to such men the heretic is even more dangerous than the non-believer. In this sense, at any rate, the surprise lies not so much in Wilson's final intervention, but rather in the strength and persistence of his moral qualms about such action. The liberal conscience ultimately broke down, but its initial resistance was greater than sometimes seems to be the case long after the crisis.

While it did not cause Wilson's change of mind, the Italian opposition to unilateral Japanese action may well have encouraged the President as he reconsidered the issue. Clearly seeking to creep in under the umbrella of the Open Door Policy, Italy made "three conditions" for its support of any Japanese move. Tokyo's action "should be satisfactory" to the United States, the intervention "should be *not* by Japan alone," and "guarantees should be given by Japan that they do not intend to hold territory."

Wilson's circular note of March 5, announcing that he now opposed unilateral Japanese intervention provides what is almost a diagram of his thinking on the general subject. He remarked first on the "most careful and anxious consideration" that he had given "to the extreme danger of anarchy" in Siberia. This social and political situation was the root cause of the crisis, and intervention might in the end be necessary to control matters before they got completely out of hand. But he was "bound in frankness to say that wisdom of intervention seems . . . most questionable." Then, in what was at once a veiled expression of his fears about Japan and his commitment to the right of self-determination, he warned that all the assurances in the world would not prevent "what Germany is doing in the West."

In conclusion, Wilson revealed that he had fallen back on the strategic estimate evolved early in December 1917. Military intervention would generate "a hot resentment" in Russia, "and that whole action might play into the hands of the enemies of Russia, and particularly the enemies of the Russian revolution, for which the Government of the United States entertains the greatest sympathy in spite of all the unhappiness and misfortune which has for the time being sprung out of it."

And to Wilson, as to American leaders in general, the Bolsheviks were both the cause and the substance of that unhappiness and misfortune. In their minds, at any rate, the Bolsheviks were not considered part of the Russian Revolution for which the United States entertained "the greatest sympathy." As Assistant Secretary of State Long put it in a personal letter to Reinsch, American policy was concerned with supporting "the original revolution."

Wilson did not abandon the idea of intervention on March 5; he merely refused to support one of-many tactics of intervening. The President continued his search for some way to go into Siberia as the dominant power in an Allied force including Japan and then begin economic and political operations in support of the anti-Bolshevik movement. There is no evidence that the discussions to evolve an effective way to accomplish this objective had been significantly influenced by the occasional rumors about German military operations in Siberia. Lansing reviewed these stories in a memorandum to Wilson on March 19, and concluded that Admiral Knight's evaluation was valid.

Knight concluded that it was "impossible" for any significant part of the military stores in Vladivostok to be destroyed; that there was "absolutely no danger" they would reach the Germans; and that there was "no evidence" of any serious German influence in Siberia. He added that Lenin and Trotsky, and their Bolshevik followers in the Far East, were revolutionaries—not German agents. And he concluded with a strong recommendation that it was "of first importance" that Japan "should not be permitted to act alone."

Lansing did become somewhat concerned, between March 21 and 24, 1918, over a new flurry of reports that the Bolsheviks were converting some German and Austrian prisoners-of-war to their radical ideology, and then using them in military operations against the anti-Bolshevik forces in Siberia. If this turned out to be true, the Secretary anticipated that "we will have a new situation in Siberia which may cause a revision of our policy." His reference to a "new situation," makes it clear that neither the Bolshevik-as-German agent theory, nor the fear of a German campaign in Siberia, was a causative factor in the discussions of intervention that took place between November 7, 1917, and March 20, 1918. Lansing's approach to the new reports, furthermore, was wholly conditional. He was merely doing what any responsible official would have done: "we should consider the problem on the hypothesis that the reports are true and be prepared to act with promptness."

Wilson commended the Secretary for his foresight, but did not think the situation called for action. "I do not find in them," he replied, "sufficient cause for altering our position." The stories reappeared from time to time, but decisions were not made on the assumption that they were true. In April, for example, both Reinsch and the Czech leader Thomas Masaryk advised Wilson and Lansing that the tales were not worth serious attention, and most certainly were not a reliable basis for policy decisions. Reinsch's estimate was based on extensive first-hand information. He put "much work" into his efforts to find out what was going on in Siberia, and his chief agent in the field, Major Walter S. Drysdale (the American military attaché in Peking) was a man with "a great deal of good sense."

An early report to Reinsch, prepared by a Colonel Speshneff on March 9, told of finding the prisoners employed "as clerks, [and] some of them work as painters, carpenters, shoemakers, tailors, hairdressers, etc." Speshneff wanted American intervention "in the internal affairs directed against the Bolsheviki," but he did not base his plea on the danger from the prisoners-of-war. He was simply against the Bolsheviks. Drysdale's review on March 19 of the evidence he had collected during a field trip was unequivocal: "not a single armed prisoner was seen and there is little probability that any of the prisoners are armed." Three weeks later, on April 10, he reaffirmed that estimate. "Some very few of the prisoners" at Chita were being converted politically, and were "fighting as workmen, for the workmen's cause, against the Bourgeoisie."

As one Austrian explained to Drysdale, "they were helping their brother laborers in Russia against Semenoff and the Bourgeoisie." This situation might with some accuracy have been described under the heading of Austrians-as-Bolsheviks, but it was positive disproof of the argument that the Bolsheviks were German agents. And, as the men on the scene reported, there were no other armed prisoners. These on-the-spot dispatches, and Reinsch's summary of them for Washington, put an end even to Lansing's conditional and hypothetical worry about the prisoners-of-war.

On the other hand, the idea of supporting the Bolsheviks against Germany continued to show life. Robins sustained his campaign for that policy to the point of antagonizing consul Summers beyond his endurance. But, when Summers asked for a transfer, Lansing promptly and effectively exerted pressure on the Red Cross directors to recall Robins from Russia. That did not put an end to the advice to collaborate with the Bolsheviks, however, for American military representatives continued to recommend the same policy after Robins was ordered to return to the United States.

These men, who had agreed with Judson's estimate of the situation in November and December 1917, had no illusions about a political honeymoon with the Bolsheviks. They understood that Lenin and Trotsky were fighting the Germans to save the revolution—not as a disinterested favor to the Allies. Some of them also have sensed, as Robins did, that the Bolsheviks were becoming aware that they—or any Russian government, for that matter—needed allies against Japan and Germany. Even before World War I, Robins had concluded from a general analysis of the world political system that an American-Russian entente offered security for both countries.

The military representatives may not have gone that far in thinking, but they did argue that short-run collaboration was the most intelligent and practical course of action. Ambassador Francis allowed them to continue their discussions with Trotsky, and even to offer some technical assistance, even though he intended that any army organized by Trotsky would be "taken from Bolshevik control" and used against the revolutionaries. He thought any agreement with the Bolsheviks would help sustain them in power, and considered that "cost will be too dear."

Sometime in the second or third week of April, at a stage when the German prisoner-of-war scare had been thoroughly discredited, President Wilson began an active search for some anti-Bolshevik group through which he could inject American power directly into the Russian situation. "I would very much value a memorandum," he advised Lansing on April 18, "containing *all* that we know about these several *nuclei* of self-governing authority . . . in Siberia. It would afford me a great deal of satisfaction to get behind the most nearly representative of them if it can indeed draw leadership and control to itself." Like the decision of December 10, 1917, to aid Kaledin in southern Russia, this letter makes it clear that American policy-makers were thinking of intervention as an anti-Bolshevik operation. The problem in the spring of 1918 was to find a winner; not only, of course, in order to defeat the Bolsheviks, but also to block the Japanese.

Further conversations between the two men seem almost certainly to have taken place during the next few days, even though no written record survives. This is strongly suggested, for example, by a dispatch Lansing sent to the American Ambassador in France on April 23. For, in briefing the Ambassador so that he would be able to discuss intervention with the French authorities, the Secretary clearly implied that such talks had occurred. Belgium and Italy, Lansing explained, had requested the United States to move a total of 450 officers and men, along with some armored cars, from Nagasaki and Vladivostok to the western front. *Acting on its own,* the American government had suggested in reply that it would be wise to leave the troops in the Far East.

That reply, Lansing explained, "was predicated upon the possibility of intervention in Siberia. It seemed inadvisable to bring away from there troops carrying flags of co-belligerents when it might be embarrassing to send back there other such troops." This action did not commit Wilson and Lansing to intervention, but it certainly indicates that they were discussing it seriously enough to keep non-Japanese troops in readiness. This conclusion is reinforced by Lansing's final cautionary word to the American Ambassador in France: "it is felt to be highly desirable that the matter should not be discussed with other persons."

Lansing and Wilson kept a sharp watch on the progress of the anti-Bolshevik leader Grigori Semenov during the ensuing month. Semenov was a Cossack who had served first as a Tsarist officer; then, after the March Revolution, he had gone to Siberia to raise a volunteer force of Mongols to battle the Germans. Caught in the east when the Bolsheviks took power, Semenov promptly began to fight them. He was vain, arrogant, and undemocratic, but his nerve and ruthlessness made him effective in the field—at least for a long enough time to attract the attention of American policy-makers. And, since neither Wilson nor Lansing favored negotiating any understanding with the Bolsheviks about intervention in Siberia, Semenov attracted their interest and concern.

The Secretary of State made it clear that he opposed any agreement with the Bolsheviks, even for the purpose of checking the Germans or the Japanese, because that "would array us against Semenov and the elements antagonistic to the Soviets." That should not be done. Wilson agreed, and on May 20 reiterated his instructions of April 18: "follow very attentively what Semenov is accomplishing and whether or not there is any legitimate way in which we can assist."

The President's clear and persistent concern to evolve some way of aiding the anti-Bolsheviks was reinforced during these weeks by an increasing campaign involving various anti-Bolshevik groups in the United States. They wanted to move in with economic aid, and then stay for a share in the post-Bolshevik economic pie. Wilson was interested in such plans, but his own thinking about intervention ran along the more narrow and specific line of aid to the anti-Bolshevik groups in their military operations. The door had to be opened, as it were, before the economic benefits—and influence—could flow through it. The President's approach of course involved economic assistance, but not in the precise form then being advocated by the various clusters of opinion in the United States. This difference between their outlooks became apparent in a second letter of May 20 from Wilson to Lansing.

A dispatch from Reinsch urging action prompted Wilson to ask the Secretary if the moment for intervention had arrived. "Situation in Siberia seems more favorable than ever," Reinsch judged on May 16, "for effective joint action of Allies and American initiative . . . Should America remain inactive longer friendly feeling is likely to fail." Lansing was definitely interested in Reinsch's argument, perhaps even partially persuaded, but not wholly convinced.

He was aware that Semenov's "policy is to keep the Siberian Railway open and overthrow the Bolsheviki," and that his successes offered "the prospect of forcing an amalgamation of all the different elements seeking reconstruction in Siberia." But the Secretary still worried about the danger of antagonizing the rank and file anti-Bolshevik Russians, even though support for Semenov could be combined with assistance to the Czecho-Slovak troops that were in Siberia. Lansing concluded, therefore, that the time was not yet "opportune" for direct intervention.

Wilson admitted the importance of not antagonizing the non-Bolshevik Russians, and of checking the Japanese, but those tactical difficulties did not lead him to abandon the search for a way to implement the strategy of anti-Bolshevism. He was prepared, as he told the British, to "go as far as intervention against the wishes of [the Russian] people knowing it was eventually for their good providing he thought the scheme had any practical chance of success." Joint intervention offered good possibilities of rallying the people against the Bolsheviks, but unilateral Japanese action would probably antagonize all the Russians "excepting for a small reactionary body who would join anybody to destroy the Bolsheviks."

Asked if this meant that the Allies should "do nothing at all," Wilson replied "No." "We must watch the situation carefully and sympathetically and be ready to move whenever the right time arrived." While waiting for an invitation to intervene from a successfully organized anti-Bolshevik group, Wilson wanted to prepare the way for effective operations by strengthening the economic situation in the non-Bolshevik areas of Siberia. Even as the President was thus reiterating his commitment to the fundamental strategy of anti-Bolshevik intervention, Lansing was modifying his tactical caution.

The Secretary received on May 26 a long letter from George Kennan, an old friend who was generally considered to be one of America's leading experts on Russian affairs. Kennan's advice and recommendations were militantly anti-Bolshevik. Lansing was impressed. "I have read the letter with especial interest because it comes from the highest authority in America on Russia." The Secretary naturally found it "gratifying that his own views were very similar" to those expressed by Kennan. The only significant disagreement concerned the "wisdom of intervention in Siberia."

Kennan was convinced that intervention was tactically workable as well as strategically desirable. Lansing wholly agreed on the strategy of anti-Bolshevism, but was "not so sure" that the tactic of direct intervention would prove successful. He explained, however, that the issue was receiving "very careful consideration" by the administration. And, because Kennan "had so clearly analyzed the state of affairs," Lansing promised to "lay it [the letter] before the President."

Lansing received more of the same kind of advice when he returned to the Department of State the next morning. A dispatch from Ambassador Page in London advised the Secretary that a League for the Regeneration of Russia in Union with Her Allies had been established in Rome, and was receiving support from Russians in England. It was militantly anti-Bolshevik, appealed directly to the United States for aid and suggested a "strong central government around which all sane elements would group themselves against Bolsheviks and Germans."

As he considered this development, the Secretary learned that the Allied ambassadors in Paris had agreed on the necessity and wisdom of intervention. They argued that it "must take place with or without the consent of the Bolshevik government," which in itself "has become far less important." Next, on May 30, Reinsch added his "urgent appeal" to act on the "extreme need for Allied action in Siberia." Russia, he explained, "is craving for order and will follow those who establish it. Only if established through Allied assistance will order be compatible with development of democracy."

All this was enough to prompt Lansing to warn Francis once again of the extreme care required in any ad hoc dealings with the Bolsheviks. "I am confident," the Secretary hopefully reminded the Ambassador, "you will appreciate the delicacy with which your actions . . . must be conducted." The Bolsheviks must not be allowed to receive or create any impression of American collaboration or assistance that would "alienate the sympathy and confidence of those liberal elements of Russian opinion which do not support Bolsheviki." As these instructions suggest, policy-makers in Washington were moving ever more rapidly toward overt intervention in support of their established anti-Bolshevism, and they wanted to rally all possible Russian support for the action.

On the next day, June 2, Lansing learned that a unit of Czecho-Slovak troops in Siberia had engaged the Bolsheviks. These men had fought with the Russians after deserting from the Austrian Army, but the Treaty of Brest-Litovsk left them without a war, and arrangements had been made by the French and the embryonic Czech government-in-exile, in negotiations with Lenin and Trotsky, for them to proceed via Siberia to the western front. Given the tensions in Russia, it would have taken a combination of great patience, extraordinary discipline, excellent communications, and unusual luck for such a contingent to avoid some clashes with the Bolshevik regional authorities. The odds against a peaceful remove to Vladivostok were simply too great, and a series of bitter outbreaks occurred along the Trans-Siberian Railway.

Lansing's first response in this situation was to assure Ambassador Page of the administration's sympathy and concern with the anti-Bolshevik League for the Regeneration of Russia. "Deeply interested in program for regeneration of Russia," he replied, "with which this Government, in the main, agrees." Then he alerted Francis to the increasing possibility of intervention through the subtle device of telling the Ambassador that the Department was "considering carefully" his own proposal of May 2 for such action. Assistant Secretary Long shortly thereafter reviewed for Lansing the advantages offered by intervention in liaison with the Czechs. They were "antagonistic to the Bolsheviks," and "available to be used as a military expedition to overcome Bolshevik influence, and under Allied guidance to restore order." As indicated by these and other dispatches of the period, American policy-makers straightforwardly discussed intervention as an anti-Bolshevik operation.

As the momentum for intervention increased among government policy-makers, Lansing became somewhat worried by a growing public discussion of the issue. The Secretary was afraid that the agitation would force the government to move before it was ready. Referring to the criticism of the government for the breakdown and failure of the aircraft construction program, Lansing warned against losing control of the intervention issue in a similar manner. "I see signs," he wrote Wilson on June 13, "in Congress and outside of a similar situation arising in connection with Russia." The Secretary's idea was to have Herbert Hoover take charge of an economic commission that would in turn provide an excellent public image of intervention. "Armed intervention to protect the humanitarian work done by the Commission," Lansing noted, "would be much preferable to armed intervention before this work had begun."

Wilson probably appreciated the political finesse inherent in Lansing's suggestion, but the President was strongly inclined to proceed first with armed intervention in support of the Czechs and other anti-Bolshevik forces. In that frame of mind, he responded favorably to Reinsch's analysis of June 13. Reinsch was very high on the Slavs: with "only slight countenance and support they could control all of Siberia against the Germans." The minister's reference to Germans did not mean that he had changed his mind about the nature of the Bolsheviks or about the danger of a German conquest of Siberia. He knew from Drysdale that the Czechs were anti-Bolshevik, and agreed with his subordinate that it was crucial to keep the Bolsheviks from mounting an effective counterattack.

The reference to Germany concerned his fear that an increasing number of prisoners-of-war might side with the Bolsheviks in view of the Czech attacks. He did not anticipate a German offensive in Siberia. Neither Wilson nor Lansing misread Reinsch's dispatch to mean that the nature of the danger had become German instead of Bolshevik. The President saw the Czechs as a strong, effective force which he could support against the Bolsheviks, and one which was also anti-Japanese and anti-German. That was precisely the kind of a nucleus he had been looking for since at least as early as the middle of April.

Wilson's central line of thought, and its anti-Bolshevik nature, was clearly revealed in his reaction to a favorable review and estimate of the All-Russian Union of Co-operative Societies. The leader of that organization, after expressing his opposition to the Bolsheviks, asked the United States to take the lead in intervention. The President's comment of June 19 on the report indicates not only his anti-Bolshevik objectives, but suggests very strongly that he had made his personal decision to intervene. The co-ops, he remarked, should be considered "instruments for what we are now planning to do in Siberia."

This interpretation is reinforced by another move Wilson made on the same day. He asked Secretary of War Baker to prepare a campaign plan for Siberia, using as a starting point a memorandum which proposed to undertake intervention by gathering and organizing support from the bourgeoisie in Siberia and the rest of Russia. The Army's reply was drafted by Chief of Staff General Peyton C. March. The war, he argued, would "be won or lost on the western front." Siberian intervention, "considered purely as a military proposition," was "neither practical nor practicable"—"a serious military mistake."

Wilson overruled this argument during a White House conference on July 6, 1918. He did so in full knowledge of the German assault on the Western Front. He also knew that the Czechs had overthrown the Bolsheviks in Vladivostok, and that they offered a general base of operations against the Bolsheviks throughout Siberia. Lansing had the same information. He noted on June 23 that the Czechs were "fighting the Red Guards along the Siberian line," and added on July 2 that they were fighting "to eject the local Soviets." As he commented in a private memo in July, the Secretary did "not think that we should consider the attitude of the Bolshevik Siberians."

The White House conference made it clear that intervention was *not* designed to establish an eastern front against the Germans. That was "physically impossible." Furthermore, the discussion of the basic "proposition and program" made no reference to aiding the Czechs against either the German or the Austrian prisoners-of-war. That phrasing appeared only as part of the "public announcement" to be made in conjunction with Japan, and in the section of the memorandum enumerating the conditions which Japan would have to meet.

Neither was there any mention of German or Austrian prisoners-of-war, or of Bolsheviks as German agents, in Wilson's aide mémoire of July 17, 1918. Though the document has often been described as rambling, fuzzy, and even contradictory, the truth of the matter is that Wilson was both lucid and candid. He discounted intervention as a maneuver to restore the eastern front, "even supposing it to be efficacious in its immediate avowed object of delivering an attack upon Germany," as "merely a method of making use of Russia." That would not help the Russians escape "from their present distress." The Bolsheviks were responsible for that distress.

As far as Wilson was concerned, the purpose of intervention was "only to help the Czecho-Slovaks consolidate their forces and get into successful cooperation with their Slavic kinsmen and to steady any efforts at self-government or self-defense in which the Russians themselves may be willing to accept assistance." The full significance of the word *only,* and of the phrase *Slavic kinsmen,* should not be missed. The *only* was a throwaway word for the simple reason that the Czechs supplied all that was necessary from the American point-of-view. For that reason, the *only* was directed at Tokyo and designed to specify American opposition to Japanese aggrandizement. In a similar vein, the phrase *Slavic kinsmen* was designed to reassure the Russians that the Japanese would be kept under control.

Since Wilson and other top American leaders knew the Bolsheviks to be radical social revolutionaries, and had repeatedly stated their opposition to them on that ground, the meaning of Wilson's aide mémoire should be clear. American intervention in Russia was a long-debated and long-delayed tactical move in support of the basic anti-Bolshevik strategy that had been established in December 1917. "I don't think you need fear of any consequences of our dealings with the Bolsheviki," he wrote Senator James Hamilton Lewis on July 24, 1918, "because we do not intend to deal with them."

Lansing added his explicit documentation a bit later. Absolutism and Bolshevism were the "two great evils at work in the world today," and the Secretary believed Bolshevism "the greater evil since it is destructive of law and order." It was, indeed, the "most hideous and monstrous thing that the human mind has ever conceived." That estimate led Lansing in 1918 to recommend a course of action that was to plague Western statesmen for at least two generations. "We must not go too far," he warned, "in making Germany and Austria impotent."

President Wilson continued to aid anti-Bolshevik forces in Russia well into 1919. For that matter, the last American troops did not leave Siberia until April 1, 1920. During those years and months, Wilson avowed his concern not only with the radicals in Russia, but also with "the dangers of Bolshevism" in the United States. "It will be necessary to be very watchful and united in the presence of such danger," he warned on the morrow of Armistice Day, 1918.

As for the difficulties which prevented intervention from attaining its objectives, both the President and Secretary Lansing left terse but sufficient comment. Wilson's explanation to Winston Churchill during a discussion of the issue at the Paris Peace Conference contained all the essentials. "Conscripts could not be sent and volunteers probably could not be obtained. He himself felt guilty in that the United States had in Russia insufficient forces, but it was not possible to increase them. It was certainly a cruel dilemma." Lansing made the same point to George Kennan in a "personal and secret" letter. "I wish you to know that it was not lack of sympathy which prevented the employment of a large active force in Siberia . . . We were bound hand and foot by the circumstances."

American intervention in Russia does not present the historian with an insuperable problem or an impenetrable mystery. It did not involve any dark conspiracy among American leaders. Considered as history, and leaving the question of its wisdom as policy for each reader to decide to his own satisfaction, the record indicates that the action was undertaken to provide direct and indirect aid to the anti-Bolshevik forces in Russia. It was thus anti-Bolshevik in origins and purpose. The men who made the decision viewed the Bolsheviks as dangerous radical social revolutionaries who threatened American interests and the existing social order throughout the world. They did not consider them to be German agents, nor did they interpret the Bolshevik Revolution as a coup engineered by the Imperial German Government.

Despite their concern to defeat Germany and to check Japan in the Far East, American leaders repeatedly refused to explore the possibility of attaining those objectives through collaboration with the Bolsheviks. *This was not a hypothetical alternative.* In spite of their theoretical doctrine, and the suspicion and hesitance it created in their minds, the Bolshevik leaders made persistent efforts to establish such co-operation. This flexibility created one of those turning points in history at which no one turned. The primary reason this opportunity was never exploited was because American leaders proved in action to be more doctrinaire and ideologically absolutist than the Bolsheviks. What might have been can never be known, but it is clear that American leaders proved less concerned with those possibilities than with the preservation of the status quo. As had so often been the case in the past, the United States defined Utopia as a linear projection of the present.

The only central question that remains unanswered about intervention concerns Wilson's personal authorization for the official publication of the infamous Sisson Documents, which purported to prove that the Bolsheviks were German agents. Neither the British Government nor the American State Department accepted the documents as proof of that allegation. Both therefore refused to publish the material. The President bears sole responsibility.

This becomes even more impressive when it is realized that *Edgar Sisson himself discounted the documents as proof that the Bolsheviks were German agents.* He said this explicitly on February 19, 1918, in a cable to George Creel, his superior in the Committee on Public Information. "These are wild internationalists," Sisson explained, "who not only in the beginning but until lately were willing to have German support for their own ends of Revolution. Germany thought she could direct the storm but the storm had no such intention."

One can only wonder, since no documentary evidence has ever been found, if Wilson knew of and read this dispatch which was transmitted through the State Department. It would certainly help to know; for, early in March, the President privately and personally ordered Sisson to proceed straight to Washington without any further discussion of the documents he had purchased in Russia. We do know that Lansing refused to accept and publish the material under the seal of the Department of State, and that Sisson was an angry man when he left his confrontation with the Secretary at the end of the first week in May. And we know that Lansing later called Sisson "a dangerous person" in a warning about dealing with him in connection with official business.

Finally, of course, we know that Sisson prevailed upon Wilson to publish the forgeries. He did so behind Lansing's back, and despite the Secretary's explicit opposition. It is possible, but unlikely, that Sisson simply persuaded the President that the documents were genuine. Wilson's own estimate of, and attitude toward, the Bolsheviks belies such an explanation. And while it is conceivable, it is highly improbable, that the decision hinged upon some personal matter between Wilson and Sisson.

Thus the evidence points toward the conclusion that Wilson underwrote the publication of the documents as a way of rationalizing his decision to intervene against the Bolsheviks despite his commitment to the principle of self-determination. The President had been intensely aware of that dilemma from the outset of the crisis, and it had caused him great torment and anguish. But he had ultimately intervened. Yet, knowing Wilson, it seems extremely unlikely that the overt act resolved the personal and ideological agony. And so, perhaps as a last effort to ease that terrible pressure, the President acquiesced in Sisson's insistent pleas. If such was the case, then it was an appropriate curtain for the tragedy of intervention.

The historian and the citizen can choose from among several arguments concerning the wisdom of intervention. He can agree with Winston Churchill that the revolutionary baby should have been strangled at birth. He can feel with Raymond Robins that the first opening to the left should have been explored; that such a course might have prevented, or at least significantly mitigated, subsequent suffering endured by the entire world. Or he can fatalistically conclude that it all would have turned out just the same no matter what had been done differently between November 1917 and April 1920.

Whatever the final evaluation, however, it does seem both more accurate and more helpful to begin the process of reflection on the consequences of intervention with the awareness that the action was anti-Bolshevik in origin and intent.

FURTHER READING

John Bradley, *Allied Intervention in Russia, 1917–1920* (1968)

Peter G. Filene, *Americans and the Soviet Experiment, 1917–1933* (1967)

Lloyd C. Gardner, ed., *Wilson and Revolutions, 1913–1921* (1976)

George F. Kennan, *The Decision to Intervene* (1958)

George F. Kennan, *Russia Leaves the War* (1956)

Arno Mayer, *Politics and Diplomacy of Peacemaking: Containment and Counter-revolution at Versailles* (1967)

John Thompson, *Russia, Bolshevism, and the Versailles Peace* (1966)

Eugene P. Trani, "Woodrow Wilson and the Decision to Intervene in Russia: A Reconsideration," *Journal of Modern History,* 48 (1976), 440–461

Betty M. Unterberger, *America's Siberian Expedition, 1918–1920* (1956)

Betty M. Unterberger, ed., *American Intervention in the Russian Civil War* (1969)

William A. Williams, *American-Russian Relations, 1781–1947* (1952)

5

Franklin D. Roosevelt
and Isolationism
Between the Wars

*The rise of European aggression in the 1930s presented Americans once
again with questions of war or peace, neutrality or alliance. Congress passed
Neutrality Acts to isolate the nation from the crises in Europe, and
President Franklin D. Roosevelt publicly concurred with the neutral position
of the United States. Remembering World War I with distaste and beset
by a terrible depression at home, many Americans endorsed what was
popularly known as isolationism. They wanted no part of European troubles,
especially because it appeared that the Europeans themselves could not
solve their own problems.*

*After the outbreak of full-scale war in October 1939, Roosevelt and the
nation gradually moved toward an interventionist posture, repealing the
arms embargo and agreeing to supply Britain with valuable military supplies
in the form of Lend-Lease.*

*The study of American foreign policy in the 1930s up to the American
entry into World War II in December 1941, and especially the diplomacy of
Franklin D. Roosevelt, has generated controversial questions: Was Roosevelt
an isolationist? Why was he so cautious in acting to assist Britain? What
role did politics play in his decisions?*

DOCUMENTS

In the first selection, Senator Gerald P. Nye explains the result of the investigation
he led into alleged business pressure on the Wilson administration to enter World
War I. His speech on May 28, 1935, reflected ideas that helped to pass the Neu-

trality Acts. In the second selection, a speech on August 14, 1936, at Chautauqua, President Franklin D. Roosevelt passionately condemns war. His abhorrence of war matched that of many isolationists. The third document is the President's address to the nation in a "fireside chat" on December 29, 1939, in which he announced that he would make the United States the "arsenal of democracy." The Lend-Lease Act was passed the following March.

In the fourth document, distinguished historian and isolationist Charles A. Beard testifies in 1941 before a Senate committee against the Lend-Lease measure as being a step toward war. The fifth and final document is the Atlantic Charter penned by Roosevelt and British Prime Minister Winston Churchill on August 14, 1941, after their summit meeting off the coast of Newfoundland. These principles were popularly considered the war objectives of the Allies.

Senator Gerald P. Nye on the Causes of War, 1935

This past year has witnessed the most intensive inquiry into the questions of arms traffic, munitions, war profits, and profits from preparedness for war that the world ever saw undertaken. It has been my privilege to work with six other Members of the United States Senate in this study. I am happy tonight to say that it grows increasingly evident that our labors have not been in vain and that truly worth-while legislation will be forthcoming to meet the frightful challenge which the inquiry disclosures have been. Largely because the people have shown tremendous interest in the subject, I am sure that substantial legislation is on the way to restrain those racketeers who find large profit in breeding hate, fear, and suspicion as a base for large preparedness programs, and who have learned that while there is large profit in preparing for war, there is larger profit for them in war itself.

But out of this year of study has come tremendous conviction that our American welfare requires that great importance be given the subject of our neutrality when others are at war.

Tonight I think we will do well to give some thought to causes behind our entry into the Great War. Those causes as well as the results which have since followed are an experience we should not soon forget.

Nineteen hundred and fourteen found America just as determined, just as anxious for peace as it is now. But less than 3 years later we were in the greatest of all wars, creating obligations and burdens which even to this day bend our backs. What was it that took us into that war in spite of our high contrary resolve?

To me there is something sinister involved in using the language of 1914 in this present pre-war year of 1935. There is, I fear, danger that the soft, evasive, unrealistic, untrue language of 21 years ago will again take root and then rise up and slay its millions as it did then, both during and after a war.

Let me make this clear. If the people of the world are told again that the next war is a political war for the noblest possible ideals, those same people will be the ones to suffer not only during the war, but also when the war is over and the peace signed on the basis of the crude, economic struggle.

Did the English or the Germans or the French in 1914 know that they were fighting the battle of commercial rivalries? No. Did the American people know that they were fighting to save the skins of the bankers who had coaxed the people into loaning $2,000,000,000 to the Allies? No. They all thought that they were fighting for national honor, for democracy, for the end of war. . . .

Let us be as frank before the next war comes as Wilson was frank after the last war was over. Let us know that it is sales and shipments of munitions and contraband, and the lure of the profits in them, that will get us into another war, and that when the proper time comes and we talk about national honor, let us know that simply means the right to go on making money out of a war.

Let us have done with all the fraud, and we will have done with all the post-war friction.

There are many who have tried to keep us from being involved in entangling foreign political alliances. But since wars are for economic causes basically, it is as important to avoid becoming involved in entangling foreign economic alliances. That is the crux of the matter. It is useless to pretend that our isolation from foreign political entanglements means anything if we open wide the gates to foreign loans and credits for munitions and spread out a network of munition ships that will be ignition points of another war.

What are the facts behind these conclusions of men familiar with the real causes of our entering the war?

From the year ending June 30, 1914, to the year ending June 30, 1916, our exports to the Allies increased almost 300 percent, or from $825,000,000 to $3,214,000,000. During the same period our exports to the Central Powers fell from $169,000,000 to $1,000,000. Long before we declared war on Germany we had ceased to have any economic interests in her fate in the war, because she was buying nothing from us.

The bulk of our sales during this pre-war period were in munitions and war materials. It must be remembered that the World War inaugurated war on the scale of whole nations pitted against nations—not simply of armies, however large, against armies. Consequently, foodstuffs and raw materials for the manufacture of items essential to modern war were declared contraband by one belligerent or another. In the year 1914 more than half of our total exports to all countries were munitions and war materials of this kind. In 1915 our sales of such materials were 179 percent greater than they had been in the preceding year and constituted 86 percent of our total exports to all countries. In 1916 our sales of these articles were 287 percent greater than in 1914 and totaled $3,700,000,000, which was 88 percent of our total exports. The growth of our sales of explosives may be taken as a single example. In the year ending June 30, 1914, we exported only $10,000,000 worth of explosives. In the year ending June 30, 1915, this figure had grown to $189,000,000, and in the next year it reached $715,000,000.

America officially regarded the right to engage in this trade as part of our neutral rights and no attempt was made to discourage it. . . .

Now, we must not forget that this enormous trade required financing also on an enormous scale. Our State Department at the outset of the war announced that "in the judgment of this Government loans by American bankers to any foreign nation which is at war are inconsistent with the true spirit of neutrality." But once we had recognized and encouraged the trade in war materials as a neutral right, it proved impossible to deny the demands for normal financing of that trade.

While the State Department was officially opposed to loans, our bankers were not. Mr. Lamont has written that J. P. Morgan & Co. was whole-heartedly in back of the Allies from the start. Mr. Davison was sent to England to place the firm's services at England's disposal. As early as February 1915 Morgan signed his first contract with the Du Pont Co. as agent for an allied power. Of the total sales by Du Pont to France and England, totalling practically half a billion dollars, over 70 percent were made through Morgan & Co., although Morgan & Co. acted as agents for the Allies only from the spring of 1915 until shortly after we entered the war—a little over 2 years.

From the early days of the war the State Department did not object to bank credits being extended to belligerents as distinguished from loans. In November 1914 France received $10,000,000 on 1-year treasury notes from the National City Bank, and in May 1915 Russia received $10,200,000 for a year from the same source. In April 1915 France received short-term credit of about $30,000,000 arranged by J. P. Morgan. Brown Bros. opened a commercial line of credit of $25,000,000 for French merchants in the summer of 1915.

In October 1915 America's bankers ceased distinguishing between credits and loans and the Government was helpless to prevent this. American investors began to finance the Allies in earnest with the flotation of the great Anglo-French loan of $500,000,000 through a huge banking syndicate headed by J. P. Morgan & Co. Similar loans followed fast, and by 1917 total loans and credits to the Allies of well over $2,000,000,000 were outstanding. Morgan & Co. had a demand loan or overdraft due from Great Britain of approximately $400,000,000, which obviously could not be paid at that time. Instead Great Britain desperately needed enormous new credits.

By this time the history of the bank credits up to October 1915 had been repeated—on a far larger scale. In the early part of 1917 it was clear that our private financial and banking resources were exhausted. Unless the great credit of the American Nation could itself be pledged, the flow of goods to Europe would end and the claims of our banks, who had made possible this flow of goods in the past, would not be paid. No one stopped to inquire whether new funds would not similarly be burned up in the holocaust of European war and would be used in the natural course of events to bail out the American banks. The facts are that by November 11, 1918, $7,000,000,000 were lent to Europe by our Government and, though most of this is still unpaid, the private loans were redeemed and the securities behind them have disappeared.

We are now discussing things that have heretofore been whispered only—things that most of us felt couldn't be true because they shouldn't be true.

But if a recognition of ugly facts will help us prevent another disaster we must discuss them openly. . . .

The experience of the last war includes the lesson that neutral rights are not a matter for national protection unless we are prepared to protect them by force. Senator Clark and I, and, I believe, Representative Maverick and other colleagues in Congress, believe that the only hope of our staying out of war is through our people recognizing and declaring as a matter of considered and fervently held national policy, that we will not ship munitions to aid combatants and that those of our citizens who ship other materials to belligerent nations must do so at their own risk and without any hope of protection from our Government. If our financiers and industrialists wish to speculate for war profits, let them be warned in advance that they are to be limited to speculation with their own capital and not with the lives of their countrymen and the fabric of their whole nation.

We must, however, frankly face the cost which this kind of decision demands. We must be realists. It requires the giving up of part at least of our present trade balance. It will mean a loss of part of our present revenue from our merchant marine and from banking. More important still, it will mean the abandonment of really vast new profits held temptingly before us.

If we cannot give up these things we cannot hope for peace. I for one believe that great though this cost is, it is insignificant compared to the catastrophe of war.

Franklin D. Roosevelt on
War, at Chautauqua, 1936

Many who have visited me in Washington in the past few months may have been surprised when I have told them personally and because of my own daily contacts with all manner of difficult situations I am more concerned and less cheerful about international world conditions than about our immediate domestic prospects.

I say this to you not as a confirmed pessimist but as one who still hopes that envy, hatred, and malice among nations have reached their peak and will be succeeded by a new tide of peace and good will. I say this as one who has participated in many of the decisions of peace and war before, during, and after the World War; one who has traveled much, and one who has spent a goodly portion of every 24 hours in the study of foreign relations.

Long before I returned to Washington as President of the United States I had made up my mind that, pending what might be called a more opportune moment on other continents, the United States could best serve the cause of a peaceful humanity by setting an example. That was why on the 4th of March, 1933, I made the following declaration:

"In the field of world policy I would dedicate this nation to the policy of the good neighbor—the neighbor who resolutely respects himself and, because he does so, respects the rights of others—the neighbor who respects his obligations and respects the sanctity of his agreements in and with a world of neighbors."

This declaration represents my purpose; but it represents more than a purpose, for it stands for a practice. To a measurable degree it has succeeded; the whole world now knows that the United States cherishes no predatory ambitions. We are strong; but less powerful nations know that they need not fear our strength. We seek no conquest: we stand for peace. . . .

But, of necessity, we are deeply concerned about tendencies of recent years among many of the nations of other continents. It is a bitter experience to us when the spirit of agreements to which we are a party is not lived up to. It is an even more bitter experience for the whole company of nations to witness not only the spirit but the letter of international agreements violated with impunity and without regard to the simple principles of honor. Permanent friendships between nations as between men can be sustained only by scrupulous respect for the pledged word.

In spite of all this we have sought steadfastly to assist international movements to prevent war. We cooperated to the bitter end—and it was a bitter end—in the work of the General Disarmament Conference. When it failed we sought a separate treaty to deal with the manufacture of arms and the international traffic in arms. That proposal also came to nothing. We participated—again to the bitter end—in a conference to continue naval limitations, and, when it became evident that no general treaty could be signed because of the objections of other nations, we concluded with Great Britain and France a conditional treaty of qualitative limitations which, much to my regret, already shows signs of ineffectiveness.

We shun political commitments which might entangle us in foreign wars; we avoid connection with the political activities of the League of Nations; but I am glad to say that we have cooperated wholeheartedly in the social and humanitarian work at Geneva. Thus we are a part of the world effort to control traffic in narcotics, to improve international health, to help child welfare, to eliminate double taxation, and to better working conditions and laboring hours throughout the world.

We are not isolationists except insofar as we seek to isolate ourselves completely from war. Yet we must remember that so long as war exists on earth there will be some danger that even the nation which most ardently desires peace may be drawn into war.

I have seen war. I have seen war on land and sea. I have seen blood running from the wounded. I have seen men coughing out their gassed lungs. I have seen the dead in the mud. I have seen cities destroyed. I have seen 200 limping, exhausted men come out of line—the survivors of a regiment of 1,000 that went forward 48 hours before. I have seen children starving. I have seen the agony of mothers and wives. I hate war.

I have passed unnumbered hours, I shall pass unnumbered hours thinking and planning how war may be kept from this nation.

I wish I could keep war from all nations, but that is beyond my power. I can at least make certain that no act of the United States helps to produce or to promote war. I can at least make clear that the conscience of America revolts against war and that any nation which provokes war forfeits the sympathy of the people of the United States. . . .

The Congress of the United States has given me certain authority to provide safeguards of American neutrality in case of war.

The President of the United States, who, under our Constitution, is vested with primary authority to conduct our international relations, thus has been given new weapons with which to maintain our neutrality.

Nevertheless—and I speak from a long experience—the effective maintenance of American neutrality depends today, as in the past, on the wisdom and determination of whoever at the moment occupy the offices of President and Secretary of State.

It is clear that our present policy and the measures passed by the Congress would, in the event of a war on some other continent, reduce war profits which would otherwise accrue to American citizens. Industrial and agricultural production for a war market may give immense fortunes to a few men; for the nation as a whole it produces disaster. It was the prospect of war profits that made our farmers in the west plow up prairie land that should never have been plowed but should have been left for grazing cattle. Today we are reaping the harvest of those war profits in the dust storms which have devastated those war-plowed areas.

It was the prospect of war profits that caused the extension of monopoly and unjustified expansion of industry and a price level so high that the normal relationship between debtor and creditor was destroyed.

Nevertheless, if war should break out again in another continent, let us not blink the fact that we would find in this country thousands of Americans who, seeking immediate riches—fools' gold—would attempt to break down or evade our neutrality.

They would tell you—and, unfortunately, their views would get wide publicity—that if they could produce and ship this and that and the other article to belligerent nations the unemployed of America would all find work. They would tell you that if they could extend credit to warring nations that credit would be used in the United States to build homes and factories and pay our debts. They would tell you that America once more would capture the trade of the world.

It would be hard to resist that clamor. It would be hard for many Americans, I fear, to look beyond, to realize the inevitable penalties, the inevitable day of reckoning that comes from a false prosperity. To resist the clamor of that greed, if war should come, would require the unswerving support of all Americans who love peace.

If we face the choice of profits or peace, the Nation will answer—must answer—"we choose peace." It is the duty of all of us to encourage such a body of public opinion in this country that the answer will be clear and for all practical purposes unanimous. . . .

We can keep out of war if those who watch and decide have a sufficiently detailed understanding of international affairs to make certain that the small decisions of each day do not lead toward war, and if, at the same time, they possess the courage to say "no" to those who selfishly or unwisely would let us go to war.

Of all the nations of the world today we are in many ways most singularly blessed. Our closest neighbors are good neighbors. If there are remoter nations that wish us not good but ill, they know that we are strong; they know that we can and will defend ourselves and defend our neighborhood.

We seek to dominate no other nation. We ask no territorial expansion. We oppose imperialism. We desire reduction in world armaments.

We believe in democracy; we believe in freedom; we believe in peace. We offer to every nation of the world the handclasp of the good neighbor. Let those who wish our friendship look us in the eye and take our hand.

Roosevelt's Fireside Chat on America as the "Arsenal of Democracy," 1940

Never before since Jamestown and Plymouth Rock has our American civilization been in such danger as now.

For, on September 27, 1940, by an agreement signed in Berlin, three powerful nations, two in Europe and one in Asia, joined themselves together in the threat that if the United States of America interfered with or blocked the expansion program of these three nations—a program aimed at world control —they would unite in ultimate action against the United States.

The Nazi masters of Germany have made it clear that they intend not only to dominate all life and thought in their own country, but also to enslave the whole of Europe, and then to use the resources of Europe to dominate the rest of the world. . . .

Does anyone seriously believe that we need to fear attack anywhere in the Americas while a free Britain remains our most powerful naval neighbor in the Atlantic? Does anyone seriously believe, on the other hand, that we could rest easy if the Axis powers were our neighbors there?

If Great Britain goes down, the Axis powers will control the continents of Europe, Asia, Africa, Australasia, and the high seas—and they will be in a position to bring enormous military and naval resources against this hemisphere. It is no exaggeration to say that all of us, in all the Americas, would be living at the point of a gun—a gun loaded with explosive bullets, economic as well as military.

We should enter upon a new and terrible era in which the whole world, our hemisphere included, would be run by threats of brute force. To survive in such a world, we would have to convert ourselves permanently into a militaristic power on the basis of war economy.

Some of us like to believe that even if Great Britain falls, we are still safe, because of the broad expanse of the Atlantic and of the Pacific.

But the width of those oceans is not what it was in the days of clipper ships. At one point between Africa and Brazil the distance is less than from Washington to Denver, Colorado—five hours for the latest type of bomber. And at the North end of the Pacific Ocean America and Asia almost touch each other.

Even today we have planes that could fly from the British Isles to New England and back again without refueling. And remember that the range of the modern bomber is ever being increased. . . .

Analyze for yourselves the future of two other places even nearer to Germany if the Nazis won. Could Ireland hold out? Would Irish freedom be permitted as an amazing pet exception in an unfree world? Or the Islands of the Azores which still fly the flag of Portugal after five centuries? You and I think of Hawaii as an outpost of defense in the Pacific. And yet, the Azores are closer to our shores in the Atlantic than Hawaii is on the other side.

There are those who say that the Axis powers would never have any desire to attack the Western Hemisphere. That is the same dangerous form of wishful thinking which has destroyed the powers of resistance of so many conquered peoples. The plain facts are that the Nazis have proclaimed, time and again, that all other races are their inferiors and therefore subject to their orders. And most important of all, the vast resources and wealth of this American Hemisphere constitute the most tempting loot in all the round world. . . .

The experience of the past two years has proven beyond doubt that no nation can appease the Nazis. No man can tame a tiger into a kitten by stroking it. There can be no appeasement with ruthlessness. There can be no reasoning with an incendiary bomb. We know now that a nation can have peace with the Nazis only at the price of total surrender. . . .

The history of recent years proves that shootings and chains and concentration camps are not simply the transient tools but the very altars of modern dictatorships. They may talk of a "new order" in the world, but what they have in mind is only a revival of the oldest and the worst tyranny. In that there is no liberty, no religion, no hope.

The proposed "new order" is the very opposite of a United States of Europe or a United States of Asia. It is not a Government based upon the consent of the governed. It is not a union of ordinary, self-respecting men and women to protect themselves and their freedom and their dignity from oppression. It is an unholy alliance of power and pelf to dominate and enslave the human race.

The British people and their allies today are conducting an active war against this unholy alliance. Our own future security is greatly dependent on the outcome of that fight. Our ability to "keep out of war" is going to be affected by that outcome.

Thinking in terms of today and tomorrow, I make the direct statement to the American people that there is far less chance of the United States getting into war, if we do all we can now to support the nations defending themselves against attack by the Axis than if we acquiesce in their defeat, submit tamely to an Axis victory, and wait our turn to be the object of attack in another war later on.

If we are to be completely honest with ourselves, we must admit that there is risk in any course we may take. But I deeply believe that the great majority of our people agree that the course that I advocate involves the least risk now and the greatest hope for world peace in the future.

The people of Europe who are defending themselves do not ask us to do their fighting. They ask us for the implements of war, the planes, the tanks, the guns, the freighters which will enable them to fight for their liberty and for our security. Emphatically we must get these weapons to them in sufficient volume and quickly enough, so that we and our children will be saved the agony and suffering of war which others have had to endure.

Let not the defeatists tell us that it is too late. It will never be earlier. Tomorrow will be later than today.

Certain facts are self-evident.

In a military sense Great Britain and the British Empire are today the spearhead of resistance to world conquest. They are putting up a fight which will live forever in the story of human gallantry.

There is no demand for sending an American Expeditionary Force outside our own borders. There is no intention by any member of your Government to send such a force. You can, therefore, nail any talk about sending armies to Europe as deliberate untruth.

Our national policy is not directed toward war. Its sole purpose is to keep war away from our country and our people.

Democracy's fight against world conquest is being greatly aided, and must be more greatly aided, by the rearmament of the United States and by sending every ounce and every ton of munitions and supplies that we can possibly spare to help the defenders who are in the front lines. It is no more unneutral for us to do that than it is for Sweden, Russia and other nations near Germany, to send steel and ore and oil and other war materials into Germany every day in the week.

We are planning our own defense with the utmost urgency; and in its vast scale we must integrate the war needs of Britain and the other free nations which are resisting aggression.

This is not a matter of sentiment or of controversial personal opinion. It is a matter of realistic, practical military policy, based on the advice of our military experts who are in close touch with existing warfare. These military and naval experts and the members of the Congress and the Administration have a single-minded purpose—the defense of the United States.

This nation is making a great effort to produce everything that is necessary in this emergency—and with all possible speed. This great effort requires great sacrifice. . . .

We must be the great arsenal of democracy. For us this is an emergency as serious as war itself. We must apply ourselves to our task with the same resolution, the same sense of urgency, the same spirit of patriotism and sacrifice as we would show were we at war.

We have furnished the British great material support and we will furnish far more in the future.

There will be no "bottlenecks" in our determination to aid Great Britain. No dictator, no combination of dictators, will weaken that determination by threats of how they will construe that determination.

The British have received invaluable military support from the heroic Greek army, and from the forces of all the governments in exile. Their strength is growing. It is the strength of men and women who value their freedom more highly than they value their lives.

I believe that the Axis powers are not going to win this war. I base that belief on the latest and best information.

We have no excuse for defeatism. We have every good reason for hope—hope for peace, hope for the defense of our civilization and for the building of a better civilization in the future.

I have the profound conviction that the American people are now determined to put forth a mightier effort than they have ever yet made to increase our production of all the implements of defense, to meet the threat to our democratic faith.

As President of the United States I call for that national effort. I call for it in the name of this nation which we love and honor and which we are privileged and proud to serve. I call upon our people with absolute confidence that our common cause will greatly succeed.

Charles A. Beard Criticizes Lend-Lease, 1941

There is no question here of sympathy for Britain; this nation is almost unanimous in its sympathy. There is no question here of aid to Britain; the Nation is agreed on that. Our immediate task is to analyze the meaning of the language employed in this bill, and to calculate as far as may be humanly possible the consequences for our country that are likely to flow from its enactment into law—to rend, if we can, some corner of the dark veil that hides the future from our vision. . . .

Unless this bill is to be regarded as a mere rhetorical flourish—and respect for its authors precludes the thought of such frivolity—then, I submit, it is a bill for waging an undeclared war. We should entertain no delusions on this point. We should now face frankly and with such knowledge and intelligence as we may have the nature and probable consequences of that war. Without indulging in recriminations, we are bound to consider that fateful prospect.

The contention that this is a war measure has been, I know, hotly denied. The bill has been called a bill to keep the United States out of war. It has been said that we are "buying peace" for ourselves, while others are fighting our war for democracy and defense. I invite your special attention to this line of argument. I confess, gentlemen of the committee, an utter inability to understand the reasoning and morals of those who use this formula. My code of honor may be antiquated, but under it I am bound to say that if this is our war for democracy and if foreign soldiers are now fighting and dying for the defense of the United States, then it is shameful for us to be buying peace with gold, when we should be offering our bodies as living sacrifices. As I am given to see things, buying peace for ourselves, if this is our war, buying it with money renders us contemptible in the eyes of the world and, if I understand the spirit of America, contemptible in our own eyes. However, that may be, there is no guaranty that this bill will buy peace and keep us out of war, despite professions to that effect.

If the bill is enacted into law and efficiently carried into execution, it will engage our government in war activities, involve us officially in the conflicts of Europe and Asia, and place in jeopardy everything we cherish in the United States. It is true that some Americans doubt this risk. They appear to be confident that they can divine the future in Europe and Asia infallibly. They seem to believe that the United States can determine the destiny of those continents without incurring the peril of war and ruin for the American people. But I am not one of those astrologers. My knowledge of Europe and Asia is less extensive than theirs. I am merely certain that Europe is old, that Asia is old; that the peoples and nations of Europe and Asia have their respective traditions, institutions, forms of government, and systems of economy; and that Europe and Asia have been torn by wars, waged under various symbols and slogans, since the dawn of recorded history.

The history of Europe and Asia is long and violent. Tenacious emotions and habits are associated with it. Can the American people, great and ingenious though they be, transform those traditions, institutions, systems, emotions, and habits by employing treasure, arms, propaganda, and diplomatic lectures? Can they, by any means at their disposal, make over Europe and Asia, provide democracy, a bill of rights, and economic security for everybody, everywhere, in the world? With all due respect for those Americans who clamor that this is the mission of the United States, I am compelled to say that, in my opinion, their exuberance is on a par with the childish exuberance of the Bolshevik internationalists who preach the gospel of one model for the whole world. And I am bound to say, furthermore, that it is an exuberance more likely to bring disasters upon our own country than to carry happiness and security to the earth's weary multitudes.

Against embarking on such a crusade, surely we are put on our guard by the history of the last World War. For public consumption and partly with a view to influencing American public opinion, several European belligerents put forth numerous formulations of war origins and war aims. Later, unexpected revolutions in Russia, Germany, and Austria ripped open the diplomatic archives of those countries. Then were revealed to us the maneuvers, negotiations, and secret treaties spread over many years, which preceded and accompanied that World War. I have spent many weary months studying these documents, and I will say, gentlemen of the committee, that these documents do not show that the European conflict was, in the aims of the great powers, a war for democracy, or for the defense of the United States, or had anything to do with protecting the interests of the United States.

And to state the case mildly, those secret agreements among the powers do not exactly square with the public statements of the belligerents respecting the origins and aims of that war. Nor indeed did the so-called settlement at Paris, in 1919, exactly square with the declared war aims of President Wilson.

This is not to say that the present war is identical with the last war or to recite that false phrase, "History repeats itself"—for it never does. Yet we do know that the present war did not spring out of a vacuum, nor merely out of the Versailles Treaty. Its origins, nature, and course are rooted in the long history of the Old World and the long conflicts of the great powers. In the light of that long history and those long conflicts, a discussion of their mere war aims shrivels into futility.

We, however, poised now on the brink of the fateful decision respecting ourselves, are under positive obligation to discuss the aims of the government of the United States in the activities which would be let loose under this bill, if enacted. Indeed it becomes the solemn duty of all members of Congress to do this. If they are not to vote thoughtlessly and recklessly, they will ask themselves certain grave questions before they vote. And I may say, gentlemen of the committee, I do not envy you that solemn task that falls upon you. Congress cannot in truth escape these questions, for it will be answering them if it passes this bill—answering them conceivably in a manner fraught with infinite tragedy for the United States.

Here are the questions:

Does Congress intend to guarantee the present extent, economic resources, and economic methods of the British Empire forever to the government of Great Britain by placing the unlimited resources of the United States forever at the disposal of the British government, however constituted?

Does Congress intend to supply money, ships, and commodities of war until the French Republic is restored? Until the integrity of its empire is assured? Until all the lands run over by Hitler are once more vested with full sovereignty? Until Russia has returned to Finland and Poland the territories wrested from them? Until democracy is reestablished in Greece? Until the King of Albania has recovered his throne?

Is Congress prepared to pour out American wealth until the Chungking government in China has conquered the Nanking government? Until Japan is expelled from the continent? Until Chinese Communists are finally suppressed? And until Soviet Russia is pushed back within the old Russian borders?

And if European or Asiatic powers should propose to make settlements without providing democracy, a bill of rights, and economic security for everybody, everywhere, will Congress insist that they keep on fighting until the President of the United States is satisfied with the results? If none of the countries deemed under the terms of this bill to be defending the United States succeeds in defeating its enemy with the material aid rendered by the United States, will Congress throw millions of boys after the billions of dollars?

Two more crucial questions are before our Nation in council. After Europe has been turned into flaming shambles, with resolutions exploding right and left, will this Congress be able to supply the men, money, and talents necessary to reestablish and maintain order and security there? Are the members of Congress absolutely sure, as they think about this bill, that the flames of war and civil commotion will not spread to our country? That when the war boom of fools' gold has burst with terrific force, Congress will be able to cope at home with the problems of unemployment and debts with which it had wrestled for years prior to this present false prosperity by borrowing money to meet the needs of distressed farmers, distressed industries, the distressed third of the nation?

As a nation in council, we should not mislead ourselves by phrases and phantoms. The present business of our Congress, it seems to me, is not to split hairs over the mere language of this bill or to try to restrict its consequences to one or two years of presidential experimentation. The present business of Congress is to decide now, in voting on this bill, whether it is prepared on a showdown to carry our country into the war in Europe and Asia, and thus set the whole world on fire, or whether it is resolved, on a showdown, to stay out to the last ditch and preserve one stronghold of order and sanity even against the gates of hell. Here, on this continent, I believe we may be secure and should make ourselves secure from the kind of conflict and terrorism in which the old worlds have indulged for such long ages of time.

The Atlantic Charter, 1941

Joint declaration of the President of the United States of America and the Prime Minister, Mr. Churchill, representing His Majesty's Government in the United Kingdom, being met together, deem it right to make known certain common principles in the national policies of their respective countries on which they base their hopes for a better future for the world.

First, their countries seek no aggrandizement, territorial or other;

Second, they desire to see no territorial changes that do not accord with the freely expressed wishes of the peoples concerned;

Third, they respect the right of all peoples to choose the form of government under which they will live; and they wish to see sovereign rights and self-government restored to those who have been forcibly deprived of them;

Fourth, they will endeavor, with due respect for their existing obligations, to further the enjoyment by all states, great or small, victor or vanquished, of access, on equal terms, to the trade and to the raw materials of the world which are needed for their economic prosperity;

Fifth, they desire to bring about the fullest collaboration between all nations in the economic field with the object of securing, for all improved labor standards, economic advancement, and social security;

Sixth, after the final destruction of the Nazi tyranny, they hope to see established a peace which will afford to all nations the means of dwelling in safety within their own boundaries, and which will afford assurance that all the men in all the lands may live out their lives in freedom from fear and want;

Seventh, such a peace should enable all men to traverse the high seas and oceans without hindrance;

Eighth, they believe that all of the nations of the world, for realistic as well as spiritual reasons, must come to the abandonment of the use of force. Since no future peace can be maintained if land, sea, or air armaments continue to be employed by nations which threaten, or may threaten, aggression outside of their frontiers, they believe, pending the establishment of a wider and permanent system of general security, that the disarmament of such nations is essential. They will likewise aid and encourage all other practicable measures which will lighten for peace-loving peoples the crushing burden of armaments.

ESSAYS

Robert A. Divine of the University of Texas argues that Franklin D. Roosevelt was a sincere isolationist who shared the views of a majority of Americans against involvement in another war. Divine surveys Roosevelt's reactions to the crises of the 1930s. On the other hand, James MacGregor Burns of Williams College, a Roosevelt biographer, thinks that Roosevelt's foreign policy was governed by the President's political ambitions, making him cautious in challenging isolationism and therefore timid as a leader. In the final essay, Arnold A. Offner of Boston University points to other factors—intra-administration divisions and Anglo-American tensions—to explain what he has called the American "appeasement" of Germany.

Roosevelt the Isolationist

ROBERT A. DIVINE

Roosevelt's foreign policy in the 1930's toward the totalitarian threat of Germany, Italy, and Japan would seem to offer little room for historical controversy. The record is clear—Roosevelt pursued an isolationist policy, refusing to commit the United States to the defense of the existing international order. He accepted a series of isolationist neutrality laws passed by Congress, objecting only to those provisions which infringed on his freedom of action as President; he acquiesced in Italy's seizure of Ethiopia, Japan's invasion of China, and Germany's takeover of Austria and the Sudetenland in Czechoslovakia. The sole exception that can be cited is the Quarantine speech in 1937, and even this apparently bold statement was so ambiguous that historians have never been able to agree on the President's precise intention.

Yet this isolationist policy does not square with the usual image of Franklin Roosevelt as a perceptive world leader who recognized the danger to the United States from Axis aggression and who eventually led his nation into war to preserve American security. Troubled by this contradiction, historians have argued that Roosevelt subordinated his own internationalist preferences and gave in to the isolationist mood of the American people. As a shrewd politician, he knew that the electorate would not tolerate an active foreign policy in the midst

Robert A. Divine, *Roosevelt and World War II* (Baltimore: Johns Hopkins University Press, 1969), pp. 5–11, 20–30, 30–37, 38–40, 43–48. Copyright © 1969 by The Johns Hopkins University Press. Reprinted by permission of The Johns Hopkins University Press.

of the depression, and so he wisely surrendered to the public will. His major desires in the mid-thirties were to achieve recovery and carry out sweeping domestic reforms; he could not jeopardize these vital goals with an unpopular foreign policy. Implicit in this interpretation is the belief that Roosevelt was an internationalist at heart. Thus Basil Rauch argues that the President acted wisely in drifting with the current in the 1930's; later in the decade, when the totalitarian threat became more intense, he was finally able to win the people over to an active policy. James MacGregor Burns is less charitable. He accuses Roosevelt of floating helplessly on a flood tide of isolationism and thus failing to fulfill his obligation of leadership. "As a foreign policy maker," Burns concludes, "Roosevelt during his first term was more pussyfooting politician than political leader."

Charles A. Beard, in his book *American Foreign Policy in the Making, 1932–1940,* offers a simpler and more convincing explanation of Roosevelt's behavior. In the 1930's, Beard contends, Roosevelt *was* an isolationist. Though Beard in a later book accuses the President of lying the nation into war, his earlier study provides a sound interpretation of Roosevelt's foreign policy. If we accept Roosevelt's own public statements at their face value, then we can dismiss the concept of two Roosevelts, one the public figure saying what the people wanted to hear, the other the private man with an entirely different set of beliefs. Equally important, we no longer have to explain Roosevelt's conduct on the basis of a devious political expediency. Instead, we can state simply that Roosevelt pursued an isolationist policy out of genuine conviction.

It is not surprising that F.D.R. shared in the isolationist temper of his times. The mood was deep and pervasive in the 1930's. The First World War had led to a profound sense of disillusion that found expression in an overwhelming national desire to abstain from future world conflicts. The generation of the thirties embraced pacifism as a noble and workable ideal—students demonstrated on college campuses every spring in massive antiwar strikes; religious and pacifist societies waged a campaign to remove ROTC units from colleges and universities; millions of Americans applauded the limited naval disarmament of the 1920's and followed with intense interest the futile disarmament conference that went on at Geneva through the early years of the decade. Feeding this pacifism was the belief that the same wicked businessmen who had destroyed the economic health of the nation were responsible for fomenting war. The Nye investigation struck a responsive chord with the airing of charges that it was merchants of death like Pierre Du Pont and J. P. Morgan who had brought the United States into the First World War. And many Americans accepted the argument that the depression was the final legacy of that war.

Roosevelt, in his speeches and letters, constantly reiterated his belief that the United States should avoid all future conflicts. In his first two years in office, he tended to ignore foreign policy as he concentrated on the problems of economic recovery at home. But in 1935, as the world crisis unfolded with Hitler's rearmament of Germany and Mussolini's attack on Ethiopia, the President began to speak out on international issues. In an Armistice Day address in 1935, after commenting on the rising danger in Europe, he said, "the primary purpose of the United States of America is to avoid being drawn into war." The nation's youth, he continued, "know that the elation and prosperity which may come from a new war must lead—for those who survive it—to economic and social collapse more sweeping than any we have experienced in the past." He concluded by stating that the proper American role was to provide an example to all mankind of the virtues of peace and democracy. In a letter to William Dodd, the American ambassador to Germany, a few weeks later, he repeated this advice, writing, "I do not know that the United States can save civilization but at least by our example we can make people think and give them the opportunity of saving themselves."

Roosevelt's initial response to the rising totalitarian threat was thus in the classic tradition of American isolationism. The United States was to play a passive role as the beacon of liberty to mankind, providing a model for the world to follow, but avoiding any active participation in a foreign conflict. In his annual message to Congress in January, 1936, for the first time he dwelt at some length on foreign policy, warning the congressmen and senators of the dangers to peace that were developing in Europe. If war came, he declared, the only course the United States could follow was neutrality, "and through example and all legitimate encouragement and assistance to persuade other Nations to return to the ways of peace and good-will." In a Dallas speech in mid-1936, he spoke again of the troubles plaguing the European nations and expressed his sympathy for their plight. "We want to help them all that we can," he stated, "but they have understood very well in these latter years that help is going to be confined to moral help, and that we are not going to get tangled up with their troubles in the days to come."

Roosevelt voiced his isolationist convictions most forthrightly in his famous Chautauqua address in August, 1936. This speech came after he had been renominated for the presidency by the Democratic Party, and it was the only speech he made in the 1936 campaign that dealt with foreign policy. Once again he concentrated on the perilous world situation, and again he reaffirmed his determination to keep the nation out of any conflict that might arise. He played on the merchants of death theme, warning that the lure of "fool's gold" in the form of trade with belligerents would lead many greedy Americans to attempt to evade the neutrality laws. "If we face the choice of profit or peace," Roosevelt demanded, "the Nation will answer—must answer—'we choose peace.'" He went on to point out how hard it would be to keep out of a major war and said that only careful day-by-day conduct of foreign policy by the Secretary of State and the President could keep the nation at peace.

The most striking passage came when Roosevelt revealed his own emotional distaste for war:

> I have seen war. I have seen war on land and sea. I have seen blood running from the wounded. I have seen men coughing out their gassed lungs. I have seen the dead in the mud. I have seen cities destroyed. I have seen two hundred limping, exhausted men come out of line—the survivors of a regiment of one thousand that went forward forty-eight hours before. I have seen children starving. I have seen the agony of mothers and wives. I hate war.

I have passed unnumbered hours, I shall pass unnumbered hours, thinking and planning how war may be kept from this nation.

Here Roosevelt laid bare the source of his isolationism. Some commentators dismissed his words as campaign rhetoric, empty phrases designed simply to win votes in the coming election. But the words carry a sense of conviction and honesty that belies such hypocrisy. Samuel Rosenman testifies to Roosevelt's sincerity, stating that the President considered the Chautauqua address one of his most important speeches. The following Christmas, after he had been safely re-elected, Roosevelt sent close friends a specially printed and inscribed copy of the speech as a holiday gift. For Roosevelt, the Chautauqua address was more than a campaign speech; it was a clear and precise statement of his innermost beliefs. He shared fully in the hatred of war that was at the root of American isolationism in the depression decade, and he was determined to insure that the United States would remain a beacon of peace and sanity in a world going mad.

Roosevelt's fundamental aversion to war determined his responses to the hostile acts committed by Italy, Japan, and Germany in the 1930's. As these totalitarian powers expanded into Ethiopia, China, and Central Europe, Roosevelt was torn between his strong distaste for their aggression and his conviction that the United States should stay out of war at any cost. In subtle ways, he tried to throw the weight of American influence against the totalitarian states, but never at the risk of American involvement.

The Italian invasion of Ethiopia in early October of 1935 touched off the first major foreign crisis that Roosevelt faced as President. The Ethiopian war had been developing for over a year, and the imminence of this conflict had goaded Congress into passing the first Neutrality Act in late August. This legislation instructed the President to apply an embargo on the export of arms to nations at war and permitted him, at his discretion, to warn American citizens against traveling on belligerent ships. The idea of preventing munitions-makers from selling weapons to countries at war appealed to Roosevelt, but he was distressed at the mandatory nature of the arms embargo, preferring discretionary power that would enable him to decide when and against whom such embargoes should be levied. Nevertheless, he decided not to veto the Neutrality Act when Congress limited it to a six-month trial period. Roosevelt realized that this legislation would not hamper him if war broke out in Africa. Italy, which had the money and ships to import arms from the United States, would be adversely affected, while Ethiopia would be no worse off.

Thus, when reporters asked him his opinion of the Neutrality Act on August 28, he could reply candidly that he found it "entirely satisfactory." "The question of embargoes as against two belligerents meets the need of the existing situation," he explained. "What more can one ask?" . . .

When Hitler announced plans for German rearmament in 1935 and then marched into the Rhineland the next year, the Roosevelt administration remained silent. In both cases, Germany was violating the Treaty of Versailles, but the fact that the United States was not a party to this agreement meant that there were no grounds for an American protest. Privately, Roosevelt did speak out, commenting to his associates that Hitler was an international gangster, a bandit who someday would have to be halted. After the German seizure of Austria in March, 1938, Cordell Hull issued a cautious statement expressing American concern over the effect of this German act on world peace. Roosevelt was also disturbed, but he was not ready to alter his policy. In a letter to the American ambassador in Ireland in April, 1938, he commented that the only hopeful sign about the world situation was "that we in the United States are still better off than the people or the governments of any other great country."

The real test of Roosevelt's policy came with the Czech crisis in September of 1938 which culminated in the Munich Conference. Moving inexorably toward his goal of uniting all German people in Europe into a Greater Third Reich, Hitler began demanding the cession of the Sudeten provinces of Czechoslovakia. The Czechs refused and turned to England and France for help. Neville Chamberlain, the British Prime Minister, flew to Germany on September 15 to confer with Hitler. A week later, England and France announced that Czechoslovakia would turn over to Hitler the districts in which Germans were in the majority. But the German dictator refused to be content with these concessions. Instead, he stepped up his demands to include areas in which the Germans were in the minority and insisted that the transfer be accomplished by October 1. British and French public opinion stiffened, and by September 25 it seemed likely that Chamberlain and Edouard Daladier, the French Premier, would fight rather than surrender completely to Hitler.

As the deadline approached, William Bullitt, the American ambassador in Paris, sent a series of urgent cables asking Roosevelt to call for an international conference to head off a major war. At one point, Bullitt even suggested that Roosevelt offer his services as a neutral arbitrator. The idea of personal diplomatic intervention appealed to the President, but Hull and other State Department advisers cautioned him against any dramatic step. Finally, on September 26, Roosevelt issued a public appeal to Hitler, Chamberlain, Daladier, and Eduard Beneš, the Czech leader, calling for a resumption of the negotiations. When Hitler sent back a negative reply, Roosevelt dispatched a personal appeal to Mussolini, asking him to do everything possible to continue the diplomatic negotiations. Then, late on September 27, the President sent a telegram to Hitler appealing once again for a peaceful solution and suggesting an international conference at some neutral spot in Europe. The next afternoon, the British and French leaders announced that they would meet with Hitler and Mussolini at Munich on September 29 to continue the quest for peace. When Roosevelt heard the news, he immediately cabled Chamberlain the brief but enthusiastic message, "Good man."

Historians still debate Roosevelt's responsibility for the Munich Conference. Basil Rauch, in a tortuous reading of the sequence of events, interprets Roosevelt's actions as an effort to bolster the willingness of Chamberlain and Daladier to stand up to Hitler! In a more carefully reasoned article, John McVickar Haight argues that Roosevelt was indeed trying to stand behind England and France, but that the French in particular misinterpreted his actions. "The president's messages," Haight concluded, "were couched in such cautious terms they were misread." William L. Langer and S. Everett Gleason deal with the Munich Conference briefly at the outset of *The Challenge to Isolation*, where they flatly state that "there is no reason to suppose that the President's appeal influenced Hitler in his decision to call the Munich Conference." James MacGregor Burns is even harsher, charging that Roosevelt pursued "a policy of pinpricks and righteous protest." "No risks, no commitments," writes Burns, "was the motto of the White House."

A careful reading of the texts of the messages Roosevelt sent on September 26 and 27 indicates that the President was genuinely perplexed by the Czech crisis. He realized that war impended; he hoped desperately to use American influence to prevent it; but he was still paralyzed by his fear of war. "Should hostilities break out, the lives of millions of men, women, and children in every country involved will most certainly be lost under circumstances of unspeakable horror," he wrote. He recognized that the United States would inevitably be affected by such a conflict, stating that "no nation can escape some measure of the consequences of such a world catastrophe." But while he urged the European leaders to come together again and seek a peaceful solution, he refrained from making any specific American commitments. Thus, in his appeal to Hitler on September 27 in which he proposed a major international conference, he made it clear that the United States would not attend. "The Government of the United States has no political involvements in Europe," Roosevelt informed Hitler, "and will assume no obligations in the conduct of the present negotiations." Nothing he might have said could have been more damaging. In effect, he gave Hitler a green light, saying that the United States would not concern itself in any meaningful way with the settlement of the gravest international crisis since the end of World War I. In that limited and indirect way, he must bear some of the responsibility for the Munich debacle.

But what is most significant is Roosevelt's inner turmoil. In a letter on September 15 to William Phillips, the American ambassador to Italy, he confessed his fear that negotiations with Hitler might only postpone "what looks to me like an inevitable conflict within the next five years." "Perhaps when it comes," he commented, "the United States will be in a position to pick up the pieces of European civilization and help them to save what remains of the wreck—not a cheerful prospect." Yet in the same letter he goes on to say, "if we get the idea that the future of our form of government is threatened by a coalition of European dictators, we might wade in with everything we have to give." A month later, after Munich, he revealed the same contradiction in his thought in a note to Canadian Prime Minister Mackenzie King. He began by saying that he rejoiced in the peaceful solution of the Czech crisis, claiming that it proved that the people of the world had a clear perception of how terrible a general European war would be. Yet, he continued, "I am still concerned, as I know you are, when we consider prospects for the future." He concluded with the fatalistic estimate that world peace depended on Hitler's continued willingness to co-operate.

It does seem clear that by the end of 1938, Roosevelt was no longer the confirmed isolationist he had been earlier in the decade. The brutal conquests by Italy, Japan, and Germany had aroused him to their ultimate threat to the United States. But he was still haunted by the fear of war that he voiced so often and so eloquently. His political opponents and subsequent historians have too readily dismissed his constant reiteration of the horrors of war as a politician's gesture toward public opinion. I contend that he was acting out of a deep and sincere belief when he declared that he hated war, and it was precisely this intense conviction that prevented him from embracing an interventionist foreign policy in the late 1930's. In the Munich crisis, he reveals himself in painful transition from the isolationist of the mid-1930's who wanted peace at almost any price to the reluctant internationalist of the early 1940's who leads his country into war in order to preserve its security.

No aspect of Roosevelt's foreign policy has been more controversial than his role in American entry into World War II. Although much of the discussion centers on the events leading to Pearl Harbor, I do not intend to enter into that labyrinth. The careful and well-researched studies by Herbert Feis, Roberta Wohlstetter, and Paul Schroeder demonstrate that while the administration made many errors in judgment, Roosevelt did not deliberately expose the fleet to a Japanese attack at Pearl Harbor in order to enter the war in Europe by a back door in the Pacific. This revisionist charge has already received far more attention than it deserves and has distracted historians from more significant issues.

What is more intriguing is the nature of Roosevelt's policy toward the war in Europe. There are a number of tantalizing questions that historians have not answered satisfactorily. Why was Roosevelt so devious and indirect in his policy toward the European conflict? When, if ever, did F.D.R. decide that the United States would have to enter the war in Europe to protect its own security? And finally, would Roosevelt have asked Congress for a declaration of war against Germany if Japan had not attacked Pearl Harbor?

In the months that followed the Munich Conference, President Roosevelt gradually realized that appeasement had served only to postpone, not to prevent, a major European war. In January, 1939, he sought to impart this fact in his annual message to Congress. He warned the representatives and senators that "philosophies of force" were loose in the world that threatened "the tenets of faith and humanity" on which the American way of life was founded. "The world has grown so small and weapons of attack so swift," the President declared, "that no nation can be safe" when aggression occurs anywhere on earth. He went on to say that the United States had "rightly" decided not to intervene militarily to prevent acts of aggression abroad and then added, somewhat cryptically, "There are many methods short of war, but stronger and more effective than mere words, of bringing home to aggressor governments the aggregate sentiments of our own people." Roosevelt did not spell out these "methods short of war," but he did criticize the existing neutrality legislation, which he suggested had the effect of encouraging aggressor nations. "We have learned," he continued, "that when we deliberately try to legislate neutrality, our neutrality laws may operate unevenly and unfairly—may actually give aid to an aggressor and deny it to the victim. The instinct of self-preservation should warn us that we ought not to let that happen any more."

Most commentators interpreted the President's speech as a call to Congress to revise the existing neutrality legislation, and in particular the arms embargo. Yet for the next two months, Roosevelt procrastinated. Finally, after Hitler's armies overran the remainder of Czechoslovakia in mid-March, Senator Key Pittman came forward with an administration proposal to repeal the arms embargo and permit American citizens to trade with nations at war on a cash-and-carry basis. The Pittman bill obviously favored England and France, since if these nations were at war with Nazi Germany, they alone would possess the sea power and financial resources to secure arms and supplies from a neutral United States. At the same time, the cash-and-carry restrictions would guard against the loss of American lives and property on the high seas and thus minimize the risk of American involvement.

Although the Pittman bill seemed to be a perfect expression of Roosevelt's desire to bolster the European democracies yet not commit the United States, the President scrupulously avoided any public endorsement in the spring of 1939. His own political stock was at an all-time low as a result of the court-packing dispute, a sharp economic recession, and an unsuccessful effort to purge dissident Democrats in the 1938 primaries. By May, Roosevelt's silence and Pittman's inept handling had led to a deadlock in the Senate. The President then turned to the House of Representatives, meeting with the leaders of the lower chamber on May 19 and telling them that passage of the cash-and-carry measure was necessary to prevent the outbreak of war in Europe. Yet despite this display of concern, Roosevelt refused to take the issue to the people, asking instead that Cordell Hull champion neutrality revision. The presidential silence proved fatal. In late June, a rebellious House of Representatives voted to retain the arms embargo and thus sabotage the administration's effort to align the United States with Britain and France.

Belatedly, Roosevelt decided to intervene. He asked the Senate Foreign Relations Committee to reconsider the Pittman bill, but in early July the Committee rebuffed the President by voting 12 to 11 to postpone action until the next session of Congress. Roosevelt was furious. He prepared a draft of a public statement in which he denounced congressional isolationists "who scream from the housetops that this nation is being led into a world war" as individuals who "deserve only the utmost contempt and pity of the American people." Hull finally persuaded him not to release this inflammatory statement. Instead, Roosevelt invited a small bipartisan group of senators to meet with him and Cordell Hull at the White House. The senators listened politely while the President and Secretary of State warned of the imminence of war in Europe and the urgent need of the United States to do something to prevent it. Senator William Borah, a leading Republican isolationist, then stunned Roosevelt and Hull by announcing categorically that there would be no war in Europe in the near future, that he had access to information from abroad that was far more reliable than the cables arriving daily at the State Department. When the other senators expressed their belief that Congress was not in the mood to revise the Neutrality Act, the meeting broke up. In a press release the next day, Roosevelt stated that the administration would accept the verdict of Congress, but he made it clear that he and Hull still believed that its failure to revise the neutrality legislation "would weaken the leadership of the United States . . . in the event of a new crisis in Europe." In a press conference three days later, Roosevelt was even blunter, accusing the Republicans of depriving him of the only chance he had to prevent the outbreak of war in Europe.

When the German invasion of Poland on September 1, 1939, touched off World War II, Roosevelt immediately proclaimed American neutrality and put the arms embargo and other restrictions into effect. In a radio talk to the American people on the evening of September 3, he voiced his determination to keep the country out of the conflict. "We seek to keep war from our firesides," he declared, "by keeping war from coming to the Americas." Though he deliberately refrained from asking the people to remain neutral in thought as Wilson had done in 1914, he closed by reiterating his personal hatred of war and pledging that, "as long as it remains within my power to prevent, there will be no blackout of peace in the United States."

President Roosevelt did not give up his quest for revision of the Neutrality Act, however. After a careful telephone canvass indicated that a majority of the Senate would now support repeal of the arms embargo, the President called Congress into special session. On September 21, Roosevelt urged the senators and representatives to repeal the arms embargo and thereby return to the traditional American adherence to international law. Calling Jefferson's embargo and the neutrality legislation of the 1930's the sole exceptions to this historic policy, he argued that the removal of the arms embargo was a way to insure that the United States would not be involved in the European conflict, and he promised that the government would also insist that American citizens and American ships be barred from entering the war zones. Denying that repeal was a step toward war, Roosevelt asserted that his proposal "offers far greater safeguards than we now possess or have ever possessed to protect American lives and property from danger . . . . There lies the road to peace." He then closed by declaring that America must stand aloof from the conflict so that it could preserve the culture of Western Europe. "Fate seems now to compel us to assume the task of helping to maintain in the western world a citadel wherein that civilization may be kept alive," he concluded.

It was an amazing speech. No less than four times the President declared that his policy was aimed at keeping the United States out of the war. Yet the whole intent of arms embargo repeal was to permit England and France to purchase arms and munitions from the United States. By basing his appeal on a return to international law and a desire to keep out of the war, Roosevelt was deliberately misleading the American people. The result was a long and essentially irrelevant debate in Congress over the administration bill to repeal the arms embargo and to place all trade with belligerents on a cash-and-carry basis. Advocates of the bill followed the President's cue, repeatedly denying that the legislation was aimed at helping Britain and France and insisting that the sole motive was to preserve American neutrality. Isolationist opponents quite logically asked, if the purpose was to insure neutrality, why did not the administration simply retain the arms embargo and add cash-and-carry for all other trade with countries at war. With heavy majorities already lined up in both houses, administration spokesmen refused to answer this query. They infuriated the isolationists by repeating with parrot-like precision the party line that the substitution of cash-and-carry for the arms embargo would keep the nation out of war.

The result was an overwhelming victory for Roosevelt. In late October the Senate, thought to be the center of isolationist strength, voted for the administration bill by more than two to one; in early November the House concurred after a closer ballot. Now Britain and France could purchase from the United States anything they needed for their war effort, including guns, tanks, and airplanes, provided only that they paid cash and carried away these supplies in their own ships.

Roosevelt expressed his thoughts most clearly in a letter to William Allen White a month later. "Things move with such terrific speed, these days," he wrote, "that it really is essential to us to think in broader terms and, in effect, to warn the American people that they, too, should think of possible ultimate results in Europe. . . . Therefore, my sage old friend, my problem is to get the American people to think of conceivable consequences without scaring the American people into thinking that they are going to be dragged into this war." In 1939, Roosevelt evidently decided that candor was still too risky, and thus he chose to pursue devious tactics in aligning the United States indirectly on the side of England and France.

The blitzkrieg that Adolf Hitler launched in Europe in the spring of 1940 aroused Americans to their danger in a way that Roosevelt never could. Norway and Denmark fell in April, and then on May 10 Germany launched an offensive thrust through the low countries into northern France that drove Holland and Belgium out of the war in less than a week and forced the British into a humiliating retreat from the continent at Dunkirk before the month was over. The sense of physical security from foreign danger that the United States had enjoyed for over a century was shattered in a matter of days. The debate over policy would continue, but from May, 1940, on, virtually all Americans recognized that the German victories in Europe imperiled the United States. . . .

In early June, the news from Europe became even worse. As he sat in his White House study one evening reading the latest dispatches, Roosevelt remarked to his wife, "All bad, all bad." He realized that a vigorous defense program was not enough—that American security depended on the successful resistance of England and France to German aggression. As Hitler's armies swept toward Paris and Mussolini moved his troops toward the exposed French frontier on the Mediterranean, Roosevelt sought to throw American influence into the balance. On June 10, he was scheduled to deliver a commencement speech at the University of Virginia in Charlottesville. Going over the State Department draft, he stiffened the language, telling a diplomat who called at the White House that morning that his speech would be a " 'tough' one—one in which the issue between the democracies and the Fascist powers would be drawn as never before." News that Italy had attacked France reached the President just before he boarded the train to Charlottesville and reinforced his determination to speak out boldly.

Addressing the graduates that evening, President Roosevelt condemned the concept of isolationism that he himself had held so strongly only a few years before. He termed the idea that the United States could exist as a lone island of peace in a world of brute force "a delusion." "Such an island," he declared, "represents to me and to the overwhelming majority of Americans today a helpless nightmare of a people without freedom—the nightmare of a people lodged in prison, handcuffed, hungry, and fed through the bars from day to day by the contemptuous, unpitying masters of other continents." In clear and unambiguous words, he declared that his sympathies lay wholly on the side of "those nations that are giving their life blood in combat" against Fascist aggression. Then, in his most significant policy statement, he announced that his administration would follow a twofold course of increasing the American defense effort and extending to England and France "the material resources of this nation."

The Charlottesville speech marks a decisive turn in Roosevelt's policy. At the time, most commentators focused on one dramatic sentence, written in at the last moment, in which he condemned the Italian attack on France by saying, "the hand that held the dagger has struck it into the back of its neighbor." But far more important was the President's pledge to defend American security by giving all-out aid to England and France. By promising to share American supplies with these two belligerents, Roosevelt was gambling that they could successfully contain Germany on the European continent and thus end the threat to American security. Given the German military advantages, the risks were enormous. If Roosevelt diverted a large portion of the nation's limited supply of weapons to England and France and then they surrendered to Hitler, the President would be responsible for leaving this country unprepared to meet a future German onslaught.

At the same time, the President's admirers have read too much into the Charlottesville speech. Basil Rauch argues that the speech ended America's status as a neutral. Robert Sherwood goes even further, claiming that at Charlottesville Roosevelt committed the United States "to the assumption of responsibility for nothing less than the leadership of the world." Samuel Rosenman is more moderate, labeling this address as "the beginning of all-out aid to the democracies," but noting that it stopped short of war. But is it even accurate to say that the speech signified all-out aid short of war? An examination of Roosevelt's subsequent steps to help France and England reveals that the President was still extremely reluctant to do anything that would directly involve the United States in the European conflict.

The French quickly discovered the limitations of the President's new policy. Heartened by Roosevelt's words at Charlottesville, Paul Reynaud, the French Premier, immediately tried to secure American military intervention to save his country. In a personal appeal to Roosevelt on June 14, Reynaud asked him to send American troops as well as American supplies in France's hour of greatest need. The next day, the President replied. The United States admired the stubborn and heroic French resistance to German aggression, Roosevelt wrote, and he promised to do all he could to increase the flow of arms and munitions to France. But there he drew the line. "I know that you will understand that these statements carry with them no implication of military commitments," the President concluded. "Only the Congress can make such commitments." On June 17, the French, now fully aware that American military involvement was out of the question, surrendered to Germany.

The British, left waging the fight alone against Germany, also discovered that Roosevelt's actions failed to live up to the promise of his words. On May 15, five days after he replaced Neville Chamberlain as Prime Minister, Winston Churchill sent an urgent message to President Roosevelt. Churchill eloquently expressed his determination to fight Hitler to the bitter end, but he warned that Britain had to have extensive aid from the United States. Above all else, England needed forty or fifty American destroyers to protect the Atlantic supply line from German submarine attacks. Churchill pointed out that England had lost thirty-two destroyers since the war began, and she needed most of her remaining sixty-eight in home waters to guard against a German invasion. "We must ask, therefore," Churchill concluded, "as a matter of life or death, to be reinforced with these destroyers."

Despite the urgency of the British request, Roosevelt procrastinated. On June 5, the President told Secretary of the Interior Harold Ickes that it would require an act of Congress to transfer the destroyers to Great Britain. Even pressure from several other cabinet members, including Henry Morgenthau and the two new Republicans Roosevelt appointed in June, Secretary of War Henry Stimson and Secretary of the Navy Frank Knox, failed to move Roosevelt. His reluctance was increased when Congress decreed on June 28 that the President could not transfer any warships to a belligerent until the Chief of Naval Operations certified that they were "not essential to the defense of the United States."

Roosevelt's inaction caused deep concern among members of the Committee to Defend America by Aiding the Allies, the pro-British pressure group headed by William Allen White. A few of the more interventionist members of White's committee developed the idea in mid-July of arranging a trade whereby the United States would give Britain the needed destroyers in return for the right to build naval and air bases on British islands in the Western Hemisphere. On August 1, a three-man delegation called at the White House to present this idea to the President, who received it noncommittally. Lord Lothian, the British ambassador, had suggested as far back as May 24 that England grant the United States the rights for bases on Newfoundland, Bermuda, and Trinidad, and in July, in talks with Secretary of the Navy Frank Knox, Lothian linked the possibility of these bases with the transfer of destroyers. Knox liked the idea, but he could not act without the President's consent. And Roosevelt remained deaf to all pleas, including one by Churchill on July 21 in which the British Prime Minister said, "Mr. President, with great respect I must tell you that in the long history of the world this is a thing to do NOW."

Churchill's appeal and the possibility of justifying the transfer of the destroyers as a trade for bases evidently persuaded Roosevelt to act. On August 2, when Frank Knox raised the issue in a cabinet meeting, Roosevelt approved the idea of giving Britain the destroyers in return for the right to build bases on British islands in the Atlantic and Caribbean, and, in addition, in return for a British pledge to send its fleet to the New World if Germany defeated England. Roosevelt still believed that the destroyer transfer would require an act of Congress, and the cabinet advised him to secure the support of Wendell Willkie, the Republican candidate for the presidency in the forthcoming campaign, to insure favorable Congressional action. Through William Allen White, who acted as an intermediary, Roosevelt received word that while Willkie refused to work actively to line up Republican support in Congress, he did agree not to make the destroyer deal a campaign issue.

Roosevelt called his advisers together on August 13 to make a final decision. With the help of Morgenthau, Knox, Stimson, and Undersecretary of State Sumner Welles, Roosevelt drafted a cable to Churchill proposing the transfer of fifty destroyers in return for eight bases and a private pledge in regard to the British fleet. The next day a joyous Churchill cabled back his acceptance of these terms, saying that "each destroyer you can spare to us is measured in rubies." But Churchill realized that the deal meant more than just help at sea. "The moral value of this fresh aid from your Government and your people at this critical time," he cabled the President, "will be very great and widely felt."

It took two more weeks to work out the details of the transaction, and during that period a group of distinguished international lawyers convinced the Attorney General that the administration could transfer the destroyers without the approval of Congress. One final hitch developed when Churchill insisted that the bases be considered free gifts from the British; Roosevelt finally agreed that two of the sites would be gifts, but that the remaining six would have to be considered a *quid pro quo* for the destroyers. On September 3, the President made the transaction public in a message to Congress in which he bore down heavily on the advantages to be gained by the United States. Barely mentioning the transfer of the destroyers, the President called the acquisition of eight naval and air bases stretching in an arc from Newfoundland to British Guiana "an epochal and far-reaching act of preparation for continental defense in the face of grave danger." Searching desperately for a historical precedent, Roosevelt described the trade as "the most important action in the reinforcement of our national defense that has been taken since the Louisiana Purchase."

What is most striking about the destroyer-for-bases deal is the caution and reluctance with which the President acted. In June he announced a policy of all-out aid to Britain, yet he delayed for nearly four months after receiving Churchill's desperate plea for destroyers. He acted only after interventionists had created strong public support, only after the transfer could be disguised as an act in support of the American defense program, only after the leader of the opposition party had agreed not to challenge him politically on this issue, and only after his legal advisers found a way to bypass Congress. What may have appeared on the surface to be a bold and courageous act by the President was in reality a carefully calculated and virtually foolproof maneuver.

It would be easy to dismiss the destroyer-for-bases deal as just another example of Roosevelt's tendency to permit political expediency to dictate his foreign policy. Certainly Roosevelt acted in this case with a careful eye on the political realities. This was an election year, and he was not going to hand Wendell Willkie and the Republicans a ready-made issue. But I believe that Roosevelt's hesitation and caution stem as much from his own uncertainty as from political calculation. He realized that the gift of vessels of war to a belligerent was a serious departure from traditional neutrality, and one that might well give Germany the grounds on which to declare war against the United States. He wanted to give England all-out aid short of war, but he was not at all sure that this step would not be an act of war. Only when he convinced himself that the destroyer-for-bases deal could be construed as a step to defend the nation's security did he give his consent. Thus his rather extravagant public defense of his action was not just a political move to quiet isolationist critics; rather it was his own deeply felt rationalization for a policy step of great importance that undoubtedly moved the United States closer to participation in the European conflict.

Perhaps even more significant is the pattern that emerges from this review of Roosevelt's policy in the spring and summer of 1940, for it is one that recurs again and again in his conduct of foreign policy. Confronted by a major crisis, he makes a bold and forthright call at Charlottesville for a policy of all-out aid short of war. But then, having pleased the interventionists with his rhetoric, he immediately retreats, turning down the French appeal for intervention and delaying on the British plea for destroyers, thus reassuring his isolationist critics. Then, as a consensus begins to form, he finally enters into the destroyer-for-bases deal and thus redeems the pledge he had made months before at Charlottesville. Like a child playing a game of giant steps, Roosevelt moved two steps forward and one back before he took the giant step ahead. Movement in a straight and unbroken line seems to have been alien to his nature—he could not go forward until he had tested the ground, studied all the reactions, and weighed all the risks. . . .

After his triumphant election to a third term, Roosevelt relaxed on a Caribbean cruise. But after only a week, a navy seaplane arrived with an urgent dispatch from Winston Churchill. The Prime Minister gave a lengthy and bleak description of the situation in Europe and then informed the President that England was rapidly running out of money for continued purchases of American goods. "The moment approaches when we shall no longer be able to pay cash for shipping and other supplies," Churchill wrote, concluding with the confident assertion that Roosevelt would find "ways and means" to continue the flow of munitions and goods across the Atlantic.

When the President returned to Washington in mid-December, he called in the press, and in his breeziest and most informal manner began to outline the British dilemma and his solution to it. His advisers were working on several plans, he said, but the one that interested him most was simply to lend or lease to England the supplies she needed, in the belief that "the best defense of

Great Britain is the best defense of the United States." Saying that he wanted to get rid of the dollar sign, Roosevelt compared his scheme to the idea of lending a garden hose to a neighbor whose house was on fire. When the fire is out, the neighbor either returns the hose or, if it is damaged, replaces it with a new one. So it would be, Roosevelt concluded, with the munitions the United States would provide Britain in the war against Nazi Germany.

In a fireside chat to the American people a few days later, Roosevelt justified this lend-lease concept on grounds of national security. Asserting that Hitler aimed not just at victory in Europe but at world domination, Roosevelt repeated his belief that the United States was in grave peril. If England fell, he declared, "all of us in the Americas would be living at the point of a gun." He admitted that the transfer of arms and munitions to Britain risked American involvement in the conflict, but he argued that "there is far less chance of the United States getting into war if we do all we can now to support the nations defending themselves against attack by the Axis than if we acquiesce in their defeat, submit tamely to an Axis victory, and wait our turn to be the object of attack in another war later on." He declared that he had no intention of sending American troops to Europe; his sole purpose was to "keep war away from our country and our people." Then, in a famous phrase, he called upon the United States to become "the great arsenal of democracy."

Congress deliberated over the lend-lease bill for the next two months, and a strong consensus soon emerged in favor of the measure. Leading Republicans, including Wendell Willkie, endorsed the bill, and most opponents objected only to the leasing provision, suggesting instead an outright loan to Britain. The House acted quickly, approving lend-lease by nearly 100 votes in February; the Senate took longer but finally gave its approval by a margin of almost two to one in early March. After the President signed the legislation into law, Congress granted an initial appropriation of seven billion dollars to guarantee the continued flow of vital war supplies to Great Britain.

Roosevelt had thus taken another giant step forward, and this time without any hesitation. His election victory made him bolder than usual, and Churchill's candid plea had convinced him that speed was essential. The granting of lend-lease aid was very nearly an act of war, for it gave Britain unrestricted access to America's enormous industrial resources. But the President felt with great sincerity that this policy would lead not to American involvement but to a British victory that alone could keep the nation out of war. . . .

In the six months preceding Pearl Harbor, Franklin Roosevelt moved slowly but steadily toward war with Germany. On July 7, he announced that he had sent 4,000 American marines to Iceland to prevent that strategic island from falling into German hands. Secretary of War Stimson, though pleased with this action, expressed disappointment over the President's insistence on describing it solely as a measure of hemispheric self-defense. Iceland was the key to defending the supply route across the Atlantic, and Stimson believed that the President should have frankly told Congress that the United States was occupying the island to insure the delivery of goods to Britain.

Once American forces landed in Iceland, Roosevelt authorized the Navy to convoy American ships supplying the marines on the island. In addition, he at first approved a naval operations plan which permitted British ships to join these convoys and thus receive an American escort halfway across the Atlantic, but in late July he reversed himself, ordering the Navy to restrict its convoys to American and Icelandic vessels. In August, at the famous Atlantic Conference with Churchill, Roosevelt once again committed himself to the principle of convoying British ships halfway across the Atlantic, but he failed to give the necessary order to the Navy after his return to Washington.

Roosevelt's hesitancy and indecision finally ended in early September when a German submarine fired a torpedo at the American destroyer *Greer*. Though subsequent reports revealed that the *Greer* had been following the U-boat for more than three hours and had been broadcasting its position to nearby British naval units, Roosevelt interpreted this incident as a clear-cut case of German aggression. In a press release on September 5, he called the attack on the *Greer* deliberate, and on the same day he told Samuel Rosenman to begin drafting a statement that would express his determination "to use any means necessary to get the goods to England." Rosenman and Harry Hopkins prepared a strongly worded speech, and after a few revisions the President delivered it over a worldwide radio network on the evening of September 11.

In biting phrases, Roosevelt lashed out against Hitler and Nazi Germany. He described the attack on the *Greer* as part of a concerted German effort to "acquire absolute control and domination of the seas for themselves." Such control, he warned, would lead inevitably to a Nazi effort to dominate the Western Hemisphere and "create a permanent world system based on force, terror, and murder." The attack on the *Greer* was an act of piracy, Roosevelt declared; German submarines had become the "rattlesnakes of the Atlantic." Then, implying but never openly saying that American ships would shoot German submarines on sight, Roosevelt declared that henceforth the United States Navy would escort "all merchant ships—not only American ships but ships of any flag—engaged in commerce in our defensive waters."

Contemporary observers and many historians labeled this the "shoot-on-sight" speech, seeing its significance primarily in the orders to American naval officers to fire at German submarines in the western Atlantic. "The undeclared war" speech would be a better label, for its real importance was that Roosevelt had finally made a firm decision on the convoy issue on which he had been hedging ever since the passage of lend-lease by Congress. Branding the Germans as "pirates" and their U-boats as "rattlesnakes" distracted the American people from the fact that the President was now putting into practice the policy of convoying British ships halfway across the ocean, and thereby assuming a significant share of the responsibility for the Battle of the Atlantic. The immediate effect was to permit the British to transfer forty destroyers from the western Atlantic to the submarine-infested waters surrounding the British Isles. In the long run, the President's decision meant war with Germany, since from this time forward there would inevitably be more and more U-boat attacks on American destroyers, increasingly heavy loss of life, and a direct challenge to the nation's honor and prestige. Only Hitler's reluctance to engage in war with the United States while he was still absorbed in the assault on Russia prevented an immediate outbreak of hostilities.

With the convoy issue now resolved, Roosevelt moved to revise the Neutrality Act. In mid-October he asked the House to permit the arming of American merchant ships with deck guns, and then later in the month he urged the Senate to remove the "carry" provision of the law so that American merchantmen could take supplies all the way across the Atlantic to British ports. When a German submarine torpedoed the destroyer *Kearney* near Iceland, Roosevelt seized on the incident to speed up action in Congress.

"America has been attacked," the President declared in a speech on October 27. "The U.S.S. *Kearney* is not just a Navy ship. She belongs to every man, woman, and child in this Nation." Describing Nazi efforts at infiltration in South America, the President bluntly charged that Germany was bent on the conquest of "the United States itself." Then, coming very close to a call for war, he asserted, "The forward march of Hitlerism can be stopped—and it will be stopped. Very simply and very bluntly—we are pledged to pull our own oar in the destruction of Hitlerism." Although he called only for the revision of the Neutrality Act, the tone of the entire address was one of unrelieved belligerency, culminating in the following peroration: "Today in the face of this newest and greatest challenge, we Americans have cleared our decks and taken our battle stations. We stand ready in the defense of our Nation and the faith of our fathers to do what God has given us the power to see as our full duty."

Two weeks later, by quite slim majorities, Congress removed nearly all restrictions on American commerce from the Neutrality Act. For the first time since the war began in 1939, American merchant vessels could carry supplies all the way across the Atlantic to British ports. The significance of this action was obscured by the Japanese attack on Pearl Harbor which triggered American entry into the war in December and gave rise to the subsequent charge that Roosevelt led the nation into the conflict via the back door. Revision of the Neutrality Act was bound to lead to war with Germany within a matter of months. Hitler could be forbearing when it was only a question of American escort vessels operating in the western Atlantic. He could not have permitted American ships to carry a major portion of lend-lease supplies to Britain without giving up the Battle of the Atlantic. With the German offensive halting before Leningrad and Moscow in December, Hitler would have been compelled to order his submarine commanders to torpedo American ships as the only effective way to hold Britain in check. And once Germany began sinking American ships regularly, Roosevelt would have had to ask Congress for a declaration of war.

The crucial question, of course, is why Roosevelt chose such an oblique policy which left the decision for peace or war in the hands of Hitler. His apologists, notably Robert Sherwood and Basil Rauch, insist that he had no choice. The isolationists were so powerful that the President could not lay the issue squarely before Congress and ask for a declaration of war. If he had, writes Basil Rauch, he would have "invited a prolonged, bitter, and divisive debate" and thereby have risked a defeat which would have discredited the administration and turned the nation back to isolationism. Sherwood sadly agrees, saying, "He had no more tricks left. The hat from which he had pulled so many rabbits was empty. The President of the United States was now the creature of circumstance which must be shaped not by his own will or his own ingenuity but by the unpredictable determination of his enemies."

In part this was true, but these sympathetic historians fail to point out that Roosevelt was the prisoner of his own policies. He had told the nation time and time again that it was not necessary for the United States to enter the war. He had propounded the doctrine that America could achieve Hitler's downfall simply by giving all-out aid to England. He had repeatedly denied that his measures would lead the nation to war. In essence, he had foreclosed to himself the possibility of going directly to the people and bluntly stating that the United States must enter the war as the only way to guarantee the nation's security. All he could do was edge the country closer and closer, leaving the ultimate decision to Germany and Japan.

We will never know at what point Roosevelt decided in his own mind that it was essential that the United States enter the war. His own personal hatred of war was deep and genuine, and it was this conviction that set him apart from men like Stimson and Morgenthau, who decided that American participation was necessary as early as the spring of 1941. William Langer and Everett Gleason believe that Roosevelt realized by the fall of 1941 that there was no other way to defeat Hitler, but they conclude that, even so, he thought the American military contribution could be limited to naval and air support and not include the dispatch of an American army to the European battlefields.

It is quite possible that Roosevelt never fully committed himself to American involvement prior to Pearl Harbor. His hesitancy was not just a catering to isolationist strength but a reflection of his own inner uncertainty. Recognizing that Hitler threatened the security of the United States, he took a series of steps which brought the nation to the brink of war, but his own revulsion at the thought of plunging his country into the most devastating conflict in history held him back until the Japanese attack left him no choice.

The Cautious Politician as Foreign Policy Maker

JAMES MACGREGOR BURNS

The record is clear. As a foreign policy maker, Roosevelt during his first term was more pussyfooting politician than political leader. He seemed to float almost helplessly on the flood tide of isolationism, rather than to seek to change both the popular attitudes and the apathy that buttressed the isolationists' strength.

He hoped that people would be educated by events; the error of this policy

Excerpted from *Roosevelt: The Lion and the Fox* © 1956 by James MacGregor Burns. Reprinted by permission of Harcourt Brace Jovanovich, Inc.

was that the dire events in Europe and Asia confirmed the American suspicion and fear of foreign involvement rather than prodding them into awareness of the need for collective action by the democracies. In short, a decisive act of interpretation was required, but Roosevelt did not interpret. At a minimum he might have avoided the isolationist line about keeping clear of joint action with other nations. Yet at a crucial moment—when he approved the Neutrality Act shortly before Italy's attack on Ethiopia—he talked about co-operating with other nations "without entanglement."

The awful implications of this policy of drift would become clear later on when Roosevelt sought to regain control of foreign policy making at home as the forces of aggression mounted abroad. But the immediate question is: Why did Roosevelt allow himself to be virtually immobilized by isolationist feeling? Why did he not, through words or action, seek to change popular attitudes and thus rechannel the pressures working on him?

The enigma deepens when Roosevelt's private views are considered. In his private role he was an internationalist. He believed, that is, in the proposition that America's security lay essentially in removing the economic and social causes of war and, if war threatened, in uniting the democracies, America included, against aggressive nations. But in his public role he talked about keeping America disentangled from the political affairs of other nations; he often talked, in short, like an isolationist.

The mystery deepens still further when one considers that the President had emphatic, though perhaps ill-defined, ideas about the need for leadership in a democracy. He must have recognized the potential in leadership when, in addressing the Woodrow Wilson Foundation at the end of 1933, he asserted roundly that the "blame for the danger to world peace lies not in the world population but in the political leaders of the population." At the same time he was concerned about the perennially weak leadership that the politicians gave France. He was perhaps aware, too, that simply following a line of policy lying at the mean between two extremes would not necessarily lead to the wisest course. In the case of Ethiopia, for instance, the British and French through their indecisive maneuverings succeeded neither in keeping Mussolini out of Germany's orbit nor in vindicating the ideals of collective security. Washington's foreign policies were equally muddled.

The reasons for the sharp divergence between Roosevelt's private and public roles in foreign policy making were several. In the first place, the President's party was cleft through the middle on international issues. The internationalist wing centered in the southern and border states was balanced by isolationists rooted in the West and Midwest. To win the nomination Roosevelt had given hostages to both groups. Part of the price of success in 1932 had been categorical opposition to United States co-operation with the collective security efforts of the League, and a cautious policy of neutrality based on nonentanglement. In the second place, Roosevelt in his campaign had so ignored foreign policy, or fuzzed the issue over when he did touch on it, that he had failed to establish popular attitudes on foreign policy that he could later evoke in support of internationalism. Moreover, during his first term the President gave first priority to domestic policies; a strong line on foreign affairs might have alienated the large number of isolationist congressmen who were supporting the New Deal. Indeed, many isolationists seemed to believe that any marked interest in foreign affairs by the President was virtually a betrayal of progressivism.

In addition, the President had surrounded himself with men from both sides. Men like Hull and Howe and Morgenthau were generally on the international end of the spectrum, but others like Moley and Hopkins and Hugh Johnson and Ickes were at the opposite end. Ickes had been so pleased by the Senate action on the World Court that he had telephoned and congratulated Hiram Johnson, whom he found "as happy as a boy." The development of the New Deal's policies of economic nationalism, tinged with the rhetoric of international good will and economic co-operation, resulted from and reinforced this division.

But the main reason for Roosevelt's caution involved the future rather than the past. The election of 1936 was approaching, and at this point he was not willing to take needless risks. It was significant that after he and Mackenzie King had signed a trade agreement in Washington—and a rather moderate one at that—Roosevelt wrote to King in April 1936 that "in a sense, we both took our political lives in our hands. . . ." The immediate goal of re-election was the supreme goal; the tasks of leadership, he hoped, could be picked up later. . . .

What was the matter? In the gravest international situation the nation had ever faced, where was the leadership of the man whose very name since 1933 had become the symbol of candor and courage?

When a leader fails to live up to the symbolic role he has come to occupy, his admirers cling to the image they love by imputing mistakes to the leader's advisers. Stories went the rounds in 1939 that Roosevelt's trouble really lay in Hull's timidity and in Kennedy's belief in appeasement. The stories were not true. Hull, to be sure, did seem to move slowly, but he was working against the embargo law before Roosevelt took a definite stand, and he was calling existing legislation "a wretched little bob-tailed, sawed-off" substitute for the established rules on international law while the President was using far softer words. As for Kennedy, Roosevelt knew that he had sympathized with the appeasement policies of Chamberlain and the so-called "Cliveden set" and to an extent valued him for this. But he would not let his ambassador get out of hand. When Kennedy submitted a draft of a talk he was to give in London, the President and Hull went over it line by line to adjust it to administration policy.

The President's tactics were his own. Another explanation for his caution lay in the nature of the opposition in Congress and among the people. Certainly the opposition to an internationalist or collective security program was not to be dismissed lightly. In a 1937 poll nineteen out of twenty people answered a flat "No" to the query whether the United States should enter another world war. Most of the people trusted Congress rather than the President to keep America out of war. They were powerfully drawn by the symbols of Peace and Neutrality—and they tended to equate the two. To be sure, these attitudes somewhat lacked stability and durability. But they had a terrible intensity. The late 1930's was the period when the famous aviatrix Laura Ingalls showered the White House with "peace" leaflets from her plane, when Father Coughlin and John L. Lewis were whipping up isolationist feeling, when to some fascism constituted the "wave of the future." Two decades of bitterness over World War I and its aftermath had left a hard, smarting scar tissue.

Any attempt by Roosevelt to override this feeling clearly would have been disastrous. His real mission as a political leader was to modify and guide this opinion in a direction closer to American interests as he saw them. To raise this question is again to confront the paradox of Roosevelt's leadership.

For under the impact of shattering events abroad, people's attitudes were slowly shifting. Most Americans, of course, clung to their "Keep-Out-of-War" position. But between Munich and the outbreak of war a great majority of the people swung over to the position of all help to Britain and France short of war. By September 1939 about 37 per cent of the people favored positive help to Britain, France, and Poland; less than half of these wanted to dispatch military help then or at any later time, while most favored sending food and materials. This 37 per cent interventionist element confronted a hard-core isolationist bloc that opposed any aid at all to either side. In the middle was a group of about 30 per cent that would refuse to sell to either side except on a cash-and-carry basis.

It was this vast middle group that offered the President his supreme opportunity. For this group was clinging to the symbol of nonentanglement while grasping the need of American help to nations under attack. This group, combined with the interventionists, would have given heavy backing to Roosevelt's all aid-short-of-war policies. Was it possible that these millions of middle-of-the-roaders thought that cash and carry in 1939 meant material help to *neither* side? No; a later poll showed that 90 per cent favored cash and carry even if in practice only Britain and France got the supplies. Without question these middle attitudes were shot through with confusions and uncertainties. But this made a real leader's opportunity all the greater, for opinions that are superficial and volatile are the most subject to influence. A situation that was an opportunity for Napoleon, A. N. Whitehead has observed, would appear as an unmanageable disorder to most of us.

Roosevelt felt that events and facts themselves would educate the public. So they did—but not quickly enough. Each time in the race between aggression and American opinion victory went to the former. The early months of 1939 were the supreme test. Roosevelt's great hope was that he could demonstrate to Hitler that America would give material aid to nations the Nazis planned to attack. The President's tactic was based on a sound proposition— the best way to keep America out of war would be to keep war out of the world. But he did not lead opinion toward a position of all aid short of war. He tagged along with opinion. Sometimes, indeed—most notably when he was frightened by the reaction to the "quarantine" speech and later by the furore over America's frontier being "on the Rhine"—he lagged behind the drift of opinion favoring more commitment by the United States to joint efforts against aggression.

The President's immediate problem was not, of course, isolationist feeling in general but the mighty isolationist phalanxes in Congress. Doubtless he feared that defeat of a crucial bill on the Hill might mean a permanent setback for his hopes to aid the democracies and might so dishearten friends of America abroad as to encourage more appeasement. If such was Roosevelt's tactic with Congress, the fate of embargo repeal in the spring of 1939 suggests that he failed. Perhaps if he had taken a position against the embargo much sooner and much more openly and consistently, he could have won repeal in the spring of 1939. But the fact is that only when he knew he had the votes on the Hill did he utter the clarion call that resulted in repeal in October of that year. Once again events, not the President, had done the job of educating —and once again the time was tragically late.

Anglophobia and Intra-Administration Debate

ARNOLD A. OFFNER

Between 1933 and 1939, Adolf Hitler's diplomacy and saber-rattling destroyed the political and military structure established at the Paris Peace Conference in 1919 and moved Germany to a position of virtual superiority in Western and Central Europe. The response of the administration of President Franklin D. Roosevelt to this dramatic shift of power was extremely cautious and aloof. Several factors were obviously responsible for this. Undeniably, Roosevelt's overriding concern throughout the decade was to deal with the Great Depression, and domestic policy took priority over foreign affairs at least until 1939.

Public and congressional attitudes also circumscribed the administration's alternatives. Revisionist literature in the 1920's had discredited traditional explanations of the origins of the First World War. Publication in 1934 of such best-selling works as Helmuth E. Engelbrecht and Frank C. Hanighen's *Merchants of Death: A Study of the International Armaments Industry,* and George Seldes's *Iron, Blood, and Profits: An Exposure of the World-Wide Munitions Racket,* combined with the publicity generated in 1934–36 by Senator George P. Nye's committee investigation of the munitions industry, challenged the propriety of relationships between bankers, munitions-makers, and government officials and the forces that might have led America to war in 1917. This sentiment manifested itself in the Neutrality Act of August 1935, which empowered the President to prohibit sale or shipment of arms, munitions, and implements of war to all parties involved in a conflict. Congress extended the law in February 1936, and in January 1937, at the administration's behest, it passed special legislation to cover the Spanish Civil War. The Neutrality Act of May 1937 allowed the President to embargo nonmilitary goods. It also contained a provision for the next two years that, if the President

From *The Origins of the Second World War: American Foreign Policy and World Politics, 1917–1941* by Arnold A. Offner. Copyright © 1975 by Praeger Publishers. Reprinted by permission of Praeger Publishers, a division of Holt, Rinehart and Winston.

had to invoke the Neutrality Act, he might also, in the name of national security, place all trade on a "cash-and-carry" basis, thereby favoring the British with their large navy and merchant marine. But the primary purpose of the 1937 law was to allow Americans to maintain their neutrality and to carry on a lucrative wartime trade without the risk that commercial debts, or the loss of ships at sea, might lead to the circumstances that had inclined the United States toward intervention on behalf of Great Britain in 1917.

Minor administration efforts at international cooperation were often stymied by ultranationalist sentiments. In January 1935, the Senate Foreign Relations Committee approved a measure proposing that the United States join the World Court, and Roosevelt sent a special message to Congress to urge its passage. But a group of senators, led by Borah, Johnson, and Huey P. Long, and then a last-minute radio and telegram campaign, led by the chauvinistic publisher William Randolph Hearst, the now anti–New Deal "radio-priest," Father Charles E. Coughlin, and the philosopher of the homespun, Will Rogers, caused crucial defections among supporters of the measure. It failed by seven votes (52–36) to gain the necessary two-thirds majority, despite the fact that the Democrats held 68 Senate seats. Secretary of the Interior Harold Ickes noted shortly thereafter that this defeat cut Roosevelt "pretty deeply," and that even the usually cautious and acquiescent Secretary of State, Cordell Hull, felt bad enough to consider an open fight with the Senate.

The administration was embarrassed in January 1938, one month after the Japanese had sunk the American gunboat *Panay* in the Yangtze River, when Representative Louis Ludlow of Indiana sought to force out of committee his proposed constitutional amendment that would have made a national referendum on a declaration of war mandatory in all instances except those involving direct attack upon the United States, its territories, or the Western Hemisphere. Roosevelt had to commit his presidential prestige to prevent the bill's discharge from committee, and the administration prevailed by only the slim margin of 209–188. The World Court and Ludlow episodes were perhaps as much symbolic as real issues, but they indicated the intense opposition the administration would meet if it sought to intervene in the growing world crisis. Roosevelt no doubt had this opposition in mind when he ruefully remarked at mid-decade that it was "a terrible thing to look over your shoulder when you are trying to lead—and to find no one there."

But neither domestic economic concerns, nor congressional and public non-interventionist attitudes, nor the neutrality legislation, sufficiently explains American foreign policy in the 1930's. The emphasis accorded to these events in the past may have obscured analysis of the way in which New Deal officials viewed European developments and the rationale that underlay their strategy and tactics. Past analysis has also overlooked two important factors: (1) intra-administration arguments between those who wished to resist German demands and those who believed that peace was possible only if Germany were properly appeased; and (2) the embittered state of Anglo-American relations, which hampered cooperation at every level and facilitated the adroit exploitation by Hitler of the fears, weaknesses, and divisions in the Western world that ultimately led to war.

Roosevelt was a patrician internationalist; he had admired cousin Theodore Roosevelt's worldly tradition, imbibed Woodrow Wilson's principles for eight years as Assistant Secretary of the Navy, and in 1920 campaigned hard for the League of Nations. By the end of the decade, he deferred to practical and Democratic party politics by urging only "wholehearted cooperation" with the League, and in 1932, to placate the Hearst faction in the Democratic party, he flatly opposed American entry, a view he reiterated before the Woodrow Wilson Foundation in December 1933. All subsequent private talks, such as with Canadian Prime Minister MacKenzie King in the summer of 1936, concerning possible American entry into the League presumed that the League Covenant would be separated from the Treaty of Versailles, which Roosevelt, along with most other American and European diplomats, believed was more the cause of international instability than any single nation or leader.

Roosevelt believed Europe's problems were basically, or exclusively, European, and that the United States could do little to resolve them other than afford moral exhortation. His speech to the Wilson Foundation in December 1933 deplored the fact that 10 per cent of the world menaced the peaceful inclinations of the other 90 per cent, and his January 1936 annual message to Congress assailed nations seeking to redress injustices springing from past wars by reverting to the "law of the sword." But, he always hastened to add, the American response to foreign conflict would always be "a well-ordered neutrality."

Reinforcing Roosevelt's unwillingness to involve the United States in European politics was his dislike or suspicion of the British, and the ambivalent state of Anglo-American relations. Roosevelt disdained the British upper classes, whose political and economic views he considered too narrow, empire-oriented, and at the root of many of the world's past and present problems. He especially disliked the financial or commercial leaders he referred to as "the Bank of England crowd," including Neville Chamberlain, who was Chancellor of the Exchequer from 1931 to May 1937 and then Prime Minister until May 1940. When Secretary of the Treasury Henry Morgenthau, Jr., asked in 1936 whether he might open talks with the British on stabilization of the exchange rate of the dollar and pound, the President replied that "the trouble is that when you sit around the table with a Britisher he usually gets 80 per cent of the deal and you get what is left. Tell them that. Tell them that if we got 45 per cent we think that would be doing well. As long as Neville Chamberlain is there we must recognize that fundamentally he thoroughly dislikes Americans." Roosevelt also believed, as he said in 1935, that the British Foreign Office needed "a little more unselfish spine," and he always suspected the British were trying to "thrust leadership on me" in order that the United States might bail them out of their European or Far Eastern difficulties, or both.

Secretary of State Cordell Hull also took a dim view of American involvement in European politics, and he, too, was suspicious of British intentions. As a congressman and senator, he had been a prominent champion of a low tariff and Wilson's League of Nations, but as Secretary of State he usually favored taking the path of least resistance at home and abroad, which often meant doing nothing or opting for neutrality. With a repetitiveness that exasperated foreign diplomats, he argued that world peace was possible only by expanding world trade through reciprocal, most-favored-nation agreements, as opposed to the exclusive agreements in the fashion of British imperial preferences or Germany's bilateral agreements with Eastern European countries. In his postwar *Memoirs,* Hull cited the failure of the United States and Great Britain to conclude a trade agreement before the autumn of 1938 (he put the onus on the British) as a major reason war was not averted. This was nearly as much his genuine conviction as retrospective blame-tossing.

Most of Hull's State Department subordinates were not as zealous as he was about increased international trade as the panacea for peace, but they shared similar viewpoints. Career diplomats such as William Phillips, Under Secretary of State from 1933 to 1936 and then ambassador to Italy until 1940, and Jay Pierrepont Moffat, Chief of the Division of Western European Affairs during 1932–35 and 1937–40, were always highly skeptical about American involvement in European affairs, except to encourage the process of appeasement. They were unhappy at Germany's announcement of rearmament in 1935 and its reoccupation of the Rhineland in 1936 but accepted these developments as inevitable. Phillips thought Chamberlain's flights to Germany in September 1938 during the crisis over Czechoslovakia were "fine and courageous," and he also favored American recognition of Italy's conquest of Ethiopia.

Even stronger views came from Hugh R. Wilson, minister to Switzerland 1927–37 (and a trusted go-between for the State Department and League officials), Assistant Secretary of State in 1937, and ambassador to Germany in 1938. Wilson's colleagues considered him a "realist," in contrast to those who held more liberal or "messianic" views and who also took a stiffer attitude toward German and Italian aggression. Not only did Wilson believe that Germany had to be economically satisfied and integrated into Europe's political mainstream, but he admired Germany's internal regimentation and was convinced that its "Strength Through Joy" program would benefit the world. Although he did not approve of German persecution of the Jews, he thought the "Jewish problem" and the American press were the reasons for increasingly bad relations between the United States and Germany. Hitler's plans, Wilson insisted in 1938, "do not necessarily involve the Western powers," and he thought the Munich settlement opened the way "to a better Europe." He also thought throughout the decade that Russia's urging resistance to German demands only endangered European peace. Three months after the Second World War had begun in Europe, he hoped the fighting would be ended so that Germany would be free to "take care of the Russian encroachment" and thereby further "the ends of civilization."

Then there was Sumner Welles, Assistant and later Under Secretary of State during 1933–43, and a close friend and confidant of Roosevelt. Welles's battles with Hull were well known and led to Hull's forcing his resignation in 1943, but their disagreements were personal and concerned diplomatic style and timing more than substantive issues. Welles and Hull agreed on American policy during the Italo-Ethiopian war, but in 1938 Welles favored recognition of Italy's conquest because he wished to appease Italy as the first step of a policy whose larger purpose was to appease Germany. In 1937 and 1938, Welles would make several proposals for achieving world peace that rested upon economic appeasement, and which, in the fashion of Hull's trade agreements, were intended to spill over into political appeasement. Hull opposed these schemes, not because he preferred a more militant stand against Germany, Japan, or Italy, but because he feared the United States was becoming too involved in world problems. Moreover, Welles also was suspicious of British purposes; for, while he would seek their approval to launch his projects, he did so more to prevent their scuttling of them than to confront anyone with an Anglo-American bloc.

By no means was the American emphasis on appeasement in the 1930's a unanimous or monolithic view. Roosevelt himself was torn with doubt about its usefulness in dealing with Nazi Germany, and as early as the spring of 1934 he asked the State Department to consider a multinational trade boycott against Germany if Germany refused to allow a commission to investigate its alleged infractions of the disarmament clauses of the Treaty of Versailles. But Moffat and Phillips persuaded the President that trade sanctions were a virtual act of war and inconsistent with a policy of neutrality. Roosevelt discussed similar proposals for sanctions or a blockade against Germany after its rearmament announcement in March 1935, and during the Rhineland crisis a year later he told an English visitor that he thought the choice was between war then and in five years.

The American Ambassador to Germany during 1933–38, William E. Dodd, was quickly disabused of the alleged redemptive, or regenerative, aspects of Nazi foreign and domestic policies, and by November 1934 he became convinced that peace would last only "until Germany can be entirely ready to command Europe." He was always pleading with Roosevelt to find some means to avoid the general war that he felt would result from acquiescence in Hitler's demands. Similarly, George S. Messersmith, consul general in Berlin in 1930–34, minister to Austria in 1934–37, and then Assistant Secretary of State, and highly regarded by all his colleagues, concluded relatively early that Germany intended war, and in July 1936 he noted that Hitler's "burning ambition is to impose his will on Europe by force of arms." Messersmith disputed the common view that Germany's more conservative elements would moderate Hitler, for "Germany's so-called conservative elements are conservative in the sense that they believe Germany is not ready and must not take any precipitate action. They are by no means conservative in the sense that they do not share the political expansionist aims of Hitler and the more radical members of the Party." Likewise, Henry Morgenthau, Jr., Secretary of the Treasury from 1934 to 1945, and Harold L. Ickes, Secretary of the Interior from 1933 to 1946, both of whom represented progressive elements in the Democratic party, deplored Nazi foreign and domestic policies (perhaps intuitively as much as analytically) and were often at odds with the State Department, while they supported policies that urged Roosevelt toward a bolder course. But in every matter of importance the forces or circumstances favoring a policy of appeasement prevailed.

Finally, it should be noted that if the Americans took a jaundiced view of British policies, the British were equally hostile toward American policies. Foreign Office personnel believed New Deal economic policies were designed to appeal to the "less responsible" elements in American life. They belittled Roosevelt's "superficial" financial and economic knowledge and his proclivity for "yes-men" and "second-rate advisers" and disparaged his diplomatic aides. Secretary Hull was a "hot gospeller," Norman Davis, Roosevelt's disarmament negotiator and ambassador-at-large, was "suspect" as an internationalist, and Welles was an intriguer who would not improve Anglo-American relations. The British almost cavalierly, and caustically, dismissed every effort Roosevelt made to find some cooperative procedure that would lead toward economic or political appeasement of Germany, partly because they feared, as they said in 1936, that they would become the "prisoner in the dock" who would be forced to bear the cost of economic appeasement. The British no doubt had real reason to dislike aspects of American trade and monetary policies, but it is also inescapable that their attitude toward their American counterparts reflected a strong element of Victorian conceit or condescension and, as in the case of Chamberlain (who loathed the American efforts no less than the Americans), a conservative Tory, or imperial, view of world affairs.

FURTHER READING

Selig Adler, *The Isolationist Impulse* (1957)
Selig Adler, *The Uncertain Giant* (1965)
Mark Chadwin, *The Hawks of World War II* (1968)
Wayne S. Cole, *America First: The Battle Against Intervention, 1940–1941* (1953)
Wayne S. Cole, *Senator Gerald P. Nye and American Foreign Relations* (1962)
James V. Compton, *The Swastika and the Eagle* (1967)
Robert A. Divine, *The Illusion of Neutrality* (1962)
Robert A. Divine, *The Reluctant Belligerent* (1965)
Jean-Baptiste Duroselle, *From Wilson to Roosevelt* (1963)
Manfred Jonas, *Isolationism in America* (1966)
Warren F. Kimball, *The Most Unsordid Act: Lend-Lease, 1939–1941* (1969)
Warren F. Kimball, ed., *Franklin Roosevelt and the World Crisis, 1937–1945* (1973)
William L. Langer and S. E. Gleason, *The Challenge to Isolation, 1937–1940* (1952)
William L. Langer and S. E. Gleason, *The Undeclared War, 1940–1941* (1953)
William E. Leuchtenburg, *Franklin D. Roosevelt and the New Deal* (1963)
Arnold Offner, *American Appeasement* (1969)
Thomas G. Paterson, "Isolationism Revisited," *The Nation*, 209 (1969), 166–169
Julius Pratt, *Cordell Hull* (1964)
Willard Range, *Franklin D. Roosevelt's World Order* (1959)
Robert Freeman Smith, "American Foreign Relations, 1920–1942," in Barton J. Bernstein, ed., *Towards a New Past* (1968)
Raymond Sontag, *A Broken World, 1919–1939* (1971)
John Wiltz, *From Isolation to War, 1931–1941* (1968)
John Wiltz, *In Search of Peace: The Senate Munitions Inquiry* (1963)

6

Japanese-American Relations and Pearl Harbor

When war came to the United States, it struck not in Europe but in the Pacific at an American naval base in the Hawaiian Islands—Pearl Harbor. For a decade before that surprise attack, the United States had protested the steady Japanese military movement through China. In 1931 Japanese forces seized Manchuria and, in 1937, after the outbreak of the "China Incident," marched through much of China. The United States began to expand its navy and did not invoke the Neutrality Acts (thereby permitting China to buy armaments in America); however, lacking adequate power in Asia, it could do little more at first than protest the aggression.

In September 1940, after Japan gained air bases in French Indochina and signed a Tripartite Pact with Germany and Italy, the United States embargoed shipments of scrap iron and steel to the island nation. In July 1941, after Japanese troops occupied French Indochina, Washington froze Japanese assets in the United States, thereby crippling Japanese-American trade and denying Japan vital petroleum imports. Proposals and counter-proposals were exchanged by Tokyo and Washington for the rest of the year, all to no avail. On December 7 Japanese pilots boldly bombed Pearl Harbor.

Historians have grappled with controversial questions in explaining the coming of World War II: Was Japan on an inexorable path of aggression? Did the United States push Japan into war? Was Pearl Harbor deliberately set up for disaster by a Roosevelt administration that wanted to get into war through the Asian "back door"? Were there alternatives to war? Should Roosevelt have met with Prince Konoye? Were American proposals realistic?

164

DOCUMENTS

On January 7, 1932, after the Japanese overran Manchuria, Secretary of State Henry L. Stimson issued what has become known as the "Stimson Doctrine," a policy of non-recognition that guided the United States for the rest of the decade. On October 5, 1937, President Franklin D. Roosevelt told a crowd in Chicago that aggressors should be "quarantined." Although he obviously directed his words at Japan, he offered no concrete plans.

The final American proposals before the outbreak of Japanese-American war were dated November 29, 1941; they sought to roll back Japanese expansion and to revive the emasculated principles of the Open Door Policy. The Japanese position is evident in Tokyo's counterproposals of December 7, 1941, which charged that the United States was uncompromising and unreasonable. Finally, President Roosevelt addressed Congress on December 8, after the "infamy" at Pearl Harbor, asking for a declaration of war.

The Stimson Doctrine, 1932

With the recent military operations about Chinchow, the last remaining administrative authority of the Government of the Chinese Republic in South Manchuria, as it existed prior to September 18th, 1931, has been destroyed. The American Government continues confident that the work of the neutral commission recently authorized by the Council of the League of Nations will facilitate an ultimate solution of the difficulties now existing between China and Japan. But in view of the present situation and of its own rights and obligations therein, the American Government deems it to be its duty to notify both the Imperial Japanese Government and the Government of the Chinese Republic that it cannot admit the legality of any situation *de facto* nor does it intend to recognize any treaty or agreement entered into between those Governments, or agents thereof, which may impair the treaty rights of the United States or its citizens in China, including those which relate to the sovereignty, the independence, or the territorial and administrative integrity of the Republic of China, or to the international policy relative to China, commonly known as the open door policy; and that it does not intend to recognize any situation, treaty or agreement which may be brought about by means contrary to the covenants and obligations of the Pact of Paris of August 27, 1928, to which Treaty both China and Japan, as well as the United States, are parties.

Roosevelt's "Quarantine" Speech, 1937

Some fifteen years ago the hopes of mankind for a continuing era of international peace were raised to great heights when more than sixty nations solemnly pledged themselves not to resort to arms in furtherance of their national aims and policies. The high aspirations expressed in the Briand-Kellogg Peace Pact and the hopes for peace thus raised have of late given way to a haunting fear of calamity. The present reign of terror and international lawlessness began a few years ago.

It began through unjustified interference in the internal affairs of other nations or the invasion of alien territory in violation of treaties; and has now reached a stage where the very foundations of civilization are seriously threatened. The landmarks and traditions which have marked the progress of civilization toward a condition of law, order and justice are being wiped away.

Without a declaration of war and without warning or justification of any kind, civilians, including vast numbers of women and children, are being ruthlessly murdered with bombs from the air. In times of so-called peace, ships are being attacked and sunk by submarines without cause or notice. Nations are fomenting and taking sides in civil warfare in nations that have never done them any harm. Nations claiming freedom for themselves deny it to others.

Innocent peoples, innocent nations, are being cruelly sacrificed to a greed for power and supremacy which is devoid of all sense of justice and humane considerations.

To paraphrase a recent author "perhaps we foresee a time when men, exultant in the technique of homicide, will rage so hotly over the world that every precious thing will be in danger, every book and picture and harmony, every treasure garnered through two millenniums, the small, the delicate, the defenseless—all will be lost or wrecked or utterly destroyed."

If those things come to pass in other parts of the world, let no one imagine that America will escape, that America may expect mercy, that this Western Hemisphere will not be attacked and that it will continue tranquilly and peacefully to carry on the ethics and the arts of civilization.

If those days come "there will be no safety by arms, no help from authority, no answer in science. The storm will rage till every flower of culture is trampled and all human beings are leveled in a vast chaos."

If those days are not to come to pass—if we are to have a world in which we can breathe freely and live in amity without fear—the peace-loving nations must make a concerted effort to uphold laws and principles on which alone peace can rest secure.

The peace-loving nations must make a concerted effort in opposition to those violations of treaties and those ignorings of humane instincts which today are creating a state of international anarchy and instability from which there is no escape through mere isolation or neutrality.

Those who cherish their freedom and recognize and respect the equal right of their neighbors to be free and live in peace, must work together for the triumph of law and moral principles in order that peace, justice and confidence may prevail in the world. There must be a return to a belief in the pledged word, in the value of a signed treaty. There must be recognition of the fact that national morality is as vital as private morality.

A bishop wrote me the other day: "It seems to me that something greatly needs to be said in behalf of ordinary humanity against the present practice of carrying the horrors of war to helpless civilians, especially women and children. It may be that such a protest might be regarded by many, who claim to be realists, as futile, but may it not be that the heart of mankind is so filled with horror at the present needless suffering that that force could be mobilized in sufficient volume to lessen such cruelty in the days ahead. Even though it may take twenty years, which God forbid, for civilization to make effective its corporate protest against this barbarism, surely strong voices may hasten the day."

There is a solidarity and interdependence about the modern world, both technically and morally, which makes it impossible for any nation completely to isolate itself from economic and political upheavals in the rest of the world, especially when such upheavals appear to be spreading and not declining. There can be no stability or peace either within nations or between nations except under laws and moral standards adhered to by all. International anarchy destroys every foundation for peace. It jeopardizes either the immediate or the future security of every nation, large or small. It is, therefore, a matter of vital interest and concern to the people of the United States that the sanctity of international treaties and the maintenance of international morality be restored.

The overwhelming majority of the peoples and nations of the world today want to live in peace. They seek the removal of barriers against trade. They want to exert themselves in industry, in agriculture and in business, that they may increase their wealth through the production of wealth-producing goods rather than striving to produce military planes and bombs and machine guns and cannon for the destruction of human lives and useful property.

In those nations of the world which seem to be piling armament on armament for purposes of aggression, and those other nations which fear acts of aggression against them and their security, a very high proportion of their national income is being spent directly for armaments. It runs from thirty to as high as fifty percent. We are fortunate. The proportion that we in the United States spend is far less—eleven or twelve percent.

How happy we are that the circumstances of the moment permit us to put our money into bridges and boulevards, dams and reforestation, the conservation of our soil and many other kinds of useful works rather than into huge standing armies and vast supplies of implements of war.

I am compelled and you are compelled, nevertheless, to look ahead. The peace, the freedom and the security of ninety percent of the population of the world is being jeopardized by the remaining ten percent who are threatening a breakdown of all international order and law. Surely the ninety percent who want to live in peace under law and in accordance with moral standards that have received almost universal acceptance through the centuries, can and must find some way to make their will prevail.

The situation is definitely of universal concern. The questions involved relate not merely to violations of specific provisions of particular treaties; they are questions of war and of peace, of international law and especially of principles of humanity. It is true that they involve definite violations of agreements, and especially of the Covenant of the League of Nations, the Briand-Kellogg Pact and the Nine Power Treaty. But they also involve problems of world economy, world security and world humanity.

It is true that the moral consciousness of the world must recognize the importance of removing injustices and well-founded grievances; but at the same time it must be aroused to the cardinal necessity of honoring sanctity of treaties, of respecting the rights and liberties of others and of putting an end to acts of international aggression.

It seems to be unfortunately true that the epidemic of world lawlessness is spreading.

When an epidemic of physical disease starts to spread, the community approves and joins in a quarantine of the patients in order to protect the health of the community against the spread of the disease.

It is my determination to pursue a policy of peace. It is my determination to adopt every practicable measure to avoid involvement in war. It ought to be inconceivable that in this modern era, and in the face of experience, any nation could be so foolish and ruthless as to run the risk of plunging the whole world into war by invading and violating, in contravention of solemn treaties, the territory of other nations that have done them no real harm and are too weak to protect themselves adequately. Yet the peace of the world and the welfare and security of every nation, including our own, is today being threatened by that very thing.

No nation which refuses to exercise forbearance and to respect the freedom and rights of others can long remain strong and retain the confidence and respect of other nations. No nation ever loses its dignity or its good standing by conciliating its differences, and by exercising great patience with, and consideration for, the rights of other nations.

War is a contagion, whether it be declared or undeclared. It can engulf states and peoples remote from the original scene of hostilities. We are determined to keep out of war, yet we cannot insure ourselves against the disastrous effects of war and the dangers of involvement. We are adopting such measures as will minimize our risk of involvement, but we cannot have complete protection in a world of disorder in which confidence and security have broken down.

If civilization is to survive, the principles of the Prince of Peace must be restored. Trust between nations must be revived.

Most important of all, the will for peace on the part of peace-loving nations must express itself to the end that nations that may be tempted to violate their agreements and the rights of others will desist from such a course. There must be positive endeavors to preserve peace.

America hates war. America hopes for peace. Therefore, America actively engages in the search for peace.

American Proposals to Japan, November 1941

SECTION I *Draft Mutual Declaration of Policy*

The Government of the United States and the Government of Japan both being solicitous for the peace of the Pacific affirm that their national policies are directed toward lasting and extensive peace throughout the Pacific area, that they have no territorial designs in that area, that they have no intention of threatening other countries or of using military force aggressively against any neighboring nation, and that, accordingly, in their national policies they will actively support and give practical application to the following fundamental principles upon which their relations with each other and with all other governments are based:

1. The principle of inviolability of territorial integrity and sovereignty of each and all nations.
2. The principle of non-interference in the internal affairs of other countries.
3. The principle of equality, including equality of commercial opportunity and treatment.
4. The principle of reliance upon international cooperation and conciliation for the prevention and pacific settlement of controversies and for improvement of international conditions by peaceful methods and processes.

The Government of Japan and the Government of the United States have agreed that toward eliminating chronic political instability, preventing recurrent economic collapse, and providing a basis for peace, they will actively support and practically apply the following principles in their economic relations with each other and with other nations and peoples:

1. The principle of non-discrimination in international commercial relations.
2. The principle of international economic cooperation and abolition of extreme nationalism as expressed in excessive trade restrictions.
3. The principle of non-discriminatory access by all nations to raw material supplies.
4. The principle of full protection of the interests of consuming countries and populations as regards the operation of international commodity agreements.
5. The principle of establishment of such institutions and arrangements of international finance as may lend aid to the essential enterprises and the continuous development of all countries and may permit payments through processes of trade consonant with the welfare of all countries.

SECTION II *Steps To Be Taken by the Government of the United States and by the Government of Japan*

The Government of the United States and the Government of Japan propose to take steps as follows:

1. The Government of the United States and the Government of Japan will endeavor to conclude a multilateral non-aggression pact among the British Empire, China, Japan, the Netherlands, the Soviet Union, Thailand and the United States.

2. Both Governments will endeavor to conclude among the American, British, Chinese, Japanese, the Netherland and Thai Governments an agreement whereunder each of the Governments would pledge itself to respect the territorial integrity of French Indochina and, in the event that there should develop a threat to the territorial integrity of Indochina, to enter into immediate consultation with a view to taking such measures as may be deemed necessary and advisable to meet the threat in question. Such agreement would provide also that each of the Governments party to the agreement would not seek or accept preferential treatment in its trade or economic relations with Indochina and would use its influence to obtain for each of the signatories equality of treatment in trade and commerce with French Indochina.

3. The Government of Japan will withdraw all military, naval, air and police forces from China and from Indochina.

4. The Government of the United States and the Government of Japan will not support—militarily, politically, economically—any government or regime in China other than the National Government of the Republic of China with capital temporarily at Chungking.

5. Both Governments will give up all extraterritorial rights in China, including rights and interests in and with regard to international settlements and concessions, and rights under the Boxer Protocol of 1901.

Both Governments will endeavor to obtain the agreement of the British and other governments to give up extraterritorial rights in China, including rights in international settlements and in concessions and under the Boxer Protocol of 1901.

6. The Government of the United States and the Government of Japan will enter into negotiations for the conclusion between the United States and Japan of a trade agreement, based upon reciprocal most-favored-nation treatment and reduction of trade barriers by both countries, including an undertaking by the United States to bind raw silk on the free list.

7. The Government of the United States and the Government of Japan will, respectively, remove the freezing restrictions on Japanese funds in the United States and on American funds in Japan.

8. Both Governments will agree upon a plan for the stabilization of the dollar-yen rate, with the allocation of funds adequate for this purpose, half to be supplied by Japan and half by the United States.

9. Both Governments will agree that no agreement which either has concluded with any third power or powers shall be interpreted by it in such a way as to conflict with the fundamental purpose of this agreement, the establishment and preservation of peace throughout the Pacific area.

10. Both Governments will use their influence to cause other governments to adhere to and to give practical application to the basic political and economic principles set forth in this agreement.

THE JAPANESE EMPIRE, 1941

The Japanese Position, 1941

Ever since the China Affair broke out owing to the failure on the part of China to comprehend Japan's true intentions, the Japanese Government has striven for the restoration of peace and it has consistently exerted its best efforts to prevent the extension of war-like disturbances. It was also to that end that in September last year Japan concluded the Tripartite Pact with Germany and Italy.

However, both the United States and Great Britain have resorted to every possible measure to assist the Chungking regime so as to obstruct the establishment of a general peace between Japan and China, interfering with Japan's constructive endeavours toward the stabilization of East Asia. Exerting pressure on the Netherlands East Indies, or menacing French Indo-China, they have attempted to frustrate Japan's aspiration to the ideal of common prosperity in cooperation with these regions. Furthermore, when Japan in accordance with its protocol with France took measures of joint defence of French Indo-China, both American and British Governments, willfully misinterpreting it as a threat to their own possessions, and inducing the Netherlands Government to follow suit, they enforced the assets freezing order, thus severing economic relations with Japan. While manifesting thus an obviously hostile attitude, these countries have strengthened their military preparations perfecting an encirclement of Japan, and have brought about a situation which endangers the very existence of the Empire. . . .

From the beginning of the present negotiation the Japanese Government has always maintained an attitude of fairness and moderation, and did its best to reach a settlement, for which it made all possible concessions often in spite of great difficulties. As for the China question which constituted an important subject of the negotiation, the Japanese Government showed a most conciliatory attitude. As for the principle of non-discrimination in international commerce, advocated by the American Government, the Japanese Government expressed its desire to see the said principle applied throughout the world, and declared that along with the actual practice of this principle in the world, the Japanese Government would endeavour to apply the same in the Pacific Area including China, and made it clear that Japan had no intention of excluding from China economic activities of third powers pursued on an equitable basis. Furthermore, as regards the question of withdrawing troops from French Indo-China, the Japanese Government even volunteered, as mentioned above, to carry out an immediate evacuation of troops from Southern French Indo-China as a measure of easing the situation.

It is presumed that the spirit of conciliation exhibited to the utmost degree by the Japanese Government in all these matters is fully appreciated by the American Government.

On the other hand, the American Government, always holding fast to theories in disregard of realities, and refusing to yield an inch on its impractical principles, caused undue delay in the negotiation. It is difficult to understand this attitude of the American Government and the Japanese Government desires to call the attention of the American Government especially to the following points:

1. The American Government advocates in the name of world peace those principles favorable to it and urges upon the Japanese Government the acceptance thereof. The peace of the world may be brought about only by discovering a mutually acceptable formula through recognition of the reality of the situation and mutual appreciation of one another's position. An attitude such as ignores realities and imposes one's selfish views upon others will scarcely serve the purpose of facilitating the consummation of negotiations.

Of the various principles put forward by the American Government as a basis of the Japanese-American Agreement, there are some which the Japanese

Government is ready to accept in principle, but in view of the world's actual conditions, it seems only a utopian ideal on the part of the American Government to attempt to force their immediate adoption.

Again, the proposal to conclude a multilateral non-aggression pact between Japan, United States, Great Britain, China, the Soviet Union, the Netherlands and Thailand, which is patterned after the old concept of collective security, is far removed from the realities of East Asia.

2. The American proposal contained a stipulation which states—"Both Governments will agree that no agreement, which either has concluded with any third power or powers, shall be interpreted by it in such a way as to conflict with the fundamental purpose of this agreement, the establishment and preservation of peace throughout the Pacific area." It is presumed that the above provision has been proposed with a view to restrain Japan from fulfilling its obligations under the Tripartite Pact when the United States participates in the War in Europe, and, as such, it cannot be accepted by the Japanese Government.

The American Government, obsessed with its own views and opinions, may be said to be scheming for the extension of the war. While it seeks, on the one hand, to secure its rear by stabilizing the Pacific Area, it is engaged, on the other hand, in aiding Great Britain and preparing to attack, in the name of self-defense, Germany and Italy, two Powers that are striving to establish a new order in Europe. Such a policy is totally at variance with the many principles upon which the American Government proposes to found the stability of the Pacific Area through peaceful means.

3. Whereas the American Government, under the principles it rigidly upholds, objects to settle international issues through military pressure, it is exercising in conjunction with Great Britain and other nations pressure by economic power. Recourse to such pressure as a means of dealing with international relations should be condemned as it is at times more inhumane than military pressure.

4. It is impossible not to reach the conclusion that the American Government desires to maintain and strengthen, in coalition with Great Britain and other Powers, its dominant position it has hitherto occupied not only in China but in other areas of East Asia. It is a fact of history that the countries of East Asia for the past hundred years or more have been compelled to observe the *status quo* under the Anglo-American policy of imperialistic exploitation and to sacrifice themselves to the prosperity of the two nations. The Japanese Government cannot tolerate the perpetuation of such a situation since it directly runs counter to Japan's fundamental policy to enable all nations to enjoy each its proper place in the world.

The stipulation proposed by the American Government relative to French Indo-China is a good exemplification of the above-mentioned American policy. Thus the six countries,—Japan, the United States, Great Britain, the Netherlands, China and Thailand,—excepting France, should undertake among themselves to respect the territorial integrity and sovereignty of French Indo-China and equality of treatment in trade and commerce would be tantamount to placing that territory under the joint guarantee of the Governments of those six countries. Apart from the fact that such a proposal totally ignores the position of France, it is unacceptable to the Japanese Government in that such an arrangement cannot but be considered as an extension to French Indo-China of a system similar to the Nine Power Treaty structure which is the chief factor responsible for the present predicament of East Asia.

5. All the items demanded of Japan by the American Government regarding China such as wholesale evacuation of troops or unconditional application of the principle of non-discrimination in international commerce ignored the actual conditions of China, and are calculated to destroy Japan's position as the stabilizing factor of East Asia. The attitude of the American Government in demanding Japan not to support militarily, politically or economically any regime other than the regime at Chungking, disregarding thereby the existence of the Nanking Government, shatters the very basis of the present negotiation. This demand of the American Government falling, as it does, in line with its above-mentioned refusal to cease from aiding the Chungking regime, demonstrates clearly the intention of the American Government to obstruct the restoration of normal relations between Japan and China and the return of peace to East Asia.

In brief, the American proposal contains certain acceptable items such as those concerning commerce, including the conclusion of a trade agreement, mutual removal of the freezing restrictions and stabilization of yen and dollar exchange, or the abolition of extra-territorial rights in China. On the other hand, however, the proposal in question ignores Japan's sacrifices in the four years of the China Affair, menaces the Empire's existence itself and disparages its honour and prestige. Therefore, viewed in its entirety, the Japanese Government regrets that it cannot accept the proposal as a basis of negotiation.

Roosevelt's War Message, 1941

Yesterday, December 7, 1941—a date which will live in infamy—the United States of America was suddenly and deliberately attacked by naval and air forces of the Empire of Japan.

The United States was at peace with that Nation and, at the solicitation of Japan, was still in conversation with its Government and its Emperor looking toward the maintenance of peace in the Pacific. Indeed, one hour after Japanese air squadrons had commenced bombing in Oahu, the Japanese Ambassador to the United States and his colleague delivered to the Secretary of State a formal reply to a recent American message. While this reply stated that it seemed useless to continue the existing diplomatic negotiations, it contained no threat or hint of war or armed attack.

It will be recorded that the distance of Hawaii from Japan makes it obvious that the attack was deliberately planned many days or even weeks ago. During the intervening time the Japanese Government has deliberately sought to deceive the United States by false statements and expressions of hope for continued peace.

The attack yesterday on the Hawaiian Islands has caused severe damage to American naval and military forces. Very many American lives have been lost.

In addition American ships have been reported torpedoed on the high seas between San Francisco and Honolulu.

Yesterday the Japanese Government also launched an attack against Malaya.

Last night Japanese forces attacked Hong Kong.

Last night Japanese forces attacked Guam.

Last night Japanese forces attacked the Philippine Islands.

Last night the Japanese attacked Wake Island.

This morning the Japanese attacked Midway Island.

Japan has, therefore, undertaken a surprise offensive extending throughout the Pacific area. The facts of yesterday speak for themselves. The people of the United States have already formed their opinions and well understand the implications to the very life and safety of our Nation.

As Commander-in-Chief of the Army and Navy I have directed that all measures be taken for our defense.

Always will we remember the character of the onslaught against us.

No matter how long it may take us to overcome this premeditated invasion, the American people in their righteous might will win through to absolute victory.

I believe I interpret the will of the Congress and of the people when I assert that we will not only defend ourselves to the uttermost but will make very certain that this form of treachery shall never endanger us again.

Hostilities exist. There is no blinking at the fact that our people, our territory, and our interests are in grave danger.

With confidence in our armed forces—with the unbounded determination of our people—we will gain the inevitable triumph—so help us God.

I ask that the Congress declare that since the unprovoked and dastardly attack by Japan on Sunday, December seventh, a state of war has existed between the United States and the Japanese Empire.

ESSAYS

In his essay, Herbert Feis, historian and long-time State Department official, reacts to criticism of the Roosevelt administration's handling of Asian affairs and defends Washington's policies as necessary in the face of Japanese aggression. In particular, he responds to charges made by historian Charles C. Tansill in the early 1950s that Roosevelt plotted to get the United States into war.

Writing in 1972 at a time when American intervention in the Vietnam War spurred a good deal of questioning about the causes of wars, past and present, political scientist Bruce M. Russett of Yale University wrote a "skeptical view" of the United States entry into World War II, titled *No Clear and Present Danger*. His thesis: war was avoidable and unnecessary. The United States, he argues, placed demands on Japan—such as full withdrawal from China—that were impossible to achieve and wrongly interpreted Japanese actions as unlimited aggression.

The Challenge from Japanese Aggression

HERBERT FEIS

Ten years after victory, we look ruefully at the way the world has gone. It is right and natural to search out any errors of judgment or faults of character that have led us to our present pass. But such self-scrutiny can go awry if governed by a wish to revile rather than a wish to understand. Unless we are alert, that could happen as a result of the suspicions that have come to cluster around the way in which the United States became engaged in the Second World War— torch-lit by the Pearl Harbor disaster.

The more recently available sources have added but little to our knowledge of the events that led to our entry into the war. The books of memoirs written by Japanese witnesses have told us something more, especially about the struggle within the Japanese Government. But in my reading, while they may improve our knowledge of details, they do not change the fundamental view of this experience or its main features. In American and British records still kept secret there may be information or explanations that would do so. But even this I doubt. With no new great revealing facts to display, and no great new insights to impart, the most useful service would seem to be to act as caretaker of what is known, and in particular to deal with certain warped comments and inferences that seasonally must feel the straightening edge of evidence.

Of all the accusations made, the one most shocking to me is that Roosevelt and his chief advisers deliberately left the Pacific Fleet and base at Pearl Harbor exposed as a lure to bring about a direct Japanese attack upon us.

This has been diffused in the face of the fact that the Japanese High Military Command conference before the Imperial Throne on September 6, 1941, resolved that "If by the early part of October there is no reasonable hope of having our demands agreed to in the diplomatic negotiations mentioned above, we will immediately make up our minds to get ready for war against America (and England and Holland)." This is September 6. The plan for the attack on Pearl Harbor was not approved and adopted until October; and Secret Operation Order #1, the execution of the plan, was not issued until November 5. The presence of the Pacific Fleet at Pearl Harbor was not a lure but an obstacle.

The literature of accusation ignores or rejects the real reasons why the Pacific Fleet was kept in Hawaii. It must do so, since one of the main reasons was the hope that its presence there would deter the Japanese from making so threatening a move south or north that American armed forces might have to join in the war. It scorns the fact that the American military plans—to be executed in the event that we became engaged in war—assigned vital tasks to this Pacific Fleet. A mind must indeed be distracted if it can believe that the American Government could, at one and the same time, use the Pacific Fleet as a target and count on having it as part of its main defending force.

A variant of this accusation, which at least does not require such a willing-

Herbert Feis, "War Came at Pearl Harbor: Suspicions Considered," *The Yale Review,* 45 (1956), 378–390. Copyright © Yale University.

ness to believe the worst, might also be noted—that despite ample knowledge that Pearl Harbor was about to be attacked, the American Government purposefully left it exposed and allowed the event to happen.

Those who do not find such an idea at odds with their view of the sense of duty and regard for human life of President Roosevelt and his chief advisers can find striking points about the occurrence that may be construed to correspond with this conception. How they glare out of the record in hindsight: Ambassador Grew's warnings; Secretary Hull's acute gleam put into words at least three times in Cabinet Councils in November that the Japanese attack might come "at any moment, anywhere"; the intercepted Japanese messages telling of the Japanese effort to secure minute information as to the location of the ships of our Pacific Fleet in the Harbor; carelessness in checking up on the protective measures taken by the local commanders; failure to use the chance to give an effective last-minute warning to Hawaii. How else, it is asked, can these be explained except in terms of secret and conscious purpose?

However, just as hindsight makes the failure of perception plain, so it also makes it understandable—but only by bringing back to mind the total circumstances. That can be done here only in the barest way. Up to then Japanese strategy had been wary, one small creeping step after another, from Manchuria to North China into China and down into Indo-China. American military circles came to take it for granted that it would go on that way. Then there was the fact that Japan's basic objectives lay to the south and southeast; there and there only it could get what it needed—raw materials, oil, and island bases to withstand the attack from the West. Expectation already set in that direction was kept there by impressive and accurate intelligence reports of movements under way. Against this flow of preconception, the signs pointing to Pearl Harbor were not heeded.

Such features of contemporary thinking within the American Government explain, though they do not excuse, the failure to discern that Pearl Harbor was going to be attacked. To think the contrary is to believe that the President and the heads of the American Army, Navy, and Air Force were given to deep deception, and in order to have us enter the war were ready to sacrifice not only the Pacific Fleet but the whole war plan for the Pacific. This, I think, is the difference between history and police court history.

I have taken note of these accusations that have been built about the disaster at Pearl Harbor because they appeal to the sense of the sinister which is so lively in our times. But I am glad to turn to ideas and interpretations of broader historical import.

The first of these is that Roosevelt and the Joint Chiefs of Staff were obligated by secret agreements with Churchill and their British colleagues to enter the war at some time or other, in one way or other. Therefore, it is further supposed, the American authors of this agreement had to cause either Germany or Japan, or both, to attack us.

This view derives encouragement from the fact that the American Government *did* enter into a secret agreement about strategy with the British. The accord, known as ABC-1 Staff Agreement, adopted at Washington in March, 1941, set down the respective missions of the British and American elements in the event that the United States should be at war with Germany or Japan, or both; and subsequently the American basic joint war plan, Rainbow-5, was adjusted to fit this combined plan of operations. An attempt was made at a similar conference in Singapore soon after to work out a more detailed United States-British-Dutch operating plan for the Pacific. This attempt failed; but the discussion that took place there left a lasting mark on American official thinking, for the conferees defined the limits on land and sea beyond which Japanese forces could not be permitted to go without great risk to the defenders.

The ABC-1 agreement did not place the Roosevelt Administration under *political* obligation to enter the war against either Germany or Japan, not even if Japan attacked British or Dutch areas in the Far East. Nor did Roosevelt give a promise to this effect to Churchill when they met at Newfoundland in August, 1941. Up to the very eve of the Japanese assault the President refused to tell the British or Dutch what we would do. In short, the Government kept itself officially free from any obligation to enter the war, certainly free of any obligation to thrust itself into the war.

But I do think this accord conveyed responsibilities of a moral sort. After ABC-1 was adopted, production of weapons in the United States and the British Commonwealth took it into account; and the allocation of weapons, troops, ships, and planes as between threatened areas was based on the expectation that the United States would carry out the assignments set down in the plan.

Thus, it may be fairly thought, Roosevelt and his administration were obligated to try to gain the consent of Congress and the American people to play the part designated in the joint plans if Japanese assaults crossed the land and sea boundaries of resistance that were defined at these joint staff conferences. In the last November weeks when the end of the diplomatic talks with Japan came into sight, and General Marshall and Admiral Stark were asked what measures should be taken in face of the threatened Japanese advances, they advised the President to declare the limits defined at Singapore, and to warn the Japanese that we would fight if these were crossed. There is much reason to think this would have been done even had the Japanese not struck at Pearl Harbor and the Philippines, and this boundary would have been the line between peace and war. But this reaffirmation was made not as a measure required to carry out a secret accord, but because it was believed to be the best course.

A variant explanation of the way we dealt with Japan runs somewhat as follows: that Roosevelt was determined to get into the war against Germany; that he had to find a release from his public promises that the United States would not enter "foreign wars" unless attacked; that his efforts to do so by unneutral aid to Britain and the Soviet Union had failed because Hitler had refused to accept the challenge; and so he sought another door into war, a back door, by inviting or compelling the Japanese attack.

This interpretation, with its kick at the end, twists the record around its own preconception. The actions taken did not flow from a settled wish to get us into war. They trailed along the rim of necessity of the true purpose—which was to sustain resistance against the Axis. How many times the American Government refused to do what the British, French, Chinese, Russians, Dutch asked it to do, because it might involve us in actual combat!

This slant of reasoning about American action passes by the course of Japanese conduct which aroused our fears and stimulated our opposition: the way in which, despite all our pleas and warnings, Japan pressed on. By not recognizing that these Japanese actions called for American counteraction, it excuses them. Thus our resistance is made to appear as nothing else but a deceitful plot to plunge us into war. Furthermore, it dismisses as insincere the patient attempt to calm Japan by diplomatic talks, by offers to join in safeguarding its security.

There were influential individuals in the Roosevelt Administration who wanted to get into the war and indifferent as to how we got into it. Of these, Secretary of the Interior Ickes was, I believe, the most candid, at any rate in his diary entries. Secretary of the Treasury Morgenthau and his staff also had a positive wish that we should engage in war—but against Germany, not against Japan, for that might have brought a diversion of forces to the Pacific. Secretary of War Stimson thought that it would not be possible for Great Britain to sustain the fight unless we entered it; but toward the very end, particularly as it was becoming plain that the Soviet Union was going to survive the Nazi assault, he began to wish for delay. However, time and time again the memoirs and diaries record the impatience of these officials, and those who thought like them, with Hull's caution and Roosevelt's watchful indirection.

The most genuine point made by those who dissent, one that merits thorough analysis, is that the American Government, in conjunction with the British and Dutch, refused to continue to supply Japan with machines and materials vital to it—especially oil. It is contended that they thereby compelled Japan to resort to war, or at least fixed a time period in which Japan was faced with the need of deciding to yield to our terms or go to war.

In reflecting upon this action, the reasons for it must not be confused with the Japanese response to it. Japan showed no signs of curbing its aggressive course. It paid no heed to repeated and friendly warnings that unless it did, the threatened countries would have to take counter-measures. As when on February 14, 1941, while the Lend-Lease Act was being argued in Congress, Dooman, Counsellor of the American Embassy in Japan and known to be a firm and straightforward friend of that country, carried back from Washington the message for the Vice-Minister for Foreign Affairs: that the American people were determined to support Britain even at the risk of war; that if Japan or any other country menaced that effort "it would have to expect to come in conflict with the United States"; and that the United States had abstained from an oil embargo in order not to impel Japan to create a situation that could only lead to the most serious outcome. Japan's answer over the following months had been to force its way further into Indo-China and threaten the Dutch East Indies.

This sustained proof that Japan was going on with its effort to dominate Asia, and the alliance pledging it to stand by Germany if that country got into war with the United States, made a continuation of trade with Japan an act of meekness on our part. Japan was concentrating its foreign purchases on products needed for war, while reducing civilian use by every means, and was thus accumulating great reserve stocks. These were enabling it to maintain its invasion of China without much strain, while continuing to expand its war-making power. Had *effective* restraints—note that I do not say *total* restraints—not been imposed, the American Government would have been in the strange position of having declared an unlimited national emergency, of calling upon the American people to strengthen their army, navy, and air force in great urgency, while at the same time nourishing the opponent that might have to be met in battle. This was a grave, if not intolerable, responsibility.

It is hard to tell how squarely the American and British Governments faced the possible consequence of their restrictive measures. My impression is that they knew the danger of war with Japan was being increased; that Japan might try to get by force the means denied it. The Japanese Government served plain warnings that this game of thrust and counterthrust might so end. These were soberly regarded, but did not weaken the will that Japan was not to have its way by threat.

Mingled with the anxiety lest these restrictive measures would make war more likely, there was a real hope that they might be a deterrent to war. Conceivably they would bring home to the Japanese people that if it came to war, they might soon run out of the means for combat, while the rapid growth of American military strength would make it clear that they could not in the end win. And, as evidence of these probabilities became plain, the conciliatory elements in the Japanese Government would prevail over the more militant ones.

This almost happened. But the reckless ones, those who would rather court fatality than accept frustration, managed to retain control of Japanese decision. The pressure applied by us did not prevent war, and may have brought the time of decision for war closer. The valid question, however, is not whether the American Government resorted to these restrictions *in order* to drive Japan to attack; it is whether the American Government failed to grasp a real chance, after the restraints had begun to leave their mark in Japanese official circles, to arrive at a satisfactory understanding that would have averted war. Twice, in the opinion of some qualified students of the subject, such a chance emerged, or at least appeared on the horizon of diplomacy. Were they real opportunities or merely mirages or decoys?

The first of these was the occasion when in the autumn of 1941, the Japanese Prime Minister, Prince Konoye, sought a personal meeting with the President. It is averred that the President's failure to respond lost a chance to avert the war without yielding any American principle or purpose. Some think the reason was that American diplomacy was inflexible, dull in its insight, and too soaked in mistrust. Others, more accusatory, explain the decision by a lack of desire for an agreement that would have thwarted the design for war.

Since there is no conclusive evidence of what Konoye intended to propose or could have achieved, comment on this subject must enter into "the boggy ground of what-might-have-been." Some observers, including Ambassador

Grew, believe that Konoye could have made a real, and an irreversible, start toward meeting American terms. It will always be possible to think that this is so. But to the Americans in authority, the chance seemed small. Konoye was a man who in every past crisis had allowed himself to flounder between criss-crossed promises; hence there was good reason to fear an attempt at deception. Such glimpses as we have of what he might have proposed do not support the view that he could have offered a suspension or end of the fight against China. His freedom to negotiate would have been subject to the conditions stated by those who had controlled Japan's course up to then—their price for allowing him to go to meet the President.

Even so, to repeat, it is possible that skilled and more daring American diplomacy might have handled the meeting so as to get a satisfactory accord; or, failing that—and this is the more likely chance—to bring about so deep a division within the Japanese circle of decision as to have prevented warlike action. These alluring historical queries will continue to roam in the land of might-have-been.

But the risks were great. The echoes of Munich and its aftermath were still loud. The American Government might have found itself forced to make a miserable choice: either to accept an accord which would have left Japan free to complete its conquest of China and menace the rest of Asia, or to face a deep division among the American people. Any understanding with Japan that was not clear and decisive would have had unpredictable consequences. The Chinese Government might have felt justified in making a deal following our own. The Soviet Union, at this time just managing with the greatest effort and agony to prevent German victory, might also have chosen to compromise with Hitler rather than to fight it out. Speculations such as these must leave the subject unsettled. But in any case I think it clear that the American decision was one of judgment, not of secret intent. Konoye was not told that the President would not meet with him; he was told that he would not do so until more progress had been made toward defining what the Japanese Government was prepared to propose.

The same basic question had to be faced in the final crisis of negotiation in November, 1941: whether to relax restraints on Japan and leave it in a position to keep on trying to control much of Asia in return for a promise not to press on farther for the time being.

The opinion that the Japanese truce offer made at this last juncture accepted the main purposes and principles for which the American Government had been standing may be summarily dismissed. It was ambiguously worded, it was silent about the alliance with Germany, and it would have required the American Government to end its support of China—for the last of its numbered five points read: "The Government of the United States undertakes to refrain from such measures and actions as will be prejudicial to the endeavors for the restoration of general peace between Japan and China." This scant and unclear proposal was at once deemed "entirely unacceptable." Furthermore, there seemed little use and much possible damage in making a counter truce-offer of the same variety. The intercepted Japanese messages stated flatly that this was

Japan's last and best offer. They told of the swift dismissal of a much more nearly acceptable one that Nomura and Kurusu asked their superiors in Tokyo to consider. A deadline had been set. Thus it was all but sure that the reduced counteroffer which had been patched together in Washington would be unheeded. But it might shake the coalition to which by then the opponents of the Axis had pledged their lives and national destinies.

This seems to have been the thought uppermost in Hull's mind in recommending to the President that the counter truce-offer be withheld. As set down in his historic memo of November 26, he had been led to this conclusion by the opposition of the Chinese, the half-hearted support or actual opposition of the British, Dutch, and Australian governments, and the further excited opposition to be expected because of lack of appreciation of the importance and value of a truce. This I believe to have been the true determining reason for a decision reluctantly taken. Even if by then Japan was genuinely ready for reform, the repentance had come too late. The situation had grown too entangled by then for minor measures, its momentum too great. Germany-Italy-Japan had forced the creation of a defensive coalition more vast than the empire of the Pacific for which Japan plotted. This was not now to be quieted or endangered by a temporary halt along the fringe of the Japanese advance.

Even though these reasons for dropping the idea of a truce may seem sufficient, they leave the question why the American Government could not have given a softer and less declaratory answer. Why had it to give one so "bleakly uncompromising"? It could have said simply that the Japanese offer did not convey the assurances that would warrant us and the alliance for which we spoke to resume the shipment of war materials to Japan and end our aid to China. Why was it deemed advisable or essential at this juncture to state fully and forcibly our maximum terms for a settlement in the Pacific? Was it foreseen that, scanned with mistrust as it would almost surely be, this would be construed as a demand for the swift abandonment of Japan's whole program? Was it done, as the accusation runs, with the deliberate intent of banning any last chance for an accord? Of propelling the Japanese attack?

That this was not the reason I am as sure as anyone can be on a matter of this sort; but I can offer only conjecture as to what the inspiring purposes were. Perhaps to vindicate past actions and decisions. Perhaps a wish to use the dramatic chance to put in the record a statement of the aims for which the risk of war was being accepted, and of the basis on which the Americans would found the peace when the time came. Such an idea was in accord with the usual mode of thought of the men in charge of the Executive Branch of the Government and of most of the American people. It gave vent to the propensity exemplified in Hull to find a base in general principles meant to be at once political standards and moral ideals. After long caution, it appealed as a defiant contradiction of the Axis program. All this, however, is surmise rather than evidenced history.

But I think it is well within the realm of evidenced history that the memo of November 26 was not in any usual sense of the word an ultimatum. It did not threaten the Japanese with war or any other form of forceful punishment if our terms were not accepted. It simply left them in the state of distress in which they were, with the prospect that they might later have to submit to our requirements. The Japanese Government could have, as Konoye and Nomura pleaded with it to do, allowed the situation to drag along, with or without resuming talks with the American Government. Its power to make war would have been depleted, but neither quickly nor crucially. The armed forces and even the position in China could have been maintained.

Notably, the final Japanese answer which ended negotiations on December 7, 1941, does not accuse the American Government of confronting it with an ultimatum, but only of thwarting the larger Japanese aims. Part 14—the clinching part of this note—reads: "Obviously it is the intention of the American Government to conspire with Great Britain and other countries to obstruct Japan's efforts toward the establishment of peace through the creation of a New Order in East Asia, and especially to preserve Anglo-American rights and interests by keeping Japan and China at war. This intention has been revealed clearly during the course of the present negotiations. Thus, the earnest hope of the Japanese Government to adjust Japanese-American relations and to preserve and promote the peace of the Pacific through coöperation with the American Government has finally been lost."

This is a more nearly accurate description of the purposes of the American Government under Roosevelt than those attributed to it by hostile and suspicious American critics. Our Government did obstruct Japanese efforts, believing them to be unjust, cruel, and a threat to our national security, especially after Japan became a partner with Hitler's Germany and Mussolini's Italy and bent its efforts toward bringing the world under their combined control.

This determination stood on the proposition that it was better to take the risks of having to share in the suffering of the war than of finding ourselves moved or compelled to fight a more desperate battle against the Axis later on. The American Government, I believe, knew how serious a risk of war was being taken. But in its addresses to the American people it chose to put in the forefront the perils we would face if the Axis won, and to leave in the background, even to camouflage, the risks of finding ourselves plunged into wars which during the election campaign it had promised would not occur. Whether any large number of Americans were fooled by this, or whether most of them, in reality, were content to have the prospect presented that way rather than in a more blunt and candid way, I do not know.

No Clear and Present Danger

BRUCE M. RUSSETT

Whatever criticisms of twentieth-century American foreign policy are put forth, United States participation in World War II remains almost entirely immune. According to our national mythology, that was a "good war," one of the few for which the benefits clearly outweighed the costs. Except for a few books pub-

Bruce M. Russett, *No Clear and Present Danger: A Skeptical View of the U.S. Entry into World War II* (New York: Harper & Row, 1972), pp. 17–23, 44–62. Copyright © 1972 by Bruce M. Russett. Reprinted by permission of Harper & Row, Publishers, Inc.

lished shortly after the war and quickly forgotten, this orthodoxy has been essentially unchallenged. The isolationists stand discredited, and "isolationist" remains a useful pejorative with which to tar the opponents of American intervention in foreign lands.

Such virtual unanimity on major policy matters is rare. World War I long ago came under the revisionists' scrutiny. The origins of the cold war have been challenged more recently, with many people asking whether the Soviet-American conflict was primarily the result of Russian aggressiveness or even whether it was the inevitable consequence of throwing together "two scorpions in a bottle." But all orthodoxy ought to be confronted occasionally, whether the result be to destroy, revise, or reincarnate old beliefs. Furthermore, this does seem an auspicious time to reexamine the standard credo about participation in World War II. Interventionism is again being questioned and Americans are groping toward a new set of principles to guide their foreign policy. Where should we intervene and where withdraw; where actively to support a "balance of power" and where husband our resources? A reexamination of the World War II experience is deliberately a look at a limiting case—an effort to decide whether, in the instance where the value of intervention is most widely accepted, the interventionist argument really is so persuasive. We should consider the World War II experience not because intervention was obvious folly, but indeed because the case for American action there is strong.

I do *not*, of course, argue that one can readily generalize from the choices of 1941 to those of 1950 or 1970. The world has changed, and many of the favorable conditions that once made isolationism or "continentalism" a plausible policy to some have vanished, perhaps forever. I feel ambivalent about the contemporary meaning of the theme developed here, in view of the manifest changes of the past 30 years and the more or less "internationalist" policy preferences that I have shared with most Americans for many years. But almost all of us do on occasion invoke the "lessons" of Manchuria, Munich, the Spanish Civil War, or Pearl Harbor; or for that matter Rome and Carthage or the Peloponnesian Wars. We therefore owe it to ourselves to look critically at this historical experience, too. I think the theme of this essay needs stating even at the risk that some people may apply it inappropriately.

Furthermore, a new look at World War II is in some real sense merely an extension of arguments that have been raised against contemporary American intervention in Southeast Asia. The intervention has been justified both on moral grounds—the need to save a small country from communist dictatorship, and on strategic grounds of American self-interest—the need to prop up dominoes and prevent the extension of a hostile power's sphere of influence.

And the opponents of that intervention have included among their arguments some that recall the debates of 1941: America cannot be the world's policeman stepping in to halt everything we might consider to be aggression or to resist governments whose philosophies or policies we consider repugnant. Nor from a pure self-interest viewpoint would such critics accept our action in South Vietnam. It is a small country, far away. Its entire national income is equivalent only to the normal *growth* of the United States national income in a single month. Communist rule in that state, or even in its immediate neighbors as well, would make but an insignificant difference to the global balance of power. In any case, the forces of nationalism render very dubious an assumption that a Communist government would represent a dependable long-term gain for China or Russia.

Thus, in an important way the record of discussion in 1940 and 1941 is being replayed now. Opponents of contemporary intervention may well find ammunition by pointing out the inflated nature of the interventionists' rhetoric preceding World War II. If in the cold light of the seventies the original arguments seem excessive, then how much more misleading must be the recent versions? Or on the contrary, if a man is sure that the Southeast Asian operation was a mistake, can he still justify the World War II experience? Perhaps his continued acceptance of the latter should cause him to rethink his extreme opposition to the American interventions of the last decade.

The theme of this brief book should already be apparent, but I will state it explicitly here before going further: American participation in World War II had very little effect on the essential *structure* of international politics thereafter, and probably did little either to advance the material welfare of most Americans or to make the nation secure from foreign military threats (the presumed goals of advocates of a "realist" foreign policy). (By structure I mean the basic balance of forces in the world, regardless of which particular nations are powerful vis-à-vis the United States.) In fact, most Americans probably would have been no worse off, and possibly a little better, if the United States had never become a belligerent. Russia replaced Germany as the great threat to European security, and Japan, despite its territorial losses, is once more a major power. The war was not clearly a mistake as most of us now consider the Vietnam War to have been. Yet it may well have been an unnecessary war that did little for us and that we need not have fought. Moreover, it set some precedents for our thinking that led too easily to later interventions—interventions that might have been challenged more quickly and more effectively in the absence of such vivid memories of World War II. . . .

Many readers surely will be uncomfortable with the book's theme, and even offended by it. For example, it can hardly be easy for a man who spent two or three of his prime years fighting World War II to think that his sacrifice had little point. Moreover, the moral outrage against Nazism that we all share makes it difficult to separate ethics from an objective assessment of the threat Germany and Japan actually posed to American national security. To suggest that the two must be kept *analytically* distinct—even if in the end one sees the former as justifying intervention after all—is to risk being considered at least a first cousin of the Beast of Belsen.

Yet it is precisely moral considerations that demand a reexamination of our World War II myths. Social scientists have accepted too many assumptions uncritically. Too few Americans, especially government officials, really looked very hard at their beliefs about the origins of the cold war before about five years ago, or seriously considered "economic" interpretations of foreign policy. Recently, however, we have been illuminated as well as blinded by an occasion we could not ignore. On watching the fireball at Alamogordo in 1945 Robert Oppenheimer mused, "I am become death, destroyer of worlds." Vietnam has been to social scientists what Alamogordo was to the physicists. Few of those who have observed it can easily return to their comfortable presumptions about America's duty, or right, to fight in distant lands.

One serious problem in reevaluating American foreign policy before World War II stems from its distance in time. How do we treat the knowledge we gain from actually observing the intervening thirty years? Is it fair to judge the friends and opponents of Franklin Roosevelt with the advantages of 20-20 hindsight? Certainly we must keep separate what they knew or could have known, and what was unavoidably hidden from them. From captured documents we now see more clearly the motivations of some Axis leaders than contemporaries could have; we know with just what strength the Soviet Union emerged in Central Europe after the elimination of German power. If they exaggerated the then-present danger how can we be too condemning?

Nevertheless, the purpose in reconsidering World War II is not to judge, but to learn. In retaining our own humility it is fair to insist on a degree of humility in our leaders of all eras. Many of those who advocated war against Germany and Japan were very sure of themselves and their visions; the same could be said of many "cold warriors." They supported acts which left millions dead and changed all our lives. Some considered Hitler not only a devil, but to have near God-like powers enabling him to walk across the water to North America. The "yellow horde" was ready to invade from the other side; I remember being told how the Japanese coveted California. Both recall more recent images of the Russians as ten feet tall. In fact, our alleged vulnerability to the Axis threat was often used to justify continued involvement and active opposition to apparent Soviet expansionism in the post-war world. Without seeking judgment or scapegoats, perhaps we still can learn by identifying even the most excusable errors of others.

My intention here is to be provocative and not to set forth revealed truth. The argument is not one subject to the principles of measurement and the strict canons of hypothesis-testing—the mode of inquiry with which I feel most comfortable. Nevertheless the subject is too important to leave untouched simply because the whole battery of modern social science cannot be brought to bear on it. Similarly, there is an intellectual dialectic, driven by the need of most thinkers to relate their ideas to established thought patterns, that requires a new view to be stated forcefully and one-sidedly. Hamlets do not make revolutions. Hence we shall proceed to the argument, though the reader—and sometimes the writer too—will doubtless have reservations.

Although I have tried to give some evidence to support the more controversial statements of fact, full documentation would be out of place in such an essay. The need is not to uncover new facts from the archives, but to look again at the old facts from a different perspective. Some of my interpretations will be challengeable, and many readers may decide that despite my arguments the war still was worthwhile. Any retrospective analysis of "might-have-beens" is subject to all the perils of conjecture. We more or less know what *did* happen as a result of American participation in the war, and can only speculate on what would otherwise have happened. But that reservation cuts two ways, since those who will disagree with this book's interpretations are also forced into speculation.

In any case, I think defenders of American intervention will find that their case ultimately rests on other, and less confident, grounds than most have previously accepted. I suspect that no reader will ever again view World War II in quite the same way as before. A new look should at least clear aside many previous exaggerations of the kind of threat foreign powers could then and now present to the United States.

If one rejects the purely moral justification of American entry into the war against Hitler, no very effective moral brief can then be made for the war in the Pacific. True, the Japanese were often unkind conquerors, though this can easily be exaggerated by American memories of the Bataan death march and other horrors in the treatment of prisoners. Japanese occupation was often welcomed in the former European colonies of Southeast Asia, and Japan retains some reservoir of good will for its assistance, late in the war, of indigenous liberation movements. In any case it is Hitler, not Tojo, who is customarily presented as the personification of evil. Possibly Americans did have some vague obligation to defend Chinese independence, but more clearly than in Europe the basis for American participation has to be *realpolitik*. The case has to be founded on a conviction that Japan was too powerful, too dangerously expansionist without any apparent restraint, to have been left alone. An extreme but widely accepted version is given by an early chronicler of the war:

> Japan in the spring and summer of 1941 would accept no diplomatic arrangement which did not give it everything that it might win in the Far East by aggression, without the trouble and expense of military campaigns.

The evidence, however, shows quite a different picture both of intent and capability. Nor is it enough simply to assert that, because Japan attacked the United States at Pearl Harbor, America took no action to begin hostilities. This is formally true, but very deceptive. The Japanese attack would not have come but for the American, British, and Dutch embargo on shipment of strategic raw materials to Japan. Japan's strike against the American naval base merely climaxed a long series of mutually antagonistic acts. In initiating economic sanctions against Japan the United States undertook actions that were widely recognized in Washington as carrying grave risk of war. To understand this requires a retracing of the events of the preceding years.

By the beginning of the 1940s Japan was involved in an exhausting and seemingly endless war on the Asian mainland. The "China incident" dated back to the Japanese seizure of Manchuria in 1931, and was greatly escalated by the clash at the Marco Polo Bridge which expanded into severe open warfare with China in 1937. Although the Army did willfully create an incident at Mukden in 1931, the Marco Polo Bridge affair seems not to have been a deliberate provocation by Tokyo. Nevertheless most Japanese military and political leaders did seek a "Co-Prosperity Sphere" of economic and political predominance.

They apparently believed that their Empire's status as an independent world power depended on military equality with Russia and the United States in the Far East; that in turn depended on a hegemonial position, preferably economic but achieved by force if necessary, in the area of China. Though this seems strange now, an adequate view of Japanese policy in its contemporary context has to remember Tokyo's position as a latecomer to colonialism, in a world where France, Britain, and the United States all had their own spheres of influence.

Japanese forces made important initial gains by occupying most of the Chinese coast and most of China's industrial capacity, but with a trickle of American aid the nationalist armies hung on in the interior. By 1941 the Japanese armies were bogged down, and their progress greatly impeded by raw material shortages. In 1940 Congress placed fuel oil and scrap iron under the new National Defense Act as goods which could not be shipped out of the Western Hemisphere without an export license. Although commerce in these products was not actually cut off for another year, the threat to Japan of a raw material scarcity was obvious, and deliberately invoked by an American government seeking to apply pressure against the Japanese campaign in China. This strategy was exercised in a series of dozens of gradually tightening economic measures—an escalation that was to drive Japan not to capitulation, as it was intended to do, but to war with the United States.

Following the July 1941 freeze on Japanese assets in America, and the consequent cessation of shipment of oil, scrap iron, and other goods from the United States, Japan's economy was in most severe straits and her power to wage war directly threatened. Her military leaders estimated that her reserves of oil, painfully accumulated in the late 1930s when the risk of just such a squeeze became evident, would last at most two years. She was also short of rice, tin, bauxite, nickel, rubber and other raw materials normally imported from the Dutch East Indies and Malaya. Negotiations with the Dutch authorities to supply these goods, plus extraordinary amounts of oil from the wells of Sumatra, had failed, ostensibly on the grounds that the Dutch feared the material would be reexported to the Axis in Europe. The United States, and the British and Dutch, made it quite clear that the embargo would be relaxed only in exchange for Japanese withdrawal from air and naval bases in Indochina (seized in order to prosecute better the war against China) and an agreement which would have meant the end of the Japanese involvement in China and the *abandonment* of any right to station troops in that country, not just a halt to the fighting. The purpose of the Western economic blockade was to force a favorable solution to the "China incident."

Under these conditions, the High Command of the Japanese navy demanded a "settlement" of one sort or another that would restore Japan's access to essential raw materials, most particularly oil. Without restored imports of fuel the fleet could not very long remain an effective fighting force. While the navy might have been willing to abandon the China campaign, it was utterly opposed to indefinite continuation of the status quo. Either raw material supplies had to be restored by a peaceful settlement with the Western powers, or access to the resources in Thailand, Malaya, and the Indies would have to be secured by force while Japan still retained the capabilities to do so.

If the navy demanded either settlement or war, most members of the Japanese elite were opposed to any settlement which would in effect have meant withdrawal from China. No serious thought was given to the possibility of peace with Chiang's government, for it would have meant the end of all hopes of empire in East Asia and even, it was thought, of influence on the continent of Asia. Moderate Foreign Minister Shigenori Togo reacted to the most forceful statement of American demands, on November 27, 1941, "Japan was asked not only to abandon all the gains of her years of sacrifice, but to surrender her international position as a power in the Far East." In his view, that surrender would have been equivalent to national suicide.

In any case, the Army High Command simply would not have tolerated any abandonment of its position in China. Its own prestige and influence had been built up step by step during the war there, and its position in China became its power base in Japanese domestic politics. General Hideki Tojo, by no means the most violent of the Army war hawks, feared that any concession on the China issue would risk an actual revolt by extremist elements in the Army. In fact, on the resignation of Prince Konoye's government in October 1941 Tojo had urged the appointment of Prince Higashi-Kuni as Premier, on the principle that, should a compromise with the United States be decided upon, only a member of the royal family would have a chance to control the Army and make peace. In the context of Japanese politics of the 1930s, when there had been several plotted coups and when one after another of the political leaders thought to be too conciliatory toward foreign elements were assassinated by extreme nationalists, this was hardly a far-fetched fear. Togo once characterized the Japanese internal political situation in these terms to Joseph C. Grew, American Ambassador to Tokyo, "If Japan were forced to give up suddenly all the fruits of the long war in China, collapse would follow." Before we judge the Japanese too harshly Americans must remember their own difficulties in terminating a stalemated war 30 years later.

Thus, for the various elements in the Japanese government, and for somewhat different reasons, a peaceful settlement ultimately become unacceptable. They could not accede to the American demands, and they could not even continue to drag out the negotiations because of the increasingly precarious nature of the war economy and especially the Navy's fuel supplies. On rejecting this unpalatable alternative they were again thrown back on the other; the necessary raw material could be obtained only by seizing Thailand, where there was rice; Malaya, with its sources of tin, nickel, and rubber; and the Dutch East Indies, with their oil. But, according to the Japanese calculations, the United States was certain to fight if British or Dutch territory in the Far East were attacked. Japanese analysts reached the latter conclusion despite the absence of any American threat or promise. At the Atlantic Conference, Roosevelt had acceded to Churchill's plea that he issue a "war warning" with regard to any further conquests by Japan in the Far East. After he returned to Washington, however, the State Department dissuaded him and no such warning was ever issued. The nearest equivalents were two statements by President Roosevelt to Ambassador Nomura in July and August of 1941. The first declared:

> If Japan attempted to seize oil supplies by force in the Netherlands East Indies, the Dutch would, without the shadow of doubt, resist, the British would immediately come to their assistance, and, in view of our policy of assisting Great Britain, an exceedingly serious situation would immediately result.

On the second occasion Roosevelt stated:

> If the Japanese Government takes any further steps in pursuance of a policy of program of military domination by force or threat of force of neighboring countries the government of the United States will be compelled to take immediately any and all steps which it may deem necessary toward safeguarding the legitimate rights and interests of the United States and American nationals and toward insuring the safety and security of the United States.

Despite its firm language, this was not an unequivocal warning. On presentation to Nomura it was, as Langer and Gleason point out, not given the status of a "written statement" or even of an "oral statement." It was merely private "reference material," for Nomura's use in communicating with his own government. No unequivocal warning could be given, simply because President Roosevelt could not be sure of American reaction in the actual event of crisis. He was fully aware of the need to secure congressional approval for war, of the strength of isolationist sentiment in the United States, of the difficulties involved in demonstrating that an attack on British and Dutch colonies was a direct threat to American interests, and of the dangers inherent in going to war with the country deeply divided.

By autumn 1941, however, opinion was crystalizing in the highest levels of the American decision-making system. In November, Roosevelt informally polled his cabinet on the question of whether the country would support war against Japan in the event of attack on Malaya or the Indies. All members responded in the affirmative. General Marshall and Admiral Stark, the Chiefs of Staff, concluded that the United States should fight if Japan attacked British or Dutch territory, or Siam west of 100 degrees East or south of 10 degrees North. In two conversations on December 1 and 3 Roosevelt assured Lord Halifax, British Ambassador to Washington, that the United States would give Britain armed support if the Japanese attacked British or Dutch territories, or if Britain went to war as a result of a Japanese landing in Siam. This assurance was communicated to London, and from there to Sir Robert Brooke-Popham, British commander in the Far East. On the morning of December 7 in Washington (before the Pearl Harbor raid, which took place at dawn, Hawaii time) Secretaries Hull (State), Knox (Navy), and Stimson (War) discussed the anticipated Japanese attack on Siam or Malaya. They agreed the United States should go to war if the British did. Roosevelt then expected to go before Congress the next day to explain why a Japanese invasion of Siam threatened the security of the United States.

These decisions came too late, however, to affect directly the Japanese deliberations. By the beginning of December their attack was irrevocably set in motion. The Japanese conviction that war could not be limited to the British and Dutch had to be based wholly on inference. Yet it was a correct analysis and a solid conviction, as shown by the otherwise inexplicable risk they took at Pearl Harbor.

Rather close links had been forged between the United States and the colonies in Malaya and the East Indies, bonds that were known to the Japanese and considered to be of great importance. The Southwest Pacific area was of undeniable economic importance to the United States—at the time most of America's tin and rubber came from there, as did substantial quantities of other raw materials. American political involvement in the area was also heavy. The United States was cooperating closely with the British and Dutch governments, and according to the Japanese evaluation, if the United States failed to defend the Indies it would lose its influence in China and endanger the Philippines. Premier Tojo even referred in this context to the approval given Pan American World Airways to establish an air route between Singapore and Manila.

Unilateral American actions to build up their military forces, both generally and in the Pacific in particular, were seen as evidence of aggressive intent. But most convincing of all were the military ties apparently being established among the ABCD (American-British-Chinese-Dutch) powers. The United States was known to be supplying munitions and arms, including aircraft, not just to China but to British and Dutch forces in the Pacific. In cooperation with the British, Dutch, Australians, New Zealanders, and the Free French (at New Caledonia), the United States had begun construction of a string of airfields to the Philippines. Furthermore, the United States had participated in staff conversations with British and Dutch military personnel at Singapore. The Japanese came to associate these conversations with an "Anglo-American policy of encirclement against Japan in the Southern Pacific Ocean." This notion of encirclement appears time and again in Japanese official documents and memoirs. The freezing of Japanese assets by the United States, British, and Netherlands East Indies governments occurred on the same day: July 26, 1941. Although that act was in direct response to Japan's occupation of southern Indo-China, her leaders nevertheless saw it as the final link in their bondage.

As early as spring 1941, in fact, the Japanese army and navy general staffs had agreed among themselves that military action in the Southwest Pacific meant war with the United States. As we have seen, no definite decision by the United States had been reached, due largely to the state of American public opinion. But President Roosevelt and Secretary Hull were quite willing to have the Japanese believe that a joint American-British-Dutch plan of defense of the Indies existed. The conviction only grew stronger with time, and was reinforced by the intelligence received from the Japanese embassy in Washington. On December 3, 1941, for example, the Washington embassy cabled Tokyo: "Judging from all indications, we feel that some joint military action between Great Britain and the United States, with or without a declaration of war, is a definite certainty in the event of an occupation of Thailand."

The American fleet in the Pacific, while inferior to the Japanese in many respects, was strong enough to endanger seriously a sustained offensive and quite possibly strong enough to postpone Japan's effective occupation of the Indies until her raw materials ran out. The oil fields might be put out of operation for many months, and in any case the shipment of these supplies to Japan under the threat of American air and naval attack would be too risky. Japan simply dared not undertake such operations while the American fleet remained intact.

Having decided against withdrawal from China, failed to negotiate a settlement with America, and decided on the necessity of seizing supplies from Southeast Asia, they were faced with the need to blunt what they regarded as the inevitable American response. Thus they launched a surprise attack on Pearl Harbor to destroy any American capability for immediate naval offensive. For all the audacity of the strike at Hawaii, its aims were limited: to destroy existing United States offensive capabilities in the Pacific by tactical surprise. The Japanese High Command hoped only to give its forces time to occupy the islands of the Southwest Pacific, to extract those islands' raw materials, and to turn the whole area into a virtually impregnable line of defense which could long delay an American counteroffensive and mete out heavy casualties when the counterattack did come. As a result of their early success the Japanese naval and military chiefs extended this line a little farther than they had first meant to do, but their original intentions were not grandiose.

In deciding to attack Pearl Harbor the Japanese took what they fully recognized to be a great risk. There is no doubt but that the Imperial government realized it could not win a long war with the United States if the Americans chose to fight such a war. Japanese strategists calculated that America's war potential was seven to eight times greater than their own; they knew that Japan could not hope to carry the war to the continental United States. General Suzuki, chairman of the Planning Board, had reported that Japan's stockpile of resources was not adequate to support a long war. Admiral Yamamoto, the brilliant inventor of the Pearl Harbor attack plan, warned: "In the first six months to a year of war against the U.S. and England I will run wild, and I will show you an uninterrupted succession of victories; I must also tell you that, should the war be prolonged for two or three years, I have no confidence in our ultimate victory."

Because the proposed attack seemed an escape from the dilemma it was grasped with more enthusiasm than it deserved. The Japanese never seriously considered exactly what would cause the United States to forego crushing Japan, or how Japan might best create the proper conditions for a negotiated peace. Certain key elements, such as the probable effect of the Pearl Harbor attack on the American will to win, were left completely unanalyzed. Japan's sole strategy involved dealing maximum losses to the United States at the outset, making the prospects of a prolonged war as grim as possible, and counting, in an extremely vague and ill-defined way, on the American people's "softness" to end the war.

Nor, certainly, can the Japanese decision be explained simply as an act of "irrationality," an impulsive act by an unstable leader. Such explanations depend either upon a situation of great stress, which would warp the actions of all or most of the participants in the decision process, or really apply only to circumstances where a single individual in fact makes the decision. Some of Hitler's most costly mistakes in World War II, for example, were highly individualistic decisions for which he alone was responsible. Typical of the pattern was his order to stand and fight at Stalingrad rather than allow his army to retreat and regroup. High stress plus the peculiarities of the Fuehrer's personality produced a command different from what other men would have given.

The Japanese decision to attack Pearl Harbor, however, was neither the decision of a single individual, where much of his behavior could be explained by his own personality, nor a decision arrived at under time pressures. It was reached incrementally and reinforced at several steps along the line. On July 2, 1941, it was decided to press ahead with expansion in Southeast Asia even though this meant a high risk of war with the United States. After deep consideration by high Japanese military and naval officials for months, a formal commitment was made at the Imperial Conference of September 6 that either negotiations must result in lifting the United States embargo on strategic raw materials, or Japan would have to fight the Americans. October 15 was set as the deadline for success in negotiation. But even though the strategic commitment (in the sense of a decision for the next move dependent upon the opponent's reaction to this one) had seemingly been made, it was the subject of a great deal of reexamination over the subsequent three months. Prince Konoye's government resigned following the expiration of the deadline, but the new cabinet formed under General Tojo took office not as a regime determined to take the nation into war, but rather as one still seeking a way out. Serious negotiation with the United States continued through November. A new secret deadline of November 25 was once set, "after which things are going to happen automatically," but it too was extended until November 30.

Whatever the nature of the decision to go to war, it was arrived at and reinforced over a long period of time, and was not the result of anyone's possibly "irrational" impulse. In any case, the decision was in no important sense the act of a single man whose peculiar traits can be used to explain it. Rather, it was a carefully—if incompletely—considered collective attempt to break out of a dilemma that no man would relish.

This analysis is meant to establish an important proposition: that the Japanese attack on Pearl Harbor, and for that matter on Southeast Asia, is not evidence of any unlimited expansionist policy or capability by the Japanese government. It was the consequence only of a much less ambitious goal, centering on an unwillingness to surrender the position that the Japanese had fought for years to establish in China. When that refusal met an equal American determination that Japan should give up many of her gains in China, the result was war. Japanese expansion into Southeast Asia originated less in strength than in weakness; it was predominantly instrumental to the China campaign, not a reach for another slice of global salami. Of course there were Japanese political and military leaders with wider ambitions, but they were not predominant in policy-making.

Throughout the 1930s the United States government had done little to resist the Japanese advance on the Asian continent. There were verbal protests, but little more. Even in early 1941 Washington apparently would have settled for a *halt* in China, and saw little danger of a much wider move into Southeast Asia. But the application of economic sanctions against Tokyo was very successful; it was obviously hurting, and the moderate Premier Prince Konoye proposed a direct meeting with Roosevelt to try to reach an understanding. At about that point the American Government seems to have been so impressed with its success that it rebuffed Konoye's approach, demanding that he agree in advance on terms of a settlement. Konoye's cabinet fell, and American observers concluded—on the basis of untestable evidence that sounded a bit like sour grapes—that he could not have enforced a "reasonable" settlement in Japanese politics anyway. Washington then raised the ante, calling for a Japanese *withdrawal* from all occupied territory in China. Several officials in the State Department proposed settling for a halt, giving China a breathing spell that would have served it better for several more years of war while America made its main effort in the Atlantic. Hull considered and then rejected their plan for such a *modus vivendi,* which rather closely resembled the second of two Japanese proposals ("Plan B") that represented Tokyo's last efforts. Economic sanctions continued to provide a warm moral glow for those who disapproved of trading with an aggressor, but they then served to make inevitable an otherwise avoidable war which was peripheral to American vital interests and for which the country was ill-prepared.

It was widely understood in Washington that the next move would probably be some sort of Japanese attack in Southeast Asia. Ambassador Grew in Tokyo had long been warning of the limited nature of Japanese goals and the consequences of resisting them. As early as 1940, Under-secretary of State Sumner Welles had cautioned that an embargo would bring Japanese occupation of the Dutch East Indies.

Why then did President Roosevelt and his advisers embark on a series of incremental pressures that had the effect of pushing the Japanese into war? In large part, of course, they decided that Japanese ambitions in China posed a long-term threat to American interests, and so they forced a confrontation. A sentimental American attitude toward China as a "ward" also must not be forgotten. From missionary days they had been a people "we had always helped," to whom there was a sense of obligation. Roosevelt had a long-time emotional attachment to China, and from his days as Assistant Secretary of the Navy had allegedly "become imbued with the Navy's conviction that Japan was America's Number One enemy."

Nor should economic, as opposed to strategic, motives be ignored as they have been in most conventional histories of the period. Beginning with Dr. Sun Yat-Sen's idea that Chinese reconstruction would have to be brought about in collaboration with other countries, the nationalist government sought foreign economic and technical assistance. Some interest was expressed in the United States, with a few loans forthcoming. Nondiscrimination in East Asian trade was almost always included in American demands on Japan. According to one analyst with a revisionist perspective:

Although the Great China Market never materialized, many American leaders in the New Deal period . . . acted upon the assumption that it would, and this gave them reason to oppose Japan's forward movement in Asia.

Another demonstrates the importance of perceived commercial possibilities in China in the first American extension of economic assistance to belligerent China. Yet another, commenting on policy toward all the Axis states, says:

The actual defense of the United States was one factor involved in the move to an "all-out aid short of war" policy, but the restoration of the Open Door world order was of at least equal importance to the Roosevelt administration.

Such considerations surely applied, and probably in greater strength, to continental Europe, where Nazi plans for autarchy threatened an American market that was quantitatively very much more important. The economic prospect of a German-Soviet dominated Europe must have seemed unattractive—though, objectively, the threat to the national interest as a whole amounted to less than two percent of American GNP for those exports and imports combined. There also was some fear of German economic penetration into South America. But as for the Far East, by embargoing Japan in 1941 the United States was giving up an export trade at least four times that with China. While one must not equate dollar volume perfectly with relative political influence, the impact of China traders can easily be exaggerated.

It is of course impossible to separate and weigh the relative importance of the various influences. Strategic considerations, however muddled, were in the forefront. Certainly the above evaluation implies no conspiracy by Roosevelt against the general welfare of the United States, but it does require us again to evaluate the military and political situation of the day, in light of what was known then and of what we know now.

On purely strategic grounds some observers might argue that the danger was not from Germany, Italy, or Japan alone, but rather from their combination in an aggressive alliance encircling the Western Hemisphere. The rhetoric of the time could suggest such a threat, but in fact the Tripartite Pact of Germany and Italy with Japan had become quite fragile. As explained in the preceding chapter, it was designed to deter United States entry into either of the then still-separate conflicts. The Japanese foreign minister in early 1941, Yosuke Matsuoka, had negotiated the Pact and was by far its strongest supporter in the cabinet. He tried to persuade his colleagues to follow the German attack on Russia with a similar act by Japan, but failed and was deposed. Thereafter the Pact faded in importance to the Tokyo government. In considering their subsequent negotiations with the United States the Japanese leaders were fully willing to sacrifice the Pact in return for the necessary economic concessions. Had Hitler managed to get himself into war with America in the Atlantic he could not successfully have invoked the Pact unless the Japanese clearly had seen war to be in their own interests.

Moreover, this drift away from Germany was, it has been well argued, adequately known to American and British officials—Ambassadors Grew and Craigie, Cordell Hull, Roosevelt and Churchill—thanks in part to American ability to crack the codes used in all Japanese secret cables. "After Matsuoka's fall . . . no Axis leader was able even to keep up the pretense of expecting Japanese intervention in behalf of Germany and Italy." In the context of late 1941, therefore, the prospects of close cooperation among Germany, Italy and Japan were not very menacing. Given their very diverse long-run interests, and Hitler's racial notions, a "permanent" alliance surely does not seem very plausible. A special irony of the situation is that Roosevelt was particularly anxious to see Hitler beaten first, and that British and Dutch colonial possessions in Southeast Asia, which seemed essential to the European war, be unmolested. His belated insistence on Japanese evacuation from China then pushed the Axis back together and endangered his other goals.

Would Japanese success in China alone, without reference to their allies, have posed such a long-term threat as has sometimes been imagined? It is easy subconsciously to invoke old Western fears that still plague American China policy. Even limited to the home islands, after two decades of spectacular growth Japan today has the world's third largest GNP. Yet it is only about one-sixth as large as that of the United States, and a third of Russia's. This third-ranking power is still manifestly weaker than the United States, as it was in 1941. From a thirty year perspective it is hard to argue that the great war made much ultimate difference either way in Japan's potential power in the world.

Firm Japanese control of all China would of course be a different matter, and would indeed have put at Tokyo's disposal an empire of awesome size. Still, really what are the prospects that Imperial Japan could effectively have ruled a population seven times larger than her own? Herbert Hoover at the time urged:

> We must remember some essentials of Asiatic life . . . that while Japan has the military ascendancy today and no doubt could take over parts or all of China, yet the Chinese people possess transcendent cultural resistance; that the mores of the race have carried through a dozen foreign dynasties over the 3,000 years . . . No matter what Japan does . . . they will not Japanify China and if they stay long enough they will be absorbed or expelled by the Chinese. For America to undertake this on behalf of China might expedite it, but would not make it more inevitable.

The Japanese War in China was going so badly in 1941 that it seems rather far-fetched to imagine firm domination ever being established. Japan was already bogged down on the Asian mainland, as other powers have done since. The Chinese nationalists, and the Communists, probably could have continued to resist for years with continuing American and Russian military assistance short of war. Maybe not, but even so it would seem that there would have been substantial warning, still allowing the United States to institute a tough policy against the Japanese later on when the evidence was clear.

FURTHER READING

Irvine H. Anderson, *The Standard-Vacuum Oil Company and United States East Asia Policy* (1975)

Harry Elmer Barnes, ed., *Perpetual War for Perpetual Peace* (1953)

Charles A. Beard, *President Roosevelt and the Coming of the War, 1941* (1948)

Dorothy Borg, *The United States and the Far Eastern Crisis of 1933–1938* (1964)

Dorothy Borg and Shumpei Okamoto, eds., *Pearl Harbor as History* (1973)

Richard Dean Burns and Edward M. Bennett, eds., *Diplomats in Crisis* (1974)

Robert J. C. Butow, *The John Doe Associates: Backdoor Diplomacy for Peace, 1941* (1974)

Robert J. C. Butow, *Tojo and the Coming of the War* (1961)

Warren I. Cohen, *America's Response to China* (1971)

Roger Dingman, *Power in the Pacific* (1976)

Herbert Feis, *The Road to Pearl Harbor* (1950)

Charles Neu, *The Troubled Encounter* (1975)

William L. Neumann, *America Encounters Japan* (1963)

Armin Rappaport, *Henry L. Stimson and Japan, 1931–1933* (1963)

Paul W. Schroeder, *The Axis Alliance and the Japanese-American Relations, 1941* (1958)

Charles C. Tansill, *Back Door to War* (1952)

Gerald E. Wheeler, *Prelude to Pearl Harbor: The United States Navy and the Far East, 1921–1931* (1963)

Robert Wohlstetter, *Pearl Harbor: Warning and Decision* (1962)

7

The Yalta Conference

During February 4–11, 1945, Franklin D. Roosevelt, Winston Churchill, and Josef Stalin met at Yalta in the Crimea to hammer out both wartime and postwar agreements on Germany, China, Japan, Poland, the United Nations, and other issues. The Big Three leaders had met before in other summits throughout the war, but this one seemed special because the war appeared to be winding down and the conferees knew they were helping to shape the contours of the postwar world. The many compromises and agreements, some of them kept secret until after the war, marked a high point in the Grand Alliance.

However, after 1945, during the onset of the Cold War, the Yalta accords became the target of critics, especially from the right wing, who believed that an ill President—he died in April— had been duped by a clever Stalin into making unnecessary concessions to the Soviets. This "sell-out" thesis has fueled an intense historical debate.

DOCUMENTS

The Yalta Protocol of Proceedings of February 11, 1945, is reprinted here, as is the agreement on Soviet entry into the Far Eastern war. An exchange between Charles E. Bohlen and Senator Homer Ferguson of Michigan during a 1953 Senate hearing highlights some of the controversial questions. A career diplomat, Bohlen was an assistant to the Secretary of State at Yalta. As is evident in Ferguson's questioning, many critics of Yalta suspected that Alger Hiss, accused in the 1940s of being a spy for the Soviets, unduly influenced the President in granting too much to Stalin. Bohlen attempts to remove that suspicion and generally defends the Yalta record.

The Yalta Protocol of Proceedings, 1945

The Crimea Conference of the Heads of the Governments of the United States of America, the United Kingdom, and the Union of Soviet Socialist Republics which took place from February 4th to 11th came to the following conclusions:

I. World Organization

It was decided:

1. that a United Nations Conference on the proposed world organization should be summoned for Wednesday, 25th April, 1945, and should be held in the United States of America.

2. the Nations to be invited to this Conference should be:

a. the United Nations as they existed on the 8th February, 1945; and

b. such of the Associated Nations as have declared war on the common enemy by 1st March, 1945. (For this purpose by the term "Associated Nations" was meant the eight Associated Nations and Turkey). When the Conference on World Organization is held, the delegates of the United Kingdom and United States of America will support a proposal to admit to original membership two Soviet Socialist Republics, i.e. the Ukraine and White Russia.

3. that the United States Government on behalf of the Three Powers should consult the Government of China and the French Provisional Government in regard to decisions taken at the present Conference concerning the proposed World Organization.

4. that the text of the invitation to be issued to all the nations which would take part in the United Nations Conference should be as follows:

Invitation

The Government of the United States of America, on behalf of itself and of the Governments of the United Kingdom, the Union of Soviet Socialist Republics, and the Republic of China and the Provisional Government of the French Republic, invite the Government of ———— to send representatives to a Conference of the United Nations to be held on 25th April, 1945, or soon thereafter, at San Francisco in the United States of America to prepare a Charter for a General International Organization for the maintenance of international peace and security.

The above named governments suggest that the Conference consider as affording a basis for such a Charter the Proposals for the Establishment of a General International Organization, which were made public last October as a result of the Dumbarton Oaks Conference, and which have now been supplemented by the following provisions for Section C of Chapter VI:

"C. Voting

"1. Each member of the Security Council should have one vote.

"2. Decisions of the Security Council on procedural matters should be made by an affirmative vote of seven members.

"3. Decisions of the Security Council on all other matters should be made by an affirmative vote of seven members including the concurring votes of the permanent members; provided that, in decisions under Chapter VIII, Section A and under the second sentence of paragraph 1 of Chapter VIII, Section C, a party to a dispute should abstain from voting."

Further information as to arrangements will be transmitted subsequently.

In the event that the Government of ——— desires in advance of the Conference to present views or comments concerning the proposals, the Government of the United States of America will be pleased to transmit such views and comments to the other participating Governments.

Territorial Trusteeship. It was agreed that the five Nations which will have permanent seats on the Security Council should consult each other prior to the United Nations Conference on the question of territorial trusteeship.

The acceptance of this recommendation is subject to its being made clear that territorial trusteeship will only apply to (a) existing mandates of the League of Nations; (b) territories detached from the enemy as a result of the present war; (c) any other territory which might voluntarily be placed under trusteeship; and (d) no discussion of actual territories is contemplated at the forthcoming United Nations Conference or in the preliminary consultations, and it will be a matter for subsequent agreement which territories within the above categories will be placed under trusteeship.

II. Declaration on Liberated Europe

The following declaration has been approved:

> The Premier of the Union of Soviet Socialist Republics, the Prime Minister of the United Kingdom and the President of the United States of America have consulted with each other in the common interests of the peoples of their countries and those of liberated Europe. They jointly declare their mutual agreement to concert during the temporary period of instability in liberated Europe the policies of their three governments in assisting the peoples of the former Axis satellite states of Europe to solve by democratic means their pressing political and economic problems.
>
> The establishment of order in Europe and the rebuilding of national economic life must be achieved by processes which will enable the liberated peoples to destroy the last vestiges of Nazism and Fascism and to create democratic institutions of their own choice. This is a principle of the Atlantic Charter— the right of all peoples to choose the form of government under which they will live—the restoration of sovereign rights and self-government to those peoples who have been forcibly deprived of them by the aggressor nations.
>
> To foster the conditions in which the liberated peoples may exercise these rights, the three governments will jointly assist the people in any European liberated state or former Axis satellite state in Europe where in their judgment conditions require (a) to establish conditions of internal peace; (b) to carry out emergency measures for the relief of distressed peoples; (c) to form interim governmental authorities broadly representative of all democratic elements in the population and pledged to the earliest possible establishment through free elections of governments responsive to the will of the people; and (d) to facilitate where necessary the holding of such elections.

The three governments will consult the other United Nations and provisional authorities or other governments in Europe when matters of direct interest to them are under consideration.

When, in the opinion of the three governments, conditions in any European liberated state or any former Axis satellite state in Europe make such action necessary, they will immediately consult together on the measures necessary to discharge the joint responsibilities set forth in this declaration.

By this declaration we reaffirm our faith in the principles of the Atlantic Charter, our pledges in the Declaration by the United Nations, and our determination to build in cooperation with other peace-loving nations world order under law, dedicated to peace, security, freedom and general well-being of all mankind.

In issuing this declaration, the Three Powers express the hope that the Provisional Government of the French Republic may be associated with them in the procedure suggested.

III. Dismemberment of Germany

It was agreed that Article 12 (a) of the Surrender Terms for Germany should be amended to read as follows:

The United Kingdom, the United States of America and the Union of Soviet Socialist Republics shall possess supreme authority with respect to Germany. In the exercise of such authority they will take such steps, including the com-

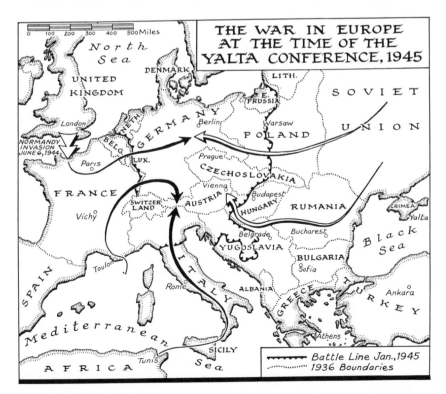

THE WAR IN EUROPE
AT THE TIME OF THE
YALTA CONFERENCE, 1945

Battle Line Jan.,1945
1936 Boundaries

plete disarmament, demilitarization and dismemberment of Germany as they deem requisite for future peace and security.

The study of the procedure for the dismemberment of Germany was referred to a Committee, consisting of Mr. Eden (Chairman), Mr. Winant and Mr. Gousev. This body would consider the desirability of associating with it a French representative.

IV. Zone of Occupation for the French and Control Council for Germany

It was agreed that a zone in Germany, to be occupied by the French Forces, should be allocated to France. This zone would be formed out of the British and American zones and its extent would be settled by the British and Americans in consultation with the French Provisional Government.

It was also agreed that the French Provisional Government should be invited to become a member of the Allied Control Council of Germany.

V. Reparation

The heads of the three governments agreed as follows:

1. Germany must pay in kind for the losses caused by her to the Allied nations in the course of the war. Reparations are to be received in the first instance by those countries which have borne the main burden of the war, have suffered the heaviest losses and have organized victory over the enemy.

2. Reparation in kind to be exacted from Germany in three following forms:

   a. Removals within 2 years from the surrender of Germany or the cessation of organized resistance from the national wealth of Germany located on the territory of Germany herself as well as outside her territory (equipment, machine-tools, ships, rolling stock, German investments abroad, shares of industrial, transport and other enterprises in Germany etc.), these removals to be carried out chiefly for purpose of destroying the war potential of Germany.

   b. Annual deliveries of goods from current production for a period to be fixed.

   c. Use of German labor.

3. For the working out on the above principles of a detailed plan for exaction of reparation from Germany an Allied Reparation Commission will be set up in Moscow. It will consist of three representatives—one from the Union of Soviet Socialist Republics, one from the United Kingdom and one from the United States of America.

4. With regard to the fixing of the total sum of the reparation as well as the distribution of it among the countries which suffered from the German aggression the Soviet and American delegations agreed as follows:

   The Moscow Reparation Commission should take in its initial studies as a basis for discussion the suggestion of the Soviet Government that the total sum of the reparation in accordance with the points (a) and (b) of the paragraph 2 should be 20 billion dollars and that 50% of it should go to the Union of Soviet Socialist Republics.

The British delegation was of the opinion that pending consideration of the reparation question by the Moscow Reparation Commission no figures of reparation should be mentioned.

The above Soviet-American proposal has been passed to the Moscow Reparation Commission as one of the proposals to be considered by the Commission.

VI. Major War Criminals

The Conference agreed that the question of the major war criminals should be the subject of enquiry by the three Foreign Secretaries for report in due course after the close of the Conference.

VII. Poland

The following Declaration on Poland was agreed by the Conference:

A new situation has been created in Poland as a result of her complete liberation by the Red Army. This calls for the establishment of a Polish Provisional Government which can be more broadly based than was possible before the recent liberation of Western part of Poland. The Provisional Government which is

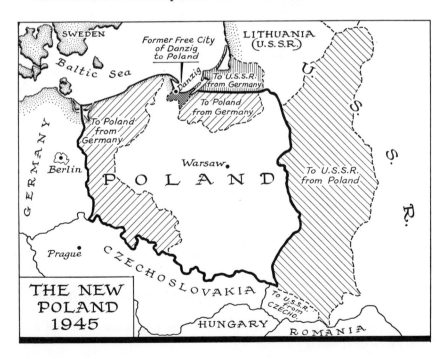

THE NEW POLAND 1945

now functioning in Poland should therefore be recognized on a broader demo-cratic basis with the inclusion of democratic leaders from Poland itself and from Poles abroad. This new Government should then be called the Polish Provisional Government of National Unity.

M. Molotov, Mr. Harriman and Sir. A. Clark Kerr are authorized as a com-mission to consult in the first instance in Moscow with members of the present Provisional Government and with other Polish democratic leaders from within Poland and from abroad, with a view to the reorganization of the present Gov-ernment along the above lines. This Polish Provisional Government of National Unity shall be pledged to the holding of free and unfettered elections as soon as possible on the basis of universal suffrage and secret ballot. In these elections all democratic and anti-Nazi parties shall have the right to take part and to put forward candidates.

When a Polish Provisional Government of National Unity has been properly formed in conformity with the above, the Government of the U.S.S.R., which now maintains diplomatic relations with the present Provisional Government of Poland, and the Government of the United Kingdom and the Government of the United States of America will establish diplomatic relations with the new Polish Provisional Government of National Unity, and will exchange Ambassadors by whose reports the respective Governments will be kept in-formed about the situation in Poland.

The three Heads of Government consider that the Eastern frontier of Poland should follow the Curzon Line with digressions from it in some regions of five to eight kilometers in favor of Poland. They recognize that Poland must re-ceive substantial accession of territory in the North and West. They feel that the opinion of the new Polish Provisional Government of National Unity should be sought in due course on the extent of these accessions and that the final delimitation of the Western frontier of Poland should therefore await the Peace Conference.

[Following this declaration, but omitted here, are brief statements on Yugo-slavia, the Italo-Yugoslav frontier and Italo-Austrian frontier, Yugoslav-Bul-garian relations, Southeastern Europe, Iran, meetings of the three Foreign Secretaries, and the Montreux Convention and the Straits.]

Agreement on Soviet Entry into the War Against Japan, 1945

The leaders of the three Great Powers—the Soviet Union, the United States of America and Great Britain—have agreed that in two or three months after Germany has surrendered and the war in Europe has terminated the Soviet Union shall enter into the war against Japan on the side of the Allies on con-dition that:

1. The *status quo* in Outer-Mongolia (The Mongolian People's Republic) shall be preserved;

2. The former rights of Russia violated by the treacherous attack of Japan in 1904 shall be restored, viz:

a. the southern part of Sakhalin as well as all the islands adjacent to it shall be returned to the Soviet Union,

b. the commercial port of Dairen shall be internationalized, the preeminent interests of the Soviet Union in this port being safeguarded and the lease of Port Arthur as a naval base of the USSR restored,

c. the Chinese-Eastern Railroad and the South-Manchurian Railroad which provides an outlet to Dairen shall be jointly operated by the establishment of a joint Soviet-Chinese Company it being understood that the preeminent interests of the Soviet Union shall be safeguarded and that China shall retain full sovereignty in Manchuria;

3. The Kuril islands shall be handed over to the Soviet Union.

It is understood, that the agreement concerning Outer-Mongolia and the ports and railroads referred to above will require concurrence of Generalissimo Chiang Kai-Shek. The President will take measures in order to obtain this concurrence on advice from Marshal Stalin.

The Heads of the three Great Powers have agreed that these claims of the Soviet Union shall be unquestionably fulfilled after Japan has been defeated.

For its part the Soviet Union expresses its readiness to conclude with the National Government of China a pact of friendship and alliance between the USSR and China in order to render assistance to China with its armed forces for the purpose of liberating China from the Japanese yoke.

Charles E. Bohlen and Senator Homer Ferguson Debate Yalta, 1953

SENATOR FERGUSON: Mr. Bohlen, you said that you were an assistant to the Secretary of State at Yalta?

MR. BOHLEN: Yes, sir.

SENATOR FERGUSON: I note that Mr. Alger Hiss was the Deputy Director, Office of Special Political Affairs, Department of State—

MR. BOHLEN: Yes, sir.

SENATOR FERGUSON (continuing): At Yalta.

MR. BOHLEN: That is true, sir.

SENATOR FERGUSON: Would you tell us what his job entailed, what his duties were?

MR. BOHLEN: Hiss was present in the delegation at the plenary sessions of the conference but took no part in them, because no one spoke except the President, or on occasion the Secretary of State. I am absolutely certain that Hiss never saw President Roosevelt in a capacity of adviser to him and never had any interviews with him except that first one when the President met the whole delegation before the opening of the Conference.

Mr. Hiss was not present at any of these discussions on the Far East between President Roosevelt and Stalin, and was at none of the private meetings with Stalin.

SENATOR FERGUSON: Do you know whether or not he prepared any data or obtained any information upon which the agreements were had?

MR. BOHLEN: If he had, it was for Mr. Stettinius, because he was attached to the State Department delegation. I was sort of betwixt and between in that I had to be with the President for interpreting purposes.

But from what I saw of Mr. Hiss' activities at Yalta, he confined himself to problems of the United Nations, the voting formula, and to matters pertaining to the establishment of the United Nations.

SENATOR FERGUSON: You have indicated that you believed that the Yalta agreement was not necessary, so far as the Far East was concerned.

MR. BOHLEN: What I meant, sir, was—what Senator Sparkman is quite right about—were the advantages of hindsight, and I might almost add the advantages of hindmyopia, because the terrific compulsions of the war are absent when you look at it 10 years afterward. The agreement at Yalta on the Far East was, as I understood it, based upon the military estimate that we were going to have to invade the Japanese Islands, which would involve very large American casualties, and that Russia's entry into the war before the landing would result in the elimination or containment, in its proper military sense, of the Kwantung Army.

SENATOR FERGUSON: Yes.

MR. BOHLEN: I say it was unnecessary, because the military development did not turn out as foreseen, but I think that in the course of a war the men who were responsible for its conduct cannot afford to underestimate the enemy, and there is a healthy and natural tendency to overestimate him because to underestimate is to court catastrophe.

SENATOR FERGUSON: The other criticism, if it was a criticism, was that Chiang Kai-shek or anyone connected with the Chinese Government was not present.

MR. BOHLEN: Yes, sir. I think that, in general, it is distasteful, to put it mildly, to do things involving another country without the representative of that country present; but there the major considerations were secrecy, and security. . . .

SENATOR FERGUSON: Was not this agreement in relation to the Far East, as far as it gave other people's rights and liberties and lands away, in violation of the Atlantic Charter?

MR. BOHLEN: I think I have answered that in saying, Senator, that the Yalta agreement in itself was not a final definitive international instrument. The definite instrument was the treaty between China and the Soviet Union of August 1945.

SENATOR FERGUSON: Yes; but we are talking about the agreement, whether it was morally right or wrong, or whether it was just a misinterpretation of the agreement that was wrong; what I want to know is whether or not the giving of this land of another power, another nation, was not in violation of the Atlantic Charter?

Did we not say there that there would be no aggrandizement? Was it not a violation of that?

MR. BOHLEN: I do not consider that the Yalta agreement, in effect, did that.

SENATOR FERGUSON: What did it do? It agreed that we would use our influence.

MR. BOHLEN: That we would support that position.

SENATOR FERGUSON: We would support that position, which was in violation of the Atlantic Charter, was it not?

MR. BOHLEN: Well, sir, I do not think that the Atlantic Charter was against any territorial adjustments between countries. Perhaps my understanding of it is erroneous. . . .

SENATOR FERGUSON: Do you know how we agreed to, as is indicated by Sherwood on Roosevelt and Hopkins when he states:

> The conclusions from the foregoing are obvious: Since Russia is the decisive factor in the war she must be given every assistance, and every effort must be made to obtain her friendship. Likewise, since without question she will dominate Europe on the defeat of the Axis, it is even more essential to develop and maintain the most friendly relations with Russia.

Did you ever hear of that before?

MR. BOHLEN: No sir; I never had until I read it in the book. I have no idea who prepared that memorandum. I think there is something in the book that says it was prepared by a military adviser for Quebec or something of that nature.

SENATOR FERGUSON: Do you know whether or not that was the basis of the agreements at Yalta and Teheran?

MR. BOHLEN: Nothing that I saw would support it that that was the basis.

SENATOR FERGUSON: Well, looking at the agreements, do you not think that is exactly what they were doing? Were they not treating Russia as being the dominant figure after the war, and were not these concessions being made to her for the purpose of allowing her to become the dominant figure?

MR. BOHLEN: No, sir; I would not say that that was the general purpose as I saw it. I think that it is, perhaps, necessary for me here to give a little background, which requires an act of memory and some imagination to put yourself back into the circumstances of the greatest war that has ever been fought.

At the time of Yalta, the Russian armies were in virtually full occupation of Poland; they were very close to the German border; offensives which had been undertaken in the latter part of January or the middle of January had brought them almost up to the German Silesian border, and there was only a small part of northeast Poland that was not under Soviet occupation.

I think the Soviet armies were very near Vienna, and were well across Hungary at the time of Yalta.

I think most of the agreements relating to Europe, therefore, were agreements which, in effect, dealt with areas which were under Soviet control, and I would like to say here that in all my experience at these conferences, the Russians were most reluctant to discuss any of the problems of Eastern Europe. They clearly would have preferred no agreement whatsoever in regard to Poland and those matters. They had physical possession by that time of Poland through their armies. They had installed their own government, which grew out of the so-called Lublin Committee in Poland, and I know that those of us who worked on Poland—and I did, myself—felt that we were trying to do everything we could to lay down some ground rules for developments in these countries and if they had been lived up to, sir, I think Eastern Europe would not now be in the enslaved condition that we find it.

SENATOR FERGUSON: Did that not bring you to the conclusion that any agreements that you made would be interpreted so as to give her absolute control of Europe, as it was indicated in the Quebec agreement that we knew that she was going to be the dominant power, and we were playing to give her the dominant power?

MR. BOHLEN: I would not from what I saw, Senator, agree with that statement. I do not know who prepared that document that is quoted in the book, but it is the first time I had ever heard of it or seen it.

SENATOR FERGUSON: Is it part of the State Department—

MR. BOHLEN: Not that I know of, sir. I think that the map of Europe, as we look at it today, and what we call the Iron Curtain is the line roughly where the armies of the Soviet Union and the armies of the western allies met, which were set by the zonal limits. . . .

SENATOR FERGUSON: Well, wouldn't you say that the Yalta agreement, the Teheran agreement, is now the basis of the situation in Europe?

MR. BOHLEN: No sir; I would not.

SENATOR FERGUSON: Both East and West?

MR. BOHLEN: I would not.

SENATOR FERGUSON: You would not?

MR. BOHLEN: I would not, sir. I believe that the map of Europe would look very much the same if there had never been the Yalta Conference at all.

SENATOR FERGUSON: You don't say then that these agreements are the cause of this enslavement?

MR. BOHLEN: I don't, sir. I say it is the violation of them.

SENATOR FERGUSON: That is what I say.

MR. BOHLEN: What I am saying, sir, I think in this business just because a policy failed doesn't mean it was a wrong one. In other words, I don't think the men who backed the League of Nations were necessarily wrong, despite the fact that the League of Nations failed to prevent World War II. . . .

SENATOR FERGUSON: Well, as it turned out now, it [Yalta Agreement] has had a great influence on what has happened in China.

MR. BOHLEN: I think that is a matter of opinion, Senator.

SENATOR FERGUSON: You don't think so?

MR. BOHLEN: I don't think it did; no, sir.

SENATOR FERGUSON: You don't think it had anything to do with what happened in China?

MR. BOHLEN: Well, everything has something to do with something, but I don't believe that it was the cause of what subsequently happened in China insofar as this treaty between the Chinese and the Soviets went, in its intended effect.

I say "intended effect" advisedly; that on the whole I think that that was a help to Chiang Kai-shek rather than a hindrance in the major business of establishing his sovereignty over China.

Now, that is a matter of opinion, and I am just giving you mine.

SENATOR FERGUSON: Did Russia agree to do anything in this agreement other than to come into the war?

MR. BOHLEN: Well, recognition of Chiang Kai-shek's sovereignty over Manchuria was the important element embodied in the treaty. I have not the text of the treaty here, but I think it says that the Soviet Government recognizes as the sole supreme authority in Manchuria the Nationalist Chinese Government, and that the representatives of that Government should be permitted to go up into that area even while the Soviet armies are in occupation.

SENATOR FERGUSON: Now, didn't this agreement in regard to Japan make the course easier for the Soviet Union in northeast Asia, especially in Manchuria and Korea, after the defeat of Japan, and thus facilitate the Communist conquest of China, and after that the Communist armed invasion of South Korea?

MR. BOHLEN: These are purely matters of opinion, Senator.

SENATOR FERGUSON: What is your opinion on it?

MR. BOHLEN: My opinion is that they did not, in this sense. I am not a Far East expert. I have no firsthand knowledge of China. I have not been engaged in that end of the business.

In this testimony, I don't want to divest myself of the slightest responsibility that I have for these matters. On the other hand, in the interest of accuracy, I don't think that I should take on responsibilities that were not mine. So, when I give you an opinion on this point, it is an opinion of a non-expert in Oriental matters.

I think the Communist conquest of China is one thing, and the terms of the treaty another. . . .

SENATOR FERGUSON: Now, do you know that after the Teheran Conference the Polish general headquarters became aware of the fact that military responsibility over Poland had been shifted to Soviet Russia? . . .

MR. BOHLEN: With regard to the question of the relief for dropping supplies to the Warsaw garrison in August 1944, we had a considerable row with the Russians over that. Mr. Harriman was Ambassador, and he had several knockdown, drag-out fights and finally they allowed one flight to go in and drop the supplies. Some flights were made there and back—

SENATOR FERGUSON: Wasn't that before Yalta?

MR. BOHLEN: Yes, sir, it was.

SENATOR FERGUSON: And, therefore, shouldn't we have understood that Russia was dominating the situation in Poland and intended to do so?

MR. BOHLEN: Yes; their armies were in Poland.

SENATOR FERGUSON: And then why would we make an agreement providing for free elections when we knew that they wouldn't carry out free elections, and that their idea of free elections was no elections at all really?

MR. BOHLEN: Do you consider, Senator, if I might, myself, ask a question, that it would have been better to have made no agreement about Poland?

SENATOR FERGUSON: It would have been better to make an agreement whereby we would have had something to say about the elections.

MR. BOHLEN: How would you do that, Senator?

SENATOR FERGUSON: Then why did you make any when you knew the Russians wouldn't carry them out?

MR. BOHLEN: I don't think you knew that for certain.

SENATOR FERGUSON: Why did we have to surrender the rights of these people and be a party to the surrender?

MR. BOHLEN: I don't consider that the agreement of Yalta involved a surrender. It involved the opposite.

Whether or not the Russians carried out, sir, is to my mind a very different question. I think the agreement on that part of the Polish agreement is about the best you could put down on paper as to what you hoped the Russians would do and they put their signature to.

The fact that they violated it I don't think means that the agreement was bad.

SENATOR FERGUSON: Then you wouldn't have been a party to an agreement that you knew or should have known was not going to be carried out.

MR. BOHLEN: I think this is an important problem.

If agreements made as written are all right and provide for the things that this country believes in, such as free elections, universal suffrage, if you have doubts as to whether the other party is going to carry them out, it still seems to me that it is worthwhile to set your opinion of what ought to happen, and if you are able to get the other fellow to agree to it, I think in the parlance of diplomacy, that that is what it is all about.

SENATOR FERGUSON: In other words, you would favor a settlement in Korea, even when anticipating that it wouldn't be carried out. In other words you want to get an agreement that would look good on paper.

MR. BOHLEN: No, sir; I don't think that is the point.

SENATOR FERGUSON: Isn't that what happened in these agreements?

MR. BOHLEN: No, sir. The point is that you were confronted at Yalta on the question of Poland which had been the subject of intense correspondence over a period of years between the Soviet, American, and British Governments. . . .

. . . The problem you were faced with at Yalta was what were you really going to do about Poland. There were three courses of action that were open.

1. You could have, by just accepting the total *fait accompli,* let it go and do nothing about it, which is what I think Stalin would have preferred by all indications.
2. To stick completely with the London government in exile, which would have meant that no member of it would have been in Poland. There wouldn't have been any entry into Poland on the part of anybody.
3. To attempt to get as many members of the Polish group in London as possible into the reorganized government.

Yes, but the other alternative was this. You had the country, Poland, which the Russians were in occupation of. The alternatives were leaving, washing your hands, so to speak, of the whole business, and leaving this complete Communist government, which would be worse.

The other alternative of just sticking with the London government amounted to almost the same thing, because you would have had an exile government in London and you would have had nothing in Poland, and they would have had nothing. . . .

SENATOR FERGUSON: And Poland was not present at these divisions.

MR. BOHLEN: That is true, but it was not possible to have Polish representatives present.

SENATOR FERGUSON: Well, no one representing Poland was present. It was just like the case of Chiang Kai-shek. No one representing China was present.

MR. BOHLEN: Well, the question is what do you do about a situation, Senator? And I think nothing would be easier if you had to do them all over again, you would probably do them with greater perfection, although in many ways under the compulsions of the times I don't know what you would have done that would have a great improvement over this. I will say this. I think more care could have been used in all of these agreements as to how they looked, that is to say, from the point of view of the record. I don't know if you were thinking of what you could do to assist Poland, which I can assure you was the major motivation in the minds as I saw it of the President and Winston Churchill—they had no other interests than that; they felt very strongly on this subject.

I think the tragic fact is that by the progress of the war, which short of some drastic revision of strategy, the map of Europe as we see it today was almost made by the war itself. I think very few people have any illusions.

SENATOR FERGUSON: We were making political agreements of division prior to the ending of the war.

MR. BOHLEN: It is true in this sense.

SENATOR FERGUSON: And we did it without consultation with our allies who were fighting in the war.

MR. BOHLEN: I think the President felt, and so did Mr. Churchill, that they were in effect trying to fight the battles for the Poles which the Poles were not able to do themselves.

Now I don't know whether these judgments were mistaken, whether there were better ways to do it, but I am utterly and totally convinced that that was the main thought. That the British had very strong feelings about Poland, had gone to war over Poland—

SENATOR FERGUSON: That is the sad part of it. They went to war over Poland, and there is no Poland today. We went to war over China and China is gone today. . . .

SENATOR FERGUSON: I think the saddest thing of all in relation to history is that we don't learn from history.

MR. BOHLEN: One of the things I have felt is these Yalta agreements obviously show imperfections, and I can assure you many of them, the one on Poland was not a happy agreement for anybody connected with it. The President spoke on that point I believe before Congress after Yalta. He was very un-happy about it.

SENATOR FERGUSON: But we agreed to it.

MR. BOHLEN: We felt it was the best we could do. The alternative of doing nothing was worse. That was the judgment.

I would like to say this: A great deal of the moral position of the United States in the leadership accepted by the free world is due to the fact that an honest attempt was made to see if any form of arrangement with the Soviet Union could be arrived at that would have any value for the future of the world. Without that attempt, it would seem to me you would have a much more divided opinion throughout the free world as to who was to blame.

People would say, "How do you know? You didn't try it." These things are all very complicated. History will deal with it and I would not undertake to say that these agreements couldn't have been done better, but I do know this much: that if there had been no Yalta Conference, I sincerely doubt very much if the map of the world would look very different.

ESSAYS

Chester Wilmot, an Englishman, wrote his book *The Struggle for Europe* in 1952. That work reflected contemporary criticism of Franklin D. Roosevelt and the Yalta Conference. Wilmot finds the President naive and too conciliatory toward Stalin, especially with regard to Asian issues. In the second essay, historian Forrest C. Pogue, a biographer of General George C. Marshall, replies to critics by arguing that they are simply not paying attention to the realities of power relationships ex-tant when the Big Three met at Yalta. What was certain, writes Pogue, was that the United States believed at the time that it needed Soviet participation in the war against Japan and that the agreements concerning Asia were struck with that goal uppermost in American decisions.

A Stalinist Victory

CHESTER WILMOT

Three days before he set out for Malta and the Crimea, Roosevelt took the oath for the fourth time as President of the United States, and, in the course of his inaugural address, declared, "We have learned to be citizens of the world, members of the human community. We have learned the simple truth, as Emerson said, 'the only way to have a friend is to be one.' "

Chester Wilmot, *The Struggle for Europe* (New York: Harper & Row, 1952), pp. 639–658. Copyright © 1952 by Chester Wilmot, reprinted by permission of Harold Matson Co. Inc.

This was the creed that Roosevelt carried to Yalta. There was, in his view, no fundamental conflict of national interest between the Soviet Union and the United States; the Russian and American peoples had so much in common that they would readily co-operate in the cause of peace and freedom if only there could be a real meeting of minds between their leaders. His trust in Stalin and his faith in his own ability to win the Soviet Union's lasting co-operation were still high, although the unhappy course of Russo-Polish relations during the past year might well have given him reason to doubt both his own personal influence and Russia's post-war intentions.

Three times since Teheran, Roosevelt had made a direct approach to Stalin in the hope of inducing him to reach a reasonable agreement with the Polish Government in London; each time he had been rebuffed and Stalin had shown no inclination whatever to allow the principles of the Atlantic Charter to apply to Poland. Nevertheless, Mikolajczyk [Premier of the Polish Government in Exile] reports—and there is no reason to disbelieve him—that, when he was in Washington in June 1944, Roosevelt told him, "Stalin is a realist, and we mustn't forget, when we judge Russian actions, that the Soviet régime has had only two years of experience in international relations. But of one thing I am certain, Stalin is not an Imperialist." Roosevelt explained to Mikolajczyk that he had not been able to take a public stand on the Polish question because it was election year, but "eventually," he said, "I will act as moderator in this problem and effect a settlement." Believing, as he had said after Teheran, that Stalin was "getatable," Roosevelt felt sure that when they met again across the conference table there would be no problem they could not solve on a "man-to-man" basis.

Roosevelt was not alone in thinking that Diplomacy by Friendship would bring a sympathetic response from Stalin. The most influential of his advisers —military and political alike—were agreed, as Hull says, that they "must and could get along with the Soviet Government," and that this would be possible if they were "patient and forbearing." The idea that they could "get along with" the Russians came more easily to the American leaders than to the British, for the United States is the great melting pot and the American people have shown an unparalleled capacity for absorbing into their own society a multitude of nationalities.

Perhaps the best exposition of Roosevelt's idea is to be found in a memorandum which Hopkins [Harry Hopkins, Roosevelt's personal adviser] wrote six months after Yalta. "We know or believe," he said, "that Russia's interests, so far as we can anticipate them, do not afford an opportunity for a major difference with us in foreign affairs. We believe we are mutually dependent upon each other for economic reasons. We find the Russians as individuals easy to deal with. The Russians undoubtedly like the American people. They like the United States. They trust the United States more than they trust any other power in the world . . . above all, they want to maintain friendly relations with us. . . . They are a tenacious, determined people who think and act just like you and I do."

Eisenhower endorsed this view of the Russian people when he wrote, "In his generous instincts, in his love of laughter, in his devotion to a comrade, and in his healthy, direct outlook on the affairs of workaday life, the ordinary Russian seems to me to bear a marked similarity to what we call an 'average American.' " Eisenhower believed too that there was a special bond between the United States and the Soviet Union, a bond that was inevitably lacking in the Anglo-American association. He felt, he says, that "in the past relations of America and Russia there was no cause to regard the future with pessimism." On the one hand, "the two peoples had maintained an unbroken friendship that dated back to the birth of the United States as an independent republic"; on the other, "both were free from the stigma of colonial empire building by force."

This remarkable statement stems straight from the Founding Fathers. It was the American way of saying that politically both peoples were free from original sin. That this was not true of either was irrelevant; it was believed, not merely by Eisenhower but also by many Americans who should have been better acquainted with their own history. This belief was implicit in Roosevelt's approach to the problems which were to be discussed at Yalta. In his eyes, Britain was an Imperial Power, bearing the "colonial stigma"; Russia was not. That assessment of his allies was a decisive factor in Roosevelt's readiness to make concessions to the Soviet Union both in Europe and Asia in order to ensure Stalin's entry into the Pacific War.

Roosevelt's intimates give two reasons for his determination to enlist the aid of Russia against Japan. His personal Chief of Staff, Admiral Leahy, says that the President was actuated by the belief that "Soviet participation in the Far East operation would insure Russia's sincere co-operation in his dream of a united, peaceful world." On the other hand, his Secretary of State, Stettinius, reports that "immense pressure [was] put on the President by our military leaders to bring Russia into the Far Eastern War. At this time the atomic bomb was still an unknown quantity and our setback in the Battle of the Bulge was fresh in the minds of all. We had not as yet crossed the Rhine. No one knew how long the European War would last nor how great the casualties would be." Stettinius adds that the American Chiefs of Staff had warned Roosevelt that "without Russia it might cost the United States a million casualties to conquer Japan" and that the Pacific War might not end until 1947.

The chief advocate of this view was Marshall [Army Chief of Staff], but Roosevelt's military advisers were by no means unanimous in the belief that it would be necessary to invade the Japanese home islands. Leahy says that at Pearl Harbour, in July 1944, both MacArthur and Nimitz (the two commanders directly concerned) had told the President that "Japan could be forced to accept our terms of surrender by the use of sea and air powers without the invasion of the Japanese homeland." Since then, at the Battle for Leyte Gulf in October, the Japanese Navy had suffered such a crushing defeat that well before Yalta Leahy considered that the war against Japan "had progressed to the point where her defeat was only a matter of time and attrition." This was also the opinion of Arnold, the Chief of the Air Staff, whose Super-Fortresses were already bombing Japan from island airfields. There was no longer any great need for air bases in the Maritime Provinces of the Soviet Union, and, after the unhappy experiment of "shuttle-bombing" in Europe, Arnold did not set much store by any facilities he might be granted in Asia. Nevertheless, the advice of Marshall and King prevailed.

The supporters of Russian intervention were considerably influenced by their estimate of the amount of help the United States would receive, or should accept, from Britain in the war against Japan. Here the colonial issue again entered American calculations. Virtually all the British and Imperial forces in the Far East were deployed in Admiral Lord Louis Mountbatten's South-East Asia Command (SEAC) for operations in Burma, and in due course Malaya and Sumatra. This deployment was dictated as much by geographical as political factors, but it was presumed in Washington that Churchill was more interested in regaining Britain's lost colonies than in bringing about the early defeat of Japan. Consequently, it came as a great surprise—to the British as much as to the American Chiefs of Staff—when at Quebec in September 1944 the Prime Minister suddenly offered to send a large part of R.A.F. Bomber Command and the main British Battle Fleet into the Central Pacific. This offer was promptly accepted by Roosevelt, but, when it was raised at the next meeting of the Combined Chiefs of Staff, "all hell broke loose"—Arnold's phrase—and King "hotly refused to have anything to do with it." Cunningham, the First Sea Lord, reports that King was sharply called to order by Leahy and "eventually gave way; but with a very bad grace."

Although there was no trace of King's Anglophobia in Marshall or Arnold, the American Chiefs of Staff had never allowed their British colleagues any voice in the conduct of the Pacific War, nor were they eager to have British forces play a major part in it lest this should give Britain the right to claim possession or trusteeship of some of the Japanese Empire. Further, they believed—and they so advised the President—that "in the interests of national defence, the Japanese mandated islands in the Pacific captured by our forces should be retained under the sovereignty of the United States and not delivered to the trusteeship of the United Nations." True to his principles, Roosevelt rejected this proposal, but those same principles made him distrustful of the activities and intentions of the British and French in South-East Asia.

Roosevelt was determined that Indo-China should not go back to France and he had refused to agree to any French military mission being accredited to SEAC. He was prepared to allow the Dutch to return to the Netherlands East Indies, because Queen Wilhelmina had promised to give them self-government, but he intended that these islands should be liberated by American forces so that he would be in a position to enforce fulfilment of this promise. Accordingly, the sole Dutch possession placed within the sphere of prospective British operations was Sumatra and this island only because of its geographical relation to Malaya. Moreover, the American Chiefs of Staff, on MacArthur's recommendation, decided that the British should not be allowed to take over the military control of the East Indies after their recapture. "The exact British intentions were not known," says Leahy, "but past experience indicated that if they did get control of some Dutch territory, it might be difficult to pry them loose." This view appears to have been shared by Roosevelt, for he told Stettinius that "the British would take land anywhere in the world even if it were only rock or a sandbar."

Roosevelt's eagerness to buy Stalin's aid in the war against Japan was principally due to his desire to save lives, but in the light of all the evidence it seems fair to say that he was also actuated by the hope that Russia's intervention would enable the United States to strike the decisive blow at Japan, and compel her surrender, before the British, French or Dutch could regain possession of their colonies. The United States would thus be able to demand that the colonies which had been liberated from the Japanese should now be liberated from the dominion of their original owners.

In due course, as it turned out, the Americans were able to achieve this purpose without the intervention of Russia. When the Japanese announced their readiness to capitulate, MacArthur, who was acting as co-ordinator of all the surrender arrangements, forbade Mountbatten to accept any local surrender in South-East Asia or to send any relief or reoccupation forces into Japanese-held areas until the overall surrender had been signed in Tokyo. Since this ceremony was not to take place for another twelve days, Mountbatten ignored his orders so far as missions of mercy were concerned, because, as he says in his dispatch, "if relief stores and personnel had not been sent in at once, the delay of twelve days imposed on me would have resulted in many more deaths each day among the prisoners [of war]."

The instructions regarding the movement of naval and military forces were observed, though these were already at sea, and the British were thus placed in the humiliating position of not being permitted to reoccupy their own colonies, until the Japanese High Command had formally acknowledged defeat to an American general on an American battleship in Tokyo Bay.

Although this particular manifestation of American anti-colonialism was not revealed until six months after Yalta, the attitude which inspired it was implicit in the policy Roosevelt pursued throughout the war.

The plenary sessions of the Yalta Conference were held at Livadia Palace overlooking the Black Sea. The ownership of this palace had changed since it was built by the Romanoffs, but the aims and ambitions of the new owners differed little from those of its former masters. The only significant difference was that the men who now sought to fulfil Russia's imperial destiny were more ruthless and more powerful.

At the opening session on Sunday, February 4th, Stalin made a gesture which was both tactful and tactical. He proposed, as he had at Teheran, that Roosevelt should take the chair, and thus once again he brought the President half-way to his side. Yet Stalin showed no early inclination to follow the chairman's lead, least of all with regard to the President's cherished plan for creating a world peace organisation based on the recognition of the sovereign rights of all nations. The first time the subject was raised, "Stalin made it quite plain," says Stettinius, "that the three Great Powers which had borne the brunt of the war should be the ones to preserve the peace." He declared, moreover, that he would "never agree to having any action of any of the Great

Powers submitted to the judgment of the small powers." In reply to this argument Churchill spoke for all the Western World in saying, "The eagle should permit the small birds to sing and care not wherefor they sang." That evening, when Stettinius and Eden discussed the outlook, they agreed that "the trend . . . seemed to be more towards a three-power alliance than anything else."

Evidently sensing that the time was not opportune to pursue the question of the world peace organisation, Roosevelt, at the start of the second plenary meeting, turned the discussion to the future of Germany. At the Moscow Conference of Foreign Ministers in November 1943 it had been decided that Germany should be completely disarmed and should pay reparations for the physical damage she had inflicted on the Soviet Union and other Allied countries. Then, and at Teheran, the question of partitioning Germany had been debated without any conclusions being reached, but it had been assumed that in any case the three powers would occupy the country, and by November 1944 they had agreed upon the actual zones of occupation and upon their joint responsibility for Berlin. At Yalta the "Big Three" confirmed their determination to demand the "Unconditional Surrender" of Germany and, for the first time, there was detailed consideration by the Russian and Anglo-American Chiefs of Staff on the military measures necessary to bring about Hitler's final defeat. On the question of post-war Germany, however, there was no such unanimity and it was soon evident that there was a considerable divergence between the British and Russian attitudes, especially with regard to the principle of partition, the extent of reparations and the right of France to share in the occupation.

The Russian view was that there should be only three occupying powers; that they should decide at Yalta to partition the Reich into a number of separate states and to include a declaration to this effect in the surrender terms; and that Germany should be deprived of eighty per cent of her heavy industry and should pay reparations in kind to the value of twenty billion dollars, half of which should go to the Soviet Union.

Churchill was not slow to realise that, if these proposals were adopted, Germany would be rendered politically impotent and economically impoverished. Although determined to ensure that Germany should not again disturb the peace of Europe, he did not wish to see her entirely neutralised as a factor in the balance of power. Accordingly, he doubted the wisdom of partitioning the Reich unless the Soviet Union would agree to the creation of a strong Danubian Confederation—and this had already been rejected by both Stalin and Roosevelt. Moreover, he did not wish to make Germany pay such severe reparations that her economy would collapse unless it were sustained by the Western Powers as it had been after the First World War. Finally, the Prime Minister wanted the French to have an equal share in both the occupation and administration of Germany so that there would be a second European voice to support Britain's in the Allied Control Commission. He was the more emphatic on this point, for the President said that the American troops would be withdrawn from Europe in "two years at the outside." Whereupon Churchill commented, without indicating what threat he feared, "Great Britain alone will not be strong enough to guard the Western approaches to the Channel."

As the discussion developed—both in the plenary sessions and at meetings of the Foreign Ministers—Roosevelt and Stettinius endeavored to take an intermediate stand on these issues. The result was that three distinct viewpoints emerged. With regard to partition, Stalin wanted a definite commitment both now and in the surrender terms; Churchill wished to make no commitments either way; and Roosevelt suggested that they should mention dismemberment in the terms without binding themselves to this policy. On the matter of reparations, Stalin demanded explicit acceptance in the Protocol of the overall figure of twenty billion dollars; Churchill opposed any mention of any figure even in a secret document; and Roosevelt inclined to the view that the Russian figure might be taken as "a basis for discussion." As for the occupation of Germany, Churchill insisted that France should have a seat on the Control Commission as well as a zone; Stalin argued against both suggestions; and Roosevelt proposed that France should have a zone but no seat.

On each of these questions the President was in fundamental agreement with the Prime Minister's stand (though not with all his reasons), but in public discussion Roosevelt played the mediator. He was not interested in upholding the balance of power concept, nor was he deeply concerned with the intrinsic merits of the German problem. To him Germany was not an issue in itself, but a bargaining point in the wider issue that was uppermost in his mind— the winning of Stalin's cooperation in the international peace organisation, and in the war against Japan.

To some extent the role of arbiter was thrust upon Roosevelt when he became chairman, but there is no doubt that he preferred it since he was thus able to preserve greater freedom of action and to avoid committing himself until he had heard the rival views. The results of the President's determination to act as mediator were twofold. On the one hand, the assertion of what were in reality Anglo-American views and principles was frequently left to the British alone—much to Churchill's annoyance; and on the other, as one of Roosevelt's closest advisers says, "the Soviet leaders did over-estimate the ultimate extent of the President's generosity and his willingness to compromise on principles."

The problem of Germany's future was still undecided when—at the third plenary session on February 6th—Roosevelt returned to the question of postwar peace and asked Stettinius to review the questions which had been in dispute at the Dumbarton Oaks Conference. There the Americans, British, Chinese and Russians had agreed on the principles and purposes of what was to become the United Nations, and had decided there should be a General Assembly, a Security Council and various other instrumentalities. The area of agreement had ended, however, when the Soviet Delegate, Gromyko, had proposed that all sixteen republics of the Soviet Union should have seats in the Assembly (a proposal which "left Stettinius and Cadogan breathless"), and had demanded that in the Security Council the Great Powers should have the right to veto any proposals, except those which related to points of procedure.

It has been alleged by some of Roosevelt's critics that the establishment of the veto power in the Security Council was a concession made by him at Yalta to induce Stalin to join the United Nations. This is not so. The basic principle of the veto was never in dispute. None of the Great Powers was prepared to submit itself and its interests unreservedly to the jurisdiction of an international security organisation. All were agreed that there must be "unqualified unanimity of the permanent members of the Council on all major decisions relating to the preservation of peace, including all economic and military enforcement measures." This was inevitable. The President, haunted by the ghost of Wilson, insisted on the veto power because he knew that the United States Senate would not surrender to an international body the right to commit American forces to military action. Churchill was equally insistent on this point because, as he said at Yalta, he would "never consent to the fumbling fingers of forty or fifty nations prying into the life's existence of the British Empire."

Although both Britain and America felt obliged to retain the right to veto any international "police action," they had no desire to curtail discussion or to prevent any small power bringing a cause of grievance to the notice of the Security Council. At Dumbarton Oaks, however, Gromyko had refused to accept this view and had told Stettinius, "The Russian position on voting in the Council will never be departed from!" Nevertheless, on December 5th, 1944, Roosevelt had sent to Stalin and Churchill a compromise formula which, while recognising the need for unanimity on matters involving the application of sanctions, provided that on questions relating to the peaceful settlement of any dispute no member of the Council would cast its vote, or exercise its veto, if it were a party to that dispute.

Now, at Yalta, after Stettinius had re-stated this formula, Churchill declared Britain's acceptance of it, and added, "We see great advantage in the three Great Powers not assuming the position of rulers of all the rest of the world without even allowing them to state their case." When Stalin spoke, however, he again emphasized the importance of unanimity, declaring that the real problem was to preserve the unity of the Great Powers and to work out a covenant that would achieve this purpose. "The danger in the future," he said, "is the possibility of conflicts among ourselves." Apologising to the President, Stalin said that he was not yet ready to pass judgment on the voting formula, because he had had "no chance to study this question in detail." Yet he proceeded to give such a concise analysis of its implications that it was obvious he must have studied it rather carefully at some time during the two months since he had received Roosevelt's draft!

After this exchange Stettinius was more confident, believing that for the first time Stalin really understood the American point of view. Byrnes, on the other hand, felt that the Russians "could not be greatly interested in the United Nations organisation," and Leahy thought it "difficult to foresee on what grounds an agreement could be reached." This impression seemed to be confirmed when, at the next meeting of the Foreign Ministers, Molotov refused even to discuss the Security Council voting procedure.

Leaving this matter for the moment, Roosevelt brought up the Polish question. He announced his readiness to accept the Curzon Line, but proposed that Stalin might agree to leave within Poland the city of Lwow and the nearby oilfields. "He pointed out," says Stettinius, "that he was merely suggesting this for consideration rather than insisting on it." In fact, the main argument he advanced in its support was that "it would have a salutary effect on American public opinion," a consideration which was hardly likely to carry much weight with the Soviet dictator. Thus, although the President's expert advisers had warned him that these oilfields were essential to the Polish economy, he did not make an issue of it, so anxious was he to preserve the role of mediator, not only on the frontier question but also in the establishment of a new Polish government.

Churchill was already committed to the Curzon Line, but he declared that if Stalin were to accept the President's Lwow plan, it would be "a magnanimous gesture" which Britain would "admire and acclaim." The Prime Minister said, however, that he was more interested in the sovereignty and independence of Poland than in the matter of frontiers, and that he, like the President, wished to see established in Warsaw a "fully representative Polish government," pledged to the holding of free elections. For Britain, having risked so much in Poland's cause, this was a question of honour.

In reply, Stalin delivered an impassioned speech. "For the Russian people," he said, "Poland is not only a question of honour but also a question of security. Throughout history Poland has been the corridor through which the enemy has passed into Russia . . . It is in Russia's interests that Poland should be strong and powerful, in a position to shut the door of this corridor by her own force." Turning to the problem of frontiers, he said that the Soviet Union must have Lwow and could not accept anything but "the line of Curzon and Clemenceau." Stalin declared: "You would drive us into shame! What will be said by the White Russians and the Ukrainians? They will say that Stalin and Molotov are far less reliable defenders of Russia than are Curzon and Clemenceau . . . I prefer the war should continue a little longer . . . to give Poland compensation in the West at the expense of the Germans. . . . I am in favour of extending the Polish Western frontier to the Neisse River."

Stalin was equally unresponsive to Roosevelt's suggestion that a new Polish Government should be formed from members of the five main political parties, including representatives of the Government in London. He stated that he did not trust the London Poles and would not recognise any administration except that already established in Lublin. "We demand order," he said, "and we do not want to be shot in the back."

Churchill joined issue vigorously with Stalin, declaring that Britain could not accept the Lublin Committee, since it did not represent more than a third of the nation; nor could he agree to extend Poland's western frontier to the River Neisse, thus giving her virtually all Silesia. "It would be a pity," he said, "to stuff the Polish goose so full of German food that he will die of indigestion." On that discordant note the meeting adjourned.

That evening Roosevelt sent Stalin a conciliatory letter, in which he reaffirmed the American opposition to the Lublin Committee, but added the assurance, "The United States will never lend its support in any way to any

provisional government in Poland which would be inimical to your interests."
Although he regarded this letter as an act of mediation, Roosevelt compromised
his own independence by telling Stalin, "I am determined there shall be no
breach between ourselves and the Soviet Union." With that statement he admitted that, if Stalin made an issue of Poland, the United States would give
way.

When the Big Three met again next afternoon (February 7th) Stalin
acknowledged receipt of the President's letter, but stated that his own reply
was not yet ready as it was being typed; in the meantime he would like to
discuss the international peace organisation. Roosevelt agreed, and Molotov
proceeded to say that the Soviet Union was "happy to accept the entire
American proposal" about voting in the Security Council, and would not press
for all sixteen Soviet Republics to be members of the United Nations. It would
be satisfactory if seats were granted to the Ukraine and White Russia. As it
had already been agreed that Britain, the four Dominions and India should have
individual representation in the General Assembly, Churchill could not oppose
this request, and, although Roosevelt did not give his consent immediately,
he told Stettinius that he "did not believe there was anything preposterous
about the Russian proposal." Indeed, he regarded it as a small price to pay for
Soviet co-operation.

The President and the Prime Minister were delighted at this manifestation
of Stalin's willingness to join the United Nations and they felt he had made
substantial concessions on two vital issues about which he had previously been
intractable. They had feared that Stalin was interested only in securing a
Three-Power Alliance, but now Roosevelt, at any rate, believed he had persuaded Stalin not only to recognise the sovereign rights of small nations, but
also to act in friendly concert with the other great Powers in maintaining peace
and extending the frontiers of freedom.

This belief was confirmed when Stalin agreed that the Soviet Union would
take part in the United Nations Conference to be held in San Francisco in
April, and would support there the right of the United States to have three
votes in the General Assembly, if the President desired to make such a claim.
It seemed to Roosevelt that these concessions were an earnest of Stalin's good
faith, for it could not be foreseen then that the Soviet Union would abuse the
veto power, as it was to do in the years after the war, employing it to prevent
discussion as well as decision and endeavouring to exercise it even on questions
of procedure. That afternoon at Yalta it appeared that Anglo-American diplomacy had gained a considerable victory, and the President felt that the long
and arduous journey had been in vain.

During the brief adjournment which followed this discussion about the
United Nations the prevailing opinion among the Western delegates was that
the concessions Stalin had made represented a decided change of heart. Considered in relation to what followed, however, these concessions appear as a
tactical manœuvre designed to make the Western delegations more receptive
to the Soviet plan for Poland which Molotov put forward while the meeting
still glowed with goodwill. This plan did little more than set out in formal

terms the attitude Stalin had so forcibly proclaimed the day before. The only hint of any readiness to meet the Western view was contained in the statement that the present Provisional Government (i.e. the Lublin Committee) might be enlarged to include "some democratic leaders from Polish *émigré* circles." Since the Russians refused to regard even Mikolajczyk, the leader of the Peasant Party, as a "democrat," that concession meant nothing. The moral of this day's proceedings was that, while Russia was willing to join the United Nations, she was not prepared to rely on it entirely. She intended to safeguard her own security in any event by ensuring that she had subservient neighbours in Europe and a commanding position in Asia.

Stalin's Asiatic ambitions were revealed on the following afternoon during a private discussion with Roosevelt about the Soviet Union's entry into the Japanese War. This discussion was conducted on a strictly Russo-American basis and in conditions of great secrecy. The only other persons present, apart from the two interpreters, were Molotov and Averell Harriman, the American Ambassador to the Soviet Union.

At the President's request, Churchill was not there and, when the negotiations were continued on the technical level by the Chiefs of Staff, the British did not take part. Even within his own entourage Roosevelt was most uncommunicative. Stettinius, though Secretary of State, was merely notified that talks were in progress. When he asked if the State Department should not be represented, Roosevelt replied that the problem was "primarily a military matter . . . and had best remain on a purely military level." This was a specious answer, for Stalin had long since committed himself on the basic military issue; the main point to be decided at Yalta was the political price of his participation.

It was in October 1943 that Stalin had first promised to join in the war against Japan after the defeat of Germany. He had made this offer to Cordell Hull, who says that it was "entirely unsolicited . . . and had no strings attached to it." At Teheran a month later, Stalin had repeated this promise virtually as a *quid pro quo* for the Second Front and for Lend-Lease. Nevertheless, Roosevelt had then volunteered to restore Russia's rights in the Manchurian port of Dairen and to ensure her free access to warm waters. Finding that the President was a "soft touch," Stalin proceeded to make this gesture his price with the paradoxical result that Soviet demands grew as the American need for Russian assistance in the Eastern War declined. During Churchill's visit to Moscow in October 1944, the Marshal said that "the Soviet Union would take the offensive against Japan three months after Germany's defeat, provided the United States would assist in building up the necessary reserve supplies and *provided the political aspects of Russia's participation had been clarified.*" During this Moscow meeting, as on five other separate occasions in 1944, Stalin gave an assurance that Russian air and naval bases in the Maritime Provinces would be made available to American forces. In December, however, this assurance was withdrawn, presumably with a view to strengthening the bargaining position of the Soviet Union at Yalta.

The course of the fateful discussions which took place behind closed doors in Livadia Palace on the afternoon of February 8th is not known in detail, for none of those who took part have publicly revealed what was said and the accounts given by Leahy, Sherwood and Stettinius, though authoritative, are second-hand. What was decided, however, is revealed only too clearly in the terms of the agreement which was subsequently signed by Stalin, Roosevelt and Churchill. This provided that "in two or three months after Germany has surrendered . . . the Soviet Union shall enter the war against Japan" on certain conditions: that "the status quo in Outer Mongolia" was to be preserved; that the Kurile Islands, north of Japan, were to be "handed over to the Soviet Union"; and that the rights Russia had lost after her defeat by Japan in 1904 were to be restored. Russia was thus to regain possession of Southern Sakhalin, the "international port" of Dairen and the naval base of Port Arthur. In addition, although China was to "retain full sovereignty in Manchuria," the principal Manchurian railways were to be "jointly operated by . . . a Soviet-Chinese Company" which was to safeguard "the pre-eminent interests of the Soviet Union." Apart from agreeing to enter the Pacific War, Stalin conceded nothing in writing. He promised Roosevelt that the United States could have bases in the Maritime Provinces, but this was not mentioned in the agreement, nor was there any reference to the one million tons of additional supplies that were to be provided by the Americans. These supplies were duly delivered, but the Russians made sure that the establishment of the bases never proceeded beyond discussions in Moscow.

The President's Chief of Staff (Admiral Leahy) says that, when the Russian terms were mentioned at a subsequent plenary session, there was "little discussion and no argument." It appears that Stalin blandly explained, "I only want to have returned to Russia what the Japanese have taken from my country"; and that Roosevelt replied, "That seems like a very reasonable suggestion from our ally. They only want to get back that which has been taken from them." Churchill must have listened a little incredulously to this exchange for he cannot have forgotten that Roosevelt had once said to him: "Winston . . . you have four hundred years of acquisitive instinct in your blood and you just don't understand how a country might not want to acquire land somewhere if they can get it. A new period has opened in the world's history and you will have to adjust yourself to it."

The British should have known, if the Americans did not, that Stalin's justification could not by any means cover all the Soviet claims. The Kuriles had never formally belonged to Russia. The reclaimed "rights" in Manchuria were those which in the nineteenth century had enabled Russia to exercise in this province a degree of dominion which seriously impinged upon Chinese sovereignty. These "rights" rested on no more substantial foundations than those extra-territorial privileges which the United States, Britain and other countries had given up in 1943 at Roosevelt's own instigation and in fulfilment of his pledge to restore and respect the independence of China. To accept the "status quo" in Outer Mongolia, which Moscow had been sedulously luring away from its allegiance to Chungking, was to acknowledge that the Soviet Union, not China, should enjoy political supremacy in that country. In short, by this agreement Russia was to become, with Anglo-American consent, the political heir of Japan in Manchuria, and thereby in North China.

No arrangement was made at Yalta with regard to the occupation of Korea and the post-war fate of that unhappy country appears to have been mentioned only incidentally. Stalin inquired whether it was to be occupied by any foreign troops. When Roosevelt replied that this was not intended, Stalin, no doubt thinking far into the future, "expressed his approval."

Upon learning the full extent of the Soviet terms, some of Churchill's advisers were deeply concerned, for they discovered that, although Stalin had made no further commitments whatever and although the most important of his claims had to be met by their ally, China, not by Japan, the President and the Prime Minister were required to declare that "these claims of the Soviet Union shall be unquestionably fulfilled after Japan has been defeated." Moreover, Stalin was insisting that for security reasons the Chinese Government should not even be informed until the Soviet Union was ready to attack. Roosevelt had undertaken to secure Chiang Kai-Shek's compliance in due course but, as Sherwood says, "if China had refused to agree to any of the Soviet claims, presumably the U.S. and Britain would have been compelled to join in enforcing them." To some of the British delegation it seemed rather incongruous that, while urging Churchill to hand Hong Kong over to China as "a gesture of good-will," Roosevelt was prepared to promise Stalin substantial concessions in Manchuria, and to do this without so much as consulting the Chinese. This point was appreciated by at least one of his staff, for Leahy reports that he warned Roosevelt, "Mr. President, you are going to lose out on Hong Kong if you agree to give the Russians half of Dairen"; and that Roosevelt replied, "Well, Bill, I can't help it."

Eden did all he could to dissuade the Prime Minister from setting his signature to the terms agreed upon by Roosevelt and Stalin. Churchill replied that he must sign, because he felt that "the whole position of the British Empire in the Far East might be at stake." The Prime Minister had good reason to fear that, since he had been excluded from the negotiations about the Japanese War, Britain might well be excluded from future discussions about the Far East if she did not stand by the United States now. Like Leahy, he may also have foreseen that, if these territorial concessions were made to Russia, Roosevelt would not be in a strong moral position to enforce his oft-repeated "threat" to reform the British Empire.

Of all the agreements reached at Yalta, this is the most controversial and would seem to be the least defensible. Yet it does not appear that the concessions, which Stalin obtained, were wrung from a reluctant Roosevelt. Sherwood records that the President had been "prepared even before the Teheran Conference . . . to agree to the legitimacy of most if not all of the Soviet claims in the Far East," although he expresses the opinion that "Roosevelt would not have agreed to the final firm commitment," if he had not been "tired and anxious to avoid further argument." Stettinius disagrees with this opinion and explains that "the Far Eastern agreement was carefully worked out and was not a snap decision made at Yalta." He endeavours to defend the concessions by asking: "What, with the possible exception of the Kuriles, did the Soviet Union receive at Yalta which she might not have taken without any agreement?"

That question does not pose the real issue which surely was: What did the Soviet Union receive at Yalta which she could not have taken without flagrantly violating the fundamental principles of the Atlantic Charter and the United Nations to which she had subscribed? The real issue for the world and for the future was not what Stalin would or could have taken but what he was given the right to take. This agreement provided Stalin with a moral cloak for his aggressive designs in Asia, and, more important, with almost a legal title enforceable at the Peace Conference to the territories and privileges which he demanded.

The President's surrender on this question is the more remarkable because it involved the sacrifice of those very principles which he had striven to uphold throughout his dealings with Churchill and Stalin. He had always insisted that he would not make any post-war commitments which would prejudice the peace treaties; he would recognise no spheres of influence, no territorial changes except those arrived at by mutual agreement, and no transfers of colonial territory except under conditions of international trusteeship. By making this agreement about the Japanese War, however, Roosevelt weakened both his mediating influence and his bargaining position in relation to problems arising out of the German War. He was not well placed to defend the sovereignty of Poland, once he had agreed to the infringement of China's sovereignty without her consent and in breach of the promise he had given to Chiang Kai-Shek at Cairo in 1943. He could not make any effective protest against the Russians' creating a sphere of influence in the Balkans, when he had acknowledged their sphere of influence in Mongolia and Manchuria. Having departed from his principles in Asia, he could not expect to be allowed to apply them in Europe; not against a realist like Stalin. Consequently, the President was now in a less favourable position than he had been at the start of the conference. Stalin's appetite had been whetted, not satisfied.

The records kept by those who were present at Yalta give the impression that the negotiations about Russia's part in the Pacific War on the Thursday afternoon marked the turning point in the week's discussions. If this was not realised by the Western delegations at the time, it seems to have been fully appreciated by Stalin. Thereafter, having gained the concessions which were to enable him to dominate China, he proceeded to consolidate politically the strategic advantages his armies had already secured in Europe. Stalin was better able to press his demands now, for he could play upon the sense of gratitude and co-operation he had built up in the Americans, and to a lesser extent in the British, by his agreement to help in the defeat of Japan and the creation of the international security organisation. The remaining negotiations were to prove the truth of the warning which had been sent to Washington two months earlier by the Head of the American Military Mission in Moscow (General Deane), an astute and not unsympathetic observer of the Soviet scene. In a letter to Marshall in December Deane had written, "We never make a request or proposal to the Soviets that is not viewed with suspicion. They simply cannot understand giving without taking, and as a result even our giving is viewed with suspicion. Gratitude cannot be banked in the Soviet Union. Each transaction is complete in itself without regard to past favours."

When the discussions about Poland were continued, as they were at each session on the last four days, the Russians gained their way on almost every point. Nothing more was heard of the President's suggestion that Poland should keep the Lwow region. The Curzon Line was accepted and this fact was duly recorded in the Protocol. With regard to Poland's western frontier, however, Stalin did not press for the formal recognition of a specific line, since he realised that neither Roosevelt nor Churchill were prepared to go beyond the Oder. He readily consented to the suggestion that "the final delimitation of the western frontier should await the Peace Conference," for in the meantime that left him free to make his own arrangements about the German territory between the Oder and the Neisse.

The negotiations about the future government of Poland were very much more protracted and involved. The essence of the argument was that the Western Powers advocated the formation of an entirely new administration representing "all democratic and anti-Fascist forces," whereas the Russians proposed merely to enlarge the Lublin Committee, and to do this in such a way that the Polish Communists could retain control. Churchill and Eden fought for four days against this proposal, insisting that Great Britain could not withdraw her recognition of the London Government unless there was "a completely new start . . . on both sides on equal terms." The British also demanded that the new government should be provisional and should be pledged to hold "free and unfettered elections as soon as possible on the basis of universal suffrage and secret ballot," and that these elections should be conducted under the supervision of the American, British and Soviet Ambassadors.

The Russians consented to the holding of free elections and Molotov told Roosevelt that these could be held "within a month." On the other hand, he bluntly rejected the supervision proposal, arguing that this would be "an affront to the pride and sovereignty of the independent people"! Eden endeavoured to insist on this safeguard, for he feared that any unsupervised elections would be a mockery, but at the final meeting of the Foreign Ministers Stettinius announced that "the President was anxious to reach agreement and that to expedite matters he was willing to make this concession." With regard to the setting up of a new administration, the three Ministers eventually decided upon a compromise formula which read: "The Provisional Government which is now functioning in Poland should be reorganised on a broader democratic basis with the inclusion of democratic leaders from Poland itself and from Poles abroad." To this end various Polish leaders from all non-Fascist parties were to be brought together in Moscow for consultations with Molotov and the British and American Ambassadors.

When this formula was adopted at the plenary session on February 10th the Western delegates, with few exceptions, believed that they had reached, as Sherwood says, "an honourable and equitable solution." They were acting in good faith and they presumed that Stalin was equally sincere, for he also set his hand to a "Declaration on Liberated Europe" which reaffirmed the principles of the Atlantic Charter. By this Declaration the three Powers bound themselves "to build . . . a world order under law, dedicated to peace, security and freedom and the general well-being of all mankind," and agreed to act in concert "in assisting the peoples liberated from the dominion of Nazi Germany and the peoples of the former Axis satellite states of Europe . . . to create democratic institutions of their own choice."

These fine phrases were to prove less important than the terms of the Polish formula, which was so loosely worded that it left the Russians ample room to manœuvre. Roosevelt certainly entertained some doubts on this score, for he concurred when Leahy said to him, "Mr. President, this is so elastic that the Russians can stretch it all the way from Yalta to Washington without ever technically breaking it." The essential fact was that, while the British and Americans started by refusing to accord any recognition whatever to the Lublin Committee, they ended by allowing it to be described in the communiqué as "the present Provisional Government of Poland." Moreover, although they had originally insisted that an entirely fresh administration should be formed, they finally agreed to the words "the Provisional Government now functioning in Poland should be reorganised." The only real difference between that formula and what Stalin had initially demanded was a change in verb; "enlarged" had become "reorganised."

Having secured virtually all he wanted in Poland, Stalin made a conciliatory gesture with regard to the occupation of Germany. When the President announced that he now believed France should have a seat on the Control Commission as well as a zone of occupation, Stalin replied simply, "I agree." So far as he was concerned, this was a minor concession, for it did not require any material sacrifice on the part of the Soviet Union. Where her interests and assets were directly concerned, however, as in the matter of reparations, he was both stubborn and persistent. On the one hand, he refused altogether to discuss the Soviet Union's right to use German manpower; on the other, he demanded that a firm agreement should be reached at Yalta on the amount of "reparations in kind" that Germany should be required to pay. Again and again, one or other of the Soviet delegates returned to their original figure of "20 billion dollars" arguing that, if this amount were accepted as "a basis for discussion," it "would not commit the Allies to that exact sum."

The Americans were inclined to accept that assurance, especially when it was repeated by Stalin, and to allow the figure to be mentioned in the Protocol. On this question, however, the British were absolutely adamant. Eden pointed out that they could not tell what Germany could afford to pay until they had discovered how much of the German economy survived the bombing and the general destruction of war. The settlement of the actual amount should be left to the Reparations Commission, which they had agreed to create. The Yalta Protocol should merely lay down principles to guide the Commission and should state that, "In establishing the amount of reparations account should be taken of arrangements made for the partitioning of Germany, the requirements of the occupying forces and Germany's need from time to time to acquire sufficient foreign currency from her export trade to pay for current imports." The British wanted it expressly stated that "Germany's industrial capacity would not be reduced to a point which would endanger the economic existence of the country." Eden argued that the Russians could not expect Germany to make large annual payments out of current production over a period of ten years, if German manufacturing capacity were reduced to the extent the Soviet Union demanded. These two objectives, he declared, were irreconcilable, as indeed they were to prove to be. "The British objective," said Eden, with marked prescience, "is to avoid a situation in which as a result of reparations we will have to finance and feed Germany." The logic of Eden's arguments was overwhelming and both Roosevelt and Stettinius agreed with it, but they did not think that the Soviet figure was unreasonable and they were strongly moved by sympathy for the terrible sufferings of the Russian people.

At the penultimate plenary session Stalin spoke with great emotion of the vast and wanton destruction which the Germans had caused in Russia and pleaded for due compensation. Churchill read a telegram from the British War Cabinet protesting that reparations to the value of 20 billion dollars was far more than Germany could afford. It seemed that a deadlock had been reached. The Russians would not accept the British principles, and the British would not accept the Russian figure, not even as "a basis for discussion." Thereupon, Roosevelt suggested that the whole problem should be left to the Reparations Commission in Moscow. Churchill and Stalin agreed, but that was not the end of the matter.

During this session Hopkins scribbled a note to Roosevelt saying, "Mr. President, the Russians have given in so much at this Conference that I do not think we should let them down. Let the British disagree if they want to—and continue their disagreement at Moscow." That night at a dinner given by the Prime Minister, Stalin tackled Churchill again, saying that he did not like to have to go back to Moscow and tell the Soviet people that owing to British opposition they would not receive adequate reparations. The combined effect of Stalin's persistence and Hopkins's intervention was that when the Protocol was signed next morning it contained the statement that "the Soviet and American delegations agreed" that the Reparations Commission "should take in its initial studies as a basis for discussion the suggestion of the Soviet Government that the total sum should be 20 billion dollars and that 50 per cent of it should go to the U.S.S.R." The British view that "no figure should be mentioned" was also recorded, but this was of little account. The figure was there—however hedged around with qualifying phrases—and it was linked to the names of the Soviet Union and the United States.

Although the very persistence of the Russians on this point might well have served as a warning, it is doubtful whether any member of the Western delegations foresaw then that, in spite of Stalin's repeated assurances, the Russians would soon be claiming that to "take as a basis for discussion" meant to "accept in principle." From this it was a short step to the claim subsequently made by Molotov that "President Roosevelt had agreed at Yalta that Soviet reparations should total at least ten billion dollars."

On that final Sunday morning at Livadia Palace neither the Americans nor the British suspected that the public communiqué and the secret protocol, so solemnly signed and endorsed with such expressions of mutual trust and good-will, would soon be distorted and violated by their Soviet Allies, and that this process of distortion and violation would begin before the Prime Minister and the President had been able to report to their respective legislatures on the conference at which, they both asserted, the Great Powers were "more closely united than ever before."

In the House of Commons on February 27th, the Prime Minister declared: "The impression I brought back from the Crimea . . . is that Marshal Stalin and the Soviet leaders wish to live in honourable friendship and equality with the Western democracies. I feel also that their word is their bond. I decline abso-lutely to embark here on a discussion about Russian good faith." That evening in Bucharest—despite the Yalta Declaration on Liberated Europe—Molotov's deputy (Andrei Vishinsky) issued to King Michael a two-hour ultimatum, de-manding the dismissal of the Rumanian Prime Minister, General Radescu, the leader of an all-party Government.

Four days later, addressing a joint session of Congress, the President said: "The Crimea Conference . . . spells—and it ought to spell—the end of the system of unilateral action, exclusive alliances, and spheres of influence, and balances of power and all the other expedients which have been tried for centu-ries and have always failed. . . . I am sure that—under the agreement reached at Yalta—there will be a more stable political Europe than ever before." That evening in Bucharest, without any reference whatever to the Allied Control Commission, Vishinsky issued to King Michael a second ultimatum, demanding that he should appoint as Prime Minister Petru Groza, the leader of the Ru-manian Communists.

Power Realities at Yalta

FORREST C. POGUE

The State Department and military advisers who drew up the briefing papers and memoranda for President Roosevelt's use at Yalta and the officials who ac-companied him to the conference did not mislead him into making wrongful concessions to the Russians. On nearly every concession made at the Crimea conference State Department advisers were more anti-Russian than Roosevelt or Churchill. Secretary of State Stettinius and his staff stood firmly against the exaggerated Soviet demands and no one did more than Ambassador Harriman to warn the President against them. Papers written by Hiss before and during the Yalta conference opposed the Russian demand for unlimited veto power in the Security Council of the proposed U.N. and contested the Soviet claim to special representation in the U.N. It is clear from the Hiss notes on the con-

Forrest C. Pogue, "Yalta in Retrospect," in *The Meaning of Yalta,* ed. John L. Snell (Baton Rouge: Louisiana State University Press, 1956), pp. 188–208.

ference and from Charles Bohlen's [State Department adviser and translator at Yalta] testimony before the Senate Foreign Relations Committee in 1953 that Hiss's role was confined almost exclusively to United Nations questions. The published record of everything that Hiss wrote and said on the subject fully reflects a concern for safeguarding American interests. Roosevelt's final approval of the extra seats for the Russians took Hiss by surprise and found him saying a few minutes before the President's approval that the Americans had not agreed to the Russian request. It is an extreme and unfounded application of the principle of guilt by association to argue that Hiss's presence at Yalta and San Francisco in some way tainted those conferences with perjury and subversion.

Yet, concessions were made to the Russians at Yalta, and the most significant thus far have been those concerning the Far East. For a variety of reasons these Far East concessions have given rise to the most pronounced denunciations of the Yalta conference. Among these reasons are the following: (1) attacks against Yalta by a coalition of proponents of Chiang Kai-shek, opponents of Roosevelt and Marshall, and the champions of MacArthur, (2) an uninformed assumption that it was Yalta that caused the downfall of Chiang Kai-shek, (3) a general prejudice against "secret diplomacy" among the American people and the fact that the agreements were reached privately by Roosevelt and Stalin, (4) the weakening of American and Japanese defenses which the concessions represented, and (5) a conviction that Roosevelt had no moral right to grant Chinese territory to the Russians.

Bohlen's arguments that Churchill was not present at the discussions on the Far East because the United States was largely responsible for that theater of the war and that China was excluded because Russia was then unwilling to be connected openly with arrangements dealing with the Far East are cogent but not conclusive. The fact that the agreement was quickly reached regarding territory belonging to neither of the conferees is hard to reconcile with Wilsonian ideals of "open covenants openly arrived at" and with the spirit of the Atlantic Charter and the Cairo Declaration.

But the suggestion that Roosevelt's promise to seek Chiang Kai-shek's agreement to concessions in the Far East brought the downfall of Nationalist China has been effectively denied by Harriman and Bohlen, and is not borne out by the facts of twentieth-century Chinese development. The willingness of Chiang to carry out these concessions in return for Russian recognition of his government has already been noted. Arguments that the United States did not properly back Chiang Kai-shek against Mao Tse-tung and that Marshall and his advisers weakened the Nationalists in insisting on compromises with the Chinese Communists should not be charged against the negotiators at Yalta, whatever their foundation in fact. Actually, in 1945 the Generalissimo thought he had a good arrangement with Stalin and for a time after the war his armies seemed to be strongly situated in parts of northern China. Overextension of supply lines, failure to get firm possession of the liberated territory, overconfidence, poor leadership, inflation, refusal to reform Kuomintang corruption, failure to satisfy the land hunger of the Chinese peasant, and, above all, the failure of Stalin to keep his promises to Chiang Kai-shek are the chief explanations for the Nationalist debacle of 1946–50. Strategically, the grant of the Kuriles and Southern Sakhalin to a potential enemy of the United States was unsound. In case of a future war between the United States and the U.S.S.R. the American position would be definitely weakened. But few Americans thought of such a war in 1945.

The moral aspects of the concessions have worried liberal supporters of Roosevelt and angered his opponents. To those who had observed the spread of late nineteenth- and early twentieth-century imperialism, concessions to the Soviet Union at the expense of China smelled of an ancient evil. The names Dairen, Port Arthur, and the South Manchurian Railway reminded the West of the Treaty of Shimonoseki, the Russo-Japanese struggle for power in Korea and Manchuria in 1904–1905, and the steady march of Japan toward control of the Far East. The 1945 grant of concessions which the czar's representatives had once won from a defenseless China smacked of a return to the breakup of China. In the disillusionment which came after 1946 many people forgot that the territory Russia gained in 1945 had not been in China's control since 1905. Within a few weeks after the war ended, the Russians held the various ports and possessions which had been promised them, without the Nationalists ever being in contact with the territory involved. Later, Stalin returned part of these areas to the technical control of the Chinese Communists, who in turn made concessions to the Russians.

Despite these extenuating arguments, and the explanations presented earlier, there is no real defense on *moral* grounds of the Far Eastern concessions to the Soviet Union. It is the one point at which Roosevelt openly went back to the type of arrangement which he and other western leaders had previously condemned. Morality and reality were in conflict; reality won. Defenders of the Far Eastern concessions can only justify them in terms of (1) the need of Russian aid against Japan to shorten the war in the Far East and save American lives, or (2) the need to prolong wartime co-operation with the U.S.S.R. into the postwar era.

Many critics of the Yalta conference have insisted that Russian participation was not needed. One group points to possession of the A-bomb and overwhelming naval and air superiority in the Pacific to prove that the United States at the beginning of February, 1945, needed no assistance to defeat Japan.

Major General Leslie R. Groves, military head of the atomic bomb project, at the end of December, 1944, notified General Marshall, Secretary Stimson, and President Roosevelt that one atomic bomb, possessing enormous destructive power, would be ready for use about the first of August, 1945, that one more would be ready toward the end of 1945, and that others would follow, apparently at shortened intervals thereafter. Colonel William S. Considine, who was assigned to the Manhattan atomic project in 1944–45, testified in 1951 that he informed Secretary Stettinius at Yalta that a successful bomb would in fact be constructed, that it would be ready about the first of August, and that such a bomb would wreck a large-sized city. These facts might well have made the military and political advisers of the President far more sanguine about their prospects of an early victory than they were. However, in the absence of an actual explosion of a bomb, there was some ground for military advisers, who had to fight until the end of the year with one bomb, to proceed on the basis that the bomb would be a bonus and not the weapon which would bring early victory.

Furthermore, the military advisers of the President were less positive concerning the value of the A-bomb than was the head of the Manhattan project. Of these the least hopeful was Admiral Leahy, Chief of Staff to the President. Leahy has frankly admitted that although General Groves in September, 1944, had made the most convincing report on the possibilities of the atomic bomb he had heard up until that time, he still did not have "much confidence in the practicability of the project." Less than a week before the actual dropping of the bomb on Hiroshima, Leahy told King George VI that he did not think it would be as effective as expected. "It sounds," he added, "like a professor's dream to me." President Truman in his memoirs has confirmed the admiral's skepticism on the subject. So far as Leahy was concerned, the development of the bomb did not affect the question of Russian aid one way or the other. His faith in 1944 and in 1945 lay in the navy; he was convinced that the fleet could defeat the Japanese without ground force help.

Fleet Admiral Ernest J. King has written that he, Leahy, Fleet Admiral Chester W. Nimitz, and other naval officers felt that the defeat of Japan could have been accomplished by sea and air power alone, without the necessity of the actual invasion of the Japanese home islands by ground forces. According to King, he and Leahy reluctantly acquiesced in the decision to attack the home islands, feeling "that in the end sea power would accomplish the defeat of Japan." Yet, on June 21, 1951, Admiral King wrote Senator William Knowland that at the time of the Yalta conference he was "agreeable" to the entry of the U.S.S.R. into the war against Japan. "Our contention," he continued, "was that blockade and bombardment could bring about Japanese capitulation, and that in connection with this course of action, engagement of the Japanese armies in Manchuria would hasten that capitulation." This throws great light on the Far Eastern concessions. No one doubted at Yalta that the Japanese would be ultimately defeated, nor that a blockade might gradually starve the Japanese islands into submission. But Americans in the spring of 1945 had no desire to leave millions of soldiers, sailors, and airmen under arms, waiting for the ultimate surrender of the Japanese, eighteen months or more in the future.

Some critics have declared that air intelligence experts knew that Japan was finished and that if General Henry H. Arnold had been well enough to attend the Yalta conference, he could have made the President aware of this fact and thus have prevented concessions to Stalin. Such a statement apparently assumes that the air force was then engaged in massive operations of such a type that air bombardment could have ended the war in the Pacific quickly without ground action. This hopeful thesis has been refuted by the arguments of General Laurence S. Kuter, who represented General Arnold at Yalta:

By March 9, 1945, only 22 small-scale B-29 strikes had been flown against Japan from the Marianas. Although the size of these strikes was steadily growing, the average number of airplanes to reach Japan from the Marianas at the time of the Yalta conference was eighty. The Yalta conference ended exactly one month before the first of the effective medium-altitude fire-bomb strikes on Japanese cities had been delivered. . . . It was sixty-five days before the first five-hundred-airplane strike could be delivered. . . .

The bad reputation now attached to Yalta, Kuter concluded in 1955, has arisen from subsequent political experience with Russia, and "to some extent from misinformation generated by partisan oratory and nourished by shaky memories."

While it was believed that American naval and air forces had gained superiority in the Pacific by February, 1945, military planners forecast that the war against Japan would likely last eighteen months after the defeat of Germany, with possible casualties, according to Secretary of War Stimson, of at least 500,000 and possibly as many as a million men. The first months of the 1945 campaigns had produced constantly mounting totals of dead and wounded. . . . Casualties at Iwo Jima and Okinawa confirmed the trend. In the spring General MacArthur himself favored Russian action in support of his offensives against the Japanese home islands. This notwithstanding, in October, 1955, General MacArthur declared that he was not consulted about concessions to the Russians and that he considered them fantastic. This argument is irrelevant. It is not the responsibility of the soldier to make political arrangements; rather it is to state what is necessary to accomplish his mission. MacArthur had only to notify Marshall of his needs, and the Chief of Staff had only to inform Roosevelt of army requirements in the Pacific. After that it was the President's duty to provide that aid on the best terms he could obtain. Had he refused to seek Soviet aid against Japan, he would almost certainly have been criticized by military commanders in 1945 instead of after his death.

It is interesting to note two contemporary reactions of Pacific veterans to the August, 1945, entry of the Russians into the war. General Robert L. Eichelberger, commander of the Eighth Army, declared: "Whether Japan surrenders in the near future or decides to fight on in a suicide finish, the entrance of Russia into the Pacific War has hastened the end of World War II." And the way the common soldier felt was revealed by the comment of Sergeant Hubert Eldridge of Kentucky, who told reporters: "I've been in the army four and a half years. Maybe those bombs and those Russians will help me get out now." The hope of getting home alive and quickly, clearly expressed in this statement, was the collective wish of the American soldiers in the Pacific; and that wish was one of the political realities that shaped the Yalta agreements.

But the western Allies need not have promised the Russians anything, say the critics; Stalin would have fought Japan without concessions. Without Russian documents, one can not say positively what the Soviet Union would have done. Stalin had made a deal with an enemy in 1939; in 1945, he might conceivably have remained true to his 1941 treaty of neutrality with Japan, or even have converted it into a pact of alliance, if the Japanese had offered him concessions which he could not obtain from China with American help. Various roads were open to Stalin in the spring and summer of 1945. He might have made a deal with Japan in return for concessions in Manchuria and Korea; he might have remained neutral in the Far East until the United States suffered heavy casualties and then entered at peak strength into the Pacific war. Either of these policies would have enabled the Red Army to dominate Europe, while the United States and Britain withdrew their forces from Germany and Italy to the Pacific. Finally, Stalin might have attacked Japan without any agreement regarding the future terms of peace.

In view of the Russian ability to take what they wanted in 1945 without Allied agreement, in view of the additional aid the Allies needed in Europe and the Pacific, and in view of what Chiang Kai-shek was willing to give in August, 1945, for what he thought to be recognition by the Soviet government, one must conclude that the Far Eastern concessions at Yalta did not seem excessive in February, 1945. Even today it is difficult to avoid the conclusion that if Stalin had not received them from Roosevelt and Churchill he would have sought them—or even greater gains—from someone else or have taken them without Allied or Chinese consent. The terms of the Yalta agreements concerning the Far East were in the nature of a Roosevelt-Stalin contract and constituted not only concessions to Stalin but also restraining limitations. It was not Roosevelt's fault that Stalin later broke the contract.

"It is a mistake," wrote Winston Churchill to Foreign Secretary Eden one month before the Yalta conference, "to try to write out on little pieces of paper what the vast emotions of an outraged and quivering world will be either immediately after the struggle is over or when the inevitable cold fit follows the hot." "These awe-inspiring tides of feeling," he added, "dominate most people's minds, and independent figures tend to become not only lonely but futile." The Prime Minister, with the prescience he so often showed, in these words pointed clearly to the problems which faced the Allies when they came to talk of the final victory and the beginnings of peace. The thirst for vengeance, the rapidly shifting desires of the public, and the unique difficulties of the democratic leader were thus graphically stated.

Churchill was aware that a responsible leader cannot escape the consequences of his acts. To mobilize the full support of the British and American people for war against Germany and Japan, he and Roosevelt had encouraged strong feelings against the aggressors. In order to maximize the war effort against the Axis states, Roosevelt and Churchill had often followed the rule of expediency in their dealings with the Soviet Union and other associated powers. Both leaders, perhaps mindful of the sneers of critics in the twenties at Wilson's World War I idealism, had tended to make their pleas at the level of self-preservation. Public demands for stern justice had been both acknowledged and spurred by the 1943 demand, which was never withdrawn, for unconditional surrender. At Yalta the free world still wanted punishment and reparation for Lidice, Rotterdam, Coventry, Nanking, Shanghai, Bataan, and Pearl Harbor. The story of the Malmedy massacre was still being circulated to troops in the field in Europe at the time of the Crimea conference. The full horrors of Buchenwald and Dachau were not yet known, but their stench was abroad.

Criticism of the actions of the Big Three at Yalta thus becomes in part an indictment of long-established Western assumptions about popular democracy. Roosevelt and Churchill were restricted in their actions at Yalta by the patterns of thought and action which their people demanded and which they themselves had laid down. As practical political leaders, they dared not go too far beyond what their followers would accept. One finds both a partial criticism and a partial explanation of the Yalta negotiations in one of the main theses of Walter Lippmann's thoughtful book, *Essays in the Public Philosophy.* "When the world wars came," Lippmann has written, "the people of the liberal democracies could not be aroused to the exertions and sacrifices of the struggle until they had been frightened by the opening disasters, had been incited to passionate hatred, and had become intoxicated with unlimited hope." The enemy had to be portrayed as evil incarnate, and the people told that when this particular opponent had been forced to unconditional surrender, "they would re-enter the golden age." Lippmann contends that the people of the western democracies have shown a compulsion to error which arises out of a time lag in democratic opinion and have compelled their governments "to be too late with too little, or too long with too much, too pacifist in peace and too bellicose in war, too neutralist or appeasing in negotiation or too intransigent."

The meaning of Yalta cannot be grasped unless the conditions under which the conference leaders worked are remembered. In February, 1945, the Allied peoples generally agreed that Germany and Japan must be severely punished and cured of aggressive tendencies. Agreement was widespread that Germany and Japan must be effectively disarmed and their heavy industries restricted in order to prevent them from making war in the future. The western powers generally acknowledged that the U.S.S.R. had suffered terribly in the war and should receive compensation from the common enemies. Thoughts of the postwar era were pervaded by a desire to counterbalance the power of Germany and Japan by the force of the "world policemen" who had co-operated to win the war. Roosevelt certainly hoped, and probably believed until the last weeks before his death, that he could sit down at a table with Stalin and Churchill and work out solutions to the problems of the world. The Big Three tended, as a result, to give smaller states little opportunity to shape their own futures. The President strongly believed that Soviet expansive tendencies would be allayed when the U.S.S.R. won security on its European and Asian frontiers.

Other assumptions likewise encouraged Roosevelt to overestimate the possibilities of postwar co-operation with the Soviet Union. Knowledge that Russia had been severely damaged in the early years of the war with Germany led him to surmise that the U.S.S.R. might require a generation to recover. Some Washington officials believed that the Soviet Union would be dependent upon postwar economic aid for her recovery, and that for this reason Stalin could be counted upon to maintain good relations with the United States. In short, one must remember both the war-born opportunism and the hopes and fears of 1945: concessions which would shorten the war and save lives would be acceptable to the people of the West; the formation of a workable United Nations organization held hope for the correction of any basic errors which might have been made in the various peace arrangements; and, more realistically, it was feared that the Soviet Union might become the center of opposition to the West unless bound as closely as possible to its wartime allies.

All these factors powerfully asserted themselves when the Big Three met in the Crimean palace of the czar in February, 1945. But yet another factor loomed large in the conference at Yalta. The disintegration of Germany meant that the force which had dominated central Europe since 1938 was gone and that its place in central-eastern Europe would be taken by the Soviet Union. A disarmed Italy and a weakened France could not be expected to balance the enormous power of the Red Army. Britain, seriously drained of her capital wealth by the heavy exactions of the war and lacking the manpower reserves to challenge a potential enemy of Russia's strength, could not hope to redress the balance of Europe as she had for two centuries. The people of the United States viewed their exertions in Europe as temporary and hoped for their early termination; they were in no state of psychological readiness to take up Britain's traditional role. The approaching defeat of Japan threatened to create a power vacuum in the Far East like that which Hitler's defeat would leave in Europe. Thus concessions at Yalta inevitably reflected the powerful position of the Soviet Union in Europe and its potential power in the Far East. Personal diplomacy at Yalta came to grips with the basic realities of a new balance of power in the world at large, and the freedom of action of the individual statesman was greatly restricted by these impersonal forces. Therein lies the overriding fact about the conference; without its comprehension, the meaning of Yalta is sure to be missed.

FURTHER READING

James M. Burns, *Roosevelt: The Soldier of Freedom* (1970)
Winston Churchill, *Triumph and Tragedy* (1953)
Diane Shaver Clemens, *Yalta* (1970)
Herbert Feis, *Churchill, Roosevelt, Stalin* (1957)
Gabriel Kolko, *The Politics of War* (1968)
William H. McNeill, *America, Britain, and Russia* (1953)
William L. Neumann, *After Victory* (1967)
Robert E. Sherwood, *Roosevelt and Hopkins* (1948)
Gaddis Smith, *American Diplomacy During the Second World War* (1965)
John L. Snell, *Illusion or Necessity* (1963)
Athan G. Theoharis, *The Yalta Myths: An Issue in U.S. Politics, 1945–1950* (1970)

8

The Atomic Bomb and Diplomacy

In August 1945 American aircraft dropped atomic bombs on the Japanese cities of Hiroshima and Nagasaki, killing over 100,000 people and injuring many more. Japan soon sued for peace and World War II ended. Ever since President Harry S. Truman made the fateful decision to unleash atomic weapons on Japan, contemporaries and historians have debated the morality, necessity, and consequences of the choice.

Truman said he authorized the use of the atomic bombs on populated areas because that was the only way to shorten the war and save American lives. Until the 1960s most historians accepted that conclusion. But recent scholarship, although not denying the argument that American lives would have been spared, has suggested that other considerations also influenced American leaders: relations with Soviet Russia, emotional revenge, momentum, and perhaps racism. Scholars today are also debating why several alternatives to military use of the bomb were not tried.

DOCUMENTS

In early May 1945, Secretary of War Henry L. Stimson appointed an Interim Committee, with himself as chairman, to advise on atomic energy and the uranium bombs the Manhattan Engineering District project was about to produce. In the committee's meeting of May 31, 1945, the decision was made to keep the bomb project a secret from the Russians and to use the atomic bomb against Japan. On June 11, 1945, a group of atomic scientists in Chicago, headed by Jerome Franck, futilely petitioned Stimson for a non-combat demonstration of the bomb in order to improve the chances for postwar international control of atomic weapons. The recommendations of the Interim Committee and the Franck Committee are reprinted here.

The Interim Committee on Military Use, 1945

Secretary Stimson explained that the Interim Committee had been appointed by him, with the approval of the President, to make recommendations on temporary war-time controls, public announcement, legislation and post-war organization. . . . He expressed the hope that the [four] scientists would feel completely free to express their views on any phase of the subject. . . .

The Secretary explained that General Marshall shared responsibility with him for making recommendations to the President on this project with particular reference to its military aspects; therefore, it was considered highly desirable that General Marshall be present at this meeting to secure at first hand the views of the scientists.

The Secretary expressed the view, a view shared by General Marshall, that this project should not be considered simply in terms of military weapons, but as a new relationship of man to the universe. This discovery might be compared to the discoveries of the Copernican theory and of the laws of gravity, but far more important than these in its effect on the lives of men. While the advances in the field to date had been fostered by the needs of war, it was important to realize that the implications of the project went far beyond the needs of the present war. It must be controlled if possible to make it an assurance of future peace rather than a menace to civilization.

The Secretary suggested that he hoped to have the following questions discussed during the course of the meeting:

1. Future military weapons
2. Future international competition
3. Future research
4. Future controls
5. Future developments, particularly non-military.

At this point *General Marshall* discussed at some length the story of charges and counter-charges that have been typical of our relations with the Russians, pointing out that most of these allegations have proven unfounded. The seemingly uncooperative attitude of Russia in military matters stemmed from the necessity of maintaining security. He said that he had accepted this reason for their attitude in his dealings with the Russians and had acted accordingly. As to the post-war situation and in matters other than purely military, he felt that he was in no position to express a view. With regard to this field he was inclined to favor the building up of a combination among like-minded powers, thereby forcing Russia to fall in line by the very force of this coalition. General Marshall was certain that we need have no fear that the Russians, if they had knowledge of our project, would disclose this information to the Japanese. He raised the question whether it might be desirable to invite two prominent Russian scientists to witness the test.

Mr. Byrnes expressed a fear that if information were given to the Russians, even in general terms, Stalin would ask to be brought into the partnership. He felt this to be particularly likely in view of our commitments and pledges of co-operation with the British. In this connection *Dr. Bush* pointed out that even the British do not have any of our blue prints on plants. *Mr. Byrnes* expressed the view, *which was generally agreed to by all present,* that the most desirable program would be to push ahead as fast as possible in production and research to make certain that we stay ahead and at the same time make every effort to better our political relations with Russia.

It was pointed out that one atomic bomb on an arsenal would not be much different from the effect caused by any Air Corps strike of present dimensions. However, *Dr. Oppenheimer* stated that the visual effect of an atomic bombing would be tremendous. It would be accompanied by a brilliant luminescence which would rise to a height of 10,000 to 20,000 feet. The neutron effect of the explosion would be dangerous to life for a radius of at least two-thirds of a mile.

After much discussion concerning various types of targets and the effects to be produced, *the Secretary expressed the conclusion, on which there was general agreement, that we could not give the Japanese any warning; that we could not concentrate on a civilian area; but that we should seek to make a profound psychological impression on as many of the inhabitants as possible. At the suggestion of Dr. Conant the Secretary agreed that the most desirable target would be a vital war plant employing a large number of workers and closely surrounded by workers' houses.*

There was some discussion of the desirability of attempting several strikes at the same time. *Dr. Oppenheimer's* judgment was that several strikes would be feasible. *General Groves,* however, expressed doubt about this proposal and pointed out the following objections: (1) We would lose the advantage of gaining additional knowledge concerning the weapon at each successive bombing; (2) such a program would require a rush job on the part of those assembling the bombs and might, therefore, be ineffective; (3) the effect would not be sufficiently distinct from our regular Air Force bombing program.

The Franck Committee on a
Non-Combat Demonstration, 1945

The way in which the nuclear weapons, now secretly developed in this country, will first be revealed to the world appears of great, perhaps fateful importance.

One possible way—which may particularly appeal to those who consider the nuclear bombs primarily as a secret weapon developed to help win the present war—is to use it without warning on an appropriately selected object in Japan. It is doubtful whether the first available bombs, of comparatively low efficiency and small size, will be sufficient to break the will or ability of Japan to resist, especially given the fact that the major cities like Tokyo, Nagoya, Osaka and Kobo already will largely be reduced to ashes by the slower process of ordinary aerial bombing. Certain and perhaps important tactical results undoubtedly can be achieved, but we nevertheless think that the question of the use of the very first available atomic bombs in the Japanese war should be weighed very carefully, not only by military authority, but by the highest political leadership of this country. If we consider international agreement on total prevention of nuclear warfare as the paramount objective, and believe that it can be achieved, this kind of introduction of atomic weapons to the world may easily destroy all our chances of success. Russia, and even allied countries which bear less mistrust of our ways and intentions, as well as neutral countries, will be deeply shocked. It will be very difficult to persuade the world that a nation which was capable of secretly preparing and suddenly releasing a weapon, as indiscriminate as the rocket bomb and a thousand times more destructive, is to be trusted in its proclaimed desire of having such weapons abolished by international agreement. We have large accumulations of poison gas, but do not use them, and recent polls have shown that public opinion in this country would disapprove of such a use even if it would accelerate the winning of the Far Eastern war. It is true, that some irrational element in mass psychology makes gas poisoning more revolting than blasting by explosives, even though gas warfare is in no way more "inhuman" than the war of bombs and bullets. Nevertheless, it is not at all certain that the American public opinion, if it could be enlightened as to the effect of atomic explosives, would support the first introduction by our own country of such an indiscriminate method of wholesale destruction of civilian life.

Thus, from the "optimistic" point of view—looking forward to an international agreement on prevention of nuclear warfare—the military advantages and the saving of American lives, achieved by the sudden use of atomic bombs against Japan, may be outweighed by the ensuing loss of confidence and wave of horror and repulsion, sweeping over the rest of the world, and perhaps dividing even the public opinion at home.

From this point of view a demonstration of the new weapon may best be made before the eyes of representatives of all United Nations, on the desert or a barren island. The best possible atmosphere for the achievement of an international agreement could be achieved if America would be able to say to the world, "You see what weapon we had but did not use. We are ready to renounce its use in the future and to join other nations in working out adequate supervision of the use of this nuclear weapon."

This may sound fantastic, but then in nuclear weapons we have something entirely new in the order of magnitude of destructive power, and if we want to capitalize fully on the advantage which its possession gives us, we must use new and imaginative methods. After such a demonstration the weapon could be used against Japan if a sanction of the United Nations (and of the public opinion at home) could be obtained, perhaps after a preliminary ultimatum to Japan to surrender or at least to evacuate a certain region as an alternative to the total destruction of this target.

It must be stressed that if one takes a pessimistic point of view and discounts the possibilities of an effective international control of nuclear weapons, then the advisability of an early use of nuclear bombs against Japan becomes even more doubtful—quite independently of any humanitarian considerations. If no international agreement is concluded immediately after the first demonstration, this will mean a flying start of an unlimited armaments race. If this race is inevitable, we have all reason to delay its beginning as long as possible in order to increase our headstart still further. . . . The benefit to the nation, and the saving of American lives in the future, achieved by renouncing an early demonstration of nuclear bombs and letting the other nations come into the race only reluctantly, on the basis of guesswork and without definite knowledge that the "thing does work," may far outweigh the advantages to be gained by the immediate use of the first and comparatively inefficient bombs in the war against Japan. At the least, pros and cons of this use must be carefully weighed by the supreme political and military leadership of the country, and the decision should not be left to considerations, merely, of military tactics.

One may point out that scientists themselves have initiated the development of this "secret weapon" and it is therefore strange that they should be reluctant to try it out on the enemy as soon as it is available. The answer to this question was given above—the compelling reason for creating this weapon with such speed was our fear that Germany had the technical skill necessary to develop such a weapon without any moral restraints regarding its use.

Another argument which could be quoted in favor of using atomic bombs as soon as they are available is that so much taxpayers' money has been invested in those projects that the Congress and the American public will require a return for their money. The above-mentioned attitude of the American public opinion in the question of the use of poison gas against Japan shows that one can expect it to understand that a weapon can sometimes be made ready only for use in extreme emergency; and as soon as the potentialities of nuclear weapons will be revealed to the American people, one can be certain that it will support all attempts to make the use of such weapons impossible.

ESSAYS

In his essay, Herbert Feis defends the decision to drop the atomic bombs on Japan with the traditional argument that leaders at the time had to be concerned primarily about saving American lives. He discounts the suggestion that the decision was made to achieve diplomatic advantage vis-à-vis Russia. Barton J. Bernstein of Stanford University surveys in detail the thinking of the Roosevelt and Truman administrations about the atomic bomb. Although he agrees that Truman hoped to save American lives, he argues that the bomb provided the United States with a "diplomatic bonus," an opportunity to bargain more forcefully with the Russians in order to gain concessions on international issues. Both authors explain why contemporaries ruled out alternative policies to military use of the bomb.

A Military Necessity

HERBERT FEIS

At the time of the event, only some contributing scientists protested the use of the atomic bomb against a vulnerable live target. The peoples fighting Japan looked upon its employment against the enemy as a natural act of war, and rejoiced at the swift ending it brought about. Any qualms they might have had over the cruel suffering of the victims were routed by the thought that if Germans or Japanese had developed this weapon they would surely have used it. Subsequently, however, as the blast and radiation effects of this new projectile were more fully appreciated, and as more and more powerful kinds were spawned, the precedent act has been regarded by many with rue.

Whether, if the United States had pledged itself as soon as the war ended to destroy the other bombs it had and dismantle the factories in which they were made other countries would have been willing to join with it in a trustworthy system of control of atomic energy, must remain forever a provocation to the speculative historian. But most probably the dismal failure to reach any restraining agreement was an inexpungable accompaniment to the suspicions, animosities, fears and hatred that have been so rampant after the war. Unable to arrive at genuine peace with each other through mutual good will, respect and understanding, they live under the common canopy of mutual terror. Little wonder then that foreboding dominates the memory of the laboratory triumphs of the physicists, the achievements of the engineers, the test at Alamogordo and the display at Hiroshima.

In the evolving discussion about the decision to use the bomb, several related but separable questions have been commingled. One of these, and by far the easiest to answer conclusively, is whether it was *essential* to do so in order to compel Japan to surrender on our terms before it was invaded.

Some of the decision-makers were confident that the invasion of the main islands of Japan would not be necessary to compel surrender quickly and unconditionally. Japan's ability to fend off our tremendous naval and air assaults was shattered. It seemed to them that the Japanese people, crowded in their small islands, with insufficient and destructible supplies of food and oil, would have to give in soon—unless bent on national suicide. Among those were Secretary of the Navy Forrestal and Under Secretary Bard and Admiral Leahy and General Spaatz, the Commander of our Strategic Air Force.

But others, especially those in the Army, remained convinced that final victory on our own terms could only be achieved on land, as it had been in the Philippines, Iwo Jima, Okinawa. Had not their military histories taught them that a hopelessly beaten Confederate Army had battled on? Had they not witnessed the refusal of the Germans under the fanatic Hitler to give up long after any chance of winning was gone, and how that people rallied from the shattering air attacks on their cities? Would the war in Europe continue many months longer, they argued, except for the combined crushing assaults of large land armies from the East, the West, the South?

To the historian, taught by the accumulated records and testimony, the answer is obvious. There cannot be a well-grounded dissent from the conclusion reached as early as 1945 by members of the U.S. Strategic Bombing Survey. After inspection of the condition to which Japan was reduced, by studies of the military position and the trend of Japanese popular and official opinion, they estimated ". . . that certainly prior to 31 December 1945, and in all probability prior to 1 November 1945, Japan would have surrendered even if the atomic bombs had not been dropped, even if Russia had not entered the war, and even if no invasion had been planned or contemplated."

If then the use of the bomb was not essential, was it justified—justified, that is, as the surest way in combination with other measures to bring about the earliest surrender? That is a harder question to answer, and a more troubling one than it was thought to be at the time of decision.

It may be contended with the grim support by history that no exceptional justification for the use of the bomb need be sought or given. For the prevalent rule of nations—except when "knighthood was in flower"—has allowed the use of any and all weapons in war except any banned by explicit agreement; and this was the prevailing view at the time, qualified only by revulsion against use of weapons and methods deemed needlessly inhumane such as poisoning of wells and torture. Did not, it should be borne in mind, every one of the contending nations strive its utmost to invent and produce more deadly weapons, faster planes of greater bomb capacity, new types of mines, rockets and buzz-bombs? And was not each and every improved sort of killing weapon brought into action without ado or reproach? For this reason alone, almost all professional military men, and those in uniform in 1945, would then have denied that any special justification for the use of the bomb was needed, and would still dispose of the subject in this way.

The more thoughtful might add that the decision to use the bomb was not really important; that the measures of permanent significance to mankind had been taken when physicists learned how to split the atom, and when scientists and engineers and builders succeeded in encasing the energy of the fissured atom in a bomb; and that after these were achieved, it made little or no difference if this novel weapon was used against Japan, since it would certainly be used in the future time unless nations renounced war. Or if it were not, other equally dreadful threats would remain; chemical and biological ways of bringing death; and these were already in the secret arsenals of nations.

The source of restraint lies in fear of consequences; fear of the fact that the enemy will use the same terrible weapon. This was, for example, why neither side used poison gas in the war. When humane feeling is allied to such fear, it may command respect, and even those striving to win a war may recognize that "virtue it is to abstain even from that which is lawful."

These considerations seem to me conclusive defenses of our right, legal and historical, for the use of the atomic bomb against Japan. Those who made the decision took them for granted. They thus felt free to make it without scruples on these scores.

Their reckoning, I believe the record clearly indicates, was governed by one reason deemed paramount: that by using the bomb the agony of war might be ended most quickly and lives be saved. It was believed with deep apprehension that many thousands, probably tens of thousands, of lives of Allied combatants would have to be spent in the continuation of our air and sea bombardment and blockade, victims mainly of Japanese suicide planes. In spite of its confidence in ultimate success, our assailant naval force felt vulnerable, because of grim and agonizing experience. Since the desperate kamikaze attacks began, suicide planes had sunk 34 American ships, including 3 aircraft carriers, and damaged 285 (including 36 carriers of all sizes and sorts, 15 battleships, 15 cruisers and 87 destroyers). During the Okinawa campaign alone, 16 of our ships had been sunk and 185 damaged (including 7 carriers, 10 battleships and 5 cruisers).

It was reliably known that the Japanese were assembling thousands of planes, of all kinds and conditions, to fling against the invasion fleet and the troop-carrying ships. Thus, should it prove necessary to carry out the plans for invasion, not only of Kyushu but also of the Tokyo Plain, it was feared by Stimson and Marshall that the American casualties alone might mount to hundreds of thousands. Our allies, it was reckoned, would suffer corresponding losses.

But the people who would have suffered most, had the war gone on much longer and their country been invaded, were the Japanese. One American incendiary air raid on the Tokyo area in March 1945 did more damage and killed and injured more Japanese than the bomb on Hiroshima. Even greater groups of American bombing planes would have hovered over Japan, consuming the land, its people and its food, with blast and fire, leaving them no place to hide, no chance to rest, no hope of reprieve. A glance at the chart kept in the Headquarters of the U.S. Strategic Air Force at Guam, with its steeply ascending record of bombing flights during the summer of 1945 and scheduled for the next month or two, leaves visions of horror of which Hiroshima is only a local illustration. Observation of the plight of the country and its people made soon after the war ended left me appalled at what those would have had to endure had the war gone on.

But the same official forecasts of what it was thought would occur if we had to fight on, gave sharper shape to the impelling reason for the development of the bomb—to end the war victoriously. Thus the decision to use the bomb seemed to be the natural culminating act for the achievement of a settled purpose as attested by its leading sponsors:

General Groves: "My mission as given to me by Secretary of War Stimson [in October 1942] was to produce this [the atomic bomb] at the earliest possible date so as to bring the war to a conclusion."

Truman: "I regarded the bomb as a military weapon and never had any doubt that it should be used."

Churchill: "The historic fact remains . . . that the decision whether or not to use the atomic bomb to compel the surrender of Japan was never even an issue. There was unanimous, automatic, unquestioned agreement around our table; nor did I ever hear the slightest suggestion that we should do otherwise."

Stimson: "Stimson believed, both at the time and later, that the dominant fact of 1945 was war, and that therefore, necessarily, the dominant objective was victory. If victory could be speeded by using the bomb, it should be used; if victory must be delayed in order to use the bomb, it should *not* be used. So far as he knew, this general view was fully shared by the President and all his associates."

Some of those men who concurred in the decision to use the bomb discerned other advantages and justifications. It is likely that Churchill, and probably also Truman, conceived that besides bringing the war to a quick end, it would improve the chances of arranging a satisfactory peace both in Europe and in the Far East. Stimson and Byrnes certainly had that thought in mind. For would not the same dramatic proof of western power that shocked Japan into surrender impress the Russians also? Might it not influence them to be more restrained? Might it not make more effective the resistance of the western allies to excessive Soviet pretensions and ventures, such as the Soviet bid for a military base in the Black Sea Straits, and a foreseen demand for a part in the occupation and control of Japan akin to that which it had in Germany? In short, the bomb, it may have been thought or hoped, would not only subdue the Japanese aggressors, but perhaps also monitor Russian behavior.

Recognition of this element in official thinking must not be distorted into an accusation that the American government engaged in what Soviet propagandists and historians have called "atomic blackmail." To the contrary, even after the American government knew that it would have the supreme weapon, it keenly sought to preserve the friendly connection with the Soviet Union. It rebuffed Churchill's proposals that the Western allies face down the Soviet government in some climactic confrontation over the outward thrust of Soviet power. After the testing of the bomb, at the Potsdam Conference, it patiently sought compromise solutions for situations in dispute. While knowledge of the successful test may have somewhat stiffened Truman's resistance to some of the furthest-reaching Soviet wishes, it did not cause him to alter American aims or terms as previously defined. In brief, and obviously, the men who determined American policy strove to achieve a stable international order by peaceful ways. They were not swayed by an excited wish to impose our will on the rest of the world by keeping atomic bombs poised over their lives. Even as the American government proceeded to use the bomb against Japan, it was brewing proposals for controlling its production and banning its use, except possibly as an international measure to enforce peace.

Had—the query continues to haunt the historian—the American government, *before* using the bomb, informed Stalin candidly of its nature and potential, and solicited his cooperation in some system of international control, might the Soviet government have reacted differently? Might it have been deflected from making the utmost effort to master the task of producing like weapons and accumulating them as a national atomic force. It is highly improbable, I think, considering Stalin's determination, as evidenced at Potsdam, to wear down Western resistance to Soviet claims, his suspicions and soaring assurance, and his belief that nations respected only strength. It would have been like him, in fact, to regard our confidential briefing as a subtle way of threatening the Soviet government, of trying to frighten it to accede to our wishes.

My best surmise is that while openness would have disarmed some foreign critics and improved the reception abroad of our later proposals for control, it would not really have influenced the Soviet policy. Nevertheless, it is regrettable that we did not take Stalin into at least the outer regions of our confidence, thereby indicating to the world that we were not intent on keeping unto ourselves a secret means of domination. After all, our secrecy and our elaborate security measures in the end were ineffectual and suffused the atmosphere with the scent of enmity.

This train of inference about other reasons for using the bomb—confluent with the wish to end the war quickly and with minimum loss of life—that may also have figured in the minds of those who made the decision, can be carried further. The scientists who served on the Scientific Panel . . . were gravely aware of the lasting and supreme significance of the achievement. Stimson, sharing their perception of its bearing upon human destiny, was impelled, despite age and fatigue, to write memo after memo expounding his conviction that every effort must be exerted to get the nations to cooperate to prevent impending mutual destruction.

These official parents of this new form of force verged toward the conclusion that it would confront the whole world with a crucial and ultimate choice: to renounce war or perish. But would the nations defer to that reality unless the horrifying power of this new weapon to destroy human life was proven by human sacrifice? Would they realize otherwise that it was imperative that they subordinate themselves to the new international security organization that had just been created in San Francisco? Would they submit to the necessary restraints unless convinced that if they did not, they would all be consumed together in the vengeful bursts of atomic explosions? Thus, even men genuinely regretful about the deaths and suffering that would be caused by the use of the bomb, could think of the act as an essential step toward the creation of a peaceful political order. And connectedly, that undeniable proof of the destructive power of atomic energy would foster a willingness to subject its development to the collectivity of nations; for unless it was so controlled, any one country with a great atomic force could defy the rest.

As recounted, there were those who believed all these purposes would be better served if the bomb was introduced in some other way. They urged that before using it against Japan its immense destructive power should be displayed to the world by dropping it in some remote, uninhabited or emptied spot—an isolated island perhaps, or over a dense forest area, or on a mountain top, or in the sea near land. All suggestions of this sort were judged impractical, ineffective and/or risky.

A genuine fear of failure persisted despite accumulated evidence that the weapon was going to bear out the scientists' prediction. It will be remembered that as early as December 1944, Groves had been sure enough that one of the two types of bomb being produced (the type that was dropped on Hiroshima) would work satisfactorily, to report to Stimson that he and presumably his technical advisers did not think a preliminary full test essential. This confidence mounted as the effort neared fruition. The physicist, Smyth, who wrote up the authorized explanation of the undertaking, entered in his notes that "the end of June [1945] finds us expecting from day to day to hear of the explosion of the first atomic bomb devised by man. All the problems are believed to have been solved at least well enough to make a bomb practicable. A sustained neutron chain reaction resulting from nuclear fission has been demonstrated; the conditions necessary to cause such a reaction to occur explosively have been established and can be achieved. . . ."

But the responsible officials and military men still had nervous fears of failure. As recalled summarily by Stimson, in explanation of the decision not to warn Japan in advance of the nature and destructive power of the weapon, "Even the New Mexico test would not give final proof that any given bomb was certain to explode when dropped from an airplane. Quite apart from the generally unfamiliar nature of atomic explosives, there was the whole problem of exploding a bomb at a predetermined height in the air by a complicated mechanism which could not be tested in the static test of New Mexico."

This uncertainty remained despite the numerous varied trials that had been made in flight with a simulated bomb casing and components. For many precautions had been conceived and taken against each and every one of these hazards; many rehearsals to enable trained mechanics and bombing crews to detect any causes of failure beforehand and to correct them.

Then there were chances of human error or accident. What if the heavily laden plane carrying the bomb and fuel needed for the long flight to the point selected for the demonstration crashed? What if the individuals entrusted with the task of turning the containing tube (in the U-235 gun type bomb that was first available for use in Japan) into an atomic weapon, faulted?

Then, also, there were chances of physical defects. Some part of the mechanism of any single specimen might turn out to be defective and malfunction.

Still another opposed reason was that the American government had so few of the new bombs. One would be consumed by the New Mexico test; another (of a different type) was promised in time for use after July 31; and it was reckoned a third by August 6th; and no others according to the schedule given to the decision-makers in June, until about August 20th. By using all—two or three—with utmost effectiveness, the desired quick end of the war might well be brought about. If one of these was misspent in a demonstration that went awry for any reason, could the trial be justified to the men in uniform whose lives were in hazard every day the war went on?

Suppose an announced demonstration had failed. Would the consequences have been serious? Stimson, and even more decidedly Byrnes and Groves, thought so. They believed that if it did not come off "as advertised," the Japanese would take fresh heart and fight on harder and longer. They feared, also, that an uproar would ensue in Congress if the demonstration fizzled or failed to budge the Japanese. They had accepted the unavoidable risks of condemnation if the project on which such vast sums had been spent turned out to be a mistaken venture. But they were not willing to widen the margin of exposure for any other purpose. They tried to dismiss their worries as did the experienced construction engineer whom Robert Patterson, the Under Secretary of War, asked to size up the operation at Oak Ridge. On his return he assured Patterson, "You have really nothing to worry about. If the project succeeds, no one will investigate what was done, and if it does not succeed, every one will investigate nothing else the rest of your life."

Such were the grave apprehensions of the decision-makers of the consequences of a failure in an attempted demonstration. I cannot refrain from remarking that I do not think they would have been as upsetting or harmful as imagined. The stimulant to Japanese military morale would have been very brief. In the United States, criticism would have faded as soon as the bomb was successfully proven—leaving admiration for a noble purpose.

However, speculation on this subject may be regarded as a professional indulgence. For, in fact, even if the decision-makers had not feared a possible failure in demonstration, they would not have tried it. For they deemed it most unlikely that a demonstration could end the war as quickly and surely as hurling the bomb on Japan; and that was their duty as they saw it. No matter what the place and setting for the demonstration, they were sure it would not give an adequate impression of its appalling destructive power, would not register its full meaning in human lives. The desired explosive impression on the Japanese, it was concluded, could be produced only by the actual awful experience. Such precursory opinion was in accord with Stimson's subsequent interpretation of why its use was so effective.

"But the atomic bomb was more than a weapon of terrible destruction; it was a psychological weapon. In March, 1945, our Air Force had launched the first incendiary raid on the Tokyo area. In this raid more damage was done and more casualties were inflicted than was the case at Hiroshima. Hundreds of bombers took part and hundreds of tons of incendiaries were dropped. Similar successive raids burned out a great part of the urban areas of Japan, but the Japanese fought on. On August 6th a B-29 dropped a single atomic bomb on Hiroshima. Three days later a second bomb was dropped on Nagasaki and the war was over."

It has since been contended, and with perseverance, that even if the drop on Hiroshima was justified by its purpose and results, that the second drop on Nagasaki was not. For the exponents of this opinion think that if right after Hiroshima the American government had made it clear, as they did later, that the Japanese authorities could retain the Emperor, they would have surrendered; and hence the destruction of Nagasaki was unnecessary.

This is a tenable judgment. But the records of happenings within Japanese ruling circles during the few days between Hiroshima and Nagasaki foster the impression that if the second bomb had not been dropped, the Japanese rulers would have delayed, perhaps for some weeks, the response which was pre-liminary to capitulation. The military heads would have been so firm in opposition that the Emperor would probably have waited until the situation became more hopeless before overruling them.

The first reports which the military investigating group that the Japanese Chief of Staff hurried to Hiroshima gave out minimized the awfulness of the effects of the bomb, describing the burns suffered from the blast by persons clothed in white and those in shelters as relatively light. Military headquarters started to issue announcements of counter measures which could be effective against the new bomb. The truth about its nature and effects, as estimated by a group of physicists after their inspection, was only made known to the Cabinet on the morning of the 9th while the mushroom cloud was over Naga-saki. Even thereafter, the Army heads accepted the decision to surrender only because the Emperor's openly declared conclusion relieved them of shame and humiliation, and lessened their fear of disobedience by their subordinates.

Thus, to repeat, it is probable that by intensifying the dread of the new weapon—of which, so far as the Japanese knew, we might have many more—the strike against Nagasaki hastened the surrender. But whether merely by a few days or few weeks is not to be known.

In summary it can be concluded that the decision to drop the bombs upon Hiroshima and Nagasaki ought not to be censured. The reasons were—under the circumstances of the time—weighty and valid enough. But a cluster of worrisome queries remain which the passage of time has coated with greater political, ethical and historical interest.

One of these—whether or not the desired quick surrender could have been induced if the American government had been more explicit in its explana-tions of how the Japanese people and Emperor would fare after surrender—was considered in the preceding chapter [of Feis's book].

Another, which has often been asked, is why ten days were allowed to pass between the receipt of information regarding the results of the test of the bomb and the issuance of our final warning. I think the delay was due to an intent to be sure that if the warning was at first unheeded, it could be driven quickly and deeply home by the bombs. Thus we waited until we knew all was in readiness to drop them. These tactics worked. But I wonder whether it might not have been wiser to issue the warning sooner, and thus to have allowed the Japanese authorities more time to ponder its meaning and acceptability. I think it not out of the question that if allowed, say, another fortnight, the Emperor might have imposed his final decision before the bomb was set for use. However, because of the blinding fury and pride of the fighting men, it is unlikely. He hardly would have dared to do so until the explosion of the atomic bomb destroyed the argument that Japan could secure a better peace if it continued to refuse to surrender unconditionally.

But what if the American government had fully revealed the results of the New Mexico test to the Japanese (and the whole world)? Could that have induced the desired quick surrender? The most promising time for such revela-tions would have been in connection with the issuance of the Potsdam Declaration; for by then the American air assaults and naval bombardments were spreading havoc everywhere, and most Japanese were aware they had no way of countering them, no good idea of how to survive them. Suppose, to be more precise, the American government had published the reports on the test which were sent by General Groves to Potsdam for Stimson and the President, such photographs of the explosion and of the mushroom cloud and the testimony of scientists about the destructive power of the weapon that were available. Might not that broadcast knowledge, prefaced by an explanation that one of our purposes was to spare the Japanese, have had enough shock effect to cause the Emperor to overrule the resistant Japanese military leaders?

Perhaps. But in order to make the disclosure as impressive as possible, it might have been necessary to postpone the issuance of the final warning—perhaps until the end of the Potsdam Conference. The test was July 16th; it would have taken time to assemble convincing accounts and photographs, and explanation. This postponement might have prolonged slightly the period of combat.

However, in retrospect, I believe that the risk should have been taken and the cost endured; for by so doing this we might have been spared the need to introduce atomic weapons into war. In the likely event that the Japanese would not have been swayed by this explicit warning of what would happen to them if they rejected our ultimatum, we as a people would be freer of any regret—I will not say remorse—at the necessity of enrolling Hiroshima and Nagasaki in the annals of history.

But the mind, circling upon itself, returns to the point of wondering whether, if the exterminating power of the bomb had not been actually displayed, the nations would have been impelled to make even as faltering an effort as they have to agree on measures to save themselves from mutual extinction by this ultimate weapon. In a novel published in 1914, H. G. Wells prophesied that nations would not recognize the impossibility of war "until the atomic bomb burst in their fumbling hands." Now, two great wars later, it remains entirely uncertain whether they will bow before its imperative.

A Diplomatic Bonus

BARTON J. BERNSTEIN

Ever since the publication in 1965 of Gar Alperovitz's *Atomic Diplomacy,* scholars and laymen have developed a new interest in the relationship of the atomic bomb to wartime and postwar diplomacy and to the origins of the Cold War. This bold book revived and sometimes recast old themes and thereby sparked renewed interest in questions that once seemed settled: Why was the atomic bomb dropped on Japan? Why weren't other alternatives

Barton J. Bernstein, "Roosevelt, Truman and the Atomic Bomb, 1943–1945: A Reinterpretation," *Political Science Quarterly,* 90 (1975), 23–24, 30–32, 34–62. Reprinted with permission from the Academy of Political Science.

vigorously pursued? How did the bomb influence American policy before and after Hiroshima? Did the dropping of the bomb and postwar American atomic policies contribute to the cold war?

Unfortunately many studies of these questions have focused exclusively on the Truman period and thereby neglected the Roosevelt administration, which bequeathed to Truman a legacy of assumptions, options, and fears. Acting on the assumption that the bomb was a legitimate weapon, Roosevelt initially defined the relationship of American diplomacy and the atomic bomb. He decided to build the bomb, to establish a partnership on atomic energy with Britain, to bar the Soviet Union from knowledge of the project, and to block any effort at international control of atomic energy. These policies constituted Truman's inheritance—one he neither wished to abandon nor could easily escape. He was restricted politically, psychologically, and institutionally from critically reassessing this legacy.

Like Roosevelt, Truman assumed that the bomb was a legitimate weapon and also understood that it could serve as a bargaining lever, a military counterweight, a threat, or a combat weapon in dealing with the Soviet Union in the postwar world. In addition to speeding the end of the war, the combat use of the bomb, the Truman administration understood, offered the United States great advantages in the postwar world. Policy makers assumed that use of the bomb would help shape the world in a desirable mold: The bomb would impress the Soviets and make them more tractable. Contrary to some contentions, this consideration about the postwar world was not the controlling reason why the United States used the bomb. Rather, it was an additional reason reinforcing an earlier analysis. Ending the war speedily was the primary purpose; impressing the Soviet Union was secondary. This secondary aim did constitute a subtle deterrent to reconsidering combat use of the bomb and to searching for alternative means of ending the war. Had the use of the bomb threatened to impair, rather than advance, American aims for the postwar peace, policy makers would have been likely to reassess their assumptions and perhaps to choose other alternatives. . . .

Running through the tangled skein of America's wartime policy on atomic energy is the persistent evidence of concern about the Soviet Union. Roosevelt knew that the Soviets were gathering information about the bomb project, and on September 9, 1943, Henry L. Stimson, the secretary of war, informed the president that spies "are already getting information about vital secrets and sending them to Russia." In late December 1944, at two sessions, they again discussed these issues. On December 31, Roosevelt told Stimson that he, too, was worried about how much the Soviets might know about the project, and they briefly discussed trading information for substantial Soviet concessions. As Stimson later summarized the conversation in his diary:

> I told him . . . that I knew they [Russia] were spying on our work but that they had not yet gotten any real knowledge of it and that, while I was troubled by the possible effect of keeping from them even now that work, I believed that it was essential not to take them into our confidence until we were sure to get a real quid pro quo from our frankness. I said I had no illusions as to the possi-

bility of keeping permanently such a secret but that I did think that it was not yet time to share it with Russia. He said he thought he agreed with me.

They did not discuss the specific nature of the concessions, and perhaps Stimson and the president would not have agreed on how to use the bomb as a bargaining lever and what to demand from the Soviet Union. Whatever their unexplored differences on these issues, they did agree to continue for a period the same policy: exclusion of the Soviets. "It was quite clear," recorded General Leslie Groves, commanding general of the Manhattan Project, "that no one present was interested in bringing Russia into the picture, at least at this time." It is less clear why Roosevelt and Stimson, faced with the realization that the Soviet Union knew about the American research, still did not want formally to notify the Soviets about the bomb project. There is no direct evidence on this subject, but probably they feared that formal disclosure would lead to explicit Soviet inquiries and then to demands for participation that American leaders were not prepared to handle. As long as the United States technically kept the project secret, the Soviets could never raise issues about the bomb without admitting their espionage.

On March 15, 1945, at their last meeting together, Stimson and Roosevelt again discussed atomic energy. Roosevelt acknowledged that he would have to choose between (1) continuing the policy of secrecy and the Anglo-American partnership that barred the Soviets or (2) moving to international control with a sharing of information. Under Roosevelt, there was no further resolution of these issues. When he died in April, American policy had not advanced beyond the point where it had been in December.

Had Roosevelt lived, perhaps he would ultimately have reversed the policy of secrecy and decided to move toward international control in return for a *quid pro quo*—perhaps on Eastern Europe which he had "ceded" at Yalta to the Soviet Union. Any consideration of what "might have happened" is, of course, a matter of speculation, since the evidence is skimpy and oblique on what Roosevelt might have done. What is clear is that he had maintained the strategy of excluding the Soviets from knowledge of the bomb and of reserving the options of using it in the future as a bargaining lever, threat, military counterweight, or even a weapon against the Soviets.

It was not that he lacked opportunities to reverse his policy. He did not want to change policy—at least not up to April. At Yalta, in February, for example, Roosevelt might have approached Stalin on the bomb, but the president neither discussed this subject nor the loan that the Soviets wanted, and thereby he simply kept open the options for the future of using economic leverage and the bomb to secure concessions. His position, then, made possible the future strategy of "atomic diplomacy"—of using the bomb as an implied or explicit threat to influence negotiations and to compel concessions from the Soviets. Would he have practiced "atomic diplomacy"? Probably. But that answer is speculative and rests principally upon the theory that he would not have wasted the options he was jealously guarding.

Roosevelt and his advisers had more clearly defined another issue: the combat use of the bomb. From the inception of the project, when it was directed primarily against Germany, they usually assumed, and most policy makers never questioned, that the bomb was a legitimate weapon to be used in combat. This assumption was phrased as policy on a number of occasions. In October 1942, for example, Stimson had directed Groves that the mission is "to produce [the bomb] at the earliest possible date so as to bring the war to a conclusion." Any time "that a single day could be saved," the general should save that day. In 1944, policy makers were also talking comfortably about *"after* S–1 [the bomb] is used." "At no time," Stimson later wrote, "did I ever hear it suggested by the President, or by any other responsible member of the government, that atomic energy should not be used in war." . . .

When Harry S. Truman became president on April 12, 1945, he was only dimly aware of the existence of the Manhattan Project and unaware that it was an atomic-bomb project. Left uninformed of foreign affairs and generally ignored by Roosevelt in the three months since the inaugural, the new president inherited a set of policies and a group of advisers from his predecessor. While Truman was legally free to reverse Roosevelt's foreign policies and to choose new advisers on foreign policy, in fact he was quite restricted for personal and political reasons. Because Truman was following a very prestigious president whom he, like a great many Americans, loved and admired, the new president was not free psychologically or politically to strike out on a clearly new course. Only a bolder man, with more self-confidence, might have tried critically to assess the legacy and to act independently. But Truman lacked the confidence and the incentive. When, in fact, he did modify policy—for example, on Eastern Europe—he still believed sincerely, as some advisers told him, that he was adhering to his predecessor's agreements and wishes. When seeking counsel on foreign affairs, he usually did not choose new advisers but simply drew more heavily upon those members of Roosevelt's staff who were more anti-Soviet and relied less upon those who were more friendly to the Soviet Union. Even in this strategy, he believed that he was adhering to the policies of his predecessor, who, in his last weeks, Truman stressed, had become more suspicious of Stalin, more distressed by Soviet action in Eastern Europe, and more committed to resisting Soviet encroachments.

In the case of the international-diplomatic policy on the bomb, Truman was even more restricted by Roosevelt's decisions, for the new president inherited a set of reasonably clear wartime policies. Because Roosevelt had already decided to exclude the Soviets from a partnership on the bomb, his successor could not *comfortably* reverse this policy during the war—unless the late president's advisers pleaded for such a reversal or claimed that he had been about to change his policy. They did neither. Consider, then, the massive personal and political deterrents that blocked Truman from even reassessing this legacy. What price might he have paid at home if Americans learned later that he had reversed Roosevelt's policy and had launched a bold new departure of sharing with the Soviets a great weapon that cost the United States $2 billion? Truman, in fact, was careful to follow Roosevelt's strategy of concealing from Congress even the dimensions of the secret partnership on atomic energy with Britain.

Truman, depending as he did upon Roosevelt's advisers, could not easily reassess the prevailing assumption that the bomb was a legitimate weapon to be used in combat against Japan. Truman lacked the will and the incentive to reexamine this assumption, and his dependence upon Roosevelt's advisers and the momentum of the project confirmed this tendency. Only one close adviser, Admiral William Leahy, may have later challenged the use of the bomb, but he was an old "war horse," an expert on explosives of another era, who had often proclaimed that the bomb would not work, that the scientists were duping the administration, and that they were squandering $2 billion. His counsel could not outweigh the continuing legacy of assumptions and commitments, of advisers and advice, that Truman had inherited from Roosevelt. It was a subtle legacy, one that infiltrated decisions and shaped actions, so that Truman accepted it as part of his unquestioned inheritance. For Truman, the question would never be how openly to challenge this legacy, only how to fulfill it, how to remain true to it.

During his first weeks in office, Truman learned about the project from Stimson and from James F. Byrnes, Roosevelt's former director of the Office of War Mobilization and Reconversion who was to become Truman's secretary of state. Byrnes, despite his recent suspicions that the project might be a scientific boondoggle, told Truman, in the president's words, that "the bomb might well put us in a position to dictate our own terms at the end of the war." On April 25, Stimson discussed issues about the bomb more fully with Truman, especially the "political aspects of the S–1 [atomic bomb's] performance." The bomb, the secretary of war explained in a substantial memorandum, would probably be ready in four months and "would be the most terrible weapon ever known in human history [for it] . . . could destroy a whole city." In the future, he warned, other nations would be able to make atomic bombs, thereby endangering the peace and threatening the world. The bomb could be either a threat to or a guarantor of peace. "[I]n the light of our present position with reference to this weapon, the question of sharing it with other nations and, if so shared, upon what terms, becomes a primary question of our foreign relations," Stimson lectured the president. If "the problem of the proper use of this weapon can be solved, we would have the opportunity to bring the world into a pattern in which the peace of the world and our civilization can be saved."

The entire discussion, judging from Stimson's diary record and Groves's memorandum, assumed that the bomb was a legitimate weapon and that it would be used against Japan. The questions they discussed were not *whether* to use the bomb, but its relationship to the Soviet Union and the need to establish postwar atomic policies. Neither Stimson nor Truman sought then to resolve these outstanding issues, and Truman agreed to his secretary's proposal for the establishment of a high-level committee to recommend "action to the executive and legislative branches of our government when secrecy is no longer in full effect." At no time did they conclude that the committee would also consider the issue of whether to use the bomb as a combat weapon. For policy makers, that was not a question; it was an operating assumption.

Nor did Stimson, in his own charge to the Interim Committee, ever *raise* this issue. Throughout the committee's meetings, as various members later noted, all operated on the assumption that the bomb would be used against Japan. They talked, for example, about drafting public statements that would be issued after the bomb's use. They did not discuss *whether* but how to use it. Only one member ultimately endorsed an explicit advance warning to Japan, and none was prepared to suggest that the administration should take any serious risks to avoid using the bomb. At lunch between the two formal meetings on May 31, some members, perhaps only at one table, briefly discussed the possibility of a noncombat demonstration as a warning to Japan but rejected the tactic on the grounds that the bomb might not explode and the failure might stiffen Japanese resistance, or that Japan might move prisoners of war to the target area.

What impact would the bomb have on Japan? At the May 31 meeting, the Interim Committee, joined by its four-member scientific advisory panel, discussed this question. Some felt, according to the minutes, that "an atomic bomb on an arsenal would not be much different in effect" from present bombing attacks. J. Robert Oppenheimer, the eminent physicist and member of the scientific panel, expecting that the bomb would have an explosive force of between 2,000 and 20,000 tons of TNT, stressed its visual effects ("a brilliant luminescence which would run to a height of 10,000 to 20,000 feet") and its deadly power ("dangerous to life for a radius of at least two-thirds of a mile"). Oppenheimer's predictions did not answer the question. There were too many unknowns—about the bomb and Japan. According to the official minutes, Stimson concluded, with unanimous support: "that we could not concentrate on a civilian area; but we should seek to make a profound psychological impression on as many of the inhabitants as possible." At Conant's suggestion, "the Secretary agreed that the most desirable target would be a vital war plant employing a large number of workers and closely surrounded by workers' houses." ("I felt," Stimson later explained, "that to extract a genuine surrender from the Emperor and his military advisers, they must be administered a tremendous shock . . . proof of our power to destroy the empire.") The Interim Committee ruled out the strategy of several atomic strikes at one time, for, according to Groves, the United States would lose the benefit of additional knowledge from each successive bombing, would have to rush in assembling bombs and court error, and also would risk the possibility that multiple nuclear attacks "would not be sufficiently distinct from our regular Air Force bombing program."

Two weeks later, after the Franck Committee recommended a noncombat demonstration, Stimson's assistant submitted this proposal to the four-member scientific advisory panel for advice. The panel promptly rejected the Franck Committee proposal: "we can propose no technical demonstration likely to bring an end to the war; we see no acceptable alternative to direct military use." Had the four scientists known that an invasion was not scheduled until November, or had they even offered their judgment after the unexpectedly impressive Alamogordo test on July 16, perhaps they would have given different counsel. But in June, they were not sure that the bomb explosion would be so dramatic, and, like many others in government, they were wary of pushing for a change in tactics if they might be held responsible for the failure of those tactics—especially if that failure could mean the loss of American lives.

A few days after the panel's report, the issue of giving Japan an advance warning about the bomb was raised at a White House meeting with the president, the military chiefs, and the civilian secretaries. On June 18, after they agreed upon a two-stage invasion of Japan, beginning on about November 1, Assistant Secretary of War John J. McCloy became clearly troubled by the omission of the bomb from the discussion and planning. When Truman invited him to speak, the assistant secretary argued that the bomb would make the invasion unnecessary. Why not warn the emperor that the United States had the bomb and would use it unless Japan surrendered? "McCloy's suggestion had appeal," the official history of the AEC later recorded, "but a strong objection developed" to warning Japan in advance, "which no one could refute—there was no assurance the bomb would work." Presumably, like the Interim Committee, they too feared that a warning, followed by a "dud," might stiffen Japan's morale. There was no reason, policy makers concluded, to take this risk.

Though the Interim Committee and high administration officials found no reason not to use the bomb against Japan, many were concerned about the bomb's impact, and its later value, in Soviet-American relations. "[I]t was already apparent," Stimson later wrote, "that the critical questions in American policy toward atomic energy would be directly connected with Soviet Russia." At a few meetings of the Interim Committee, for example, members discussed informing the Soviets of the bomb before its use against Japan. When the issue first arose, Bush and Conant estimated that the Soviet Union could develop the bomb in about four years and argued for informing the Soviets before combat use as a preliminary to moving toward international control and thereby avoiding a postwar nuclear arms race. Conant and Bush had been promoting this strategy since the preceding September. Even though Roosevelt had cast them to the side in 1943, when he cemented the Anglo-American alliance, the two scientist-administrators had not abandoned hope for their notions. They even circulated to the Interim Committee one of their memoranda on the subject. But at the meetings of May 18 and 31 they again met defeat. General Groves, assuming that America was far more advanced technologically and scientifically and also that the Soviet Union lacked uranium, argued that the Soviets could not build a bomb for about twenty years. He contributed to the appealing "myth" of the atomic secret—that there was a secret and it would long remain America's monopoly. James Byrnes, with special authority as secretary of state-designate and Truman's representative on the committee, accepted Groves's analysis and argued for maintaining the policy of secrecy—which the committee endorsed. Byrnes was apparently very pleased, and Stimson agreed, as he told Truman on June 6, "There should be no revelation to Russia or anyone else of our work on S–1 [the atomic bomb] until the first bomb has been laid successfully on Japan."

At a later meeting on June 21, the Interim Committee, including Byrnes, reversed itself. Yielding to the pleas of Bush and Conant, who were strengthened by the scientific panel's recommendations, the Interim Committee advised Truman to inform the Soviets about the bomb before using it in combat. Like the Franck Committee, the Interim Committee concluded (as the minutes record):

> In the hope of securing effective future control and in view of the fact that general information concerning the project would be made public shortly after the [Potsdam] conference, the Committee *agreed* that there would be considerable advantage, if suitable opportunity arose, in having the President advise the Russians that we were working on this weapon with every prospect of success and that we expected to use it against Japan.
>
> The President might say further that he hoped this matter might be discussed some time in the future in terms of insuring that the weapon would become an aid to peace.

Because of this recommendation, and perhaps also because of the continuing prodding of Bush and Conant, Stimson reversed his own position. He concluded that if the United States dropped the bomb on Japan without first informing the Soviet Union, that act might gravely strain Soviet-American relations. Explaining the committee's position to Truman, Stimson proposed that if the president "thought that Stalin was on good terms with him" at the forthcoming Potsdam conference, he would inform Stalin that the United States had developed the bomb, planned to use it against Japan, knew the Soviets were working on the bomb, and looked forward to discussing international control later. This approach left open the option of "atomic diplomacy."

The issues of the bomb and the Soviet Union had already intruded in other ways upon policy and planning. Awaiting the bomb, Truman had postponed the Potsdam conference, delayed negotiations with Russia, and hoped that atomic energy would pry some concessions from Russia. Truman explained in late May to Joseph Davies, an advocate of Soviet-American friendship, and in early June to Stimson that he was delaying the forthcoming Potsdam conference until the Alamogordo test, when he would know whether the United States had a workable atomic bomb—what Stimson repeatedly called the "master card." Truman also told some associates that he was delaying because he wanted to work out budget matters, but it is unlikely that the budget was the controlling reason. Certainly, there was no reason that he should have told Davies, who, unlike Stimson, was not counseling delay of the conference, that he was waiting for the bomb. Stimson's counsel of caution, offered on May 15, had apparently triumphed: it would be "a terrible thing to gamble with such high stakes in diplomacy without having your master card in your hand. . . . Over [the] tangled wave of problems the S–1 secret would be dominant." This was not the counsel for a "delayed showdown," as some have wrongly argued, but for no showdown and for delaying some negotiations until the bomb test so that policy makers could determine whether they would have to make concessions to the Soviet Union.

For the administration, the atomic bomb, if it worked, had great potential value. It could reduce the importance of early Soviet entry into the war and make American concessions unnecessary. It could also be a lever for extracting concessions from the Soviet Union. On June 6, for example, Stimson discussed with Truman "quid pro quos which should be established for our taking them [Russia] into [a nuclear] partnership. He [Truman] said that he had been thinking of the same things that I was thinking of, namely the settlement of the Polish, Rumanian, Yugoslavian, and Manchurian problems." There is no evidence that they were planning explicitly to threaten the Soviets to gain these concessions, but, obviously, they realized that the Soviets would regard an American nuclear monopoly as threatening and would yield on some issues in order to terminate that monopoly and thereby reduce, or eliminate, the threat. Neither Stimson nor Truman discussed brandishing the bomb or using it explicitly as a threat to compel concessions. "Atomic diplomacy," as a conception, advanced no further than the notion of possibly trading in the future an atomic partnership, which was still undefined, for Soviet concessions.

For policy makers, the atomic weapons scheduled for combat use against Japan were intimately connected with the problem of Russia. In recent years some historians have focused on this relationship and raised troubling questions: Did the bomb, for policy makers, constitute an alternative to Soviet intervention in the Pacific war? Did they delay or even try to prevent Soviet entry because the bomb made it unnecessary? If so, did they do this in order to use the bomb? Was the bomb dropped on Japan primarily to influence Russia? Did the bomb influence American policy at Potsdam?

At Yalta, Roosevelt had granted the Soviet Union concessions in China in order to secure Soviet entry into the Pacific war, which Stalin promised, within two to three months after V-E Day (May 8). Stalin made it clear that Soviet entry would await a Sino-Soviet pact ratifying these concessions. At the time of Yalta, American military planners were counting on a Soviet attack in Manchuria to pin down the Kwantung army there and hence stop Japan from shifting these forces to her homeland to meet an American invasion.

But by April, war conditions changed and military planners revised their analysis: Japan no longer controlled the seas and therefore could not shift her army, so Soviet entry was not essential. In May, the State Department asked Stimson whether Soviet participation "at the earliest possible moment" was so necessary that the United States should abide by the Far East section of the Yalta agreement. Stimson concluded that the Soviets would enter the war for their own reasons, at their schedule, and with little regard to any American action, that the Yalta concessions would be largely within the grasp of Soviet military power, and that Soviet assistance would be useful, but not essential, if an American invasion was necessary. If there is an invasion, "Russian entry," he wrote, "will have a profound military effect in that almost certainly it will materially shorten the war and thus save American lives." But if the bomb worked, he implied in other discussions, then an invasion would probably not be necessary and Soviet help would be less important. As a result, he urged a delay in settling matters with Russia on the Far East until after the Alamogordo test, and the president apparently followed this counsel.

On June 18, when the joint chiefs of staff, the civilian secretaries, and the president discussed plans for an American invasion of Kyushu on about November 1 and of Honshu during the following March, the issue of Soviet intervention again received attention. General George Marshall, the army chief of staff and the military leader Truman most admired, presented as his own views a JCS memorandum:

> It seems that if the Japanese are ever willing to capitulate short of complete military defeat in the field they will do it when faced by the completely hopeless prospect occasioned by (1) destruction already wrought by air bombardment and sea blockade, coupled with (2) a landing on Japan indicating the firmness of our resolution, and also perhaps coupled with (3) the entry or threat of Russian entry into the war.
>
> With reference to clean-up of the Asiatic mainland, our objective should be to get the Russians to deal with the Japs [sic] in Manchuria (and Korea).…
>
> An important point about Russian participation in the war is that the impact of Russian entry on the already hopeless Japanese *may well be the decisive action* levering them into capitulation at that time or shortly thereafter *if we land in Japan.* [Emphasis added.]

Marshall's counsel was ambiguous and should have raised questions at this meeting. In one place, he said that Soviet entry, when combined with an invasion and other continued destruction, might lead to Japan's capitulation. In another place, he suggested that Soviet entry alone, or followed by an American invasion, might lead to Japan's capitulation. And he was unclear whether Russia's "clean-up of the Asiatic mainland" was necessary if Japan surrendered without an invasion.

None apparently noted the ambiguities or raised questions about Marshall's meaning. After the group approved plans for an invasion of Kyushu on about November 1, with possibly 30,000 casualties in the first thirty days, Truman indicated that one of his "objectives [at Potsdam] . . . would be to get from Russia all the assistance in the war that was possible." Admiral Ernest L. King, chief of Naval Operations, pointed out, according to the minutes, that the Soviets "were not indispensable and he did not think we should go as far as to beg them to come in. While the cost of defeating Japan would be greater, there was no question in his mind but that we should handle it alone. . . . [R]ealization of this fact should greatly strengthen the President's hand" at Potsdam. Admiral Leahy also expressed a "jaundiced view" of the need for Soviet participation.

Truman claimed that he went to Potsdam to secure Soviet entry and that he never changed his position. The first part of that claim is correct, but the second part is dubious, for Truman did nothing substantive at Potsdam to encourage Soviet intervention and much to delay or prevent it. The successful test at Alamogordo emphasized to policy makers that prompt Soviet entry was no longer necessary and that the United States might even be able to end the war without Soviet entry. After the unexpectedly glowing report of the test, Truman wanted to know whether Marshall considered Soviet entry necessary. "Marshall felt," Stimson recorded, "that now with our new weapon we would not need the assistance of the Russians to conquer Japan." "The bomb as a merely probable weapon had seemed a weak reed on which to rely, but the bomb as a colossal reality was very different," Stimson later explained. From Potsdam on July 23, Churchill cabled London: "It is quite clear that the United States do not at the present time desire Russian participation in the war against Japan." The bomb had eliminated the importance of Russia's prompt entry, since the planned American invasion no longer seemed necessary. Invasion and the bomb were the likely alternatives. As a result, Truman had no reason to offer concessions to secure early Soviet entry.

Could the United States keep the Soviet Union out of the war? Did policy makers try to do this? In mid-July Soviet troops were stationed on the Manchurian border and would soon be ready to intervene. Marshall concluded that even if Japan surrendered on American terms before Soviet entry, Russia could still march into Manchuria and take virtually whatever she wanted there in the surrender terms. Truman, if he believed Marshall's analysis, had nothing to gain politically from deterring Soviet entry, unless he feared, as did Stimson, that the Soviets might try to reach the Japanese homeland and put in a "claim to occupy and help rule it." Perhaps Truman followed the counsel of Stimson and Byrnes, who, for slightly different reasons, were eager to restrain the Soviets.

Byrnes, unlike Stimson, was sometimes naively optimistic. Part of the time he hoped to keep the Soviet Union out of the war, and not simply delay her entry, in order to protect China. On July 28, he explained to Secretary of the Navy James Forrestal (in Forrestal's words): "Byrnes said he was most anxious to get the Japanese affair over with before the Russians got in, with particular reference to Dairen and Port Arthur." These were the areas that both Stimson and Marshall acknowledged the Soviets could seize. Walter Brown, the friend who accompanied the secretary to Potsdam, recorded in his diary notes for July 20 Byrnes's strategy: "JFB determined to outmaneuver Stalin on China. Hopes Soong [the Chinese foreign minister] will stand firm and then Russians will not go in war. Then he feels Japan will surrender before Russia goes to war and this will save China." On July 24, four days later, Brown noted that Byrnes was linking the bomb and Japan's surrender but was less optimistic about excluding Russia: "JFB still hoping for time, believing after atomic bombing Japan will surrender and Russia will not get in so much on the kill, thereby [not] being in a position to press for claims against China."

Byrnes purposely impeded Sino-Soviet negotiations in order to *prevent* the Soviets from entering the war. Did Truman support Byrnes for the *same* reasons?—as Byrnes claimed later and as Truman obliquely denied. Perhaps. But, more likely, Truman supported his secretary's strategy for a different reason: the early entry of the Soviets was no longer important and, therefore, Truman did not want Chiang to make the required concessions, which could later weaken Chiang's government. In addition, Truman *may* have concluded that Russia's delayed entry would weaken her possible claims for a role in the postwar occupation government in Japan.

Why didn't Truman invite Stalin to sign the Potsdam Proclamation of July 26 calling for Japan's surrender? Some analysts argued later that this omission was part of a devious strategy: that Truman wanted to use the bomb and feared that

Stalin's signature, tantamount to a declaration of war, might catapult Japan to surrender, thereby making a nuclear attack impossible. The major difficulty with this interpretation is that it exaggerates occasional, sometimes ambiguous, statements about the *possible* impact of Soviet entry and ignores the fact that this possible shock was not a persistent or important theme in American planning. Truman did not exclude the Soviets from the Proclamation in order to use the bomb. The skimpy, often oblique evidence *suggests* a different, more plausible explanation and a less devious pattern: he wanted to avoid requesting favors from the Soviets. As a result, he did not try this one possible, but not very likely, way of ending the war without using atomic weapons.

At Potsdam, on July 24, Truman told Stalin casually that the United States had developed "a new weapon of unusual destructive force" for use against Japan but did not specify an atomic weapon. Why didn't Truman explicitly inform Stalin about the atomic bomb? Was Truman, as some have suggested, afraid that the news would prompt Stalin to hasten Soviet intervention and therefore end the war and make combat use of the bomb impossible? Did Truman simply want to delay Soviet entry and did he, like Byrnes, fear that his news would have the opposite effect? Did Truman think that the destruction wrought by the bomb would not impress the Soviets as forcefully if they were informed in advance? Why did Truman reject the counsel of the Interim Committee, of Stimson, and even of Churchill, who, after the flowing news of the Alamogordo test, "was not worried about giving the Russians information on the matter but was rather inclined to use it as an argument in our favor in the negotiations"?

Many of these questions cannot be definitively answered on the basis of the presently available evidence, but there is enough evidence to refute one popular interpretation: that Truman's tactic was part of an elaborate strategy to prevent or retard Soviet entry *in order* to delay Japan's surrender and *thereby* make combat use of the bomb possible. That interpretation claims too much. Only the first part can be supported by some, albeit indirect, evidence: that he was probably seeking to delay or prevent Soviet entry. Byrnes later said that he feared that Stalin would order an immediate Soviet declaration of war if he realized the importance of this "new weapon"—advice Truman dubiously claimed he never received. Truman was not trying to postpone Japan's surrender *in order* to use the bomb. In addition to the reasonable theory that he was seeking to prevent or retard Soviet entry, there are two other plausible, complementary interpretations of Truman's behavior. First, he believed, as had some of his advisers earlier, that a combat demonstration would be more impressive to Russia without an advance warning and therefore he concealed the news. Second, he was also ill-prepared to discuss atomic energy with Stalin, for the president had not made a decision about postwar atomic policy and how to exploit the bomb, and probably did not want to be pressed by Stalin about sharing nuclear secrets. Perhaps all three theories collectively explain Truman's evasive tactics.

Even without explicit disclosure, the bomb strengthened American policy at Potsdam. The Alamogordo test stiffened Truman's resolve, as Churchill told Stimson after the meeting of the Big Three on July 22: "Truman was evidently much fortified . . . and . . . he stood up to the Russians in a most emphatic and decisive manner, telling them as to certain demands that they absolutely could not have." Probably, also, the bomb explains why Truman pushed more forcefully at Potsdam for the Soviets to open up Eastern Europe. It is less clear whether the bomb changed the substance of American policy at Potsdam. Probably Byrnes endorsed a reparations policy allowing the division of Germany because the bomb replaced Germany as a potential counterweight to possible Soviet expansion.

Not only did the bomb strengthen American resolve in dealing with the Soviets, but Stimson and Truman linked the bomb and the Soviet Union in another way: the selection of targets for atomic attacks. Kyoto, a city of religious shrines, was originally on the list, but Stimson removed it, with Truman's approval. Truman "was particularly emphatic in agreeing with my suggestion," Stimson wrote, because

> the bitterness . . . caused by such a wanton act might make it impossible during the long post war period to reconcile the Japanese to us in that area rather than to the Russians. It might thus, I pointed out, be the means of preventing what our policy demanded, namely, a sympathetic Japan to the United States in case there should be any aggression by Russia in Manchuria.

Scholars and laymen have criticized the combat use of the atomic bomb. They have contended, among other points, that the bombs were not necessary to end the war, that the administration knew or should have known this, that the administration knew that Japan was on the verge of defeat and *therefore* close to surrender, and that the administration was either short-sighted or had other controlling international-political motives (besides ending the war) for using the bomb. These varying contentions usually focus on the alleged failure of the United States to pursue five alternatives, individually or in combination, in order to achieve Japanese surrender before using the bomb: (1) awaiting Soviet entry, a declaration of war, or a public statement of intent (already discussed); (2) providing a warning and/or a noncombat demonstration (already discussed); (3) redefining unconditional surrender to guarantee the Imperial institution; (4) pursuing Japan's "peace feelers"; or (5) relying upon conventional warfare for a longer period. These contentions assume that policy makers were trying, or should have tried, to avoid using atomic bombs—precisely what they were not trying to do.

In examining these contentions, analysts must carefully distinguish between those writers (like Alperovitz) who maintain that there were ulterior motives for rejecting alternatives and those (like Hanson Baldwin) who regard policy makers as dangerously short sighted but without ulterior motives. It is logically possible to agree with Alperovitz and not Baldwin, or vice versa; but it is impossible logically to endorse both positions.

There were powerful reasons why the fifth alternative—the use of conventional weapons for a longer period *before* using atomic bombs—seemed undesirable to policy makers. The loss of American lives, while perhaps not great, would have been unconscionable and politically risky. How could policy makers have justified to themselves or to other Americans delaying the use of this great weapon and squandering American lives? Consider the potential political cost at home. In contrast, few Americans were then troubled by the mass killing of enemy citizens, especially if they were yellow. The firebombings of Tokyo, of other Japanese cities, and even of Dresden had produced few cries of outrage in the United States. There was no evidence that most citizens would care that the atomic bomb was as lethal as the raids on Dresden or Tokyo. It was unlikely that there would be popular support for relying upon conventional warfare and not using the atomic bomb. For citizens and policy makers, there were few, if any, moral restraints on what weapons were acceptable in war.

Nor were there any powerful advocates within the high councils of the administration who wanted to delay or not use the bomb and rely instead upon conventional warfare—a naval blockade, continued aerial bombings, or both. The advocates of conventional warfare were not powerful, and they did not directly oppose the use of the bomb. Admiral Ernest L. King, chief of Naval Operations, did believe that the invasion and the atomic bomb were not the only alternative tactics likely to achieve unconditional surrender. A naval blockade, he insisted, would be successful. The army, however, he complained, had little faith in sea power and, hence, Truman did not accept his proposal. Leahy had serious doubts about using the bomb, but as an old explosives expert who had long claimed that the bomb would never work, he carried little weight on this matter. Surprisingly, perhaps, he did not forcefully press his doubts on the president. Had Marshall plumped for the strategy of stepping up conventional warfare and delaying or not using the bomb, he might have been able to compel a reassessment. He had the respect and admiration of the president and could command attention for his views. But Marshall had no incentive to avoid the use of the bomb, prolong the war, and expend American lives. For him, nuclear weapons and invasion were likely alternatives, and he wanted to avoid invasion. If the bomb was used as quickly as possible, the invasion might be unnecessary and American lives would be saved.

For policy makers, the danger was not simply the loss of a few hundred American lives *prior* to the slightly delayed use of the bombs if the United States relied upon conventional warfare for a few more weeks. Rather the risk was that, if the nuclear attacks were even slightly delayed, the scheduled invasion of Kyushu, with perhaps 30,000 casualties in the first month, would be necessary. After the war, it became fashionable to assume that policy makers clearly foresaw and comfortably expected that an atomic bomb or two would shock Japan into a speedy surrender. But the evidence does not support this view. "The abrupt surrender of Japan came more or less as a surprise," Henry H. Arnold, commanding general of the air force, later explained. Policy makers were planning, if necessary, to drop at least three atomic bombs in August, with the last on about August 24, and more in September. Before Hiroshima, only occasionally did some policy makers imply (but never state explicitly) that one bomb or a few bombs might shock Japan into a prompt surrender: capitulation within a few days or weeks. Usually they were less optimistic, sometimes even pessimistic. They often assumed that the war might drag on after the nuclear attacks. Faced with this prospect, policy makers were unprepared to take risks and delay using the bombs. So unsure was Truman of the likelihood of a speedy surrender after the first atomic attack that he left domestic officials unprepared for the surrender and thereby seriously weakened his stabilization program and lost political support at home. Because policy makers feared that the attack on Hiroshima might not speedily end the war, they continued conventional bombing and also dropped the second bomb. Their aim was to end the war without a costly invasion of Kyushu. According to their analysis, atomic weapons, if employed promptly and combined with conventional attacks, were likely to achieve that goal. Delay was unconscionable, as Stimson later explained.

There have also been criticisms of the administration for failing to pursue two other alleged opportunities: (1) redefining the unconditional surrender demands before Hiroshima to guarantee the Imperial institution; and (2) responding to Japan's "peace feelers," which stressed the need for this guarantee. Byrnes and apparently Truman, however, were fearful at times that concessions might strengthen, not weaken, the Japanese military and thereby prolong, not shorten, the war. Some critics imply that Byrnes and Truman were not sincere in presenting this analysis and that they rejected concessions consciously in order to use the bomb. That is incorrect. Other critics believe that these policy makers were sincere but disagree with their assessment—especially since some intelligence studies implied the need for concessions on peace terms to shorten the war. Probably the administration was wrong, and these latter critics right, but either policy involved risks and some were very unattractive to Truman.

Truman, as a new president, was not comfortable in openly challenging Roosevelt's policy of unconditional surrender and modifying the terms. That was risky. It could fail and politically injure him at home. Demanding unconditional surrender meant fewer risks at home and, according to his most trusted advisers at times, fewer risks in ending the war speedily. Had his most powerful and trusted advisers pushed for a change in policy, perhaps he might have found reason and will to modify Roosevelt's policy well before Hiroshima. But most of Truman's closest advisers first counseled delay and then some moved into opposition. As a result, he too shifted from delay to opposition. At Potsdam, when Stimson pushed unsuccessfully for providing the guarantee in the Proclamation, Truman refused but told Stimson that he would carefully watch Japan's reactions on this issue and implied that he would yield if it seemed to be the only impediment to surrender. After August 10, when Japan made the guarantee the only additional condition, Truman yielded on the issue. He deemed it a tactical problem, not a substantive one. But even then, Byrnes was wary of offering this concession, despite evidence that it would probably end the war promptly —precisely what he wanted in order to forestall Soviet gains in the Far East.

Within the administration, the issue of redefining the terms of surrender was a subject of discussion for some months before Hiroshima. Since at least April, Joseph Grew, undersecretary of state and at times acting secretary of state, urged the administration to redefine unconditional surrender to permit a guarantee of the Imperial institution. He argued that these moderate terms would speed Japan's surrender and perhaps make an invasion unnecessary. Within the

Department of State, he met opposition from some high-ranking officials, including Dean Acheson and Archibald MacLeish, both assistant secretaries, who regarded the emperor as the bulwark of Japan's feudal-military tradition, which all wanted to destroy, and who feared that the American press and public opinion would be enraged by Grew's proposed concession. Hirohito, Japan's emperor, like Hitler and Mussolini, had become a wartime symbol of a hated enemy, of depravity, of tyranny, and of inhumanity.

On May 28, President Truman, perhaps then sympathetic to Grew's proposal, told him to discuss it with Stimson, Forrestal, Marshall, and King. Unlike Acheson and MacLeish, these military leaders approved the principle but apparently agreed with Marshall that publication of softened terms at that time would be premature. Grew later explained, "for certain military reasons, not divulged, it was considered inadvisable for the President to make such a statement just now. The question of timing was the nub of the whole matter according to the views of those present." Though Grew knew about the atomic bomb, its connection with the delay never seemed to occur to him, and he thought that Marshall and others were concerned *only* about the impact of the announcement on the fighting on Okinawa. In his diary, Stimson explained the opposition more fully: "It was an awkward meeting because there were people present . . . [before] whom I could not discuss the real features which would govern the whole situation, namely S–1 [the atomic bomb]." Stimson never revealed this to Grew, who reported to Truman that they decided to postpone the statement—a position that the president endorsed.

Some analysts have argued, wrongly, that this evidence indicates that Stimson and the others blocked the statement *because* they wanted to use the bomb and did not want to risk a peace before the bomb could be used. That is incorrect. In view of Stimson's frequent judgments that the United States would issue a warning *after* the atomic bombing but before the scheduled attack on Kyushu, his objection was what Grew reported—an issue of timing. On July 2, for example, when Stimson proposed as part of the warning a guarantee of the Imperial institution, he was apparently assuming, as he stated explicitly a week earlier, that he hoped "to get Japan to surrender by giving her a warning after she had been sufficiently *pounded possibly with S–1.*" Not until July 16, when Stimson learned of "the recent news of attempted approaches" by Japan for peace did he shift and call for a prompt warning *before* the atomic attacks.

"There was a pretty strong feeling" by mid-June, Stimson wrote in his diary, "that it would be deplorable if we have to go through [with] the military program with all its stubborn fighting to a finish." On June 18, Grew again went to Truman with his proposal, and the president told him, in Grew's words, that he "liked the idea [but] he had decided to hold this up until it could be discussed at the Big Three meeting" starting on July 16. Grew properly lamented that the government was missing an opportunity but did not speculate on whether the president had ulterior motives. Truman did not. A few hours later, he uneasily told associates that he, too, thought the requirement of unconditional surrender might drag out the war; that with "that thought in mind . . . [he] had left the door open for Congress to take appropriate action . . . [but] he did not feel that he could take any action at this time to change public opinion on the matter." Truman, apparently uneasy about departing from Roosevelt's policy, later explained that he delayed the guarantee until what he regarded as a more propitious time—the Potsdam conference, when the allies, by signing the proclamation, could forcefully demonstrate their "united purpose."

Had Cordell Hull, former secretary of state, Byrnes, and the JCS not intervened, Truman probably would have included in the Potsdam Proclamation a provision guaranteeing the Imperial institution. The provision was in early drafts. But Byrnes deleted it when Hull warned that it might stiffen Japan's resistance, and, if it failed, it could create serious political problems for the administration at home. The military chiefs, perhaps independently, also moved to delete the provision. Unlike Hull, they feared, among other problems, that the "guarantee would make it difficult or impossible to utilize the authority of the Emperor to direct a surrender of the Japanese forces in the outlying areas as well as in Japan proper." The guarantee, then, was not removed for ulterior purposes (because the administration wanted to use the bomb) but because advisers, with more power than Stimson and Grew, triumphed. Neither of these older men was close to Truman. Grew was headed for a quick retirement and was left behind in Washington when the president and top policy makers journeyed to Potsdam. Stimson, also headed for retirement, had so little influence by July that he was compelled to beg and scheme to attend the Potsdam conference and, while there, he was shunted to the side and seldom informed of negotiations.

Grew long maintained that America could have achieved peace without using atomic bombs if the United States had modified its demands and guaranteed the Imperial institution. In 1948, Stimson provided some support for this position: "It is possible, in the light of the final surrender, that a clearer and earlier exposition of American willingness to retain the Emperor would have produced an earlier ending to the war. Only on this question did [Stimson] . . . later believe," he wrote in his "autobiography," "that history might find that the United States, by its delay in stating its position, had prolonged the war." By implication, he was also criticizing the wartime fear—that he sometimes shared with Byrnes and most military advisers—that conciliatory offers would be interpreted in Japan "as an indication of [American] weakness" and thereby prolong the war. Probably policy makers were wrong in not acting earlier.

Let us look at the remaining, but connected, alternative—pursuing Japan's "peace feelers." Japan's so-called peace feelers were primarily a series of messages from the foreign minister to his nation's ambassador in Moscow, who was asked to investigate the possibility of having the Soviets serve as intermediaries in negotiating a peace. American intelligence intercepted and decoded all the messages. Most, if not all, were sent on to Potsdam, where Truman and Byrnes had access to them. Both men showed little interest in them, and may not even have read all of them, apparently because the proposed concessions were insufficient to meet American demands and because Truman and Byrnes had already decided that the peace party in Japan could not succeed until American attacks—including atomic bombs—crushed the military's hopes. The intercepted and decoded messages fell short of American expectations. Not only did Japan's foreign minister want to retain the Imperial institution, which was acceptable to some policy makers, but he also wanted a peace that would maintain his nation's "honor and existence," a phrase that remained vague. As late as July 27, the day after the Potsdam Proclamation, when Japan's foreign minister was planning a special peace mission to Russia, he was still unwilling or unable to present a "concrete proposal" for negotiations. What emerges from his decoded correspondence is a willingness by some elements in Japan's government to move toward peace, their fear of opposition from the military, and their inability to be specific about terms. Strangely, perhaps, though they feared that Stalin might be on the verge of entering the war, they never approached the United States directly to negotiate a peace settlement. For Truman and Byrnes, Japan was near defeat but not near surrender when the three powers issued the Potsdam Proclamation on July 26. When Japan's premier seemed to reject it, the president and secretary of state could find confirmation for their belief that the peace party could not triumph in Japan without more American "aid"— including nuclear attacks.

Given the later difficulties of Japan's peace party, even after the atomic bombings, after Soviet entry, and after more large-scale conventional bombings, top American policy makers could find evidence in the ambiguous record for their assessment that Japan's leaders were not ready to surrender before Hiroshima. More troubling were American policy makers' wartime convictions that any concessions or pursuit of unsure "peace feelers" might stiffen resistance. Most American leaders were fearful of softening demands. War had bred an attitude that any efforts at compromise might indicate to the enemy America's flaccidity of spirit and weakness of will. Toughness, for most policy makers, seemed to promise success.

Looking back upon these years, Americans may well lament the unwillingness of their leaders to make some concessions at this time and to rely upon negotiations before using the bombs. That lament, however, is logically separable from the unfounded charges that policy makers consciously avoided the "peace feelers" *because* they wanted to drop the bombs in order to intimidate the Soviets. It is true that American leaders did not cast policy in order to avoid using the atomic bombs. Given their analysis, they had no reason to avoid using these weapons. As a result, their analysis provokes ethical revulsion among many critics, who believe that policy makers should have been reluctant to use atomic weapons and should have sought, perhaps even at some cost in American lives, to avoid using them.

Truman inherited the assumption that the bomb was a legitimate weapon to use to end the war. No policy maker ever effectively challenged this conception. If the combat use of the bomb deeply troubled policy makers morally or politically, they might have been likely to reconsider their assumption and to search ardently for other alternatives. But they were generally inured to the mass killing of civilians and much preferred to sacrifice the lives of Japanese civilians to those of American soldiers. As a result, they were committed to using the bomb *as soon as possible* to end the war. "The dominant objective was victory," Stimson later explained. "If victory could be speeded by using the bomb, it should be used; if victory must be delayed in order to use the bomb, it should *not* be used. So far as . . . [I] knew, this general view was fully shared by the President and his associates." The morality of war confirmed the dictates of policy and reinforced the legacy that Truman had inherited. Bureaucratic momentum added weight to that legacy, and the relatively closed structure of decision making served also to inhibit dissent and to ratify the dominant assumption.

Had policy makers concluded that the use of the bomb would impair Soviet-American relations and make the Soviets intransigent, they might have reconsidered their assumption. But their analysis indicated that the use of the bomb would aid, not injure, their efforts to secure concessions from the Soviets. The bomb offered a bonus. The promise of these likely advantages probably constituted a subtle deterrent to any reconsideration of the use of the atomic bomb. Policy makers rejected the competing analysis advanced by the Franck Committee:

> Russia, and even allied countries which bear less mistrust of our ways and intentions, as well as neutral countries, will be deeply shocked. It will be very difficult to persuade the world that a nation which was capable of secretly preparing and suddenly releasing . . . [the bomb] is to be trusted in its proclaimed desire of having such weapons abolished by international agreement.

Instead, policy makers had come to assume that a combat demonstration would advance, not impair, the interests of peace—a position shared by Conant, Oppenheimer, Arthur H. Compton, Nobel laureate and director of the Chicago Metallurgical Laboratory, and Edward Teller, the physicist and future father of the hydrogen bomb. In explaining the thinking of the scientific advisory panel in recommending combat use of the bomb, Oppenheimer later said that one of the two "overriding considerations . . . [was] the effect of our actions on the stability . . . of the postwar world." Stimson's assistant, Harvey H. Bundy, wrote in 1946, that some thought "that unless the bomb were used it would be impossible to persuade the world that the saving of civilization in the future would depend on a proper international control of atomic energy." The bomb, in short, would impress the Soviets.

In addition, there was another possible advantage to using the bomb: retribution against Japan. A few days after Nagasaki, Truman hinted at this theme in a private letter justifying the combat use of the bombs:

> Nobody is more disturbed over the use of Atomic bombs than I am but I was greatly disturbed over the unwarranted attack by the Japanese on Pearl Harbor. The only language they seem to understand is the one that we have been using to bombard them. When you have to deal with a beast you have to treat him as a beast. It is most regrettable but nevertheless true.

In this letter, one can detect strains of the quest for retribution (the reference to Pearl Harbor), and some might even find subtle strains of racism (Japan was "a beast"). The enemy was a beast and deserved to be destroyed. War, as some critics would stress, dehumanized victors and vanquished, and justified inhumanity in the name of nationalism, of justice, and even of humanity.

In assessing the administration's failure to challenge the assumption that the bomb was a legitimate weapon to be used against Japan, we may conclude that Truman found no reason to reconsider, that it would have been difficult for him to challenge the assumption, and that there were also various likely benefits deterring a reassessment. For the administration, in short, there was no reason to avoid using the bomb and many reasons making it feasible and even attractive. The bomb was used primarily to end the war *promptly* and thereby to save American lives. There were other ways to end the war, but none of them seemed as effective. They would not produce victory as promptly and seemed to have greater risks. Even if Russia had not existed, the bombs would have been used in the same way. How could Truman, in the absence of overriding contrary reasons, justify not using the bombs, or even delaying their use, and thereby prolonging the war and sacrificing American lives?

Some who have searched for the causes of Truman's decision to use atomic weapons have made the error of assuming that the question was ever open, that the administration ever carefully faced the problem of *whether* to use the bombs. It was not a carefully weighed decision but the implementation of an assumption. The administration devoted thought to how, not whether, to use them. As Churchill later wrote, "the decision whether or not to use the atomic bomb to compel the surrender of Japan was never even an issue."

FURTHER READING

Gar Alperovitz, *Atomic Diplomacy* (1965)
Paul R. Baker, ed., *The Atomic Bomb* (1976)
Barton J. Bernstein, ed., *The Atomic Bomb* (1975)
Robert J. C. Butow, *Japan's Decision to Surrender* (1954)
Richard Hewlett and Oscar Anderson, *The New World* (1962)
Gabriel Kolko, *The Politics of War* (1968)
Lisle Rose, *After Yalta* (1973)
Martin Sherwin, *A World Destroyed* (1975)

9

The Origins of the Cold War

*The Big Three alliance of World War II, often strained during the war
itself, quickly splintered as the victors began to plan the peace. Questions of
territorial boundaries, spheres of influence, atomic weaponry, trade, economic
reconstruction, political principles, and international organizations divided
Britain, the United States, and the Soviet Union. In Germany, Iran, Eastern
Europe, China—indeed, on a global scale—the major powers, especially
America and Russia, competed for postwar influence, using the economic,
political, military, and ideological means available to them. The result was
the Cold War.*

*Why the Cold War developed with such divisiveness is a topic of spirited
debate among scholars and surviving participants of this postwar antagonism.
Were the causes to be found in the flawed and broken international system
itself? Or in a totalitarian Communist Russia bent on aggression? Or in a
powerful, expansionist United States? These questions suggest one-dimensional
answers. However, recent scholarship makes clear that there is no single
explanation for the origins of the Cold War and that the historian's task
is not to pin blame on one antagonist or the other, but to probe for the
complex national and international tensions and drives that pitted nation
against nation.*

DOCUMENTS

In May 1945 President Harry S. Truman sent a special representative to Moscow to
speak with Josef Stalin. Harry Hopkins, who for years had advised President
Franklin D. Roosevelt, already knew the Soviet Marshal and they talked frankly

about a host of issues, including the abrupt American termination of Lend-Lease
aid to Russia and the repressive Soviet presence in Poland. Portions of a memorandum of their conversation on May 27 constitute the first document. The second
document, from the gifted pen of George F. Kennan, is the famous and influential
"long telegram" of February 22, 1946, which Kennan, then attaché in the Moscow
Embassy, sent to Washington to spell out what he thought were the underlying
sources of Soviet behavior.

The third document is former British Prime Minister Winston S. Churchill's
"iron curtain" speech of March 5, 1946, delivered in Fulton Missouri. The next
document, a memorandum sent to the President in July 1946, was written by Secretary of Commerce Henry A. Wallace, a critic of Truman's "get tough" policies.
The President removed Wallace from office in September. And, finally, the "Truman
Doctrine" address by the President to Congress on March 12, 1947, is an outline of
the basic principle of containment, which thereafter guided American foreign policy.

Harry Hopkins and Josef Stalin Discuss Lend-Lease and Poland, 1945

Mr. Hopkins said that last night the Marshal had indicated that there were a
number of questions concerning the United States which were worrying him.
He asked Marshal Stalin if he would perhaps care to begin with these
questions.

Marshal Stalin said he would not attempt to use Soviet public opinion as a
screen but would speak of the feeling that had been created in Soviet governmental circles as a result of recent moves on the part of the United States
Government. He said these circles felt a certain alarm in regard to the attitude
of the United States Government. It was their impression that the American
attitude towards the Soviet Union had perceptibly cooled once it became
obvious that Germany was defeated, and that it was as though the Americans
were saying that the Russians were no longer needed. He said he would give
the following examples: . . .

[1] 3. The attitude of the United States Government towards the Polish question. He said that at Yalta it had been agreed that the existing government was
to be reconstructed and that anyone with common sense could see that this
meant that the present government was to form the basis of the new. He said
no other understanding of the Yalta Agreement was possible. Despite the fact
that they were simple people the Russians should not be regarded as fools
which was a mistake the West frequently made, nor were they blind and could
quite well see what was going on before their eyes. It is true that the Russians
are patient in the interests of a common cause but that their patience has its
limits.

[2] 4. The manner in which Lend Lease had been curtailed. He said that if
the United States was unable to supply the Soviet Union further under Lend
Lease that was one thing but that the manner in which it had been done had

been unfortunate and even brutal. For example, certain ships had been un-loaded and while it was true that this order had been cancelled the whole manner in which it had been done had caused concern to the Soviet Govern-ment. If the refusal to continue Lend Lease was designed as pressure on the Russians in order to soften them up then it was a fundamental mistake. He said he must tell Mr. Hopkins frankly that [if] the Russians were approached frankly on a friendly basis much could be done but that reprisals in any form would bring about the exact opposite effect. . . .

Mr. Hopkins said he first of all wished to express his appreciation of the frankness with which Marshal Stalin had exposed his worries. He said that insofar as he and Ambassador Harriman were able they would answer equally frankly and if on certain points they did not have full information they would endeavor to obtain it. . . .

Mr. Hopkins then said on the subject of Lend Lease he thought it had been clear to the Soviet Union that the end of the war with Germany would necessitate a reconsideration of the old program of Lend Lease to the Soviet Union.

Marshal Stalin said that was entirely understandable.

Mr. Hopkins continued that the history of Lend Lease showed that although in certain cases we had not always been able to meet every Soviet request we had nonetheless freely accepted commitments which we had done our best to carry out in spirit as well as in fact.

Marshal Stalin said that was undoubtedly true.

Mr. Hopkins stated that even prior to the end of the war in Europe we had made an agreement with the Soviet Union known as Annex 3 to Protocol 1 [IV], which involved delivery of supplies which might be of use in the Far East. He said that this grew out of recent conferences in which Far Eastern matters had been discussed. He emphasized that this commitment was accepted in full by the United States and we were in the process of carrying it out. In regard to the unloading of the ships he said that that was a technical mis-understanding and did not in any sense represent a decision of policy on the part of the United States. That it had been the action of one government agency involved in Lend Lease and that it had been countermanded promptly within twenty-four hours. He said that no one who was responsible for Lend Lease policy or American Government policy had had anything to do with that mis-taken order. The only question which had to be reconsidered was the program of deliveries to the Soviet Union which had been based on the needs of the war against Germany and that it had been made clear that on the basis of this reconsideration we would be glad to reconsider any Soviet requests and that he thought some were now being considered. He said he wished to emphasize that he had seen no tendency on the part of those responsible for American policy to handle the question of future Lend Lease to the Soviet Union in an arbitrary fashion. It was in fact a question of law, since the basic Lend Lease Act made it clear that materials could only be delivered which would be useful in the process of the war. The United States Government, however, had interpreted this in its broadest sense and had included in addition to munitions of war foodstuffs and other non-military items.

Marshal Stalin said this was true.

Mr. Hopkins concluded by saying that there had naturally been considerable confusion in the United States Government as to the status of Lend Lease towards Russia at the end of the war and that there had been varying legal interpretations but that he wished to emphasize that the incident to which Marshal Stalin referred did not have any fundamental policy significance.

Marshal Stalin said he wished to make it clear that he fully understood the right of the United States to curtail Lend Lease shipments to the Soviet Union under present conditions since our commitments in this respect had been freely entered into. Even two months ago it would have been quite correct for the United States to have begun to curtail shipments but what he had in mind was the manner and form in which it was done. He felt that what was after all an agreement between the two Governments had been ended in a scornful and abrupt manner. He said that if proper warning had been given to the Soviet Government there would have been no feeling of the kind he had spoken of; that this warning was important to them since their economy was based on plans. He added that they had intended to make a suitable expression of gratitude to the United States for the Lend Lease assistance during the war but the way in which this program had been halted now made that impossible to do.

Mr. Hopkins replied that what disturbed him most about the Marshal's statement was the revelation that he believed that the United States would use Lend Lease as a means of showing our displeasure with the Soviet Union. He wished to assure the Marshal that however unfortunate an impression this question had caused in the mind of the Soviet Government he must believe that there was no attempt or desire on the part of the United States to use it as a pressure weapon. He said the United States is a strong power and does not go in for those methods. Furthermore, we have no conflict of immediate interests with the Soviet Union and would have no reason to adopt such practices.

Marshal Stalin said he believed Mr. Hopkins and was fully satisfied with his statement in regard to Lend Lease but said he hoped Mr. Hopkins would consider how it had looked from their side.

Ambassador Harriman then suggested that he and Mr. Molotov might go into the details of the whole Lend Lease matter together with Mr. Mikoyan the following day.

Mr. Hopkins concluded the discussions of Lend Lease by stating that he thought it would be a great tragedy if the greatest achievement in cooperation which the Soviet Union and the United States had on the whole worked out together on the basis of Lend Lease were to end on an unsatisfactory note. He said he wished to add that we had never believed that our Lend Lease help had been the chief factor in the Soviet defeat of Hitler on the eastern front. That this had been done by the heroism and blood of the Russian Army. . . .

Mr. Hopkins then said with the Marshal's permission he would like to review the position of the United States in regard to Poland. He said first of all he wished to assure the Marshal that he had no thought or indeed any right to attempt to settle the Polish problem during his visit here in Moscow, nor was he intending to hide behind American public opinion in presenting the position of the United States.

Marshal Stalin said he was afraid that his remark concerning Soviet public opinion has cut Mr. Hopkins to the quick and that he had not meant to imply that Mr. Hopkins was hiding behind the screen of American public opinion. In fact he knew Mr. Hopkins to be an honest and frank man.

Mr. Hopkins said that he wished to state this position as clearly and as forcibly as he knew how. He said the question of Poland per se was not so important as the fact that it had become a symbol of our ability to work out problems with the Soviet Union. He said that we had no special interests in Poland and no special desire to see any particular kind of government. That we would accept any government in Poland which was desired by the Polish people and was at the same time friendly to the Soviet Government. He said that the people and Government of the United States felt that this was a problem which should be worked out jointly between the United States, the Soviet Union and Great Britain and that we felt that the Polish people should be given the right to free elections to choose their own government and their own system and that Poland should genuinely be independent. The Government and people of the United States were disturbed because the preliminary steps towards the reestablishment of Poland appeared to have been taken unilaterally by the Soviet Union together with the present Warsaw Government and that in fact the United States was completely excluded. He said he hoped that Stalin would believe him when he said that this feeling was a fact. Mr. Hopkins said he urged that Marshal Stalin would judge American policy by the actions of the United States Government itself and not by the attitudes and public expressions of the Hearst newspapers and the *Chicago Tribune*. He hoped that the Marshal would put his mind to the task of thinking up what diplomatic methods could be used to settle this question keeping in mind the feeling of the American people. He said he himself was not prepared to say how it could be done but that he felt it must be done. Poland had become a symbol in the sense that it bore a direct relation to the willingness of the United States to participate in international affairs on a world-wide basis and that our people must believe that they are joining their power with that of the Soviet Union and Great Britain in the promotion of international peace and the well being of humanity. Mr. Hopkins went on to say that he felt the overwhelming majority of the people of the United States felt that the relations between the United States and the U.S.S.R. could be worked out in a spirit of cooperation despite the differences in ideology and that with all these factors in its favor he wished to appeal to the Marshal to help find a way to the solution of the Polish problem.

Marshal Stalin replied that he wished Mr. Hopkins would take into consideration the following factors: He said it may seem strange although it appeared to be recognized in United States circles and Churchill in his speeches also recognized it, that the Soviet Government should wish for a friendly

Poland. In the course of twenty-five years the Germans had twice invaded Russia via Poland. Neither the British nor American people had experienced such German invasions which were a horrible thing to endure and the results of which were not easily forgotten. He said these German invasions were not warfare but were like the incursions of the Huns. He said that Germany had been able to do this because Poland had been regarded as a part of the *cordon sanitaire* around the Soviet Union and that previous European policy had been that Polish Governments must be hostile to Russia. In these circumstances either Poland had been too weak to oppose Germany or had let the Germans come through. Thus Poland had served as a corridor for the German attacks on Russia. He said Poland's weakness and hostility had been a great source of weakness to the Soviet Union and had permitted the Germans to do what they wished in the East and also in the West since the two were mixed together. It is therefore in Russia's vital interest that Poland should be both strong and friendly. He said there was no intention on the part of the Soviet Union to interfere in Poland's internal affairs, that Poland would live under the parliamentary system which is like Czechoslovakia, Belgium and Holland and that any talk of an intention to Sovietize Poland was stupid. He said even the Polish leaders, some of whom were communists, were against the Soviet system since the Polish people did not desire collective farms or other aspects of the Soviet system. In this the Polish leaders were right since the Soviet system was not exportable—it must develop from within on the basis of a set of conditions which were not present in Poland. He said all the Soviet Union wanted was that Poland should not be in a position to open the gates to Germany and in order to prevent this Poland must be strong and democratic. Stalin then said that before he came to his suggestion as to the practical solution of the question he would like to comment on Mr. Hopkins's remarks concerning future United States interests in the world. He said that whether the United States wished it or not it was a world power and would have to accept world-wide interests. Not only this war but the previous war had shown that without United States intervention Germany could not have been defeated and that all the events and developments of the last thirty years had confirmed this. In fact the United States had more reason to be a world power than any other state. For this reason he fully recognized the right of the United States as a world [power] to participate in the Polish question and that the Soviet interest in Poland does not in any way exclude those of England and the United States. Mr. Hopkins had spoken of Russian unilateral action in Poland and United States public opinion concerning it. It was true that Russia had taken such unilateral action but they had been compelled to. He said the Soviet Government had recognized the Warsaw Government and concluded a treaty with it at a time when their Allies did not recognize this government. These were admittedly unilateral acts which would have been much better left undone but the fact was they had not met with any understanding on the part of their Allies. The need for these actions had arisen out of the presence of Soviet troops in Poland and it would have been impossible to have waited until such time as the Allies had come to an agreement on Poland. The logic of the war against Germany demanded that the Soviet rear be assured and the Lublin Committee had been of great assistance to the Red Army at all times and it was for this reason that these actions had been taken by the Soviet Government. He said it was contrary to the Soviet policy to set up [a] Soviet administration on foreign soil since this would look like occupation and be resented by the local inhabitants. It was for this reason that some Polish administration had to be established in Poland and this could be done only with those who had helped the Red Army. He said he wished to emphasize that these steps had not been taken with any desire to eliminate or exclude Russia's Allies. He must point out however that Soviet action in Poland had been more successful than British action in Greece and at no time had they been compelled to undertake the measures which they had done in Greece. Stalin then turned to his suggestion for the solution of the Polish problem.

Marshal Stalin said that he felt that we should examine the composition of the future Government of National Unity. He said there were eighteen or twenty ministries in the present Polish Government and that four or five of these portfolios could be given representatives of other Polish groups taken from the list submitted by Great Britain and the United States (Molotov whispered to Stalin who then said he meant four and not five posts in the government). He said he thought the Warsaw Poles would not accept more than four ministers from other democratic groups. He added that if this appears a suitable basis we could then proceed to consider what persons should be selected for these posts. He said of course that they would have to be friendly to the U.S.S.R. and to the Allies. He added that Mikolajczyk had been suggested and he thought he was acceptable and that the question was now who else. He inquired of Mr. Hopkins whether possibly Professor Lange might be willing to join the government.

Mr. Hopkins said he doubted whether Professor Lange, who was an American citizen could be induced to give up his American citizenship for this purpose but that of course was only a private opinion.

Marshal Stalin then said it might be wise to ask some of the Warsaw leaders to come to Moscow now and to hear what they had to say and to learn more of what had been decided. He added that if we are able to settle the composition of the new government he felt that no differences remained since we were all agreed on the free and unfettered elections and that no one intended to interfere with the Polish people.

Mr. Hopkins said he would like to have some time to consider the Marshal's suggestion.

George F. Kennan's "Long Telegram," 1946

At bottom of Kremlin's neurotic view of world affairs is traditional and instinctive Russian sense of insecurity. Originally, this was insecurity of a peaceful agricultural people trying to live on vast exposed plain in neighborhood of fierce nomadic peoples. To this was added, as Russia came into contact with economically advanced West, fear of more competent, more powerful, more highly organized societies in that area. But this latter type of insecurity was one which afflicted rather Russian rulers than Russian people; for Russian rulers have invariably sensed that their rule was relatively archaic in form, fragile and artificial in its psychological foundation, unable to stand comparison or contact with political systems of Western countries. For this reason they have always feared foreign penetration, feared direct contact between Western world and their own, feared what would happen if Russians learned truth about world without or if foreigners learned truth about world within. And they have learned to seek security only in patient but deadly struggle for total destruction of rival power, never in compacts and compromises with it.

It was no coincidence that Marxism, which had smouldered ineffectively for half a century in Western Europe, caught hold and blazed for first time in Russia. Only in this land which had never known a friendly neighbor or indeed any tolerant equilibrium of separate powers, either internal or international, could a doctrine thrive which viewed economic conflicts of society as insoluble by peaceful means. After establishment of Bolshevist regime, Marxist dogma, rendered even more truculent and intolerant by Lenin's interpretation, became a perfect vehicle for sense of insecurity with which Bolsheviks, even more than previous Russian rulers, were afflicted. In this dogma, with its basic altruism of purpose, they found justification for their instinctive fear of outside world, for the dictatorship without which they did not know how to rule, for cruelties they did not dare not to inflict, for sacrifices they felt bound to demand. In the name of Marxism they sacrificed every single ethical value in their methods and tactics. Today they cannot dispense with it. It is fig leaf of their moral and intellectual respectability. Without it they would stand before history, at best, as only the last of that long succession of cruel and wasteful Russian rulers who have relentlessly forced country on to ever new heights of military power in order to guarantee external security of their internally weak regimes. This is why Soviet purposes must always be solemnly clothed in trappings of Marxism, and why no one should underrate importance of dogma in Soviet affairs. Thus Soviet leaders are driven [by?] necessities of their own past and present position to put forward a dogma which [apparent omission] outside world as evil, hostile and menacing, but as bearing within itself germs of creeping disease and destined to be wracked with growing internal convulsions until it is given final *coup de grace* by rising power of socialism and yields to new and better world. This thesis provides justification for that increase of military and police power of Russian state, for that isolation of Russian population from outside world, and for that fluid and constant pressure to extend limits of Russian police power which are together the natural and instinctive urges of Russian rulers. Basically this is only the steady advance of uneasy Russian nationalism, a centuries old movement in which conceptions of offense and defense are inextricably confused. But in new guise of international Marxism, with its honeyed promises to a desperate and war torn outside world, it is more dangerous and insidious than ever before.

It should not be thought from above that Soviet party line is necessarily disingenuous and insincere on part of all those who put it forward. Many of them are too ignorant of outside world and mentally too dependent to question [apparent omission] self-hypnotism, and who have no difficulty making themselves believe what they find it comforting and convenient to believe. Finally we have the unsolved mystery as to who, if anyone, in this great land actually receives accurate and unbiased information about outside world. In atmosphere of oriental secretiveness and conspiracy which pervades this Government, possibilities for distorting or poisoning sources and currents of information are infinite. The very disrespect of Russians for objective truth—indeed, their disbelief in its existence—leads them to view all stated facts as instruments for furtherance of one ulterior purpose or another. There is good reason to suspect that this Government is actually a conspiracy within a conspiracy; and I for one am reluctant to believe that Stalin himself receives anything like an objective picture of outside world. Here there is ample scope for the type of subtle intrigue at which Russians are past masters. Inability of foreign governments to place their case squarely before Russian policy makers—extent to which they are delivered up in their relations with Russia to good graces of obscure and unknown advisers whom they never see and cannot influence—this to my mind is most disquieting feature of diplomacy in Moscow, and one which Western statesmen would do well to keep in mind if they would understand nature of difficulties encountered here. . . .

In summary, we have here a political force committed fanatically to the belief that with US there can be no permanent *modus vivendi,* that it is desirable and necessary that the internal harmony of our society be disrupted, our traditional way of life be destroyed, the international authority of our state be broken, if Soviet power is to be secure. This political force has complete power of disposition over energies of one of world's greatest peoples and resources of world's richest national territory, and is borne along by deep and powerful currents of Russian nationalism. In addition, it has an elaborate and far flung apparatus for exertion of its influence in other countries, an apparatus of amazing flexibility and versatility, managed by people whose experience and skill in underground methods are presumably without parallel in history. Finally, it is seemingly inaccessible to considerations of reality in its basic reactions. For it, the vast fund of objective fact about human society is not, as with us, the measure against which outlook is constantly being tested and re-formed, but a grab bag from which individual items are selected arbitrarily and tendenciously to bolster an outlook already preconceived. This is admittedly not a pleasant picture. Problem of how to cope with this force in [*is*] undoubtedly greatest task our diplomacy has ever faced and probably greatest it will ever have to face. It should be point of departure from which our political general staff work at present juncture should proceed. It should be approached with same thoroughness and care as solution of major strategic problem in war, and if necessary, with no smaller outlay in planning effort. I cannot attempt to suggest all answers here. But I would like to record my conviction that problem is within our power to solve—and that without recourse to any general military conflict. And in support of this conviction there are certain observations of a more encouraging nature I should like to make:

1. Soviet power, unlike that of Hitlerite Germany, is neither schematic nor adventuristic. It does not work by fixed plans. It does not take unnecessary risks. Impervious to logic of reason, and it is highly sensitive to logic of force. For this reason it can easily withdraw—and usually does—when strong resistance is encountered at any point. Thus, if the adversary has sufficient force and makes clear his readiness to use it, he rarely has to do so. If situations are properly handled there need be no prestige-engaging showdowns.

2. Gauged against Western World as a whole, Soviets are still by far the weaker force. Thus, their success will really depend on degree of cohesion, firmness and vigor which Western World can muster. And this is factor which it is within our power to influence.

3. Success of Soviet system, as form of internal power, is not yet finally proven. It has yet to be demonstrated that it can survive supreme test of successive transfer of power from one individual or group to another. Lenin's death was first such transfer, and its effects wracked Soviet state for 15 years. After Stalin's death or retirement will be second. But even this will not be final test. Soviet internal system will now be subjected, by virtue of recent territorial expansions, to series of additional strains which once proved severe tax on Tsardom. We here are convinced that never since termination of civil war have mass of Russian people been emotionally farther removed from doctrines of Communist Party than they are today. In Russia, party has now become a great and—for the moment—highly successful apparatus of dictatorial administration, but it has ceased to be a source of emotional inspiration. Thus, internal soundness and permanence of movement need not yet be regarded as assured.

4. All Soviet propaganda beyond Soviet security sphere is basically negative and destructive. It should therefore be relatively easy to combat it by any intelligent and really constructive program.

For these reasons I think we may approach calmly and with good heart problem of how to deal with Russia. As to how this approach should be made, I only wish to advance, by way of conclusion, following comments:

1. Our first step must be to apprehend, and recognize for what it is, the nature of the movement with which we are dealing. We must study it with same courage, detachment, objectivity, and same determination not to be emotionally provoked or unseated by it, with which doctor studies unruly and unreasonable individual.

2. We must see that our public is educated to realities of Russian situation. I cannot over-emphasize importance of this. Press cannot do this alone. It must be done mainly by Government, which is necessarily more experienced and better informed on practical problems involved. In this we need not be deterred by [ugliness?] of picture. I am convinced that there would be far less hysterical anti-Sovietism in our country today if realities of this situation were

better understood by our people. There is nothing as dangerous or as terrifying as the unknown. It may also be argued that to reveal more information on our difficulties with Russia would reflect unfavorably on Russian-American relations. I feel that if there is any real risk here involved, it is one which we should have courage to face, and sooner the better. But I cannot see what we would be risking. Our stake in this country, even coming on heels of tremendous demonstrations of our friendship for Russian people, is remarkably small. We have here no investments to guard, no actual trade to lose, virtually no citizens to protect, few cultural contacts to preserve. Our only stake lies in what we hope rather than what we have; and I am convinced we have better chance of realizing those hopes if our public is enlightened and if our dealings with Russians are placed entirely on realistic and matter-of-fact basis.

3. Much depends on health and vigor of our own society. World communism is like malignant parasite which feeds only on diseased tissue. This is point at which domestic and foreign policies meet. Every courageous and incisive measure to solve internal problems of our own society, to improve self-confidence, discipline, morale and community spirit of our own people, is a diplomatic victory over Moscow worth a thousand diplomatic notes and joint communiqués. If we cannot abandon fatalism and indifference in face of deficiencies of our own society, Moscow will profit—Moscow cannot help profiting by them in its foreign policies.

4. We must formulate and put forward for other nations a much more positive and constructive picture of sort of world we would like to see than we have put forward in past. It is not enough to urge people to develop political processes similar to our own. Many foreign peoples, in Europe at least, are tired and frightened by experiences of past, and are less interested in abstract freedom than in security. They are seeking guidance rather than responsibilities. We should be better able than Russians to give them this. And unless we do, Russians certainly will.

5. Finally we must have courage and self-confidence to cling to our own methods and conceptions of human society. After all, the greatest danger that can befall us in coping with this problem of Soviet communism, is that we shall allow ourselves to become like those with whom we are coping.

Winston S. Churchill's "Iron Curtain" Speech, 1946

The United States stands at this time at the pinnacle of world power. It is a solemn moment for the American democracy. With primacy in power is also joined an awe-inspiring accountability to the future. As you look around you, you feel not only the sense of duty done but also feel anxiety lest you fall below the level of achievement. Opportunity is here now, clear and shining, for both our countries. To reject it or ignore it or fritter it away will bring upon us all the long reproaches of the after-time. It is necessary that constancy of mind, persistency of purpose, and the grand simplicity of decision shall guide and rule the conduct of the English-speaking peoples in peace as they did in war. We must and I believe we shall prove ourselves equal to this severe requirement. . . .

Before we cast away the solid assurances of national armaments for self-preservation, we must be certain that our temple is built, not upon shifting sands or quagmires, but upon the rock. Anyone with his eyes open can see that our path will be difficult and also long, but if we persevere together as we did in the two World Wars—though not, alas, in the interval between them— I cannot doubt that we shall achieve our common purpose in the end.

I have, however, a definite and practical proposal to make for action. Courts and magistrates cannot function without sheriffs and constables. The United Nations Organization must immediately begin to be equipped with an international armed force. In such a matter we can only go step by step; but we must begin now. I propose that each of the powers and states should be invited to dedicate a certain number of air squadrons to the service of the world organization. These squadrons would be trained and prepared in their own countries but would move around in rotation from one country to another. They would wear the uniform of their own countries with different badges. They would not be required to act against their own nation but in other respects they would be directed by the world organization. This might be started on a modest scale and a grow [sic] as confidence grew. I wished to see this done after the First World War and trust it may be done forthwith.

It would nevertheless be wrong and imprudent to entrust the secret knowledge or experience of the atomic bomb, which the United States, Great Britain, and Canada now share, to the world organization, while it is still in its infancy. It would be criminal madness to cast it adrift in this still agitated and un-united world. No one in any country has slept less well in their beds because this knowledge and the method and the raw materials to apply it are at present largely retained in American hands. I do not believe we should all have slept so soundly had the positions been reversed and some Communist or neo-Fascist state monopolized, for the time being, these dread agencies. The fear of them alone might easily have been used to enforce totalitarian systems upon the free democratic world, with consequences appalling to human imagination.

God has willed that this shall not be, and we have at least a breathing space before this peril has to be encountered, and even then, if no effort is spared, we should still possess so formidable a superiority as to impose effective deterrents upon its employment or threat of employment by others. Ultimately when the essential brother of man is truly embodied and expressed in a world organization, these powers may be confided to it. . . .

There is . . . an important question we must ask ourselves. Would a special relationship between the United States and the British Commonwealth be inconsistent with our overriding loyalties to the world organization? I reply that on the contrary, it is probably the only means by which that organization will achieve its full stature and strength. There are already the special United

States relations with Canada and between the United States and the South American republics. We also have our twenty years' treaty of collaboration and mutual assistance with Soviet Russia. I agree with Mr. Bevin that it might well be a fifty-year treaty. We have an alliance with Portugal unbroken since 1384. None of these clash with the general interest of a world agreement. On the contrary they help it. "In my Father's house are many mansions." Special associations between members of the United Nations which have no aggressive point against any other country, which harbor no design incompatible with the charter of the United Nations, far from being harmful, are beneficial and, as I believe, indispensable. . . .

A shadow has fallen upon the scenes so lately lighted by the Allied victory. Nobody knows what Soviet Russia and its Communist international organization intends to do in the immediate future, or what are the limits, if any, to their expansive and proselytizing tendencies. I have a strong admiration and regard for the valiant Russian people and for my wartime comrade, Marshal Stalin. There is sympathy and good will in Britain—and I doubt not here also —toward the peoples of all the Russias and a resolve to persevere through many differences and rebuffs in establishing lasting friendships.

We understand the Russian need to be secure on her western frontiers from all renewal of German aggression. We welcome her to her rightful place among the leading nations of the world. Above all, we welcome constant, frequent, and growing contacts between the Russian people and our own people on both sides of the Atlantic. It is my duty, however, to place before you certain facts about the present position in Europe.

From Stettin in the Baltic to Trieste in the Adriatic, an iron curtain has descended across the continent. Behind that line lie all the capitals of the ancient states of Central and Eastern Europe. Warsaw, Berlin, Prague, Vienna, Budapest, Belgrade, Bucharest, and Sofia, all these famous cities and the populations around them lie in the Soviet sphere and all are subject, in one form or another, not only to Soviet influence but to a very high and increasing measure of control from Moscow. Athens alone, with its immortal glories, is free to decide its future at an election under British, American, and French observation.

The Russian-dominated Polish government has been encouraged to make enormous and wrongful inroads upon Germany, and mass expulsions of millions of Germans on a scale grievous and undreamed of are now taking place. The Communist parties, which were very small in all these eastern states of Europe, have been raised to preeminence and power far beyond their numbers and are seeking everywhere to obtain totalitarian control. Police governments are prevailing in nearly every case, and so far, except in Czechoslovakia, there is no true democracy.

Turkey and Persia are both profoundly alarmed and disturbed at the claims which are made upon them and at the pressure being exerted by the Moscow government. An attempt is being made by the Russians in Berlin to build up a quasi-Communist party in their zone of occupied Germany by showing special favors to groups of left-wing German leaders. At the end of the fighting last June, the American and British Armies withdrew westward, in accordance with an earlier agreement, to a depth at some points of 150 miles on a front of nearly 400 miles, to allow the Russians to occupy this vast expanse of territory which the Western democracies had conquered.

If now the Soviet government tries, by separate action, to build up a pro-Communist Germany in their areas, this will cause new serious difficulties in the British and American zones, and will give the defeated Germans the power of putting themselves up to auction between the Soviets and the Western democracies. Whatever conclusions may be drawn from these facts—and facts they are—this is certainly not the liberated Europe we fought to build up. Nor is it one which contains the essentials of permanent peace.

In front of the iron curtain which lies across Europe are other causes for anxiety. In Italy the Communist party is seriously hampered by having to support the Communist-trained Marshall Tito's claims to former Italian territory at the head of the Adriatic. Nevertheless, the future of Italy hangs in the balance. Again, one cannot imagine a regenerated Europe without a strong France. . . .

However, in a great number of countries, far from the Russian frontiers and throughout the world, Communist fifth columns are established and work in complete unity and absolute obedience to the directions they receive from the Communist center. Except in the British Commonwealth, and in the United States, where communism is in its infancy, the Communist parties or fifth columns constitute a growing challenge and peril to Christian civilization. These are somber facts for anyone to have to recite on the morrow of a victory gained by so much splendid comradeship in arms and in the cause of freedom and democracy, and we should be most unwise not to face them squarely while time remains.

The outlook is also anxious in the Far East and especially in Manchuria. The agreement which was made at Yalta, to which I was a party, was extremely favorable to Soviet Russia, but it was made at a time when no one could say that the German war might not extend all through the summer and autumn of 1945 and when the Japanese war was expected to last for a further eighteen months from the end of the German war. In this country you are all so well informed about the Far East and such devoted friends of China that I do not need to expatiate on the situation there. . . .

Our difficulties and dangers will not be removed by closing our eyes to them; they will not be removed by mere waiting to see what happens; nor will they be relieved by a policy of appeasement. What is needed is a settlement, and the longer this is delayed, the more difficult it will be and the greater our dangers will become. From what I have seen of our Russian friends and allies during the war, I am convinced that there is nothing they admire so much as strength, and there is nothing for which they have less respect than for military weakness. For that reason the old doctrine of a balance of power is unsound. We cannot afford, if we can help it, to work on narrow margins, offering temptations to a trial of strength. If the Western democracies stand together in strict adherence to the principles of the United Nations Charter, their influence for furthering these principles will be immense and no one is likely to molest them. If, however, they become divided or falter in their duty, and if these all-important years are allowed to slip away, then indeed catastrophe may overwhelm us all.

Last time I saw it all coming, and cried aloud to my own fellow countrymen and to the world, but no one paid any attention. Up till the year 1933 or even 1935, Germany might have been saved from the awful fate which has overtaken her and we might all have been spared the miseries Hitler let loose upon mankind.

There never was a war in all history easier to prevent by timely action than the one which has just desolated such great areas of the globe. It could have been prevented without the firing of a single shot, and Germany might be powerful, prosperous, and honored today, but no one would listen and one by one we were all sucked into the awful whirlpool.

We surely must not let that happen again. This can only be achieved by reaching now, in 1946, a good understanding on all points with Russia under the general authority of the United Nations and by the maintenance of that good understanding through many peaceful years, by the world instrument, supported by the whole strength of the English-speaking world and all its connections.

Henry A. Wallace Questions the "Get Tough" Policy, 1946

How do American actions since V-J Day appear to other nations? I mean by actions the concrete things like $13 billion for the War and Navy Departments, the Bikini tests of the atomic bomb and continued production of bombs, the plan to arm Latin America with our weapons, production of B-29s and planned production of B-36s, and the effort to secure air bases spread over half the globe from which the other half of the globe can be bombed. I cannot but feel that these actions must make it look to the rest of the world as if we were only paying lip service to peace at the conference table. These facts rather make it appear either (1) that we are preparing ourselves to win the war which we regard as inevitable or (2) that we are trying to build up a predominance of force to intimidate the rest of mankind. How would it look to us if Russia had the atomic bomb and we did not, if Russia had ten thousand-mile bombers and air bases within a thousand miles of our coast lines and we did not?

Some of the military men and self-styled "realists" are saying: "What's wrong with trying to build up a predominance of force? The only way to preserve peace is for this country to be so well armed that no one will dare attack us. We know that America will never start a war."

The flaw in this policy is simply that it will not work. In a world of atomic bombs and other revolutionary new weapons, such as radioactive poison gases and biological warfare, a peace maintained by a predominance of force is no longer possible.

Henry A. Wallace, "The Path to Peace with Russia," *New Republic*, 115 (1946), 401–406.

Why is this so? The reasons are clear:

First. Atomic warfare is cheap and easy compared with old-fashioned war. Within a very few years several countries can have atomic bombs and other atomic weapons. Compared with the cost of large armies and the manufacture of old-fashioned weapons, atomic bombs cost very little and require only a relatively small part of a nation's production plant and labor force.

Second. So far as winning a war is concerned, having more bombs—even many more bombs—than the other fellow is no longer a decisive advantage. If another nation had enough bombs to eliminate all of our principal cities and our heavy industry, it wouldn't help us very much if we had ten times as many bombs as we needed to do the same to them.

Third. The most important, the very fact that several nations have atomic bombs will inevitably result in a neurotic, fear-ridden, itching-trigger psychology in all the peoples of the world, and because of our wealth and vulnerability we would be among the most seriously affected. Atomic war will not require vast and time-consuming preparations, the mobilization of large armies, the conversion of a large proportion of a country's industrial plants to the manufacture of weapons. In a world armed with atomic weapons, some incident will lead to the use of those weapons.

There is a school of military thinking which recognizes these facts, recognizes that when several nations have atomic bombs, a war which will destroy modern civilization will result and that no nation or combination of nations can win such a war. This school of thought therefore advocates a "preventative war," an attack on Russia now, before Russia has atomic bombs. This scheme is not only immoral but stupid. It we should attempt to destroy all the principal Russian cities and her heavy industry, we might well succeed. But the immediate countermeasure which such an attack would call forth is the prompt occupation of all continental Europe by the Red Army. Would we be prepared to destroy the cities of all Europe in trying to finish what we had started? This idea is so contrary to all the basic instincts and principles of the American people that any such action would be possible only under a dictatorship at home.

Thus the "predominance of force" idea and the notion of a "defensive attack" are both unworkable. The only solution is the one which you have so wisely advanced and which forms the basis of the Moscow statement on atomic energy. That solution consists of mutual trust and confidence among nations, atomic disarmament and an effective system of enforcing that disarmament.

There is, however, a fatal defect in the Moscow statement, in the Acheson report, and in the American plan recently presented to the United Nations Atomic Energy Commission. That defect is the scheme, as it is generally understood, of arriving at international agreements by "easy stages," of requiring other nations to enter into binding commitments not to conduct research into the military uses of atomic energy and to disclose their uranium and thorium resources while the United States retains the right to withhold its technical knowledge of atomic energy until the international control and inspection system is working to our satisfaction. In other words, we are telling the Russians that if they are "good boys" we may eventually turn over our knowledge of atomic energy to them and to the other nations. But there is no objective standard of what will qualify them as being "good" nor any specified time for sharing our knowledge.

Is it any wonder that the Russians did not show any great enthusiasm for our plan? Would we have been enthusiastic if the Russians had a monopoly of atomic energy, and offered to share the information with us at some indefinite time in the future at their discretion if we agreed now not to try to make a bomb and give them information on our secret resources of uranium and thorium? I think we should react as the Russians appear to have done. We would have put up counterproposal for the record, but our real effort would go into trying to make a bomb so that our bargaining position would be equalized. . . .

Insistence on our part that the game must be played our way will only lead to a deadlock. The Russians will redouble their efforts to manufacture bombs, and they may also decide to expand their "security zone" in a serious way. Up to now, despite all our outcries against it, their efforts to develop a security zone in Eastern Europe and in the Middle East are small change from the point of view of military power as compared with our air bases in Greenland, Okinawa and many other places thousands of miles from our shores. We may feel very self-righteous if we refuse to budge on our plan and the Russians refuse to accept it, but that means only one thing—the atomic armament race is on in deadly earnest.

I am convinced therefore that if we are to achieve our hopes of negotiating a treaty which will result in effective international atomic disarmament we must abandon the impractical form of the "step-by-step" idea which was presented to the United Nations Atomic Energy Commission. We must be prepared to reach an agreement which will commit us to disclosing information and destroying our bombs at a specific time or on terms of specified actions by other countries, rather than at our unfettered discretion. If we are willing to negotiate on this basis, I believe the Russians will also negotiate seriously with a view to reaching an agreement.

There can be, of course, no absolute assurance the Russians will finally agree to a workable plan if we adopt this view. They may prefer to stall until they also have bombs and can negotiate on a more equal basis, not realizing the danger to themselves as well as the rest of the world in a situation in which several nations have atomic bombs. But we must make the effort to head off the atomic bomb race. We have everything to gain by doing so, and do not give up anything by adopting this policy as the fundamental basis for our negotiation. During the transition period toward full-scale international control we retain our technical know-how, and the only existing production plants for fissionable materials and bombs remain within our borders. . . .

Our basic distrust of the Russians, which has been greatly intensified in recent months by the playing up of conflict in the press, stems from differences in political and economic organizations. For the first time in our history defeatists among us have raised the fear of another system as a successful rival to democracy and free enterprise in other countries and perhaps even our own. I am convinced that we can meet that challenge as we have in the past by demonstrating that economic abundance can be achieved without sacrificing personal, political and religious liberties. We cannot meet it, as Hitler tried to, by an anti-Comintern alliance.

It is perhaps too easy to forget that despite the deep-seated differences in our culture and intensive anti-Russian propaganda of some twenty-five years' standing, the American people reversed their attitudes during the crisis of war. Today, under the pressure of seemingly insoluble international problems and continuing deadlocks, the tide of American public opinion is again turning against Russia. In this reaction lies one of the dangers to which this letter is addressed.

I should list the factors which make for Russian distrust of the United States and of the Western world as follows: The first is Russian history, which we must take into account because it is the setting in which Russians see all actions and policies of the rest of the world. Russian history for over a thousand years has been a succession of attempts, often unsuccessful, to resist invasion and conquest—by the Mongols, the Turks, the Swedes, the Germans and the Poles. The scant thirty years of the existence of the Soviet government has in Russian eyes been a continuation of their historical struggle for national existence. The first four years of the new regime, from 1917 through 1921, were spent in resisting attempts at destruction by the Japanese, British and French, with some American assistance, and by the several White Russian armies encouraged and financed by the Western powers. Then, in 1941, the Soviet state was almost conquered by the Germans after a period during which the Western European powers had apparently acquiesced in the rearming of Germany in the belief that the Nazis would seek to expand eastward rather than westward. The Russians, therefore, obviously see themselves as fighting for their existence in a hostile world.

Second, it follows that to the Russians all of the defense and security measures of the Western powers seem to have an aggressive intent. Our actions to expand our military security system—such steps as extending the Monroe Doctrine to include the arming of the Western Hemisphere nations, our present monopoly of the atomic bomb, our interest in outlying bases and our general support of the British Empire—appear to them as going far beyond the requirements of defense. I think we might feel the same if the United States were the only capitalistic country in the world and the principal socialistic countries were creating a level of armed strength far exceeding anything in their previous history. From the Russian point of view, also, the granting of a loan to Britain and the lack of tangible results on their request to borrow for rehabilitation purposes may be regarded as another evidence of strengthening of an anti-Soviet bloc.

Finally, our resistance to her attempts to obtain warm water ports and her own security system in the form of "friendly" neighboring states seems, from the Russian point of view, to clinch the case. After twenty-five years of isolation and after having achieved the status of a major power, Russia believes that she is entitled to recognition of her new status. Our interest in establishing democracy in Eastern Europe, where democracy by and large has never existed, seems to her an attempt to reestablish the encirclement of unfriendly neighbors which was created after the last war and which might serve as a springboard of still another effort to destroy her.

If this analysis is correct, and there is ample evidence to support it, the action to improve the situation is clearly indicated. The fundamental objective of such action should be to allay any reasonable Russian grounds for fear, suspicions and distrust. We must recognize that the world has changed and that today there can be no "one world" unless the United States and Russia can find some way of living together. For example, most of us are firmly convinced of the soundness of our position when we suggest the internationalization and defortification of the Danube or of the Dardanelles, but we would be horrified and angered by any Russian counterproposal that would involve also the internationalizing and disarming of Suez or Panama. We must recognize that to the Russians these seem to be identical situations.

We should ascertain from a fresh point of view what Russia believes to be essential to her own security as a prerequisite to the writing of the peace and to cooperation in the construction of a world order. We should be prepared to judge her requirements against the background of what we ourselves and the British have insisted upon as essential to our respective security. We should be prepared, even at the expense of risking epithets of appeasement to agree to reasonable Russian guarantees of security. . . .

We should also be prepared to enter into economic discussions without demanding that the Russians agree in advance to discussion of a series of what are to them difficult and somewhat unrelated political and economic concessions. Although this is the field in which my department is most directly concerned, I must say that in my opinion this aspect of the problem is not as critical as some of the others, and certainly is far less important than the question of atomic energy control. But successful negotiation in this field might help considerably to bridge the chasm that separates us. The question of a loan should be approached on economic and commercial grounds and should be dissociated as much as possible from the current misunderstandings which flow from the basic differences between their system and ours. You have already clearly dissociated yourself and the American people from the expressions of anti-Soviet support for the British loan. If we could have followed up your statement on signing the British loan bill with a loan to the USSR on a commercial basis and on similar financial terms, I believe that it would have clearly demonstrated that this country is not attempting to use its economic resources in the game of power politics. In the light of the present Export-Import Bank situation it is now of the greatest importance that we undertake general economic discussions at an early date.

It is of the greatest importance that we should discuss with the Russians in a friendly way their long-range economic problems and the future of our cooperation in matters of trade. The reconstruction program of the USSR and the plans for the full development of the Soviet Union offers tremendous opportunities for American goods and American technicians.

American products, especially machines of all kinds, are well established in the Soviet Union. For example, American equipment, practices and methods are standard in coal mining, iron and steel, oil and nonferrous metals.

Nor would this trade be one-sided. Although the Soviet Union has been an excellent credit risk in the past, eventually the goods and services exported from this country must be paid for by the Russians by exports to us and to other countries. Russian products which are either definitely needed or which are noncompetitive in this country are various nonferrous metal ores, furs, linen products, lumber products, vegetable drugs, paper and pulp and native handicrafts. . . .

Many of the problems relating to the countries bordering on Russia could more readily be solved once an atmosphere of mutual trust and confidence is established and some form of economic arrangements is worked out with Russia. These problems also might be helped by discussions of an economic nature. Russian economic penetration of the Danube area, for example, might be countered by concrete proposals for economic collaboration in the development of the resources of this area, rather than by insisting that the Russians should cease their unilateral penetration and offering no solution to the present economic chaos there.

This proposal admittedly calls for a shift in some of our thinking about international matters. It is imperative that we make this shift. We have little time to lose. Our postwar actions have not yet been adjusted to the lessons to be gained from experience of Allied cooperation during the war and the facts of the atomic age.

It is certainly desirable that, as far as possible, we achieve unity on the home front with respect to our international relations; but unity on the basis of building up conflict abroad would prove to be not only unsound but disastrous. I think there is some reason to fear that in our earnest efforts to achieve bipartisan unity in this country we may have given away too much to isolationism masquerading as tough realism in international affairs.

The Truman Doctrine, 1947

The gravity of the situation which confronts the world today necessitates my appearance before a joint session of the Congress.

The foreign policy and the national security of this country are involved.

One aspect of the present situation, which I present to you at this time for your consideration and decision, concerns Greece and Turkey.

The United States has received from the Greek Government an urgent appeal for financial and economic assistance. Preliminary reports from the American Economic Mission now in Greece and reports from the American Ambassador in Greece corroborate the statement of the Greek Government that assistance is imperative if Greece is to survive as a free nation. . . .

The British Government has informed us that, owing to its own difficulties, it can no longer extend financial or economic aid to Turkey.

As in the case of Greece, if Turkey is to have the assistance it needs, the United States must supply it. We are the only country able to provide that help.

I am fully aware of the broad implications involved if the United States extends assistance to Greece and Turkey, and I shall discuss these implications with you at this time.

One of the primary objectives of the foreign policy of the United States is the creation of conditions in which we and other nations will be able to work out a way of life free from coercion. This was a fundamental issue in the war with Germany and Japan. Our victory was won over countries which sought to impose their will, and their way of life, upon other nations.

To ensure the peaceful development of nations, free from coercion, the United States has taken a leading part in establishing the United Nations. The United Nations is designed to make possible lasting freedom and independence for all its members. We shall not realize our objectives, however, unless we are willing to help free peoples to maintain their free institutions and their national integrity against aggressive movements that seek to impose upon them totalitarian regimes. This is no more than a frank recognition that totalitarian regimes imposed upon free peoples, by direct or indirect aggression, undermine the foundations of international peace and hence the security of the United States.

The peoples of a number of countries of the world have recently had totalitarian regimes forced upon them against their will. The Government of the United States has made frequent protests against coercion and intimidation, in violation of the Yalta agreement, in Poland, Rumania, and Bulgaria. I must also state that in a number of other countries there have been similar developments.

At the present moment in world history nearly every nation must choose between alternative ways of life. The choice is too often not a free one.

One way of life is based upon the will of the majority, and is distinguished by free institutions, representative government, free elections, guarantees of individual liberty, freedom of speech and religion, and freedom from political oppression.

The second way of life is based upon the will of a minority forcibly imposed upon the majority. It relies upon terror and oppression, a controlled press and radio, fixed elections, and the suppression of personal freedoms.

I believe that it must be the policy of the United States to support free peoples who are resisting attempted subjugation by armed minorities or by outside pressures.

I believe that we must assist free peoples to work out their own destinies in their own way.

I believe that our help should be primarily through economic and financial aid which is essential to economic stability and orderly political processes.

The world is not static, and the *status quo* is not sacred. But we cannot allow changes in the *status quo* in violation of the Charter of the United Nations by such methods as coercion, or by such subterfuges as political infiltration. In helping free and independent nations to maintain their freedom, the United States will be giving effect to the principles of the Charter of the United Nations.

It is necessary only to glance at a map to realize that the survival and integrity of the Greek nation are of grave importance in a much wider situation. If Greece should fall under the control of an armed minority, the effect upon its neighbor, Turkey, would be immediate and serious. Confusion and disorder might well spread throughout the entire Middle East.

Moreover, the disappearance of Greece as an independent state would have a profound effect upon those countries in Europe whose peoples are struggling against great difficulties to maintain their freedoms and their independence while they repair the damages of war.

It would be an unspeakable tragedy if these countries, which have struggled so long against overwhelming odds, should lose that victory for which they sacrificed so much. Collapse of free institutions and loss of independence would be disastrous not only for them but for the world. Discouragement and possibly failure would quickly be the lot of neighboring peoples striving to maintain their freedom and independence.

Should we fail to aid Greece and Turkey in this fateful hour, the effect will be far reaching to the West as well as to the East.

We must take immediate and resolute action.

I therefore ask the Congress to provide authority for assistance to Greece and Turkey in the amount of $400,000,000 for the period ending June 30, 1948. In requesting these funds, I have taken into consideration the maximum amount of relief assistance which would be furnished to Greece out of the $350,000,000 which I recently requested that the Congress authorize for the prevention of starvation and suffering in countries devastated by the war.

In addition to funds, I ask the Congress to authorize the detail of American civilian and military personnel to Greece and Turkey, at the request of those countries, to assist in the tasks of reconstruction, and for the purpose of supervising the use of such financial and material assistance as may be furnished. I recommend that authority also be provided for the instruction and training of selected Greek and Turkish personnel.

Finally, I ask that the Congress provide authority which will permit the speediest and most effective use, in terms of needed commodities, supplies, and equipment, of such funds as may be authorized.

If further funds, or further authority, should be needed for the purposes indicated in this message, I shall not hesitate to bring the situation before the Congress. On this subject the Executive and Legislative branches of the Government must work together.

This is a serious course upon which we embark.

I would not recommend it except that the alternative is much more serious.

The United States contributed $341,000,000,000 toward winning World War II. This is an investment in world freedom and world peace.

The assistance that I am recommending for Greece and Turkey amounts to little more than $\frac{1}{10}$ of 1 percent of this investment. It is only common sense that we should safeguard this investment and make sure that it was not in vain.

The seeds of totalitarian regimes are nurtured by misery and want. They spread and grow in the evil soil of poverty and strife. They reach their full growth when the hope of a people for a better life has died.

We must keep that hope alive.

The free peoples of the world look to us for support in maintaining their freedoms.

If we falter in our leadership, we may endanger the peace of the world— and we shall surely endanger the welfare of this Nation.

Great responsibilities have been placed upon us by the swift movement of events.

I am confident that the Congress will face these responsibilities squarely.

ESSAYS

Arthur M. Schlesinger, Jr., a contemporary of the early days of the Cold War, spoke out strongly in the 1940s against Communism at home and abroad. A distinguished historian and politician who served as an adviser to President John F. Kennedy in the early 1960s, Schlesinger believes that Soviet ideology and the paranoia of Josef Stalin caused the Cold War and that there was little the United States could have done to avert the shattering of the alliance and the onset of postwar controversy. He represents the "traditional" or "orthodox" view of the Cold War.

Thomas G. Paterson of the University of Connecticut holds "revisionist" views, as the selection from his book *Soviet-American Confrontation* attests. Paterson acknowledges Soviet intransigence, but stresses that the United States held the predominant power in the postwar world and followed an expansionist diplomacy that helped to exacerbate friction. He discusses ideology, economic needs, personalities, lessons of the past, and other factors that together influenced American foreign policy.

Soviet Ideology and Stalinist Paranoia

ARTHUR M. SCHLESINGER, JR.

The orthodox American view, as originally set forth by the American government and as reaffirmed until recently by most American scholars, has been that the Cold War was the brave and essential response of free men to com-

Arthur Schlesinger, Jr., "Origins of the Cold War," *Foreign Affairs,* 46 (1967), 23–25, 26–27, 28–30, 32–50, 52. Reprinted by permission from *Foreign Affairs,* October 1967. Copyright 1967 by Council on Foreign Relations, Inc.

munist aggression. Some have gone back well before the Second World War to lay open the sources of Russian expansionism. Geopoliticians traced the Cold War to imperial Russian strategic ambitions which in the nineteenth century led to the Crimean War, to Russian penetration of the Balkans and the Middle East and to Russian pressure on Britain's "lifeline" to India. Ideologists traced it to the Communist Manifesto of 1848 ("the violent overthrow of the bourgeoisie lays the foundation for the sway of the proletariat"). Thoughtful observers (a phrase meant to exclude those who speak in Dullese about the unlimited evil of godless, atheistic, militant communism) concluded that classical Russian imperialism and Pan-Slavism, compounded after 1917 by Leninist messianism, confronted the West at the end of the Second World War with an inexorable drive for domination.

The revisionist thesis is very different. In its extreme form, it is that, after the death of Franklin Roosevelt and the end of the Second World War, the United States deliberately abandoned the wartime policy of collaboration and, exhilarated by the possession of the atomic bomb, undertook a course of aggression of its own designed to expel all Russian influence from Eastern Europe and to establish democratic-capitalist states on the very border of the Soviet Union. As the revisionists see it, this radically new American policy —or rather this resumption by Truman of the pre-Roosevelt policy of insensate anti-communism—left Moscow no alternative but to take measures in defense of its own borders. The result was the Cold War. . . .

Peacemaking after the Second World War was not so much a tapestry as it was a hopelessly raveled and knotted mess of yarn. Yet, for purposes of clarity, it is essential to follow certain threads. One theme indispensable to an understanding of the Cold War is the contrast between two clashing views of world order: the "universalist" view, by which all nations shared a common interest in all the affairs of the world, and the "sphere-of-influence" view, by which each great power would be assured by the other great powers of an acknowledged predominance in its own area of special interest. The universalist view assumed that national security would be guaranteed by an international organization. The sphere-of-interest view assumed that national security would be guaranteed by the balance of power. While in practice these views have by no means been incompatible (indeed, our shaky peace has been based on a combination of the two), in the abstract they involved sharp contradictions.

The tradition of American thought in these matters was universalist—*i.e.* Wilsonian. Roosevelt had been a member of Wilson's subcabinet; in 1920, as candidate for Vice President, he had campaigned for the League of Nations. It is true that, within Roosevelt's infinitely complex mind, Wilsonianism warred with the perception of vital strategic interests he had imbibed from Mahan. Moreover, his temperamental inclination to settle things with fellow princes around the conference table led him to regard the Big Three—or Four—as trustees for the rest of the world. On occasion, as this narrative will show, he was beguiled into flirtation with the sphere-of-influence heresy. But in principle he believed in joint action and remained a Wilsonian. His hope for Yalta, as he told the Congress on his return, was that it would "spell the end of the system of unilateral action, the exclusive alliances, the spheres of influence, the balances of power, and all the other expedients that have been tried for centuries—and have always failed."

Whenever Roosevelt backslid, he had at his side that Wilsonian fundamentalist, Secretary of State Cordell Hull, to recall him to the pure faith. After his visit to Moscow in 1943, Hull characteristically said that, with the Declaration of Four Nations on General Security (in which America, Russia, Britain and China pledged "united action . . . for the organization and maintenance of peace and security"), "there will no longer be need for spheres of influence, for alliances, for balance of power, or any other of the special arrangements through which, in the unhappy past, the nations strove to safeguard their security or to promote their interests."

Remembering the corruption of the Wilsonian vision by the secret treaties of the First World War, Hull was determined to prevent any sphere-of-influence nonsense after the Second World War. He therefore fought all proposals to settle border questions while the war was still on and, excluded as he largely was from wartime diplomacy, poured his not inconsiderable moral energy and frustration into the promulgation of virtuous and spacious general principles. . . .

It is true that critics, and even friends, of the United States sometimes noted a discrepancy between the American passion for universalism when it applied to territory far from American shores and the preëminence the United States accorded its own interests nearer home. Churchill, seeking Washington's blessing for a sphere-of-influence initiative in Eastern Europe, could not forbear reminding the Americans, "We follow the lead of the United States in South America;" nor did any universalist of record propose the abolition of the Monroe Doctrine. But a convenient myopia prevented such inconsistencies from qualifying the ardency of the universalist faith.

There seem only to have been three officials in the United States Government who dissented. One was the Secretary of War, Henry L. Stimson, a classical balance-of-power man, who in 1944 opposed the creation of a vacuum in Central Europe by the pastoralization of Germany and in 1945 urged "the settlement of all territorial acquisitions in the shape of defense posts which each of these four powers may deem to be necessary for their own safety" in advance of any effort to establish a peacetime United Nations. Stimson considered the claim of Russia to a preferred position in Eastern Europe as not unreasonable: as he told President Truman, "he thought the Russians perhaps were being more realistic than we were in regard to their own security." Such a position for Russia seemed to him comparable to the preferred American position in Latin America; he even spoke of "our respective orbits." Stimson was therefore skeptical of what he regarded as the prevailing tendency "to hang on to exaggerated views of the Monroe Doctrine and at the same time butt into every question that comes up in Central Europe." Acceptance of spheres of influence seemed to him the way to avoid "a head-on collision."

A second official opponent of universalism was George Kennan, an eloquent advocate from the American Embassy in Moscow of "a prompt and clear recognition of the division of Europe into spheres of influence and of a policy based on the fact of such division." Kennan argued that nothing we could do would possibly alter the course of events in Eastern Europe; that we were deceiving ourselves by supposing that these countries had any future but Russian domination; that we should therefore relinquish Eastern Europe to the Soviet Union and avoid anything which would make things easier for the Russians by giving them economic assistance or by sharing moral responsibility for their actions.

A third voice within the government against universalism was (at least after the war) Henry A. Wallace. As Secretary of Commerce, he stated the sphere-of-influence case with trenchancy in the famous Madison Square Garden speech of September 1946 which led to his dismissal by President Truman:

> On our part, we should recognize that we have no more business in the *political* affairs of Eastern Europe than Russia has in the *political* affairs of Latin America, Western Europe, and the United States. . . . Whether we like it or not, the Russians will try to socialize their sphere of influence just as we try to democratize our sphere of influence. . . . The Russians have no more business stirring up native Communists to political activity in Western Europe, Latin America, and the United States than we have in interfering with the politics of Eastern Europe and Russia.

Stimson, Kennan and Wallace seem to have been alone in the government, however, in taking these views. They were very much minority voices. Meanwhile universalism, rooted in the American legal and moral tradition, overwhelmingly backed by contemporary opinion, received successive enshrinements in the Atlantic Charter of 1941, in the Declaration of the United Nations in 1942 and in the Moscow Declaration of 1943.

The Kremlin, on the other hand, thought *only* of spheres of interest; above all, the Russians were determined to protect their frontiers, and especially their border to the west, crossed so often and so bloodily in the dark course of their history. These western frontiers lacked natural means of defense—no great oceans, rugged mountains, steaming swamps or impenetrable jungles. The history of Russia had been the history of invasion, the last of which was by now horribly killing up to twenty million of its people. The protocol of Russia therefore meant the enlargement of the area of Russian influence. Kennan himself wrote (in May 1944), "Behind Russia's stubborn expansion lies only the age-old sense of insecurity of a sedentary people reared on an exposed plain in the neighborhood of fierce nomadic peoples," and he called this "urge" a "permanent feature of Russian psychology." . . .

Teheran in December 1943 marked the high point of three-power collaboration. Still, when Churchill asked about Russian territorial interests, Stalin replied a little ominously, "There is no need to speak at the present time about any Soviet desires, but when the time comes we will speak." In the next weeks, there were increasing indications of a Soviet determination to deal unilaterally with Eastern Europe—so much so that in early February 1944 Hull cabled Harriman in Moscow:

Matters are rapidly approaching the point where the Soviet Government will have to choose between the development and extension of the foundation of international cooperation as the guiding principle of the postwar world as against the continuance of a unilateral and arbitrary method of dealing with its special problems even though these problems are admittedly of more direct interest to the Soviet Union than to other great powers.

As against this approach, however, Churchill, more tolerant of sphere-of-influence deviations, soon proposed that, with the impending liberation of the Balkans, Russia should run things in Rumania and Britain in Greece. Hull strongly opposed this suggestion but made the mistake of leaving Washington for a few days; and Roosevelt, momentarily free from his Wilsonian conscience, yielded to Churchill's plea for a three-months' trial. Hull resumed the fight on his return, and Churchill postponed the matter.

The Red Army continued its advance into Eastern Europe. In August the Polish Home Army, urged on by Polish-language broadcasts from Moscow, rose up against the Nazis in Warsaw. For 63 terrible days, the Poles fought valiantly on, while the Red Army halted on the banks of the Vistula a few miles away, and in Moscow Stalin for more than half this time declined to coöperate with the Western effort to drop supplies to the Warsaw Resistance. It appeared a calculated Soviet decision to let the Nazis slaughter the anti-Soviet Polish underground; and, indeed, the result was to destroy any substantial alternative to a Soviet solution in Poland. The agony of Warsaw caused the most deep and genuine moral shock in Britain and America and provoked dark forebodings about Soviet postwar purposes.

Again history enjoins the imaginative leap in order to see things for a moment from Moscow's viewpoint. The Polish question, Churchill would say at Yalta, was for Britain a question of honor. "It is not only a question of honor for Russia," Stalin replied, "but one of life and death. . . . Throughout history Poland had been the corridor for attack on Russia." A top postwar priority for any Russian régime must be to close that corridor. The Home Army was led by anti-communists. It clearly hoped by its action to forestall the Soviet occupation of Warsaw and, in Russian eyes, to prepare the way for an anti-Russian Poland. In addition, the uprising from a strictly operational viewpoint was premature. The Russians, it is evident in retrospect, had real military problems at the Vistula. The Soviet attempt in September to send Polish units from the Red Army across the river to join forces with the Home Army was a disaster. Heavy German shelling thereafter prevented the ferrying of tanks necessary for an assault on the German position. The Red Army itself did not take Warsaw for another three months. None the less, Stalin's indifference to the human tragedy, his effort to blackmail the London Poles during the ordeal, his sanctimonious opposition during five precious weeks to aerial resupply, the invariable coldness of his explanations ("the Soviet command has come to the conclusion that it must dissociate itself from the Warsaw adventure") and the obvious political benefit to the Soviet Union from the destruction of the Home Army—all these had the effect of suddenly dropping the mask of wartime comradeship and displaying to the West the hard face of Soviet policy.

In now pursuing what he grimly regarded as the minimal requirements for the postwar security of his country, Stalin was inadvertently showing the irreconcilability of both his means and his ends with the Anglo-American conception of the peace.

Meanwhile Eastern Europe presented the Alliance with still another crisis that same September. Bulgaria, which was not at war with Russia, decided to surrender to the Western Allies while it still could; and the English and Americans at Cairo began to discuss armistice terms with Bulgarian envoys. Moscow, challenged by what it plainly saw as a Western intrusion into its own zone of vital interest, promptly declared war on Bulgaria, took over the surrender negotiations and, invoking the Italian precedent, denied its Western Allies any role in the Bulgarian Control Commission. In a long and thoughtful cable, Ambassador Harriman meditated on the problems of communication with the Soviet Union. "Words," he reflected, "have a different connotation to the Soviets than they have to us. When they speak of insisting on 'friendly governments' in their neighboring countries, they have in mind something quite different from what we would mean." The Russians, he surmised, really believed that Washington accepted "their position that although they would keep us informed they had the right to settle their problems with their western neighbors unilaterally." But the Soviet position was still in flux: "the Soviet Government is not one mind." The problem, as Harriman had earlier told Harry Hopkins, was "to strengthen the hands of those around Stalin who want to play the game along our lines." The way to do this, he now told Hull, was to

> be understanding of their sensitivity, meet them much more than half way, encourage them and support them wherever we can, and yet oppose them promptly with the greatest of firmness where we see them going wrong. . . . The only way we can eventually come to an understanding with the Soviet Union on the question of non-interference in the internal affairs of other countries is for us to take a definite interest in the solution of the problems of each individual country as they arise.

As against Harriman's sophisticated universalist strategy, however, Churchill, increasingly fearful of the consequences of unrestrained competition in Eastern Europe, decided in early October to carry his sphere-of-influence proposal directly to Moscow. Roosevelt was at first content to have Churchill speak for him too and even prepared a cable to that effect. But Hopkins, a more rigorous universalist, took it upon himself to stop the cable and warn Roosevelt of its possible implications. Eventually Roosevelt sent a message to Harriman in Moscow emphasizing that he expected to "retain complete freedom of action after this conference is over." It was now that Churchill quickly proposed— and Stalin as quickly accepted—the celebrated division of southeastern Europe: ending (after further haggling between Eden and Molotov) with 90 percent Soviet predominance in Rumania, 80 percent in Bulgaria and Hungary, fifty-fifty in Jugoslavia, 90 percent British predominance in Greece.

Churchill in discussing this with Harriman used the phrase "spheres of influence." But he insisted that these were only "immediate wartime arrangements" and received a highly general blessing from Roosevelt. Yet, whatever Churchill intended, there is reason to believe that Stalin construed the percentages as an agreement, not a declaration; as practical arithmetic, not algebra. For Stalin, it should be understood, the sphere-of-influence idea did not mean that he would abandon all efforts to spread communism in some other nation's sphere; it did mean that, if he tried this and the other side cracked down, he could not feel he had serious cause for complaint. As Kennan wrote to Harriman at the end of 1944:

> As far as border states are concerned the Soviet government has never ceased to think in terms of spheres of interest. They expect us to support them in whatever action they wish to take in those regions, regardless of whether that action seems to us or to the rest of the world to be right or wrong. . . . I have no doubt that this position is honestly maintained on their part, and that they would be equally prepared to reserve moral judgment on any actions which we might wish to carry out, i.e., in the Caribbean area.

In any case, the matter was already under test a good deal closer to Moscow than the Caribbean. The communist-dominated resistance movement in Greece was in open revolt against the effort of the Papandreou government to disarm and disband the guerrillas (the same Papandreou whom the Greek colonels have recently arrested on the claim that he is a tool of the communists). Churchill now called in British Army units to crush the insurrection. This action produced a storm of criticism in his own country and in the United States; the American Government even publicly dissociated itself from the intervention, thereby emphasizing its detachment from the sphere-of-influence deal. But Stalin, Churchill later claimed, "adhered strictly and faithfully to our agreement of October, and during all the long weeks of fighting the Communists in the streets of Athens not one word of reproach came from *Pravda* or *Izvestia*," though there is no evidence that he tried to call off the Greek communists. Still, when the communist rebellion later broke out again in Greece, Stalin told Kardelj and Djilas of Jugoslavia in 1948, "The uprising in Greece must be stopped, and as quickly as possible."

No one, of course, can know what really was in the minds of the Russian leaders. The Kremlin archives are locked; of the primary actors, only Molotov survives, and he has not yet indicated any desire to collaborate with the Columbia Oral History Project. We do know that Stalin did not wholly surrender to sentimental illusion about his new friends. In June 1944, on the night before the landings in Normandy, he told Djilas that the English "find nothing sweeter than to trick their allies. . . . And Churchill? Churchill is the kind who, if you don't watch him, will slip a kopeck out of your pocket. Yes, a kopeck out of your pocket! . . . Roosevelt is not like that. He dips in his hand only for bigger coins." But whatever his views of his colleagues it is not unreasonable to suppose that Stalin would have been satisfied at the end of the war to secure what Kennan has called "a protective glacis along Russia's western border," and that, in exchange for a free hand in Eastern Europe, he was prepared to give the British and Americans equally free hands in their zones of vital interest, including in nations as close to Russia as Greece (for the British) and, very probably—or at least so the Jugoslavs believe—China (for the United States). In other words, his initial objectives were very probably not world conquest but Russian security.

It is now pertinent to inquire why the United States rejected the idea of stabilizing the world by division into spheres of influence and insisted on an East European strategy. One should warn against rushing to the conclusion that it was all a row between hard-nosed, balance-of-power realists and starry-eyed Wilsonians. Roosevelt, Hopkins, Welles, Harriman, Bohlen, Berle, Dulles and other universalists were tough and serious men. Why then did they rebuff the sphere-of-influence solution?

The first reason is that they regarded this solution as containing within itself the seeds of a third world war. The balance-of-power idea seemed inherently unstable. It had always broken down in the past. It held out to each power the permanent temptation to try to alter the balance in its own favor, and it built this temptation into the international order. It would turn the great powers of 1945 away from the objective of concerting common policies toward competition for postwar advantage. As Hopkins told Molotov at Teheran, "The President feels it essential to world peace that Russia, Great Britain and the United States work out this control question in a manner which will not start each of the three powers arming against the others." "The greatest likelihood of eventual conflict," said the Joint Chiefs of Staff in 1944 (the only conflict which the J.C.S., in its wisdom, could then glimpse "in the foreseeable future" was between Britain and Russia), ". . . would seem to grow out of either nation initiating attempts to build up its strength, by seeking to attach to herself parts of Europe to the disadvantage and possible danger of her potential adversary." The Americans were perfectly ready to acknowledge that Russia was entitled to convincing assurance of her national security—but not this way. "I could sympathize fully with Stalin's desire to protect his western borders from future attack," as Hull put it. "But I felt that this security could best be obtained through a strong postwar peace organization."

Hull's remark suggests the second objection: that the sphere-of-influence approach would, in the words of the State Department in 1945, "militate against the establishment and effective functioning of a broader system of general security in which all countries will have their part." The United Nations, in short, was seen as the alternative to the balance of power. Nor did the universalists see any necessary incompatibility between the Russian desire for "friendly governments" on its frontier and the American desire for self-determination in Eastern Europe. Before Yalta the State Department judged the general mood of Europe as "to the left and strongly in favor of far-reaching economic and social reforms, but not, however, in favor of a left-wing totalitarian regime to achieve these reforms." Governments in Eastern Europe could be sufficiently to the left "to allay Soviet suspicions" but sufficiently representative "of the center and *petit bourgeois* elements" not to seem a prelude to communist dictatorship. The American criteria were therefore that the government "should be dedicated to the preservation of civil liberties" and "should favor social and economic reforms." A string of New Deal states—of Finlands and Czechoslovakias—seemed a reasonable compromise solution.

Third, the universalists feared that the sphere-of-interest approach would be what Hull termed "a haven for the isolationists," who would advocate America's participation in Western Hemisphere affairs on condition that it did not participate in European or Asian affairs. Hull also feared that spheres of interest would lead to "closed trade areas or discriminatory systems" and thus defeat his cherished dream of a low-tariff, freely trading world.

Fourth, the sphere-of-interest solution meant the betrayal of the principles for which the Second World War was being fought—the Atlantic Charter, the Four Freedoms, the Declaration of the United Nations. Poland summed up the problem. Britain, having gone to war to defend the independence of Poland from the Germans, could not easily conclude the war by surrendering the independence of Poland to the Russians. Thus, as Hopkins told Stalin after Roosevelt's death in 1945, Poland had "become the symbol of our ability to work out problems with the Soviet Union." Nor could American liberals in general watch with equanimity while the police state spread into countries which, if they had mostly not been real democracies, had mostly not been tyrannies either. The execution in 1943 of Ehrlich and Alter, the Polish socialist trade union leaders, excited deep concern. "I have particularly in mind," Harriman cabled in 1944, "objection to the institution of secret police who may become involved in the persecution of persons of truly democratic convictions who may not be willing to conform to Soviet methods."

Fifth, the sphere-of-influence solution would create difficult domestic problems in American politics. Roosevelt was aware of the six million or more Polish votes in the 1944 election; even more acutely, he was aware of the broader and deeper attack which would follow if, after going to war to stop the Nazi conquest of Europe, he permitted the war to end with the communist conquest of Eastern Europe. As Archibald MacLeish, then Assistant Secretary of State for Public Affairs, warned in January 1945, "The wave of disillusionment which has distressed us in the last several weeks will be increased if the impression is permitted to get abroad that potentially totalitarian provisional governments are to be set up without adequate safeguards as to the holding of free elections and the realization of the principles of the Atlantic Charter." Roosevelt believed that no administration could survive which did not try everything short of war to save Eastern Europe, and he was the supreme American politician of the century.

Sixth, if the Russians were allowed to overrun Eastern Europe without argument, would that satisfy them? Even Kennan, in a dispatch of May 1944, admitted that the "urge" had dreadful potentialities: "If initially successful, will it know where to stop? Will it not be inexorably carried forward, by its very nature, in a struggle to reach the whole—to attain complete mastery of the shores of the Atlantic and the Pacific?" His own answer was that there were inherent limits to the Russian capacity to expand—"that Russia will not have an easy time in maintaining the power which it has seized over other people in Eastern and Central Europe unless it receives both moral and material assistance from the West." Subsequent developments have vindicated Kennan's argument. By the late forties, Jugoslavia and Albania, the two East European states farthest from the Soviet Union and the two in which communism was imposed from within rather than from without, had declared their independence of Moscow. But, given Russia's success in maintaining centralized control over the international communist movement for a quarter of a century, who in 1944 could have had much confidence in the idea of communist revolts against Moscow?

Most of those involved therefore rejected Kennan's answer and stayed with his question. If the West turned its back on Eastern Europe, the higher probability, in their view, was that the Russians would use their security zone, not just for defensive purposes, but as a springboard from which to mount an attack on Western Europe, now shattered by war, a vacuum of power awaiting its master. "If the policy is accepted that the Soviet Union has a right to penetrate her immediate neighbors for security," Harriman said in 1944, "penetration of the next immediate neighbors becomes at a certain time equally logical." If a row with Russia were inevitable, every consideration of prudence dictated that it should take place in Eastern rather than Western Europe.

Thus idealism and realism joined in opposition to the sphere-of-influence solution. The consequence was a determination to assert an American interest in the postwar destiny of all nations, including those of Eastern Europe. In the message which Roosevelt and Hopkins drafted after Hopkins had stopped Roosevelt's initial cable authorizing Churchill to speak for the United States at the Moscow meeting of October 1944, Roosevelt now said, "There is in this global war literally no question, either military or political, in which the United States is not interested." After Roosevelt's death Hopkins repeated the point to Stalin: "The cardinal basis of President Roosevelt's policy which the American people had fully supported had been the concept that the interests of the U.S. were worldwide and not confined to North and South America and the Pacific Ocean."

For better or worse, this was the American position. It is now necessary to attempt the imaginative leap and consider the impact of this position on the leaders of the Soviet Union who, also for better or for worse, had reached the bitter conclusion that the survival of their country depended on their unchallenged control of the corridors through which enemies had so often invaded their homeland. They could claim to have been keeping their own side of the sphere-of-influence bargain. Of course, they were working to capture the resistance movements of Western Europe; indeed, with the appointment of Oumansky as Ambassador to Mexico they were even beginning to enlarge underground operations in the Western Hemisphere. But, from their viewpoint, if the West permitted this, the more fools they; and, if the West stopped it, it was within their right to do so. In overt political matters the Russians were scrupulously playing the game. They had watched in silence while the British shot down communists in Greece. In Jugoslavia Stalin was urging Tito (as Djilas later revealed) to keep King Peter. They had not only acknowledged Western preëminence in Italy but had recognized the Badoglio régime; the

Italian Communists had even voted (against the Socialists and the Liberals) for the renewal of the Lateran Pacts.

They would not regard anti-communist action in a Western zone as a *casus belli;* and they expected reciprocal license to assert their own authority in the East. But the principle of self-determination was carrying the United States into a deeper entanglement in Eastern Europe than the Soviet Union claimed as a right (whatever it was doing underground) in the affairs of Italy, Greece or China. When the Russians now exercised in Eastern Europe the same brutal control they were prepared to have Washington exercise in the American sphere of influence, the American protests, given the paranoia produced alike by Russian history and Leninist ideology, no doubt seemed not only an act of hypocrisy but a threat to security. To the Russians, a stroll into the neighborhood easily became a plot to burn down the house: when, for example, damaged American planes made emergency landings in Poland and Hungary, Moscow took this as attempts to organize the local resistance. It is not unusual to suspect one's adversary of doing what one is already doing oneself. At the same time, the cruelty with which the Russians executed their idea of spheres of influence—in a sense, perhaps, an unwitting cruelty, since Stalin treated the East Europeans no worse than he had treated the Russians in the thirties—discouraged the West from accepting the equation (for example, Italy = Rumania) which seemed so self-evident to the Kremlin.

So Moscow very probably, and not unnaturally, perceived the emphasis on self-determination as a systematic and deliberate pressure on Russia's western frontiers. Moreover, the restoration of capitalism to countries freed at frightful cost by the Red Army no doubt struck the Russians as the betrayal of the principles for which *they* were fighting. "That they, the victors," Isaac Deutscher has suggested, "should now preserve an order from which they had experienced nothing but hostility, and could expect nothing but hostility . . . would have been the most miserable anti-climax to their great 'war of liberation.' " By 1944 Poland was the critical issue; Harriman later said that "under instructions from President Roosevelt, I talked about Poland with Stalin more frequently than any other subject." While the West saw the point of Stalin's demand for a "friendly government" in Warsaw, the American insistence on the sovereign virtues of free elections (ironically in the spirit of the 1917 Bolshevik decree of peace, which affirmed "the right" of a nation "to decide the forms of its state existence by a free vote, taken after the complete evacuation of the incorporating or, generally, of the stronger nation") created an insoluble problem in those countries, like Poland (and Rumania) where free elections would almost certainly produce anti-Soviet governments.

The Russians thus may well have estimated the Western pressures as calculated to encourage their enemies in Eastern Europe and to defeat their own minimum objective of a protective glacis. Everything still hung, however, on the course of military operations. The wartime collaboration had been created by one thing, and one thing alone: the threat of Nazi victory. So long as this threat was real, so was the collaboration. In late December 1944, von Rundstedt launched his counter-offensive in the Ardennes. A few weeks later, when

Roosevelt, Churchill and Stalin gathered in the Crimea, it was in the shadow of this last considerable explosion of German power. The meeting at Yalta was still dominated by the mood of war.

Yalta remains something of an historical perplexity—less, from the perspective of 1967, because of a mythical American deference to the sphere-of-influence thesis than because of the documentable Russian deference to the universalist thesis. Why should Stalin in 1945 have accepted the Declaration on Liberated Europe and an agreement on Poland pledging that "the three governments will jointly" act to assure "free elections of governments responsive to the will of the people"? There are several probable answers: that the war was not over and the Russians still wanted the Americans to intensify their military effort in the West; that one clause in the Declaration premised action on "the opinion of the three governments" and thus implied a Soviet veto, though the Polish agreement was more definite; most of all that the universalist algebra of the Declaration was plainly in Stalin's mind to be construed in terms of the practical arithmetic of his sphere-of-influence agreement with Churchill the previous October. Stalin's assurance to Churchill at Yalta that a proposed Russian amendment to the Declaration would not apply to Greece makes it clear that Roosevelt's pieties did not, in Stalin's mind, nullify Churchill's percentages. He could well have been strengthened in this supposition by the fact that *after* Yalta, Churchill himself repeatedly reasserted the terms of the October agreement as if he regarded it, despite Yalta, as controlling.

Harriman still had the feeling before Yalta that the Kremlin had "two approaches to their postwar policies" and that Stalin himself was "of two minds." One approach emphasized the internal reconstruction and development of Russia; the other its external expansion. But in the meantime the fact which dominated all political decisions—that is, the war against Germany—was moving into its final phase. In the weeks after Yalta, the military situation changed with great rapidity. As the Nazi threat declined, so too did the need for coöperation. The Soviet Union, feeling itself menaced by the American idea of self-determination and the borderlands diplomacy to which it was leading, skeptical whether the United Nations would protect its frontiers as reliably as its own domination in Eastern Europe, began to fulfill its security requirements unilaterally.

In March Stalin expressed his evaluation of the United Nations by rejecting Roosevelt's plea that Molotov come to the San Francisco conference, if only for the opening sessions. In the next weeks the Russians emphatically and crudely worked their will in Eastern Europe, above all in the test country of Poland. They were ignoring the Declaration on Liberated Europe, ignoring the Atlantic Charter, self-determination, human freedom and everything else the Americans considered essential for a stable peace. "We must clearly recognize," Harriman wired Washington a few days before Roosevelt's death, "that the Soviet program is the establishment of totalitarianism, ending personal liberty and democracy as we know and respect it."

At the same time, the Russians also began to mobilize communist resources in the United States itself to block American universalism. In April 1945

Jacques Duclos, who had been the Comintern official responsible for the Western communist parties, launched in *Cahiers du Communisme* an uncompromising attack on the policy of the American Communist Party. Duclos sharply condemned the revisionism of Earl Browder, the American Communist leader, as "expressed in the concept of a long-term class peace in the United States, of the possibility of the suppression of the class struggle in the postwar period and of establishment of harmony between labor and capital." Browder was specifically rebuked for favoring the "self-determination" of Europe "west of the Soviet Union" on a bourgeois-democratic basis. The excommunication of Browderism was plainly the Politburo's considered reaction to the impending defeat of Germany; it was a signal to the communist parties of the West that they should recover their identity; it was Moscow's alert to communists everywhere that they should prepare for new policies in the postwar world.

The Duclos piece obviously could not have been planned and written much later than the Yalta conference—that is, well before a number of events which revisionists now cite in order to demonstrate American responsibility for the Cold War: before Allen Dulles, for example, began to negotiate the surrender of the German armies in Italy (the episode which provoked Stalin to charge Roosevelt with seeking a separate peace and provoked Roosevelt to denounce the "vile misrepresentations" of Stalin's informants); well before Roosevelt died; many months before the testing of the atomic bomb; even more months before Truman ordered that the bomb be dropped on Japan. William Z. Foster, who soon replaced Browder as the leader of the American Communist Party and embodied the new Moscow line, later boasted of having said in January 1944, "A post-war Roosevelt administration would continue to be, as it is now, an imperialist government." With ancient suspicions revived by the American insistence on universalism, this was no doubt the conclusion which the Russians were reaching at the same time. The Soviet canonization of Roosevelt (like their present-day canonization of Kennedy) took place after the American President's death.

The atmosphere of mutual suspicion was beginning to rise. In January 1945 Molotov formally proposed that the United States grant Russia a $6 billion credit for postwar reconstruction. With characteristic tact he explained that he was doing this as a favor to save America from a postwar depression. The proposal seems to have been diffidently made and diffidently received. Roosevelt requested that the matter "not be pressed further" on the American side until he had a chance to talk with Stalin; but the Russians did not follow it up either at Yalta in February (save for a single glancing reference) or during the Stalin-Hopkins talks in May or at Potsdam. Finally the proposal was renewed in the very different political atmosphere of August. This time Washington inexplicably mislaid the request during the transfer of the records of the Foreign Economic Administration to the State Department. It did not turn up again until March 1946. Of course this was impossible for the Russians to believe; it is hard enough even for those acquainted with the capacity of the American government for incompetence to believe; and it only strengthened Soviet suspicions of American purposes.

The American credit was one conceivable form of Western contribution to Russian reconstruction. Another was lend-lease, and the possibility of reconstruction aid under the lend-lease protocol had already been discussed in 1944. But in May 1945 Russia, like Britain, suffered from Truman's abrupt termination of lend-lease shipments—"unfortunate and even brutal," Stalin told Hopkins, adding that, if it was "designed as pressure on the Russians in order to soften them up, then it was a fundamental mistake." A third form was German reparations. Here Stalin in demanding $10 billion in reparations for the Soviet Union made his strongest fight at Yalta. Roosevelt, while agreeing essentially with Churchill's opposition, tried to postpone the matter by accepting the Soviet figure as a "basis for discussion"—a formula which led to future misunderstanding. In short, the Russian hope for major Western assistance in postwar reconstruction foundered on three events which the Kremlin could well have interpreted respectively as deliberate sabotage (the loan request), blackmail (lend-lease cancellation) and pro-Germanism (reparations).

Actually the American attempt to settle the fourth lend-lease protocol was generous and the Russians for their own reasons declined to come to an agreement. It is not clear, though, that satisfying Moscow on any of these financial scores would have made much essential difference. It might have persuaded some doves in the Kremlin that the U.S. government was genuinely friendly; it might have persuaded some hawks that the American anxiety for Soviet friendship was such that Moscow could do as it wished without inviting challenge from the United States. It would, in short, merely have reinforced both sides of the Kremlin debate; it would hardly have reversed deeper tendencies toward the deterioration of political relationships. Economic deals were surely subordinate to the quality of mutual political confidence; and here, in the months after Yalta, the decay was steady.

The Cold War had now begun. It was the product not of a decision but of a dilemma. Each side felt compelled to adopt policies which the other could not but regard as a threat to the principles of the peace. Each then felt compelled to undertake defensive measures. Thus the Russians saw no choice but to consolidate their security in Eastern Europe. The Americans, regarding Eastern Europe as the first step toward Western Europe, responded by asserting their interest in the zone the Russians deemed vital to their security. The Russians concluded that the West was resuming its old course of capitalist encirclement; that it was purposefully laying the foundation for anti-Soviet régimes in the area defined by the blood of centuries as crucial to Russian survival. Each side believed with passion that future international stability depended on the success of its own conception of world order. Each side, in pursuing its own clearly indicated and deeply cherished principles, was only confirming the fear of the other that it was bent on aggression.

Very soon the process began to acquire a cumulative momentum. The impending collapse of Germany thus provoked new troubles: the Russians, for example, sincerely feared that the West was planning a separate surrender of the German armies in Italy in a way which would release troops for Hitler's eastern front, as they subsequently feared that the Nazis might succeed in surrendering Berlin to the West. This was the context in which the atomic bomb now appeared. Though the revisionist argument that Truman dropped the bomb less to defeat Japan than to intimidate Russia is not convincing, this thought unquestionably appealed to some in Washington as at least an advantageous side-effect of Hiroshima.

So the machinery of suspicion and counter-suspicion, action and counteraction, was set in motion. But, given relations among traditional national states, there was still no reason, even with all the postwar jostling, why this should not have remained a manageable situation. What made it unmanageable, what caused the rapid escalation of the Cold War and in another two years completed the division of Europe, was a set of considerations which this account has thus far excluded.

Up to this point, the discussion has considered the schism within the wartime coalition as if it were entirely the result of disagreements among national states. Assuming this framework, there was unquestionably a failure of communication between America and Russia, a misperception of signals and, as time went on, a mounting tendency to ascribe ominous motives to the other side. It seems hard, for example, to deny that American postwar policy created genuine difficulties for the Russians and even assumed a threatening aspect for them. All this the revisionists have rightly and usefully emphasized.

But the great omission of the revisionists—and also the fundamental explanation of the speed with which the Cold War escalated—lies precisely in the fact that the Soviet Union was *not* a traditional national state. This is where the "mirror image," invoked by some psychologists, falls down. For the Soviet Union was a phenomenon very different from America or Britain; it was a totalitarian state, endowed with an all-explanatory, all-consuming ideology, committed to the infallibility of government and party, still in a somewhat messianic mood, equating dissent with treason, and ruled by a dictator who, for all his quite extraordinary abilities, had his paranoid moments.

Marxism-Leninism gave the Russian leaders a view of the world according to which all societies were inexorably destined to proceed along appointed roads by appointed stages until they achieved the classless nirvana. Moreover, given the resistance of the capitalists to this development, the existence of any noncommunist state was *by definition* a threat to the Soviet Union. "As long as capitalism and socialism exist," Lenin wrote, "we cannot live in peace: in the end, one or the other will triumph—a funeral dirge will be sung either over the Soviet Republic or over world capitalism."

Stalin and his associates, whatever Roosevelt or Truman did or failed to do, were bound to regard the United States as the enemy, not because of this deed or that, but because of the primordial fact that America was the leading capitalist power and thus, by Leninist syllogism, unappeasably hostile, driven by the logic of its system to oppose, encircle and destroy Soviet Russia. Nothing the United States could have done in 1944–45 would have abolished this mistrust, required and sanctified as it was by Marxist gospel—nothing short of the conversion of the United States into a Stalinist despotism; and even this would not have sufficed, as the experience of Jugoslavia and China soon showed, unless it were accompanied by total subservience to Moscow. So long as the United States remained a capitalist democracy, no American policy, given Moscow's theology, could hope to win basic Soviet confidence, and every American action was poisoned from the source. So long as the Soviet Union remained a messianic state, ideology compelled a steady expansion of communist power.

It is easy, of course, to exaggerate the capacity of ideology to control events. The tension of acting according to revolutionary abstractions is too much for most nations to sustain over a long period: that is why Mao Tse-tung has launched his Cultural Revolution, hoping thereby to create a permanent revolutionary mood and save Chinese communism from the degeneration which, in his view, has overtaken Russian communism. Still, as any revolution grows older, normal human and social motives will increasingly reassert themselves. In due course, we can be sure, Leninism will be about as effective in governing the daily lives of Russians as Christianity is in governing the daily lives of Americans. Like the Ten Commandments and the Sermon on the Mount, the Leninist verities will increasingly become platitudes for ritual observance, not guides to secular decision. There can be no worse fallacy (even if respectable people practiced it diligently for a season in the United States) than that of drawing from a nation's ideology permanent conclusions about its behavior.

A temporary recession of ideology was already taking place during the Second World War when Stalin, to rally his people against the invader, had to replace the appeal of Marxism by that of nationalism. ("We are under no illusions that they are fighting for us," Stalin once said to Harriman. "They are fighting for Mother Russia.") But this was still taking place within the strictest limitations. The Soviet Union remained as much a police state as ever; the régime was as infallible as ever; foreigners and their ideas were as suspect as ever. "Never, except possibly during my later experience as ambassador in Moscow," Kennan has written, "did the insistence of the Soviet authorities on isolation of the diplomatic corps weigh more heavily on me . . . than in these first weeks following my return to Russia in the final months of the war. . . . [We were] treated as though we were the bearers of some species of the plague"— which, of course, from the Soviet viewpoint, they were: the plague of skepticism.

Paradoxically, of the forces capable of bringing about a modification of ideology, the most practical and effective was the Soviet dictatorship itself. If Stalin was an ideologist, he was also a pragmatist. If he saw everything through the lenses of Marxism-Leninism, he also, as the infallible expositor of the faith, could reinterpret Marxism-Leninism to justify anything he wanted to do at any given moment. No doubt Roosevelt's ignorance of Marxism-Leninism was inexcusable and led to grievous miscalculations. But Roosevelt's efforts to work on and through Stalin were not so hopelessly naïve as it used to be fashionable to think. With the extraordinary instinct of a great political leader, Roosevelt intuitively understood that Stalin was the *only* lever available to the West against the Leninist ideology and the Soviet system. If Stalin could be reached, then alone was there a chance of getting the Russians to act contrary to the prescriptions of their faith. The best evidence is that Roosevelt retained a certain capacity to influence Stalin to the end; the nominal Soviet acquiescence in American universalism as late as Yalta was perhaps an indication of that. It is in this way that the death of Roosevelt was crucial—not in the vulgar sense that his policy was then reversed by his successor, which did not happen, but in the sense that no other American could hope to have the restraining impact on Stalin which Roosevelt might for a while have had.

Stalin alone could have made any difference. Yet Stalin, in spite of the impression of sobriety and realism he made on Westerners who saw him during the Second World War, was plainly a man of deep and morbid obsessions and compulsions. When he was still a young man, Lenin had criticized his rude and arbitrary ways. A reasonably authoritative observer (N. S. Khrushchev) later commented, "These negative characteristics of his developed steadily and during the last years acquired an absolutely insufferable character." His paranoia, probably set off by the suicide of his wife in 1932, led to the terrible purges of the mid-thirties and the wanton murder of thousands of his Bolshevik comrades. "Everywhere and in everything," Khrushchev says of this period, "he saw 'enemies,' 'double-dealers' and 'spies.' " The crisis of war evidently steadied him in some way, though Khrushchev speaks of his "nervousness and hysteria . . . even after the war began." The madness, so rigidly controlled for a time, burst out with new and shocking intensity in the postwar years. "After the war," Khrushchev testifies,

> the situation became even more complicated. Stalin became even more capricious, irritable and brutal; in particular, his suspicion grew. His persecution mania reached unbelievable dimensions. . . . He decided everything, without any consideration for anyone or anything.
>
> Stalin's wilfulness showed itself . . . also in the international relations of the Soviet Union. . . . He had completely lost a sense of reality; he demonstrated his suspicion and haughtiness not only in relation to individuals in the USSR, but in relation to whole parties and nations.

A revisionist fallacy has been to treat Stalin as just another Realpolitik statesman, as Second World War revisionists see Hitler as just another Stresemann or Bismarck. But the record makes it clear that in the end nothing could satisfy Stalin's paranoia. His own associates failed. Why does anyone suppose that any conceivable American policy would have succeeded?

An analysis of the origins of the Cold War which leaves out these factors—the intransigence of Leninist ideology, the sinister dynamics of a totalitarian society and the madness of Stalin—is obviously incomplete. It was these factors which made it hard for the West to accept the thesis that Russia was moved only by a desire to protect its security and would be satisfied by the control of Eastern Europe; it was these factors which charged the debate between universalism and spheres of influence with apocalyptic potentiality.

Leninism and totalitarianism created a structure of thought and behavior which made postwar collaboration between Russia and America—in any normal sense of civilized intercourse between national states—inherently impossible. The Soviet dictatorship of 1945 simply could not have survived such a collaboration. Indeed, nearly a quarter-century later, the Soviet régime, though it has meanwhile moved a good distance, could still hardly survive it without risking the release inside Russia of energies profoundly opposed to communist despotism. As for Stalin, he may have represented the only force in 1945 capable of overcoming Stalinism, but the very traits which enabled him to win absolute power expressed terrifying instabilities of mind and temperament and hardly offered a solid foundation for a peaceful world. . . .

In retrospect, if it is impossible to see the Cold War as a case of American aggression and Russian response, it is also hard to see it as a pure case of Russian aggression and American response. "In what is truly tragic," wrote Hegel, "there must be valid moral powers on both the sides which come into collision. . . . Both suffer loss and yet both are mutually justified." In this sense, the Cold War had its tragic elements. The question remains whether it was an instance of Greek tragedy—as Auden has called it, "the tragedy of necessity," where the feeling aroused in the spectator is "What a pity it had to be this way" —or of Christian tragedy, "the tragedy of possibility," where the feeling aroused is "What a pity it was this way when it might have been otherwise."

Once something has happened, the historian is tempted to assume that it had to happen; but this may often be a highly unphilosophical assumption. The Cold War could have been avoided only if the Soviet Union had not been possessed by convictions both of the infallibility of the communist word and of the inevitability of a communist world. These convictions transformed an impasse between national states into a religious war, a tragedy of possibility into one of necessity. One might wish that America had preserved the poise and proportion of the first years of the Cold War and had not in time succumbed to its own forms of self-righteousness. But the most rational of American policies could hardly have averted the Cold War. Only today, as Russia begins to recede from its messianic mission and to accept, in practice if not yet in principle, the permanence of the world of diversity, only now can the hope flicker that this long, dreary, costly contest may at last be taking on forms less dramatic, less obsessive and less dangerous to the future of mankind.

American Expansionism and Power

THOMAS G. PATERSON

United States diplomats who witnessed the outbreak of World War II and its ultimate costs naturally looked to the interwar years for explanations. Persuasive historical analyses sounded the common theme that economic catastrophe and extreme nationalism corroded world peace. Americans studied their own "mistakes"—their rejection of the League of Nations, high tariffs, and restrained involvement in international crises—all of which tugged at the national conscience after 1939. Woodrow Wilson's unfulfilled pleas for a stable world

Thomas G. Paterson, *Soviet-American Confrontation: Postwar Reconstruction and the Origins of the Cold War* (Baltimore: Johns Hopkins University Press, 1973), pp. 1–3, 8–14, 260–267. Copyright © 1973 by The Johns Hopkins University Press.

order of self-determination and nondiscriminatory trade were taken up anew. Cordell Hull, Franklin D. Roosevelt's secretary of state for over a decade, articulated a relationship between economics and war and the lessons of the past more effectively than most Americans. In his autobiography, published in 1948, he recalls that as early as World War I he had become convinced that "unhampered trade dovetailed with peace; high tariffs, trade barriers, and unfair economic competition, with war." The "economic dissatisfaction that breeds war" had to be eliminated. With the opening of World War II, after years of depression, repressive politics, and inconclusive diplomacy, these ideas took on new importance. Leaders pledged to eradicate economic deprivation and war through their reconstruction policies.

A legion of wartime State Department and interdepartmental committees had contemplated the contours of the economically hobbled postwar world. To guide them was a set of principles developed over a period of two centuries. Foremost was the principle of nondiscrimination or equal opportunity in foreign trade, investment, and navigation. In the late nineteenth century this principle became enshrined in the words "open door." "Private enterprise," as opposed to government ownership or state-conducted foreign commerce, was another popular tenet. In the twentieth century, United States leaders increasingly subscribed to the principle of "multilateralism," or cooperation among several nations to encourage free-flowing world trade, and to the "most-favored-nation" principle, whereby signatories agree to extend to each other any commercial favors either grants to a third state. Cherishing these principles, although it sometimes contradicted them in practice, the United States tremendously expanded its foreign commerce and became the world's greatest trader.

In the 1930s Hull created institutions to realize these doctrines. The Reciprocal Trade Agreements program and the Export-Import Bank were devoted to overcoming barriers to world trade. When the wartime committees met, they looked to these institutions and to the ideas of the past. They decided to tackle economic programs first because the principles were already established and widely accepted, because of their recent experience in the depression years, and because great areas of the world lay in ruins. They expected to encounter the least domestic opposition to economic foreign policy: many citizens did not understand the technicalities and were content to leave such policymaking to government experts. The task of the postwar planners, then, was not the creation of doctrines and agencies but their elaboration.

The hope that world war would never erupt again if the United States insisted upon an open political and economic world was often offered as a counter to the somber battle reports. During the war this hope joined with national self-interest in efforts to free world trade from the shackles of the 1930s. The Atlantic Charter of 1941 was an early document illustrating the belief that economic issues and peace were linked. Roosevelt and Winston Churchill forswore territorial aggrandizement and championed self-determination and disarmament, but achievement of these goals alone would not ensure a peaceful world. Economic collaboration to improve living standards, freedom of the seas, and the right of all nations to "access, on equal terms, to the trade and to the raw materials of the world which are needed for their economic prosperity" were the other stated purposes of the Charter. In numerous wartime agreements and official statements, Washington emphatically urged its principles of multilateral nondiscriminatory foreign trade and investment as the guide for the postwar world.

Just before his death Roosevelt informed Congress that "we cannot succeed in building a peaceful world unless we build an economically healthy world." His successor, Harry S. Truman, although lacking practical experience in diplomacy, was an enthusiastic New Deal Democrat committed to Roosevelt's programs and the traditional principles of the open door. A self-proclaimed student of history, the often brash president drew the same lessons from the past as did Cordell Hull. The day after Roosevelt's burial, Truman nervously addressed a session of Congress, asserting that national security in the future would not lie behind "geographical barriers." Rather, mutual cooperation through the machinery of the United Nations and enlarged international trade would produce a lasting peace. The United States, he proclaimed, "may well lead the world to peace and prosperity."

When Truman, like Roosevelt, expressed the postwar ideology of "peace and prosperity," those simple words meant more than their catchy phraseology would suggest. This ideology drew upon the past and enjoyed wide acceptance among most segments of the political spectrum, from the liberal magazine *New Republic* to the conservative National Association of Manufacturers. It constituted a rejection of the shortcomings of the 1930s and a belief that the United States possessed the wherewithal and commitment to vanquish economic and political disorder. With the tenets of "peace and prosperity" ever on their minds, Americans emerged from World War II only to enter a new international confrontation. Desperate to explain why cooperation crumbled so quickly, many called upon history and became convinced that the 1940s were potentially a replay of the 1930s, with Soviet Russia replacing Nazi Germany as the unwelcome challenger to an open world. This assumption made all the more urgent the fulfillment of the goals of "peace and prosperity." . . .

Not only were United States leaders aware of the realities of an interdependent world, they also recognized their own comparative strength. And they intended to use it. The country possessed an enviable set of credentials. National power derived from popular support at home, which consistently applauded the exercise of that collective power. The United States unquestionably emerged from World War II as the foremost international power. One scholar has concluded that it held the "prime weapon of *de*struction—the atomic bomb —and the prime weapon of *recon*struction—such wealth as no nation hitherto had possessed."

The United States military establishment ranked supreme in the early Cold War period. Its air force was the largest and most capable; its navy was first with twelve hundred warships and fifty thousand supporting and landing craft; its troops occupied territory and bases across the globe, including Japan, Germany, Austria, and new outposts in the Pacific. Public pressure for demobilization forced the Truman administration to reduce military forces faster than it wished to (from 12 million in 1945 to 1.5 million in 1947), but defense needs and security were not impaired because other nations were heavily devastated and the Soviet Union also demobilized (from 12 million to 3 to 4 million). Then, too, the military expenditures for fiscal years 1947 and 1948 represented one-third of the total United States budget as compared to its miniscule defense budget and might in the 1930s. The United States after 1945 was a military giant, and few denied it. While the U.S.S.R. held power confined largely to one region, eastern Europe, the United States had become a global power.

Most officials recognized before 1947 that Russia was, as George F. Kennan put it, the "weaker force." In early 1946 Secretary of the Navy James Forrestal received a memorandum on Soviet capabilities from one of his aides:

> The Red Fleet is incapable of any important offensive or amphibious operations. . . . a strategic air force is practically non-existent either in materiel or concept. . . . economically, the Soviet Union is exhausted. The people are undernourished, industry and transport are in an advanced state of deterioration, enormous areas have been devastated, thirty percent of the population has been dislocated. . . . Maintenance of large occupation forces in Europe is dictated to a certain extent by the necessity of "farming out" millions of men for whom living accommodations and food cannot be spared in the USSR during the current winter. This also aids the popular opinion that the USSR is a tremendous military power, thereby influencing political decisions to a degree out of proportion to the USSR's actual present offensive potential. . . . The USSR is not expected to take any action during the next five years which might develop into hostilities with Anglo-Americans.

The nation's military superiority and its effects on diplomacy were spelled out by President Truman in October, 1945, when he asserted that through its military strength the United States would "enforce the peace of the world." "We have learned," he said, "the bitter lesson that the weakness of this great Republic invites men of ill-will to shake the very foundations of civilization all over the world." When asked by Senator Claude Pepper where the American fleet would sail, Forrestal replied, "wherever there is a sea." The dramatic dispatch of warships to the Mediterranean in 1946 and 1947 was only one example of this global perception.

The awesome atomic bomb had a potential rather than real place in the military arsenal. After Hiroshima and Nagasaki, many officials hoped that the ghastly demonstration of this weapon's destructive power, combined with the United States monopoly of it, would constitute enough of a threat to force some diplomatic concessions. Its presence was always implicit at the conference table, even though United States negotiators never overtly threatened its use. Secretary of War Henry L. Stimson recorded in his diary that Secretary of State James F. Byrnes "wished to have the implied threat of the bomb" at the London Foreign Ministers meeting (September, 1945). Indeed, Byrnes "looks to having the presence of the bomb in his pocket" at the conference. Both Britain and Russia were immediately alarmed by this unilateral handling of the bomb, and the Soviets ordered their scientists to speed up their atomic development project. Not until they exploded their atomic bomb in 1949 did the United States lose its monopoly. But that monopoly never meant much as a diplomatic device. In essence, it created fear and anxiety and loomed in the background as a symbol of United States technological genius and destructive ability to which other nations would aspire.

Closely linked to this military prominence was international political power. In control of Japan, Italy, and parts of Korea and Germany after the war, the United States could greatly shape their internal history. In Japan General Douglas MacArthur excluded the Soviets from joint participation, wrote a new constitution, established a representative government, and built a base at Okinawa. Thus Japan was securely placed within the United States sphere of influence for years. United States interference in the internal affairs of Latin America remained a part of western hemispheric relations after the war. Through the Act of Chapultepec (1945) and the Rio Pact (1947), and continued aid to military governments, poltical strength and "friends" were acquired.

In the United Nations Organization, which was constructed by the great powers as an instrument to reflect their control of world affairs, the United States frequently won its way through bloc voting. In essence, it possessed a "hidden veto" because a majority of the members were "friends" of or dependent upon Washington. Almost twenty Latin American governments repeatedly voted with Washington on important questions. Using its majority, Washington could avoid the veto which an outnumbered Moscow employed time and time again. When the Soviets did veto a Security Council action, the United States could often circumvent it by utilizing alternative machinery such as the General Assembly. Also effective were threats of a "financial veto" because the United States paid a sizeable share of the organization's operating budget. The Soviets, however unenviable their own practices, sharply criticized this decisive United States hold on the United Nations.

Joined to this military and political pre-eminence was the overwhelming economic power of the United States. Its businesses owned or controlled 59 percent of the world's total known oil reserves by 1947; its automobile production then was eight times that of France, England, and Germany combined, and four years later it turned out seven million cars, compared to Russia's 65,000. It was the largest producer and consumer of coal and steel in the world and at mid-century held one-third of the world's merchant fleet (gross tonnage). General Motors president Charles Wilson bragged in 1948 that with only 6 percent of the world's area and 7 percent of its population, the United States had 46 percent of the world's electric power, 48 percent of its radios, 54 percent of its telephones, and 92 percent of its modern bathtubs. The economic power of American bathtubs may have been lost on foreigners, but that of its capital and durable goods manufacturing was not. Countries in dire need of economic rehabilitation could not ignore the fact that in 1948 the United States produced about 41 percent of the goods and services in the world and was the source of almost half its total industrial output. Secretary Forrestal tied this economic power to other elements of national strength: "As long as we can out-produce the world, can control the sea and can strike with the atomic bomb, we can assume certain risks otherwise unacceptable in an effort to restore world trade, to restore the balance of power—military power—and to eliminate some of the conditions which breed war."

American leaders used words like "giant," "center," and "pivot" to describe their country's economic position. Leo Crowley, head of the Foreign Economic Administration, noted in early 1945 that the president "is now in a better bargaining position in dealing with our Allies than he is likely to be either before or after the end of the war," because other nations are "heavily dependent" upon the United States for both war and postwar materiel. Even earlier, in 1944, Harriman wrote that "economic assistance is one of the most effective weapons" with which to influence events in eastern Europe. . . . Government officials understood their nation's exclusive power and without much reluctance attempted to exploit their advantage.

Other governments, especially in European countries desperately in need of reconstruction aid, recognized this power. Soviet officials constantly remarked on United States economic strength while at the same time predicting, on the basis of rigid and distorting dogma, that the capitalist nations were heading for depression. Philip Mosely has confirmed that "when the Soviet leaders look at America, they think primarily of its great economic power." Foreign Minister V. M. Molotov dipped into the *World Almanac* in 1946 to point out how World War II had strengthened the United States economy, and asked what "equal opportunity" in foreign trade and investment would really mean when the United States had no peers. Then, too, American economic power and the willingness to employ it for diplomatic leverage reinforced in the Soviet mind the Communist teaching that capitalist countries are acquisitive and aggressive and that imperialism results from their drive to expand economically to evade depressions at home.

The record is replete with examples of American diplomatic forcefulness sustained by a self-conscious awareness of power. The Truman administration was not helpless, defensive, drifting, or ignorant in its Cold War diplomacy. The most famous example of its position is the White House confrontation between Truman and Molotov in April, 1945, when the president, less than two weeks in office, vigorously chided the shocked Russian diplomat and warned that no reconstruction aid would be forthcoming unless the Soviets accepted the American interpretation of the Yalta accords. Truman in fact told his advisers just before this meeting that "if the Russians did not wish to join us [in establishing the United Nations] they could go to hell." Shortly after the incident, Truman informed Joseph Davies, former ambassador to Russia, "I gave it to him straight 'one-two to the jaw.' I let him have it straight."

This language amounted to more than mere rhetoric or an exuberant style; the tough words were backed by a growing confidence in United States power. Less than a month after the Potsdam Conference Secretary Byrnes drew a lesson: "the only way to negotiate with the Russians is to hit them hard, and then negotiate." The president, declaring the United States the "greatest naval power on earth" and meaning it, insisted in the fall of 1945 that "we shall not give our approval to any compromise with evil." And in September, 1946, when Byrnes was having a difficult time with the stubborn Russians over peace treaties with the German satellites, Truman cabled him in Paris: "Do everything you can to continue but in the final analysis do whatever you think is right and tell them [the Russians] to go to hell if you have to." Although its leaders had a sense of their powerful rank in world affairs and were not reluctant to flex their muscles, both rhetorically and actually . . . the influence of the United States ultimately never reached as far as its power, and many of its hopes for the postwar period went unfulfilled. . . .

The national security and economic wellbeing of countries touched by the destructive force of World War II depended upon a successful recovery from its devastation, and the most conspicuous fact in the postwar period was that the United States alone possessed the necessary resources—the economic power —to resolve the recovery crisis. American military and atomic power also existed, but their influence on international affairs after the war was limited, whereas there was no doubt about the exceptional economic power of the United States. It seemed an unusual opportunity for Americans to fulfill their dream of a political and economic open world, a world so different from that of the depression years. Few international leaders underestimated the power of the United States, and most expected it to be used for diplomatic advantage. The question was how—whether as a diplomatic tool to reach mutually satisfactory agreements or as a weapon to compel compliance with American positions on international issues.

The question was quickly answered. Coercion characterized United States reconstruction diplomacy, and the Russians, British, and French, among others, resented it. It is obvious that the reconstruction crisis and diplomatic use of American economic power cannot alone explain the origins of the Cold War. Important factors were the long-standing Soviet anti-capitalist and American anti-Communist sentiments dating from 1917, the troubled relations before and after diplomatic recognition of the Soviet Union in 1933, and the strained alliance between the two in World War II. In 1945 and after, Soviet expansion into eastern Europe and rude diplomatic conduct aroused understandable hostility in Washington. Yet, as the evidence in this book has suggested, United States diplomatic maneuvers helped trigger some reprehensible Soviet actions, and United States diplomats exaggerated the impact of many others. Because the United States was maneuvering from an uncommonly powerful position and on a global scale, its foreign policy often was haughty, expansionist, and uncompromising. Washington attempted to exploit Europe's weaknesses for its advantage and must share a substantial responsibility for the division of the world into competing blocs. This is not to ignore or excuse the Soviet grip on eastern Europe, but as the preceding discussion has indicated, Soviet policy was flexible in the immediate postwar years. Use of economic power as a weapon served to encourage further Soviet intrusions and thereby reduced the independence of the eastern European nations.

All of Europe groaned under the burdens of reconstruction. Economies were paralyzed, populations uprooted, helpless millions left hungry, communications severed, and governments tottering. The mass bombings, scorched-earth campaigns, and deliberate destruction of people and property left much of the continent dazed and dependent. After six years of war thirty million Europeans were dead. Russia suffered most, with fifteen to twenty million killed. Poland lost 15 percent of its population, or 5.8 million. Germany counted 4.5 million dead, France 600,000, Czechoslovakia 415,000, and the United Kingdom 400,000. Another sixteen million displaced persons were wandering in unfamiliar lands.

The survivors' prospects were dreary. Major cities had been reduced to heaps of rubble; 75 percent of the houses in Berlin were uninhabitable, and twenty-five million Russians were homeless. Food shortages were acute. European grain harvests in 1945 were half those of 1939. Across Europe industrial plants were closed and would require new machinery, raw materials, and extensive repairs. The Rhine was blocked by collapsed bridges, and everywhere telephone lines, canals, and railroads were unusable. Both Russia and Britain had lost one-fourth of their prewar wealth. Europe was an appalling picture of ruin.

The postwar picture of the United States provided a stark contrast. Its wartime death count of approximately 300,000 appeared merciful when set against European figures. Its countryside untrampled by armies and its economy booming, it had become an "economic giant," as President Truman proudly noted. "For most Americans World War II spelled neither hardship nor suffering but a better way of life," Richard Polenberg has recently concluded. During the war the gross national product climbed from $91 billion to $166 billion; industry grew in "hothouse fashion," sending Lend-Lease goods valued at $30 billion to the Allies. Observers spoke of the performance as a "production miracle." Such economic power, combined with European reconstruction needs, afforded an unprecedented opportunity to influence postwar international affairs, and United States diplomats knew it. As early as March, 1944, Ambassador Averell Harriman informed the State Department: "I am impressed with the consideration that economic assistance is one of the most effective weapons at our disposal to influence European political events in the direction we desire. . . ."

By denying a postwar loan, abruptly terminating Lend-Lease, limiting Russian-American trade, severing eastern Europe from loans and trade, and halting UNRRA relief supplies to eastern Europe, White Russia, and the Ukraine, the United States tried to force Soviet concessions on American terms, but failed to orient eastern Europe toward the United States. Reconstruction diplomacy was more successful elsewhere. Britain and western Europe were drawn closer to American foreign policy positions. Western Germany was rehabilitated as the "vital center" of a revived western Europe, and Greece, Turkey, and Iran became bulwarks against the Soviet Union and Communism. The World Bank, International Monetary Fund, and United Nations became instruments of American diplomacy. The Truman Doctrine established the guiding principle and the Marshall Plan the model for foreign aid. The developing American sphere of influence in the Near East, the Middle East, and western Europe did rebuild. The United States had sought world peace and prosperity, but the world of 1947 resembled that of the 1930s more than Americans wished to admit.

Interwoven in the fabric of American diplomacy were several strands which together explain this determination to use United States power assertively. The outward-looking ideology of peace and prosperity, with its stress on foreign trade, and the very existence of great power itself were prominent. Another strand was the American reading of history. The Bolshevik Revolution of 1917 and the turmoil of the decade leading to World War II cast long shadows. Communism and Nazism were historical evils which had been in large part responsible for the twentieth-century cycle of war and peace, at least so Americans believed. When the postwar period brought tension rather than peace, an explanation was drawn from history: Soviet Russia was replacing Nazi Germany as the major disrupter of a stable, pacific international order. Therefore, the United States must isolate the evil and avert the cyclical recurrence of war. As Gaddis Smith has described Dean Acheson's historical understanding, "only the United States had the power to grab hold of history and make it conform."

The particular style and personality of Harry S. Truman and many of his advisers constitutes another strand in the diplomatic fabric. The president's impatient "get tough" and "give 'em hell" style complemented and reflected the power he represented. His acerbity and quick temper seemed all the more dramatic and meaningful because he could back up his tough language. He, Harriman, Byrnes, and Acheson, as well as diplomats like Lane and Steinhardt, were in agreement that lecturing the Russians was a proper procedure because the Soviets understood only assertiveness and direct pressure. Giving Molotov a "straight 'one-two to the jaw' " meant more than a verbal lashing in 1945; it united Truman's hard-hitting style and a national awareness of unmatched power. The president's frequently extreme and alarmist statements also helped garner support from Congress for his foreign aid legislation. His White House assistants believed that Truman was at his best and most persuasive when "he's been mad," and they cited the Truman Doctrine speech as a prime example.

A sense of moral superiority and a conviction of the universality and attainability of American ideals also played a part. "Most nations, probably all," Stephen Ambrose has written, "believe in the moral goodness of their ideals, but few have had the conceit to imagine, much less constantly proclaim, that their particular ideals are universal." Thus a double standard was created which often obscured the disparity between professions of political democracy and the open door behavior. American expansion into Iran, for example, buttressed world peace, while Soviet attempts to gain influence there were tagged "aggression." Because United States goals were noble and "right," its exercise of power could not be naked or raw, despite what many foreigners might believe. When President Truman reminisced in 1948 that American diplomacy stood as "a record of action in behalf of peace without parallel in history," he was not being deliberately deceitful: he was espousing the truth as the nation defined it.

What made American foreign policy so exceptional in the postwar period was the combination of these factors—the peace and prosperity ideology, the presence and awareness of power, "get tough" leaders, a particular reading of history, and the notion of American superiority. American diplomacy was not accidental or aimless: rather, it was self-consciously expansionist. An essential element in that expansion, expressed in the peace and prosperity ideology, was economic: the growth of foreign trade and investments and the acquisition of raw materials. But there was more to this expansionism than its economic aspects, nor can it be explained simply as a singular effort to sustain capitalism at home and to reform it abroad. The United States was capitalist, but it was also arrogant, Christian, militarist, racist, highly technological, chauvinistic, and industrialized. To argue that these traits all stem from capitalist roots is to make the term "capitalist" so elastic and all-encompassing as to be meaningless. It should be kept in mind, truism though it may be, that the United States had become a world power of uncommon dimensions, not just a capitalist power, and behaved like other great powers through history—it exploited opportunities. Although Washington preferred a capitalist world, it learned in the postwar period that it could live securely and profitably with a socialist government in Britain, feudal Middle Eastern sheikdoms, and a Communist regime in Yugoslavia. What seems to describe United States expansionism best is the "will to dominate," which is motivated by the strands discussed above.

There was bound to be conflict in the postwar period, but whether the Cold War, with its strident rhetoric, simplistic analyses, sacred myths, ideological battles, rigid alliances, military competition, blocs, and interrupted trade relations, was inevitable is questionable. Washington was free to make different choices or, at the very least, to pursue its reconstruction policies less coercively. To suggest that Americans (and Russians) could not have acted otherwise is to blind oneself to the options available, some of which were exercised (as, for example, in the treatment accorded Finland as opposed to Czechoslovakia). Many alternatives were ignored or rejected because Washington decided self-confidently to use its power to expand.

Few restraints inhibited the exercise of American power. Fears of a postwar depression, uncertainty about the magnitude of the plight of western Europe, and alarm about the "Russian menace" caused great concern in the United States. The bureaucracy at home did not always function smoothly; State and Treasury tangled over Germany, and the Export-Import Bank often moved slowly, for example. The Truman administration had to deal with a Congress which harbored a few recalcitrant isolationists, parsimonious budget-watchers, and many Republicans, and "public opinion" had to be marshaled behind Truman's foreign aid programs. Yet despite all this, Washington acted with a remarkable degree of confidence and cohesion, and one could suggest that their fears and anxieties actually encouraged Americans not to "retreat" from problems in foreign affairs but to "solve" them. It should further be noted that objects which can be easily moved or bypassed cannot be labeled restraints. The phrase "public opinion" suggests that the "people," or at least a majority of them, express opinions on most issues. Yet studies have demonstrated that only a small number of voting Americans (no more than 25 percent) in the early

Cold War years were attentive to foreign policy questions. The real "foreign policy public" or "opinion leaders" were a minority, most of them professional people, businessmen, and members of organized interest groups. Evidence from the period 1945 to 1950 indicates that these people, especially businessmen, labor leaders, journalists, intellectuals, and citizens' groups, substantially endorsed Truman's foreign policy. Most foreign policy debates centered on how much to spend, not whether to spend. When United States diplomats told foreign officials that they could not make a certain decision because the "American people" would not countenance it, such statements often served more as diplomatic ploys than as expressions of real apprehension.

In masterful fashion the Truman administration quieted or isolated most critics of its foreign policy. The historian must be impressed by the president's ability to shape the "public opinion" he wanted to hear and to discredit the opposition. Henry Wallace, for one, was successfully identified by Truman and his advisers as "pro-Soviet," if not actually a Communist. Conservative critics feared the isolationist label, with its negative connotations from the rejected 1930s. Administration-backed citizens' groups like the Committee for the Marshall Plan generated widespread support. Truman's technique of presenting Congress with an accomplished fact while arousing patriotic fervor through inflammatory public pronouncements undercut his critics. Dissenters could develop only small followings. Most Democratic liberals joined the anti-Communist crusade at home and abroad by forming the Americans for Democratic Action. The Socialist Party and the peace movement were weak, and even Norman Thomas frequently applauded Cold War diplomacy.

As for the Congress, at times it made Truman work hard for his legislation, but it trimmed budgets only slightly and usually left him free to exercise American power as he wished in the early Cold War years. Bipartisanship characterized the Congress until 1948. Senator Arthur Vandenberg congratulated himself on its maintenance, as did John Foster Dulles, a respected Republican adviser to the State Department. In both 1944 and 1948 Dulles was able to prevent conservatives from shaping the foreign policy platform of the Republican Party. Not until after the 1948 Republican debacle did bipartisanship begin to erode. During the 1948 campaign foreign policy was only marginally debated and Truman's effective explanations for the Czech coup and the Berlin Blockade helped gain him support. Vandenberg had persuaded leading Republicans to refrain from an open attack on the Truman administration's diplomacy. For most of the early Cold War years Dean Acheson took pride in his ability to flatter and manipulate Vandenberg into doing the administration's bidding. Vandenberg himself told a Detroit audience in early 1949 that "during the last two years, when the Presidency and Congress represented different parties, America could only speak with unity. . . . So-called bipartisan foreign policy provided the connecting link. It did not apply to everything—for example, not to Palestine or China. But it did apply generally elsewhere. It helped to formulate foreign policy before it ever reached the legislative stage." He concluded, "our Government did not splinter. It did not default. It was strong in the presence of its adversaries."

Governed by bipartisanship and Vandenberg's commitment to it, aroused by Truman's alarmist appeals, disarmed by faits accomplis, and influenced by opinion leaders who applauded American diplomacy, Congress voted the president his requests. Although there was always some congressional opposition in this period, the Senate votes on Bretton Woods (61 to 16), on Truman Doctrine assistance to Greece and Turkey (67 to 23), on Interim Aid (86 to 3), and on the Marshall Plan (69 to 17) demonstrate its acquiescence in administration policy. There were exceptions: the vote on the British loan (46 to 33) was close, and Truman had to veto the Wool Act of 1947, which was embarrassing in view of his appeals for multilateral trade. But, on the whole, Truman got what he wanted from Congress, and Congress did not control foreign policy. When its reaction was very critical, as over the issues of UNRRA and Soviet-American trade, that criticism itself paralleled existing administration thinking. It may be that Truman spoke to Congress in alarmist tones and simplified the issues not necessarily because he had to persuade a reluctant legislature to his point of view but simply because this style had worked political magic for him throughout a long career.

In these years immediately after the war foreign aid became an integral part of the United States arsenal of weapons. American interests were world-wide, and the Truman Doctrine offered a principle by which the new global responsibilities could be understood. The crushing of the Greek civil war became a much-cited precedent to justify intervention in other countries. The Marshall Plan's place in history has been assured by those foreign aid advocates who point to the success of the ERP in combating Communism. The manipulation of international organizations became a feature of the Cold War. The declining influence of Congress on diplomacy and the curtailment of the debate at home on foreign policy were features of the early Cold War experience which have also persisted. The quest for raw materials, investments, and markets has been pursued vigorously, especially after attempts to create an open world had failed and trade blocs had been formed. Notions of American superiority and arrogance toward weaker states have dogged American diplomacy and have continued to obscure the gap between ideals and actions.

The most significant survival from this period is Washington's disdain for diplomacy as a means of solving disputes and avoiding confrontations. Walter Lippmann sensed this new attitude when he pointed out the shortcomings of the containment doctrine in 1947. There seemed to be little faith in negotiations with the Soviet Union, especially after the breakdown of the Yalta agreements and the inconclusive Foreign Ministers meetings in the fall of 1945. Convinced that their interpretations of international agreements were alone the correct ones, depicting Stalin as Hitler's replacement, and fearful of charges of "appeasement," United States officials attempted to fulfill their goals through the unilateral application of the power they knew they possessed. Reconstruction would proceed on their terms. The tragic result of this attitude was the division of the world into hostile spheres and the emasculation of the goal of peace and prosperity that postwar Americans so eagerly hoped to fulfill.

FURTHER READING

Les K. Adler and Thomas G. Paterson, "Red Fascism," *American Historical Review,* 75 (1970), 1046–1064

Stephen Ambrose, *Rise to Globalism* (1976)

Richard J. Barnet, *Intervention and Revolution* (1972)

Barton J. Bernstein, ed., *Politics and Policies of the Truman Administration* (1970)

Lynn Etheridge Davis, *The Cold War Begins* (1974)

Herbert Feis, *From Trust to Terror* (1970)

Denna F. Fleming, *The Cold War and Its Origins* (1961)

Richard Freeland, *The Truman Doctrine and the Origins of McCarthyism* (1971)

John L. Gaddis, *The United States and the Origins of the Cold War* (1972)

Lloyd C. Gardner, *Architects of Illusion* (1970)

John Gimbel, *The American Occupation of Germany* (1968)

Louis Halle, *The Cold War as History* (1967)

George Herring, *Aid to Russia, 1941–1946* (1973)

Richard Kirkendall, ed., *The Truman Period as a Research Field* (1974)

Gabriel Kolko and Joyce Kolko, *The Limits of Power* (1972)

Walter LaFeber, *America, Russia, and the Cold War* (1976)

Walter Lippmann, *The Cold War* (1947)

Lynn H. Miller and Ronald W. Pruessen, eds., *Reflections on the Cold War* (1974)

Thomas G. Paterson, ed., *Cold War Critics* (1971)

Thomas G. Paterson, ed., *The Origins of the Cold War* (1974)

Lisle Rose, *Dubious Victory* (1973)

John Spanier, *American Foreign Policy Since World War II* (1977)

Robert W. Tucker, *The Radical Left and American Foreign Policy* (1971)

Adam Ulam, *The Rivals* (1971)

Richard Walton, *Henry Wallace, Harry Truman and the Cold War* (1976)

Daniel Yergin, *Shattered Peace* (1977)

10

The Korean War

Before the outbreak of the Korean War in June 1950, the United States had launched a number of Cold War programs—the Truman Doctrine, the Marshall Plan, and NATO—and had weathered several crises: in Iran, Greece, and Berlin, for example. Yet in Asia, the American policy of containment faltered in China, where Mao Tse-tung's Communists after years of war unseated Chiang Kai-shek's Nationalists in late 1949 and created the People's Republic of China. Americans considered the new Chinese government a Soviet puppet.

Another shock wave hit the United States in August 1949, when the Soviet Union successfully exploded a nuclear device, thereby ending the American atomic monopoly. Many Americans jumped to the conclusion that the United States was losing the Cold War. The phenomenon of McCarthyism began in early 1950. Then the Korean War erupted. The Truman administration quickly decided to intervene—to draw the containment line.

Since then, questions have challenged scholars and contemporaries alike: Why did the Truman administration intervene? Should the United States have intervened? What were the comparative benefits of intervention or non-intervention? Was the Korean War an example of global Communist aggression? Or was it essentially a Korean civil war? Did Russia plan and order the North Korean invasion? What exactly was China's role, and why did it intervene? Why was General Douglas MacArthur fired? Should the Americans have conducted a "limited" war, as they did? The recent declassification of formerly closed documents permits historical scholarship on the Korean War to move increasingly from tentative answers to substantiated conclusions.

DOCUMENTS

On January 12, 1950, Secretary of State Dean Acheson delivered a speech, re-printed here, on United States policy toward Asia and therein defined the American defense perimeter, which excluded Korea. Critics later charged that that omission gave the Soviet Union the incentive to use its North Korean stooges to attack South Korea. During the opening days of the Korean crisis, President Harry S. Truman met with key advisers at Blair House, a building across the street from the White House. Reproduced here is a record of the June 26, 1950, "Blair House Meeting," wherein Secretary Acheson recommended several important policies not only for Korea, but for the Philippines, Formosa, and Indochina as well.

The third document is a dramatic speech by President Truman, dated April 11, 1951, and delivered shortly after he relieved General MacArthur of his command in Korea. Truman defends "limited" war in Korea and reveals that his administration thought Communism was an omnipresent, monolithic, global menace. The concluding document is MacArthur's rebuttal of April 19, 1951. In this speech to Congress, the General argues that there is "no substitute for victory."

Dean Acheson on the Defense Perimeter in Asia, 1950

I hear almost every day someone say that the real interest of the United States is to stop the spread of communism. Nothing seems to me to put the cart before the horse more completely than that. Of course we are interested in stopping the spread of communism. But we are interested for a far deeper reason than any conflict between the Soviet Union and the United States. We are interested in stopping the spread of communism because communism is a doctrine that we don't happen to like. Communism is the most subtle instrument of Soviet foreign policy that has ever been devised, and it is really the spearhead of Russian imperialism which would, if it could, take from these people what they have won, what we want them to keep and develop, which is their own national independence, their own individual independence, their own development of their own resources for their own good and not as mere tributary states to this great Soviet Union.

Now, it is fortunate that this point that I made does not represent any real conflict. It is an important point because people will do more damage and create more misrepresentation in the Far East by saying our interest is merely to stop the spread of communism than any other way. Our real interest is in those people as people. It is because communism is hostile to that interest that we want to stop it. But it happens that the best way of doing both things is to do just exactly what the peoples of Asia want to do and what we want to help them to do, which is to develop a soundness of administration of these new governments and to develop their resources and their technical skills so that they are not subject to penetration either through ignorance, or because they believe these false promises, or because there is real distress in their areas. If we can help that development, if we can go forward with it, then we have brought about the best way that anyone knows of stopping this spread of communism.

It is important to take this attitude not as a mere negative reaction to communism but as the most positive affirmation of the most affirmative truth that we hold, which is in the dignity and right of every nation, of every people, and of every individual to develop in their own way, making their own mistakes, reaching their own triumphs but acting under their own responsibility. That is what we are pressing for in the Far East, and that is what we must affirm and not get mixed up with purely negative and inconsequential statements.

Now, let me come to another underlying and important factor which determines our relations and, in turn, our policy with the peoples of Asia. That is the attitude of the Soviet Union toward Asia, and particularly towards those parts of Asia which are contiguous to the Soviet Union, and with great particularity this afternoon, to north China.

The attitude and interest of the Russians in north China, and in these other areas as well, long antedates communism. This is not something that has come out of communism at all. It long antedates it. But the Communist regime has added new methods, new skills, and new concepts to the thrust of Russian imperialism. This Communistic concept and techniques have armed Russian imperialism with a new and most insidious weapon of penetration. Armed with these new powers, what is happening in China is that the Soviet Union is detaching the northern provinces [areas] of China from China and is attaching them to the Soviet Union. This process is complete in outer Mongolia. It is nearly complete in Manchuria, and I am sure that in inner Mongolia and in Sinkiang there are very happy reports coming from Soviet agents to Moscow. This is what is going on. It is the detachment of these whole areas, vast areas— populated by Chinese—the detachment of these areas from China and their attachment to the Soviet Union.

I wish to state this and perhaps sin against my doctrine of nondogmatism, but I should like to suggest at any rate that this fact that the Soviet Union is taking the four northern provinces of China is the single most significant, most important fact, in the relation of any foreign power with Asia.

What does that mean for us? It means something very, very significant. It means that nothing that we do and nothing that we say must be allowed to obscure the reality of this fact. All the efforts of propaganda will not be able to obscure it. The only thing that can obscure it is the folly of ill-conceived adventures on our part which easily could do so, and I urge all who are thinking about these foolish adventures to remember that we must not seize the unenviable position which the Russians have carved out for themselves. We must not undertake to deflect from the Russians to ourselves the righteous anger, and the wrath, and the hatred of the Chinese people which must develop. It would be folly to deflect it to ourselves. We must take the position we have always taken—that anyone who violates the integrity of China is the enemy of China and is acting contrary to our own interest. That, I suggest to you this afternoon, is the first and the greatest rule in regard to the formulation of American policy toward Asia.

I suggest that the second rule is very like the first. That is to keep our own purposes perfectly straight, perfectly pure, and perfectly aboveboard and do not get them mixed-up with legal quibbles or the attempt to do one thing and really achieve another.

The consequences of this Russian attitude and this Russian action in China are perfectly enormous. They are saddling all those in China who are proclaiming their loyalty to Moscow, and who are allowing themselves to be used as puppets of Moscow, with the most awful responsibility which they must pay for. Furthermore, these actions of the Russians are making plainer than any speech, or any utterance, or any legislation can make throughout all of Asia, what the true purposes of the Soviet Union are and what the true function of communism as an agent of Russian imperialism is. These I suggest to you are the fundamental factors, fundamental realities of attitude out of which our relations and policies must grow.

Now, let's in the light of that consider some of these policies. First of all, let's deal with the question of military security. I deal with it first because it is important and because, having stated our policy in that regard, we must clearly understand that the military menace is not the most immediate.

What is the situation in regard to the military security of the Pacific area, and what is our policy in regard to it?

In the first place, the defeat and the disarmament of Japan has placed upon the United States the necessity of assuming the military defense of Japan so long as that is required, both in the interest of our security and in the interests of the security of the entire Pacific area and, in all honor, in the interest of Japanese security. We have American—and there are Australian—troops in Japan. I am not in a position to speak for the Australians, but I can assure you that there is no intention of any sort of abandoning or weakening the defenses of Japan and that whatever arrangements are to be made either through permanent settlement or otherwise, that defense must and shall be maintained.

This defensive perimeter runs along the Aleutians to Japan and then goes to the Ryukyus. We hold important defense positions in the Ryukyu Islands, and those we will continue to hold. In the interest of the population of the Ryukyu Islands, we will at an appropriate time offer to hold these islands under trusteeship of the United Nations. But they are essential parts of the defensive perimeter of the Pacific, and they must and will be held.

The defensive perimeter runs from the Ryukyus to the Philippine Islands. Our relations, our defensive relations with the Philippines are contained in agreements between us. Those agreements are being loyally carried out and will be loyally carried out. Both peoples have learned by bitter experience the vital connections between our mutual defense requirements. We are in no doubt about that, and it is hardly necessary for me to say an attack on the Philippines could not and would not be tolerated by the United States. But I hasten to add that no one perceives the imminence of any such attack.

So far as the military security of other areas in the Pacific is concerned, it must be clear that no person can guarantee these areas against military attack. But it must also be clear that such a guarantee is hardly sensible or necessary within the realm of practical relationship.

Should such an attack occur—one hesitates to say where such an armed attack could come from—the initial reliance must be on the people attacked to resist it and then upon the commitments of the entire civilized world under the Charter of the United Nations which so far has not proved a weak reed to lean on by any people who are determined to protect their independence against outside aggression. But it is a mistake, I think, in considering Pacific and Far Eastern problems to become obsessed with military considerations. Important as they are, there are other problems that press, and these other problems are not capable of solution through military means. These other problems arise out of the susceptibility of many areas, and many countries in the Pacific area, to subversion and penetration. That cannot be stopped by military means. . . .

That leads me to the other thing that I wanted to point out, and that is the limitation of effective American assistance. American assistance can be effective when it is the missing component in a situation which might otherwise be solved. The United States cannot furnish all these components to solve the question. It can not furnish determination, it can not furnish will, and it can not furnish the loyalty of a people to its government. But if the will and if the determination exists and if the people are behind their government, then, and not always then, is there a very good chance. In that situation, American help can be effective and it can lead to an accomplishment which could not otherwise be achieved. . . .

Korea. In Korea, we have taken great steps which have ended our military occupation, and in cooperation with the United Nations, have established an independent and sovereign country recognized by nearly all the rest of the world. We have given that nation great help in getting itself established. We are asking the Congress to continue that help until it is firmly established, and that legislation is now pending before the Congress. The idea that we should scrap all of that, that we should stop half way through the achievement of the establishment of this country, seems to me to be the most utter defeatism and utter madness in our interests in Asia. . . .

So after this survey, what we conclude, I believe, is that there is a new day which has dawned in Asia. It is a day in which the Asian peoples are on their own, and know it, and intend to continue on their own. It is a day in which the old relationships between east and west are gone, relationships which at their worst were exploitation, and which at their best were paternalism. That relationship is over, and the relationship of east and west must now be in the Far East one of mutual respect and mutual helpfulness. We are their friends. Others are their friends. We and those others are willing to help, but we can help only where we are wanted and only where the conditions of help are really sensible and possible. So what we can see is that this new day in Asia, this new day which is dawning, may go on to a glorious noon or it may darken and it may drizzle out. But that decision lies within the countries of Asia and within the power of the Asian people. It is not a decision which a friend or even an enemy from the outside can decide for them.

"Blair House Meeting," June 26, 1950

GENERAL [HOYT S.] VANDENBERG reported that the First Yak plane had been shot down.

THE PRESIDENT remarked that he hoped that it was not the last.

GENERAL VANDENBERG read the text of the orders which had been issued to our Air Forces calling on them to take "aggressive action" against any planes interfering with their mission or operating in a manner unfriendly to the South Korean forces. He indicated, however, that they had been avoiding combat where the direct carrying-out of their mission was not involved.

MR. [DEAN] ACHESON suggested that an all-out order be issued to the Navy and Air Force to waive all restrictions on their operations in Korea and to offer the fullest possible support to the South Korean forces, attacking tanks, guns, columns, etc., of the North Korean forces in order to give a chance to the South Koreans to reform.

THE PRESIDENT said he approved this.

MR. [FRANK] PACE inquired whether this meant action only south of the 38th parallel.

MR. ACHESON said this was correct. He was making no suggestion for any action across the line.

GENERAL VANDENBERG asked whether this meant also that they should not fly over the line.

MR. ACHESON said they should not.

THE PRESIDENT said this was correct; that no action should be taken north of the 38th parallel. He added "not yet".

MR. PACE said that care should be used to avoid hitting friendly forces.

GENERAL [J. LAWTON] COLLINS agreed but suggested that the orders themselves should not put restrictions on the operation.

MR. ACHESON said that if it was considered useful the orders could add that the purpose which the orders would implement is to support South Korean forces in conformity with the resolution of the Security Council.

MR. ACHESON said that the second point he wished to bring up was that orders should be issued to the Seventh Fleet to prevent an attack on Formosa.

THE PRESIDENT said he agreed.

MR. ACHESON continued that at the same time the National Government of China should be told to desist from operations against the mainland and that the Seventh Fleet should be ordered to see that those operations would cease.

MR. ACHESON said his third point was an increase in the United States military forces in the Philippines and an acceleration of aid to the Philippines in order that we might have a firm base there.

THE PRESIDENT said he agreed.

MR. ACHESON said his fourth point was that aid to Indochina should be stepped up and that a strong military mission should be sent.

He suggested that on all these matters if orders were issued tonight it would be desirable for the President to make a statement tomorrow. He handed the President a rough draft of the type of statement which might be issued.

THE PRESIDENT said he would work on the statement tonight. The President continued that he wished consideration given to taking Formosa back as part of Japan and putting it under MacArthur's Command.

MR. ACHESON said that he had considered this move but had felt that it should be reserved for later and should not be announced at this time. It required further study.

THE PRESIDENT said that he had a letter from the Generalissimo about one month (?) ago to the effect that the Generalissimo might step out of the situation if that would help. He said this was a private letter and he had kept it secret. He said that we might want to proceed along those lines in order to get Chinese forces helping us. He thought that the Generalissimo might step out if MacArthur were put in.

MR. ACHESON said that the Generalissimo was unpredictable and that it was possible that he might resist and "throw the ball game". He said that it might be well to do this later.

THE PRESIDENT said that was alright. He himself thought that it was the next step.

MR. [LOUIS A.] JOHNSON said that the proposals made by the Secretary of State pleased him very much. He thought that if we hold the line as indicated that that was alright.

MR. ACHESON added in regard to the Formosan situation that he thought it undesirable that we should get mixed up in the question of the Chinese administration of the Island.

THE PRESIDENT said that we were not going to give the Chinese "a nickel" for any purpose whatever. He said that all the money we had given them is now invested in United States real estate.

MR. JOHNSON added or in banks in the Philippine Islands.

ADMIRAL [FORREST P.] SHERMAN said that the Command of the Seventh Fleet could be either under Admiral Radford at Pearl Harbor or under General MacArthur. He said that under the orders issued yesterday the Seventh Fleet had been ordered to proceed to Japan and placed under General MacArthur's Command. He said that the orders in regard to Formosa would be issued from the Joint Chiefs of Staff to General MacArthur so to employ the forces allocated by Admiral Radford to General MacArthur.

No objection was raised to this statement.

MR. ACHESON said that the Security Council would meet tomorrow afternoon and that the Department had prepared a further resolution for adoption. Our reports were that we would get full support. He noted that even the Swedes were now supporting us.

MR. [JOHN D.] HICKERSON read the draft of the Security Council resolution recommending that UN members render such assistance as was needed to Korea to repel the attack.

THE PRESIDENT said that was right. He said we wanted everyone in on this, including Hong Kong.

GENERAL [OMAR] BRADLEY reported that British Air Marshall Tedder had come to see him, was generally in accord with our taking the firm position, and gave General Bradley a full report of the forces which the British have in that area.

MR. [DEAN] RUSK pointed out that it was possible the Russians would come to the Security Council meeting and cast a veto. In that case we would still take the position that we could act in support of the Charter.

THE PRESIDENT said that was right. He rather wished they would veto. He said we needed to lay a base for our action in Formosa. He said that he would work on the draft of his statement tonight and would talk to the Defense and State Departments in the morning regarding the final text.

MR. RUSK pointed out that it was Mr. Kennan's estimate that Formosa would be the next likely spot for a Communist move.

SECRETARY JOHNSON reported that SCAP's guess was that the next move would be on Iran. He thought there should be a check on this.

GENERAL COLLINS said that SCAP did not have as much global information as they have in Washington. He and Mr. Pace stated that they have asked for full reports all over the world in regard to any developments, particularly of Soviet preparations.

SECRETARY JOHNSON suggested to Mr. Acheson that it would be advisable to have some talks with the UK regarding possible action in Iran.

MR. ACHESON said he would talk with both the British and French.

MR. ACHESON asked Admiral Sherman whether he desired that any action should be taken regarding the utilization of the Sakishimas, south of Okinawa.

ADMIRAL SHERMAN said he would leave this to General MacArthur.

MR. ACHESON said it would be better to put any necessary supporting air forces on these Islands than to try to put them on Formosa itself.

MR. PACE inquired whether the State Department would inform Ambassador Muccio concerning the orders which were being given.

MR. ACHESON said from latest reports it would probably be impossible for us to contact Ambassador Muccio.

GENERAL COLLINS reported that they were in contact with Seoul through a ham radio operator there.

MR. PACE said that they could pass a message to Ambassador Muccio through General MacArthur.

MR. ACHESON suggested that the President might wish to get in Senator Connally and other members of the Senate and House and tell them what had been decided.

THE PRESIDENT said that he had a meeting scheduled for 10:00 tomorrow morning with the Big Four and that he would get in any others that the Secretary thought should be added. He suggested that Secretaries Acheson and Johnson should also be there.

MR. JOHNSON suggested that the majority and minority members of the two Armed Services Committees be included.

After the discussion it was agreed to set the meeting for 11:30.

THE PRESIDENT then read the following list of persons to be included in the meeting:

The Big Four (Lucas, Rayburn, McCormack—the Vice President will be out of town), Senators Connally, Wiley, George, Alexander Smith, Thomas of Utah, Tydings and Bridges; Congressmen Kee, Eaton, Vinson and Short.

MR. JOHNSON referred again to the draft statement for the President, said that it was very forthright, that he liked it very much and that the Joint Chiefs would consider it during the evening and make any suggestions in the morning.

GENERAL COLLINS stated that the military situation in Korea was bad. It was impossible to say how much our air can do. The Korean Chief of Staff has no fight left in him.

MR. ACHESON stated that it was important for us to do something even if the effort were not successful.

MR. JOHNSON said that even if we lose Korea this action would save the situation. He said this action "suits me". He then asked whether any of the military representatives had any objection to the course of action which had been outlined. There was no objection.

GENERAL VANDENBERG, in response to a question from Mr. Finletter, said that he bet a tank would be knocked out before dark.

THE PRESIDENT said he had done everything he could for five years to prevent this kind of situation. Now the situation is here and we must do what we can to meet it. He had been wondering about the mobilization of the National Guard and asked General Bradley if that was necessary now. If it was he must go to Congress and ask for funds. He was merely putting the subject on the table for discussion. He repeated we must do everything we can for the Korean situation—"for the United Nations".

GENERAL BRADLEY said that if we commit our ground forces in Korea we cannot at the same time carry out our other commitments without mobilization. He wondered if it was better to wait now on the question of mobilization of the National Guard. He thought it would be preferable to wait a few days.

THE PRESIDENT said he wished the Joint Chiefs to think about this and to let him know in a few days time. He said "I don't want to go to war".

GENERAL COLLINS stated that if we were going to commit ground forces in Korea we must mobilize.

MR. ACHESON suggested that we should hold mobilization in reserve.

MR. JOHNSON said he hoped these steps already authorized will settle the Korean question.

THE PRESIDENT said the next question would be the mobilization of the Fleet Reserve.

ADMIRAL SHERMAN said there must be a degree of balance.

THE PRESIDENT noted that there is some pretty good air in the National Guard. He had never been in favor of this and thought it should be like the Naval Reserve.

GENERAL VANDENBERG said he was very glad to hear the President say this.

ADMIRAL SHERMAN asked whether MacArthur could anchor the fleet in Formosan ports if necessary.

THE PRESIDENT asked Mr. Acheson what he thought about this.

MR. ACHESON said that they should go ahead and do it.

ADMIRAL SHERMAN said this would be the best procedure.

GENERAL COLLINS remarked that if we had had standing orders we could have stopped this. We must consider this problem for the future.

THE PRESIDENT said he agreed.

MR. JOHNSON said that if there was danger of a Russian veto in the Security Council the President's statement should be put out before the Security Council meets tomorrow.

MR. ACHESON agreed.

Harry S. Truman Defends United States Policy, 1951

I want to talk plainly to you tonight about what we are doing in Korea and about our policy in the Far East.

In the simplest terms, what we are doing in Korea is this: We are trying to prevent a third world war.

I think most people in this country recognized that fact last June. And they warmly supported the decision of the Government to help the Republic of Korea against the Communist aggressors. Now, many persons, even some who applauded our decision to defend Korea, have forgotten the basic reason for our action.

It is right for us to be in Korea. It was right last June. It is right today.

I want to remind you why this is true.

The Communists in the Kremlin are engaged in a monstrous conspiracy to stamp out freedom all over the world. If they were to succeed, the United States would be numbered among their principal victims. It must be clear to everyone that the United States cannot—and will not—sit idly by and await foreign conquest. The only question is: When is the best time to meet the threat and how?

The best time to meet the threat is in the beginning. It is easier to put out a fire in the beginning when it is small than after it has become a roaring blaze.

And the best way to meet the threat of aggression is for the peace-loving nations to act together. If they don't act together, they are likely to be picked off, one by one.

If they had followed the right policies in the 1930's—if the free countries had acted together, to crush the aggression of the dictators, and if they had acted in the beginning, when the aggression was small—there probably would have been no World War II.

If history has taught us anything, it is that aggression anywhere in the world is a threat to peace everywhere in the world. When that aggression is supported by the cruel and selfish rulers of a powerful nation who are bent on conquest, it becomes a clear and present danger to the security and independence of every free nation.

This is a lesson that most people in this country have learned thoroughly. This is the basic reason why we joined in creating the United Nations. And since the end of World War II we have been putting that lesson into practice— we have been working with other free nations to check the aggressive designs of the Soviet Union before they can result in a third world war.

That is what we did in Greece, when that nation was threatened by the aggression of international communism.

The attack against Greece could have led to general war. But this country came to the aid of Greece. The United Nations supported Greek resistance. With our help, the determination and efforts of the Greek people defeated the attack on the spot.

Another big Communist threat to peace was the Berlin blockade. That too could have led to war. But again it was settled because free men would not back down in an emergency.

The aggression against Korea is the boldest and most dangerous move the Communists have yet made.

The attack on Korea was part of a greater plan for conquering all of Asia. . . .

They want to control all Asia from the Kremlin.

This plan of conquest is in flat contradiction to what we believe. We believe that Korea belongs to the Koreans, that India belongs to the Indians—that all the nations of Asia should be free to work out their affairs in their own way. This is the basis of peace in the Far East and everywhere else.

The whole Communist imperialism is back of the attack on peace in the Far East. It was the Soviet Union that trained and equipped the North Koreans for aggression. The Chinese Communists massed 44 well-trained and well-equipped divisions on the Korean frontier. These were the troops they threw into battle when the North Korean Communists were beaten.

The question we have had to face is whether the Communist plan of conquest can be stopped without general war. Our Government and other countries associated with us in the United Nations believe that the best chance of stopping it without general war is to meet the attack in Korea and defeat it there.

That is what we have been doing. It is a difficult and bitter task.

But so far it has been successful.

So far, we have prevented World War III.

So far, by fighting a limited war in Korea, we have prevented aggression from succeeding and bringing on a general war. And the ability of the whole free world to resist Communist aggression has been greatly improved.

We have taught the enemy a lesson. He has found out that aggression is not cheap or easy. Moreover, men all over the world who want to remain free have been given new courage and new hope. They know now that the

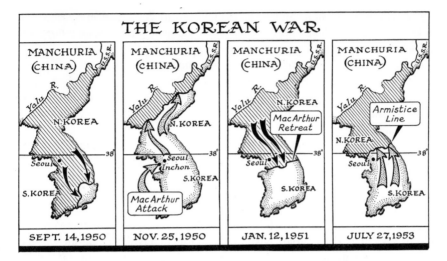

champions of freedom can stand up and fight and that they will stand up and fight.

Our resolute stand in Korea is helping the forces of freedom now fighting in Indochina and other countries in that part of the world. It has already slowed down the timetable of conquest.

In Korea itself, there are signs that the enemy is building up his ground forces for a new mass offensive. We also know that there have been large increases in the enemy's available air forces.

If a new attack comes, I feel confident it will be turned back. The United Nations fighting forces are tough and able and well equipped. They are fighting for a just cause. They are proving to all the world that the principle of collective security will work. We are proud of all these forces for the magnificent job they have done against heavy odds. We pray that their efforts may succeed, for upon their success may hinge the peace of the world.

The Communist side must now choose its course of action. The Communist rulers may press the attack against us. They may take further action which will spread the conflict. They have that choice, and with it the awful responsibility for what may follow. The Communists also have the choice of a peaceful settlement which could lead to a general relaxation of tensions in the Far East. The decision is theirs, because the forces of the United Nations will strive to limit the conflict if possible.

We do not want to see the conflict in Korea extended. We are trying to prevent a world war—not to start one. The best way to do that is to make it plain that we and the other free countries will continue to resist the attack.

But you may ask: Why can't we take other steps to punish the aggressor? Why don't we bomb Manchuria and China itself? Why don't we assist Chinese Nationalist troops to land on the mainland of China?

If we were to do these things we would be running a very grave risk of starting a general war. If that were to happen, we would have brought about the exact situation we are trying to prevent.

If we were to do these things, we would become entangled in a vast conflict on the continent of Asia and our task would become immeasurably more difficult all over the world.

What would suit the ambitions of the Kremlin better than for our military forces to be committed to a full-scale war with Red China?

It may well be that, in spite of our best efforts, the Communists may spread the war. But it would be wrong—tragically wrong—for us to take the initiative in extending the war.

The dangers are great. Make no mistake about it. Behind the North Koreans and Chinese Communists in the front lines stand additional millions of Chinese soldiers. And behind the Chinese stand the tanks, the planes, the submarines, the soldiers, and the scheming rulers of the Soviet Union.

Our aim is to avoid the spread of the conflict.

The course we have been following is the one best calculated to avoid an all-out war. It is the course consistent with our obligation to do all we can to maintain international peace and security. Our experience in Greece and Berlin shows that it is the most effective course of action we can follow.

First of all, it is clear that our efforts in Korea can blunt the will of the Chinese Communists to continue the struggle. The United Nations forces have put up a tremendous fight in Korea and have inflicted very heavy casualties on the enemy. Our forces are stronger now than they have been before. These are plain facts which may discourage the Chinese Communists from continuing their attack.

Second, the free world as a whole is growing in military strength every day. In the United States, in Western Europe, and throughout the world, free men are alert to the Soviet threat and are building their defenses. This may discourage the Communist rulers from continuing the war in Korea—and from undertaking new acts of aggression elsewhere.

If the Communist authorities realize that they cannot defeat us in Korea, if they realize it would be foolhardy to widen the hostilities beyond Korea, then they may recognize the folly of continuing their aggression. A peaceful settlement may then be possible. The door is always open.

Then we may achieve a settlement in Korea which will not compromise the principles and purposes of the United Nations.

I have thought long and hard about this question of extending the war in Asia. I have discussed it many times with the ablest military advisers in the country. I believe with all my heart that the course we are following is the best course.

I believe that we must try to limit the war to Korea for these vital reasons: to make sure that the precious lives of our fighting men are not wasted; to see that the security of our country and the free world is not needlessly jeopardized; and to prevent a third world war.

A number of events have made it evident that General MacArthur did not agree with that policy. I have therefore considered it essential to relieve General MacArthur so that there would be no doubt or confusion as to the real purpose and aim of our policy.

It was with the deepest personal regret that I found myself compelled to take this action. General MacArthur is one of our greatest military commanders. But the cause of world peace is more important than any individual.

General Douglas MacArthur's "No Substitute for Victory" Speech, 1951

I do not stand here as advocate for any partisan cause, for the issues are fundamental and reach quite beyond the realm of partisan consideration. They must be resolved on the highest plane of national interest if our course is to prove sound and our future protected. I trust, therefore, that you will do me the justice of receiving that which I have to say as solely expressing the considered viewpoint of a fellow American. I address you with neither rancor nor bitterness in the fading twilight of life with but one purpose in mind, to serve my country. . . .

While I was not consulted prior to the President's decision to intervene in the support of the Republic of Korea, that decision from a military standpoint proved a sound one. As I say, a brief and sound one as we hurled back the invaders and decimated his forces. Our victory was complete and our objectives within reach when Red China intervened with numerically superior ground forces. This created a new war and an entirely new situation, a situation not contemplated when our forces were committed against the North Korean invaders, a situation which called for new decisions in the diplomatic sphere to permit the realistic adjustment of military strategy. Such decisions have not been forthcoming.

While no man in his right mind would advocate sending our ground forces into continental China—and such was never given a thought—the new situation did urgently demand a drastic revision of strategic planning if our political aim was to defeat this new enemy as we had defeated the old.

Apart from the military need as I saw it to neutralize sanctuary, protection given to the enemy north of the Yalu, I felt that military necessity in the conduct of the war made necessary:

First, the intensification of our economic blockade against China.

Second, the imposition of a naval blockade against the China coast.

Third, removal of restrictions on air reconnaissance of China's coastal areas and of Manchuria.

Fourth, removal of restrictions on the forces of the Republic of China on Formosa with logistical support to contribute to their effective operation against the Chinese mainland.

For entertaining these views all professionally designed to support our forces committed to Korea and bring hostilities to an end with the least possible delay and at a saving of countless American and Allied lives, I have been severely criticized in lay circles, principally abroad, despite my understanding that from a military standpoint the above views have been fully shared in the past by practically every military leader concerned with the Korean campaign, including our own Joint Chiefs of Staff.

I called for reinforcements, but was informed that reinforcements were not available. I made clear that if not permitted to utilize the friendly Chinese force of some 600,000 men on Formosa; if not permitted to blockade the China coast to prevent the Chinese Reds from getting succor from without; and if there were to be no hope of major reinforcements, the position of the command from the military standpoint forbade victory. We could hold in Korea by constant maneuver and at an approximate area where our supply advantages were in balance with the supply line disadvantages of the enemy, but we could hope at best for only an indecisive campaign, with its terrible and constant attrition upon our forces if the enemy utilized his full military potential. I have constantly called for the new political decisions essential to a solution. Efforts have been made to distort my position. It has been said in effect that I was a warmonger. Nothing could be further from the truth. I know war as few other men now living know it, and nothing to me is more revolting. . . .

But once war is forced upon us, there is no other alternative than to apply every available means to bring it to a swift end. War's very object is victory—not prolonged indecision. In war, indeed, there can be no substitute for victory.

There are some who for varying reasons would appease Red China. They are blind to history's clear lesson. For history teaches with unmistakable emphasis that appeasement but begets new and bloodier war. It points to no single instance where the end has justified that means—where appeasement has led to more than a sham peace. Like blackmail, it lays the basis for new and successively greater demands, until, as in blackmail, violence becomes the only other alternative. Why, my soldiers asked of me, surrender military advantages to an enemy in the field? I could not answer. Some may say to avoid spread of the conflict into an all-out war with China; others, to avoid Soviet intervention. Neither explanation seems valid. For China is already engaging with the maximum power it can commit and the Soviet will not necessarily mesh its actions with our moves. Like a cobra, any new enemy will more likely strike whenever it feels that the relativity in military or other potential is in its favor on a world-wide basis.

The tragedy of Korea is further heightened by the fact that as military action is confined to its territorial limits, it condemns that nation, which it is our purpose to save, to suffer the devastating impact of full naval and air bombardment, while the enemy's sanctuaries are fully protected from such attack and devastation. Of the nations of the world, Korea alone, up to now, is the sole one which has risked its all against communism. The magnificence of the courage and fortitude of the Korean people defies description. They have chosen to risk death rather than slavery. Their last words to me were "Don't scuttle the Pacific."

I have just left your fighting sons in Korea. They have met all tests there and I can report to you without reservation they are splendid in every way. It was my constant effort to preserve them and end this savage conflict honorably and with the least loss of time and a minimum sacrifice of life. Its growing bloodshed has caused me the deepest anguish and anxiety. Those gallant men will remain often in my thoughts and in my prayers always.

I am closing my 52 years of military service. When I joined the Army even before the turn of the century, it was the fulfillment of all my boyish hopes and dreams. The world has turned over many times since I took the oath on the plain at West Point, and the hopes and dreams have long since vanished. But I since remember the refrain of one of the most popular barrack ballads of that day which proclaimed most proudly that—

"Old soldiers never die; they just fade away." And like the old soldier of that ballad, I now close my military career and just fade away—an old soldier who tried to do his duty as God gave him the light to see that duty.

Good-by.

ESSAYS

David F. Trask of the Department of State's Historical Office surveys the events preceding, during, and following the Korean War. He sees the issue largely as another crisis in the Cold War and writes that Russia engineered the North Korean attack. In discussing the Truman-MacArthur tussle over "limited" war, he sides with the President on this issue.

The other essay, by Robert R. Simmons, a political scientist, investigates the subject very differently. In a selection drawn from the introduction and later chapters of his book, *The Strained Alliance,* Simmons finds the origins of the Korean conflict not in the Cold War, but in Korean politics, both North and South. In short, he urges us to interpret it as the Korean *civil* war. He studies the role of Russia and suggests that Moscow was surprised by the timing of the Northern invasion of the South and was a reluctant supporter throughout the conflict. Like Trask, he assesses the long-term impact of the war on American foreign policy.

The Korean War and the Cold War

DAVID F. TRASK

While the United States and the Soviet Union concentrated on Europe, a crisis gradually built up in East Asia. The defeat of Japan and China's debility left another power vacuum, which America moved quickly to fill. After Japan surrendered in 1945, General Douglas MacArthur assumed direction of the American occupation. As vigorous in his proconsular role as in his wartime

From *The Ordeal of World Power: American Diplomacy Since 1900* by Samuel F. Wells, Jr., Robert H. Ferrell, and David F. Trask, pp. 276–287. Copyright © 1975, 1973 by Little, Brown and Company (Inc.). Reprinted by permission.

leadership, the autocratic MacArthur set about to demilitarize and democratize Japan, and in these endeavors he achieved considerable success. Under his tutelage the Japanese people developed a constitution that provided for permanent disarmament and Western parliamentary government. Trade unions were founded to improve the lot of urban workers, and land reform wrought improvements in country life. Energetic activity in Japan revealed that the United States did not intend to withdraw from East Asia, as did the policy of retaining strategic islands in the Pacific seized during the war. Friendly relations with disarmed Japan became a cardinal component of the nation's Asian policy, particularly after the Chinese Communists rose to power in Peking. Japan, of course, benefited from the onset of the cold war and American patronage; it received both protection and economic assistance in good measure. As in the case of Germany, the United States recognized that vengeance was both unsatisfying and dangerous.

The Soviet Union had entered the Far Eastern war during its last days, but the United States prevented its participation in the postwar occupation of Japan, just as the Kremlin excluded Washington from Eastern Europe after 1945. On the other hand, the Russians capitalized on the Yalta pledges, which permitted them to recover the territory they had lost to Japan in 1905, including their old sphere of influence in Manchuria and Outer Mongolia. They also occupied Korea north of the thirty-eighth parallel. Honoring his engagements at Yalta, Stalin established friendly relations with Nationalist China despite a powerful Chinese Communist movement.

President Roosevelt had sponsored the Nationalist government of Chiang Kai-shek as an eventual replacement for Japan in the Asian balance of political forces, but this project never came to fruition. Chiang received extensive diplomatic and economic support from the United States, but mismanagement, corruption, and lack of popular support laid Nationalist China open to conquest by the Communist armies of Mao Tse-tung. After World War II, President Truman sent General Marshall to China to facilitate negotiations between Chiang and Mao, but his good offices came to nothing. Neither side was prepared to bargain in good faith because each believed that it could destroy the other. Marshall's failure precipitated Washington's decision to let events take their course. Nothing short of initiatives such as those being developed in Europe appeared likely to influence the outcome in China, but the Truman administration assumed, correctly, that the American people at the time were unwilling to subsidize Asian projects comparable to the Marshall Plan and NATO. Like the United States, the Soviet Union concentrated on European questions, so that Chinese realities rather than outside influences largely determined the outcome of the struggle between the Nationalists and the Communists. Acheson in 1949 summarized the denouement accurately, asserting that the Communist victory was "the product of internal Chinese forces, forces which this country tried to influence but could not."

When Mao's armies forced Chiang to flee from the mainland to Formosa in 1949, the American people reacted in shock. Chiang's fall came at about the same time that the Soviet Union exploded its first atomic device. Both events aroused anger and fear in the United States, contributing to a raging Red Scare after disclosures of espionage that had conveyed information about the atomic bomb to the Soviet Union. Trading on this concatenation of events, members of the United States Congress and other opportunists soon began to advance the spurious thesis that high government officials had betrayed the United States from within. No exponent of this view made more capital out of it than Senator Joseph R. McCarthy, Republican of Wisconsin, who gave his name to the practice of issuing unsupported allegations of disloyalty against government officials and others who supposedly had sold out China to the "Reds." He reserved his greatest scorn for the State Department, which, he stoutly maintained, was "thoroughly infested with Communists."

Meanwhile a crisis was building in the small country of Korea, traditionally an outlying part of the Chinese empire but since 1910 a Japanese colony. When World War II ended, Korea was divided at the thirty-eighth parallel into Russian and American zones of occupation, pending elections designed to choose a government for the entire country. Unhappily for the Koreans, the cold war intervened. After the United Nations failed in an attempt to arrange elections, separate regimes appeared in the two zones. Voters to the south placed the conservative Korean nationalist Syngman Rhee at the head of the Republic of Korea. As in Germany, the Soviet Union sponsored a Communist nation in North Korea—the Democratic People's Republic. Russia energetically built up North Korea, particularly its armed forces, but the United States, attempting to minimize its involvement, had withdrawn its combat troops from South Korea by late 1949. Some economic help went to Rhee, but no extensive arrangements were made to protect South Korea against possible invasion from the north. During 1949 General MacArthur specifically excluded Korea as well as Formosa from the perimeter of American defenses in East Asia; he defined the line of demarcation as running from the Philippines through the Ryukyu Islands to Japan and thence to Alaska. Secretary Acheson may have conveyed the false impression that the United States might not defend Korea when in January 1950 he reiterated MacArthur's description of the perimeter and stated that in the event of aggression in the region "initial reliance must be on the people attacked to resist it and upon the commitments of the entire civilized world under the Charter of the United Nations."

Six months later, on June 24 (local time), 1950, North Korean troops swept across the thirty-eighth parallel into South Korea. Insufficient evidence exists to explain the reasons for the invasion, but apparently Stalin masterminded it, assuming that the United States would not use force and that the well-armed North Koreans could triumph easily. A conquest would recoup at least some of the prestige the Soviet Union had lost because of setbacks in Europe. Miscalculations of this nature, on both sides, have occurred all too frequently during the cold war.

Despite its earlier vagueness, the United States acted with remarkable energy; the Korean War became a test of containment in East Asia. President Truman arranged an emergency meeting of the Security Council, which passed a resolution branding the North Korean action "a breach of peace." (The Soviet delegate was not present to cast a veto; he was boycotting the Security Council because after Mao's victory the United States had refused to seat Communist China in place of Nationalist China.) The President instructed General MacArthur to provide naval and air support to South Korea and ordered the Seventh Fleet into the Straits of Formosa to prevent the Chinese Nationalists and Communists from attacking each other. After this decisive step, the United States sought sanction for its actions from the United Nations. When on June 27 the Security Council approved a proposal to resist the North Korean aggression, the United Nations accepted sponsorship of military operations to be conducted primarily by the armed forces of the United States and South Korea, acting as policemen for the world organization—hence the term "police action" as a description of the conflict. MacArthur soon recommended deployment of American ground, air, and naval units. The President ordered them into action on June 30.

In his memoirs Truman described his thoughts when he made the decision to resist the North Korean invasion, citing a historical analogy almost invariably invoked during other cold war crises: "In my generation, this was not the first occasion when the strong had attacked the weak. I recalled some earlier instances: Manchuria, Ethiopia, Austria. I remembered how each time that the democracies failed to act it had encouraged the aggressors to keep going ahead." What would happen if the United States failed to act? "I felt certain that if South Korea was allowed to fall Communist leaders would be emboldened to override nations closer to our own shores." Failure to control Communist aggression in Asia would lead to a third world war, just as appeasement in Europe had led to World War II. "It was also clear to me," the President wrote, "that the foundations and the principles of the United Nations were at stake unless this unprovoked attack on Korea could be stopped."

America's intervention frustrated an early North Korean success, but the conflict at first went badly for the United Nations command. By September, General MacArthur's forces had been corralled within a perimeter around Pusan on the extreme southeastern coast. Fortunately, reinforcements finally arrived, permitting a remarkable recovery. Brilliant landing operations near the thirty-eighth parallel at Inchon on the west coast of Korea in October, coordinated with a breakout at Pusan, virtually destroyed the North Korean forces. The aggressor had been contained. This victory raised difficult questions. Should the United Nations force stand at the thirty-eighth parallel? Or should it invade North Korea in order to reunify the peninsula by force of arms? Fatefully, the United States decided to support a move northward, a step that led to vast "escalation" of the war. The General Assembly of the United Nations approved a somewhat ambiguous resolution that was taken as authority to unify Korea by force. On October 11 President Truman conferred on Wake Island with his field commander. MacArthur, ignoring indications that the Chinese Communists might intervene in the struggle if his troops approached the Korean-Manchurian border, talked of victory by Thanksgiving. He told the President that the Red Army was not likely to act, but, "if the Chinese tried to get down to Pyongyang [North Korea's capital], there would be the greatest slaughter."

Despite the general's confident appraisal, his attacks to the north of the thirty-eighth parallel, some of which approached the Yalu River flowing between North Korea and the Chinese province of Manchuria, provoked an all-out intervention by Communist China. On November 26, the American Eighth Army began a precipitate retreat after it encountered a huge Chinese force. Almost immediately, MacArthur appealed for massive reinforcements, admitting that "the situation here must be viewed on the basis of an entirely new war against an entirely new power of great military strength and under entirely new conditions." By January 1951, the Eighth Army managed to establish a defensible position well below the thirty-eighth parallel.

These developments led to a serious conflict, long in the making, between General MacArthur and his superiors in Washington. The humiliated theater commander called for total victory, a stance that implied use of nuclear weapons. He also wanted to deploy Formosan forces against the Chinese Communist army. After tasting defeat, the general seemed to forget his earlier opposition to extensive land warfare in Asia. Truman and the Joint Chiefs of Staff proved much more cautious, favoring a limited war for limited objectives. General Omar Bradley later described MacArthur's strategy as "the wrong war, at the wrong place, at the wrong time, with the wrong enemy." This view precluded the use of nuclear weapons against the Chinese and also air raids against enemy bases on the Manchurian side of the Yalu River. MacArthur called these locations "privileged sanctuaries." When the administration refused to accept MacArthur's recommendations, the general became insubordinate. He failed to support the President's desire to seek a negotiated end of the war as the Eighth Army gradually regained control of South Korea to the thirty-eighth parallel. On April 5, 1951, a Congressman read to the House of Representatives a letter from MacArthur that bluntly criticized the policy of limited war. Truman, who had decided to act earlier, used this occasion to remove the general summarily from his duties. The discomfited commander returned to the United States amid a tumultuous public welcome. In New York huge crowds turned out for a parade in his honor.

MacArthur touched off a "great debate" when he presented his views to a joint session of Congress on April 19, 1951. Asia, he thought, should not have been placed second to Europe in American planning: "You cannot appease or otherwise surrender to Communism in Asia without simultaneously undermining our efforts to halt its advance in Europe." He had approved the decision to defend South Korea, but when the Chinese intervened he had assumed that new strategic departures were called for. Besides authority to bomb the enemy's "privileged sanctuaries" in Manchuria, he advocated more effective means of inhibiting the Chinese economy, improved naval blockade of the China coast, extensive air reconnaissance over China and Manchuria, and military operations against the Chinese mainland by Chiang Kai-shek's forces. Denying that he was a warmonger, MacArthur implied that the President's refusal to accept his counsel represented appeasement. Those who disagreed with him were "blind to history's clear lesson, for history teaches, with unmistakable emphasis, that appeasement but begets new and bloodier war." He closed his address with a sentimental reference that brought tears to the eyes of some legislators. He remembered an old barracks ballad that proclaimed: " 'Old soldiers never die; they just fade away.' And like the old soldier of that ballad, I now close my military career and just fade away, an old soldier who tried to do his duty as God gave him the light to see that duty. Good-by."

Spokesmen for the administration replied vigorously before congressional investigators. General Bradley maintained that MacArthur vastly underestimated the likelihood that expanding the limited war in Korea would lead to global conflict. Local commanders often make such errors, but the Joint Chiefs of Staff had to consider each theater in relation to all others. Bradley maintained that "a policy of patience and determination without provoking world war, while we improve our military power, is one we believe we must continue to follow." Any other approach would play into the hands of the Russians, the real enemy, because it would "tie down additional forces . . . while the Soviet Union would not be obliged to put a single man into the conflict."

By the time that Congress concluded its extended discussion of the war, public opinion had rallied behind the policies of the administration. Although the American people admired MacArthur, they did not accept his call for a wider war, however much they disliked the idea of limited struggle. The necessity to avoid total victory proved a hard pill to swallow. It was difficult to endure the frustrations of not using all the power at the command of the nation, including, of course, the nuclear arsenal.

In American mythology, when conflict occurs between "good" and "evil," the solution, so often depicted in western films, is a shoot-out at high noon, producing a clear decision—for virtue. The western is a kind of American passion play, summarizing the approved national method for dealing with scoundrels. Truman's decision to pursue limited warfare precluded a triumph for virtue. It flew in the face of attitudes that found expression in General MacArthur's statement before Congress: "Once war is forced upon us, there is no other alternative than to apply every available means to bring it to a swift end. War's very object is victory—not prolonged indecision. In war, indeed, there can be no substitute for victory. . . . Why, my soldiers asked of me, surrender military advantages to an enemy in the field? I could not answer." MacArthur's emotional appeal derived largely from his portrayal of the international situation as a confrontation between good and evil, an approach that most Americans found congenial. Prudence dictated adherence to President Truman's middle course in Korea, but Washington's defense of limited warfare did not satisfy the people.

Widespread disillusion expressed itself in a burst of public antipathy toward Truman, Acheson, and other representatives of a party that had been in power since 1933. Senator McCarthy, hopeful of public support for his anti-Communist crusade, seized upon the occasion to elaborate the thesis that the Democratic Party had committed twenty years of treason. Senator Robert Taft of Ohio, widely accepted as Mr. Republican by his supporters because of his ascendancy in the conservative wing of the GOP, lent prestige to this notion when he stated, "The Korean War and the problems which arise from it are the final result of the continuous sympathy toward communism which inspired American policy." Much of this partisan onslaught, of course, reflected efforts to profit during the approaching presidential election from disturbing domestic developments. Frustrations abroad combined with internal dissatisfactions to discredit the administration.

During June 1951, the United Nations indicated its willingness to accept an armistice in Korea based on a territorial division between the contending forces roughly following the thirty-eighth parallel. The Chinese had good reason to negotiate because by this time many thousands of their troops were being chewed up in General Matthew B. Ridgway's "meat-grinder offensive." China and North Korea responded favorably to the proposal, and truce talks began on July 7. Hopes for an early settlement disappeared when the conferees bogged down over several controversial questions, of which the most ticklish were procedures for prisoner exchange and Syngman Rhee's insistence on a settlement that would unify Korea under his leadership. When negotiators failed to announce an early armistice, public opposition to the conflict intensified further in the United States, particularly in response to casualty lists resulting from bloody positional warfare at so-called Heartbreak Hill and other parts of the front.

The American electorate in 1952 chose the Republican Party's candidate for the presidency, General Eisenhower, shortly after "Ike" promised to "go to Korea." He did just that, but his assessment of the situation confirmed that of the leaders he had been chosen to displace. Deciding against military action to unify the Korean peninsula under one government, Eisenhower instead hinted that the United States might use nuclear weapons if the armistice negotiations failed to produce a settlement. This tactic must have impressed the Chinese. Another event, the death of Stalin in March 1953, may have had some influence. The new Russian leaders appeared willing to lessen international tensions while making domestic adjustments required by Stalin's demise. In any event, a Korean armistice was finally agreed upon, taking effect on July 27, 1953, establishing a buffer zone close to the thirty-eighth parallel. Both sides developed fortifications adjacent to this demilitarized area, pending a permanent political settlement. No peace conference materialized, and antagonistic governments continued to function in North and South Korea. In subsequent years the United States maintained about 50,000 troops near the demilitarized zone along with important naval and air contingents, and Russia and China underwrote a buildup of North Korean forces.

The Korean War of 1950–1953 stimulated a series of initiatives that institutionalized containment in East Asia. This process began in 1951, when the United States and the other nations that had fought in the Far East during World War II, excluding the Soviet Union and India, signed a treaty with Japan. The United States also arranged a bilateral defense agreement with the former enemy. During the same period Washington made arrangements with Australia and New Zealand (ANZUS) to protect the southwestern Pacific and worked out a military accord with the Philippines. A comparable pact was negotiated with South Korea in October 1953. The chain of alliances in East Asia became complete when a bilateral treaty was negotiated in 1954 with

Chiang Kai-shek's Republic of China on Formosa. These extraordinary departures, sounding as they did the death knell of "no entangling alliances," committed the United States to a political-military role in the western Pacific that was without national precedent. The conviction that expansive communism in the Orient constituted overwhelming dangers to national security had entered the American consciousness between 1950 and 1954, and this belief controlled Washington's Asian policy for many years to come.

The Korean War became a turning point in the history of American foreign relations because it raised the question of what role the nation would play outside the Atlantic region. Its settlement helped bring about a short-lived détente with the Soviet Union, but the rise of Mao's China posed the gloomy prospect of continuing conflict with another Communist opponent in world politics. Washington persisted in refusal to extend diplomatic recognition to the People's Republic of China or to support Peking's admission into the United Nations, maintaining that the Communists refused to accept obligations under the United Nations Charter appropriate to a peace-loving nation, particularly those that forbade aggression against neighbors. In regions of the Pacific where the United States had conquered during World War II, American power had been asserted. Similarly, the Soviet Union consolidated control of Asian regions turned over by the Yalta agreement. In mainland China, where neither of the superpowers had intervened, Mao's successful revolution against the Nationalists determined the future. As in Europe, political tensions caused occasional crises along the line from Japan to the Philippines, but the barrier that separated the American sphere of influence in East Asia from that of the Sino-Soviet bloc had been defined. Contentions in the region soon shifted to Southeast Asia, where anticolonial warfare, particularly in French Indochina, threatened the status quo.

America's experience in Korea reinforced attitudes toward the cold war and the means of waging it, even if the conditions that had produced the conflict had altered. Most important, events both in Europe and in East Asia had largely eliminated the power vacuums over which Russia and America had contended for eight years. Classical containment dogma assumed a globe divided into two camps—free world and Communist bloc—but new centers of power exerted influence on international politics. The bipolarity of 1945 was a thing of the past by 1953. Innovations in policy seemed necessary in order to cope with the changing situation.

The Korean *Civil* War

ROBERT R. SIMMONS

The proper study of the Korean war should, while recognizing that both Moscow and Peking were intimately involved, emphasize its civil nature. The causes of the war must be sought on the Korean peninsula itself, an intensely nation-

Reprinted with permission of Macmillan Publishing Co., Inc. from *The Strained Alliance* by Robert R. Simmons. Copyright © 1975 by The Free Press, A Division of Macmillan Publishing Co., Inc.

alistic land whose people had been arbitrarily divided at the end of World War II. The opposing nature of the ideologies resident in the two halves of the nation served only to reinforce the passionate desire for reunification. In short, the proper appellation for the conflict is the Korean Civil War.

Conventional wisdom regarding the Korean Civil War has hitherto suggested that Korea between 1945 and 1959 should be seen primarily as an integral part of the Cold War, and that the origins of the war should thus be sought outside the peninsula. Behind this assumption is the belief that the genesis of the conflict is to be found in the largely unified wishes of the Soviet Union, China, and North Korea, with most of the control emanating from Moscow.

On the contrary, however, it is our contention that we can better gauge the fount of the beginnings of the war, the relationship between the three communist states during the war, and the war's termination by rejecting these shibboleths. An investigation of the war which neglects the internal situation on the peninsula, the patterns formed by Asian history relevant to Korea's relations with its two giant neighbors, and the nature of the ties between these three countries is incomplete and inconclusive.

Because the stress previously has been upon American strategic actions and reactions, most studies have largely ignored the communist side during the war. The political context which actually formed and framed the Korean Civil War is usually pictured as mere background when, in reality, politics was almost always in the foreground.

Related to this is the common impression that the United States was merely *reacting* in the course of the war, and to a united, monolithic enemy. Actually, in goals and purposes the three allied communist states were frequently at odds with each other—a fact which has been largely neglected in the belief that the war and the armistice negotiations that ended it were directed by a monolithic foe. Conceivably, a realization of these allies' differing motivations might have led to other negotiating or military postures on the part of the United States. Washington, it should be further noted, was not simply "reacting" to the war, but rather took positive stances of its own to which the communist states felt impelled to reply.

Because social scientists are permitted partial access to the antechambers of power only to take notes, their summations are usually incomplete, and often distorted. This problem is compounded when dealing not merely with one state, but, as here, with three diverse, authoritarian regimes. A thorough study of the Korean Civil War is made even more difficult because not only have the archives of Moscow, Peking, and P'yŏngyang remained closed, but so also have the more sensitive files of the United States Government. We are, for example, as yet incompletely informed on American activities on the Korean peninsula directed by General MacArthur between 1949 and 1951, and on the messages and signals exchanged by Washington and the three communist states throughout the war. . . .

Because international crises are seldom divorced from past geopolitics, our first chapter briefly sketches the background of the Korean peninsula in Northeast Asian history. Several important conclusions emerge from this short survey, all relevant to an understanding of the twentieth-century war. One is that Korea has traditionally been a battleground between China, Russia, and Japan, each of which considered Korea vital to its security. Consequently, each has sought to control events on the peninsula. This was accomplished either by military occupation or by exerting influence on Korea's politically fragmented domestic factions.

Interestingly, the United States had become involved in Korean politics in the late 1800s, by promising to protect Korea's fragile neutrality between her neighbors. The United States–Korean agreement, however, turned out to be impotent; that memory might well have prompted Koreans in 1950 to expect that America would not intervene in their civil war.

The overriding fact of Korean history has been the keen nationalism felt throughout the peninsula. Factions aligned with foreign powers for the purpose of preserving both their own authority and Korea's independence. Within this context, Kim Il-sŏng's (and Syngman Rhee's) association with an external power should be seen as an extension of a pattern well understood on the peninsula.

Building upon this history, the second chapter then examines the political system of North Korea between 1945 and 1950. This system was in many ways an extension of the earlier pattern. Politics were both factionalized and highly nationalistic. The background of the war must be considered in the light of these factional struggles. This explanation underscores the domestic causes of the war, while stressing the fact that Kim Il-sŏng's authority was in large measure born of his nationalist credentials combined with the support of the Soviet occupation army.

Also vital to an understanding of events after June, 1950, is an appreciation of the general strains between China and the Soviet Union, including their struggle for influence on the peninsula. Chapters 3 and 4 shift focus away from the peninsula in an effort to explain several of the differences between its two giant neighbors. Chapter 3 presents some of the available evidence indicating that the ultimate alliance between China and the Soviet Union, sealed by the Korean Civil War, was not inevitable. The Chinese Communist Party had suggested its interest in maintaining communication and compromise with the United States before the war began. This was in part because of the strains that had existed historically both between Russia and China and between the Communist parties of the two states.

The following chapter presents an example of the causes of stress between the two states. This section contends that the Soviet Union deliberately froze China out of the United Nations in January of 1950 in a calculated effort to cut off all of China's potential contacts with the West. These two chapters, together, suggest that there was a strong possibility that if not for the Korean Civil War and the subsequent conflict which it brought about between China and the United States, these two states might well have reached a rapprochement, similar in some respects to the one which they have achieved in the 1970s.

Chapter 5 returns the center of attention to events on the Korean peninsula.

In examining the fierce factional fighting between North Korean leaders in the post–World War II period, this chapter argues that the timing of the beginning of the war was chosen by Kim Il-sŏng as a result of these internal divisions combined with fears of a South Korean invasion.

This chapter is the most speculative of the book; there is little hard primary data on exactly why the war began on June 25, 1950. On the other hand, the customary interpretations of the causes of the war have so far unsatisfactorily answered such questions as why the Soviet Union was absent from the United Nations at the time, why China did not take Taiwan before the beginning of the war, or why P'yŏngyang did not receive more aid from its allies. The hypothesis presented here has the value of focusing attention upon the *Korean* bases of the war, a most important aspect of a conflict which is usually viewed as being largely a Cold War battle. Although the hypothesis is founded largely upon circumstantial evidence, it has the advantage of being the most parsimonious explanation available to answer several hitherto puzzling factors associated with the war. Moreover, it encourages the introduction of data which are often not taken into account when considering the beginning of the war.

Chapter 6 discusses the hesitation with which China entered the war. Crucial to an understanding of Peking's attitude is the fact that the celebrated American naval "interdiction" of the Taiwan Straits in the summer of 1950 was almost entirely a merely *verbal* one. China was therefore hopeful that President Truman would reverse his formal statement—meant largely for domestic American consumption—once Washington realized that China was not involved in the war. Instead, of course, the United States acted in a reverse manner and appeared to be threatening an invasion of China as the war entered the fall of 1950.

Both China and North Korea hoped that the Soviet Union would assist P'yŏngyang as the tide of battle turned. The usual interpretation of China's entrance into the war has been that it was done cautiously, in an effort to protect her territorial security. While this idea is accurate insofar as it goes, it is an insufficient explanation of the circumstances surrounding China's crossing the Yalu. These can be fully understood only in the context of the interrelationship between the three communist states.

The Soviet Union was as concerned as was China about the possibility of an American invasion of its territory as General MacArthur advanced north along the Korean peninsula in the fall of 1950. Although most studies of the war recognize that U.S. troops were threatening China, they neglect the significant fact that these forces were also approaching the *Soviet* border. Moscow therefore encouraged China's intervention, but Peking entered the war only when it became obvious that Russia steadfastly refused the use of its own troops on the peninsula. Consequently, the Sino-Soviet Treaty of Mutual Assistance, conceived in Moscow in February of 1950, was aborted on the Korean peninsula in October of the same year.

Koreans, moreover, learned not to expect altruistic aid from either neighbor when their national survival was at stake. This last goes a long way toward explaining North Korea's "sudden" display of independence from both China and the Soviet Union after the mid-1950s. And it applies equally forcefully to the lesson which China learned about the nature of Russian assistance during a crisis. In fact, the serious split between the two communist allies may be dated from China's unsatisfactory experience with Soviet aid during the Korean Civil War.

The next two chapters examine the causes of the strains between the three communist allies during the war. In particular, these pages point up the fact that Moscow consistently supplied its two neighbors with second-line military equipment that was inadequate to overcome American technology. Similarly, Soviet economic aid was not considered sufficient by either China or North Korea. Meanwhile, the Soviet Union dictated most of the political decisions affecting the war. For example, the initiatives for the beginning of the P'anmunjŏm armistice negotiations apparently came as a surprise to both Peking and P'yŏngyang when they were first proposed by Moscow. P'yŏngyang's influence upon the tactics of these talks, in particular, was nil.

The last substantive chapter argues that, beginning in the late spring of 1952, China and North Korea brought pressure to bear upon the Soviet Union to accede to their desire to leave the war. By the fall of that year, as a result of the combination of her allies' entreaties and its own domestic politics, the Soviet Union began to signal its own decision to reach a compromise solution at P'anmunjŏm.

The wartime coalition, in short, was a strained alliance. But just what is an "alliance?" How and why does one come into existence? Does an alliance evolve? Why does it end? Can we examine one particular alliance and draw some conclusions that will apply generally to this type of international relationship? The ubiquitous and ambiguous term "alliance" presents a problem, because its nearly universal use masks the fact that interstate relationships are dynamic events.

States enter into alliances for reasons of military security in the face of a present or imminently expected crisis. Because each state enters the alliance for different purposes and propelled by differing histories, and each is willing to expend a different proportion of its national resources for the common effort, there is an inevitable tension within the alliance. Each state is anxious that it receive the maximum possible aid from its allies, and is affronted when expected aid is not forthcoming.

The final chapter examines various types of alliances and advances the idea that different states within an alliance may well perceive the alliance differently. This asymmetry of goals and expectations leads to strains between the alliance partners. This is, in fact, what occurred to North Korea, China, and the Soviet Union. Each was involved in the war for different purposes, and each had conflicting expectations of support from the other two. It was a strained alliance; the strains made manifest during the war (and present in the relationship before the war) were to become clearer to us in later years. . . .

Concealed within the still-obscure origins of the Korean Civil War lies a hinge of the Sino-Soviet relationship. Vitally important to an understanding of the schism between these two neighbors in the late 1950s are the lessons which each learned from its experiences in the war. The full significance of these lessons, however, can be grasped only if the origins of the war are known. So far, well over two decades after the events, these beginnings remain shrouded in uncertainties.

The literature of the Korean crisis of the summer of 1950 has customarily described it as occurring in the context of a tight, bipolar world. The predominant view of the causes of the war has been that the Soviet Union completely controlled the North Korean invasion of June 25. A much less accepted variant of the bipolar concept states that the responsibility for the North Korean attack rests with the PRC. Neither hypothesis, however, is sufficient to explain satisfactorily the events of the summer of 1950 and their consequences.

Most observers of this period have seen the North Korean regime as a satellite of the Soviet Union, and Kim Il-sŏng as a mere hireling of the Russians. Stalin, so this version runs, pulled the trigger that started the war. Such a metaphor, of course, neglects the "gun" itself: viz., the government in P'yŏngyang. Because the origins of the war have been placed in Moscow, research on its Korean paternity has been largely neglected. . . . The factional divisions within the P'yŏngyang government . . . had an immediate bearing upon the initiation of the war. . . . The Kim Il-sŏng regime of 1950 was neither a passive "gun" for an itchy Soviet trigger finger, nor a monolithic system subservient to Moscow. Hence, analysis of its own internal factional components is necessary in order to explain the origins of the war.

Although the Russians certainly armed the North Koreans, and did expect a war, . . . the *timing* of the war—which was primarily a *civil* conflict—can best be understood in terms of the indigenous conditions on the Korean peninsula.

All Koreans were united in their urgent desire for an early reunification. However, the specific timing of the June 25 invasion was caused by intense intra-Korean Workers' Party (KWP) rivalry in the north, combined with appeals from South Korean–based guerrillas who had powerful supporters in the north. These pressures forced Kim Il-sŏng into a war date earlier than the one which his Soviet mentors and he had probably agreed upon. This hypothesis, based upon a fresh reconstruction of the available evidence, leads to conclusions which more satisfactorily account for previously unresolved enigmas, viz.: 1) the nature of the triangular bonds between Peking, P'yŏngyang, and Moscow; 2) the reactions of China and the Soviet Union to the North Korean attack; and 3) the effect of the Korean Civil War on the Sino-Soviet relationship.

The DPRK declared itself an independent state on September 9, 1948, with Kim Il-sŏng as Premier. Soon thereafter, the southern regime of Syngman Rhee carried out a stringent purge of the South Korean Communist Party; many of the party's leaders, foremost among them Pak Hŏn-yŏng, fled to the north. This was followed by the fusion of the North and South Korean Communist Parties into the Korean Workers' Party on June 24, 1949 (one year plus one day before the beginning of the war, Korean time). Because of his de facto control of the north, Kim Il-sŏng remained as Premier; according to one scholar, the merger "appeared more like an incorporation of the Workers' party of the South into the Workers' Party of the North than a unification of the two." Pak, however, still enjoyed widespread support among the newly unified KWP. His arrival in the north undoubtedly spurred North Korean irredentist feelings toward the south. Both as a symbol of the repression in the south and as a respected spokesman voicing the view that the Rhee government could be easily overthrown, Pak encouraged a drive south.

On June 25, 1949 (one year to the day before the war's initiation), Pak helped organize the Democratic Front for the Unification of the Fatherland (DFUF), which carried out guerrilla activities in the south. Concurrently, he was also the supervisor of the Kang-Dong Political Institute, on the outskirts of P'yŏngyang, which trained the guerrillas sent to the south. From these two positions, he monitored and encouraged revolutionary actions in the south. Accordingly, his influence in the north rose and fell largely according to how well the anti-Syngman Rhee movement was doing in the south. (In a loose analogy, Pak's position is reminiscent of Le Duan's situation in North Vietnam between 1954 and 1964.) Pak was also concurrently the Vice-Chairman of the KWP, a Vice-Premier of the DPRK, and its Foreign Minister.

Both the DPRK's ambassador to Peking, Yi Chu-yŏn, and the ambassador to Moscow, Chu Nyŏng-ha, had been comrades of Pak Hŏn-yŏng. Through them Pak was both quickly aware of thinking in those two capitals of the DPRK's allies and was also able, perhaps, to speak to those allies on his own authority. Pak accompanied Kim to the Moscow conference between Russian and Korean leaders in March, 1949, and took part in the meetings with Stalin. In short, although Pak Hŏn-Yŏng occupied positions in the DPRK below Kim Il-sŏng, his very important posts and connections ensured his continued prestige and potential as a rival to Kim.

In July, 1949, the DFUF called for nationwide elections for September 15, 1949, but this demand was simply dropped on that date. That this attempt at a September reunification aborted was probably due to the south's largely successful policy of obstructing the DFUF's guerrillas. This failure of the DFUF was undoubtedly a setback for Pak within the factional maze of P'yŏngyang.

Another possible explanation is that the DPRK was prohibited by its allies from attempting a drive south in September, 1949. U.S. Senator H. Alexander Smith later recounted that during a fall, 1949, inspection trip to South Korea he had been told that:

> the north Koreans had endeavoured to enlist the aid of the Chinese Communists in order to take over and conquer the South Koreans, but the Chinese Communists turned them down on the grounds that they had too many responsibilities in other parts of China. . . . They also tried to get the Russians to intervene directly in taking over South Korea but the Russian reply was that they did not wish to initiate World War Three by creating an incident in a minor area like Korea.

On June 7, 1950, the DFUF abruptly released an appeal for reunification combined with a proposal for nationwide elections to be held on August 5–8.

A national conference would be held in either Haeju or Kaesŏng on June 15–17 to discuss the mechanics of carrying out the election. The all-Korean legislature resulting from these elections would then meet in Seoul on August 15, the fifth anniversary of liberation from Japanese rule. This appeal, however, was issued not by the government of the DPRK but rather by the DFUF, indicating, perhaps, that this plan was under the immediate direction of Pak Hŏn-yŏng. That the Russians were aware of the importance of the August 15 date is suggested by an *Izvestiya* article of June 10, 1950, which declared that "on the fifth anniversary of the liberation of Korea, the people of South and North Korea can and should mark this day by celebrating it in the folds of one united, democratic state."

On June 19, 1950, P'yŏngyang made another proposal, this one originating from the Supreme People's Assembly of the DPRK government. Directed toward the South Korean National Assembly, it suggested the merging of the South and North Korean parliaments into one all-Korean legislative body, the reorganization of the Korean military bodies into one unit, and an agreement that the Korean United Nations Commission leave South Korea. These three measures were to be completed by August 15.

Why would the anti–Syngman Rhee program now be transferred from the DFUF to the Supreme People's Assembly? There are at least two, partially contradictory, hypotheses. Both hypotheses emphasize the domestic determinants of the Korean Civil War. Although there was certainly some congruence of plans made in Moscow and P'yŏngyang, the final stamp on the war nonetheless reads "made in Korea."

The first conjecture is that the Kapsan faction, either with or without Soviet approval, launched the invasion under the charter authorized by the Supreme People's Assembly, the Kim Il-sŏng group thus outmaneuvering Pak Hŏn-yŏng by weakening the DFUF's claim to the authorship of the liberation of South Korea. What we know of Kim's personal predilections would seem to support this idea:

> Those of the Kapsan faction, directly under Kim Il-sŏng, were principally guerilla fighters and underground organizers. The members of all these groups were essentially revolutionaries accustomed to small group activities and to destructive operations rather than to orderly, structured functioning. Those from the Soviet Union, on the other hand, were born and raised in a relatively stable and highly bureaucratic environment where affairs of the Party were routinized. In short, the men from the Soviet Union already belonged to the second generation.

On the other hand, of course, this description of the Kapsan faction also largely fits Pak's Domestic faction, since it had also operated as a guerrilla and clandestine organization during the long, harsh Japanese occupation. In contrast, the above description would argue, the Soviet faction would both be cautious about the actual beginnings of the Korean Civil War and would most likely be opposed by both Kim and Pak's factions as not being truly representative of revolutionary Korean interests. Indeed, by June, 1950, the Soviet-

Korean faction was beginning to be displaced by Kim and Pak's men within the KWP:

> Although the Soviet-Koreans held key posts, by the start of the war they were no longer proportionately a very large number in a party numbering 750,000, or an army of 198,380 men. This meant that their position was vulnerable if opposition on the part of other party members could be galvanized against them. *This is in fact what happened during the Korean War.*

The launching of the war as a *nationalist* crusade (rather than merely as a product of Soviet foreign policy) would thus benefit both Kim and Pak's factions. The first hypothesis, then, concludes that Kim launched the invasion in order to preempt his major rival, Pak, who was calling for an early invasion of the south. Kim Il-sŏng's credentials to legitimacy rested upon his nationalist claims, his "guerrilla-hero" status. When he had returned to Korea in 1945, his first public speeches had been not about communism but rather about the nationalist aspirations held by all Koreans, for the reunification of an independent Korea. In 1950, this young (aged 38) leader, in a nation where age is thought to be correlated with respect and wisdom, needed to present himself as out-nationalizing any political rival, particularly Pak Hŏn-yŏng, who held most impressive nationalist credentials and was urging the early reunification of the Fatherland.

Kim's pre-June 25 actions toward the weakened South Korean Communist Party would seem to validate the idea that he might have planned to use the invasion to undermine Pak's position in the south. Since Pak's main strength remained in the south, Kim Il-sŏng, a few weeks before the invasion, sent Kapsan-faction personnel south to take control of the remaining apparatus of the South Korean Communist Party. It was Kapsan men who were now to run the southern party; Kim, aware of Pak's residual strength in the south, which might coalesce to form an active opposition, acted to control it before Pak could reactivate his followers after June 25.

The second hypothesis relating to the switching of the North Korean program toward the south from the DFUF to the Supreme People's Assembly in mid-June suggests that it was Pak himself who triggered the invasion with Kim's reluctant consent, which the last-minute approval by the Supreme People's Assembly might indicate. Because Pak's nationalist credentials within the KWP were stronger than Kim Il-sŏng's—and because Kim himself was a fervent believer in the desirability of an early Korean reunification—this view postulates that Pak outflanked Kim by questioning his independence from his Russian supporters. "What kind of leader is this," Pak may have asked the KWP, "who waits upon the word of his Masters before giving the signal for the quick and inevitable overthrow of the corrupt Syngman Rhee regime?"

Pak was in a pivotal position to influence the tactical judgment to initiate hostilities by virtue of his near-monopoly of information on conditions in the south. Information on favorable dates for an invasion and the likelihood for the success of an attack was funneled to the KWP by virtue of Pak's position both as head of the guerrilla training school which sent agents south and then collected military/political data from them, and concurrently as de facto head of the remaining communist apparatus in the south. That Pak utilized these positions to press for an early invasion date is indicated by the charges which were publicly brought against him on the day after the signing of the armistice in July, 1953. Item no. 5 of the indictment stated: "In the June 25 war, he indulged in circulating a false report that in South Korea the South Korean Labor Party had an underground organization of 500,000 members, who were ready to take action in concert with the north." North Korean agents who went south, it was charged, returned with reports that these 500,000 were most eager for the war's beginning. "This was a major reason why the Kapsan faction decided to attack South Korea."

One knowledgeable observer of what happened during this period summarized conditions within the KWP in June, 1950 as follows:

> Pak thought that the party members he had left in South Korea would be saved only by a war, and that if all Korea were unified, he would be sure to win much more support than Kim Il-sŏng in view of his popularity with the people. Since his entry into the north, he had been asking Kim Il-sŏng to invade the south. As a condition for an absolute victory, he emphasized that the 500,000 South Korean Labor Party members were standing by to fight, and as evidence he presented reports from the agents trained at Kumgang School [Kang-Dong Political Institute]. He preached that the south should be invaded as soon as possible ... and thought that the time had ripened for the invasion of the south. He calculated that the whole of Korea would be completely liberated in two months or even that the day of liberation would be August 15. In regard to Pak Hŏn-yŏng and the South Korean Labor Party, he thought that he would be victorious over them even after reunification so long as he controlled the Party's main-current faction and the People's Army.

Kim Il-sŏng and Pak Hŏn-yŏng (as well as Syngman Rhee) shared a moral imperative to reunify the nation. It appears likely, however, that some of the tactics of the civil war, and particularly the timing of it, were dictated in part by the Kim-Pak rivalry.

The leaders of the DPRK (and of the Republic of Korea) remembered their history: intruding powers on the peninsula could not be completely trusted. Although there were factional divisions within the leadership, all of the groups agreed on the desire for an early Korean reunification. The Russians, who had operated an unpopular occupation policy, did not control this irredentist urge. In sum, an understanding of the war must take into consideration both the "images" which all of the participants held of the significance of the peninsula, and the domestic factional infighting which led to the war.

In September, 1947, the United States Joint Chiefs of Staff, reacting to the dispersal of American troops around the world, recommended the withdrawal of American forces from South Korea, and added that Korea was not essential for the security of the United States. General MacArthur, in a March, 1949, newspaper interview, traced an American line of defense which left out both Taiwan and Korea, on the assumption that in an all-out war (the expected type) they would be strategic liabilities. In his famous speech of January 12,

1950, which was a summary of accepted Washington wisdom on the topic, Secretary of State Dean Acheson also left Taiwan and South Korea out of the American vital defense perimeter—although, as noted before, Acheson's celebrated speech was more ambiguous in its strategic implications than his later critics would allow. In late April, 1950, Senator Tom Connally, the Chairman of the Senate Foreign Relations Committee, reiterated the American public position: "Korea is not an essential part of America's defense strategy, and Russia could overrun it whenever it takes a notion."

However, the speeches, as messages in and of themselves to the North Koreans and their allies were superfluous pronouncements. The repeated cuts in U.S. troop deployments and defense budgets were sufficient signals. Of particular significance to the Korean peninsula was the fact that the American military occupation force in Japan was both understrength and "soft."

There seemed to be little doubt that the peninsula was ripe for irredentist impulses from both sides. After the cancellation of the DFUF-sponsored elections of 1949, Kim Il-sŏng wrote to United Nations Secretary-General Trygvie Lie an assurance of his determination to continue his labors:

> The Korean people will not abandon the struggle and will reserve for itself the right to continue by any maneuvers at its disposal the struggle . . . for the final unification of the country by its own forces into a unified democratic state.

There were constant and sizeable armed clashes and border incursions between the north and the south for over a year before the final crisis. A U.S. State Department official in April, 1950, stated that "the boundary at the 38th parallel . . . is a real front line. There is constant fighting. . . . There are very real battles, involving perhaps one or two thousand men." Koreans were accustomed to the fighting; each side believed that an early reunification was worth a war. The south was as intense in this yearning as the north.

Syngman Rhee, even as he apparently planned to mount an invasion of the north, consolidated his control of the south, his regime becoming increasingly autocratic. The judiciary, for example, was an "instrument of executive predominance, not the defender of rights or instrument of balance of forces. . . . [It] became even more active than under colonial rule." In 1946 the north had redistributed 2.3 million acres of land to 600,000 households; over 50% of North Korea's land and 70% of its farm families were affected. The P'yŏngyang government profited in popularity. Seoul, however, did not carry out land reform until 1950; its regime was less popular and there were sporadic revolts.

Between September 4, 1948, and April 30, 1949, over 80,710 people were arrested in the south. During this same period, more than one-third of the officers of the South Korean army were discharged as procommunists. By October of 1949, 7 percent of the South Korean National Assembly had been jailed by Syngman Rhee's police.

At the end of October, 1949, the South Korean Defense Minister was quoted as saying: "If we had our own way we would, I'm sure, have started up already. But we had to wait until they [the Americans] are ready. They keep telling us, 'No, no, no, wait. You are not ready.' " Washington, aware that Rhee might attempt to begin a war and then entangle the United States in it, was leery of granting arms. William Sebald, State Department representative in Japan during this time, later wrote of Rhee's belligerency: "It was feared that, properly armed for offense, Rhee promptly would punch northward across the 38th parallel." While it has frequently been remarked in military histories of the war that the North Korean army possessed greater firepower than the south, and that some blame should therefore be attached to the United States for failing to protect its client state, the official history of the American advisor force in Korea presents a supplementary view of why heavy tanks and more powerful artillery were not supplied to Seoul. Rather than an apprehension about Rhee's northern intentions, "it is much more likely that terrain factors and dollar limitations were actually responsible for the United States' failure to supply this type of equipment."

Although Washington was not parsimonious in its financial support of Seoul, it was wary of granting arms. The Syngman Rhee regime received $495.7 million in military and economic aid between the end of World War II and the beginning of the Korean War: $53.7 million was economic assistance, while the rest was military. Moreover, the American army maintained a 482-man military assistance mission in South Korea. Under the guidance of this permanent American military advisor mission, Syngman Rhee in 1949–50 was in the process of rapidly expanding his military forces. At the end of 1948 the South Korean army had consisted of 60,000 men; when the war began it had grown to approximately 100,000. The American advisors were attached to thirteen military training schools.

Rhee's air force also began to increase. The Korean Military Advisory Group's (KMAG) semiannual report of December 31, 1949, requested forty F-51 fighter aircraft, ten T-6 trainers, two C-47 cargo planes, and $225,000 for supporting equipment. It is, of course, true that Rhee's air force was not a solid weapon as of June 25, 1950. It appears, however, that in not very much time it would have become a potent force. During the first months of 1950, for example, the air force rapidly expanded from a few hundred men to 1,865 officers and men. Before the war began, Rhee reportedly was seeking a ninety-nine plane air force.

In April of 1950 Rhee decided to create twenty-one combat police battalions with 1,200 men in each. Meanwhile, the U.S. Congress had on March 15, 1950, voted a grant of $10,970,000 in additional aid for Seoul. Consequently, although by June 25 neither Rhee's air force nor his police battalions had been operationalized, it seemed only a matter of time before they would be. After the war began, United States Army Brigadier General William L. Roberts, head of the American advisor mission, was quoted as saying: "The only real flaw in KMAG's plan [in preparing the South Korean military] was that time ran out." Considering the rapid growth of the South Korean military, this view is understandable. In fact, less than three weeks before the war began, General Roberts assured Seoul that "the passage of military aid to the Republic of Korea looks slow because it was extended by appropriations of many committees in the U.S. However, the earnest [sic] aid will be extended from July."

As it was, the North Korean army actually invaded the south with a numerically smaller force than the one Seoul commanded. The south controlled a 95,000-man army and a national police force of 48,000 that was essentially an arm of the military. P'yŏngyang, on the other hand, invaded with an army of 103,800 infantry and 18,600 police. Probably a contributory factor in P'yŏngyang's decision to invade was a desire to disarm Rhee's military machine before—as seemed likely to happen in the near future—it became too powerful to contend with. Two scholars, noting that the North Korean army had not been fully mobilized by June 25, and that the South Korean elections held three weeks before had returned an anti–Syngman Rhee National Assembly, suggest the possibility that Kim Il-sŏng meant only to take Seoul and then "open negotiations with the new assembly on favorable terms." In short, the North Korean victory was caused not by the size of its invading force, but rather by a combination of superior fire power (tanks, artillery, and planes), the element of surprise, and a greater morale.

Events in South Korea seemed to augur increasingly well for a successful invasion from the north. The black market in Seoul in January, 1950, listed the *won* at 4,200 to one U.S. dollar; the official rate was 600 *won*. The price of rice in the south jumped 30 percent in the first three weeks of June, 1950. The elections of May 30, 1950, to the South Korean National Assembly (postponed by the unpopular government and conducted only under pressure from Washington) resulted in a massive display of discontent with the Syngman Rhee regime: out of 210 seats in the National Assembly, only 47 were now held by Rhee supporters. Guerrillas were active, and South Korean dislike for American G.I.'s was very much in evidence.

It was this combination of anti–Syngman Rhee sentiment and widespread desire for reunification that led one responsible observer to declare that:

> Considering the relative strength and combat readiness of the forces that faced each other across the thirty-eighth parallel in June 1950, it was a miracle that the North Korean armies were delayed at all in their desire to overrun all of South Korea . . . it was as if a few troops of Boy Scouts with hand weapons had undertaken to stop a panzer unit.

Seoul apparently held similar expectations with regard to a quick triumph over its enemy. It was also anxious to engage in hostilities, and felt restrained only by the Americans' limited grant of armaments. In March, 1950, Syngman Rhee promised an early armed reunification: "even though some of our friends across the sea tell us that we must not cherish thoughts of attacking the foreign puppet who stifles the liberties of our people in the North. . . . We shall respond to the cries of our brothers in distress."

In a private letter dated June 14, 1950, to his chief adviser, Dr. Oliver, President Rhee said:

> I am going to say a few words about the Korean situation. I think now is the best time for us to take on the offensive to mop up the guerrillas in P'yŏngyang.

> We will drive Kim Il-sŏng and his bandit to remote mountains and make them starve there in order to make the Tumen and Yalu rivers our defense line. . . . Our people are desiring for an action against the north. And Koreans in the north are also fervently looking forward to our action. . . .

A South Korean scholar comments that "a look at President Syngman Rhee's letter indicates that he had a foray into the north in mind, while his top Army commander was fully prepared to translate his design into action."

For its part, P'yŏngyang, listening to Seoul's provocative rhetoric and observing the burgeoning capabilities of the ROK's military, must have been concerned about Rhee's martial plans. Professor Robert Jervis has described a phenomenon of perception relevant to the manner in which a regime such as P'yŏngyang's would probably assess the situation:

> The evidence from both psychology and history overwhelmingly supports the view (which may be labeled hypothesis 1) that decision-makers tend to fit incoming information into their existing theories and images. Indeed, their theories and images play a large part in determining what they notice.

From P'yŏngyang's perspective, then, its invasion *may have been* launched as a preemptive strike in the expectation of an early South Korean attack.

Although it is certain that the Soviet Union armed the North Korean army, there is evidence that the North Koreans were not as well armed in June as they would be in late July. In fact, until the end of 1949 the North Korean army had been, to quote an official U.S. military history of the war, a "defensive-type army." This military history further stated that it was only when Seoul's army began to bulge, and Rhee loudly announced his intentions of marching north in the not-too-distant future, that P'yŏngyang began receiving large amounts of weapons from the Soviet Union. Indeed, the North Korean army had not reached its war mobilization level in June:

> The North Korean Army had not carried out its mobilization plan at the time the war began on June 25, but now, despite heavy losses, has raised its strength to about 200,000 men, a spokesman for the American intelligence staff (in Tokyo) said today. He asserted that only six full divisions had been ready for combat when the invasion started, although the North Korean war plans called for thirteen to fifteen.

Of course, an alternative interpretation might argue that mobilization might have tipped the north's hand, thus losing the element of surprise. Moreover, mobilization may have been thought unnecessary, given the perceived vulnerability of the south. As indicated below, I consider these suggestions less persuasive than the interpretation which sees the north as having speeded up its invasion date. There are also strong indications that the Russians themselves were not prepared to work with their ally in the field in July of 1950:

> Over a period of four weeks, systematic investigation into what went on in Seoul and the conquered areas during the Communist occupation has not revealed more than a handful of lesser Russian military officials or any political agents seen by South Koreans. . . . this, coupled with the reportedly confused

and disorganized interim in Seoul while the Communists held power, is taken as indicating either that *the Russians had not as much control over the Korean Communists as supposed* or had not intended to move in until the military conquest of South Korea was complete.

Since the conquest was expected to take a matter of days, however, the Russian advisers reasonably would have been present with their organizational plans and advice. Their absence suggests that they were surprised by the early date of the invasion.

On the day of the invasion, Lee Sang-jo, Chief of North Korean Military Intelligence, was in Moscow. It would seem unlikely that a Soviet-planned attack with a definite June 25 date would take place while this vital official was outside of the peninsula; he would presumably have been stationed in North Korea, monitoring data on the rapidly changing situation.

There were 100,000 North Korean troops in the ranks of the Chinese People's Liberation Army (PLA) in 1949. Only 12,000 of them had been returned to North Korea before June 25. It is reasonable to assume that the bulk of these battle-hardened 100,000 would have been returned to North Korea before the invasion as a core of the invasion force, if the invasion had taken place as scheduled on a previously planned date.

A "harder" indication that June 25 was not the prearranged date is the fact that in late April, 1950, at a conference of the communist Korean League in Japan, a North Korean invasion was spoken of in these terms: "To facilitate the achievement of this objective, we will engage in guerrilla activities directed at the destruction of imperialistic industry. Our operations are scheduled, until further notice, for August." At least as late as the end of April, then, Koreans in Japan anticipated an August invasion. All of these factors indicate that the decision for war was made rather suddenly by the P'yŏngyang leadership.

We dealt earlier with the pressures bearing on Kim Il-sŏng to initiate an invasion of South Korea as early as possible. It seems that the initiative for the war lay with Kim, rather than with Stalin. Nikita Khrushchev, for one, allegedly later declared: "I must stress that the war wasn't Stalin's idea, but Kim Il-sŏng's. Kim was the initiator."

Part of the basis for the general belief that Stalin could closely monitor the thoughts and actions of Kim Il-sŏng, and would thus be aware of all of the developing plans for the beginning of the war, is the fact that a key influential adviser to Kim was a Soviet Major General, Rebezev, who "followed Kim Il-sŏng like a shadow, living, eating, and sleeping in the same house." Rebezev, however, was posted to Kim Il-sŏng's staff *after* the war began; he was undoubtedly *then* a factor in North Korea's diminished political autonomy.

There is also the possibility that the Russian proconsul in North Korea, operating under what he considered to be general orders from Moscow (a "blank check"), collaborated with Kim's timing for the invasion, while keeping Moscow only loosely informed. The war, after all, was expected to be brief and successful. A former Lieutenant Colonel in the Russian internal police later wrote that it was Colonel General and Ambassador to P'yŏngyang, Terenty F. Shtykov who sold Stalin on the idea of the war. Shtykov therefore held a proprietary interest in the strategy of the invasion; since there were few Soviet advisers in North Korea, he probably held a free rein in his communications with Moscow. In 1951 Shtykov was deprived of rank and sent to a Russian province in disgrace for low-level work.

Interestingly, the Americans had a potentially analagous situation with respect to General MacArthur. *If* the United States had given Rhee a "blank check" for the invasion of the north, *if* Rhee's victory had seemed assured, and *if* communications between the White House and MacArthur had been lax, one wonders whether the General would have insisted that Rhee wait for an invasion date six weeks hence when all conditions on the peninsula itself said "go." (In fact, while the analogy must necessarily be loose, General MacArthur did have a somewhat similar experience of operating on his own authority, without Washington's knowledge, in drafting and proclaiming the Japanese constitution in 1946.)

Would it have been physically possible for P'yŏngyang to have begun the attack earlier than the Soviet Union expected? The usual assumptions regarding Soviet control of North Korea and its influence on the beginnings of the Korean Civil War would deny this possibility. As suggested above, however, what is known about the factional infighting within the North Korean regime casts doubt upon these assumptions. Moreover, weapons for the invasion were still coming through the Soviet "pipeline" in June, which would indicate an invasion plan for sometime later than June 25, when all of the military preparations would have been completed. The absence of Soviet military advisers with the North Korean army also indicates Soviet unpreparedness. (A less likely explanation would be the Russian hesitation to become involved. Given the Russian mistrust of the North Koreans and Moscow's behavior in similar crises, however, it would seem more likely that the Soviet Union would have been quite anxious to supervise directly the actions of its client state.)

"But," an objection to this hypothesis might be voiced, "surely the Russian advisers attached to the North Korean army prior to June 25 would have prevented an unauthorized attack." The surprising rejoinder is that as of the June 25 invasion date there were very few Russian advisers present to counsel against an independent North Korean decision. In 1948 there were 150 Soviet advisers in each North Korean army division (approximately one per company); in 1949 this number was reduced to 20 per division; by the spring of 1950 there were only between 3 and 8 per division. An alleged Russian defector who served in North Korea shortly before the Korean Civil War began later stated that the Soviet Union's military adviser group numbered only 40 before June 25. With such a small group of Russians posted to the North Korean army, it is entirely possible that events could have taken place without Moscow's foreknowledge. Not only the Russians but much of the North Korean leadership itself were apparently prevented from learning intimate details of the invasion:

Top secret work plans of the Standing Committee of the Labor Party headquarters dated January-June 1950 make absolutely no reference to the forthcoming invasion, although covering in some detail all other aspects of government policy. Second, a number of fairly highly placed North Korean officers that were interviewed, including the Chiefs of Staff of two divisions, stated that they had only the barest presentiment of the coming of hostilities, and that they were given no concrete indication of their onset until approximately one week before the invasion took place.

This would suggest, again, that the initiation of hostilities came as a rather precipitous move on the part of the inner core of the P'yŏngyang government.

So far, three elements are evident in the puzzling story of the origins of the war: 1) the underlying assumption in almost all Western accounts is that the war was caused by external machinations, within which the role of the North Koreans themselves was minimal; 2) despite the American occupation of P'yŏngyang in the fall of 1950 and the interrogation of high-ranking North Korean and Chinese prisoners throughout the war, we have no "hard" data to back up this assumption; and 3) there are a number of circumstances from which one can tenably argue that it was the North Korean government which chose the actual June 25 invasion date.

Does it in fact make any significant difference whether or not the Korean Civil War was expected by the Russians to begin on June 25? Perhaps the best way to answer this question is to propose an alternative expected date: given the information available, that date would have been about August 7. It will be remembered that the June, 1950, election proposals put forward by P'yŏngyang, and endorsed by Moscow, called for those elections to have been completed by August 8, with the resultant all-Korean legislature to meet in Seoul on August 15, the fifth anniversary of Korea's liberation from Japanese rule.

Russian and American foreign policy had at least one characteristic in common: a compulsion for legitimacy. Stalin, regardless of his tactical moves on the international chess board, was intensely interested in garbing his actions in an aura of legitimate behavior. Following this pattern, it would have suited Stalin's style to have called for an election which he knew would be forbidden by the Syngman Rhee regime in South Korea. Then, at the very moment when these "rightful" elections had been scheduled to have taken place, the people in the south, in righteous indignation and anger at this refusal of their basic right to peaceful all-Korean elections, would rise up against the dictator. At this point, such a scenario would run, their North Korean compatriots would feel compelled to aid their brothers in the south to gain victory over the hated dictator and reunion with the north. The people of the world would, of course, recognize reunion as a popular and inevitable development; the corrupt Rhee regime would, in effect, have condemned itself by refusing to listen to the will of the people in elections and reunification would follow as a natural result, with a little help from the north.

As we have seen . . . , one section of Secretary of State Acheson's January 12 speech foresaw an American appeal to the United Nations in such a crisis

as the Korean Civil War. Consequently, the Soviet Union could have anticipated that an American response to the beginning of the war, at least for the
purpose of legitimizing any U.S. actions in aiding South Korea—and such
actions were expected to be mostly propagandistic—would have involved the
United Nations.

In previous crises of the Cold War, regardless of the West's ordering of
priorities or perception of provocation, the Soviet Union had not hesitated to
engage in vitriolic debate in the United Nations (e.g., the Northern Iran and
Greek Crises of 1946–47).

Why should they absent themselves now that an established satellite was
being attacked with the approval of the United Nations?

In fact, the Soviet Union issued no public pronouncements, not even *pro
forma* declarations in support of its ally, for thirty-six hours after the beginning of the war. Moreover, the first full official statement of Russian attitudes
was not released until July 4. There were no mass meetings in support of North
Korea, even though the Soviet Union was at this time in the midst of a major
"world peace campaign" which would have lent itself ideally to such demonstrations, until July 3. Moscow Radio's domestic service commented on July
2 that "the most important event which has had great influence on the international situation during the last week is the collection of signatures for the
Stockholm Peace Appeal which has been started in the Soviet Union." The
Soviet Union's public reaction may well have been testimony to its surprise
at the timing of the invasion.

If the fiction of the action being a *South* Korean invasion were to be created
and maintained, the Soviet government should logically have addressed notes
of protest to the U.S. and the U.N. immediately after the beginning of the war.
But no such messages were delivered; instead, in its June 29 reply to an American note of June 27 the Soviet Union disavowed any responsibility, merely
indicating instead that its information was that it was South Korea who had
been the aggressor. This mild Soviet note could just as easily have been issued
on June 25. Subsequently, the Soviet government elaborated its response to
the fluid situation on the Korean battlefield only after some delay. Until July
3, the news from Korea was tucked in the back pages of the Soviet press.
Nothing suggested to the Soviet reader that a major world crisis had just
erupted.

In looking for an analogous situation, one notes that during the 1948 Berlin
Blockade, Soviet response to each American action was very rapid. While a
detailed knowledge of the P'yŏngyang-Peking-Moscow relationship in the
summer of 1950 remains unobtainable, a review of the available evidence
suggests that the reason that the Soviet Union was absent from the United
Nations during the early stages of the Korean Civil War was its surprise at the
actual event of June 25.

By regular rotation, the Soviet Union was scheduled to have its delegate
assume the president's seat in the United Nations Security Council in August.
It had been boycotting that body since January, 1950, ostensibly in protest
against the Council's failure to seat the PRC . . . ; but on August 1 it resumed

its seat on the Council. As president for the month, it was able to prevent any U.N. business concerning Korea from being accomplished.

The inference which may be drawn from these circumstances is that the Soviet Union—if it had had control over the beginning of the Korean Civil War—would have "scheduled" it for a date after it was to assume the Council presidency and after South Korea had, as expected, prohibited the all-Korea elections that had been proposed for August 5–8. . . .

The intervention of the United States in the Korean Civil War had disastrous consequences both for America and for the Korean peninsula. A potentially swift and relatively bloodless reunification was converted into a carnage. For Korea, both north and south, the devastation was awesome. By the end of September, 1950, for example, the U.S. Air Force had dropped 97,000 tons of bombs and 7.8 million gallons of napalm. The results of the bombings rivaled Dante's *Inferno*. P'yŏngyang's population, for instance, was 400,000 when the war started, 80,000 when the war ended. Only two public buildings in the capital remained intact by 1953. In 1949 the North Korean population was 9,622,000; by 1953 it had declined to 8,491,000. Incredibly, the peninsula's total population in 1950 had been 30 million.

The United States suffered 142,091 casualties in the war, including 33,629 killed. The DPRK's military casualties have been estimated at 500,000, with 1 million civilians missing. The ROK's situation was similar; their military casualty list officially reads 300,000, with 1 million dead civilians. At the end of the war, 2½ million refugees roamed the south, and another 5 million people were living on some form of relief. It may be assumed that the bulk of North Korea's population was living at a subsistence level in 1953. In short, the 1950–53 war was one of the most destructive conflicts in history.

From an American perspective, nonintervention would have brought welcome consequences. First, the Chinese civil war would have ended with the liberation of Taiwan. Thereupon, in all probability, Washington and Peking would have reached a working relationship, averting China's forced alliance with the Soviet Union. Secondly, without the continuing identification of nationalism and communism that America's entrance into the Korean Civil War reinforced, it is possible that the Indochina adventure might have been forestalled.

In the first three months of the war, the entire peninsula was largely devastated. General Emmett (Rosie) O'Donnell, head of the Bomber Command in the Far East, put it succinctly:

> I would say that the entire, almost the entire Korean peninsula, is just a terrible mess. Everything is destroyed. There is nothing standing worthy of the name. . . . Just before the Chinese came in we were grounded. There were no more targets in Korea.

Considering the next civil war in which the United States was to intervene, Indochina, perhaps the most unsettling legacy of the war for North Americans is that many of the shibboleths about the conflict are still accepted, while its lessons have often been only partially learned.

FURTHER READING

Frank Baldwin, ed., *Without Parallel* (1975)
Ronald J. Caridi, *The Korean War and American Politics* (1969)
Allen Guttmann, ed., *Korea: Cold War and Limited War* (1972)
David McLellan, *Dean Acheson* (1976)
Glenn D. Paige, *The Korean Decision* (1968)
Glenn D. Paige, ed., *1950: Truman's Decision* (1970)
David Rees, *Korea: The Limited War* (1964)
Gaddis Smith, *Dean Acheson* (1972)
John W. Spanier, *The Truman-MacArthur Controversy* (1959)
I. F. Stone, *The Hidden History of the Korean War* (1962)
Allen Whiting, *China Crosses the Yalu* (1960)

11

The Eisenhower-Dulles Foreign Policy

In 1953 the leadership of the two major antagonists of the Cold War changed hands. In Soviet Russia, Josef Stalin died and Nikita Khrushchev eventually took command. In the United States, Dwight D. Eisenhower won the 1952 election, entered the White House, and named John Foster Dulles his Secretary of State. The problems they faced were familiar: Korea, Indochina, Berlin, China, Eastern Europe, and the nuclear arms race. But new problems arose in the Third World, as emerging nations asserted their independence. The Middle East and Latin America became more unsettled and hence more dangerous to international stability.

The Eisenhower-Dulles team had to respond to both the old Cold War issues and the new realities. Their response has prompted questions about the foreign policy of the 1950s: Was there continuity or discontinuity between Truman diplomacy and Eisenhower-Dulles diplomacy? Who was most responsible for shaping foreign policy—Eisenhower or Dulles? How realistic was their diplomacy? How moralistic? Did the Eisenhower administration restrain or exacerbate the Cold War? How skillfully did American leaders handle the crises in Guatemala, Indochina, Lebanon, and elsewhere? Why were alternative policies rejected?

DOCUMENTS

Before taking office, Secretary of State John Foster Dulles told the Senate Foreign Relations Committee that he favored the "liberation" of China and Eastern Europe from Communist domination. Neither his statement of January 15, 1953, nor others by him explained how he would accomplish this.

In 1954, when a leftist Guatemalan government under Jacobo Arbenz Guzmán expropriated lands owned by the mammoth United Fruit Company, President Eisenhower ordered the Central Intelligence Agency to topple Arbenz and to begin a public campaign to discredit the Guatemalan reformer by dubbing him a Communist. Guatemala's Guillermo Toriello Garido defended the integrity of his nation in a speech on March 5, 1954, to the Organization of American States, reprinted here. On June 30 of the same year, after Arbenz had been forced from office by CIA-backed rebels, Dulles cheered the change and explained it as a victory over "international communism."

The fourth document is a portion of President Eisenhower's press conference of April 7, 1954, wherein he spelled out what he meant by the "domino theory" and its relationship to war in Indochina. The next document is Premier Nikita Khrushchev's momentous speech to the Twentieth Party Congress in Moscow on February 25, 1956. With his denunciation of the "cult of the individual," he launched a "de-Stalinization" program, sparking rebellions in Hungary and elsewhere in Eastern Europe and seemingly providing Dulles with an opportunity to fulfill his "liberation" policy.

In early 1958, one of the architects of containment, George F. Kennan, urged the "disengagement" of American and Russian troops from Central Europe and the establishment of a nuclear-free zone there. His arguments, reprinted here, aroused considerable debate but little action. The last document is Eisenhower's farewell address of January 17, 1961, which surprised many by including a warning against a "military-industrial complex."

John Foster Dulles on Liberation, 1953

THE CHAIRMAN: I am particularly interested in something I read recently, to the effect that you stated you were not in favor of the policy of containment. I think you advocated a more dynamic or positive policy.

Can you tell us more specifically what you have in mind? . . .

MR. DULLES: There are a number of policy matters which I would prefer to discuss with the committee in executive session, but I have no objection to saying in open session what I have said before: namely, that we shall never have a secure peace or a happy world so long as Soviet communism dominates one-third of all of the peoples that there are, and is in the process of trying at least to extend its rule to many others.

These people who are enslaved are people who deserve to be free, and who, from our own selfish standpoint, ought to be free because if they are the servile instruments of aggressive despotism, they will eventually be welded into a force which will be highly dangerous to ourselves and to all of the free world.

Therefore, we must always have in mind the liberation of these captive peoples. Now, liberation does not mean a war of liberation. Liberation can be accomplished by processes short of war. We have, as one example, not an ideal example, but it illustrates my point, the defection of Yugoslavia, under Tito from the domination of Soviet communism. Well, that rule of

Tito is not one which we admire, and it has many aspects of despotism, itself; but at least it illustrates that it is possible to disintegrate this present monolithic structure which, as I say, represents approximately one-third of all the people that there are in the world.

The present tie between China and Moscow is an unholy arrangement which is contrary to the traditions, the hopes, the aspirations of the Chinese people. Certainly we cannot tolerate a continuance of that, or a welding of the 450 million people of China into the servile instruments of Soviet aggression.

Therefore, a policy which only aims at containing Russia where it now is, is, in itself, an unsound policy; but it is a policy which is bound to fail because a purely defensive policy never wins against an aggressive policy. If our only policy is to stay where we are, we will be driven back. It is only by keeping alive the hope of liberation, by taking advantage of that wherever opportunity arises, that we will end this terrible peril which dominates the world, which imposes upon us such terrible sacrifices and so great fears for the future. But all of this can be done and must be done in ways which will not provoke a general war, or in ways which will not provoke an insurrection which would be crushed with bloody violence, such as was the case, for example, when the Russians instigated the Polish revolt, under General Bor, and merely sat by and watched them when the Germans exterminated those who were revolting.

It must be and can be a peaceful process, but those who do not believe that results can be accomplished by moral pressures, by the weight of propaganda, just do not know what they are talking about.

I ask you to recall the fact that Soviet communism itself, has spread from controlling 200 million people some 7 years ago to controlling 800 million people today, and it has done that by methods of political warfare, psychological warfare and propaganda, and it has not actually used the Red Army as an open aggressive force in accomplishing that.

Surely what they can accomplish, we can accomplish. Surely if they can use moral and psychological force, we can use it; and, to take a negative defeatest attitude is not an approach which is conducive to our own welfare, or in conformity with our own historical ideas.

Guillermo Toriello Garido Defends
Guatemala's Reforms, 1954

The people of Guatemala are enormously disturbed to find that a respected people, freed of brutal tyrannies, eager to progress and to put in practice the most noble postulates of democracy; determined to put an end to the abuses of the past, trying to wipe out feudalism and colonial procedures and the iniquitous exploitation of its most humble citizens, finds itself faced with the dismaying reality that those who boast of encouraging other peoples to travel the road to economic and political liberty decide to bring them to a halt, only because the decisions and the efforts of these peoples injure unjust interests and because the highest interest of these peoples is incompatible with the maintenance of privileges granted by tyrants in evil times as a means of achieving impunity and a guarantee that they not be moved from the throne of their despotism. And these privileges are so important for the satisfaction of intemperate ambitions and the privileged ones are so powerful that, despite the noble postulates of Pan Americanism, they have unleashed against Guatemala the most iniquitous campaign, and have been unashamed to have recourse to the most cowardly weapons to defame, to deceive, to discredit one of the purest movements that this hemisphere has ever witnessed. . . .

What is the reason for this campaign of defamation? What is the real and effective reason for describing our Government as communist? From what source comes the accusation that we threaten continental solidarity and security? Why do they wish to intervene in Guatemala?

The answers are simple and evident. The plan of national liberation being carried out with firmness by my Government has necessarily affected the privileges of the foreign enterprises that are impeding the progress and the economic development of the country. The highway to the Atlantic, besides connecting the important productive zones it traverses, is destroying the monopoly of internal transportation to the ports now held by the Ferrocarriles Internacionales de Centro América (an enterprise controlled by the United Fruit Company), in order to increase foreign trade free of grievous and discriminatory charges. With construction of national ports and docks, we are putting an end to the monopoly of the United Fruit Company, and we will thus make it possible for the nation to increase and to diversify its foreign trade through the use of maritime transport other than the White Fleet, also belonging to the United Fruit Company, which now controls this essential instrument of our international commercial relations.

With the realization of the plan of national electrification, we shall put and [sic] end to foreign monopoly of electric power, indispensable to our industrial development, which has been delayed by the lack, the scarcity, or the distribution failures of that important means of production.

With our Agrarian Reform, we are abolishing the latifundia, including those of the United Fruit Company itself. Following a dignified policy, we have refused to broaden the concessions of that company. We have insisted that foreign investment be in accordance with our laws, and we have recovered and maintained absolute independence in our foreign policy. . . .

These bases and purposes of the Guatemalan revolution cannot be catalogued within a Communist ideology or policy: a political-economic platform like that put forward by the government of Guatemala, which is settling in rural areas thousands of individual landowners, individual farmers, can never be conceived of as a Communist plan. Far from that, we believe that raising the standard of living and the income of rural and urban workers alone stimulates the capitalistic economic development of the country and the sociological bases of a genuinely Guatemalan functional democracy. . . .

International reaction, at the same time it is pointing out Guatemala as a "threat to continental solidarity", is preparing vast interventionist plans, such as the one recently denounced by the Guatemalan government. The published documents—which the Department of State at Washington hastened to call Moscow propaganda—unquestionably show that the foreign conspirators and monopolistic interests that inspired and financed them sought to permit armed intervention against our country, as "a noble undertaking against communism." Let us emphasize before this Conference the gravity of these events. Non-intervention is one of the most priceless triumphs of Pan Americanism and the essential basis of inter-American unity, solidarity, and cooperation. It has been fully supported in various inter-American instruments, and specifically in Article 15 of the Charter of the Organization of American States. The Secretary General of the Organization, Dr. Alberto Lleras Camargo, in his report on the Ninth International Conference of American States, in commenting on this article, states categorically that with it "the doubt that seemed to arise recently, as to whether intervention carried out collectively would be so considered, has thus been dispelled".

Dulles Condemns "International Communism" in Guatemala, 1954

For several years international communism has been probing here and there for nesting places in the Americas. It finally chose Guatemala as a spot which it could turn into an official base from which to breed subversion which would extend to other American Republics.

This intrusion of Soviet despotism was, of course, a direct challenge to our Monroe Doctrine, the first and most fundamental of our foreign policies. . . .

In Guatemala, international communism had an initial success. It began 10 years ago, when a revolution occurred in Guatemala. The revolution was not without justification. But the Communists seized on it, not as an opportunity for real reforms, but as a chance to gain political power.

Communist agitators devoted themselves to infiltrating the public and private organizations of Guatemala. They sent recruits to Russia and other Communist countries for revolutionary training and indoctrination in such institutions as the Lenin School at Moscow. Operating in the guise of "reformers" they organized the workers and peasants under Communist leadership. Having gained control of what they call "mass organizations," they moved on to take over the official press and radio of the Guatemalan Government. They dominated the social security organization and ran the agrarian reform program. Through the technique of the "popular front" they dictated to the Congress and the President.

The judiciary made one valiant attempt to protect its integrity and independence. But the Communists, using their control of the legislative body, caused the Supreme Court to be dissolved when it refused to give approval to a Communist-contrived law. Arbenz, who until this week was President of Guatemala, was openly manipulated by the leaders of communism.

Guatemala is a small country. But its power, standing alone, is not a measure of the threat. The master plan of international communism is to gain a solid political base in this hemisphere, a base that can be used to extend Communist penetration to the other peoples of the other American Governments. It was not the power of the Arbenz government that concerned us but the power behind it.

If world communism captures any American State, however small, a new and perilous front is established which will increase the danger to the entire free world and require even greater sacrifices from the American people.

This situation in Guatemala had become so dangerous that the American States could not ignore it. At Caracas last March the American States held their Tenth Inter-American Conference. They then adopted a momentous statement. They declared that "the domination or control of the political institutions of any American State by the international Communist movement . . . would constitute a threat to the sovereignty and political independence of the American States, endangering the peace of America."

There was only one American State that voted against this declaration. That State was Guatemala.

This Caracas declaration precipitated a dramatic chain of events. From their European base the Communist leaders moved rapidly to build up the military power of their agents in Guatemala. In May a large shipment of arms moved from behind the Iron Curtain into Guatemala. The shipment was sought to be secreted by false manifests and false clearances. Its ostensible destination was changed three times while en route.

At the same time, the agents of international communism in Guatemala intensified efforts to penetrate and subvert the neighboring Central American States. They attempted political assassinations and political strikes. They used consular agents for political warfare.

Many Guatemalan people protested against their being used by Communist dictatorship to serve the Communists' lust for power. The response was mass arrests, the suppression of constitutional guaranties, the killing of opposition leaders, and other brutal tactics normally employed by communism to secure the consolidation of its power.

In the face of these events and in accordance with the spirit of the Caracas declaration, the nations of this hemisphere laid further plans to grapple with the danger. The Arbenz government responded with an effort to disrupt the inter-American system. Because it enjoyed the full support of Soviet Russia, which is on the Security Council, it tried to bring the matter before the Security Council. It did so without first referring the matter to the American regional organization as is called for both by the United Nations Charter itself and by the treaty creating the American organization.

The Foreign Minister of Guatemala openly connived in this matter with the Foreign Minister of the Soviet Union. The two were in open correspondence and ill-concealed privity. The Security Council at first voted overwhelmingly to refer the Guatemala matter to the Organization of American States. The vote was 10 to 1. But that one negative vote was a Soviet veto. . . .

Throughout the period I have outlined, the Guatemalan Government and Communist agents throughout the world have persistently attempted to obscure the real issue—that of Communist imperialism—by claiming that the United States is only interested in protecting American business. We regret that there have been disputes between the Guatemalan Government and the United Fruit Company. We have urged repeatedly that these disputes be submitted for settlement to an international tribunal or to international arbitration. That is the way to dispose of problems of this sort. But this issue is relatively unimportant. All who know the temper of the U.S. people and Government must realize that our overriding concern is that which, with others, we recorded at Caracas, namely, the endangering by international communism of the peace and security of this hemisphere.

The people of Guatemala have now been heard from. Despite the armaments piled up by the Arbenz government, it was unable to enlist the spiritual cooperation of the people.

Led by Colonel Castillo Armas, patriots arose in Guatemala to challenge the Communist leadership—and to change it. Thus, the situation is being cured by the Guatemalans themselves.

Dwight D. Eisenhower Explains the "Domino Theory," 1954

QUESTION. Robert Richards, *Copley Press:* Mr. President, would you mind commenting on the strategic importance of Indochina to the free world? I think there has been, across the country, some lack of understanding on just what it means to us.

THE PRESIDENT: You have, of course, both the specific and the general when you talk about such things.

First of all, you have the specific value of a locality in its production of materials that the world needs.

Then you have the possibility that many human beings pass under a dictatorship that is inimical to the free world.

Finally, you have broader considerations that might follow what you would call the "falling domino" principle. You have a row of dominoes set up, you knock over the first one, and what will happen to the last one is the certainty that it will go over very quickly. So you could have a beginning of a disintegration that would have the most profound influences.

Now, with respect to the first one, two of the items from this particular area that the world uses are tin and tungsten. They are very important. There are others, of course, the rubber plantations and so on.

Then with respect to more people passing under this domination, Asia, after all, has already lost some 450 million of its peoples to the Communist dictatorship, and we simply can't afford greater losses.

But when we come to the possible sequence of events, the loss of Indochina, of Burma, of Thailand, of the Peninsula, and Indochina following, now you begin to talk about areas that not only multiply the disadvantages that you would suffer through loss of materials, sources of materials, but now you are talking really about millions and millions and millions of people.

Finally, the geographical position achieved thereby does many things. It turns the so-called island defensive chain of Japan, Formosa, of the Philippines and to the southward; it moves in to threaten Australia and New Zealand.

It takes away, in its economic aspects, that region that Japan must have as a trading area or Japan, in turn, will have only one place in the world to go—that is, toward the Communist areas in order to live.

So, the possible consequences of the loss are just incalculable to the free world.

QUESTION. Raymond Brandt, *St. Louis Post-Dispatch:* Mr. President, what response has Secretary Dulles and the administration got to the request for united action in Indochina?

THE PRESIDENT: So far as I know, there are no positive reactions as yet, because the time element would almost forbid.

The suggestions we have, have been communicated; and we will have communications on them in due course, I should say.

QUESTION. Robert G. Spivack, *New York Post:* Mr. President, do you agree with Senator Kennedy that independence must be guaranteed the people of Indochina in order to justify an all-out effort there?

THE PRESIDENT: Well, I don't know, of course, exactly in what way a Senator was talking about this thing.

I will say this: for many years, in talking to different countries, different governments, I have tried to insist on this principle: no outside country can come in and be really helpful unless it is doing something that the local people want.

Now, let me call your attention to this independence theory. Senator Lodge, on my instructions, stood up in the United Nations and offered one country independence if they would just simply pass a resolution saying they wanted it, or at least said, "I would work for it." They didn't accept it. So I can't say that the associated states want independence in the sense that the United States is independent. I do not know what they want.

I do say this: the aspirations of those people must be met, otherwise there is in the long run no final answer to the problem.

QUESTION. Joseph Dear, Madison *Capital Times:* Do you favor bringing this Indochina situation before the United Nations?

THE PRESIDENT: I really can't say. I wouldn't want to comment at too great a length at this moment, but I do believe this: this is the kind of thing that must not be handled by one nation trying to act alone. We must have a concert of opinion, and a concert of readiness to react in whatever way is necessary.

Of course, the hope is always that it is peaceful conciliation and accommodation of these problems.

QUESTION. James Patterson, New York *Daily News:* Mr. President, as the last resort in Indochina, are we prepared to go it alone?

THE PRESIDENT: Again you are bringing up questions that I have explained in a very definite sense several times this morning.

I am not saying what we are prepared to do because there is a Congress, and there are a number of our friends all over this world that are vitally engaged.

I know what my own convictions on this matter are; but until the thing has been settled and properly worked out with the people who also bear responsibilities, I cannot afford to be airing them everywhere, because it sort of stultifies negotiation which is often necessary.

Nikita Khrushchev on "De-Stalinization," 1956

Comrades! In the report of the Central Committee of the Party of the XXth Congress, in a number of speeches by delegates to the Congress, as also formerly during the plenary CC/CPSU sessions, quite a lot has been said about the cult of the individual and about its harmful consequences.

After Stalin's death the Central Committee of the Party began to implement a policy of explaining concisely and consistently that it is impermissible and foreign to the spirit of Marxism-Leninism to elevate one person, to transform him into a superman possessing supernatural characteristics akin to those of a god. Such a man supposedly knows everything, sees everything, thinks for everyone, can do anything, is infallible in his behavior. . . .

Stalin was a very distrustful man, sickly suspicious; we knew this from our work with him. He could look at a man and say: "Why are your eyes so shifty today," or "Why are you turning so much today and avoiding to look me directly in the eyes?" The sickly suspicion created in him a general distrust even toward eminent Party workers whom he had known for years. Everywhere and in everything he saw "enemies," "two-facers" and "spies."

Possessing unlimited power he indulged in great willfulness and choked a person morally and physically. A situation was created where one could not express one's own will. . . .

When the Fascist armies had actually invaded Soviet territory and military operations began, Moscow issued the order that the German fire was not to be returned. Why? It was because Stalin, despite evident facts, thought that the war had not yet started, that this was only a provocative action on the part of several undisciplined sections of the German army, and that our reaction might serve as a reason for the Germans to begin the war. . . .

As you see, everything was ignored: warnings of certain army commanders, declarations of deserters from the enemy army, and even the open hostility of the enemy. Is this an example of the alertness of the Chief of the Party and of the state at this particularly significant historical moment?

And what were the results of this carefree attitude, this disregard of clear facts? The result was that already in the first hours and days the enemy had destroyed in our border regions a large part of our air force, artillery and other military equipment; he annihilated large numbers of our military cadres and disorganized our military leadership; consequently we could not prevent the enemy from marching deep into the country.

Very grievous consequences, especially in reference to the beginning of the war, followed Stalin's annihilation of many military commanders and political workers during 1937–1941 because of his suspiciousness and through slanderous accusations. During these years repressions were instituted against certain parts of military cadres beginning literally at the company and battalion commander level and extending to the higher military centers; during this time the cadre of leaders who had gained military experience in Spain and in the Far East was almost completely liquidated. . . .

We must state that after the war the situation became even more complicated. Stalin became even more capricious, irritable and brutal; in particular his suspicion grew. His persecution mania reached unbelievable dimensions. Many workers were becoming enemies before his very eyes. After the war Stalin separated himself from the collective even more. Everything was decided by him alone without any consideration for anyone or anything. . . .

The willfulness of Stalin showed itself not only in decisions concerning the internal life of the country but also in the international relations of the Soviet Union. . . .

I recall the first days when the conflict between the Soviet Union and Yugoslavia began artificially to be blown up. Once, when I came from Kiev to Moscow, I was invited to visit Stalin who, pointing to the copy of a letter lately sent to Tito, asked me, "Have you read this?" Not waiting for my reply he answered, "I will shake my little finger—and there will be no more Tito. He will fall." . . .

You see to what Stalin's mania for greatness led. He had completely lost consciousness of reality; he demonstrated his suspicion and haughtiness not only in relation to individuals in the USSR, but in relation to whole parties and nations. . . .

We should in all seriousness consider the question of the cult of the individual. We cannot let this matter get out of the Party, especially not to the press. It is for this reason that we are considering it here at a closed Congress session. We should know the limits; we should not give ammunition to the enemy; we should not wash our dirty linen before their eyes. I think that the delegates to the Congress will understand and assess properly all these proposals.

George F. Kennan Advocates "Disengagement," 1958

Never in history have nations been faced with a danger greater than that which now confronts us in the form of the atomic weapons race. Except in instances where there was a possibility of complete genocide, past dangers have generally

Specified excerpts from "A Chance to Withdraw Our Troops in Europe," as it appeared in *Harper's Magazine*, February 1958. Abridged and adapted from *Russia, the Atom and the West* by George F. Kennan. Copyright © 1958 by George F. Kennan. Reprinted by permission of Harper & Row, Publishers, Inc.

threatened only the existing generation. Today it is everything which is at stake —the kindliness of our natural environment to the human experience, the genetic composition of the race, the possibilities of health and life for future generations.

Not only is this danger terrible, but it is immediate. Efforts toward composition of major political differences between the Russians and ourselves have been practically abandoned. Belief in the inevitability of war—itself the worst disservice to peace—has grown unchecked. We have a world order marked by extreme instability. In the Middle East alone, for example, we have a situation where any disturbance could now easily involve us all in an all-out war.

To me it is a source of amazement that there are people who still see the escape from this danger in our continued multiplication of the destructiveness and speed of delivery of the major atomic weapons. These people seem unable to wean themselves from the belief that if the Russians gain the slightest edge in the capacity to wreak massive destruction at long range, they will immediately use it—regardless of our capacity for retaliation—whereas, if we can only contrive to get a tiny bit ahead of the Russians, we shall in some way have won; our salvation will be assured; the road will then be paved for a settlement on our own terms. This cast of thought seems to have been much encouraged, in the U.S. at least, by the shock of the launching of the Russian earth satellites.

I scarcely need say that I see no grounds whatsoever in this approach. The hydrogen bomb, admittedly, has a certain sorry value to us today as a deterrent. When I say this, I probably do not mean exactly what many other people mean when they say it. I have never thought that the Soviet government wanted a general world war at any time since 1945, or that it would have been inclined, for any rational political reason, to inaugurate such a war, even had the atomic weapon never been invented. I do not believe, in other words, that it was our possession of the atomic bomb which prevented the Russians from overrunning Europe in 1948 or at any other time. In this I have disagreed with some very important people.

But now that the capacity to inflict this fearful destruction *is* mutual, and now that this premium *has* been placed on the element of surprise, I am prepared to concede that the atomic deterrent has its value as a stabilizing factor until we can evolve some better means of protection. And so long as we are obliged to hold it as a deterrent, we must obviously see to it that it is in every way adequate to that purpose—in destructiveness, in speed of delivery, in security against a sudden preventive blow, and in the alertness of those who control its employment. But I can see no reason why we should indulge ourselves in the belief that the strategic atomic weapon can be anything more than a temporary and regrettable expedient, tiding us over a dangerous moment. . . .

The beginning of understanding rests, in this appalling problem, with the recognition that the weapon of mass destruction is a sterile and hopeless weapon which may for a time serve as an answer of sorts to itself, as an uncertain sort of a shield against utter cataclysm, but which cannot in any way serve the purposes of a constructive and hopeful foreign policy. The true end of political action is, after all, to effect the deeper convictions of men; this the A-bomb cannot do. The suicidal nature of this weapon renders it unsuitable both as a sanction of diplomacy and as the basis of an alliance. There can be no coherent relations between such a weapon and the normal objects of national policy. A defense posture built around a weapon suicidal in its implications can serve in the long run only to paralyze national policy, to undermine alliances, and to drive everyone deeper and deeper into the hopeless exertions of the weapons race. . . .

Is there, then, any reasonable hopeful alternative to the unpromising path along which we are now advancing? I must confess that I see only one. This is precisely the opposite of the attempt to incorporate the tactical atomic weapon into the defense of Western Europe. It is, again, the possibility of separating geographically the forces of the great nuclear powers, of excluding them as direct factors in the future development of political relationships on the continent, and of inducing the Europeans, by the same token, to accept a higher level of responsibility for the defense of the Continent than they have recently borne.

This is still a possibility. We have not yet taken the fatal step. The continental countries have not yet prejudiced their usefulness for the solution of continental problems, as we have ours, by building their defense establishments around the atomic weapon. If they could be induced to refrain from doing this—and if there could be a general withdrawal of American, British, and Russian armed power from the heart of the Continent—there would be at least a chance that Europe's fortunes might be worked out, and the competition between two political philosophies carried forward, in a manner disastrous neither to the respective peoples themselves nor to the cause of world peace.

Eisenhower on the
"Military-Industrial Complex," 1961

A vital element in keeping the peace is our military establishment. Our arms must be mighty, ready for instant action, so that no potential aggressor may be tempted to risk his own destruction.

Our military organization today bears little relation to that known by any of my predecessors in peacetime, or indeed by the fighting men of World War II or Korea.

Until the latest of our world conflicts, the United States had no armaments industry. American makers of plowshares could, with time and as required, make swords as well. But now we can no longer risk emergency improvisation of national defense; we have been compelled to create a permanent armaments industry of vast proportions. Added to this, three and a half million men and women are directly engaged in the defense establishment. We annually spend on military security more than the net income of all United States corporations.

This conjunction of an immense military establishment and a large arms industry is new in the American experience. The total influence—economic, political, even spiritual—is felt in every city, every State house, every office of the Federal government. We recognize the imperative need for this development.

Yet we must not fail to comprehend its grave implications. Our toil, resources and livelihood are all involved; so is the very structure of our society.

In the councils of government, we must guard against the acquisition of unwarranted influence, whether sought or unsought, by the military-industrial complex. The potential for the disastrous rise of misplaced power exists and will persist.

We must never let the weight of this combination endanger our liberties or democratic processes. We should take nothing for granted. Only an alert and knowledgeable citizenry can compel the proper meshing of the huge industrial and military machinery of defense with our peaceful methods and goals, so that security and liberty may prosper together.

Akin to, and largely responsible for the sweeping changes in our industrial-military posture, has been the technological revolution during recent decades.

In this revolution, research has become central; it also becomes more formalized, complex, and costly. A steadily increasing share is conducted for, by, or at the direction of, the Federal government.

Today, the solitary inventor, tinkering in his shop, has been overshadowed by task forces of scientists in laboratories and testing fields. In the same fashion, the free university, historically the fountainhead of free ideas and scientific discovery, has experienced a revolution in the conduct of research. Partly because of the huge costs involved, a government contract becomes virtually a substitute for intellectual curiosity. For every old blackboard there are now hundreds of new electronic computers.

The prospect of domination of the nation's scholars by Federal employment, project allocations, and the power of money is ever present—and is gravely to be regarded.

Yet, in holding scientific research and discovery in respect, as we should, we must also be alert to the equal and opposite danger that public policy could itself become the captive of a scientific-technological elite.

It is the task of statesmanship to mold, to balance, and to integrate these and other forces, new and old, within the principles of our democratic system—ever aiming toward the supreme goals of our free society. . . .

Down the long lane of the history yet to be written America knows that this world of ours, ever growing smaller, must avoid becoming a community of dreadful fear and hate, and be, instead, a proud confederation of mutual trust and respect.

Such a confederation must be one of equals. The weakest must come to the conference table with the same confidence as do we, protected as we are by our moral, economic, and military strength. That table, though scarred by many past frustrations, cannot be abandoned for the certain agony of the battlefield.

Disarmament, with mutual honor and confidence, is a continuing imperative. Together we must learn how to compose differences, not with arms, but with intellect and decent purpose. Because this need is so sharp and apparent I confess that I lay down my official responsibilities in this field with a definite sense of disappointment. As one who has witnessed the horror and the lingering sadness of war—as one who knows that another war could utterly destroy this civilization which has been so slowly and painfully built over thousands of years—I wish I could say tonight that a lasting peace is in sight.

Happily, I can say that war has been avoided. Steady progress toward our ultimate goal has been made. But, so much remains to be done. As a private citizen, I shall never cease to do what little I can to help the world advance along that road.

ESSAYS

Townsend Hoopes, a Defense Department official in the 1960s and author of *The Devil and John Foster Dulles*, believes that Dulles was the chief architect of the foreign policy of the 1950s. Hoopes critically probes Dulles' thought, finds him excessively moralistic, faults him for ignoring opportunities for negotiations, and compares his diplomacy unfavorably to that of Dean Acheson and Harry S. Truman.

Stephen E. Ambrose of Louisiana State University, an Eisenhower biographer, questions this harsh indictment. Although critical of the Eisenhower administration for failing to adjust sympathetically to nationalist movements in the Third World, Ambrose thinks the cautious President restrained the Cold War (and John Foster Dulles), essentially followed the policies set by the Truman administration, placed a lid on military expenditures, and kept the United States out of wars. Although the Eisenhower-Dulles team used vociferous rhetoric, Ambrose concludes, that rhetoric was not matched by comparable action.

A Critique of the Prime Mover
John Foster Dulles

TOWNSEND HOOPES

There were few people who held indifferent opinions of John Foster Dulles. President Eisenhower called him, in retrospect, "the greatest Secretary of State I have ever known," and added, "his calm approach, his comprehension of the important factors in every problem, his firm conclusions, and his moral courage were majestic." Winston Churchill called him "the only bull I know who carries his china closet with him"; and, noting the garrulous insistence on dominating the moving diplomatic dialogue, Churchill added: "Mr. Dulles makes a speech every day, holds a press conference every other day, and preaches on Sundays. All this tends to rob his utterances of any real significance." Alastair Buchan thought him "one of the most unattractive figures in modern history." Elliott Bell admitted that his friend Dulles was "not a man with a great deal of come-hither." Sir Oliver Franks, the British Ambassador to Washington in the early

Townsend Hoopes, "God and John Foster Dulles." *Foreign Policy*, no. 13 (1973), pp. 154–161, 161–162, 165–177. Reprinted with permission from *Foreign Policy* 13. Copyright 1973 by National Affairs, Inc.

1950's, said: "Three or four centuries ago, when Reformation and Counter-Reformation divided Europe into armed camps, in an age of wars of religion, it was not so rare to encounter men of the type of Dulles. Like them he came to unshakable convictions of a religious and theological order. Like them he saw the world as an arena in which forces of good and evil were continuously at war." James Reston thought that, like many crusaders, Dulles possessed "a wide streak of hypocrisy," reflected in "the constant contradiction" between the "moralistic man" and the "shrewd political and diplomatic operator."

I might say a passing word on why I decided to spend two years thinking and writing about this man. In early 1968, when the Tet offensive and then Lyndon Johnson's withdrawal from further political combat tore away the final veil hiding the misperception and failure of America's freedom-defending and nation-building in South Vietnam, I faced, along with many others, the dawning realization that an era in American foreign policy had ended—an era of more than 20 years' duration in which the American people had found a large measure of their political *raison d'être,* as well as much moral comfort, in fusing their perception of the national interest with what seemed an unarguable ideological imperative: namely, the absolute need to confront and defeat (or at least oppose) every manifestation of Communism at every point on the globe. In 1970, amid the crumbled premises of that posture, it seemed necessary for one to ask how and why America had come to press its quite legitimate concern for freedom and world order to extremes that increasingly failed to meet the test of interest or reason, proportion or morality. The question led backward in time to a reexamination of the roots and tendrils and spreading branches of the cold war—hardly a new subject for reappraisal.

Yet, at least one element of truth seemed to have been overlooked or under-appreciated in earlier appraisals. It was that, while the Truman Administration responded with boldness to the serious Russian threats to Western and Southern Europe, and to the attack on South Korea, in the main its efforts were guided by a conscious rhetorical restraint, by a determined effort to avoid setting in motion the runaway locomotive of a global ideological crusade. And that, conversely, it was in the ensuing period of the Eisenhower Presidency that the spirit, the policies, and the supporting deployments of the cold war spread pervasively in the United States. The Eisenhower years thus seemed the necessary place to look for answers to the basic question of why American foreign policy had lost its sense of proportion. An examination of the Eisenhower foreign policy led, of course, straight to an appraisal of John Foster Dulles. For while Eisenhower knew his own mind in foreign policy, and indeed demonstrated at critical junctures a humane and practical wisdom, and a firm restraint in the face of bellicose advice, Dulles was indisputably the conceptual fount and prime mover—the initiator, formulator, energizer, negotiator and operator—of American foreign policy during those years. Moreover, as he came not only to dominate but to personify this policy, it was in largest measure *his* legacy that was bequeathed to Presidents Kennedy and Johnson. To Americans under 30, Dulles is only a name in history. But his legacy cast a long shadow upon successive Presidents, foreign policy practitioners at every level, and the national psyche. And that legacy was formed in large part out of the character and personality of the man.

Born in 1888, John Foster Dulles grew up in the small northern village of Watertown, New York, near the St. Lawrence River, the oldest of five children. His father was a Presbyterian minister descended from a long line of vigorous churchmen and missionaries, one of whom had sailed 123 days in an open boat to carry God's word to the heathen in the Indian state of Madras and had stayed in South Asia long enough to be buried in Ceylon. His mother was the daughter of John W. Foster, a soldier, lawyer, and diplomat who served as Secretary of State during the last eight months of President Benjamin Harrison's Administration. Previously he had been Minister (which is to say, Ambassador) to Mexico, Spain, and Russia. He was a worldly and affluent man, and the fact that his daughter had grown up in the relative glitter of the international diplomatic swim was a strong source of her own ambition for her two sons, John Foster and Allen. Dulles was thus marked by both aspects of his dual heritage throughout the course of his life. On his father's side was the simple, devout, moderately intellectual, unmoneyed life of a small upstate parsonage. On his mother's side were relative affluence and sophistication—a fine house in Washington that saw the comings and goings of ambassadors, senators, congressmen, and other men of the world. There is no doubt that it was Grandfather Foster who proved the decisive influence on his life, both as an example and as a source of moral and financial support at each of several junctures. The twin aspects of his family heritage were not, however, easy to reconcile, and the inner conflict between them deeply affected Dulles' personality and manner.

He went to Princeton because all of his theological Dulles relations had gone there. (His uncle Joseph, who had baptized him, was librarian of the Princeton Theological Seminary when Dulles entered the university in 1904.) It was assumed, certainly by his father, probably by his mother, that his purpose at Princeton was to prepare for the ministry. He was only 16 years old when he arrived. At Princeton, at least until well into his senior year, Dulles was an obscure member of the undergraduate body—serious, shy, poor, and notably younger than those around him. And a number of colleagues and observers of his later life attribute the rigid, grave, and graceless manner with which he moved through most of his relationships to the strain of his circumstances at Princeton and later at law school. His tender years, they said, his puritanical background, his lack of spending money, had all made it very hard for him to make friends on an equal basis; and the pain and chagrin caused by these were deepened by a fierce awareness, indeed a subjective enlargement, of his heritage, which he considered not merely an upstate parsonage but the corridors of diplomatic power. Needing defenses to hide the gap between his sense of who he was and the apparent facts of the situation, he built up heavy layers of reserve. Arthur Krock, one of his Princeton classmates, remembered that Dulles "kept greatly to himself," gave intense concentration to his intellectual studies (which were mainly philosophical), and played chess. Such social and psychological pressures had the effect of forcing him to grow up unevenly and rather too fast, and made him a man of persisting social unease—devoid of a sound sense of situational nuance, and with a manner combining shyness and suspicion with arrogance. He could express warmth and a rather Victorian sentimentality with a few close and trusted friends. But he was notable for a flat hardness and striking insensitivity to other people.

Thrown in with older men during the years of his early manhood—not only in college and law school, but later in his law firm, and especially during his service at Versailles in 1919, where he served as legal counsel to Bernard Baruch, the United States representative on the Reparations Commission— Dulles further developed a manner of grave reserve and an operating style that managed to combine an attitude of moral superiority with the cold blankness of a professional poker player. Physically imposing, he conveyed in negotiations the impression of massive immovability, technical mastery, and (hovering just beneath the surface) an instinct for the jugular. He also developed, no doubt inadvertently, an extraordinary manner of speaking—slow, almost tortured, with long pauses in mid-sentence while he blinked his eyes and opened and closed his mouth, groping for the precise word or phrase. His friend Elliott Bell said that Dulles vividly conveyed the impression that cerebration is an intense physical act. Although the performance made his auditors uncomfortable, it appeared to give Dulles no embarrassment. Finally would come forth a well-formulated, carefully phrased comment that seemed to reflect the sense of the meeting, resolve the major issues, and lay out the logical next steps. Carefully dissected, these Dullesian formulations were found to be simple in conception, confined to basic issues, more tactical than fundamental in their approach to action, and cast in almost banal language. What gave them decisive weight with the men who heard them, however, was the sense of passionate conviction with which they were propounded, an impression reinforced by the evident physical labor that accompanied their gestation.

This gift for logical synthesis made him an effective advocate and arbiter, though hardly a dazzling public speaker. In small groups he was supreme; speaking at a rostrum before a large audience, he seemed merely wooden. The gift also led to a reputation for compulsive oversimplification. He was never guilty of complex legal formulations, and his law firm, Sullivan and Cromwell, possessed several better legal theoreticians. In a true sense, the law for Dulles was a vehicle for the growth and self-expression of a powerful mind and personality—powerful in logic, powerful in practicality, but quite narrow in range, and seeking always an immediate and a tangible result. Combined with an instinct to dominate, this cast of mind made him an advocate with an ever-present tendency to overstate his case, and it was a tendency he did not confine to the law, but extended readily to theology and foreign affairs. Reinhold Niebuhr was later to complain that "Mr. Dulles' moral universe makes everything quite clear, too clear. . . . self-righteousness is the inevitable fruit of simple moral judgments."

The ease of his accommodation to the values of Wall Street seemed another reflection of this simplicity, suggesting that the theological baggage Dulles brought with him from the Watertown parsonage was a good deal lighter than some had supposed. There was no reason to doubt the genuineness of his religious beliefs, but they boiled down to three rather thin elements: a generalized faith in a "universal moral law," which he failed anywhere to define, yet assumed every man could grasp and should obey; a conviction in the supreme worth of the individual; and a belief that religion has a role to play in the political process. The theologian John Coleman Bennett thought Dulles had evolved his own form of "secularized Calvinism." In his many speeches over the years on the subject of religion, and in the steady stream of his moralistic utterances as Secretary of State, Dulles rarely referred to the central theological problem of sin, made no admission that ethical decisions are fraught with moral ambiguity, and evidenced no understanding that the dimension of self-interest and self-preservation is implicit in every exercise of power. What he lacked in theology, however, he more than made up for in a self-certitude that seemed to grow steadily out of his mounting worldly success. As the years passed, and especially following his categorical commitment to anti-Communism, this quality seemed to fuse with his thin but firm religious tenets in an awesome self-righteousness, as though, someone said, he were acting as the agent of a Higher Power.

A case can be made for the view that a healthy percentage of Dulles' moral utterances were calculated and pragmatic appeals to the sanctified American myths of God and Motherhood, designed to secure public support for his policies. Yet if pressed too far, this theory founders on the truth—evidenced by the striking similarity of his public and private statements—that Dulles was not merely a pragmatist, but also a genuine religionist and ideologue. On the plane of goals and premises, he was a true moral believer; on the plane of action, he was a rather thoroughly amoral tactician.

A major point in understanding Dulles is to grasp the fact that he was an intellectual loner, a man who relied not merely in the last resort, but almost exclusively, in large matters and in small, on his own counsel. He appeared to develop his views through some elaborate, structured, yet wholly internalized process, whose result thus stood at the end of a long chain of logic. When finally arrived at, they were not easily reversed. Moreover, resistance to reversal was reinforced by Dulles' almost unlimited confidence in his own reasoning, his own judgment, and his own power of persuasion. . . .

As Secretary of State, Dulles performed like a one-man band, causing wide circulation of the cliché that he "carried the State Department in his hat." A loyal inner circle of subordinates fiercely disputed this, insisting that he conferred with all relevant sectors of the department. The truth is, he conferred very selectively and the consultations were of a rather special sort. His ideas being largely self-developed, he needed facts, and relished debate with those he considered informed and tough enough to defend their positions. But the purpose of the process was to produce, at most, minor refinements of his own handiwork. He was not much interested in ideas that failed to mesh with his own (Ambassador Bohlen once said, "You could almost hear the click as he turned off the mental hearing aid"), and he could be discourteous in dealings with very high people.

Many officers in the Department of State, finding him forbidding and unapproachable, could hardly avoid the contrast between the new Secretary and his immediate predecessor. Both Dulles and Dean Acheson were men of exceptional intellectual power and purpose, and tough inner fiber; there the similarity ended. Acheson projected the long lines and aristocratic bearing of a thoroughbred horse, a self-assured grace, an acerbic elegance of mind, and a charm whose chief attraction was perhaps its penetrating candor. Dulles projected the heavy opaqueness of a large bear—massive in physique, in energy, in capacity for work, in self-certitude. Where Acheson was swift-flowing and direct, Dulles was ponderous and Jesuitical; where Acheson was perceived as an eighteenth century rationalist ready to apply an irreverent wit to matters public and private, Dulles came across as an austere nineteenth century moralist, a one-dimensional man who could not relieve the self-conscious gravity of his every public utterance. . . .

In the period 1946–1950, Dulles became a fervent anti-Communist. For him, the world struggle had now moved from a sort of economic determinism to a sort of spiritual determinism; the principal source of war was now to be found in a confrontation of universalist faiths: Christianity vs. Communism. While millions of his angry and fearful countrymen shared this view, Dulles held a measurably more absolute, more vigorously logical, more uncompromising posture.

When Stalin died on March 4, 1953, opening up the prospect of a major shift toward what Malenkov, his immediate successor, called "peaceful coexistence and competition," the event found Dulles girded for uncompromising, permanent, global struggle. Indeed he seemed to require, temperamentally, a form of Communist opposition whose goal was not less than the total conquest of the world in the most literal and physical sense. The effort to formulate an American response revealed profound differences of instinct and feeling between Dulles and Eisenhower. The President stood instinctively on the side of hope, seeing in the new situation an opportunity for renewed appeal to common aspirations on both sides of the Iron Curtain. The Secretary of State stood sternly on the side of moral rectitude, seeing in the new situation an opportunity to pursue, indeed to reinforce, a policy of global pressure and liberation. Eisenhower saw hopeful signals in the Malenkov speeches; Dulles saw exploitable weakness and uncertainty in the Kremlin. When the President nevertheless decided to make a speech in April, taking note of Stalin's death as marking the end of an era, and appealing to the Russians for a mutual reduction of strategic nuclear arms, Dulles was opposed, feeling the United States would be taking the baited hook of a new Communist peace offensive. He feared and suspected any manifestation of American-Russian agreement, thinking it could only be a ruse that would cause the free world to "let down its guard," as well as a fatal discouragement to peoples in Eastern Europe.

The President's speech of April 16, before the American Society of Newspaper Editors and Publishers, was very favorably received. The New York Times called it "a magnificent and deeply moving initiative," and both Pravda and Isvestia reprinted it verbatim, which was both unusual and unusually favorable in the context of 1953. Dulles, whose relations with the President were not yet intimate, and who had accordingly muted his opposition to the speech during its formulation, now moved boldly to fit the President's speech within the frame of his own policy of pressure. Speaking to the same audience two days later, he said:

> When President Eisenhower first took office, a plea for peace such as he made this week might have been interpreted as a sign of weakness or a mere gesture of sentimentality . . . it was first necessary to demonstrate the will and capacity to develop foreign policies so firm, so fair, so just that Soviet leaders might find it expedient to live with these policies rather than to live against them.

This statement amounted to the unreal claim that the policies of the new Administration had transformed the international situation in the space of its first two months in office! Of graver import than the rather crass effort at credit-taking was the cynical distortion of Eisenhower's generous impulse. Believing Eisenhower naive, Dulles gave the clear signal that only a policy of pressure had made the President's speech possible, and that a policy of pressure would continue.

Bureaucratic resistance to change was formidable on both sides of the Iron Curtain, and Eisenhower's speech was thus a paper boat launched against the tide. But Charles Bohlen, who assumed his post as Ambassador in Moscow that same month, believed in retrospect that the spring of 1953 had presented a rare opportunity for Western diplomacy. There were serious rumors in Moscow that the Russians were considering "the possibility of giving up East Germany," and these tended to be confirmed by Khrushchev's later charge that both Malenkov and Beria had "plotted" such a policy. Bohlen thought that if the United States had accepted Churchill's plea for a quick and flexible Summit meeting in 1953, it could have led to "a very fruitful period" for Western diplomacy, and perhaps to "a radical solution in our favor on the German question." Dulles was absolutely opposed to such a Summit, and his stone-bottomed resistance prevailed.

Dulles' famous "massive retaliation" speech of January 12, 1954 was, on one level, the Administration's considered public announcement of the so-called "New Look" approach to defense. In essence, this emphasized the threat of nuclear punishment against centers of Communist power, and de-emphasized local efforts to block or contain Russian or Chinese Communist expansion at the peripheries. The primary consideration for the new approach was budgetary, President Eisenhower and his principal advisors being gravely concerned that a logical extension of American defense efforts on the scale of the Korean war would lead to American bankruptcy. On another level, however, the Dulles speech was a strikingly personal interpretation of the new policy, couching the threat of nuclear retaliation in far more vivid terms than it was formulated in the underlying policy document (NSC 162/2) and drawing almost verbatim from an article he had written nearly two years before.

It was necessary, Dulles said, "for the free world to develop the will and organize the means to retaliate instantly against open aggression by Red Armies

. . . by means of our choosing." As nuclear retaliation was, however, already a vital component of the containment strategy (and the Strategic Air Command a force in being), Dulles was not really calling on the free world to "organize the means" for nuclear retaliation, but rather to "develop the will" to use it "instantly." Taken at face value, this was a proposal to transform the awesome nuclear hitting power from an instrument of last resort to one of first resort. Whether this was a sensible or credible proposition, four years after the Soviet Union had exploded its own nuclear weapons, was a question Dulles did not choose to explore. His argument was a lawyer's brief, more presentation than analysis, and avoided the logical weaknesses in his own case. It concentrated entirely on what the United States could do to an enemy, ignoring what an enemy could do in return to the United States, or indeed what a nuclear exchange would mean for peoples and nations who happened to be located near the presumed points of nuclear conflict. The public reaction was, not surprisingly, an uproar of confusion, consternation, and disbelief. Yet Dulles applied the new doctrine of nuclear retaliation to a variety of situations over the next five years.

The basic elements of what came to be the standard Dulles formula for brinkmanship were four: (1) an overstatement of the threat; (2) the development of an elaborate framework of authority (involving proxy commitments given in advance by Congress or allies) within which the President could take or avoid action at his absolute discretion; (3) ambiguous public warnings as to the likelihood of such action; and (4) extreme vagueness as to the military means that might be employed. The indispensable added ingredient came to be ambiguity, which permitted not only a possible carrying out of the dire threat, but also a practical withdrawal from an untenable situation.

During the Indochina crisis of March-April 1954, for example, Dulles sought to persuade Britain and France to sign on to an ambiguous formulation he called "united action." It was never clear whether this envisioned Americans fighting beside the French in an allied coalition, or a warning of American air attack against China if the Chinese directly entered the struggle, or merely an organizing point for a regional security alliance in Southeast Asia. Dulles vigorously avoided definition of the term, and its meaning thus ranged up and down the scale of potential action over the next three months, causing confusion and irritation almost everywhere. Ironically, he had started out in 1950 deploring the ambiguity of the Truman posture. It was not hard or clear enough, as he saw it, to avoid the serious risk that an enemy might miscalculate the American reaction to its intended depredation (e.g., the North Korean attack on South Korea). His overriding aim was thus to make United States intentions "crystal clear" so that a "potential aggressor" would not "miscalculate" the certainty and strength of the American response. Dulles probably drew a distinction between the certainty of an American response if a clear-cut warning were ignored, and the desirable ambiguity regarding the character of such a response. Yet when he came to his own formulations—"united action," the Formosa Resolution, the Eisenhower Doctrine—the distinction was lost and the result was a compounding of the uncertainties for friend and foe alike.

The underlying reasons were not hard to discover. Once the Russians had acquired a respectable nuclear striking power of their own, the certainty of any American response could not be assumed. Moreover, to make categorical threats against them was not credible, for the growing public awareness of the reality of nuclear stalemate generated heated political resistance to the use of such threats. In a sense, then, Dulles was forced (in the absence of an abandonment of a first resort nuclear retaliation policy) to manipulate not only the ambiguity of means but the ambiguity of whether American power would react at all in a particular crisis. Broadly speaking, Dulles and a majority of the Joint Chiefs of Staff (General Matthew Ridgway of the Army being a notable dissenter) were more ready to react than was President Eisenhower.

Twenty years after he entered office as Secretary of State and fourteen years after his death in 1959, what does John Foster Dulles look like? An impressive, headstrong man who was unquestionably the principal architect of foreign policy during the Eisenhower period, he nonetheless left behind no very distinguished or enduring monuments to his diplomatic handiwork, with the notable exception of the Japanese Peace Treaty (and that was fashioned while he was a consultant to the Truman Administration). In fairness, it must be said that the basic architecture of the postwar world—the containment strategy, the Truman Doctrine, the Marshall Plan, NATO, the philosophy of foreign economic and military aid—was already in place when the Eisenhower Administration came to office. And while there was no doubt room for new conceptions and new structures, the works of the Truman Administration proved to have been soundly built, leaving Dulles little choice but to accept and utilize major elements of the legacy. He tried hard to disguise this fact, employing a dramatic rhetoric and a hyperthyroid activism to convey an impression of his own bold innovation, but he succeeded chiefly in institutionalizing the attitudes and structures of the cold war in American life. Moved by his self-righteous and apocalyptic style, the country set out to ring the Soviet Union and China with a comprehensive set of multilateral and bilateral anti-Communist alliances, whose development led in turn to a proliferation of American military bases overseas and a dramatic rise in the flow of American military equipment for foreign armies. Bases must be manned and client armies trained and advised. In 1950, we had a few occupation troops in Germany, Austria, Japan, and Korea, and a few military base rights (with Iceland and Saudi Arabia). By 1959, more than a million American officials, military and otherwise, including their servitors and dependents, were stationed in some 42 countries. This vast formation represented unprecedented imperial power, yet that fact remained largely beyond the recognition of the American people, who were now thoroughly conditioned by the doctrinaire tendency of their leaders to elevate every issue of foreign policy to the level of deadly clash between opposed moral absolutes. Dulles had led in the building of a powerful posture of anti-Communist "deterrence." As he quit the scene, there was as yet only the first glimmering awareness that this posture also defined the limits of Dullesian diplomacy, that he possessed neither the perception of the opportunity, nor the will to move beyond it.

Today the essence of his legacy is more apparent. The slogans that have clung to his name—"agonizing reappraisal," "liberation," "massive retaliation," "brinkmanship"—all share the same sad connotation of emptiness, indeed of semifraud. The collective security alliances he planned or put together—SEATO and CENTO—were in the 1950's not very different from the makeshift arrangements they appear today; at no time did they significantly strengthen the Western posture or enhance the diplomatic landscape, and their continued survival today, in a moribund state, is attributable largely to the extraordinary strength of bureaucratic inertia. The Formosa Resolution and the Eisenhower Doctrine appear in retrospect as onetime devices formulated in haste to meet problems that were substantially misperceived (or misrepresented), and to generate congressional support for potential American actions that seemed unclear even in the minds of Dulles and the President. There is an *ad hoc* quality to the whole record.

Much of this may be explained by the fact that Dulles was far more a tactician than a systematic strategist and planner, but it is important to understand that he was a tactician who operated on fixed moral or religious premises. Moved by strong, but highly generalized, articles of faith, and lacking the managerial instinct to develop an orderly or systematic plan of operation, he showed a marked tendency to move directly from the faith to the tactic, from an abstract premise to its direct application in a very specific situation. As his premises appeared to him too basic to warrant reexamination, and as his preference was for action, he expended most of his intellectual and physical energy on the short-term tactical requirements of a problem. Lawyerlike, he applied formidable powers of concentration to a suddenly urgent or dangerous development, yet rarely aimed at more than temporary repair; and as he was insensitive to the interdependence of problems, he would frequently say or do things to help the immediate case, only dimly aware of the adverse effects he was producing on other, often more important, cases.

One key premise was that the Communist system was not only morally inferior to the West (which few doubted), but also inherently inferior in material terms (which a good many doubted). Impelled by faith in this premise, Dulles continued to pursue a policy of global pressure aimed at isolating, weakening, and eventually bringing down the major Communist adversaries in the world arena, trusting (as West German Ambassador Albrecht von Kessel said of him) "that Bolshevism was a product of the Devil and that God would wear out the Bolsheviks in the long run." He resisted any earnest search for accommodation, for his goal was not really coexistence based on calculated compromise and a balance of force; it was superiority and mastery based on a vague expectation that the West would maintain a permanent power preponderance. There may have been a real opportunity to negotiate a détente with the Soviet Union in the fluid period immediately following Stalin's death, and with the Chinese Communists in the long lull between mid-1955 and mid-1958. But Dulles was geared, ideologically and intellectually, for interminable struggle with the Devil, and he refused to reexamine his premise of inherent Western superiority long after the Soviet Union had developed military and industrial strength and exportable economic surplus of magnitudes that made his policy unrealistic and unproductive.

By 1957, for example, most of the major trading countries, including Japan, were moving toward normal economic relations with Communist China. This action by other countries reduced America's "total embargo" on China trade to a symbolic gesture, yet Dulles clung stubbornly to his shop-worn posture of total exclusion. "Whatever others may do," he said, the United States "ought not build up the military power of its potential enemy." Similarly, he refused to use the opportunity afforded by the long lull in the Formosa Strait (1955–1958) to clarify the U.S. commitment to the offshore islands, or to take any other measures that might prevent or mitigate a second, predictable explosion over those tiny bits of territory nearly touching the Chinese mainland. With regard to Peking, he remained totally inflexible, asserting (June 28, 1957) that "neither recognition, nor trade, nor cultural relations, nor all three would favorably influence the evolution of affairs in China." On the contrary, U.S. recognition of Peking would simply "enhance their ability to hurt us and our friends"; admission of Communist China to the United Nations would implant in that organization "the seeds of its own destruction." He deeply deplored the rising sentiment for change in U.S. China policy that emanated from the universities, the newspapers, and the moderate and liberal sectors of the Congress. In exasperation, he declared, "If Communism is stubborn for the wrong, let us be steadfast for the right." As a consequence of this mulish resistance to the fast-changing realities of the mid-1950's (which also included a rising determination of the Third World to achieve a position of genuine independence between the two major power blocs), the confident architect of pressure in the first Eisenhower term became the exhausted fire-fighter in the second, dashing distractedly from one blaze to another in a frenzied effort to stifle the flames of national rebellion and revolution in the Third World.

The tragedy of this situation is that there might well have been a different outcome. For the domestic political situation in the second Eisenhower term might well have sustained a different approach to the Third World, including China. Through a demonstration of trustworthiness and practical wisdom, and the exercise of ultimate control over several dangerous foreign policy crises, Eisenhower, by the end of 1956, had persuaded most of the congressional Republicans (who had oscillated between isolationism and imperialism) to support the foreign policies of an internationalist Republican President, and indeed to assume a measure of personal responsibility for them. Except for a few incorrigibles, the Republican party was being brought out of isolation to the threshold of responsible international behavior. The stage seemed set for constructive diplomacy. But the popular President suffered a diffusion of purpose and a waning of energy, while the unpopular Secretary of State continued to pursue his phantom goals.

The result was that Dulles imposed a tenacious continuity on U.S. policy at a time when conditions, at home and abroad, cried out for a searching reappraisal of basic premises, and when bold, clearheaded political leadership might have produced far-reaching change in American relations with the Soviet

Union and China, at least as significant as that finally achieved by the Nixon-Kissinger initiatives of 1972. Philosophically, for example, Dulles was a strong anti-colonialist, but as Russian and Chinese offers of trade and aid gave Third World countries a greater leverage vis-à-vis the West in their determined efforts to achieve unfettered independence, he continued in sterile opposition to neutralism and nonalignment. Neutralism, he reasoned, had adverse implications for regional alliance arrangements and American military base rights, and these were the main ingredients of his policy of pressure and encirclement. Also, because he failed to see the practical limits for Russian and Chinese imperialism in its encounters with the resistant strength of nationalism (including Communist manifestations of nationalism) in the newly independent countries, he continued to fear that *any* Communist presence among weak and backward peoples would lead to forms of subversion and takeover that could only enhance the power and influence of the Soviet Union or China at the expense of the United States.

There was, however, no doubting his dominant influence. Conviction, intellect, knowledge, and power of advocacy gave him a preeminent place with the President, the Cabinet, and in the wider public forums across the country and the world. His was the informing mind on American foreign policy; his speeches and policy statements—stamped with personal conviction, tight logic and moral fervor—provided a uniquely authoritative assessment of allies, adversaries, crises, and proposed courses of action. He was the undisputed spokesman on foreign policy, and because he spoke so often, because his words were frequently amplified by dramatic activity or dramatic inactivity, it is fair to say that what the average American citizen thought about the Communist system in the 1950's—the threats it posed, and how the United States should respond in a world of complexity and danger—was derived in no small part, directly or indirectly, from Dulles. For six years, his simple, fervent sermons and his bluntly righteous approach to defense in Western Europe, liberation in Eastern Europe, Russian influence in the Middle East, Peking's claim to Taiwan, and Communism's threat to Southeast Asia, strongly shaped American attitudes and cast a long shadow upon the decade of the 1960's. The attitudes and convictions he engendered, if not his diplomatic achievements, were enduring. To his credit (although greater credit was due to President Eisenhower's firm restraint), he avoided actual war, yet his strident approach to nearly every crisis divided the nation, weakened the trust and support of allies, and led at times to the almost total diplomatic isolation of the United States.

The rigidity of his moral stance and the power of his advocacy also defined the limits of his constructive statesmanship. And in the longer perspective, as history is ultimately measured, it is these qualities that seem likely to deny him a place among the greatest American or foreign statesmen. For his real gift lay in adversary proceedings, in tactics, in handling the urgent problem at hand, a problem not infrequently exacerbated by his own previous tactics. He lacked, in large measure, the statesman's vision, especially the statesman's dispassionate courage to peer across the angry divide to the bristling trenches of alien ideology, to identify there, and then to build upon, the hidden elements of possible reconciliation. On the whole, he was too much the believer, too much the advocate, too much the prudent political partisan to venture very far beyond the near-term interest of his client, or to perceive the wisdom of yielding minor outposts for the sake of reconciling an enemy or of building greater stability into the larger situation. Where he thought morality or ideology were engaged, he was a compulsive and righteous combatant (though not always in the end an unyielding one), and he had also concluded that in such a public stance lay his surest hope of retaining office. As one diplomat, who knew him well, put it, with more truth than tact or elegance, "Dulles was a curious cross between a 'Christer' and a shrewd and quite ruthless lawyer."

The Cold War Restrained

STEPHEN E. AMBROSE

"We can never rest," General Eisenhower declared during his 1952 campaign for the Presidency, "until the enslaved nations of the world have in the fulness of freedom the right to choose their own path, for then, and then only, can we say that there is a possible way of living peacefully and permanently with communism in the world." Like most campaign statements, Eisenhower's bowed to both sides of the political spectrum. For the bold he indicated a policy of liberation, while the cautious could take comfort in his willingness to someday live peacefully with the communists. Since the Americans believed, however, that no one would freely choose communism, Eisenhower's statement had a major internal contradiction.

The emphasis, therefore, was on liberation. John Foster Dulles, the Republican expert on foreign policy, author of the Japanese peace treaty, and soon to be Secretary of State, was more explicit than Eisenhower. Containment, he charged, was a treadmill policy "which, at best might perhaps keep us in the same place until we drop exhausted." It cost far too much in taxes and loss of civil liberties and was "not designed to win victory conclusively". One plank in the Republican platform damned containment as "negative, futile and immoral", for it abandoned "countless human beings to a despotism and Godless terrorism". It hinted that the Republicans, once in power, would roll back the atheistic tide, a hint that Dulles made into a promise when in a campaign speech he said that Eisenhower, as President, would use "all means to secure the liberation of Eastern Europe". Rollback would come not only in East Europe but also in Asia. The platform denounced the "Asia last" policy of the Democrats and said, "We have no intention to sacrifice the East to gain time for the West."

Stephen E. Ambrose, *Rise to Globalism: American Foreign Policy, 1938–1976* (rev. ed.; New York: Penguin Books, 1976). Volume 8 of *The Pelican History of the United States*, General Editor: Robert A. Divine. Copyright © Stephen E. Ambrose, 1971, 1976. Reprinted by permission of Penguin Books.

The Eisenhower landslide of 1952 was a compound of many factors, the chief being the General's enormous personal popularity. Corruption in the Truman administration, and the McCarthy charges of communist infiltration into the government ("There are no Communists in the Republican Party," a platform plank began), also helped. So did Eisenhower's promise to go to Korea and end the war there, not through victory but through negotiation. But one of the major appeals of the Eisenhower-Dulles team was its rejection of containment. The Republican pledge to do something about communist enslavement— it was never very clear exactly what—brought millions of former Democratic voters into the Republican fold, especially those of East European descent. Eisenhower reaped where McCarthy sowed. Far from rejecting internationalism and retreating to isolationism, the Republicans were proposing to go beyond containment. They would be more internationalist than Truman.

Republican promises to liberate the enslaved, like nineteenth-century abolitionist programs to free the Negro slaves, logically led to only one policy. Since the slave-holders would not voluntarily let the oppressed go, and since the slaves were too tightly controlled to stage their own revolution, those who wished to see them freed would have to fight. In the second half of the twentieth century, however, war was a much different proposition than it had been a hundred years earlier. Freeing the slaves would lead to the destruction of much of the world; most of the slaves themselves would die in the process.

There was another major constraint on action. The Republicans had accepted some of the New Deal, but essentially they were wedded to conservative fiscal views that stressed the importance of balancing the budget and cutting taxes. All of Eisenhower's leading cabinet figures, save Dulles, were businessmen who believed that an unbalanced federal budget was immoral. Government expenditures could be reduced significantly, however, only by cutting the Defense Department budget, which the Republicans proceeded to do. The cuts made liberation even more difficult.

In practice, then, Eisenhower and Dulles continued the policy of containment. There was no basic difference between their foreign policy and that of Truman and Acheson. Their campaign statements frequently haunted them, but they avoided embarrassment over their lack of action through their rhetoric. "We can never rest," Eisenhower had said, but rest they did, except in their speeches, which expressed perfectly the assumptions and desires of millions of Americans.

Better than anyone else, Dulles described the American view of communism. A devout Christian, highly successful corporate lawyer, something of a prig, and absolutely certain of his own and his nation's goodness, Dulles's unshakeable beliefs were based on general American ideas. They differed hardly at all from those of Truman, Acheson, Main Street in Iowa, or Madison Avenue in New York City. All the world wanted to be like America; the common people everywhere looked to America for leadership; communism was unmitigated evil imposed by a conspiracy on helpless people, whether it came from the outside as in East Europe or from the inside as in Asia; there could be no permanent reconciliation with communism for "this is an irreconcilable conflict". In

January 1953, Dulles told the Senate Foreign Relations Committee that communism "believes that human beings are nothing more than somewhat superior animals . . . and that the best kind of a world is that world which is organized as a well-managed farm is organized, where certain animals are taken out to pasture, and they are fed and brought back and milked, and they are given a barn as shelter over their heads." This was somewhat more sophisticated than the way Eisenhower usually described the ideology that had millions of adherents, and far more sophisticated than the description employed by newspaper editors and television commentators, but it accurately summed up the American view of communism.

The Eisenhower administration, like its predecessor, based its policy on the lessons of history, or at least on one lesson, which was that appeasement was a disaster. The verbiage of the thirties helped shape the policies of the fifties. When the Chinese moved to capture tiny islands held by Chiang, for example, and America's N.A.T.O. allies indicated that they did not want to start World War III over such a trifling matter, Eisenhower talked incessantly about Munich and compared the Russian and Chinese leaders to Hitler. He could never understand why the Europeans could not see the threat as clearly as he did.

The Eisenhower-Dulles speeches helped hide the fact that they did nothing about their promise to liberate the enslaved, but perhaps more important to their popularity was their unwillingness to risk American lives, for here too they were expressing the deepest sentiments of their countrymen. On occasion the Republicans rattled the saber and always they filled the air with denunciations of the communists, but they also shut down the Korean War, cut corporate taxes, and reduced the size of the armed forces. Despite intense pressure and great temptation, they entered no wars. They were willing to supply material, on a limited scale, to others so that they could fight the enemy, but they would not commit American boys to the struggle. Like Truman they did their best to contain communism; unlike him they did not use American troops to do so. They were unwilling to make peace but they would not go to war. Their speeches provided emotional satisfaction but their actions failed to liberate a single slave. No one had a right to complain that the Republicans had been misleading, however, for the policy had been clearly spelled out in the campaign. The vague and militant talk about liberation was balanced by specific promises to end the war in Korea—without liberating North Korea, much less China—and balance the budget.

When General Marshall was Secretary of State he had complained that he had no muscle to back up his foreign policy. Truman agreed and did all he could to increase the armed forces. Dulles did not make such complaints. He worked with what was available—which was, to be sure, far more than Marshall had at hand in 1948—for he shared the Republican commitment to fiscal soundness.

The extent of the commitment was best seen in the New Look, the term Eisenhower coined to describe his military policy. It combined domestic, military, and foreign considerations. The New Look rejected the premiss of N.S.C. 68 that the United States could spend up to 20 per cent of its G.N.P. on arms;

it rejected deficit financing; it maintained that enough of N.S.C. 68 had been implemented to provide security for the United States and to support a policy of containment. It came into effect at a time of lessening tension. The Korean War had ended and Stalin's death (March 1953) made the world seem less dangerous. The New Look was based in large part on the success of the N.S.C. 68 program, for the first two years of the New Look were the high-water mark of relative American military strength in the Cold War. As Samuel Huntington has noted, "The basic military fact of the New Look was the overwhelming American superiority in nuclear weapons and the means of delivering them." Between 1953 and 1955 the United States could have effectively destroyed the Soviet Union with little likelihood of serious reprisal. The fact that America did not do so indicated the basic restraint of the Eisenhower administration, as opposed to its verbiage.

The New Look became fixed policy during a period of lessened tensions and American military superiority, but it did not depend on either for its continuation. In its eight years of power, the Eisenhower administration went through a series of war scares and it witnessed the development of Soviet long-range bombers, ballistic missiles, and nuclear weapons. Throughout, however, Eisenhower held to the New Look. His Defense Department expenditures remained in the $35 to $40 billion range. . . .

The key to the New Look was the American ability to build and deliver nuclear weapons. Put more bluntly, Eisenhower's military policy rested on America's capacity to destroy the Soviet Union. Soviet strides in military technology gave them the ability to retaliate, but not to defend Russia, which was the major reason Eisenhower could accept sufficiency. The United States did not have to be superior to the Soviet Union to demolish it. . . .

The New Look shaped foreign policy. Since it was almost his only weapon, Dulles had to flash a nuclear bomb whenever he wanted to threaten the use of force. To make the threat believable, the United States developed smaller atomic weapons that could be used tactically on the battlefield. Dulles then attempted to convince the world that the United States would not hesitate to use them. The fact that the N.A.T.O. forces were so small made the threat persuasive, for there was no other way to stop the Red Army in Europe. Both Dulles and Eisenhower made this explicit. If the United States were engaged in a major military confrontation, Dulles said, "those weapons would come into use because, as I say, they are becoming more and more conventional and replacing what used to be called conventional weapons." Eisenhower added, "Where these things are used on strictly military targets . . . I see no reason why they shouldn't be used just exactly as you would use a bullet or anything else."

Dulles called the policy massive retaliation. In a speech in January 1954, he quoted Lenin and Stalin to show that the Soviets planned to overextend the free world and then destroy it with one blow. Dulles held that the United States should counter the strategy by maintaining a great strategic reserve in the United States and that the free world should be "willing and able to respond vigorously at places and with means of its own choosing". The Eisenhower administration had made a decision "to depend primarily upon a great capacity to retaliate, instantly, by means and at places of our own choosing".

Dulles used massive retaliation as the chief instrument of containment. In 1956 he called his overall method brinksmanship, which he explained in an article in *Life* magazine. "You have to take chances for peace, just as you must take chances in war. Some say that we were brought to the verge of war. Of course we were brought to the verge of war. The ability to get to the verge without getting into the war is the necessary art. . . . If you try to run away from it, if you are scared to go to the brink, you are lost. We've had to look it square in the face. . . . We walked to the brink and we looked it in the face. We took strong action."

Dulles implicitly recognized the limitations on brinksmanship. He never tried to use it for liberation and he used it much more sparingly after the Soviets were able to threaten the United States itself with destruction. It was a tactic to support containment at an acceptable cost, within a limited time span under a specific set of military circumstances, not a strategy for protracted conflict. . . .

Vietnam also illustrated the continuity of policy between the Truman and Eisenhower administrations, based as they were on the same assumptions. In December 1952, the lame-duck Truman administration approved $60 million for support of the French effort against Ho Chi Minh's Vietminh. Truman, and later Eisenhower, labeled Ho a communist agent of Peking and Moscow, characterizing the war in Vietnam as another example of communist aggression.

When Eisenhower moved into the White House, the State Department presented him with a background paper on Vietnam that succinctly summed up the American position not only on Vietnam but on the entire Third World. In 1949 France had broken up Indochina and granted Laos, Cambodia, and Vietnam "independence within the French Union". All objective observers recognized this as a heavy-handed attempt to buy off the Vietminh without giving anything of substance in return. Even the U.S. State Department could not totally ignore the obvious sham, but it did its best to dismiss it.

In the background presentation to Eisenhower, the State Department said that "certain symbols of the former colonial era remain". These "certain symbols" included total French control over "foreign and military affairs, foreign trade and exchange, and internal security. France continues to maintain a near monopoly in the economic life" of Vietnam. The State Department told Eisenhower that French control of the reality of power in its former colonies was "disliked by large elements of the native population", but said it was "justified" because the French were bearing the major burden of "defending the area". But the only non-native troops in Vietnam were French and even State admitted that the bulk of the population "disliked" French rule. American policy was to encourage an end to colonialism; yet in the face of all this State could still seriously assert that France retained "certain symbols" of power and was "defending the area". Against whom, and for what?

Such nonsense could have meaning only to those who believed that the challenge to French rule came not from the Vietnamese but from the Chinese

communists, acting in turn as proxies for the Kremlin, with the ultimate purpose of world conquest. If these beliefs were true, there was little point in fighting what Eisenhower called the tail of the snake, the Vietminh. Better to cut off
the neck in Peking, or even the head in Moscow. Dulles tried that, warning
the Chinese that if their troops entered Vietnam the United States would use
nuclear weapons against China. The Chinese sent no troops, but they had never
planned to anyway and Dulles's threat had absolutely no effect on the war
in Vietnam.

While he served as Supreme Commander at N.A.T.O. Headquarters in
Europe, and again in his first year in the White House, Eisenhower continually
urged the French to state unequivocally that they would give complete independence to Vietnam upon the conclusion of hostilities. He made "every kind
of presentation" to the French to "put the war on an international footing",
i.e., to make it a clear Cold War struggle rather than a revolt against colonialism. If France promised independence, and Ho continued to fight, Eisenhower
reasoned that the Vietminh could no longer pretend to be national liberators
and would stand revealed as communist stooges. At that point, Britain and the
United States could enter the conflict to halt aggression.

Eisenhower was badly confused about the nature of the war, but the French
were not. Like Rhee, they were willing enough to talk about the communist
menace in order to receive American aid, but they had no intention of giving
up Vietnam. They knew perfectly well that their enemies were in the interior
of Vietnam, not in Peking or Moscow, and they were determined to retain the
reality of power. If the Americans wanted to fight communists, that was fine
with the French; their concern was with continuing the exploitation of the
Vietnamese.

Unfortunately the war did not go well for the French. By early 1954 the
Vietminh controlled over half the countryside. The French put their best
troops into an isolated garrison north of Hanoi, called Dien Bien Phu, and
dared the Vietminh to come after them. They assumed that in open battle the
Asians would crumble. The results, however, were the other way around, and
by April it was the garrison at Dien Bien Phu that was in trouble. War weari-
ness in France was by then so great, and the French had attached so much
prestige to Dien Bien Phu, that it was clear that the fall of the garrison would
mean the end of French rule in Vietnam. Eisenhower and Dulles saw such an
outcome as a victory for communist aggression and a failure of containment.

On 3 April 1954, Dulles and Radford met with eight Congressional leaders.
The administration wanted support for a congressional resolution authorizing
American entry into the war. The Congressmen, including Senator Lyndon B.
Johnson of Texas, the Senate majority leader, were aghast. They remembered
all too well the difficulties of the Korean War and they were disturbed because
Dulles had found no allies to support intervention. Congressional opposition
hardened when they discovered that one of the other three Joint Chiefs dis-
agreed with Radford's idea of saving Dien Bien Phu through air strikes.

Eisenhower was as adamant as the Congressional leaders about allies. He
was anxious to shore up the French but only if they promised complete inde-

pendence and only if Britain joined the United States in intervening. Unless these conditions were met he would not move, but he was worried about what would happen if the French lost. On 7 April he introduced a new political use for an old word when he explained that all Southeast Asia was like a row of dominoes. If you knocked over the first one what would happen to the last one was "the certainty that it would go over very quickly".

To make sure the dominoes stood, Eisenhower went shopping for allies. He wanted "the U.S., France, United Kingdom, Thailand, Australia, and New Zealand et al. to begin conferring at once on means of successfully stopping the Communist advances in Southeast Asia". He proposed to use the bulk of the French army already there, while "additional ground forces should come from Asiatic and European troops". America would supply the material, but not the lives. The policy had little appeal to Britain, Australia, New Zealand, et al., but it was consistent with the approach of both Eisenhower's predecessors. The trouble was it had no chance of success. The proposed allies figured that if America would not fight in Korea, they would not fight in Vietnam. Even when Eisenhower wrote Churchill and compared the threat in Vietnam to the dangers of "Hirohito, Mussolini and Hitler", the British would not budge.

The Vice President, Richard M. Nixon, then tried another tack. On 16 April he said that "if to avoid further Communist expansion in Asia and Indochina, we must take the risk now by putting our boys in, I think the Executive has to take the politically unpopular decisions and do it". Nixon was evidently confused about the premises of the New Look, which made his suggestion impossible, since there were no troops available. In any case, the storm that followed his speech was so fierce that the possibility of using "our boys" in Vietnam immediately disappeared from the suggestion pile. Eisenhower would never have supported it anyway, and his Army Chief of Staff, Matthew Ridgway, was firmly opposed to rushing into another ground war in Asia.

What to do? The question was crucial because a conference on Vietnam was scheduled to begin in Geneva on 26 April. Like Truman in Korea, the Eisenhower administration was flatly opposed to a negotiated peace at Geneva which would give Ho Chi Minh any part of Vietnam. The United States was paying 75 per cent of the cost of the war, an investment too great simply to abandon. But the French position at Dien Bien Phu was deteriorating rapidly. Air Force Chief of Staff Nathan Twining had a solution. He wanted to drop three small atomic bombs on the Vietminh around Dien Bien Phu "and clean those Commies out of there and the band could play the Marseillaise and the French would come marching out . . . in fine shape". Eisenhower was opposed to using atomic bombs for the second time in a decade against Asians, but he did consider a conventional air strike. Dulles flew to London a week before the Geneva Conference to get Churchill's approval. Churchill would not approve, and Eisenhower did not act. Brinksmanship had failed.

On 7 May 1954, Dien Bien Phu fell. Still there was no immediate progress in Geneva and the Americans withdrew from the conference. At the insistence of the N.A.T.O. allies Eisenhower eventually sent his close friend, Walter B. Smith, as an observer. Dulles himself refused to return and the negotiations dragged on. The break came when the French government fell and, in mid-June, the Radical-Socialist Pierre Mendès-France assumed the position of Foreign Minister as well as of Premier. On the strength of his pledge to end the war or resign by 20 July, he had a vote of confidence of 419 to 47. Mendès-France immediately met Chinese Premier Chou En-lai privately at Berne, which infuriated the Americans, and progress towards peace began. Eisenhower, Dulles, and Smith were helpless bystanders. On 20–21 July two pacts were signed, the Geneva Accords and the Geneva Armistice Agreement.

The parties agreed to a truce and to a temporary partition of Vietnam at the 17th parallel, with the French withdrawing south of that line. Neither the French in south Vietnam nor Ho Chi Minh in the north could join a military alliance or allow foreign military bases on their territory. There would be elections, supervised by a joint commission of India, Canada, and Poland, within two years to unify the country. France would stay in the south to carry out the elections. The United States did not sign either of the pacts, nor did any South Vietnamese government. The Americans did promise that they would support "free elections supervised by the United Nations" and would not use force to upset the agreements. Ho Chi Minh had been on the verge of taking all of Vietnam, but he accepted only the northern half because he needed time to repair the war damage and he was confident that when the elections came he would win a smashing victory. All Western observers agreed with his prediction on how the vote would go.

Desperate to save something from the débâcle, in July 1954 Dulles, Radford and Twining, along with others at the Pentagon, worked out an invasion scheme calling for a landing at Haiphong and a march to Hanoi, which American troops would then liberate. Again, Ridgway opposed, arguing that the adventure would require at least six divisions even if the Chinese did not intervene, and again Eisenhower refused to act.

The New Look had tied Dulles's hands in Vietnam, so after Geneva and Eisenhower's refusal to invade North Vietnam the Secretary of State moved in two ways to restore some flexibility to American foreign policy. One of the major problems had been the lack of allies for an intervention. Dulles tried to correct this before the next crisis came by signing up the allies in advance. In September 1954, he persuaded Britain, Australia, New Zealand, France, Thailand, Pakistan, and the Philippines to join the Southeast Asian Treaty Organization (S.E.A.T.O.), in which the parties agreed to consult if any signatory felt threatened. They would act together to meet an aggressor if they could unanimously agree on designating him and if the threatened state agreed to action on its territory. Protection for Cambodia, Laos, and South Vietnam was covered in a separate protocol. Thus quickly did the United States undermine the Geneva Accords by implicitly bringing the former French colonies into an alliance system. The absence of India, Burma, and Indonesia was embarrassing, as was the presence of so many white men. Clearly this was no N.A.T.O. for Southeast Asia, but rather a Western—especially American—effort to regulate the affairs of Asia from the outside. Once again the hoary old Monroe Doctrine had been extended. The United States, as Dulles put it, had "declared that an intrusion [in Southeast Asia] would be dangerous to our peace and security", and America would fight to prevent it. . . .

Eisenhower's decision to go to the summit [in 1955] meant the end of any American dreams of winning the Cold War by military means. The Russians had come so far in nuclear development that Eisenhower himself warned the nation that an atomic war would ruin the world. There could be no "possibility of victory or defeat", only different degrees of destruction. As James Reston reported in the *New York Times,* "Perhaps the most important single fact in world politics today is that Mr. Eisenhower has thrown the immense authority of the American Presidency against risking a military solution of the cold war". Since Eisenhower would not lead the nation into a nuclear war, and since he did not have the troops to fight a limited war, nor could he get them from his allies, and since the Republicans were more determined to balance the budget and enjoy the fruits of capitalism than they were to support a war machine, the only alternative left was peace of some kind with the Russians. Eisenhower was not willing to give in on any of the crucial questions, like the unification of Germany or Vietnam or Korea, but he was willing to talk with the new Russian leaders. . . .

On 18 July 1955 the summit meeting began. It had been called in response to the arms race and it was no surprise that there was no progress towards political settlements. What Dulles had feared most, however, did happen— there emerged a "spirit of Geneva". Before the meeting, Dulles had warned Eisenhower to maintain "an austere countenance" when being photographed with Bulganin. He pointed out that any pictures taken of the two leaders smiling "would be distributed throughout the Soviet satellite countries", signifying "that all hope of liberation was lost and that resistance to communist rule was henceforth hopeless". But the pictures were taken, and "Ike" could not restrain his famous grin, and the photographs were distributed.

Dulles had been unable to prevent this symbolic recognition of the failure of Republican promises for liberation of communist satellites. The Soviets had almost caught up militarily and brinksmanship was dead. Geneva did not mean the end of the Cold War but it did put it on a different basis. The West had admitted that it could not win the Cold War, that a thermonuclear stalemate had developed, and that the *status quo* in Europe and China (where tensions quickly eased) had to be substantially accepted.

Dulles was bitter but helpless. He was especially infuriated because the battleground now shifted to the areas of economic and political influence in the Third World, a battleground on which Russia had enormous advantages. Dulles warned the N.A.T.O. Foreign Ministers in December 1955 that the Soviets would hereafter employ "indirect" threats "primarily developed in relations to the Near and Middle East and South Asia". To fight back, Dulles needed two things—money, and an American willingness to accept radicalism in the emerging nations. He had neither. Republicans who resented giving money to West Europe through the Marshall Plan were hardly likely to approve significant sums for non-white revolutionaries. . . .

The overwhelming first impression of American foreign policy from 1956 to 1961 was one of unrelieved failure. Eisenhower and Dulles were unable to contain the Russians, who succeeded in their centuries-old dream of establishing themselves in the Mediterranean and the Middle East. America's inability to do anything at all to aid Hungary's rebels made a mockery of the Republican calls for liberation. Spectacular Soviet successes in rocketry, beginning with Sputnik, sent the United States into a deep emotional depression. Russia seemed to have won the arms race and in 1959 it was Khrushchev who played at brinksmanship from a position of strength. After Suez the French, and to a lesser extent the British, would never trust the United States again. In Southeast Asia, communist guerrillas in South Vietnam and Laos threatened to upset the delicate balance there in favor of the communists. In Latin America, the Eisenhower administration was helpless in the face of a revolution in Cuba, which soon allowed the Russians to extend their influence to within ninety miles of the United States. Only in Africa did the Soviets fail to gain new Third World adherents, although even there this was less because of American actions and more because the Russians, like the Americans, did not have a clear understanding of what was happening in black Africa.

Surface appearances, however, reveal only surface truths. After he retired, Eisenhower said his greatest disappointment was his failure to bring real peace to the world. Given his attitudes towards communism, peace—in the sense of mutual co-operation with the Soviets to solve the world's problems—was never a strong possibility. Eisenhower's outstanding achievement was the negative one of avoiding war. However irresponsible Republican emotional appeals to the anti-communist vote may have been, and despite the Russian shift to the offensive in the Cold War, Eisenhower refused to engage American troops in armed conflict. He was not immune to intervention, nor to provocative rhetoric, nor to nuclear testing, nor to the arms race (within strict limits), but he did set his face against war. It became the Democrats' turn to complain that the United States was not "going forward", that it was not "doing enough", that America was "losing the Cold War".

But despite the Democratic complaints, and although Dulles's sermonizing and moralizing and baffling shifts of position drove America's allies to distraction, the United States emerged from the Eisenhower years in a spectacularly good position. The American G.N.P. went up, without dangerous inflation. The Western European economy continued to boom. N.A.T.O. stood more or less intact. Anglo-American oil interests in the Middle East were secure. The Latin American economy remained under American domination. American military bases in the Pacific were safe. Chiang remained in control of Formosa. And the United States, although Eisenhower was spending only about two-thirds the amount that the Democrats wanted him to on defense, was in fact strategically superior to the Soviet Union.

Eisenhower had been unable to contain the communists, much less liberate East Europe, and he remained wedded to the clichés of the Cold War, but he was a man of moderation and caution with a clear view of what it would cost the United States to resist communist advances everywhere. He thought the

American economy could not pay the price, which was the fundamental distinction between Eisenhower and his Democratic successors. Because of Eisenhower's fiscal conservatism, Dulles's hands were tied. The Secretary of State was reduced to vapid fulminations which provided emotional satisfaction but kept the budget balanced. . . .

At the 20th Party Congress in February 1956, Khrushchev shocked the world by denouncing Stalin for his crimes, confessing that there could be several roads to communism, and indicating that Stalinist restrictions would be loosened. Two months later the Russians dissolved the Cominform. Ferment swept through East Europe. Riots in Poland forced Khrushchev to disband the old, Stalinist Politburo and allow Wladyslaw Gomulka, an independent communist, to take power (20 October 1956). Poland remained communist and a member of the Warsaw Pact, but it won substantial independence and set an example for the other satellites.

The excitement spread to Hungary, before the war the most fascist of the East European states and the one where Stalin's imposition of communism had been most alien. On 23 October Hungarian students took to the streets to demand that the Stalinist rulers be replaced with Imre Nagy. Workers joined the students and the riot spread. Khrushchev agreed to give power to Nagy, but that was no longer enough. The Hungarians demanded the removal of the Red Army from Hungary and the creation of an anti-communist political party. By 28 October the Russians had given in and begun to withdraw their tanks from around Budapest.

Liberation was at hand. Eisenhower was careful in his campaign speeches to use only the vaguest of phrases, although the Voice of America and Radio Free Europe did encourage the rebels. So did Dulles, who promised economic aid to those who broke with the Kremlin. At the decisive moment, however, just as it seemed that the European balance of power was about to be drastically altered, the Israeli Army struck Egypt. In a matter of hours it nearly destroyed Nasser's Army and took most of the Sinai peninsula. Britain and France then issued an ultimatum, arranged in advance with the Israelis, warning the Jews and the Egyptians to stay away from the Suez Canal. When Nasser rejected the note, the Europeans began bombing Egyptian military targets and prepared to move troops into Suez, under the cover of keeping the Jews and Arabs apart.

On 31 October, the day after the bombing in Egypt began, Nagy announced that Hungary was withdrawing from the Warsaw Pact. The Russians, certain that events in Egypt and the American Presidential campaign would paralyze the United States, and unwilling in any event to let the Warsaw Pact disintegrate, decided to move. Russian tanks crushed the Hungarian rebels, although only after bitter street fighting that left 7,000 Russians and 30,000 Hungarians dead. The emotional impact on the United States was exemplified by the angry tears of thousands of American students who met and passed resolutions in support of the Hungarians. Radio pleas for help from Hungary made the tragedy even more painful: "Any news about help? Quickly, quickly, quickly!" And the last, desperate cry, on a teletype message to the Associated Press:

"Help!—help!—help!—SOS!—SOS!—SOS! They just brought us a rumor that the American troops will be here within one or two hours. . . . We are well and fighting."

There would never be any American troops. Eisenhower did not even consider giving military support to the Hungarians and he would not have done so even had there been no concurrent Middle Eastern crisis. Under no conceivable circumstances would he risk World War III for East Europe. Liberation was a sham; it had always been a sham. All Hungary did was to expose it to the world. However deep Eisenhower's hatred of communism, his fear of war was deeper. Even had this not been so, the armed forces of the United States were not capable of driving the Red Army out of Hungary, except through a nuclear holocaust that would have left all Hungary and most of Europe devastated. The Hungarians, and the other Eastern European peoples, learned that there would be no liberation, that they could not look forward to tying themselves to the West, that their traditional policy of playing East against West was finished. They would have to make the best deal they could with the Soviets. The Russian capture and execution of Nagy made the point brutally clear.

In Egypt, meanwhile, the British and French had bungled. They blew their cover story almost immediately. The Israeli advance was so rapid that they could not pretend that their invasion was one by a disinterested third party designed to keep the Jews and Egyptians apart. Eisenhower was upset at their use of nineteenth-century colonial tactics; he was livid at their failure to inform him of their intentions. The Americans backed a resolution in the General Assembly urging a truce, then cut off oil supplies desperately needed in Britain and France. Khrushchev, meanwhile, rattled his rockets, warning the British and French on 5 November to withdraw before he destroyed them. Although they were only hours away from taking the canal, the Anglo-French governments agreed to a cease-fire and pullback.

It had been quite a week for lessons. The British and French learned that they no longer stood on the center of the world stage—they were second-rate powers incapable of independent action. Henceforth they could either operate within the American orbit or try to create European unity with Germany and without the United States, thereby allowing Europe to play a world role. American politicians learned to stop their irresponsible prattling about liberation. The Russians learned just how strong a force nationalism was in East Europe, while the Israelis saw that they would have to make it on their own in their conflict with the Arabs. United States and United Nations pressure soon forced the Jews to give up their gains in Sinai. The Egyptians learned to look at the Soviet Union for support—encouraged by Nasser, they believed that the Russian ultimatum, not the United States' action in the United Nations, had saved them.

Dulles seemed to be losing the Third World, but from his point of view things were not that bad. To be sure the Russians were taking over the great Western military base in Egypt, but the oil-rich countries stayed in the Anglo-American orbit. To solidify this hold, Dulles and Eisenhower pushed through Congress (January 1957) the Eisenhower Doctrine, which gave the President the right to intervene in the Middle East whenever a legitimate government said it was threatened by communism and asked for aid. Simultaneously, Eisenhower broke all diplomatic precedents and went to the airport to meet King Saud of Saudi Arabia (the mayor of New York City had just refused to meet the King, who was violently anti-Israel), and in the talks that followed gave the King extensive military aid in return for an American air base at Dhahran. Eisenhower went so far as to assure the King that no American Jew would serve in the U.S. Air Force in Saudi Arabia.

In April 1957, when pro-Nasser officers tried to oust King Hussein of Jordan, Eisenhower dispatched the U.S. Sixth Fleet from the French Riviera to the Eastern Mediterranean and gave $20 million to Hussein in military aid. There were sardonic references in Britain and France about unilateral action and gunboat diplomacy, but it worked. The three feudal Arab monarchies, Jordan, Saudi Arabia, and Iraq, were now wedded to the United States. A year later, when Russia began to move into Syria, and Iraq moved towards Nasser, thereby threatening its neighbor, Lebanon, Eisenhower rushed troops to that Christian Arab country (14 July 1958). The Russians may have gained bases in the Mediterranean, but the United States still had the oil.

The intervention in Lebanon illustrated Eisenhower's methods. It was a unilateral action that risked general war in support of a less than democratic government threatened by pro-Nasser Arabs. Eisenhower tried to tie the action into great historic precedents by invoking Greece and the 1947 Truman Doctrine. He emphasized the danger by mentioning the communist takeovers in Czechoslovakia and China, and he explained that the United States "had no intention of replacing the United Nations in its primary responsibility of maintaining international peace and security". The United States had acted alone merely "because only swift action would suffice".

The rhetoric was grand, the intervention itself less sweeping. The Joint Chiefs wanted American troops to overrun all of Lebanon, but Eisenhower ordered the men to limit themselves to taking the airfield and the capital. If the government could not survive even after American soldiers had secured the capital, Eisenhower said, "I felt we were backing up a government with so little popular support that we probably should not be there." The British used the occasion to send troops into Jordan to prop up King Hussein and to make sure their oil interests in Iraq were not damaged. The British then asked the Americans to join them in occupying Jordan. Although many administration officials wanted to take advantage of the request in order to extend American influence, Eisenhower flatly refused. As always, he wanted to limit the risks and America's commitment.

The Russians, too, were unwilling to take drastic action. Nasser flew to Moscow to beg for aid; Khrushchev turned him down. The Soviet ruler knew that Eisenhower acted to protect Western oil holdings and he knew how vital those holdings were to the West. As long as Eisenhower was willing to hold down the scope of the intervention, Khrushchev would not interfere.

Khrushchev's caution surprised many observers, since the Russians were generally believed to have achieved military superiority. On 4 October 1957, the Soviet Union successfully launched the world's first man-made satellite,

Sputnik. Two months earlier they had fired the world's first intercontinental ballistic missile (I.C.B.M.). Americans were frustrated, angry, ashamed, and afraid all at once. As Walter LaFeber puts it, " 'gaps' were suddenly discovered in everything from missile production to the teaching of arithmetic at the pre-school level". Eisenhower dispersed Strategic Air Force units and installed medium-range ballistic missiles in Turkey and Italy, but this was hardly enough to assuage the sudden fear. When the Russians began trumpeting about their average increase in their G.N.P. (7 per cent, nearly twice the American rate), the pressure on Eisenhower to "get the country moving again" became almost irresistible.

Eisenhower refused to panic, even when in late 1957 the newspapers discovered and published the findings and recommendations of a committee headed by H. Rowan Gaither, Jr., of the Ford Foundation, which painted an exceedingly dark picture of the future of American security. The Gaither Report, as Eisenhower typically understated it, included "some sobering observations". It found that the Soviet G.N.P. was indeed increasing at a much faster rate than that of the United States, that the Russians were spending as much on their armed forces and heavy industry as the Americans were, that the Soviets had enough fissionable material for 1,500 nuclear weapons, with 4,500 jet bombers, 300 long-range submarines and an extensive air defense system, that they had been producing ballistic missiles with a 700-mile range, that by 1959 the Soviets might be able to launch an attack against the United States with 100 I.C.B.M.'s carrying megaton-sized nuclear warheads, and that if such an attack should come the civilian population and the American bombers in S.A.C. would be vulnerable.

The Gaither Report was similar to N.S.C. 68 in its findings, and like N.S.C. 68 it recommended a much improved defense. The committee wanted fallout shelters built on a massive scale, an improvement of America's air defense capability, a vast increase in S.A.C.'s offensive power, a build-up of conventional forces capable of fighting limited war, and another reorganization of the Pentagon. As a starter, the Gaither Report (and a somewhat similar study done by the Rockefeller Foundation) urged an increase in defense spending to $48 billion.

Eisenhower said no. "We could not turn the nation into a garrison state," he explained in his memoirs, adding as an afterthought that the Gaither Report was "useful; it acted as a gadfly . . .". He kept the Defense budget under $40 billion, quietly rejected the demands for fallout shelters and increased conventional war capability, and dropped one more Army division and a number of tactical air wings from active duty. He did disperse S.A.C. bombers and he speeded up the ballistic missile programs, although Congress had to appropriate more funds than the administration requested for the I.C.B.M. and Polaris to get those programs into high gear.

Democrats charged that the Republicans were allowing their Neanderthal fiscal views to endanger the national security, but Eisenhower knew what he was doing. The C.I.A., in one of the great intelligence coups of all time, had in 1956 inaugurated a series of flights over the Soviet Union in high-altitude airplanes, called U-2s. The photographs that resulted from the flights revealed, as Eisenhower later put it, "proof that the horrors of the alleged 'bomber gap' and the later 'missile gap' were nothing more than imaginative creations of irresponsibility". The United States still had a substantial lead in strategic weapons.

One of the most important points about the U-2 flights was that Khrushchev knew they were taking place (none of the Russian fighter airplanes could reach the altitude the U-2s flew at, so they could not knock them down), which meant that Khrushchev knew that Eisenhower knew how hollow were the Soviet boasts about strategic superiority. The fact that Eisenhower made no strong statements about Soviet inferiority during the American domestic controversy about the missile gap tended to reassure the Soviets and convince them that the President really was a man of moderation who was sincerely interested in some sort of *modus vivendi*. The flights, the information they produced, and Eisenhower's rejection of the Gaither Report, all indicated to the Soviets that Eisenhower had accepted the fundamental idea that neither side could win a nuclear war and that both would lose in an arms race.

The events in the year following Sputnik had the effect of establishing ground rules for the Cold War. By staying out of the Lebanon situation the Soviets indicated that they recognized and would not challenge the West's vital interests. By refusing to take the easy way out of the missile gap controversy, Eisenhower indicated that he did not want an arms race and was eager to establish a *modus vivendi*. Through their negative signals, both sides showed that they would keep the threshold of conflict low. The years of Eisenhower's second term marked the height of bipolarity, for as the British, French, Israelis, and Egyptians could testify, what the Big Two wanted, they got. Whether they could continue to control their allies, especially France and China, much less the Third World, was an open question. Indeed, it was not at all clear that Eisenhower and Khrushchev could control the hard-liners in their own countries. . . .

In a limited and halting but nevertheless real way, Eisenhower had opted for peace. Throughout his second term he warned of the danger of turning America into a garrison state and of the need to learn to live with the communists. As a professional soldier of the old school, Eisenhower felt his first responsibility was the nation's security, which he realized could never be enhanced by an arms race in the nuclear age. If the United States built more bombers and missiles, the Russians also would build more. American security would be lowered, not increased. Negotiation with the Russians was a more effective way to enhance the nation's security. Democrats thought the primary reason for Eisenhower's concern was his commitment to a balanced budget, and it was true that he had decided the cost of the Cold War was more than America could bear, but there was something else. By 1958 Eisenhower realized that he had only two more years on the world stage, that if he were to leave any lasting gift to the world he would have to do it soon. His deepest personal desire was to leave mankind the gift of peace.

Eisenhower and Khrushchev were anxious to solidify the concept of peaceful co-existence, each for his own reasons, but by 1959 the Cold War had gone on for so long that calling it off was no easy task. Both men had to fend off hard-liners at home, both had troubles with their allies, and both were beset by Third World problems that they could neither understand nor control. Eisenhower had trouble with the Democrats, who were unhampered by orthodox fiscal views and who did want an arms race. In their view, government spending would help, not hurt, the economy. The Democrats, led by Senators John F. Kennedy, Lyndon B. Johnson, and Hubert H. Humphrey, were impatient with Eisenhower's conservatism, yearned for a dynamic President, and talked in-cessantly about America's loss of prestige. They wanted to restore America to world leadership, which in practice meant extending American commitments and increasing American arms. On the other side, Eisenhower was beset by Republicans who wanted to hear more about liberation and getting tough with the communists, and the President himself had by no means escaped fully from the patterns of thought of the Cold War.

Neither had Khrushchev, who also had hardliners in Moscow pushing him towards the brink. In addition, Mao had become as much a problem for Khrushchev as Chiang was for Eisenhower. Khrushchev's refusal to support Mao's call for wars of national liberation, a basic cause of the Sino-Russian split, signified to Mao that the Russians had joined the have powers against the have-nots. There was other evidence, such as Khrushchev's trip to the United States, his willingness to go to Geneva again, and the cooling of the Berlin crisis. As the Chinese saw it, the Soviets were selling out both communism and the Third World. They accused Khrushchev of appeasement. Mao's propa-ganda increasingly warned of winds blowing from the east instead of the west and of a world-wide revolt of the rural peoples against the urbanites, among whom the Chinese counted the Russians. Mao's radicalism, heightened by his emphasis on racism, appealed strongly to the Third World and made it almost as difficult for the Soviets to influence development in Southeast Asia and Africa as it was for the United States. Mao challenged, directly and success-fully, Khrushchev's leadership of the communist world. Indirectly, he chal-lenged bipolarity. The world was simply too large, with too much diversity, to be controlled by the two super powers, no matter how closely together they marched (Mao would soon discover, in Africa, that the world could not be controlled by three powers either).

Khrushchev and Eisenhower, in short, had gone too far towards co-existence for the Cold Warriors in their own countries and for their allies. Khrushchev was in the weaker position at home, since Eisenhower was almost immune to criticism, especially on military matters. When the Air Force and certain Con-gressmen demanded that one-third of S.A.C.'s bombers be airborne at all times, for example, Eisenhower dismissed the proposal as too costly and not necessary. As one Senator, who was an Air Force supporter, put it, "How the hell can I argue with 'Ike' Eisenhower on military matters?" Khrushchev did not have such prestige and he found it increasingly difficult to ward off those in the Kremlin who wanted more arms and something done about Berlin. He also had to face the Chinese challenge for communist leadership.

Khrushchev badly needed a Cold War victory, for internal political reasons and to compete with China for followers. He may have felt that Eisenhower, who would shortly be leaving office and who had no pressing need for a resounding triumph, would be willing to allow him a victory. Whatever his reasoning, Khrushchev announced on 5 May 1960, on the eve of the Geneva summit meeting, that a Russian surface-to-air missile (S.A.M.) had knocked down an American U-2 spy plane inside Russia.

The event illustrated more than Khrushchev's flair for the dramatic, for it also showed how entrenched Cold War interests could block any move towards peace. Having finally achieved the ability to knock down the U-2s, the Soviets could have waited for the results of the Geneva meeting to actually do it. On the other side, the C.I.A. could have suspended the flights in the period preceding the meeting. Or Khrushchev could have kept quiet about the entire affair, hoping that the C.I.A. had learned the lesson and would cease and desist thereafter. Instead, he deliberately embarrassed the President. Khrushchev boasted about the performance of the S.A.M.s but concealed the pilot's survival in order to elicit an American explanation that could be demolished by producing the pilot. When Eisenhower fell into the trap, Khrushchev crowed over his discomfort and demanded an apology or a repudiation of presidential responsibility. He had misjudged the man. Eisenhower stated instead that the United States had the right to spy on the Soviet Union and took full personal responsibility for the flight. The summit conference was ruined. The best hope for an agreement on Berlin was gone, although Khrushchev did abandon his effort to change the *status quo* there. He said he would wait for the new President to take office before he brought it up again.

Khrushchev had improved his position at home, and with the Chinese, but not much. Eisenhower had tried but in the end he was unable to bring the Cold War to a close. Despite the U-2 and the wrecked summit meeting, he had improved Russian-American relations. He had failed to liberate any communist slaves—had indeed been forced to acquiesce in the coming of communism to Indochina and in the establishment of a Russian base in the Mediterranean—but he had avoided war and kept the arms race at a low level. He had tried, insofar as he was capable, to ease the policy of permanent crisis he had inherited from Truman.

Eisenhower's major weakness was that he was an old man, head of an old party, surrounded by old advisers. He dealt with old problems. His image, deliberately promoted by the Republicans, was that of a kindly grandfather. He could not anticipate new problems, nor adjust to the winds of change that Mao always talked about and which were, indeed, blowing across the world. Domestically as well as abroad, the revolution of rising expectations more or less escaped notice. . . .

In January 1961, Eisenhower delivered his farewell address to the people. He was concerned about the internal cost of the Cold War. His ideals were those of the small town in the Middle West where he grew up. He was afraid that big government and the regimentation of private life were threatening the old American values. He had no precise idea of what could be done about the dangers, for he knew that both were necessary to carrying on the Cold War, but he did want to warn his countrymen. He pointed out that the "conjunction of an immense military establishment and a large arms industry, . . . new in American experience", exercised a "total influence . . . felt in every city, every state house, every office of the federal government. . . . In the councils of government, we must guard against the acquisition of unwarranted influence, whether sought or unsought, by the military-industrial complex."

The Democrats paid no attention. In the campaign, and in his inaugural address, Kennedy emphasized that a new generation was coming to power in America. Hardened by the Cold War, it was prepared to deal with all the tough problems. He promised to replace Eisenhower's tired, bland leadership with new ideas and new approaches. Since these generalities were not reinforced by any specific suggestions, it was difficult to tell what the new directions would be. What was clear was that a forward-looking, offensive spirit had come to America. Action was about to replace inaction. Kennedy promised to get the country moving again. Where to, no one knew precisely.

FURTHER READING

Charles Alexander, *Holding the Line* (1975)
Louis Gerson, *John Foster Dulles* (1968)
Richard Gould-Adams, *Time of Power* (1962)
Michael Guhin, *John Foster Dulles* (1972)
Townsend Hoopes, *The Devil and John Foster Dulles* (1973)
Emmet J. Hughes, *The Ordeal of Power* (1963)
Walter LaFeber, *America, Russia, and the Cold War* (1976)
Peter Lyon, *Eisenhower* (1974)
Herbert S. Parmet, *Eisenhower and the Great Crusades* (1972)
Thomas G. Paterson, ed., *Containment and the Cold War* (1973)
I. F. Stone, *The Haunted Fifties* (1963)

12

The Cuban Missile Crisis

In October 1962, American U-2 reconnaissance planes photographed Soviet missile sites in Cuba. For several days a chilling war scare gripped Washington and the world. The Cuban Missile Crisis became one of the most dangerous Cold War confrontations, bringing the world perilously close to nuclear holocaust. After installation of an American naval blockade, a dramatic television address by President John F. Kennedy, and an exchange of letters between Kennedy and Soviet Premier Nikita Khrushchev, an agreement was reached whereby Russia pledged to withdraw its missiles from Cuba and the United States promised never again to invade Cuba (as it had done in April 1961 at the Bay of Pigs).

Questions persist, and the answers will remain tentative until both Soviet and American documentary archives are opened to scholars: Why did the Soviets place missiles in Cuba? Were they offensive or defensive? Did the missiles affect seriously the strategic balance of power? Why did Kennedy shun private negotiations? What alternatives existed, and why was the blockade selected? What lessons were drawn from the experience? What impact did the crisis have thereafter on international relations?

DOCUMENTS

The first document was written by White House assistant Theodore C. Sorensen for President Kennedy on October 17, 1962, two days after the missiles were discovered in Cuba. The memorandum summarizes the alternatives and questions considered by the Executive Committee that Kennedy organized to manage the crisis. The second document is President Kennedy's October 22 television address to the nation, wherein he strongly criticized Russia and announced American retaliatory actions, including a naval "quarantine" of the Caribbean island.

The final document is Nikita Khrushchev's October 27 letter offering proposals to defuse the crisis. The President ignored this letter, which asked that American missiles be removed from Turkey, and answered an earlier, more moderate letter from the Soviet leader which had not mentioned such a swap.

Theodore C. Sorensen's Memorandum on Executive Committee Discussions, 1962

1. It is generally agreed that Soviet MRBM's—offensive weapons—are now in Cuba. While only one complex of three sites and no nuclear warheads have been spotted, it must be assumed that this is the beginning of a larger build-up.

2. It is generally agreed that these missiles, even when fully operational, do not significantly alter the balance of power—i.e., they do not significantly increase the potential megatonnage capable of being unleashed on American soil, even after a surprise American nuclear strike. The Soviet purpose in making this move is not understood—whether it is for purposes of diversion, harassment, provocation or bargaining.

3. Nevertheless it is generally agreed that the United States cannot tolerate the known presence of offensive nuclear weapons in a country 90 miles from our shore, if our courage and our commitments are ever to be believed by either allies or adversaries. Retorts from either our European allies or the Soviets that we can become as accustomed as they to accepting the nearby presence of MRBM's have some logic but little weight in this situation.

4. It is also agreed that certain of our NATO allies would be notified but not consulted immediately prior to any action by the United States; that certain Latin nations would at least be notified; and that, if there is to be military action, the President would hold announcing the existence of the missiles and the justification of our action until after that action had been completed.

5. The following possible tracks or courses of action have each been considered. Each has obvious diplomatic and military disadvantages, but none others as yet occur.

> Track A: Political action, pressure and warning, followed by a military strike if satisfaction is not received.
> Track B: A military strike without prior warning, pressure or action, accompanied by messages making clear the limited nature of this action.
> Track C: Political action, pressure and warning, followed by a total naval blockade, under the authority of the Rio Pact and either a Congressional Declaration of War on Cuba or the Cuban Resolution of the 87th Congress.
> Track D: Full-scale invasion, to "take Cuba away from Castro."

Obviously any one of these could lead to one of the others—but each represents a distinguishable approach to the problem.

6. Within Tracks A and C, the political actions, pressures and warnings could include one or more of the following:

    a. Letter to Khrushchev

        —Stating if ever offensive bases exist, they will be struck; or

        —Warning that we know they exist, and must be dismantled or they will be struck; or

        —Summoning him to a Summit, offering to withdraw our MRBM's from Turkey, etc.

    b. Letter to Castro

        —Warning him of action if bases not dismantled; and/or

        —Seeking to separate him from Soviets on grounds that they are willing to see him destroyed

    c. Take this threat to the peace before the UN, requesting inspection team, etc.

    d. Take this threat to the Hemisphere to the OAS and obtain authorization for action.

7. Within Tracks A and B, the most likely military alternatives aside from blockade and invasion include the following:

    a. A 50 sortie, 1 swoop air strike limited to the missile complex, followed by open surveillance and announcement that future missile sites would be similarly struck.

    b. Broadened air strikes to eliminate all Cuban air power or other retaliatory capacity, up to 200 sortie (one day's activities).

    c. Not yet considered: Commando raid, under air cover, by helicopter or otherwise, to take out missiles with bullets, destroy launches, and leave.

    d. Note: It is generally agreed that we must also be prepared to take further action to protect Guantanamo, from which dependents will have to be evacuated in advance.

8. Other questions or points of disagreement

    a. Whether Soviet reaction would be more intense to Tracks A, B, C or D

    b. Whether Moscow would be either able or willing to prevent Soviet missile commanders from firing on United States when attacked, or Castro and/or his Air Force or any part of it attacking U.S. mainland. This includes the further question of whether, if a military strike is to take place, it must take place before these missiles become operational in the next 2 weeks or so.

    c. Whether Soviets would make, or threaten in response to any note, an equivalent attack on U.S. missiles in Turkey or Italy—or attack Berlin or somewhere else—or confine themselves to stirring up UN and world opinion.

    d. What our response would be to such a Soviet attack—or a Soviet defiance of blockade—and what their response would be to our response

    e. Whether Castro would risk total destruction by sending planes to U.S. mainland—or be able to control all his planes

    f. Whether any Congressmen should be consulted, whether war need be declared, whether the President should cancel all remaining speeches

    g. Whether NATO allies should be briefed at highest level by high-level spokesman

    h. Fate of the 1100 prisoners under any alternative

    i. Whether it would be helpful to obtain a public (UN) and private (Gromyko) denial

    j. To what extent any advance notice—through political notes or pressure, etc.—makes more difficult the military's task, if in the meantime
       —the missiles are concealed; or
       —the missiles become operational

    k. Whether, if missiles are taken out, the Soviets would bring in additional missiles—or, if aware of continued surveillance, would find "their bayonets had struck steel instead of mush" and therefore desist

    l. Whether reservists call-up, National Emergency, or Declaration of War by a reconvened Congress are necessary

    m. How successful we would be in justifying to world military action against Cuba

    n. Whether the effect on our allies would be worse if we do strike or if we do not.

John F. Kennedy's Television Address, 1962

This Government, as promised, has maintained the closest surveillance of the Soviet military buildup on the island of Cuba. Within the past week unmistakable evidence has established the fact that a series of offensive missile sites is now in preparation on that imprisoned island. The purpose of these bases can be none other than to provide a nuclear strike capability against the Western Hemisphere.

Upon receiving the first preliminary hard information of this nature last Tuesday morning [October 16] at 9:00 A.M., I directed that our surveillance be stepped up. And having now confirmed and completed our evaluation of the evidence and our decision on a course of action, this Government feels obliged to report this new crisis to you in fullest detail.

The characteristics of these new missile sites indicate two distinct types of installations. Several of them include medium-range ballistic missiles capable of carrying a nuclear warhead for a distance of more than 1,000 nautical miles. Each of these missiles, in short, is capable of striking Washington, D.C., the Panama Canal, Cape Canaveral, Mexico City, or any other city in the southeastern part of the United States, in Central America, or in the Caribbean area.

Additional sites not yet completed appear to be designed for intermediate-range ballistic missiles capable of traveling more than twice as far—and thus capable of striking most of the major cities in the Western Hemisphere, ranging as far north as Hudson Bay, Canada, and as far south as Lima, Peru. In addition, jet bombers, capable of carrying nuclear weapons, are now being uncrated and assembled in Cuba, while the necessary air bases are being prepared.

This urgent transformation of Cuba into an important strategic base—by the presence of these large, long-range, and clearly offensive weapons of sudden mass destruction—constitutes an explicit threat to the peace and security of all the Americas, in flagrant and deliberate defiance of the Rio Pact of 1947, the traditions of this nation and hemisphere, the Joint Resolution of the 87th Congress, the Charter of the United Nations, and my own public warnings to the Soviets on September 4 and 13.

This action also contradicts the repeated assurances of Soviet spokesmen, both publicly and privately delivered, that the arms buildup in Cuba would retain its original defensive character and that the Soviet Union had no need or desire to station strategic missiles on the territory of any other nation.

The size of this undertaking makes clear that it has been planned for some months. Yet only last month, after I had made clear the distinction between any introduction of ground-to-ground missiles and the existence of defensive antiaircraft missiles, the Soviet Government publicly stated on September 11 that, and I quote, "The armaments and military equipment sent to Cuba are designed exclusively for defensive purposes," and, and I quote the Soviet Government, "There is no need for the Soviet Government to shift its weapons for a retaliatory blow to any other country, for instance Cuba," and that, and I quote the Government, "The Soviet Union has so powerful rockets to carry these nuclear warheads that there is no need to search for sites for them beyond the boundaries of the Soviet Union." That statement was false.

Only last Thursday, as evidence of this rapid offensive buildup was already in my hand, Soviet Foreign Minister Gromyko told me in my office that he was instructed to make it clear once again, as he said his Government had already done, that Soviet assistance to Cuba, and I quote, "pursued solely the purpose of contributing to the defense capabilities of Cuba," that, and I quote him, "training by Soviet specialists of Cuban nationals in handling defensive armaments was by no means offensive," and that "if it were otherwise," Mr. Gromyko went on, "the Soviet Government would never become involved in rendering such assistance." That statement also was false.

Neither the United States of America nor the world community of nations can tolerate deliberate deception and offensive threats on the part of any nation, large or small. We no longer live in a world where only the actual firing of weapons represents a sufficient challenge to a nation's security to constitute maximum peril. Nuclear weapons are so destructive and ballistic missiles are so swift that any substantially increased possibility of their use or any sudden change in their deployment may well be regarded as a definite threat to peace.

For many years both the Soviet Union and the United States, recognizing this fact, have deployed strategic nuclear weapons with great care, never upsetting the precarious *status quo* which insured that these weapons would not be used in the absence of some vital challenge. Our own strategic missiles have never been transferred to the territory of any other nation under a cloak of secrecy and deception; and our history, unlike that of the Soviets since the end of World War II, demonstrates that we have no desire to dominate or conquer any other nation or impose our system upon its people. Nevertheless, American citizens have become adjusted to living daily on the bull's eye of Soviet missiles located inside the U.S.S.R. or in submarines.

In that sense missiles in Cuba add to an already clear and present danger— although it should be noted the nations of Latin America have never previously been subjected to a potential nuclear threat.

But this secret, swift, and extraordinary buildup of Communist missiles— in an area well known to have a special and historical relationship to the United States and the nations of the Western Hemisphere, in violation of Soviet assurances, and in defiance of American and hemispheric policy—this sudden, clandestine decision to station strategic weapons for the first time outside of Soviet soil—is a deliberately provocative and unjustified change in the *status quo* which cannot be accepted by this country if our courage and our commitments are ever to be trusted again by either friend or foe.

The 1930's taught us a clear lesson: Aggressive conduct, if allowed to grow unchecked and unchallenged, ultimately leads to war. This nation is opposed to war. We are also true to our word. Our unswerving objective, therefore, must be to prevent the use of these missiles against this or any other country and to secure their withdrawal or elimination from the Western Hemisphere.

Our policy has been one of patience and restraint, as befits a peaceful and powerful nation, which leads a worldwide alliance. We have been determined not to be diverted from our central concerns by mere irritants and fanatics. But now further action is required—and it is underway; and these actions may only be the beginning. We will not prematurely or unnecessarily risk the costs of worldwide nuclear war in which even the fruits of victory would be ashes in our mouth—but neither will we shrink from that risk at any time it must be faced.

Acting, therefore, in the defense of our own security and of the entire Western Hemisphere, and under the authority entrusted to me by the Constitution as endorsed by the resolution of the Congress, I have directed that the following *initial* steps be taken immediately:

> *First:* To halt this offensive buildup, a strict quarantine on all offensive military equipment under shipment to Cuba is being initiated. All ships of any kind bound for Cuba from whatever nation or port will, if found to contain cargoes of offensive weapons, be turned back. This quarantine will be extended, if needed, to other types of cargo and carriers. We are not at this time, however, denying the necessities of life as the Soviets attempted to do in their Berlin blockade of 1948.
>
> *Second:* I have directed the continued and increased close surveillance of Cuba and its military buildup. The Foreign Ministers of the OAS in their communique of October 3 rejected secrecy on such matters in this hemisphere. Should these offensive military preparations continue, thus increasing the threat to the hemisphere, further action will be justified. I have directed the Armed

Forces to prepare for any eventualities; and I trust that, in the interest of both the Cuban people and the Soviet technicians at the sites, the hazards to all concerned of continuing this threat will be recognized.

Third: It shall be the policy of this nation to regard any nuclear missile launched from Cuba against any nation in the Western Hemisphere as an attack by the Soviet Union on the United States, requiring a full retaliatory response upon the Soviet Union.

Fourth: As a necessary military precaution I have reinforced our base at Guantanamo, evacuated today the dependents of our personnel there, and ordered additional military units to be on a standby alert basis.

Fifth: We are calling tonight for an immediate meeting of the Organ of Consultation, under the Organization of American States, to consider this threat to hemispheric security and to invoke articles 6 and 8 of the Rio Treaty in support of all necessary action. The United Nations Charter allows for regional security arrangements—and the nations of this hemisphere decided long ago against the military presence of outside powers. Our other allies around the world have also been alerted.

Sixth: Under the Charter of the United Nations, we are asking tonight that an emergency meeting of the Security Council be convoked without delay to take action against this latest Soviet threat to world peace. Our resolution will call for the prompt dismantling and withdrawal of all offensive weapons in Cuba, under the supervision of U.N. observers, before the quarantine can be lifted.

Seventh and finally: I call upon Chairman Khrushchev to halt and eliminate this clandestine, reckless, and provocative threat to world peace and to stable relations between our two nations. I call upon him further to abandon this course of world domination and to join in an historic effort to end the perilous arms race and transform the history of man. He has an opportunity now to move the world back from the abyss of destruction—by returning to his Government's own words that it had no need to station missiles outside its own territory, and withdrawing these weapons from Cuba—by refraining from any action which will widen or deepen the present crisis—and then by participating in a search for peaceful and permanent solutions.

This nation is prepared to present its case against the Soviet threat to peace, and our own proposals for a peaceful world, at any time and in any forum—in the OAS, in the United Nations, or in any other meeting that could be useful—without limiting our freedom of action.

We have in the past made strenuous efforts to limit the spread of nuclear weapons. We have proposed the elimination of all arms and military bases in a fair and effective disarmament treaty. We are prepared to discuss new proposals for the removal of tensions on both sides—including the possibilities of a genuinely independent Cuba, free to determine its own destiny. We have no wish to war with the Soviet Union, for we are a peaceful people who desire to live in peace with all other peoples.

But it is difficult to settle or even discuss these problems in an atmosphere of intimidation. That is why this latest Soviet threat—or any other threat which is made either independently or in response to our actions this week—must and will be met with determination. Any hostile move anywhere in the world against the safety and freedom of peoples to whom we are committed—including in particular the brave people of West Berlin—will be met by whatever action is needed.

Finally, I want to say a few words to the captive people of Cuba, to whom this speech is being directly carried by special radio facilities. I speak to you as a friend, as one who knows of your deep attachment to your fatherland, as one who shares your aspirations for liberty and justice for all. And I have watched and the American people have watched with deep sorrow how your nationalist revolution was betrayed and how your fatherland fell under foreign domination. Now your leaders are no longer Cuban leaders inspired by Cuban ideals. They are puppets and agents of an international conspiracy which has turned Cuba against your friends and neighbors in the Americas—and turned it into the first Latin American country to become a target for nuclear war, the first Latin American country to have these weapons on its soil.

These new weapons are not in your interest. They contribute nothing to your peace and well-being. They can only undermine it. But this country has no wish to cause you to suffer or to impose any system upon you. We know that your lives and land are being used as pawns by those who deny you freedom.

Many times in the past the Cuban people have risen to throw out tyrants who destroyed their liberty. And I have no doubt that most Cubans today look forward to the time when they will be truly free—free from foreign domination, free to choose their own leaders, free to select their own system, free to own their own land, free to speak and write and worship without fear or degradation. And then shall Cuba be welcomed back to the society of free nations and to the associations of this hemisphere.

My fellow citizens, let no one doubt that this is a difficult and dangerous effort on which we have set out. No one can foresee precisely what course it will take or what costs or casualties will be incurred. Many months of sacrifice and self-discipline lie ahead—months in which both our patience and our will will be tested, months in which many threats and denunciations will keep us aware of our dangers. But the greatest danger of all would be to do nothing.

The path we have chosen for the present is full of hazards, as all paths are; but it is the one most consistent with our character and courage as a nation and our commitments around the world. The cost of freedom is always high— but Americans have always paid it. And one path we shall never choose, and that is the path of surrender or submission.

Our goal is not the victory of might but the vindication of right—not peace at the expense of freedom, but both peace *and* freedom, here in this hemisphere and, we hope, around the world. God willing, that goal will be achieved.

Nikita Khrushchev's Letter to the President, 1962

I understand your concern for the security of the United States, Mr. President, because this is the first duty of the president. However, these questions are also uppermost in our minds. The same duties rest with me as chairman of the USSR Council of Ministers. You have been worried over our assisting Cuba with arms designed to strengthen its defensive potential—precisely defensive potential—because Cuba, no matter what weapons it had, could not compare with you since these are different dimensions, the more so given up-to-date means of extermination.

Our purpose has been and is to help Cuba, and no one can challenge the humanity of our motives aimed at allowing Cuba to live peacefully and develop as its people desire. You want to relieve your country from danger and this is understandable. However, Cuba also wants this. All countries want to relieve themselves from danger. But how can we, the Soviet Union and our government, assess your actions which, in effect, mean that you have surrounded the Soviet Union with military bases, surrounded our allies with military bases, set up military bases literally around our country, and stationed your rocket weapons at them? This is no secret. High-placed American officials demonstratively declare this. Your rockets are stationed in Britain and in Italy and pointed at us. Your rockets are stationed in Turkey.

You are worried over Cuba. You say that it worries you because it lies at a distance of 90 miles across the sea from the shores of the United States. However, Turkey lies next to us. Our sentinels are pacing up and down and watching each other. Do you believe that you have the right to demand security for your country and the removal of such weapons that you qualify as offensive, while not recognizing this right for us?

You have stationed devastating rocket weapons, which you call offensive, in Turkey literally right next to us. How then does recognition of our equal military possibilities tally with such unequal relations between our great states? This does not tally at all.

It is good, Mr. President, that you agreed for our representatives to meet and begin talks, apparently with the participation of U.N. Acting Secretary General U Thant. Consequently, to some extent, he assumes the role of intermediary, and we believe that he can cope with the responsible mission if, of course, every side that is drawn into this conflict shows good will.

I think that one could rapidly eliminate the conflict and normalize the situation. Then people would heave a sigh of relief, considering that the statesmen who bear the responsibility have sober minds, an awareness of their responsibility, and an ability to solve complicated problems and not allow matters to slide to the disaster of war.

This is why I make this proposal: We agree to remove those weapons from Cuba which you regard as offensive weapons. We agree to do this and to state this commitment in the United Nations. Your representatives will make a statement to the effect that the United States, on its part, bearing in mind the anxiety and concern of the Soviet state, will evacuate its analogous weapons from Turkey. Let us reach an understanding on what time you and we need to put this into effect.

After this, representatives of the U.N. Security Council could control on-the-spot the fulfillment of these commitments. Of course, it is necessary that the Governments of Cuba and Turkey would allow these representatives to come to their countries and check fulfillment of this commitment, which each side undertakes. Apparently, it would be better if these representatives enjoyed the trust of the Security Council and ours—the United States and the Soviet Union—as well as of Turkey and Cuba. I think that it will not be difficult to find such people who enjoy the trust and respect of all interested sides.

We, having assumed this commitment in order to give satisfaction and hope to the peoples of Cuba and Turkey and to increase their confidence in their security, will make a statement in the Security Council to the effect that the Soviet Government gives a solemn pledge to respect the integrity of the frontiers and the sovereignty of Turkey, not to intervene in its domestic affairs, not to invade Turkey, not to make available its territory as a place d'armes for such invasion, and also will restrain those who would think of launching an aggression against Turkey either from Soviet territory or from the territory of other states bordering on Turkey.

The U.S. Government will make the same statement in the Security Council with regard to Cuba. It will declare that the United States will respect the integrity of the frontiers of Cuba, its sovereignty, undertakes not to intervene in its domestic affairs, not to invade and not to make its territory available as place d'armes for the invasion of Cuba, and also will restrain those who would think of launching an aggression against Cuba either from U.S. territory or from the territory of other states bordering on Cuba.

Of course, for this we would have to reach agreement with you and to arrange for some deadline. Let us agree to give some time, but not to delay, two or three weeks, not more than a month.

The weapons on Cuba, that you have mentioned and which, as you say, alarm you, are in the hands of Soviet officers. Therefore any accidental use of them whatsoever to the detriment of the United States of America is excluded. These means are stationed in Cuba at the request of the Cuban Government and only in defensive aims. Therefore, if there is no invasion of Cuba, or an attack on the Soviet Union, or other of our allies then, of course, these means do not threaten anyone and will not threaten. For they do not pursue offensive aims.

If you accept my proposal, Mr. President, we would send our representatives to New York, to the United Nations, and would give them exhaustive instructions to order to come to terms sooner. If you would also appoint your men and give them appropriate instructions, this problem could be solved soon.

Why would I like to achieve this? Because the entire world is now agitated and expects reasonable actions from us. The greatest pleasure for all the peoples would be an announcement on our agreement, on nipping in the bud the conflict that has arisen. I attach a great importance to such understanding because it might be a good beginning and, specifically, facilitate a nuclear test ban agreement. The problem of tests could be solved simultaneously, not linking one with the other, because they are different problems. However, it is important to reach an understanding to both these problems in order to make a good gift to the people, to let them rejoice in the news that a nuclear test ban agreement has also been reached and thus there will be no further contamination of the atmosphere. Your and our positions on this issue are very close.

All this, possibly, would serve as a good impetus to searching for mutually acceptable agreements on other disputed issues, too, on which there is an exchange of opinion between us. These problems have not yet been solved but they wait for an urgent solution which would clear the international atmosphere. We are ready for this.

These are my proposals, Mr. President.

ESSAYS

Walt W. Rostow of the University of Texas was a State Department official during the Cuban Missile Crisis. Formerly an economist at the Massachusetts Institute of Technology and later, from 1966 to 1969, an influential special assistant to President Lyndon B. Johnson, Rostow holds strong opinions on the events of the hectic 1960s. In the first essay, from his book *Diffusion of Power,* Rostow applauds what he considers the cool-headedness of the American response to the missiles and explains why they were placed in Cuba: Khrushchev was "at bay."

Political scientist James A. Nathan of the University of Delaware is skeptical that the handling of the crisis was Kennedy's finest hour. Nathan doubts that the crisis was managed well, suggests that domestic political considerations helped to determine the President's diplomacy, emphasizes the importance of "appearances," and concludes that American civilian leaders were so impressed with their performance that "toughness" thereafter became their watchword.

The Genius of the American Response

WALT W. ROSTOW

The Cuba missile crisis is clearly one of the bench marks in modern history. All its consequences cannot, even now, be assessed; for example, the subsequent gross expansion of Soviet nuclear and naval capabilities. It is also a crisis about which, at the American end, a great deal is known. The purpose here is not to rehearse the details but to try to put the crisis into perspective as Khrushchev's climactic effort in the post-Sputnik offensive and to lay a basis for analyzing its subsequent wide-ranging effects within both the communist and noncommunist worlds.

While the literature on the missile crisis itself is ample, there is still ambiguity, debate, and unavoidable ignorance about why, when, and how Khrushchev and his colleagues decided to risk putting the missiles into Cuba.

Elie Abel, a competent and vivid chronicler of the crisis, explains its origins essentially on the grounds that Kennedy's performance down to October 22,

1962, had persuaded Khrushchev that he lacked the fiber to force the removal of the missiles once they were secretly installed. He points to the Bay of Pigs, Kennedy's failure to knock down the Berlin Wall, and Khrushchev's alleged assessment of Kennedy in Vienna. Something like Abel's view is the conventional judgment.

Before the event, as well as during and after, I took a somewhat different view. I judged that Khrushchev, in the spring of 1962, was under extremely powerful pressures to retrieve a waning situation. On August 20, 1962, I gave a speech at the National War College entitled "Khrushchev at Bay"; and it was in similar terms that I initiated discussion of the situation during the following week in meetings with my fellow planners throughout Washington and my colleagues in the State Department, including Dean Rusk.

Why was Khrushchev at bay? He was at bay because by the spring of 1962 his initial post-Sputnik hopes and dispositions had grossly failed: he had greatly committed himself on Berlin but had been unable to shift the Western position; he had failed to achieve a foothold in the Congo; Castro was isolated and neutralized by the OAS, and the Alliance for Progress dimmed longer-run prospects for communist expansion in Latin America; prospects in Southeast Asia were reduced by the July 1962 Geneva Accords on Laos and Kennedy's commitment to Vietnam after the Taylor mission.

On the strategic level, the image of the missile gap had been reversed and the Berlin crisis had triggered a substantial expansion of American arms. This, in turn, increased pressure on Khrushchev for expanded Soviet military outlays to which he had to accede at some cost to economic growth. Aside from increased military outlays, the Soviet economy was slowing down (and there was acute difficulty in agriculture) at a time when American growth was accelerating. Finally, the Moscow meeting at the end of 1960 had failed either to unify the communist movement or to isolate Peking.

All this translated into real political pressures on Khrushchev as the Soviet leader.

Those pressures were evident at the Twenty-Second Party Congress, which opened on October 17, 1961. Out of the Congress emerged a situation where Khrushchev, continuing to use de-Stalinization as a political weapon, failed to eliminate some of his opponents; and he found his power further hedged about by the new constitution of the Presidium, as it had been since the aftermath of the U-2 incident. He was also denied by the decisions of the Congress the resources he wished to invest in agriculture and the expansion of civil consumption. The military had clearly found allies at the Congress and successfully asserted their interests. A whole range of constraints on civil consumption was put into effect in the spring of 1962, including a rise of 20–30 percent in the price of meat and butter.

Khrushchev was under unrelenting ideological pressure from Peking (and Albania) to move forward more decisively against "the imperialists," and Ulbricht had not been fully satisfied by the Wall.

Thus, in the spring of 1962, Khrushchev was looking for a quick success which would enhance his political prestige and power in Soviet politics; enhance his authority in the international communist movement and reduce the pressures on him from Ulbricht as well as the Chinese; redress the military balance cheaply in terms of resources, and thereby permit more Russian resources to flow into civil investment and consumption; and provide leverage for the resolution of the Berlin problem he had sought without success since 1958.

Khrushchev's rationale after the missile crisis was couched in terms of an alleged Cuban request for the missiles to fend off an alleged impending invasion by the United States: a view Castro promptly denied and then elaborated at length in a speech of March 13, 1965, reprinted in *Pravda*. Khrushchev's memoir, nevertheless, tries to perpetuate his initial rationale. But he also acknowledges that he sought, with MRBM's already available, to equalize the nuclear balance of power.

> In addition to protecting Cuba, our missiles would have equalized what the West likes to call "the balance of power." The Americans had surrounded our country with military bases and threatened us with nuclear weapons, and now they would learn just what it feels like to have enemy missiles pointing at you; we'd be doing nothing more than giving them a little of their own medicine. And it was high time America learned what it feels like to have her own land and her own people threatened. We Russians have suffered three wars over the last half century: World War I, the Civil War, and World War II. America has never had to fight a war on her own soil, at least not in the past fifty years. She's sent troops abroad to fight in the two World Wars—and made a fortune as a result. America has shed a few drops of her own blood while making billions by bleeding the rest of the world dry.

Khrushchev dates the time when the idea seized him—when "all these thoughts kept churning in my head"—to his visit to Bulgaria, completed on May 21. He then describes how he came back to Moscow and persuaded his colleagues to launch the plan, making clear it was collectively approved.

Khrushchev may or may not be precise about timing. His dating of events in his memoir is notably fuzzy. He evidently did not have his files with him in his dacha after retirement. In any case, a good deal was happening in the spring of 1962 in Moscow. In late April two Soviet marshals, associated with the missile command, were relieved of their posts, to be restored only in November. Possibly they opposed the Cuban venture, which may have been discussed at a Presidium meeting at the time of the Supreme Soviet, April 22–25. The tone of Soviet statements about Berlin began to harden, after a quiet interval, on May 3 when *Pravda* carried a major article on Berlin warning the West that "whoever sows the wind will reap the whirlwind." The Soviet-Bulgarian communique of May 21 revived the threat of a separate peace treaty. The June Warsaw Pact communique promised the West "a bitter awakening."

On April 28, in the week when the hardening on Berlin could be noted, Cuban Minister of Public Works Osmani Cienfuegos was seen by Khrushchev, who also saw the Cuban ambassador on May 5. At the beginning of June, Khrushchev spoke of a new flow of arms to Cuba which might have a salutary "effect on the minds of those who are thinking of starting a new war." At just this period Washington was receiving reports from Moscow that Chinese diplomats were going about town saying they were quite pleased with the Russians who had found a "new way" to solve the Berlin problem. Raul Castro arrived in Moscow on July 2, and enlarged flows of military equipment moved to Cuba during that month, continuing through August. With the scale of the operation impossible to conceal, increased arms deliveries to Cuba were formally announced September 3, on the occasion of Che Guevara's stay in Moscow. Khrushchev then undertook his campaign to deceive Kennedy on the character of the shipments and to "reassure" him on Berlin.

On September 12 *Pravda* carried the following statement:

> The Soviet Government has authorized Tass to declare that the Soviet Union does not need to ship to any country, to Cuba for instance, any actual equipment in order to repel aggression and deal a retaliatory blow. The explosive force of our nuclear capabilities is so powerful and the Soviet Union has such a large number of powerful rockets for the delivery of these atomic warheads that there is no need to seek any site for their installation outside the borders of the Soviet Union.

Six days earlier Dobrynin had sought out Sorensen and dictated the following personal message from Khrushchev to Kennedy:

> Nothing will be undertaken before the American Congressional elections that could complicate the international situation or aggravate the tension in the relations between our two countries . . . provided there are no actions taken on the other side which would change the situation. This includes a German peace settlement and West Berlin. . . .

To the flow of visitors through Moscow that summer, Khrushchev reaffirmed that the question of Berlin and a German peace settlement would be quiet until after the American election in November; but if the West did not accept his position, there would be serious trouble thereafter. He linked such talk to the possibilities that might open for negotiation upon the occasion of his visit to New York.

Khrushchev's objectives were, then, quite clear: to present Kennedy with the installation of the missiles as a fait accompli under the cover of an enlarged flow of conventional arms; and to come to New York after the congressional elections in November and bargain on Berlin, bases, and other matters from a position of strength cheaply achieved: MRBM's under the American radar screen targeted at the major American cities. As he had underlined at Vienna (in talking about his treaty with East Germany), the situation Khrushchev planned to create in Cuba was one where Kennedy would have to start the war.

At the time, my own crystal ball was by no means that clear; but it was not wholly opaque. The minutes summarizing my presentation to Rusk and my colleagues on August 28 include this passage, following on a description of the frustration of the post-Sputnik offensive and the hopeful prospects it might open up:

> . . . before things get better they may get worse. We must view the present and immediate future as a time of special danger. Khrushchev may seek to break out of his frustrations. Three areas appear to merit special watchfulness:

The arms race: Khrushchev may stake heavily on an important breakthrough that would furnish a hard military base for a renewed offensive.

Berlin: Khrushchev may feel under strong compulsion to achieve at least one success to which he can point, and may be prepared to step up the risk rate over Berlin.

Cuba: Khrushchev may be unwilling to accept as final the failure of Cuba to produce automatic gains in Latin America and may decide to increase substantially Soviet outlays and risks to secure a payoff from Cuba.

Why did Khrushchev believe the Cuba missile plan might work? Why, if Berlin was a major objective, did he not take greater risks there? [Michel] Tatu responds to these questions as follows:

The lengthy negotiations conducted with the West for years had convinced him [Khrushchev] that the Atlantic camp would regard any violation of freedom of access to West Berlin as a *casus belli.* By placing his rockets in Cuba, on the other hand, Khrushchev was doing nothing illegal and was on the contrary forcing his opponent to act illegally if he wished to react at all. . . . In 1961 Kennedy had in fact appeared much firmer on Berlin—where he held out against the very violent pressure of that summer by taking military measures, and so forth—than on Cuba, where he had not dared push his Bay of Pigs operation to its logical conclusion. As seen by the resolute gambler in Moscow, Cuba was the weak spot.

I rather doubt Tatu's observation on the Bay of Pigs. Soviet missiles in Cuba were a different matter than a Cuban refugee operation against Castro. Kennedy at Vienna could not have been more explicit about how he would react to an effort to shift the balance of power; and this, in the most literal sense, is what Khrushchev set out to do.

But I agree with Tatu that it must have seemed attractive to Khrushchev to be acting legally while putting Kennedy in the position of having to initiate military action with no legal basis except some OAS resolutions Khrushchev had probably never read. Looked at from Moscow, the installation of missiles in Cuba must have seemed, in one sense, as legal as the placing of American missiles in Turkey. Khrushchev knew, of course, what Kennedy had said at Vienna about shifting the balance of power. He knew of the Monroe Doctrine and the OAS posture generalized from it, which would deny the legitimacy of extra-continental military intrusion in the hemisphere. What he did not assess correctly is the depth of feeling and determination his act would evoke from Kennedy (or, in my judgment, from any other American President) and the unanimity of the hemispheric response.

As rumors of offensive missiles in Cuba spread, Kennedy set about trying to disabuse Khrushchev of the notion that he would remain passive if offensive missiles turned up. On September 4 he said "the gravest issues" would arise if their presence was established; and on September 13 he volunteered this carefully drafted statement:

If at any time the Communist buildup in Cuba were to endanger or interfere with our security in any way, including our base at Guantanamo, our passage to the Panama Canal, our missile and space activities at Cape Canaveral, or the lives of American citizens in this country, or if Cuba should ever attempt to export its aggressive purposes by force or the threat of force against any nation in this hemisphere, or become an offensive military base of significant capacity for the Soviet Union, then this country will do whatever must be done to protect its own security and that of its allies.

It was a quite complete formulation of the functional approach to Cuba which had emerged since the Bay of Pigs.

As September unfolded, Khrushchev may have had doubts; for example, he never committed himself publicly to go to the U.N. General Assembly. But the operation was rolling, and he was going to see what would happen.

I remember recalling in September 1962 the biography of Khrushchev we had read in galley proofs before Vienna. In a vivid chapter it described the substantial engineering risks Khrushchev took in building the Moscow subway to meet his tight deadline. He was a gambler. If, in fact, he felt at bay, I thought he would go out with a bang rather than a whimper. With the missiles moving across the Atlantic in September, he was embarked on the greatest gamble of his career. I suspect he relished those days. There is even a flavor of pleasurable excitement as he recalls in his memoir the days of most acute crisis: "[I] slept on my couch in the office—and I kept my clothes on. I didn't want to be like that Western minister [Guy Mollet] who was caught literally with his pants down by the Suez events of 1956 and who had to run around in his shorts until the emergency was over." But I believe the Soviet plan was written in such a way as to exclude war with the United States. Khrushchev's statement on this point carries conviction: "I want to make one thing absolutely clear: when we put our ballistic missiles in Cuba, we had no desire to start a war." At no stage during the crisis did the Soviet armed forces go on an alert equivalent to that which governed American forces. The Presidium had acquiesced in Khrushchev's plan; but it had also decided that the gamble would involve Khrushchev's political career, not all the Soviets had achieved since 1917.

The high-level Washington scene from Monday, October 15, to Sunday, October 28, has been about as fully described as any time and place in modern history. In essence, there were these distinct moments of decision: Khrushchev's decision not to force the blockade on October 24; Khrushchev's decision to cease erecting the missiles and to withdraw them on October 28; Castro's decision to reject inspection (circa October 30); Khrushchev's decision to withdraw the IL-14 bombers on November 20.

Once it was decided in Moscow that the blockade would not be forced, Khrushchev had to see what might be salvaged. Kennedy had to see that nothing of substance was salvaged while minimizing Khrushchev's humiliation. The quiet but real buildup of conventional military power in Florida and elsewhere was decisive. I took part in the discussions of October 27 on the appropriate scale of the air strike (which probably would have occurred on Tuesday, October 30) and supported McNamara's case for a limited attack rather than a total assault embracing all the Cuban air bases and antiaircraft installations. Khrushchev smelled the seriousness of all this, and, essentially, his letter of the next day ended the matter, although weeks of tangled diplomacy followed.

I have little to add to knowledge of the mechanics of these events, among other reasons because of my limited part in the day-to-day unfolding of the crisis. I was in Europe during most of the week of deliberations preceding Kennedy's speech of October 22, attending a meeting of the Atlantic Policy Advisory Group, the NATO planners' club created to expand the area of political consultation. I also went to Berlin to see how the viability program was coming along in the face of the Wall. Landing in New York on Friday the 19th, I was told to return promptly to Washington rather than to a Camp David session that had been arranged previously. My first official contact with the crisis was a session in the White House Situation Room on Sunday night, October 21, to go over the draft of Kennedy's speech of the next day. Subsequently, I managed a planning group set up in support of the ExCom (Executive Committee of the NSC). Our contributions were in the form of written reports and the various enterprises we spawned in the form of military plans and diplomatic initiatives. I attended only a few of the ExCom sessions, but I was there on the memorable occasion (October 24) when news arrived that Soviet ships had stopped outside the quarantine area and Rusk made his famous remark on eyeballs and the first blink. As a planner at the time, and in historical retrospect, I would make only a few observations.

First, the genius of Kennedy's blockade—"selective quarantine," as it was termed—was, in part, that it required Khrushchev to initiate military action. It was the obverse of the dilemma posed for the United States by Soviet interference with Allied traffic to Berlin. Khrushchev had to start the war if his merchant ships were to go through. One had the feeling that Soviet contingency planners had never done the kind of laborious work Western planners carried out on the questions of harassment of the Berlin routes. It is even possible that Moscow never anticipated a quarantine or blockade as one of Kennedy's options.

Second, the rallying of the Latin Americans during the missile crisis carried elements of conviction and credibility that were not wholly anticipated. The unanimity of the OAS was an impressive political fact in Moscow, at the United Nations, and elsewhere; and the evoking of the Punta del Este Resolution II of January 1962 gave Kennedy a solid legal basis for his action, urging, as it did, "member states to take those steps they may consider appropriate for their individual or collective self-defense, and to cooperate, as may be necessary or desirable, to strengthen their capacity to counteract threats or acts of aggression, subversion, or other dangers to peace and security resulting from the continued intervention in this hemisphere of Sino-Soviet powers. . . ."

Third, there were real differences of view in the administration as to how dangerous the situation really was; that is, on whether Khrushchev was conducting a hair-raising, precarious probe or whether the Soviet Union had decided to put real muscle behind the endeavor. From any perspective, it was an exceedingly dangerous interval; but one's judgment of Soviet motivation and intent mattered a good deal in assessing how near we all actually were to nuclear war. It was one thing to view Khrushchev's initiative as a full-fledged, deeply meant Russian strategic challenge in the Caribbean; another, to regard it as an

incredibly risky gamble by a man at bay, who would back down if he met resolute force. These differences, intensely felt, came to rest on the question of
whether Kennedy should negotiate out the Turkish missiles to achieve a settlement. Kennedy carried a liability he had earlier tried to liquidate; but he preserved the integrity of NATO by not bargaining a European asset against a
direct American interest. In so doing, I suspect his assessment of the risks was
somewhat higher than that of those who had concluded that Khrushchev's gamble was a desperate effort to retrieve a waning situation but not a determined
Soviet strategic thrust to shift the balance of power.

Fourth, the Washington bureaucracy was remarkably light on its feet, more
generally responsive, alert, and effective than I had seen it in the twenty years or
so over which I had observed or participated in its workings. It operated less
like a governmental machine than like a regimental command post in combat,
despite the extraordinarily complex military and diplomatic enterprise under
way. There was, throughout, a sense of direct and personal command by the
President.

The planning group over which I presided, representing some of the best
minds in the second level of government, was quite like-minded in interpreting
the crisis, its origins, and the implications for the future. We had been meeting
without fail every week on one concrete problem after another, followed by a
lunch in which we would exchange wider perspectives. We had the advantage of
time to reflect at length on the meaning of the sharpening Soviet position on
Berlin since the spring. In the wake of my War College talk, "Khrushchev at
Bay," we had canvassed the possibilities of a convulsive effort by Khrushchev
to retrieve his waning position. We thought his three major options were: Berlin,
an orbiting weapon in space, Cuba. As I recall, Ray Cline of the CIA was the
most perceptive among us. I closed the meeting on August 21 by observing we
might be about to see the greatest act of risk-taking since the war. Cline said:
"Maybe we're seeing it right now in Cuba." But none of us thought Moscow was
about to risk nuclear war. Therefore, our individual and collective advice, from
the beginning to the end of the crisis, was to keep the pressure on Moscow until
the missiles and bombers were out. The only thing we thought had to be bar-
gained away was the quarantine imposed on October 22.

The planners met for some weeks after the peak of the crisis had passed to
probe at its implications.

We all were conscious that the tactical situation in the Caribbean had peculiar
advantages for the United States, given the preponderance of naval, conventional air, and ground strength that could be brought to bear relative to that
which Moscow could mount. We did not believe the outcome of the crisis justified an exuberant or casual application of American military power to resolve
other issues in dispute.

One recommendation was to see if Khrushchev was prepared to move along
the other fork in the nuclear road: toward a nuclear test ban.

In the longer run we judged that Moscow would conduct a fundamental review of its military strategy. The upshot might be: a revision in military doctrine
which would not rule out limited clashes of United States and Soviet military

power, accompanied by a buildup in Soviet conventional military strength; a radical long-term expansion in Soviet ICBM capabilities to achieve a solid balance in United States–Soviet nuclear power; a second effort to achieve an economical shift in the nuclear balance (e.g., weapons orbiting in space); a serious Soviet move toward arms control.

In fact, the Soviet Union did move in the post-Cuba missile crisis years toward a radical buildup in strategic nuclear strength; and it eased cautiously toward the negotiation of a missile agreement as its nuclear strength came into balance with the United States. It also appears to have drawn Mahanist conclusions from its experience with American naval power in the Caribbean. The Cuba missile crisis, in effect, rendered anachronistic current Soviet military doctrine. The great post-Stalin review of Soviet military strategy organized by Marshal V. A. Sokolovsky (published May 1962) had shifted doctrine, to a degree, toward missiles, leaving a diminished though still large role for conventional ground forces. No naval officer contributed to Sokolovsky's volume. The debate Sokolovsky straddled was between "radicals" (like Khrushchev) who believed nuclear missiles permitted a sharp reduction in conventional ground force and naval strength, and "conservatives" who thought in terms of protracted war in Europe, on the ground, in continuity with the sweep of Russian history. On the eve of the Cuba missile crisis, the Sokolovsky volume tended to favor the position of the "radicals," but its moderation tempered the more sweeping pronouncements of Khrushchev, leaving ample place for conventional forces and military claims on the Soviet budget.

But the Sokolovsky doctrine did not fit the case of Cuba. More generally, it did not match a Soviet policy of seeking power and influence in the developing regions, across seas over which Russian military power had never sought to project itself, except in the disastrous Russo-Japanese War. The setback of the Cuba missile crisis dramatized that gap between Soviet policy and its military force structure. It undoubtedly led to the buildup of Soviet naval (as well as strategic nuclear) strength in the 1960s; and, by demonstrating the advantages of logistical proximity, the Cuba missile crisis may well have introduced Moscow to concentrate its expansionist zeal for a time in the Middle East.

Politically, the outcome of the crisis had two major effects in the communist world: it undercut Khrushchev's already eroded power base in Moscow; and it led to a new phase of violent and open polemic between Moscow and Peking.

Tatu cites impressive evidence that Khrushchev began to lose power and status within the collective leadership from as early as October 23, the day after Kennedy announced his response to the challenge. The signs were both symbolic and substantive. They included the renaming on October 25 of the town of Khrushchev to Kremges; oblique attacks on Khrushchev's use of de-Stalinization as a political instrument against his opponents; a shift away from economic liberalism in November; and increased pressure on Soviet intellectuals and artists. A low point came in February–March 1963 when Khrushchev appeared somewhat helpless and disheartened. On February 28 he referred to the fact that he would soon be sixty-nine years old and *Pravda* published his concluding remark: "Thank you for having gathered here to cheer me up, as it were." This was also a time when Moscow made a serious effort to play down the quarrel with Peking, which had accused Khrushchev of first taking excessive risk in launching the Cuba missile crisis and then failing to back his play.

At this point, it appeared that Kozlov, backed by the anti-Khrushchev group in the Presidium, would soon emerge as his successor. But about April 10 Kozlov suffered a severe heart attack; and by the end of the month Khrushchev was engaged in a limited but vigorous comeback. On April 20, 1963, he was confident enough to tell an Italian newspaper director: "... there are times when the rule of one far-seeing man is better than that of several who cannot see."

On this basis he moved to the test ban treaty and revived his campaign against Stalinism. But, while he had gained a transient tactical victory in Kremlin politics, his post-Sputnik strategy was in a shambles. As 1963 drew to a close, nuclear blackmail as a means of pressure on western Europe was, for the time, a discredited device; nowhere in the developing world did he have effective leverage; the Soviet economy was in evident disarray, with a bad harvest requiring large grain imports; and relations with Peking had never been worse.

The Tragic Enshrinement of Toughness

JAMES A. NATHAN

Historians know there is a rhythm to their craft. Events are examined and orthodoxies are established. Then comes a chipping away of previously held convictions. New understandings emerge and stand, at least for a while; and then comes another tide of re-evaluation. The Kennedy Administration's shimmering hour—the Cuban missile crisis—has just begun to have its luster tarnished by critics. Yet few have subjected the event to a complex review of its meaning in terms of the assumptions, policy processes, and relationships of the cold war.

My contention is that the crisis became something of a misleading "model" of the foreign policy process. There are seven central tenets of this model, each of which was "confirmed" by the "lessons" of the Cuban crisis:

1. Crises are typical of international relations. The international environment is a constant collision of wills that is a surrogate of war and, at the same time, takes place at the doorstep of war. Crises are objective elements of the international system—but they also have a profoundly psychological element of "will" and "resolve."

2. Crises are assumed to be manageable. The skills of personality, training, and organizational expertise that have been developed in the national security machinery during the past twenty-five years can be orchestrated by a vast bureaucracy in controlled and responsive movements.

3. Although crises are a characteristic of the international system, the domestic system is one of order and consensus, and is insulated from the neces-

James A. Nathan, "The Missile Crisis: His Finest Hour Now," *World Politics,* 27 (1975), 256–281. Reprinted by permission of Princeton University Press.

sities of international politics. Public opinion can be controlled to lend support for a particular foreign policy; but rarely do appurtenances of the domestic sector have their own imperatives.

4. Diplomacy is a mixture of the instrumentation of force and bargaining. An essential element of crisis management is the ability to reconcile the inherent forward dynamic of violence, threats of violence, and the instruments of violence with negotiation.

5. The United States can control the process of crisis negotiation to "win." "Winning" results in the conclusion of the events themselves. Political crises therefore terminate by definition, almost like medical crises.

6. The Soviets seldom negotiate serious matters except under extreme duress.

7. Military questions are too critical to be left in the hands of strictly military men and organizations that are not in step with the needs of crisis management. Crisis management can and must be a civilian enterprise.

After the Cuban missile crisis, there were the beginnings of détente with the Soviet Union. The test-ban treaty, the hot line, and a more civil exchange between the two powers are widely believed to stem from the favorable resolution of the missile crisis. Yet the model and the usual inherent assumptions on the meaning of Cuba can be challenged. Nevertheless, the Cuban missile crisis stands as a watershed of the cold war and in the history of the contemporary international system.

By far the most intense experience in East-West relations occurred in October 1962, when the Russians were discovered to have placed forty-two medium-range missiles in Cuba. In Khrushchev's apt description, it was a time when "a smell of burning hung heavy" in the air. Kennedy's apparently controlled and masterful way of forcing Khrushchev to withdraw the missiles in the thirteen-day crisis has become a paradigmatic example of the way force can be harnessed to a policy by an elaborate manipulation of threats and gambits, negotiation and intimidation. Academic and government analysts have viewed Kennedy's response as a highly calibrated dissection of alternatives instead of seeing his actions as largely an intuitive response to a threat to his administration's electoral future, pride, and strategic posture. As Hans J. Morgenthau, the eminent scholar and a critic of the Kennedy Administration, concluded: "The Cuban Crisis of 1962 . . . was the distillation of a collective intellectual effort of a high order, the like of which must be rare in history." Much of this analysis—so drenched in the cool light of hindsight—bears a suspicious resemblance to the logical and psychological fallacy of reasoning, *post hoc, ergo propter hoc.* Nevertheless, the dominant lesson Americans have drawn from the Cuban experience has been a joyous sense of the United States regaining mastery over history.

For many years Americans had felt threatened by the Soviet challenge to world order—especially since that challenge had been reinforced by growing Russian strategic capability. But after Cuba, the fears of precipitate expansion of a Soviet-American dispute into a final paroxysm of nuclear dust were dissipated. After Cuba, "escalation" became the *idée fixe* of academics and policy-makers —a vision of a ladder of force with rungs separated by equivalent spaces of destruction, each with its own "value," running out toward darkness. Escalation became the dominant metaphor of American officialdom. Each rung could be ascended or descended with the proper increment of will and control. Events and military machines could be mastered for diplomatic ends. As Robert McNamara exalted after the exciting and frightening Cuban climax: "There is no longer any such thing as strategy, only crisis management." Dennis Healy, the British Labor Party "shadow" Defense Minister called the Kennedy Administration's performance a "model in any textbook on diplomacy." Journalist Henry Pachter described Kennedy's execution of crisis management as "a feat whose technical elegance compelled the professionals' admiration." Similarly, the Wohlstetters made Cuba into a general historical principle about the use of force in times of great stress: "where the alternative is to be ruled by events with such enormous consequences, the head of a great state is likely to examine his acts of choice in crisis and during it to subdivide these possible acts in ways that make it feasible to continue exercising choice."

The decisions as to what steps should be taken to deal with the implantation of the missiles were hammered out in the ExCom meetings. Although court chroniclers of the Kennedy Administration have pored over each detail, the impression now is not one of all choices having been carefully weighed and considered. Rather, in retrospect, there appears to have been a gripping feeling of uncertainty and pressure. Robert Kennedy, for instance, at the height of the crisis, looked across at his brother and almost fainted at the horror of what they were contemplating: "Inexplicably, I thought of when he was ill and almost died; when he lost his child, when we learned that our oldest brother had been killed; of personal times of strain and hurt. The voices droned on, but I didn't seem to hear anything. . . ."

There were reports that one Assistant Secretary was so disconcerted and fatigued that he drove into a tree at 4 a.m. Robert Kennedy recalled, "The strain and the hours without sleep were beginning to take their toll. . . . That kind of pressure does strange things to a human being, even to brilliant, self-confident, mature, experienced men." And President Kennedy, although deliberately pacing himself, wondered if some of his principal advisors had not suffered mental collapse from the long hours and pressure. Tense, fearful, and exhausted men planned and held together the American policy response to the Russian missiles.

The consensus of most behavioral research is that men operating under such acute stress are scarcely capable of considered judgment. Strain and fatigue commonly produce actions which are "caricatures of day-to-day behavior." Although the stress of crisis decision-making concentrates and focuses the collective mind, it does not allow for the kind of elegant dissection of events that is now read into the Cuban affair. Events can take charge of decision-makers; on October 25, 1962, Robert Kennedy reported that he felt, as Soviet ships drew near the edge of the American quarantine, that "[W]e were on the edge of a precipice with no way off. . . . President Kennedy had initiated the course of events, but he no longer had control over them." John F. Kennedy's calm public face, discipline, and cool control gave a sense of intellectual engagement in the crisis which yielded no hint of the mute wasteland he was contemplating. But his private anxiety is well recorded, and a case can be made that dispassionate analysis or problem-solving was all but precluded by the psychology of the situation.

It was very close. The military and the "hawks"—a term coined by journalistic descriptions of the ExCom deliberations—were pushing for actions ranging from a "surgical strike" to an all-out invasion of Cuba. Such options would have demanded the stark choice of an even greater Soviet humiliation or a Soviet response in kind. Ironically, a "surgical strike" was not really practical, for there was no guarantee that more than 90 percent of the missiles could be extirpated. Even after an American air attack, some of the missiles could have survived and been launched. And "surgical" always was a misnomer to describe an estimated 25,000 Cuban fatalities, not to speak of the 500 sorties which American planes would have had to run in order to "take out" the Soviet missiles and bombers. Nevertheless, if six out of fourteen members of the ExCom group had had their way, the blockade of Cuba would have been an attack, which Bobby Kennedy called a "Pearl Harbor in reverse." It is no wonder that President Kennedy estimated the world's chance of avoiding war at between one out of three and even.

The illusion of control derived from the crisis was perniciously misleading. Although many Americans shared the belief of historian Schlesinger that the Cuban crisis displayed to the "whole world . . . the ripening of an American leadership unsurpassed in the responsible management of power . . . [a] combination of toughness . . . nerve and wisdom, so brilliantly controlled, so matchlessly calibrated that [it] dazzled the world," President Kennedy's control was in fact far from complete. For example, the main instrument of pressure was the blockade run by the Navy. Following the suggestion of British Ambassador Ormsby-Gore, Kennedy decided to move the blockade closer to Cuba, from 800 miles to 500 miles, in order to give the Russian ships heading toward Cuba more time. The order was given but never carried out. The blockade remained at 800 miles.

McNamara had sensed the Navy's lack of responsiveness to civilian commands and had gone to the "Flag Plot," or Naval Operations Center, where he could talk to ship commanders directly by voice-scrambled radio. McNamara pointed to a map symbol indicating that a ship was in a spot where he had not wanted it. "What's that ship doing there?" he asked. Anderson confessed, "I don't know, but I have faith in my officers." McNamara's unease with the apparent lack of responsiveness of the Navy to civilian command prompted him to inquire what would happen if a Soviet captain refused to divulge his cargo to a boarding American officer. Chief of Naval Operations Anderson picked up a Manual of Naval Regulations and rose to defend the Navy against any implied slight about Navy procedure. "It's all in there," Anderson asserted. McNamara retorted, "I don't give a damn what John Paul Jones would have done. I want to know what you are going to do, now!" The last word—again, however—was the Navy's: Admiral Anderson patronizingly soothed the fuming Defense Secretary, "Now, Mr. Secretary, if you and your deputy will go to your offices, the Navy will run the blockade." As McNamara and his entourage turned to leave,

Anderson called to him, "Don't worry, Mr. Secretary, we know what we are doing here."

Just when the first Soviet-American encounter at sea seemed imminent, William Knox, the president of Westinghouse International, who happened to be in Moscow, was surprised by an abrupt summons from Premier Khrushchev. The voluble Soviet leader, perhaps half-convinced that Wall Street really manipulated American policy, gave a frightening summary of the strategic situation in the Caribbean. He warned that if the U.S. Navy began stopping Soviet ships, the Soviet subs would start sinking American ships. That, Khrushchev explained, would lead to World War III.

Only a little later, the Navy began to force Soviet subs to the surface in order to defend its blockade—well before Kennedy had authorized contact with surface vessels. Kennedy was appalled when he learned that military imperatives are distinct from diplomatic necessities and can, all too often, conflict. When he found out that the Navy was intent on surfacing ships, he was horrified: "Isn't there some way we can avoid having our first exchange with a Russian submarine—almost anything but that?" McNamara replied, "No, there's too much danger to our ships. There is no alternative." The President's brother wrote that "all six Russian submarines then in the area or moving toward Cuba from the Atlantic were followed and harassed and, at one time or another, forced to surface in the presence of U.S. military ships." One can only wonder what would have happened if one of the Russian subs had refused to surface and had instead turned on its pursuers.

Events were only barely under control when at the height of the crisis, on October 26, an American U-2 plane fixed on the wrong star and headed back from the North Pole to Alaska via Siberia. To compound matters the Alaskan Air Command sent fighter-bombers to escort the plane home, and the U.S. fighters and the spy plane met over Soviet territory before proceeding back. To survive a Strangelove series of incidents like these, even given the assumptions of the day, can hardly be characterized as more than luck. It would not seem to be the mastery that Schlesinger and other court scribes delight in recalling and extolling.

Why was there a crisis in the first place? The answer is found, in part, in one of the unacknowledged necessities in the conduct of American international affairs—domestic political considerations. The Kennedy Administration's sense of its own precarious electoral position, the coming of the November mid-term elections, and the place Cuba had occupied in public debate, all augured for an immediate and forceful response, no matter what the strategic reality was of having Russian missiles near American borders. The imperatives of American domestic politics during an election year had been building for some time. On August 27, 1962, for example, Republican Senator Homer E. Capehart of Indiana declared, "It is high time that the American people demand that President Kennedy quit 'examining the situation' and start protecting the interests of the United States." Former Vice President Nixon, on the gubernatorial campaign stump in California, proposed that Cuban communism be "quarantined" by a naval blockade. Republicans in both Houses had warned the administration that Cuba would be "the dominant issue of the 1962 campaign." The chairman of the Republican National Committee jabbed at Kennedy's most sensitive spot—his concern for foreign policy "resolve": "If we are asked to state the issue in one word, that word would be Cuba—symbol of the tragic irresolution of the administration."

The pressure mounted. As the political campaign began, one observer spotted a sign at a Kennedy rally in Chicago which read, "Less Profile—More Courage." The widely respected and conservative *London Economist* reported that America had become "obsessed" by the "problem" of Cuba; and I. F. Stone despaired in his *Weekly* that Cuba was a bogey which shook Americans, in the autumn of 1962, even more than the thought of war. The domestic pressure on the American President was so intense that one member of Camelot, former Ambassador John Kenneth Galbraith, wrote: "once they [the missiles] were there, the political needs of the Kennedy administration urged it to take almost any risk to get them out." This skeptical view was shared by none other than former President Eisenhower, who suspected "that Kennedy might be playing politics with Cuba on the eve of Congressional elections."

Nor, as Ronald Steel pointed out, were the "principals"—the ExCom—insulated from domestic considerations in their deliberations. One Republican member of the crisis planners sent Theodore Sorensen—Kennedy's alter ego—a note that read: "Ted—have you considered the very real possibility that if we allow Cuba to complete installation and operational readiness of missile bases, the next House of Representatives is likely to have a Republican majority?" Similarly, McGeorge Bundy, chief advisor to two presidents, wondered, when the missiles were first reported, whether action could be deferred until after the election. If the missile installations were completed earlier, there would be, arguably, both a strategic and an electoral problem facing the administration.

What was the worrisome substance of change in the strategic balance represented by the placement of forty-two missiles? To Robert McNamara, the Secretary of Defense, it seemed that "A missile is a missile. It makes no great difference whether you are killed by a missile from the Soviet Union or from Cuba." About two weeks later, on television, Deputy Secretary of Defense Roswell Gilpatrick confirmed the debatable meaning of the missiles: "I don't believe that we were under any greater threat from the Soviet Union's power, taken in totality, after this than before." Indeed, Theodore Sorensen wrote in a memorandum to the President on October 17, 1962—five days before the blockade was ordered—that the presence of missiles in Cuba did not "significantly alter the balance of power." Sorensen explained, "They do not significantly increase the potential megatonnage capable of being unleashed on American soil, even after a surprise American nuclear strike." Sorensen confessed, in conclusion, that "Soviet motives were not understood."

To Khrushchev, the missiles offered the appearance of what former State Department analyst Roger Hilsman called a "quick fix" to the Soviet problem of strategic inferiority. Khrushchev was under enormous pressure from the Russian military who rejected his "goulash communism" and were pushing for a vast increase in the Soviet arms budget. The Cuban missile ploy was probably Khrushchev's response to the prospect of Russian strategic inferiority which was reported by the Kennedy Administration as it admitted that the Democratic preelection charge of a "missile gap" had not been based on fact. The American announcement that the "gap" had been closed was accompanied by a Defense Department plan, dated October 19, 1961, for production of over one thousand missiles by 1964.

One purpose of the Soviet moves in Cuba was, therefore, to gain the *appearance* of parity with the Americans. The employment of twenty-four MRBM's and eighteen IRBM's *seemed* to be a dramatic movement in that direction. But such an increase posed no real threat to American retaliatory strength, or to increasing American superiority. As Henry Kissinger noted at the time, "The bases were of only marginal use in a defensive war. In an offensive war their effectiveness was reduced by the enormous difficulty—if not impossibility —of coordinating a first strike from the Soviet Union and Cuba."

The U.S. Administration knew that the Soviets were not striving for more than an appearance of strategic equality. As Kennedy later reflected, they were not "intending to fire them, because if they were going to get into a nuclear struggle, they have their own missiles in the Soviet Union. But it would have politically changed the balance of power. It would have appeared to, and appearances contribute to reality." In the 1970's, by contrast, "appearances" were less important while the Americans were arranging a complex international order which verged on duopoly. Indeed, beginning in 1970, Soviet submarines and tenders began to visit Cuban ports. And by 1973, Soviet submarines with Polaris-type missiles were regularly stopping in Cuba. What protest there was by the Nixon Administration seemed so muted as to be almost inaudible.

Why was Kennedy so concerned about "appearances"? Perhaps he felt that the American people demanded an energetic response, given their purported frustration over Cuba. The administration's evaluation of the public mood supported the notion that firmness was a requisite of policy. Although repeated Gallup polls before the crisis showed 90 per cent of Americans opposing actual armed intervention in Cuba, Kennedy's own sense was, as his brother pointed out, that if he did not act, he would have been impeached.

Another explanation for Kennedy's concern that he would not "appear credible" to Khrushchev dates from the time, less than two years earlier, when he decided not to use air support for the Bay of Pigs invasion. According to James Reston's impression upon seeing Kennedy ten minutes after the two leaders had met in Vienna, "Khrushchev had studied the events of the Bay of Pigs; he would have understood if Kennedy had left Castro alone or destroyed him; but when Kennedy was rash enough to strike at Cuba but not bold enough to finish the job, Khrushchev decided he was dealing with an inexperienced young leader who could be intimidated and blackmailed." Similarly, George F. Kennan, then the United States Ambassador to Yugoslavia, met the President after the Vienna summit session and reported that he found Kennedy "strangely tongue-tied" during these talks. Later, he recalled for a Harvard oral history interviewer:

> I felt that he had not acquitted himself well on this occasion and that he had permitted Khrushchev to say many things which should have been challenged right there on the spot.
> I think this was definitely a mistake. I think it definitely misled Khrushchev; I think Khrushchev failed to realize on that occasion what a man he was up against and also that he'd gotten away with many of these talking points; that he had placed President Kennedy in a state of confusion where he had nothing to say in return.

Kennedy expressed concern to Reston and others that Khrushchev considered him but a callow, inexperienced youth and that he soon expected a "test." "It will be a cold winter," he was heard to mutter as he left the Vienna meeting. Khrushchev may indeed have been surprised at the forceful reaction of Kennedy, particularly after the young President had accepted the Berlin Wall in August 1961 with no military response and had temporized in Laos in 1961 and 1962.

Perhaps, as Hilsman has argued, the Soviets assumed that the fine American distinctions between "offensive and defensive" missiles were really a *de facto* acknowledgment of the Soviet effort in Cuba. One could conjecture that this was what led Khrushchev to promise, and to believe that Kennedy understood, that no initiatives would be taken before the elections. In any case, Kennedy's concern about his "appearance" and the national appearance of strength kept him from searching very far for Soviet motivation. His interpretation was that it was a personal injury to him and his credibility, as well as to American power. He explained this sentiment to *New York Post* reporter James Wechsler:

> What worried him was that Khrushchev might interpret his reluctance to wage nuclear war as a symptom of an American loss of nerve. Some day, he said, the time might come when he would have to run the supreme risk to convince Khrushchev that conciliation did not mean humiliation. "If Khrushchev wants to rub my nose in the dirt," he told Wechsler, "it's all over." But how to convince Khrushchev short of a showdown? "That son of a bitch won't pay any attention to words," the President said bitterly on another occasion. "He has to see you move."

The missile crisis illuminates a feature of the American character that came to be considered a requisite personality trait of the cold war: being "tough." Gritty American determination had become the respected and expected stance of American statesmen under stress in confrontations with the Soviets from the earliest days of the cold war. When Truman, for example, dispatched an aircraft carrier, four cruisers, a destroyer flotilla, and the battleship Missouri to counter Soviet pressure on the Turkish Straits, he told Acheson, "We might as well find out whether the Russians [are] bent on world conquest now as in five or ten years." Clark Clifford gave more formal expression to this sentiment when he advised Harry Truman, in a memo, in late 1946: "The language of military power is the only language which disciples of power politics understand. The United States must use that language in order that Soviet leaders will realize that our government is determined to uphold the interest of its citizens and the rights of small nations. Compromise and concessions are considered, by the Soviets, to be evidence of weakness and they are encouraged by our 'retreats' to make new and greater demands."

The American concern with its appearance of strength was a mark of the Kennedy Administration. One White House aide recalled that, especially after the failure of the Bay of Pigs, "Nobody in the White House wanted to be soft. . . . Everybody wanted to show they were just as daring and bold as everybody else."

In the Cuban crisis, the cold-war ethic of being "tough" exacerbated the discrepancies between the necessities of force and the necessities of diplomacy and negotiation. As a result, diplomacy was almost entirely eclipsed. In fact, it was hardly tried. According to Adam Yarmolinsky, an inside observer of the Executive Committee of the National Security Council, "90 per cent of its time" was spent "studying alternative uses of troops, bombers and warships. Although the possibility of seeking withdrawal of the missiles by straightforward diplomatic negotiation received some attention within the State Department, it seems hardly to have been aired in the Ex-Com." Yarmolinsky confesses that it is curious that no negotiations were considered. Nor were economic pressures ever suggested by the foreign affairs bureaucracy. Only a series of military plans emerged, and they varied from a blockade to a preemptive strike.

Kennedy knew the Russians had deployed missiles on October 16. But, instead of facing Soviet Foreign Secretary Gromyko with the evidence while the Russian was giving the President false assurances that missiles were not being installed, the President blandly listened without comment. Whether or not the Russians believed that Kennedy must have known, the effect of the charade was an absence of serious negotiations. Instead of using private channels to warn the Russians that he knew and intended to act, Kennedy chose to give notice to the Russians in a nationwide TV address. After that, a Soviet withdrawal had to be in public and it almost had to be a humiliation. When the Soviets attempted nonetheless to bargain for a graceful retreat, their path was blocked. Kennedy refused Khrushchev's offer of a summit meeting "until Khrushchev first accepted, as a result *of our deeds* as well as our statements, the U.S. determination in the matter." A summit meeting, Kennedy concluded, had to be rejected; for he was intent on offering the Russians "nothing that would tie our hands." We would only negotiate with that which would "strengthen our stand." If there were to be any deals, Kennedy wanted them to seem a part of American munificence. He did not want a compromise to be tied to the central issue of what he conceived to be a test of American will and resolve. "[W]e must stand absolutely firm now. Concessions must come at the end of negotiation, not at the beginning," Robert Kennedy cautioned.

In other words, the Soviets had to submit to American strength before any real concessions could take place. When Khrushchev offered to exchange the Cuban missiles for the Jupiter missiles stationed in Turkey, Kennedy refused, even though he had ordered the missiles out months earlier; in fact, he had thought they were out when Khrushchev brought them to his attention. (The Jupiters were all but worthless. A marksman with a high-powered rifle could knock them out. They took a day to ready for firing and the Turks did not want them.) Kennedy, however, did not want to appear to yield to Soviet pressure even when he might give little and receive a great deal. An agreement would have confounded the issue of "will." As Kennedy's Boswell put it, the President wanted to "concentrate on a single issue—the enormity of the introduction of the missiles and the absolute necessity of their removal."

In the final act of the crisis, Kennedy accepted one of two letters sent almost simultaneously by Khrushchev. One contained the demand for removal of the Turkish missiles; the other did not. Kennedy accepted the latter. Khrushchev's second letter began with a long, heartfelt, personal communication and made no mention of a *quid pro quo*. Kennedy's response was a public letter to Khrushchev, temperate in tone, in which he accepted the more favorable terms he preferred and further detailed American conditions. It is said that Kennedy published his response "in the interests of both speed and psychology." But this procedure of publishing the private terms of an interchange with another head of state was a considerable departure from diplomacy. It was not negotiation; it was, in this context, a public demand. Public statements during a crisis lack flexibility. Compromise is almost foreclosed by such a device, because any bargaining after the terms have been stated seems to be a retreat which would diminish a statesman's reputation. Since reputation was the stake in Cuba as much as anything else, Kennedy's response was hardly more than a polite ultimatum. In private, Kennedy was even more forceful. Robert Kennedy told Soviet Ambassador Dobrynin, "We had to have a commitment by tomorrow that those bases would be removed. . . . If they did not remove those bases, we would remove them. . . . Time was running out. We had only a few more hours—we needed an answer immediately from the Soviet Union. . . . We must have it the next day."

As a result of the crisis, force and toughness became enshrined as instruments of policy. George Kennan observed, as he left forty years of diplomatic service: "There is no presumption more terrifying than that of those who would blow up the world on the basis of their personal judgment of a transient situation. I do not propose to let the future of mankind be settled, or ended, by a group of men operating on the basis of limited perspectives and short-run calculations."

In spite of occasional epistles from the older diplomatists, the new managers who proliferated after Cuba routed those who most favored negotiations. In an article in the *Saturday Evening Post,* one of the last "moderates" of the Kennedy Administration, Adlai Stevenson, was attacked for advocating "a Munich." The source of the story, it was widely rumored, was President Kennedy himself.

The policy of toughness became dogma to such an extent that nonmilitary solutions to political problems were excluded. A "moderate" in this circumstance was restricted to suggesting limited violence. Former Under Secretary of State Ball explained his "devil advocacy" in Vietnam, in which he suggested that there be a troop ceiling of 70,000 men and bombing be restricted to the South: "What I was proposing was something which I thought had a fair chance of being persuasive . . . if I had said let's pull out overnight or do something of this kind, I obviously wouldn't have been persuasive at all. They'd have said 'the man's mad.' "

This peculiar search for the middle ground of a policy defined in terms of force was abetted by the sudden sense on the part of Kennedy's national security managers that the military was filled with Dr. Strangeloves. There was some warrant for this fear. Time and time again, during the crisis, the military seemed obsessed by the opportunity to demonstrate its potential. When asked what the Soviet reaction would be to a surgical raid on their missiles and men, General Lemay snapped, "There will be no reaction." When the crisis ended on Sunday, October 25th, one of the Joint Chiefs suggested that they go ahead with a massive bombing the following Monday in any case. "[T]he military are mad," concluded President Kennedy. Robert Kennedy recalled acidly that "many times . . . I heard the military take positions which, if wrong, had the advantage that no one would be around at the end to know."

In part, it was as a result of the Cuban crisis that the civilians of the American defense and foreign policy bureaucracy grew to despise the military. Hilsman reports that later in the Kennedy Administration, an official prepared a mock account of a high-level meeting on Vietnam in which Averell Harriman "stated that he had disagreed for twenty years with General [Brute] Krulak [Commandant of the Marines] and disagreed today, reluctantly, more than ever; he was sorry to say that he felt General Krulak was a fool and had always thought so." It is reported that President Kennedy roared with laughter upon reading this fictitious account. Hilsman also delighted in telling a story about General Lemnitzer, Chairman of the Joint Chiefs of Staff, who once briefed President Kennedy on Vietnam: "This is the Mekong Valley. Pointer tip hit the map. Hilsman, watching, noticed something, the point tip was not on the Mekong Valley, it was on the Yangtze Valley." Hilsman's recollection of the general's error became a common office story.

Ironically, while the military was increasingly thought to be rather loutish and ill-prepared, civilians were starting to rely more and more on military instrumentalities in the application of which, with few exceptions, they were not trained, and whose command structure they despised as being second-rate at best. Civilian "crisis managers" felt, after Cuba, that they should have control and that the military could not be trusted and had to be made more responsive to the political and civilian considerations of policy. To many observers, as well as to these managers, the "failures" of the Cuban missile crisis were not failures of civilian judgment but of organizational responsiveness. The intelligence establishment, for instance, had not discovered the missiles until the last minute. McNamara never really secured control over the Navy. U-2 flights were sent near the Soviet Union to "excite" Soviet radar at the height of the crisis; until Kennedy ordered their dispersal, American fighters and bombers were wing to wing on the ground, almost inviting a preemptive Soviet blow. Moreover, American tactical nuclear weapons and nuclear-tipped

IRBM's in Turkey and Italy were discovered to be unlocked and lightly guarded. All this led observers and policy-makers to believe that crisis management demanded the President's organizational dominance and control, because the military and intelligence organizations were inept and their judgment was not reliable or at times even sane.

After Cuba, confidence in the ability of U.S. armed superiority to command solutions to "crises" in a way that would favor American interests expanded in such a way that Americans again began to speak of the American century. For a period before the crisis there had been a national reexamination. There were fears of national decline in the face of startling Soviet economic growth. Advances in Russian rocketry had led Americans to believe that not only were they in a mortal competition with the Soviets, but that the outcome was uncertain. Now, however, most of these doubts seemed to have dissipated.

The Cuban missile crisis revived the sense of the American mission. Henry R. Luce once rhapsodized in a widely circulated *Life* editorial that Americans must "accept wholeheartedly our duty and opportunity as the most powerful and vital nation in the world and in consequence to exert upon the world the full impact of our influence for such purposes as we see fit, and by such means as we see fit." After the crisis, Arthur Schlesinger could lyrically resurrect this tradition: "But the ultimate impact of the missile crisis was wider than Cuba, wider than even the western hemisphere. . . . Before the missile crisis people might have feared that we would use our power extravagantly or not use it at all. But the thirteen days gave the world—even the Soviet Union—a sense of American determination and responsibility in the use of power which, if sustained, might indeed become a turning point in the history of the relations between east and west."

Similarly, Professor Zbigniew Brzezinski, then a member of the Planning Council of the Department of State, proclaimed that American paramountcy was the lesson of Cuba. Brzezinski explained, "The U.S. is today the only effective global military power in the world."

In contrast to the United States, Brzezinski declared, the Soviets were not a global power. Although Khrushchev may at one time have believed otherwise, the Cuban crisis demonstrated the limits of Soviet capabilities. "The Soviet leaders were forced, because of the energetic response by the United States, to the conclusion that their apocalyptic power [nuclear deterrent power] was insufficient to make the Soviet Union a global power. Faced with a showdown, the Soviet Union didn't dare to respond even in an area of its regional predominance—in Berlin. . . . It had no military capacity to fight in Cuba, or in Vietnam, or to protect its interests in the Congo." No doubt the historic American sense of divine purpose and the almost Jungian need to be the guarantor of global order received a strong fillip from the Cuban crisis. Brzezinski concluded: "What should be the role of the United States in this period? To use our power responsibly and constructively so that when the American paramountcy ends, the world will have been launched on a constructive pattern of development towards international stability. . . . The ultimate objective ought to be the shaping of a world of cooperative communities."

The overwhelming belief of policy-makers in American superiority seriously eroded deterrence. The Soviet Union reached the same conclusion as the United States—that a preponderance of military power, ranging across the spectrum of force from PT craft to advanced nuclear delivery systems, was the *sine qua non* of the successful exercise of political will. Before fall of 1962, Khrushchev's strategic policy, in the words of a Rand Kremlinologist, "amounted to settling for a second-best strategic posture." The missile crisis, however, manifestly demonstrated Soviet strategic weakness and exposed every Soviet debility that Khrushchev's verbal proclamation of superiority had previously covered.

After Cuba, the Soviet military, responding to the humiliating American stimulus, demanded a higher priority to strategic arms and a cutback on the agricultural and consumer sectors of the Soviet economy. Although Khrushchev and Kennedy were by then moving toward a détente—best symbolized by the signing of the test-ban accords of mid-1963—many in the Kremlin saw this as but a breathing spell in which the Chinese might be isolated and Soviet arms could catch up. Naval preparations, especially the building of Polaris-type submarines, were intensified. Soviet amphibian landing capability— something in which the Soviets had shown little interest before—was revitalized and expanded. As Wolfe noted, "From the time of the first test-launching ... of 1957 to mid-1961 only a handful of ICBM's had been deployed.... After Cuba, the pace of deployment picked up, bringing the total number of operational ICBM launchers to around 200 by the time of Khrushchev's ouster." Although the West still outnumbered the Russians by four to one in numbers of launchers at the time, the Russians worked furiously, and by September 1968, they commanded a larger force than the United States. Worldwide "blue water" Soviet submarine patrols were initiated; and a decision was taken under Brezhnev and Kosygin to extend the Soviet navy to "remote areas of the world's oceans previously considered a zone of supremacy of the fleets of the imperialist powers."

After the missile crisis, the cold-war establishmentarian John McCloy, representing President Kennedy, was host to Soviet Deputy Foreign Minister V. V. Kuznetzov. McCloy secured an affirmation from Kuznetzov that the Soviets would indeed observe their part of the agreement to remove the missiles and bombers from Cuba. But the Soviet leader warned, "Never will we be caught like this again."

The Soviets were to yield again to U.S. strength in Vietnam and the Middle-East. But each time, the usable strategic leverage of the United States grew weaker. Thus, the structure of the international system and international stability was shaken in three ways.

First, the United States became confident that its power would prevail because global politics had become "unifocal." But American military primacy began to erode as soon as it was proclaimed, when the Soviets fought to gain at least a rough strategic parity.

Second, nations, once cowed, are likely to be less timid in the next confrontation. As Kennedy admitted some time later, referring to the Cuban missile crisis, "You can't have too many of those." Just as Kennedy feared he had appeared callow and faint-hearted in successive Berlin crises, and thus had to be tough over Cuba, the Soviets were likely to calculate that they must appear as the more rigid party in future confrontations or risk a reputation of "capitulationism." For weeks after the missile crisis, the Chinese broadcast their charges of Russian stupidity and weakness to the four corners of the globe. The Chinese labeled Khrushchev an "adventurist" as well as a "capitulationist," and therefore not fit for world Communist leadership. The Russian answer was to accuse the Chinese of being even "softer" than they for tolerating the Western enclaves of Macao and Hong Kong. The charge of who was the most capitulationist, the Chinese or the Russians, grew almost silly; but these puerile exchanges had their own dangers in terms of deterrence.

Third, once a threat is not carried out—even after an appearance of a willingness to carry it out has been demonstrated—the ante is upped just a bit more. Morgenthau described a two-step process in nuclear gamesmanship, "diminishing credibility of the threat and even bolder challenges to make good on it. . . . [T]he psychological capital of deterrence has been nearly expended and the policy of deterrence will be close to bankruptcy. When they reach that point, the nations concerned can choose one of three alternatives: resort to nuclear war, retreat, or resort to conventional war."

Morgenthau's observation captured the dilemma of American policy-makers after Cuba. The problem was that nuclear superiority had been useful, but each succeeding threat (since no nuclear threat has ever been carried out) would necessarily be weaker than the last. Yet, how could security managers translate military power into political objectives without such threats? Daniel Ellsberg recalled the quandary of U.S. security managers:

> McNamara's tireless and shrewd efforts in the early sixties, largely hidden from the public to this day, [were to] gradually control the forces within the military bureaucracy that pressed for the threat and use of nuclear weapons. [He had] a creditable motive for proposing alternatives to nuclear threats. . . . [I]n this hidden debate, there was strong incentive—indeed it seemed necessary—for the civilian leaders to demonstrate that success was possible in Indochina without the need either to compromise Cold War objectives or to threaten or use nuclear weapons.
>
> Such concerns remained semi-covert: (for it was seen as dangerous to lend substance to the active suspicions of military staffs and their Congressional allies that there were high Administration officials who didn't love the Bomb). . . .

But after the Cuban crisis, the option of "low-level violence" became more and more attractive. Conventional and limited deployments of force became increasingly necessary as conventional force was considered less forbidding than the nuclear abyss. After all, the symbolic or "psychological capital" of deterrence rested on the notion of resolve. And one way to demonstrate political will was through the resurrection of conventional force as an instrument of demonstrating "commitment"—a commitment whose alternative form was a threat of nuclear holocaust. The latter was bound to deteriorate with the advent of a viable Soviet retaliatory capability and the knowledge that the Soviets had collapsed once under a nuclear threat and might not be willing to be quite so passive again. Many national security managers found they could navigate between the Scylla of nuclear war and the Charybdis of surrender with the serendipitous discovery of the "lifeboat" of the 1960's—limited war. It would not prove to be a sturdy craft.

Of course, the assumptions of the planners of limited war—as they emerged victorious from the Cuban crisis—were as old as the cold war. They dated from the Truman Doctrine's Manichean presentation of a bipolar global confrontation where a gain to one party necessarily would be a loss to the other. A world order of diverse centers of power, with elements of superpower cooperation, where gains and losses would be less easily demonstrable, was not so demanding of military remedy. A multipolar world would be less congenial to the belief that the only options available to policy-makers were either military force or retreat. Maneuver and negotiation, in such a world, would again become part of diplomacy. But such a development was to come about only after the tragic failure of the military remedy had been demonstrated in Vietnam.

There were other effects related to the exuberant reaction to the Cuban crisis. As the United States began to feel that power and force were successful solvents to the more sticky problems of the cold war, the role of international law declined precipitously.

Moral pontifications appeared increasingly hypocritical after Cuba. But after all, hypocrisy, in the words of H. L. Mencken, "runs, like a hair in a hot dog, through the otherwise beautiful fabric of American life." The participants in the crisis knew the blockade was an act of war that had little basis in international law. After the crisis was over, even lawyers began to see law as but another instrumentality of American policy. The conclusion reached by American academics was that "International law is . . . a tool, not a guide to action. . . . It does not have a valid life of its own; it is a mere instrument, available to political leaders for their own ends, be they good or evil, peaceful or aggressive. . . . [The Cuban missile crisis] merely reconfirms the irrelevance of international law in major political disputes."

Dean Acheson summarized the code of the cold war as it was confirmed by the Cuban experience: "The power, prestige and position of the United States had been challenged. . . . Law simply does not deal with such questions of ultimate power. . . . The survival of states is not a matter of law."

George Ball, former Under Secretary of State, wrote: "No one can seriously contend that we now live under a universal system or, in any realistic sense, under the 'rule of law.' We maintain the peace by preserving a precarious balance of power between ourselves and the Soviet Union—a process we used to call 'containment' before the word went out of style. It is the preservation of that balance which, regardless of how we express it, is the central guiding principle of American foreign policy."

The UN was used in the Cuban Crisis, not as Kennedy had told the General Assembly the year before, as "the only true alternative to war," but as a platform where Adlai Stevenson, the eloquent American representative, could deal "a final blow to the Soviet case before world opinion."

Epitomized by Cuba, crisis after crisis pointed out the stark irony: Americans, who had so long stroked the talisman of international law, now seemed to do so only when their interests were not jeopardized. Otherwise, law became merely a rhetorical flourish of United States policy. International law was still a part of the admonition that "armed aggression" and "breaches of the peace" cease and desist. But, in back of these legalistic and moralistic injunctions, the armed cop became more and more apparent. As General de Gaulle had observed earlier, the conclusion that American idealism was but a reflection of the American will to power became almost inescapable after the Cuban crisis. Few obeisances about the need for law in international society disguised the sense that America had abandoned her ancient, liberal inheritance in the zesty pursuit of world order.

Another effect of the crisis was to differentiate the "great powers"—the United States and the Soviet Union—from other states which were literally frozen out of a major role in structuring global politics. After all, the major "chips" of big-power poker were simply not accessible to other governments—even those with modest and nominally independent nuclear forces. For no other nations had the capability of making even plausible calculations of either preemptive or second-strike blows against a great power, much less basing national strategies on such possibilities. As a result, Europeans were offered the appearance of some control in their nuclear lot with the ill-fated MLF. But the nuclear trigger was still in the hands of the United States, and so was the final squeeze. Not only were the weapons of great-power diplomacy increasingly inaccessible to other states, but the other tools of statecraft also receded from the grasp of those with modest resources. The spy, for instance, was largely replaced by satellite reconnaissance. Intellectual musings on great-power conflict became differentiated from other strategic thinking. Gradually, the Soviets and the Americans created a shared private idiom of force; and a curious dialogue began between the congressional budget messages of the Secretary of Defense and the periodic revisions of *Strategy* by Marshal Sokolovsky. Allies became mere appurtenances of power whose purpose, in the duopolistic structure of international society, was increasingly symbolic. Thus, for example, the OAS was asked to validate the U.S. blockade at the same time the American quarantine was announced.

Similarly, Dean Acheson flew to Paris and other European capitals to confer with American allies about the coming confrontation over Cuba.

"Your President does me great honor," de Gaulle said, "to send me so distinguished an emissary. I assume the occasion to be of appropriate importance." Acheson delivered President Kennedy's letter, with the text of the speech to be delivered at P-hour, 7 P.M. Washington time. He offered to summarize it. De Gaulle raised his hand in a delaying gesture that the long-departed Kings of France might have envied. "May we be clear before you start," he said. "Are you consulting or informing me?" Acheson confessed that he was there to inform, not to consult. "I am in favor of independent decisions," de Gaulle acknowledged.

For the Europeans, Gaullists and Leftists alike, it appeared that there was a high likelihood of nuclear annihilation without representation. In spite of European gestures of support, the alliance received a shock from which it did not recover. The British, in the midst of a vicious internal debate about whether or not to abandon nuclear weapons, decided they were necessary to buy even minimum consideration from their American allies. The French did not debate; they accelerated their nuclear programs while withdrawing from a military role in the alliance.

On the Soviet side, it was equally apparent that Russian interests would not be sacrificed to sister socialist states. Castro was plainly sold out. The weak promise tendered by the Kennedy Administration not to invade the island was probably cold comfort as Castro saw his military benefactors beat a hasty retreat from American power. Embarrassingly, Castro began to echo the "capitulationist" theme of Chinese broadcasts. Privately Castro said that if he could, he would have beaten Khrushchev to within an inch of his life for what he did. Soviet Foreign Minister Mikoyan was dispatched to Cuba and stayed there for weeks, not even returning to the bedside of his dying wife, but Castro's fury was unabated. Whatever the motive for Khrushchev's moves in Cuba, the Chinese were also enraged. Any attempts the Soviets had made prior to October 1962 to dissuade the Chinese from assuming a nuclear role lost their validity when it became obvious that the Russians would not risk their own destruction for an associate.

By 1963, a new era of East-West relations was unfolding. The United States still cultivated the asymmetrical assumptions of the cold war, but the Soviet Union was at least admitted as a junior partner in a duopolistic international system which began to be characterized as détente. The relaxation was favorable to Kennedy, who wanted to begin to deal with the Soviets without the ideological rancor that had poisoned previous relations, and who had a vision of Soviet "responsibility" which was to be enlarged upon by succeeding administrations. The Soviets, too, sought a détente. Given their acknowledged strategic inferiority, they could hardly expect to be successful in another series of confrontations. Moreover, the Chinese began to present formidable ideological and political difficulties for the Russians, whose new interest in improved relations with the United States caused intense fears in China of American-Soviet collusion. At the same time, the Soviets began to fear a Sino-American agreement that would be detrimental to their interests. As Michael Suslov, chief ideologue of the Soviet Union, explained in early 1964, "With a stubbornness worthy of a better cause the Chinese leaders attempt to prevent the improvement of Soviet-American relations, representing this as 'plotting with the imperialists.' At the same time the Chinese government makes feverish attempts to improve relations with Britain, France, Japan, West Germany, and Italy. It is quite clear that they would not refuse to improve relations with the United States but as yet do not see favorable circumstances for such an endeavor."

Thus, by 1964, the crisis had precipitated a change in the global structure of power. American paramountcy had been self-proclaimed; the seeds of détente had been sown by a shared vision of nuclear oblivion; and the ingredients for a great-power condominium were becoming clear. If it had not been for the war in Vietnam, the present framework of international affairs might have been with us ten years earlier. Tragically and ironically, the "lessons" of the Cuban missile crisis—that success in international crisis was largely a matter of national guts; that the opponent would yield to superior force; that presidential control of force can be "suitable," "selective," "swift," "effective," and "responsive" to civilian authority; and that crisis management and execution are too dangerous and events move too rapidly for anything but the tightest secrecy—all these inferences contributed to President Johnson's decision to use American air power against Hanoi in 1965. The Cuban crisis changed the international environment but riveted American expectations to the necessities of the diplomacy of violence. Even the language of the Gulf of Tonkin Resolution was almost identical to that which Kennedy's legal advisors had drawn up for the OAS in October of 1962. Although the Cuban crisis created substantial changes in distinguishing superpowers from other states, the realization of the equality of the superpowers and of the indications that they could join in a relationship which had some elements of condominium and some elements of the classic balance of power was suppressed until the American agony in Vietnam drew to a close.

FURTHER READING

Elie Abel, *The Missile Crisis* (1966)

Graham Allison, *Essence of Decision* (1971)

Barton J. Bernstein, "The Week We Almost Went to War," *Bulletin of the Atomic Scientists,* 30 (1976), 13–21

Abram Chayes, *The Cuban Missile Crisis: International Crisis and the Role of Law* (1974)

Herbert Dinerstein, *The Making of a Missile Crisis: October 1962* (1976)

Robert A. Divine, ed., *The Cuban Missile Crisis* (1971)

Jim Heath, *Decade of Disillusionment* (1975)

Robert F. Kennedy, *Thirteen Days* (1969)

Henry M. Pachter, *Collision Course* (1963)

Arthur M. Schlesinger, Jr., *A Thousand Days* (1965)

Ronald Steel, "Endgame," *New York Review of Books,* March 13, 1969, pp. 15–22

Richard Walton, *Cold War and Counterrevolution* (1972)

13

The War in Vietnam

For thirty years after World War II, the United States was involved in the Indo-chinese country of Vietnam. In 1945 America tolerated the reimposition of French colonialism there; in 1950 the United States began giving massive aid to the French to quell the Vietnamese insurgency; from 1954 to 1961 America helped to organize and maintain a non-Communist regime in the South; in 1961 American military personnel began to fight in Vietnamese jungles; in 1964 American bombers began a tremendous campaign of raids against North Vietnam; in 1968 peace talks began; in 1973 a peace settlement was reached and the United States continued to support the South Vietnamese regime; and in 1975 the remaining Americans were driven pell-mell from Vietnam when the Viet Cong and North Vietnamese seized the southern capital of Saigon, renaming it Ho Chi Minh City. Over 56,000 American servicemen died in Vietnam, and the United States spent about $155 billion in Southeast Asia between 1950 and 1975.

In the 1960s, when the American military intervention escalated, peace demonstrations and debates swept the United States, putting pressure on politicians to reverse American policy and withdraw from the war. The question posed in the 1960s is the same as that asked by recent scholars: Why did the United States become so deeply involved in Vietnam for so long? The answers have varied greatly: security, containment of Communism, economic needs, lessons of the past, maintenance of international stature as the "number one" power, rampant globalism, imperialism, arrogance of power, immorality, inadvertence (the "quagmire" thesis), an imperial presidency, manipulation of public opinion, and bureaucratic imperatives.

It is not surprising that America's longest war in history should produce so many explanations, for the causes of the Vietnamese conflict were less clear-cut than those of previous wars in which the United States fought.

DOCUMENTS

The Tonkin Gulf Resolution, which passed the Senate on August 10, 1964, with only two dissenting votes, authorized the President to use the force he deemed necessary in Vietnam. President Lyndon B. Johnson's vigorous speech at The Johns Hopkins University on April 7, 1965, summarizes the reasons why the United States was fighting in Vietnam. The third document is a portion of Chinese General Lin Piao's 1965 statement that "people's war" would overcome American imperialism in the "testing ground" of Vietnam. J. William Fulbright, chairman of the Senate Foreign Relations Committee, became a vocal opponent of the Vietnam War. In a speech on May 5, 1966, he protested American "arrogance of power." The next document is a transcript of a November 24, 1969, interview between Mike Wallace of the Columbia Broadcasting System and Vietnam veteran Private Paul Meadlo, who participated in the 1968 massacre at My Lai. In the final document, a speech delivered in Texas on April 30, 1972, President Richard M. Nixon defends the American presence in Indochina, including the extensive United States bombing sorties in that area.

The Tonkin Gulf Resolution, 1964

To promote the maintenance of international peace and security in southeast Asia.

Whereas naval units of the Communist regime in Vietnam, in violation of the principles of the Charter of the United Nations and of international law, have deliberately and repeatedly attacked United States naval vessels lawfully present in international waters, and have thereby created a serious threat to international peace; and

Whereas these attacks are part of a deliberate and systematic campaign of aggression that the Communist regime in North Vietnam has been waging against its neighbors and the nations joined with them in the collective defense of their freedom; and

Whereas the United States is assisting the peoples of southeast Asia to protect their freedom and has no territorial, military or political ambitions in that area, but desires only that these peoples should be left in peace to work out their own destinies in their own way: Now, therefore, be it *Resolved by the Senate and House of Representatives of the United States of America in Congress assembled,* That the Congress approves and supports the determination of the President, as Commander in Chief, to take all necessary measures to repel any armed attack against the forces of the United States and to prevent further aggression.

SEC. 2. The United States regards as vital to its national interest and to world peace the maintenance of international peace and security in southeast Asia. Consonant with the Constitution of the United States and the Charter of the United Nations and in accordance with its obligations under the Southeast

Asia Collective Defense Treaty, the United States is, therefore, prepared, as the President determines, to take all necessary steps, including the use of armed force, to assist any member or protocol state of the Southeast Asia Collective Defense Treaty requesting assistance in defense of its freedom.

SEC. 3. This resolution shall expire when the President shall determine that the peace and security of the area is reasonably assured by international conditions created by action of the United Nations or otherwise, except that it may be terminated earlier by concurrent resolution of the Congress.

Lyndon B. Johnson Explains
Why Americans Fight in Vietnam, 1965

Why must this nation hazard its ease, its interest, and its power for the sake of a people so far away?

We fight because we must fight if we are to live in a world where every country can shape its own destiny, and only in such a world will our own freedom be finally secure.

This kind of world will never be built by bombs or bullets. Yet the infirmities of man are such that force must often precede reason and the waste of war, the works of peace.

We wish that this were not so. But we must deal with the world as it is, if it is ever to be as we wish.

The world as it is in Asia is not a serene or peaceful place.

The first reality is that North Viet-Nam has attacked the independent nation of South Viet-Nam. Its object is total conquest.

Of course, some of the people of South Viet-Nam are participating in attack on their own government. But trained men and supplies, orders and arms, flow in a constant stream from North to South.

This support is the heartbeat of the war.

And it is a war of unparalleled brutality. Simple farmers are the targets of assassination and kidnaping. Women and children are strangled in the night because their men are loyal to their government. And helpless villages are ravaged by sneak attacks. Large-scale raids are conducted on towns, and terror strikes in the heart of cities.

The confused nature of this conflict cannot mask the fact that it is the new face of an old enemy.

Over this war—and all Asia—is another reality: the deepening shadow of Communist China. The rulers in Hanoi are urged on by Peking. This is a regime which has destroyed freedom in Tibet, which has attacked India and has been condemned by the United Nations for aggression in Korea. It is a nation which is helping the forces of violence in almost every continent. The contest in Viet-Nam is part of a wider pattern of aggressive purposes.

Why are these realities our concern? Why are we in South Viet-Nam?

We are there because we have a promise to keep. Since 1954 every American President has offered support to the people of South Viet-Nam. We have helped to build, and we have helped to defend. Thus, over many years, we have made a national pledge to help South Viet-Nam defend its independence. And I intend to keep that promise.

To dishonor that pledge, to abandon this small and brave nation to its enemies, and to the terror that must follow, would be an unforgivable wrong.

We are also there to strengthen world order. Around the globe from Berlin to Thailand are people whose well being rests in part on the belief that they can count on us if they are attacked. To leave Viet-Nam to its fate would shake the confidence of all these people in the value of an American commitment and in the value of America's word. The result would be increased unrest and instability, and even wider war.

We are also there because there are great stakes in the balance. Let no one think for a moment that retreat from Viet-Nam would bring an end to conflict. The battle would be renewed in one country and then another. The central lesson of our time is that the appetite of aggression is never satisfied. To withdraw from one battlefield means only to prepare for the next. We must say in Southeast Asia—as we did in Europe—in the words of the Bible: "Hitherto shalt thou come, but no further."

There are those who say that all our effort there will be futile—that China's power is such that it is bound to dominate all Southeast Asia. But there is no end to that argument until all of the nations of Asia are swallowed up.

There are those who wonder why we have a responsibility there. Well, we have it there for the same reason that we have a responsibility for the defense of Europe. World War II was fought in both Europe and Asia and when it ended we found ourselves with continued responsibility for the defense of freedom.

Our objective is the independence of South Viet-Nam and its freedom from attack. We want nothing for ourselves—only that the people of South Viet-Nam be allowed to guide their own country in their own way.

We will do everything necessary to reach that objective and we will do only what is absolutely necessary.

In recent months attacks on South Viet-Nam were stepped up. Thus, it became necessary for us to increase our response and to make attacks by air. This is not a change of purpose. It is a change in what we believe that purpose requires.

We do this in order to slow down aggression.

We do this to increase the confidence of the brave people of South Viet-Nam who have bravely borne this brutal battle for so many years with so many casualties.

And we do this to convince the leaders of North Viet-Nam—and all who seek to share their conquest—of a simple fact:

We will not be defeated.

We will not grow tired.

We will not withdraw, either openly or under the cloak of a meaningless agreement.

We know that air attacks alone will not accomplish all of these purposes. But it is our best and prayerful judgment that they are a necessary part of the surest road to peace.

We hope that peace will come swiftly. But that is in the hands of others besides ourselves. And we must be prepared for a long continued conflict. It will require patience as well as bravery—the will to endure as well as the will to resist.

I wish it were possible to convince others with words of what we now find it necessary to say with guns and planes: armed hostility is futile—our resources are equal to any challenge—because we fight for values and we fight for principle, rather than territory or colonies, our patience and our determination are unending.

Once this is clear, then it should also be clear that the only path for reasonable men is the path of peaceful settlement. . . .

These countries of Southeast Asia are homes for millions of impoverished people. Each day these people rise at dawn and struggle through until the night to wrestle existence from the soil. They are often wracked by diseases, plagued by hunger, and death comes at the early age of forty.

Stability and peace do not come easily in such a land. Neither independence nor human dignity will ever be won though by arms alone. It also requires the works of peace. The American people have helped generously in times past in these works, and now there must be a much more massive effort to improve the life of man in that conflict-torn corner of our world.

The first step is for the countries of Southeast Asia to associate themselves in a greatly expanded co-operative effort for development. We would hope that North Viet-Nam would take its place in the common effort just as soon as peaceful co-operation is possible.

The United Nations is already actively engaged in development in this area, and as far back as 1961 I conferred with our authorities in Viet-Nam in connection with their work there. And I would hope tonight that the Secretary General of the United Nations could use the prestige of his great office and his deep knowledge of Asia to initiate, as soon as possible, with the countries of that area, a plan for co-operation in increased development.

For our part I will ask the Congress to join in a billion dollar American investment in this effort as soon as it is underway.

And I would hope that all other industrialized countries, including the Soviet Union, will join in this effort to replace despair with hope and terror with progress.

The task is nothing less than to enrich the hopes and existence of more than a hundred million people. And there is much to be done.

The vast Mekong River can provide food and water and power on a scale to dwarf even our own T.V.A.

The wonders of modern medicine can be spread through villages where thousands die every year from lack of care.

Schools can be established to train people in the skills needed to manage the process of development.

And these objectives, and more, are within the reach of a cooperative and determined effort.

I also intend to expand and speed up a program to make available our farm surpluses to assist in feeding and clothing the needy in Asia. We should not allow people to go hungry and wear rags while our own warehouses overflow with an abundance of wheat and corn and rice and cotton.

So I will very shortly name a special team of outstanding, patriotic, and distinguished Americans to inaugurate our participation in these programs. This team will be headed by Mr. Eugene Black, the very able former president of the World Bank.

This will be a disorderly planet for a long time. In Asia, and elsewhere, the forces of the modern world are shaking old ways and uprooting ancient civilizations. There will be turbulence and struggle and even violence. Great social change—as we see in our own country—does not always come without conflict.

We must also expect that nations will on occasion be in dispute with us. It may be because we are rich, or powerful, or because we have made some mistakes, or because they honestly fear our intentions. However, no nation need ever fear that we desire their land, or to impose our will, or to dictate their institutions.

But we will always oppose the effort of one nation to conquer another nation.

We will do this because our own security is at stake.

But there is more to it than that. For our generation has a dream. It is a very old dream. But we have the power, and now we have the opportunity to make that dream come true.

For centuries nations have struggled among each other. But we dream of a world where disputes are settled by law and reason. And we will try to make it so.

For most of history men have hated and killed one another in battle. But we dream of an end to war. And we will try to make it so.

For all existence most men have lived in poverty, threatened by hunger. But we dream of a world where all are fed and charged with hope. And we will help to make it so.

Lin Piao on People's War, 1965

Ours is the epoch in which world capitalism and imperialism are heading for their doom and socialism and communism are marching to victory. Comrade Mao Tse-tung's theory of people's war is not only a product of the Chinese revolution, but has also the characteristics of our epoch. The new experience gained in the people's revolutionary struggles in various countries since World War II has provided continuous evidence that Mao Tse-tung's thought is a common asset of the revolutionary people of the whole world. This is the great international significance of the thought of Mao Tse-tung.

Since World War II, U.S. imperialism has stepped into the shoes of German, Japanese, and Italian fascism and has been trying to build a great American empire by dominating and enslaving the whole world. It is actively fostering Japanese and West German militarism as its chief accomplices in unleashing a world war. Like a vicious wolf, it is bullying and enslaving various peoples, plundering their wealth, encroaching upon their countries' sovereignty and interfering in their internal affairs. It is the most rabid aggressor in human history and the most ferocious common enemy of the people of the world. Every people or country in the world that wants revolution, independence and peace cannot but direct the spearhead of its struggle against U.S. imperialism.

Just as the Japanese imperialists' policy of subjugating China made it possible for the Chinese people to form the broadest possible united front against them, so the U.S. imperialists' policy of seeking world domination makes it possible for the people throughout the world to unite all the forces that can be united and form the broadest possible united front for a converging attack on U.S. imperialism.

At present, the main battlefield of the fierce struggle between the people of the world on the one side and U.S. imperialism and its lackeys on the other is the vast area of Asia, Africa, and Latin America. In the world as a whole, this is the area where the people suffer worst from imperialist oppression and where imperialist rule is most vulnerable. Since World War II, revolutionary storms have been rising in this area, and today they have become the most important force directly pounding U.S. imperialism. The contradiction between the revolutionary peoples of Asia, Africa, and Latin America and the imperialists headed by the United States is the principal contradiction in the contemporary world. The development of this contradiction is promoting the struggle of the people of the whole world against U.S. imperialism and its lackeys.

Since World War II, people's war has increasingly demonstrated its power in Asia, Africa, and Latin America. The peoples of China, Korea, Vietnam, Laos, Cuba, Indonesia, Algeria and other countries have waged people's wars against the imperialists and their lackeys and won great victories. The classes leading these people's wars may vary, and so may the breadth and depth of mass mobilization and the extent of victory, but the victories in these people's wars have very much weakened and pinned down the forces of imperialism, upset the U.S. imperialist plan to launch a world war, and become mighty factors defending world peace.

Today, the conditions are more favorable than ever before for the waging of people's wars by the revolutionary peoples of Asia, Africa, and Latin America against U.S. imperialism and its lackeys.

Since World War II and the succeeding years of revolutionary upsurge, there has been a great rise in the level of political consciousness and the degree of organization of the people in all countries, and the resources available to them for mutual support and aid have greatly increased. The whole capitalist-imperialist system has become drastically weaker and is in the process of increasing convulsion and disintegration. After World War I, the imperialists lacked the power to destroy the new-born socialist Soviet state, but they were still able to suppress the people's revolutionary movements in some countries in the parts of the world under their own rule and so maintain a short period of comparative stability. Since World War II, however, not only have they been unable to stop a number of countries from taking the socialist road, but they are no longer capable of holding back the surging tide of the people's revolutionary movements in the areas under their own rule.

U.S. imperialism is stronger, but also more vulnerable, than any imperialism of the past. It sets itself against the people of the whole world, including the people of the United States. Its human, military, material and financial resources are far from sufficient for the realization of its ambition of dominating the whole world. U.S. imperialism has further weakened itself by occupying so many places in the world, overreaching itself, stretching its fingers out wide and dispersing its strength, with its rear so far away and its supply lines so long. As Comrade Mao Tse-tung has said, "Wherever it commits aggression, it puts a new noose around its neck. It is besieged ring upon ring by the people of the whole world."

When committing aggression in a foreign country, U.S. imperialism can only employ part of its forces, which are sent to fight an unjust war far from their native land and therefore have a low morale, and so U.S. imperialism is beset with great difficulties. The people subjected to its aggression are having a trial of strength with U.S. imperialism neither in Washington nor New York, neither in Honolulu nor Florida, but are fighting for independence and freedom on their own soil. Once they are mobilized on a broad scale, they will have inexhaustible strength. Thus superiority will belong not to the United States but to the people subjected to its aggression. The latter, though apparently weak and small, are really more powerful than U.S. imperialism.

The struggles waged by the different peoples against U.S. imperialism reinforce each other and merge into a torrential world-wide tide of opposition to U.S. imperialism. The more successful the development of people's war in a given region, the larger the number of U.S. imperialist forces that can be pinned down and depleted there. When the U.S. aggressors are hard pressed in one place, they have no alternative but to loosen their grip on others. Therefore, the conditions become more favorable for the people elsewhere to wage struggles against U.S. imperialism and its lackeys.

Everything is divisible. And so is this colossus of U.S. imperialism. It can be split up and defeated. The peoples of Asia, Africa, Latin America and other regions can destroy it piece by piece, some striking at its head and others at its feet. That is why the greatest fear of U.S. imperialism is that people's wars will be launched in different parts of the world, and particularly in Asia, Africa and Latin America, and why it regards people's war as a mortal danger.

U.S. imperialism relies solely on its nuclear weapons to intimidate people. But these weapons cannot save U.S. imperialism from its doom. Nuclear weapons cannot be used lightly. U.S. imperialism has been condemned by the people of the whole world for its towering crime of dropping two atom bombs on Japan. If it uses nuclear weapons again, it will become isolated in the extreme. Moreover, the U.S. monopoly of nuclear weapons has long been broken; U.S. imperialism has these weapons, but others have them too. If it threatens other countries with nuclear weapons, U.S. imperialism will expose its own country to the same threat. For this reason, it will meet with strong opposition not only from the people elsewhere but also inevitably from the people in its own country. Even if U.S. imperialism brazenly uses nuclear weapons, it cannot conquer the people, who are indomitable.

However highly developed modern weapons and technical equipment may be and however complicated the methods of modern warfare, in the final analysis the outcome of a war will be decided by the sustained fighting of the ground forces, by the fighting at close quarters on battlefields, by the political consciousness of the men, by their courage and spirit of sacrifice. Here the weak points of U.S. imperialism will be completely laid bare, while the superiority of the revolutionary people will be brought into full play. The reactionary troops of U.S. imperialism cannot possibly be endowed with the courage and the spirit of sacrifice possessed by the revolutionary people. The spiritual atom bomb which the revolutionary people possess is a far more powerful and useful weapon than the physical atom bomb.

Vietnam is the most convincing current example of a victim of aggression defeating U.S. imperialism by a people's war. The United States has made South Vietnam a testing ground for the suppression of people's war. It has carried on this experiment for many years, and everybody can now see that the U.S. aggressors are unable to find a way of coping with people's war. On the other hand, the Vietnamese people have brought the power of people's war into full play in their struggle against the U.S. aggressors. The U.S. aggressors are in danger of being swamped in the people's war in Vietnam. They are deeply worried that their defeat in Vietnam will lead to a chain reaction. They are expanding the war in an attempt to save themselves from defeat. But the more they expand the war, the greater will be the chain reaction. The more they escalate the war, the heavier will be their fall and the more disastrous their defeat. The people in other parts of the world will see still more clearly that U.S. imperialism can be defeated, and that what the Vietnamese people can do, they can do too.

History has proved and will go on proving that people's war is the most effective weapon against U.S. imperialism and its lackeys. All revolutionary people will learn to wage people's war against U.S. imperialism and its lackeys. They will take up arms, learn to fight battles and become skilled in waging people's war, though they have not done so before. U.S. imperialism, like a mad bull dashing from place to place, will finally be burned to ashes in the blazing fires of the people's wars it has provoked by its own actions.

Senator J. William Fulbright on the Arrogance of Power, 1966

The attitude above all others which I feel sure is no longer valid is the arrogance of power, the tendency of great nations to equate power with virtue and major responsibilities with a universal mission. The dilemmas involved are preeminently American dilemmas, not because America has weaknesses that others do not have but because America is powerful as no nation has ever been before and the discrepancy between its power and the power of others appears to be increasing. . . .

We are now engaged in a war to "defend freedom" in South Vietnam. Unlike the Republic of Korea, South Vietnam has an army which [is] without notable success and a weak, dictatorial government which does not command the loyalty of the South Vietnamese people. The official war aims of the United States Government, as I understand them, are to defeat what is regarded as North Vietnamese aggression, to demonstrate the futility of what the communists call "wars of national liberation," and to create conditions under which the South Vietnamese people will be able freely to determine their own future. I have not the slightest doubt of the sincerity of the President and the Vice President and the Secretaries of State and Defense in propounding these aims. What I do doubt—and doubt very much—is the ability of the United States to achieve these aims by the means being used. I do not question the power of our weapons and the efficiency of our logistics; I cannot say these things delight me as they seem to delight some of our officials, but they are certainly impressive. What I do question is the ability of the United States, or France or any other Western nation, to go into a small, alien, undeveloped Asian nation and create stability where there is chaos, the will to fight where there is defeatism, democracy where there is no tradition of it and honest government where corruption is almost a way of life. Our handicap is well expressed in the pungent Chinese proverb: "In shallow waters dragons become the sport of shrimps."

Early last month demonstrators in Saigon burned American jeeps, tried to assault American soldiers, and marched through the streets shouting "Down with the American imperialists," while one of the Buddhist leaders made a speech equating the United States with the communists as a threat to South Vietnamese independence. Most Americans are understandably shocked and angered to encounter such hostility from people who by now would be under the rule of the Viet Cong but for the sacrifice of American lives and money. Why, we may ask, are they so shockingly ungrateful? Surely they must know that their very right to parade and protest and demonstrate depends on the Americans who are defending them.

The answer, I think, is that "fatal impact" of the rich and strong on the poor and weak. Dependent on it though the Vietnamese are, our very strength is a reproach to their weakness, our wealth a mockery of their poverty, our success a reminder of their failures. What they resent is the disruptive effect of our strong culture upon their fragile one, an effect which we can no more avoid than a man can help being bigger than a child. What they fear, I think rightly, is that traditional Vietnamese society cannot survive the American economic and cultural impact. . . .

The cause of our difficulties in southeast Asia is not a deficiency of power but an excess of the wrong kind of power which results in a feeling of importance when it fails to achieve its desired ends. We are still acting like boy scouts dragging reluctant old ladies across the streets they do not want to cross. We are trying to remake Vietnamese society, a task which certainly cannot be accomplished by force and which probably cannot be accomplished by any means available to outsiders. The objective may be desirable, but it is not feasible. . . .

If America has a service to perform in the world—and I believe it has—it is in large part the service of its own example. In our excessive involvement in the affairs of other countries, we are not only living off our assets and denying our own people the proper enjoyment of their resources; we are also denying the world the example of a free society enjoying its freedom to the fullest. This is regrettable indeed for a nation that aspires to teach democracy to other nations, because, as Burke said, "Example is the school of mankind, and they will learn at no other." . . .

There are many respects in which America, if it can bring itself to act with the magnanimity and the empathy appropriate to its size and power, can be an intelligent example to the world. We have the opportunity to set an example of generous understanding in our relations with China, of practical cooperation for peace in our relations with Russia, of reliable and respectful partnership in our relations with Western Europe, of material helpfulness without moral presumption in our relations with the developing nations, of abstention from the temptations of hegemony in our relations with Latin America, and of the all-around advantages of minding one's own business in our relations with everybody. Most of all, we have the opportunity to serve as an example of democracy to the world by the way in which we run our own society; America, in the words of John Quincy Adams, should be "the well-wisher to the freedom and independence of all" but "the champion and vindicator only of her own." . . .

If we can bring ourselves so to act, we will have overcome the dangers of the arrogance of power. It will involve, no doubt, the loss of certain glories, but that seems a price worth paying for the probable rewards, which are the happiness of America and the peace of the world.

Private Paul Meadlo Explains
the My Lai Massacre, 1969

MEADLO: Captain Medina had us all in a group, and oh, he briefed us, and I can't remember all the briefing.

WALLACE: How many of them were you?   A. Well, with the mortar platoon, I'd say there'd be about 60–65 people, but the mortar platoon wasn't with us, and I'd say the mortar platoon had about 20–25—about 25 people in the mortar platoon. So we didn't have the whole company in the Pinkville [My Lai], no we didn't.

Q. There weren't about 40–45—   A. . . . right. . . .

Q. —that took part in all of this?   A. Right.

Q. Now you took off from your base camp.   A. . . . yes—Dolly.

New York Times, November 25, 1969. © 1969 by The New York Times Company. Reprinted by permission.

Q. . . . Dolly. At what time?   A. I wouldn't know what time it was. . . .

Q. . . . in the early morning. . . .   A. . . . In the early morning. It was—it would have been a long time ago.

Q. And what had you been briefed to do when you got to Pinkville?

A. To search and to make sure that there weren't no N.V.A. in the village and expecting to fight—when we got there. . . .

Q. To expect to fight?   A. To expect to fight.

Q. Un-huh. So you took off and—in how many choppers?

A. Well, I'd say the first wave was about four of us—I mean four choppers, and. . . .

Q. How many men aboard each chopper?

A. Five of us. And we landed next to the village, and we all got in line and we started walking toward the village. And there was one man, one gook in the shelter, and he was all huddled up down in there, and the man called out and said there's a gook over here.

Q. How old a man was this? I mean was this a fighting man or an older man?

A. An older man. And the man hauled out and said that there's a gook over here, and then Sergeant Mitchell hollered back and said shoot him.

Q. Sergeant Mitchell was in charge of the 20 of you?   A. He was in charge of the whole squad. And so then the man shot him. So we moved on into the village, and we started searching up the village and gathering people and running through the center of the village.

Q. How many people did you round up?   A. Well, there was about 40–45 people that we gathered in the center of the village. And we placed them in there, and it was like a little island, right there in the center of the village, I'd say. And—

Q. What kind of people—men, women, children?

A. Men, women, children.

Q. Babies?

A. Babies. And we all huddled them up. We made them squat down, and Lieutenant Calley came over and said you know what to do with them, don't you? And I said yes so I took it for granted that he just wanted us to watch them. And he left, and came back about 10 to 15 minutes later, and said, how come you ain't killed them yet? And I told him that I didn't think you wanted us to kill them, that you just wanted us to guard them. He said, no, I want them dead. So—

Q. He told this to all of you, or to you particularly?

A. Well, I was facing him. So, but, the other three, four guys heard it and so he stepped back about 10, 15 feet, and he started shooting them. And he told me to start shooting. So I started shooting, I poured about four clips into the group.

Q. You fired four clips from your . . . .   A. M-16.

Q. And that's about—how many clips—I mean how many—

A. I carried seventeen rounds to each clip.

Q. So you fired something like 67 shots—   A. Right.

Q. And you killed how many? At that time?

A. Well, I fired them on automatic, so you can't—you just spray the area on them and so you can't know how many you killed 'cause they were going fast. So I might have killed ten or fifteen of them.

Q. Men, women and children?   A. Men, women and children.

Q. And babies?

A. And babies.

Q. Okay, then what?   A. So we started to gather them up, more people, and we had about seven or eight people, that we was gonna put into the hootch, and we dropped a hand grenade in there with them.

Q. Now you're rounding up more?

A. We're rounding up more, and we had about seven or eight people. And we was going to throw them in the hootch, and well, we put them in the hootch and then we dropped a hand grenade down there with them. And somebody holed up in the ravine, and told us to bring them over to the ravine, so we took them back out, and led them over to—and by that time, we already had them over there, and they had about 70–75 people all gathered up. So we threw ours in with them and Lieutenant Calley told me, he said, Meadlo, we got another job to do. And so he walked over to the people, and he started pushing them off and started shooting. . . .

Q. Started pushing them off into the ravine?

A. Off into the ravine. It was a ditch. And so we started pushing them off and we started shooting them, so altogether we just pushed them all off, and just started using automatics on them. And then—

Q. Again—men, women, children?   A. Men, women and children.

Q. And babies?

A. And babies. And so we started shooting them and somebody told us to switch off to single shot so that we could save ammo. So we switched off to single shot and shot a few more rounds. And after that, I just—we just—the company started gathering up again. We started moving out, and we had a few gooks that was in—as we started moving out, we had gooks in front of us that was taking point, you know.

Q. Uh-huh.   A. —and as we walked—

Q. Taking point. You mean out in front? To take any fire that might come.

A. Right. And so we started walking across that field. And so later on that day, they picked them up, and gooks we had, and I reckon they took them to Chu Lai or some camp that they was questioning them, so I don't know what they done with them. So we set up [indistinct] the rest of the night, and the next morning we started leaving, leaving the perimeter, and I stepped on a land mine next day, next morning.

Q. And you came back to the United States.   A. I came back to the United States, and lost a foot out of it.

Q. You feel—

A. I feel cheated because the V.A. cut my disability like they did, and they said that my stump is well healed, well padded, without tenderness. Well, it's well healed, but it's a long way from being well padded. And without tenderness? It hurts all the time. I got to work eight hours a day up on my foot, and at the end of the day I can't hardly stand it. But I gotta work because I gotta make a living. And the V.A. don't give me enough money to live on as it is.

Q. Veterans Administration.   A. Right. So—

Q. Did you feel any sense of retribution to yourself the day after?

A. Well, I felt that I was punished for what I'd done, the next morning. Later on in that day, I felt like I was being punished.

Q. Why did you do it?   A. Why did I do it? Because I felt like I was ordered to do it, and it seemed like that, at the time I felt like I was doing the right thing, because like I said I lost buddies. I lost a damn good buddy, Bobby Wilson, and it was on my conscience. So after I done it, I felt good, but later on that day, it was getting to me.

Q. You're married?   A. Right.

Q. Children?   A. Two.

Q. How old?   A. The boy is two and a half, and the little girl is a year and a half.

Q. Obviously, the question comes to my mind . . . the father of two little kids like that . . . how can he shoot babies?   A. I didn't have the little girl. I just had a little boy at the time.

Q. Uh-huh. How do you shoot babies?   A. I don't know. It's just one of them things.

Q. How many people would you imagine were killed that day?   A. I'd say about 370.

Q. How do you arrive at that figure?   A. Just looking.

Q. You say, you think, that many people, and you yourself were responsible for how many of them?   A. I couldn't say.

Q. Twenty-five? Fifty?   A. I couldn't say . . . just too many.

Q. And how many men did the actual shooting?   A. Well, I really couldn't say that, either. There was other . . . there was another platoon in there and . . . but I just couldn't say how many.

Q. But these civilians were lined up and shot? They weren't killed by cross-fire?

A. They weren't lined up . . . they [were] just pushed in a ravine or just sitting, squatting . . . and shot.

Q. What did these civilians—particularly the women and children, the old men —what did they do? What did they say to you?   A. They weren't much saying to them. They [were] just being pushed and they were doing what they was told to do.

Q. They weren't begging or saying, "No . . . no," or—   A. Right, they were begging and saying, "No, no." And the mothers was hugging their children and, but they kept right on firing. Well, we kept right on firing. They was waving their arms and begging. . . .

Q. Was that your most vivid memory of what you saw?   A. Right.

Q. And nothing went through your mind or heart?   A. Many a times . . . many a times. . . .

Q. While you were doing it?   A. Not while I was doing it. It just seemed like it was the natural thing to do at the time. I don't know . . . I was getting relieved from what I'd seen earlier over there.

Q. What do you mean?   A. Well, I was getting . . . like the . . . my buddies getting killed or wounded or—we weren't getting no satisfaction from it, so what it really was, it was just mostly revenge.

Q. You call the Vietnamese "gooks?"   A. Gooks.

Q. Are they people to you? Were they people to you?

A. Well, they were people. But it was just one of them words that we just picked up over there, you know. Just any word you pick up. That's what you call people, and that's what you been called.

Q. Obviously, the thought that goes through my mind—I spent some time over there, and I killed in the second war, and so forth. But the thought that goes through your mind is, we've raised such a dickens about what the Nazis did, or what the Japanese did, but particularly what the Nazis did in the second world war, the brutalization and so forth, you know. It's hard for a good many Americans to understand that young, capable, American boys could line up old men, women and children and babies and shoot them down in cold blood. How do you explain that?

A. I wouldn't know.

Q. Did you ever dream about all of this that went on in Pinkville?

A. Yes, I did . . . and I still dream about it.

Q. What kind of dreams?   A. About the women and children in my sleep. Some days . . . some nights, I can't even sleep. I just lay there thinking about it.

Richard M. Nixon Defends
American Policy, 1972

[THE PRESIDENT:] Let me tell you the reasons why I feel that it is vitally important that the United States continue to use its air and naval power against targets in North Vietnam, as well as in South Vietnam, to prevent a Communist takeover and a Communist victory over the people of South Vietnam.

First, because there are 69,000 Americans still in Vietnam—that will be reduced to 49,000 by the first of July—and I, as Commander in Chief, have a responsibility to see to it that their lives are adequately protected, and I, of course, will meet that responsibility.

Second, because as we consider the situation in Vietnam, we must remember that if the North Vietnamese were to take over in South Vietnam as a result of our stopping our support in the air and on the sea—we have no ground support whatever; there are no American ground forces in action in South Vietnam, and none will be—but when we consider that situation, if there were such a takeover, we must consider the consequences.

There is first the consequence to the people of South Vietnam. We look back to what happened historically. In 1954, when the North Vietnamese took over in North Vietnam, the Catholic Bishop of Da Nang estimated that at least 500,000 people in North Vietnam who had opposed the Communist takeover in the North were either murdered or starved to death in slave labor camps.

I saw something of that when Mrs. Nixon and I were in there in 1956, when we visited refugee camps where over a million North Vietnamese fled from the Communist tyranny to come to the South. If, at this particular point, the Communists were to take over in South Vietnam, you can imagine what would happen to the hundreds of thousands of South Vietnamese who sided with their own government and with the United States against the Communists. It would be a bloodbath that would stain the hands of the United States for time immemorial.

That is bad enough. I know there are some who say we have done enough, what happens to the South Vietnamese at this particular time is something that should not be our concern. We have sacrificed enough for them. So let's put it in terms of the United States alone, and then we really see why the only decision that any man in the position of President of the United States can make is to authorize the necessary air and naval strikes that will prevent a Communist takeover.

In the event that one country like North Vietnam, massively assisted with the most modern technical weapons by two Communist superpowers—in the event that that country is able to invade another country and conquer it, you can see how that pattern would be repeated in other countries throughout the world: in the Mideast, in Europe, and in others as well.

If, on the other hand, that kind of aggression is stopped in Vietnam and fails there, then it will be discouraged in other parts of the world. Putting it quite directly then, what is on the line in Vietnam is not just peace for Vietnam, but peace in the Mideast, peace in Europe, and peace not just for the five or six or seven years immediately ahead of us, but possibly for a long time in the future.

As I put it last Wednesday night, I want and all America wants to end the war in Vietnam. I want and all Americans want to bring our men home from Vietnam. But I want, and I believe all Americans want, to bring our men home and to end this war in a way that the younger brothers and the sons of the men who have fought and died in Vietnam won't be fighting in another Vietnam five or ten years from now. That is what this is all about.

Q. May we raise our glasses and pay tribute to the courage of the President of the United States.

THE PRESIDENT: I am most grateful for that toast. Incidentally, I hope the champagne holds out for the evening.

But I do want to say that in the final analysis, what is really on the line here, of course, is the position of the United States of America as the strongest free-world power, as a constructive force for peace in the world.

Let us imagine for a moment what the world would be like if the United States were not respected in the world. What would the world be like if friends of the United States throughout the non-Communist world lost confidence in the United States? It would be a world that would be much less safe. It would be a world that would be much more dangerous, not only in terms of war but in terms of the denial of freedom, because when we talk about the United States of America and all of our faults, let us remember in this country we have never used our power to break the peace, only to restore it or keep it,

and we have never used our power to destroy freedom, only to defend it.

Now, I think that is a precious asset for the world. I also feel one other thing, and I will close this rather long answer on this point: John Connally has referred to the office of the presidency of the United States. Earlier this evening I talked to President Johnson on the phone. We are of different parties. We both served in this office. While I had my political differences with him, and he with me, I am sure he would agree that each of us in his way tries to leave that office with as much respect and with as much strength in the world as he possibly can—that is his responsibility—and to do it the best way that he possibly can.

Let me say in this respect I have noted that when we have traveled abroad to 18 countries, particularly even when we went to the People's Republic of China, the office of President, not the man but the office of President of the

United States is respected in every country we visited. I think we will find that same respect in Moscow. But if the United States at this time leaves Vietnam and allows a Communist takeover, the office of President of the United States will lose respect; and I am not going to let that happen.

Q. Mr. President, may I ask you about strategic targets in North Vietnam? I have been told for years by the pilots that there are dams up there that would be very much defeating to the North Vietnamese, who have defied what you have tried to prove in the way of peace. Is this true or false? Has this crossed your mind?

THE PRESIDENT: The question is with regard to the targets in North Vietnam, and particularly with regard to the dams and the dikes, which many of the pilots believe would be very effective strategic targets.

I would say on that score that we have, as you know, authorized strikes, and we have made them over the past four weeks, since the Communist offensive began, in the Hanoi-Haiphong area.

I have also indicated, as this offensive continues, if it does continue, that we will continue to make strikes on military targets throughout North Vietnam.

Now, the problem that is raised with regard to dams or dikes is that while it is a strategic target, and indirectly a military target, it would result in an enormous number of civilian casualties. That is something that we want to avoid. It is also something we believe is not needed.

Just let me say that as far as the targets in North Vietnam are concerned, that we are prepared to use our military and naval strength against military targets throughout North Vietnam, and we believe that the North Vietnamese are taking a very great risk if they continue their offensive in the South.

I will just leave it there, and they can make their own choice.

ESSAYS

Eugene V. Rostow, like his brother Walt, was a maker of foreign policy in the 1960s. A law professor from Yale University, he has always vigorously and positively explained intervention in Vietnam as the pursuit of America's national interest. He places the struggle in the wider context of a post-1945 threat from global Communism. James C. Thomson, Jr., now of Harvard University, was also an Asian policy-maker; he served in both the State Department and the White House from 1961 to 1966. Yet he became a dissenter and offers far different explanations for intervention, stressing such factors as lessons from the past, bureaucratic inertia, lack of expertise, and miscalculation.

Thomson's autopsy of the subject differs from the radical perspective of Gabriel Kolko of York University. Kolko does not believe that the war was a mistake on the part of the United States or that Washington was simply acting according to the containment doctrine—to check the advance of Communism. He argues that the United States deliberately intervened in Southeast Asia in order to maintain its economic hegemony in the Third World. Vietnam, Kolko concludes, became a symbolic test case of America's ability to continue its economic colonialism in the face of leftist opposition.

The Containment of Communism

EUGENE V. ROSTOW

The situation in Southeast Asia which President Johnson inherited in 1963 was not without hope, if the Soviet Union could be persuaded to cooperate in enforcing the agreements for the neutralization of Laos it had made with us the year before. But that hope, like so many others, proved illusory.

The basic elements of the problem are well known, but they bear restatement.

The Geneva agreements of 1954 undertook to end the hostilities in Indochina and make it possible for the peoples of that area to develop their independence in peace. The Vietminh was to withdraw its forces from Laos and Cambodia, and from the area south of the seventeenth parallel in Vietnam. French Union forces were to withdraw from Vietnam north of the seventeenth parallel. For Laos and Cambodia, this amounted to recognition of the existing royal governments as the sole legal authorities. For Vietnam, in effect, the agreement meant that in the northern zone Ho Chi Minh's Democratic Republic of Vietnam became the de facto government. In the southern zone, Emperor Bao Dai's State of Vietnam was able to consolidate its authority. It was then in the final stages of attaining full independence from France and later was to become a republic.

The agreements provided the possibility that North and South Vietnam could be united as a single state if the peoples of both states, through free elections under international supervision, expressed the wish to be reunited. It was also clear, however, that for the time being the two parts of Vietnam were to be distinct political entities, as was the case in Germany and Korea. Provision was made to allow individuals to migrate from one area to the other, in the expectation of a division of the country which some thought might last for a considerable time. The regimes in Saigon and Hanoi were "governments" in every practical sense, exercising the normal authority of governments, although they were not universally recognized.

The United States made certain basic positions explicit in 1954. We were not a party to the Geneva Accords, but we were far from indifferent to their content. It was clear at the time that there were some outcomes we could not accept. Further, we stated that we should view any aggression in violation of the Geneva Accords with concern, as seriously threatening international peace and security. And third, we took the same position on the reunification of South and North Vietnam that we took in regard to other "nations now divided against their will," that is to say, Germany and Korea. Our policy was that in Vietnam,

Reprinted from *Law, Power, and the Pursuit of Peace* by Eugene V. Rostow by permission of University of Nebraska Press. Copyright © 1968 by University of Nebraska Press.

as in Germany and Korea, we should continue to favor unity by peaceful means, and ultimately through free elections supervised by the United Nations, but that reunification through the use of force was inadmissible. It was manifestly impossible in 1956 to hold free elections under international supervision in North Vietnam, where thousands of dissidents had already been liquidated. It was not conceivable that North Vietnam would permit supervision for elections that could be called free. The government of South Vietnam therefore concluded that the referendum provisions of the Geneva Accords could not be carried out as scheduled. The United States acquiesced in this decision, as most responsible observers did under the circumstances. The Soviet Union did not object.

In 1954, we sought to give formal structure to a coalition among ourselves, some of our allies, and a number of the non-Communist states of Southeast Asia. The result was the SEATO Treaty. In that document, we and our allies underwrote the provisions against direct and indirect aggression in the Geneva Accords. The new government of South Vietnam and its territory were expressly protected by a protocol to the SEATO Treaty, which aimed more widely to safeguard the security of the Southeast Asian signatories, and the other successor states of Indochina. Thus the United States was formally committed as guarantor of the peace in Southern Asia, as it had been committed five years earlier in Europe.

These steps derived from President Eisenhower's considered judgment about the nature of American interests in protecting the integrity and assisting the development of the independent nations of Southeast Asia. We undertook these successive obligations for the same reasons which led us to safeguard the security of Japan, Korea, and the Republic of China. As a Pacific power, we have a national security interest in preventing the transfer of the area, or large parts of it, to Communist control achieved by subversion and aggression. Such conquests would mean a major addition to the power status of hostile and aggressive Communist Chinese and North Vietnamese regimes. It would alter the expectations of many other nations, in Asia, in Europe, and in the Middle East, which rely for their security on an American guaranty. And it would doom our plans for constructive political and economic progress toward stability and development in the region.

There is the view, of course, that it is hopeless to intervene in these explosive situations—that Southeast Asia, South America, and Africa are destined to go through revolutionary turmoil of many kinds, and that nothing can be done to stem the flood.

The simplest answer to this opinion is the accomplishments of many developing states, often achieved in the face of threats both from within and without: Iran, for example, and Thailand, Israel, South Korea, Taiwan, and Malaysia. India and Pakistan have made notable advances in recent years, against formidable obstacles. Others, like Indonesia, have turned sharply from adventurism to policies of peace and economic development. All over the world countries are choosing their own paths to development, based upon their national traditions and their perception of the enlightened methods of modern capitalism, which have brought about the social revolutions of the Free World since 1945

—by all odds the most progressive and successful revolutions of the century.

South Vietnam, on the other hand, has had little chance. Starting in 1957, or at least in 1959, the government of North Vietnam began systematically to initiate and to support guerrilla hostilities against the government of South Vietnam. That effort, steadily increasing in scale and tempo, was part of a deliberate plan to unite Vietnam by force under Communist domination. Its significance to world politics was exactly the same as if attempts had been made by either side to unify Germany or Korea by force. There, too, after all, unification had been promised through free elections; and there, too, elections had not been held.

By 1961, the guerrilla aggression against South Vietnam had made ominous progress. President Kennedy decided to enlarge the program of political, economic, and military aid which President Eisenhower had started. He increased the number of our military advisers, and sent in pilots and other supporting military personnel to assist the armed forces of the South Vietnamese government. Their number rose gradually to 25,000.

This then was the situation which President Johnson found when he became President: a treaty commitment to protect South Vietnam, made by President Eisenhower and ratified by the Senate, and a process of military participation under that treaty, which had been maintained and greatly strengthened by President Kennedy.

North Vietnam intensified its effort, and, as early as 1964, sent its own regular troops to supplement the guerrilla forces organized, trained, and infiltrated from the North. In the same period, attacks were made directly on American naval vessels in the Tonkin Gulf, and on American installations in South Vietnam. These episodes of escalation took place in 1964—a moment in time when Indonesia, under strong Communist influence, was attacking Malaysia, and recurrent trouble threatened India as well. President Johnson ordered retaliatory action in the Tonkin Gulf, and presented the situation to the Congress.

On August 7, 1964, Congress passed a resolution which not only approved retaliatory action in the Tonkin Gulf but reiterated the basic policy decisions taken since 1954 in asserting America's security interest in the defense of Southeast Asia. The second operative part of the resolution reads as follows:

> The United States regards as vital to its national interest and to world peace the maintenance of international peace and security in South East Asia. Consonant with the Constitution and the Charter of the United Nations and in accordance with its obligations under the South East Collective Defense Treaty, the United States is, therefore, prepared, as the President determines, to take all necessary steps, including the use of armed force, to assist any member or protocol state of the South East Asia Collective Defense Treaty requesting assistance in defense of its freedom.

The language of that resolution, and the discussion of its meaning in the Congress, make its significance crystal clear. When Congress and the President act together, the full weight of the nation is placed behind policy. In this instance, the position President Eisenhower took at Geneva in 1954, and in the SEATO Treaty, was solemnly reaffirmed. And American military participation in the war in Vietnam was fully authorized. The joint resolution has the same constitutional status, though not the same international and legal consequences, as a joint resolution declaring that a state of war exists.

Early in 1965, President Johnson made the basic decisions to bomb targets in North Vietnam, and to send American troops into combat. It was clear at the time that if he had not taken this step South Vietnam would have fallen. Would such an event have proved the guarantees of the SEATO Treaty worthless? Would the strong Chinese and North Vietnamese threat to Southeast Asia have multiplied in strength?

The President and other spokesmen for the Administration have explained the purpose of our actions in Vietnam on many occasions. The policy was fully stated in President Johnson's speech at Baltimore in April, 1965. We are in Vietnam, he said, for the same reason that we have a responsibility in Europe —because great interests in world order are in balance and therefore our own security is at stake. The "deepening shadow of Communist China" is the reality behind the contest in Vietnam, which "is part of a wider pattern of aggressive intention." We are there, he went on, because "we have a promise to keep," and it would shake confidence "from Berlin to Thailand" if an American commitment were proved worthless.

> Our objective is the independence of South Viet-Nam, and its freedom from attack. We want nothing for ourselves—only that the people of South Viet-Nam be allowed to guide their own country in their own way.
>
> We will do everything necessary to reach that objective. And we will do only what is absolutely necessary.

The legal and political basis for our course in Vietnam is clear.

Whatever view one takes of the disputed origins of the war in Vietnam— whether it is considered simply an insurrection against the authority of the South Vietnamese state aided by North Vietnam, or an infiltration and invasion from North Vietnam—the issue of international law and politics is the same. In either view of the facts, North Vietnam is waging war against South Vietnam. And South Vietnam has the right to ask for the help of the international community in resisting the North Vietnamese attack. No state has the right to assist an insurrection against another. The international law on the subject has been agreed for centuries, and it is confirmed by the Charter of the United Nations.

Nor can it be contended for this purpose that all of Vietnam is one country, so that the North Vietnamese attempt to conquer South Vietnam should be considered a civil war, and therefore an internal affair of the Vietnamese nation. The argument proves too much. It would license a unification of Germany and of Korea by force. And it is denied by the facts. There is no Vietnamese state; on the contrary, the two political entities governed from Hanoi and Saigon are in fact separate states, so acknowledged by the international community, by the SEATO Treaty, and by many other acts of recognition. Both regimes raise taxes and armies, conduct foreign relations, and exercise all the normal activities of governments within their boundaries.

Neither South Vietnam nor the United States is interested in conquering North Vietnam, or in overturning its Communist regime. The only issue of the war is whether North Vietnam will be allowed forcibly to impose its system on South Vietnam.

But, men ask, does the United States have any national interest in South Vietnam? Does the conflict in Vietnam threaten the general balance of power, or otherwise justify intervention? Or is it the kind of local conflict, unfortunate for the participants, which the world should pass by on the other side?

From the point of view of the national interests of the United States, there are several answers to the question.

The first is the obligation of the SEATO Treaty. The commitments of that treaty are expressly addressed to the risk which in fact materialized—the risk, that is, that North Vietnam would resume the war.

Secondly, the obligations of the United Nations Charter are not suspended when permanent members of the Security Council disagree. The principles of the Charter are binding on signatories as rules of international law, even though neither the Security Council nor the Assembly has been willing as yet to act officially. Those principles condemn the attack of North Vietnam on South Vietnam, and authorize the members of the organization to offer South Vietnam assistance in its efforts of self-defense.

Thirdly, it has been the judgment of three Presidents and several Congresses that the independence of South Vietnam was directly related to the fate of Southeast Asia as a whole, and therefore to our national interests in a stable balance of power. If South Vietnam were to be forcibly taken over, the parallel expansionist designs of Communist China and North Vietnam would surely be encouraged, and the resistance to these designs seriously weakened throughout the area, and perhaps beyond. Responsible opinion throughout Southeast Asia is agreed that the stakes in Vietnam involve the most drastic alternatives for Southeast Asia and for Asia as a whole. As these lines are written, during the spring of 1968, the pace of guerrilla intrusions in Laos, Thailand, and Burma are increasing, and increasing ominously. The imposition of a Communist government in South Vietnam would menace all hopes of building a strong coalition for peaceful progress in Southeast Asia, and elsewhere as well. It would be a signal for a policy of *sauve qui peut*—and Devil take the hindmost.

Finally, it is obvious that both the Soviet Union and China regard the conflict in Vietnam as a test for a technique of revolution. As Soviet spokesmen have made clear, nuclear warfare is unthinkable, and massed frontal attacks of the Korean type are too dangerous to be tried. The spread of Communism, they have said, must therefore depend on what they call "wars of national liberation," that is to say, insurrections supported from abroad or the proxy wars which they incite. On their present scale, the hostilities in Vietnam could hardly continue for any length of time without large-scale aid from China and the Soviet Union. De-escalation of the fighting should follow logically if that aid were to be reduced.

So far, however, the Soviet Union has not responded either to proposals of this kind, or to requests that it join with the United Kingdom in reactivating the enforcement procedures for the Geneva agreements dealing with Laos or Vietnam.

Thus the attack on South Vietnam involves the principle of the Truman Doctrine—the challenge we decided to confront in Greece, in Berlin, and in Korea, an attempt to change the boundary between the two systems by force. If this effort prevailed, all that has been gained at such cost in previous tests of the Truman Doctrine would be in doubt. And the instability of the world would increase.

In a fundamental sense, the controversies over the origins of the war in Vietnam are irrelevant. Whether President Eisenhower and the Senate were right or wrong in ratifying the SEATO Treaty; whether President Kennedy made a mistake in beginning to send in large numbers of American troops to enforce that commitment—these issues are of less significance than the dilemma President Johnson has had to confront.

Our presence in South Vietnam has made it possible for the South Vietnamese to create for themselves a constitutional system and the beginnings of national political development, which are by far the most hopeful they have ever had. Most South Vietnamese have committed themselves to this path, and are daily increasing their ability to defend it.

Our commitment to South Vietnam has made it possible for the South Vietnamese to take these steps, steps which offer promise of a truly unified South Vietnam, in which the Vietnamese themselves could make a successful Communist "war of national liberation" an improbability, short of open invasion, such as that of Czechoslovakia. To abandon our commitment at this time would be to undermine this process before it could hope to succeed.

Such an abandonment would be more than a simple act of folly; it would cast a shadow of doubt over the whole network of our security arrangements, the central nervous system of world politics. There would be little security to protect our interests anywhere if America's promise faltered or failed when the going got rough. Such an event would weaken the deterrent influence of our security commitments, which are crucial to the very possibility of world peace.

As President Kennedy once said: "The 1930's taught us a clear lesson: aggressive conduct, if allowed to go unchecked and unchallenged, ultimately leads to war. The nation is opposed to war. We are also true to our word."

If aggression succeeds in South Vietnam it would open a Pandora's box for wars of national liberation, especially in the struggling and disoriented world of the developing countries. If it fails, there is some hope that China will come in time to accept the wisdom of the Truman Doctrine. As President Bourguiba of Tunisia has recently said:

> ... the problem of Vietnam is not as simple as one thinks. It is a serious problem, involving the equilibrium of the world. ... An analysis of the events leads to the conclusion that the struggle in Vietnam is taking place between America and China behind the scenes. ... For Mao Tse-tung the object is to prove that the United States can be brought to capitulation. ... Things are far from simple, and what is called "imperialism" often is only a matter of opinion. To humanity's misfortune, it happens that peace is founded on the balance of power. ... I am not seeking to spare anyone or to please any nation when I say that the world would be in danger the day that, in response to a trend of public opinion,

America decided to go back to her former isolationism. . . . China would seize control of all the countries in the region and would wrest leadership of the Communist world from Moscow. And that would be the end of world peace. . . . Hence the conflict we are witnessing has a scope and significance that goes beyond Vietnam.

The continuance of the war, President Bourguiba contends, threatens the modus vivendi on which the chance of peace turns. "One can imagine," he writes, "the mortal danger to which the world would be exposed if East Germany or West Germany were to attempt to achieve, for its own benefit, the unification of the country, as in Vietnam." After each Soviet attempt since the war to extend its sphere of influence, he points out, the Soviets returned to the demarcation line of their sphere of influence. No solution in Vietnam is conceivable without threatening "the balance of the world," President Bourguiba argues, other than the preservation of a South Vietnam free to choose its own course.

Accepting this reasoning, President Johnson has persisted in a course of measured resistance to North Vietnamese aggression, using limited force, and seeking to persuade Moscow, Peking, and Hanoi to live in accordance with the logic of coexistence.

The President has linked the military campaign in Vietnam to three concurrent political campaigns.

The first is addressed to the Soviet Union, and is designed to accomplish two purposes: (1) to reassure the Soviets that our exclusive and limited military goal is to protect South Vietnam, and not to destroy or conquer North Vietnam or to weaken Soviet influence in that country; and (2) to enlist the cooperation of the Soviet Union in persuading the regime in Hanoi to desist from its attempt to unite Vietnam by force. The President accepts the interest of the Soviet Union in helping North Vietnam defend itself. That interest is parallel to our own in the defense of South Vietnam. His concern, in note after note, and in talk after talk, is to invoke the joint responsibility of the two leading powers in the world for the ultimate protection of the peace. The basis of his appeal is the principle of the Truman Doctrine, that in situations like those in Vietnam, Korea, or Germany, the use of force is simply too dangerous to be tolerated.

The President's second diplomatic effort pursues every opportunity to engage the regime in Hanoi in negotiations based on the principles of the Geneva Accords of 1954 and of 1962. In this process, American officials have talked with many representatives of many governments in almost every country of the world, including direct and indirect exchanges with Hanoi.

Three principal lines of approach have been taken by President Johnson.

First, in carrying out his commitment to "unconditional negotiations," we have responded affirmatively to the repeated public appeals of world leaders for peace talks.

Second, we have acted unilaterally on five separate occasions to stop the bombing in order to meet the contention that North Vietnam would move toward peace if we stopped bombing the North.

And, finally, we have approached Hanoi—both directly and through intermediaries—in a serious effort to achieve a settlement or, at least, to bring about reciprocal steps to reduce the level of fighting.

The events of the winter of 1966–1967 illustrate the President's methods in his continuing quest for a peaceful resolution of the Vietnam conflict.

When in December, 1966, efforts through an intermediary to arrange meetings with Hanoi failed, and the bombing pauses over the Christmas and New Year's period resulted only in dramatic increases in infiltration into South Vietnam, direct contacts were established with the North Vietnamese. The substantive exchanges of repeated contacts in January and early February were summarized in messages we conveyed in early February to Chairman Kosygin and Prime Minister Wilson, heads of the Soviet and British governments, the Co-Chairmen of the Geneva Conference, who were meeting in London.

We informed the British and Soviet representatives that we were ready to stop the bombing of North Vietnam if Hanoi would agree to stop infiltration of the South. In addition, we would also promise not to increase the size of our forces in the South. These assurances could be exchanged secretly, so that the continued suspension of the bombing would appear to be unilateral. We said we should welcome British and Soviet support for this approach.

Although Hanoi had known of this basic position of the United States government for at least three months, on February 8, in an effort to avoid misunderstanding, President Johnson reiterated it in a letter to President Ho Chi Minh, emphasizing that these acts of restraint on both sides would make it possible to conduct serious private discussions leading toward an early peace. Such a meeting, the President stated, could take place in Moscow, Burma, or elsewhere.

Ho Chi Minh's reply on February 15 was harsh and unyielding—halt the bombing "definitely and unconditionally," cease all other acts of war, withdraw all American forces from Vietnam, recognize the Liberation Front as the sole legitimate representatives of the South Vietnamese people, and let the Vietnamese settle their problems themselves. In short, it was a formula for turning South Vietnam over to the Communists and to Hanoi's control.

To slam the door more completely, Hanoi then published President Johnson's letter, though not the communications which had preceded it.

Despite this provocation, President Johnson has refused thus far to publish the documents. His purpose has been to preserve the secrecy of the channel, in the hope that it could someday be used again.

Finally, on March 31, 1968, President Johnson succeeded in obtaining a sign that Hanoi might be ready to discuss the possibility of peace. Our unilateral halt in bombing above the twentieth parallel, coupled with the President's withdrawal from the election of 1968, proved to be a volcanic event, dislodging resistance, at least for a time, to the appearance of negotiation. The result was the start of talks with Hanoi in Paris, and a partial, if temporary, consolidation of national opinion at home.

Our third campaign in Southeast Asia consists in encouraging the non-

Communist Asian governments to work together for mutual security and peaceful development. In the Vietnam war itself, there are now more forces sent by our allies than there were in Korea.

Behind the shield of American commitment, the non-Communist governments of Asia have begun to move in new directions. Japan, Australia, New Zealand, Thailand, Malaysia, the Philippines, Singapore, the Republic of Korea, and the Republic of China are evolving toward a broader view of their responsibilities for collective security and development. Indonesia has turned from pro-Communist adventures to a businesslike nationalist government. South Vietnam itself, through five elections in eighteen months, has created a new constitutional base for its national life.

In Asia as in Europe, the Truman Doctrine has encouraged regional forces of cooperation to come into being. Their effect should be felt for many years after the war in Vietnam is brought to a conclusion.

Against this background, it is difficult to translate the furious political arguments of 1967–1968 about our Vietnam policy into words tangible enough to permit analysis. Hostilities in Vietnam, the American people have been told repeatedly on high authority, are an immoral act on the part of the United States, contrary to our national tradition. But those who make such claims never explain why it is immoral for a great power to remain loyal to its treaties, and help a small people resist aggression. The critics protest American bombing, but never elucidate the moral difference between bombing and other forms of warfare, or the indiscriminate terrorism of the Vietcong operations in South Vietnam. Nor do they explain how we could hope to establish conditions of peace in the world without stopping the process of Communist expansion at a given point, and obtaining Soviet and Chinese acceptance of the principle of equilibrium. They never attempt to demonstrate how unilateral withdrawal in Vietnam would affect the credibility of our guarantees elsewhere, or make it politically possible for us to resume the struggle on a more favorable field, short of nuclear war, when aggression against a free country is attempted again, directly or indirectly, with the support of the Soviet Union or China.

Historical Legacies and Bureaucratic Procedures

JAMES C. THOMSON, JR.

As a case study in the making of foreign policy, the Vietnam War will fascinate historians and social scientists for many decades to come. One question that will certainly be asked: How did men of superior ability, sound training, and high ideals—American policy-makers of the 1960s—create such costly and divisive policy?

As one who watched the decision-making process in Washington from 1961

James C. Thomson, Jr., "How Could Vietnam Happen? An Autopsy," *Atlantic Monthly*, 221 (1968), 47–53.

to 1966 under Presidents Kennedy and Johnson, I can suggest a preliminary answer. I can do so by briefly listing some of the factors that seemed to me to shape our Vietnam policy during my years as an East Asia specialist at the State Department and the White House. I shall deal largely with Washington as I saw or sensed it, and not with Saigon, where I have spent but a scant three days, in the entourage of the Vice President, or with other decision centers, the capitals of interested parties. Nor will I deal with other important parts of the record: Vietnam's history prior to 1961, for instance, or the overall course of America's relations with Vietnam.

Yet a first and central ingredient in these years of Vietnam decisions does involve history. The ingredient was *the legacy of the 1950s*—by which I mean the so-called "loss of China," the Korean War, and the Far East policy of Secretary of State Dulles.

This legacy had an institutional by-product for the Kennedy Administration: in 1961 the U.S. government's East Asian establishment was undoubtedly the most rigid and doctrinaire of Washington's regional divisions in foreign affairs. This was especially true at the Department of State, where the incoming Administration found the Bureau of Far Eastern Affairs the hardest nut to crack. It was a bureau that had been purged of its best China expertise, and of far-sighted, dispassionate men, as a result of McCarthyism. Its members were generally committed to one policy line: the close containment and isolation of mainland China, the harassment of "neutralist" nations which sought to avoid alignment with either Washington or Peking, and the maintenance of a network of alliances with anti-Communist client states on China's periphery.

Another aspect of the legacy was the special vulnerability and sensitivity of the new Democratic Administration on Far East policy issues. The memory of the McCarthy era was still very sharp, and Kennedy's margin of victory was too thin. The 1960 Offshore Islands TV debate between Kennedy and Nixon had shown the President-elect the perils of "fresh thinking." The Administration was inherently leery of moving too fast on Asia. As a result, the Far East Bureau (now the Bureau of East Asian and Pacific Affairs) was the last one to be overhauled. Not until Averell Harriman was brought in as Assistant Secretary in December, 1961, were significant personnel changes attempted, and it took Harriman several months to make a deep imprint on the bureau because of his necessary preoccupation with the Laos settlement. Once he did so, there was virtually no effort to bring back the purged or exiled East Asia experts.

There were other important by-products of this "legacy of the fifties":

The new Administration inherited and somewhat shared *a general perception of China-on-the-march*—a sense of China's vastness, its numbers, its belligerence; a revived sense, perhaps, of the Golden Horde. This was a perception fed by Chinese intervention in the Korean War (an intervention actually based on appallingly bad communications and mutual miscalculation on the part of Washington and Peking; but the careful unraveling of that tragedy, which scholars have accomplished, had not yet become part of the conventional wisdom).

The new Administration inherited and briefly accepted *a monolithic con-*

ception of the Communist bloc. Despite much earlier predictions and reports by outside analysts, policy-makers did not begin to accept the reality and possible finality of the Sino-Soviet split until the first weeks of 1962. The inevitably corrosive impact of competing nationalisms on Communism was largely ignored.

The new Administration inherited and to some extent shared *the "domino theory" about Asia.* This theory resulted from profound ignorance of Asian history and hence ignorance of the radical differences among Asian nations and societies. It resulted from a blindness to the power and resilience of Asian nationalisms. (It may also have resulted from a subconscious sense that, since "all Asians look alike," all Asian nations will act alike.) As a theory, the domino fallacy was not merely inaccurate but also insulting to Asian nations; yet it has continued to this day to beguile men who should know better.

Finally, the legacy of the fifties was apparently compounded by an uneasy sense of a worldwide Communist challenge to the new Administration after the Bay of Pigs fiasco. A first manifestation was the President's traumatic Vienna meeting with Khrushchev in June, 1961; then came the Berlin crisis of the summer. All this created an atmosphere in which President Kennedy undoubtedly felt under special pressure to show his nation's mettle in Vietnam —if the Vietnamese, unlike the people of Laos, were willing to fight.

In general, the legacy of the fifties shaped such early moves of the new Administration as the decisions to maintain a high-visibility SEATO (by sending the Secretary of State himself instead of some underling to its first meeting in 1961), to back away from diplomatic recognition of Mongolia in the summer of 1961, and most important, to expand U.S. military assistance to South Vietnam that winter on the basis of the much more tentative Eisenhower commitment. It should be added that the increased commitment to Vietnam was also fueled by a new breed of military strategists and academic social scientists (some of whom had entered the new Administration) who had developed theories of counterguerrilla warfare and were eager to see them put to the test. To some, "counter-insurgency" seemed a new panacea for coping with the world's instability.

So much for the legacy and the history. Any new Administration inherits both complicated problems and simplistic views of the world. But surely among the policy-makers of the Kennedy and Johnson Administrations there were men who would warn of the dangers of an open-ended commitment to the Vietnam quagmire?

This raises a central question, at the heart of the policy process: Where were the experts, the doubters, and the dissenters? Were they there at all, and if so, what happened to them?

The answer is complex but instructive.

In the first place, the American government was sorely *lacking in real Vietnam or Indochina expertise.* Originally treated as an adjunct of Embassy Paris, our Saigon embassy and the Vietnam Desk at State were largely staffed from 1954 onward by French-speaking Foreign Service personnel of narrowly European experience. Such diplomats were even more closely restricted than the normal embassy officer—by cast of mind as well as language—to contacts with Vietnam's French-speaking urban elites. For instance, Foreign Service linguists in Portugal are able to speak with the peasantry if they get out of Lisbon and choose to do so; not so the French speakers of Embassy Saigon.

In addition, the *shadow of the "loss of China"* distorted Vietnam reporting. Career officers in the Department, and especially those in the field, had not forgotten the fate of their World War II colleagues who wrote in frankness from China and were later pilloried by Senate committees for critical comments on the Chinese Nationalists. Candid reporting on the strengths of the Viet Cong and the weaknesses of the Diem government was inhibited by the memory. It was also inhibited by some higher officials, notably Ambassador Nolting in Saigon, who refused to sign off on such cables.

In due course, to be sure, some Vietnam talent was discovered or developed. But a recurrent and increasingly important factor in the decision-making process was *the banishment of real expertise.* Here the underlying cause was the "closed politics" of policy-making as issues become hot: the more sensitive the issue, and the higher it rises in the bureaucracy, the more completely the experts are excluded while the harassed senior generalists take over (that is, the Secretaries, Undersecretaries, and Presidential Assistants). The frantic skimming of briefing papers in the back seats of limousines is no substitute for the presence of specialists; furthermore, in times of crisis such papers are deemed "too sensitive" even for review by the specialists. Another underlying cause of this banishment, as Vietnam became more critical, was the replacement of the experts, who were generally and increasingly pessimistic, by men described as "can-do guys," loyal and energetic fixers unsoured by expertise. In early 1965, when I confided my growing policy doubts to an older colleague on the NSC staff, he assured me that the smartest thing both of us could do was to "steer clear of the whole Vietnam mess"; the gentleman in question had the misfortune to be a "can-do guy," however, and is now highly placed in Vietnam, under orders to solve the mess.

Despite the banishment of the experts, internal doubters and dissenters did indeed appear and persist. Yet as I watched the process, such men were effectively neutralized by a subtle dynamic: *the domestication of dissenters.* Such "domestication" arose out of a twofold clubbish need: on the one hand, the dissenter's desire to stay aboard; and on the other hand, the nondissenter's conscience. Simply stated, dissent, when recognized, was made to feel at home. On the lowest possible scale of importance, I must confess my own considerable sense of dignity and acceptance (both vital) when my senior White House employer would refer to me as his "favorite dove." Far more significant was the case of the former Undersecretary of State, George Ball. Once Mr. Ball began to express doubts, he was warmly institutionalized: he was encouraged to become the inhouse devil's advocate on Vietnam. The upshot was inevitable: the process of escalation allowed for periodic requests to Mr. Ball to speak his piece; Ball felt good, I assume (he had fought for righteousness); the others felt good (they had given a full hearing to the dovish option); and there was minimal unpleasantness. The club remained intact; and it is of course possible that matters would have gotten worse faster if Mr. Ball had kept silent, or left before his final departure in the fall of 1966. There was also, of course, the case of the last institutionalized doubter, Bill Moyers. The President is said to have greeted his arrival at meetings with an affectionate, "Well, here comes Mr. Stop-the-Bombing . . ." Here again the dynamics of domesticated dissent sustained the relationship for a while.

A related point—and crucial, I suppose, to government at all times—was the "effectiveness" trap, the trap that keeps men from speaking out, as clearly or often as they might, within the government. And it is the trap that keeps men from resigning in protest and airing their dissent outside the government. The most important asset that a man brings to bureaucratic life is his "effectiveness," a mysterious combination of training, style, and connections. The most ominous complaint that can be whispered of a bureaucrat is: "I'm afraid Charlie's beginning to lose his effectiveness." To preserve your effectiveness, you must decide where and when to fight the mainstream of policy; the opportunities range from pillow talk with your wife, to private drinks with your friends, to meetings with the Secretary of State or the President. The inclination to remain silent or to acquiesce in the presence of the great men—to live to fight another day, to give on this issue so that you can be "effective" on later issues—is overwhelming. Nor is it the tendency of youth alone; some of our most senior officials, men of wealth and fame, whose place in history is secure, have remained silent lest their connection with power be terminated. As for the disinclination to resign in protest: while not necessarily a Washington or even American specialty, it seems more true of a government in which ministers have no parliamentary back-bench to which to retreat. In the absence of such a refuge, it is easy to rationalize the decision to stay aboard. By doing so, one may be able to prevent a few bad things from happening and perhaps even make a few good things happen. To exit is to lose even those marginal chances for "effectiveness."

Another factor must be noted: as the Vietnam controversy escalated at home, there developed a preoccupation with Vietnam public relations as opposed to Vietnam policy-making. And here, ironically, internal doubters and dissenters were heavily employed. For such men, by virtue of their own doubts, were often deemed best able to "massage" the doubting intelligentsia. My senior East Asia colleague at the White House, a brilliant and humane doubter who had dealt with Indochina since 1954, spent three quarters of his working days on Vietnam public relations: drafting presidential responses to letters from important critics, writing conciliatory language for presidential speeches, and meeting quite interminably with delegations of outraged Quakers, clergymen, academics, and housewives. His regular callers were the late A. J. Muste and Norman Thomas; mine were members of the Women's Strike for Peace. Our orders from above: keep them off the backs of busy policy-makers (who usually happened to be nondoubters). Incidentally, my most discouraging assignment in the realm of public relations was the preparation of a White House pamphlet entitled Why Vietnam, in September, 1965; in a gesture toward my conscience, I fought—and lost—a battle to have the title followed by a question mark.

Through a variety of procedures, both institutional and personal, doubt, dissent, and expertise were effectively neutralized in the making of policy. But what can be said of the men "in charge"? It is patently absurd to suggest that they produced such tragedy by intention and calculation. But it is neither absurd nor difficult to discern certain forces at work that caused decent and honorable men to do great harm.

Here I would stress the paramount role of *executive fatigue*. No factor seems to me more crucial and underrated in the making of foreign policy. The physical and emotional toll of executive responsibility in State, the Pentagon, the White House, and other executive agencies is enormous; that toll is of course compounded by extended service. Many of today's Vietnam policy-makers have been on the job for from four to seven years. Complaints may be few, and physical health may remain unimpaired, though emotional health is far harder to gauge. But what is most seriously eroded in the deadening process of fatigue is freshness of thought, imagination, a sense of possibility, a sense of priorities and perspective—those rare assets of a new Administration in its first year or two of office. The tired policy-maker becomes a prisoner of his own narrowed view of the world and his own clichéd rhetoric. He becomes irritable and defensive—short on sleep, short on family ties, short on patience. Such men make bad policy and then compound it. They have neither the time nor the temperament for new ideas or preventive diplomacy.

Below the level of the fatigued executives in the making of Vietnam policy was a widespread phenomenon: *the curator mentality* in the Department of State. By this I mean the collective inertia produced by the bureaucrat's view of his job. At State, the average "desk officer" inherits from his predecessor our policy toward Country X; he regards it as his function to keep that policy intact— under glass, untampered with, and dusted—so that he may pass it on in two to four years to his successor. And such curatorial service generally merits promotion within the system. (Maintain the status quo, and you will stay out of trouble.) In some circumstances, the inertia bred by such an outlook can act as a brake against rash innovation. But on many issues, this inertia sustains the momentum of bad policy and unwise commitments—momentum that might otherwise have been resisted within the ranks. Clearly, Vietnam is such an issue.

To fatigue and inertia must be added the factor of internal confusion. Even among the "architects" of our Vietnam commitment, there has been persistent *confusion as to what type of war we were fighting* and, as a direct consequence, *confusion as to how to end that war.* (The "credibility gap" is, in part, a reflection of such internal confusion.) Was it, for instance, a civil war, in which case counterinsurgency might suffice? Or was it a war of international aggression? (This might invoke SEATO or UN commitment.) Who was the aggressor —and the "real enemy"? The Viet Cong? Hanoi? Peking? Moscow? International Communism? Or maybe "Asian Communism"? Differing enemies dictated differing strategies and tactics. And confused throughout, in like fashion, was the question of American objectives; your objectives depended on whom you were fighting and why. I shall not forget my assignment from an Assistant Secretary of State in March, 1964: to draft a speech for Secretary McNamara which would, *inter alia,* once and for all dispose of the canard that the Vietnam conflict was a civil war. "But in some ways, of course," I mused, "it *is* a civil war." "Don't play word games with me!" snapped the Assistant Secretary.

Similar confusion beset the concept of "negotiations"—anathema to much of official Washington from 1961 to 1965. Not until April, 1965, did "unconditional discussions" become respectable, via a presidential speech; even then the Secretary of State stressed privately to newsmen that nothing had changed, since "discussions" were by no means the same as "negotiations." Months later that issue was resolved. But it took even longer to obtain a fragile internal agreement that negotiations might include the Viet Cong as something other than an appendage to Hanoi's delegation. Given such confusion as to the whos and whys of our Vietnam commitment, it is not surprising, as Theodore Draper has written, that policy-makers find it so difficult to agree on how to end the war.

Of course, one force—a constant in the vortex of commitment—was that of *wishful thinking.* I partook of it myself at many times. I did so especially during Washington's struggle with Diem in the autumn of 1963 when some of us at State believed that for once, in dealing with a difficult client state, the U.S. government could use the leverage of our economic and military assistance to make good things happen, instead of being led around by the nose by men like Chiang Kai-shek and Syngman Rhee (and, in that particular instance, by Diem). If we could prove that point, I thought, and move into a new day, with or without Diem, then Vietnam was well worth the effort. Later came the wishful thinking of the air-strike planners in the late autumn of 1964; there were those who actually thought that after six weeks of air strikes, the North Vietnamese would come crawling to us to ask for peace talks. And what, someone asked in one of the meetings of the time, if they don't? The answer was that we would bomb for another four weeks, and that would do the trick. And a few weeks later came one instance of wishful thinking that was symptomatic of good men misled: in January, 1965, I encountered one of the very highest figures in the Administration at a dinner, drew him aside, and told him of my worries about the air-strike option. He told me that I really shouldn't worry; it was his conviction that before any such plans could be put into effect, a neutralist government would come to power in Saigon that would politely invite us out. And finally, there was the recurrent wishful thinking that sustained many of us through the trying months of 1965–1966 after the air strikes had begun: that surely, somehow, one way or another, we would "be in a conference in six months," and the escalatory spiral would be suspended. The basis of our hope: "It simply can't go on."

As a further influence on policy-makers I would cite the factor of *bureaucratic detachment.* By this I mean what at best might be termed the professional callousness of the surgeon (and indeed, medical lingo—the "surgical strike" for instance—seemed to crop up in the euphemisms of the times). In Washington the semantics of the military muted the reality of war for the civilian policy-makers. In quiet, air-conditioned, thick-carpeted rooms, such terms as "systematic pressure," "armed reconnaissance," "targets of opportunity," and even "body count" seemed to breed a sort of games-theory detachment. Most memorable to me was a moment in the late 1964 target planning when the question under discussion was how heavy our bombing should be, and how extensive our strafing, at some midpoint in the projected pattern of systematic pressure. An Assistant Secretary of State resolved the point in the following words: "It seems to me that our orchestration should be mainly violins, but with periodic touches of brass." Perhaps the biggest shock of my return to Cambridge, Massachusetts, was the realization that the young men, the flesh and blood I taught and saw on these university streets, were potentially some of the numbers on the charts of those faraway planners. In a curious sense, Cambridge is closer to this war than Washington.

There is an unprovable factor that relates to bureaucratic detachment: the ingredient of *crypto-racism*. I do not mean to imply any conscious contempt for Asian loss of life on the part of Washington officials. But I do mean to imply that bureaucratic detachment may well be compounded by a traditional Western sense that there are so many Asians, after all; that Asians have a fatalism about life and a disregard for its loss; that they are cruel and barbaric to their own people; and that they are very different from us (and all look alike?). And I *do* mean to imply that the upshot of such subliminal views is a subliminal question whether Asians, and particularly Asian peasants, and most particularly Asian Communists, are really people—like you and me. To put the matter another way: would we have pursued quite such policies—and quite such military tactics—if the Vietnamese were white?

It is impossible to write of Vietnam decision-making without writing about language. Throughout the conflict, words have been of paramount importance. I refer here to the impact of *rhetorical escalation* and to the *problem of oversell*. In an important sense, Vietnam has become of crucial significance to us *because we have said that it is of crucial significance*. (The issue obviously relates to the public relations preoccupation described earlier.)

The key here is domestic politics: the need to sell the American people, press, and Congress on support for an unpopular and costly war in which the objectives themselves have been in flux. To sell means to persuade, and to persuade means rhetoric. As the difficulties and costs have mounted, so has the definition of the stakes. This is not to say that rhetorical escalation is an orderly process; executive prose is the product of many writers, and some concepts—North Vietnamese infiltration, America's "national honor," Red China as the chief enemy—have entered the rhetoric only gradually and even sporadically. But there is an upward spiral nonetheless. And once you have *said* that the American Experiment itself stands or falls on the Vietnam outcome, you have thereby created a national stake far beyond any earlier stakes.

Crucial throughout the process of Vietnam decision-making was a conviction among many policy-makers: that Vietnam posed a *fundamental test of America's national will*. Time and again I was told by men reared in the tradition of Henry L. Stimson that all we needed was the will, and we would then prevail. Implicit in such a view, it seemed to me, was a curious assumption that Asians lacked will, or at least that in a contest between Asian and Anglo-Saxon wills, the non-Asians must prevail. A corollary to the persistent belief in will was a *fascination with power* and an awe in the face of the power America possessed as no nation or civilization ever before. Those who doubted our role in Vietnam were said to shrink from the burdens of power, the obligations of power, the uses of power, the responsibility of power. By implication, such men were soft-headed and effete.

Finally, no discussion of the factors and forces at work on Vietnam policy-makers can ignore the central fact of *human ego investment*. Men who have participated in a decision develop a stake in that decision. As they participate in further, related decisions, their stake increases. It might have been possible to dissuade a man of strong self-confidence at an early stage of the ladder of decision; but it is infinitely harder at later stages since a change of mind there usually involves implicit or explicit repudiation of a chain of previous decisions.

To put it bluntly: at the heart of the Vietnam calamity is a group of able, dedicated men who have been regularly and repeatedly wrong—and whose standing with their contemporaries, and more important, with history, depends, as they see it, on being proven right. These are not men who can be asked to extricate themselves from error.

The various ingredients I have cited in the making of Vietnam policy have created a variety of results, most of them fairly obvious. Here are some that seem to me most central:

Throughout the conflict, there has been *persistent and repeated miscalculation* by virtually all the actors, in high echelons and low, whether dove, hawk, or something else. To cite one simple example among many: in late 1964 and early 1965, some peace-seeking planners at State who strongly opposed the projected bombing of the North urged that, instead, American ground forces be sent to South Vietnam; this would, they said, increase our bargaining leverage against the North—our "chips"—and would give us something to negotiate about (the withdrawal of our forces) at an early peace conference. Simultaneously, the air-strike option was urged by many in the military who were dead set against American participation in "another land war in Asia"; they were joined by other civilian peace-seekers who wanted to bomb Hanoi into early negotiations. By late 1965, we had ended up with the worst of all worlds: ineffective and costly air strikes against the North, spiraling ground forces in the South, and no negotiations in sight.

Throughout the conflict as well, there has been *a steady give-in to pressures for a military solution* and only minimal and sporadic efforts at a diplomatic and political solution. In part this resulted from the confusion (earlier cited) among the civilians—confusion regarding objectives and strategy. And in part this resulted from the self-enlarging nature of military investment. Once air strikes and particularly ground forces were introduced, our investment itself had transformed the original stakes. More air power was needed to protect the ground forces; and then more ground forces to protect the ground forces. And needless to say, the military mind develops its own momentum in the absence of clear guidelines from the civilians. Once asked to save South Vietnam, rather than to "advise" it, the American military could not but press for escalation. In addition, sad to report, assorted military constituencies, once involved in Vietnam, have had a series of cases to prove: for instance, the utility not only of air power (the Air Force) but of supercarrier-based air power (the Navy). Also, Vietnam policy has suffered from one ironic byproduct of Secretary McNamara's establishment of civilian control at the Pentagon: in the face of such control, interservice rivalry has given way to a united front among the military—reflected in the new but recurrent phenomenon of JCS unanimity. In conjunction with traditional congressional allies (mostly Southern senators and representatives) such a united front would pose a formidable problem for any President.

Throughout the conflict, there have been *missed opportunities, large and small, to disengage ourselves from Vietnam on increasingly unpleasant but still acceptable terms.* Of the many moments from 1961 onward, I shall cite only one, the last and most important opportunity that was lost: in the summer of 1964 the President instructed his chief advisers to prepare for him as wide a range of Vietnam options as possible for postelection consideration and decision. He explicitly asked that all options be laid out. What happened next was, in effect, Lyndon Johnson's slow-motion Bay of Pigs. For the advisers so effectively converged on one single option—juxtaposed against two other, phony options (in effect, blowing up the world, or scuttle-and-run)—that the President was confronted with unanimity for bombing the North from all his trusted counselors. Had he been more confident in foreign affairs, had he been deeply informed on Vietnam and Southeast Asia, and had he raised some hard questions that unanimity had submerged, this President could have used the largest electoral mandate in history to de-escalate in Vietnam, in the clear expectation that at the worst a neutralist government would come to power in Saigon and politely invite us out. Today, many lives and dollars later, such an alternative has become an elusive and infinitely more expensive possibility.

In the course of these years, another result of Vietnam decision-making has been *the abuse and distortion of history.* Vietnamese, Southeast Asian, and Far Eastern history has been rewritten by our policy-makers, and their spokesmen, to conform with the alleged necessity of our presence in Vietnam. Highly dubious analogies from our experience elsewhere—the "Munich" sellout and "containment" from Europe, the Malayan insurgency and the Korean War from Asia—have been imported in order to justify our actions. And more recent events have been fitted to the Procrustean bed of Vietnam. Most notably, the change of power in Indonesia in 1965–1966 has been ascribed to our Vietnam presence; and virtually all progress in the Pacific region—the rise of regionalism, new forms of cooperation, and mounting growth rates—has been similarly explained. The Indonesian allegation is undoubtedly false (I tried to prove it, during six months of careful investigation at the White House, and had to confess failure); the regional allegation is patently unprovable in either direction (except, of course, for the clear fact that the economies of both Japan and Korea have profited enormously from our Vietnam-related procurement in these countries; but that is a costly and highly dubious form of foreign aid).

There is a final result of Vietnam policy I would cite that holds potential danger for the future of American foreign policy: *the rise of a new breed of American ideologues who see Vietnam as the ultimate test of their doctrine.* I have in mind those men in Washington who have given a new life to the missionary impulse in American foreign relations: who believe that this nation, in this era, has received a threefold endowment that can transform the world. As they see it, that endowment is composed of, first, our unsurpassed military might; second, our clear technological supremacy; and third, our allegedly invincible benevolence (our "altruism," our affluence, our lack of territorial aspirations). Together, it is argued, this threefold endowment provides us with the opportunity and the obligation to ease the nations of the earth toward modernization and stability: toward a full-fledged *Pax Americana Technocratica.* In reaching toward this goal, Vietnam is viewed as the last and crucial test. Once we have succeeded there, the road ahead is clear. In a sense, these men are our counterpart to the visionaries of Communism's radical left: they are technocracy's own Maoists. They do not govern Washington today. But their doctrine rides high.

Long before I went into government, I was told a story about Henry L. Stimson that seemed to me pertinent during the years that I watched the Vietnam tragedy unfold—and participated in that tragedy. It seems to me more pertinent than ever as we move toward the election of 1968.

In his waning years Stimson was asked by an anxious questioner, "Mr. Secretary, how on earth can we ever bring peace to the world?" Stimson is said to have answered: "You begin by bringing to Washington a small handful of able men who believe that the achievement of peace is possible.

"You work them to the bone until they no longer believe that it is possible.

"And then you throw them out—and bring in a new bunch who believe that it is possible."

To Master the Third World

GABRIEL KOLKO

There is no comprehensive theory of the contemporary world crisis. That both conventional academic or Left scholars have failed or been unable to assess the causes and meaning of the most significant events of our time in large part reflects their unwillingness to confront directly the nature of American interest and power. Theories of imperialism are now the dry-as-dust topics of academic

Gabriel Kolko, *The Roots of American Foreign Policy: An Analysis of Power and Purpose* (Boston: Beacon Press, 1969), pp. 48–55, 83–86, 88–90. Copyright © 1969 by Gabriel Kolko. Reprinted by permission of Beacon Press.

tomes, and all too few have made a serious effort to scratch beneath the ideology of American expansion to define its larger needs, imperatives, and functions as a system.

Earlier studies of imperialism left no doubt as to what one had to examine in order to comprehend the role of a state in the world. Whether it was imperialist rivalries for economic and strategic power, the atavism of feudal ideologies, reaction and counterrevolution, or the desire to integrate and stabilize a world economy, the study of foreign policy was specific, real, and discounted the notion of error, myth, and exuberance as the sources of conduct as explanations sufficient only for national patriots. American scholars have not translated their ability to perceive correctly the roots of diplomacy in the past into a description of contemporary American policy, even though the same categories and analogies may be equally relevant today.

To understand the unique economic interests and aspirations of the United States in the world, and the degree to which it benefits or loses within the existing distribution and structure of power and the world economy, is to define a crucial basis for comprehending as well as predicting its role overseas. The nature of the international crisis, and the limited American responses to it, tell us why the United States is in Vietnam and why in fact American intervention inevitably colors the direction of the vast changes in the world political and social system which are the hallmarks of modern history. In brief, the manner in which the United States has expanded its problems and objectives overseas, transforming the American crisis into a global one, also explains its consistent interventionism.

It is critical, as part of a comprehensive theory of the world crisis, to study the control and organization of the international economy, who gains and who loses in it, and how we have arrived at the present impasse. We should neither dismiss nor make too much of the issue of ideology or the less systematic belief, as former Secretary of Defense James Forrestal once put it, that ". . . our security is not merely the capacity or ability to repel invasion, it is our ability to contribute to the reconstruction of the world. . . ." For American ideology is a vague synthesis that embodies, once its surface is scratched, economic and strategic objectives and priorities that a thin rhetoric rationalizes into doctrines more interesting for what they imply than for what they state. . . . I shall deal only with the structure and the material components of the world economy that set the context for the repeated local interventions and crises that are the major characteristics of the modern world scene.

The role of raw materials is qualitative rather than merely quantitative, and neither volume nor price can measure their ultimate significance and consequences. The economies and technologies of the advanced industrial nations, the United States in particular, are so intricate that the removal of even a small part, as in a watch, can stop the mechanism. The steel industry must add approximately thirteen pounds of manganese to each ton of steel, and though the weight and value of the increase is a tiny fraction of the total, a modern diversified steel industry *must* have manganese. The same analogy is true of the entire relationship between the industrial and so-called developing nations:

The nations of the Third World may be poor, but in the last analysis the industrial world needs their resources more than these nations need the West, for poverty is nothing new to peasantry cut off from export sectors, and trading with industrial states has not ended their subsistence living standards. In case of a total rupture between the industrial and supplier nations, it is the population of the industrial world that proportionately will suffer the most.

Since the Second World War the leaders of the United States have been acutely aware of their vital reliance on raw materials, and the fact, to quote Paul G. Hoffman, former Marshall Plan administrator, that ". . . our own dynamic economy has made us dependent on the outside world for many critical raw materials." Successive Administrations have been incessantly concerned over the ability and necessity of the United States to develop these resources everywhere, given the paucity of local capital and technology, and their interest extends far beyond short-term profits of investment. In areas such as Africa this obsession has defined American policy on every major issue.

At the beginning of this century the United States was a net earner in the export of minerals and commodities, but by 1926–30 it had a vast annual deficit of crude materials, and in 1930 imported 5 percent of its iron ore, 64 percent of its bauxite (aluminum), 65 percent of its copper, 9 percent of its lead, and 4 percent of its zinc. Imports of these five critical metals by 1960 had increased to 32 percent for iron ore, 98 percent for bauxite, 35 percent for lead, and 60 percent for zinc, and only in the case of copper declined to 46 percent. As a percentage of the new supply, the United States in 1956 imported at least 80 percent of thirty-nine necessary commodities, 50 to 79 percent of fifteen commodities, 10 to 49 percent of twenty commodities, and less than 10 percent of another twenty-three—all with a total import value of $6.6 billion. There was no doubt, as one Senate report concluded in 1954, that Washington knew that should the mineral-rich nations cut off these sources, "To a very dangerous extent, the vital security of this Nation is in serious jeopardy."

By 1956–60 the United States was importing over half of all its required metals and almost 60 percent of its wool. It imported all tropical foodstuffs, such as cocoa, coffee, and bananas, as well as over half the sugar supply. When, in 1963, Resources for the Future completed its monumental survey of raw materials and projected American needs for the next forty years, it predicted a vast multiplication of American demands that made imperative, in its estimate, ". . . that in the future even larger amounts of certain items will have to be drawn from foreign sources if demand is to be satisfied without marked increases in cost." Its medium projections suggested immensely increased needs for nearly all metals, ranging as high as nine times for molybdenum to about two and one-half times for lead. Within three years, however, all of the critical output, consumption, and population assumptions upon which the Resources for the Future experts based their speculations proved to be far too conservative, the omnivorous demands of the economy were far greater than they had expected.

A critical shift in the location of the world's most vital mineral output and reserves has accompanied the imperative need for raw materials in the United States. In 1913 the developing nations accounted for 3 percent of the world's total iron ore output and 15 percent of its petroleum, as opposed to 37 percent and 65 percent, respectively, in 1965. Its share of bauxite output increased from 21 percent in 1928 to 69 percent in 1965. The United States share of world oil output fell from 61 percent in 1938 to 29 percent in 1964, as the known world reserves shifted toward the Middle East.

Despite the introduction of synthetics between 1938 and 1954, which reduced by about one-fifth the quantity of natural raw materials needed for the average constant quantity of goods produced in the industrial nations, the vast increase in world industrial output has more than compensated for the shift and greatly increased pressures on raw materials supplies from the industrial nations. In effect, the United States has become more dependent on imported raw materials as its share of the consumption of the world's total has declined sharply in the face of European and Japanese competition for supplies. The United States, which consumed slightly less than half of the world's total output of copper, lead, zinc, aluminum, and steel in 1948–50, consumed slightly over one-quarter in 1960, save for aluminum, where the percentage decline was still great. This essentially European demand, which has grown far more rapidly than in the United States, has challenged the American predominance in the world raw materials trade in a manner which makes the maintenance and expansion of existing sources in the ex-colonial regions doubly imperative to it.

American and European industry can find most of these future sources of supply, so vital to their economic growth, only in the continents in upheaval and revolution. Over half of United States iron ore imports in 1960 came from Venezuela and three equally precarious Latin American countries. Over half the known world reserves of manganese are in Russia and China, and most of the remainder is in Brazil, India, Gabon, and South Africa. South Africa and Rhodesia account for nearly all the world's chromium reserves, Cuba and New Caledonia for half the nickel, China for over two-thirds the tungsten, and Chile, Northern Rhodesia, Congo, and Peru for well over two-thirds of the foreign copper reserves. Guyana has about six times the American reserves of bauxite, and China has three times, while Malaya, Indonesia, and Thailand alone have two-thirds of the world tin reserves, with Bolivia and the Congo possessing most of the balance. Only zinc and lead, among the major metals, are in politically stable regions, from the American viewpoint.

It is extraordinarily difficult to estimate the potential role and value of these scarce minerals to the United States, but certain approximate definitions are quite sufficient to make the point that the future of American economic power is too deeply involved for this nation to permit the rest of the world to take its own political and revolutionary course in a manner that imperils the American freedom to use them. Suffice it to say, the ultimate significance of the importation of certain critical raw materials is not their cost to American business but rather the end value of the industries that *must* employ these materials, even in small quantities, or pass out of existence. And in the larger sense, confident access to raw materials is a necessary precondition for industrial expansion into new or existing fields of technology, without the fear of limiting shortages which the United States' sole reliance on its national resources would entail. Intangibly, it is really the political and psychological assurance of total freedom of development of national economic power that is vital to American economic growth. Beyond this, United States profits abroad are made on overseas investments in local export industries, giving the Americans the profits of the suppliers as well as the consumer. An isolated America would lose all this, and much more.

It is not enough, therefore, to state that nonfood raw materials imports doubled in value between 1953 and 1966, and that $16.6 billion in imports for the food and industrial users in 1966 was vitally necessary to American prosperity. More relevant is the fact that in 1963 the Census valued the iron and steel industry's shipments at $22.3 billion, the aluminum's at $3.9 billion, metal cans at $2.1 billion, copper at $3.1 billion, asbestos at a half billion, zinc at a half billion, coffee at $1.9 billion, sugar and chocolate at $1.7 billion—and that all of these industries and many others, to some critical extent, depended on their access to the world's supply of raw materials. Without the availability of such goods for decades, at prices favorable to the United States, the American economy would have been far different—and much poorer.

To suggest that the United States could solve its natural shortages by attempting to live within its raw materials limits would also require a drastic reduction in its exports of finished goods, and this the leaders of the American system would never voluntarily permit, for it would bring profound economic repercussions for a capitalist economy in the form of vast unemployment and lower profits. While only four or five percent of American steel mill products went to exports in 1955–60, this proportion reached nearly one-quarter in the aluminum and one-fifth in the copper industries. In this context the United States has become a processor of the world's raw materials in a number of fields not simply to satisfy domestic needs but also its global export trade and military ambitions. At home, a policy of self-sufficiency would, in the case of aluminum, seriously affect the building construction industry, consumer and producer durables, and transport industries. The same is true for copper, which is critical for producer durables, building construction, communications, and electric power. Minor metals, of which the United States is largely deficient, are essential to any technologically advanced nation, especially to the chemical, electrical, and electronics industries.

America's ability to procure at will such materials as it needs, and at a price it can afford, is one of the keystones of its economic power in this century. The stakes are vast, and its capacity to keep intact something like the existing integrated but unequal relations between the poor, weak nations and the United States is vital to the future of its mastery of the international economy.

The dominant interest of the United States is in world economic stability, and anything that undermines that condition presents a danger to its present hegemony. Countering, neutralizing and containing the disturbing political and social trends thus becomes the most imperative objective of its foreign policy. . . .

In their brilliant essay on the political economy of nineteenth century British imperialism, John Gallagher and Ronald Robinson have described a process that parallels the nature of United States expansion after 1945:

> Imperialism, perhaps, may be defined as a sufficient political function of this process of integrating new regions into the expanding economy; its character is largely decided by the various and changing relationships between the political and economic elements of expansion in any particular region and time. Two qualifications must be made. First, imperialism may be only indirectly connected with economic integration in that it sometimes extends beyond areas of economic development, but acts for their strategic protection. Secondly, although imperialism is a function of economic expansion, it is not a necessary function. Whether imperialist phenomena show themselves or not, is determined not only by the factors of economic expansion, but equally by the political and social organization of the regions brought into the orbit of the expansive society, and also by the world situation in general.
>
> It is only when the politics of these new regions fail to provide satisfactory conditions for commercial or strategic integration and when their relative weakness allows, that power is used imperialistically to adjust those conditions. Economic expansion, it is true, will tend to flow into the regions of maximum opportunity, but maximum opportunity depends as much upon political considerations of security as upon questions of profit. Consequently, in any particular region, if economic opportunity seems large but political security small, then full absorption into the extending economy tends to be frustrated until power is exerted upon the state in question. Conversely, in proportion as satisfactory political frameworks are brought into being in this way, the frequency of imperialist intervention lessens and imperialist control is correspondingly relaxed. It may be suggested that this willingness to limit the use of paramount power to establishing security for trade is the distinctive feature of the British imperialism of free trade in the nineteenth century, in contrast to the mercantilist use of power to obtain commercial supremacy and monopoly through political possession.

In today's context, we should regard United States political and strategic intervention as a rational overhead charge for its present and future freedom to act and expand. One must also point out that however high that cost may appear today, in the history of United States diplomacy specific American economic interests in a country or region have often defined the national interest on the assumption that the nation can identify its welfare with the profits of some of its citizens—whether in oil, cotton, or bananas. The costs to the state as a whole are less consequential than the desires and profits of specific class strata and their need to operate everywhere in a manner that, collectively, brings vast prosperity to the United States and its rulers.

Today it is a fact that capitalism in one country is a long-term physical and economic impossibility without a drastic shift in the distribution of the world's income. Isolated, the United States would face those domestic backlogged economic and social problems and weaknesses it has deferred confronting for over two decades, and its disappearing strength in a global context would soon open the door to the internal dynamics which might jeopardize the very existence of liberal corporate capitalism at home. It is logical to regard

Vietnam, therefore, as the inevitable cost of maintaining United States imperial power, a step toward saving the future in something akin to its present form by revealing to others in the Third World what they too may encounter should they also seek to control their own development. That Vietnam itself has relatively little of value to the United States is all the more significant as an example of America's determination to hold the line as a matter of principle against revolutionary movements. What is at stake, according to the "domino" theory with which Washington accurately perceives the world, is the control of Vietnam's neighbors, Southeast Asia and, ultimately, Latin America.

The contemporary world crisis, in brief, is a by-product of United States response to Third World change and its own definitions of what it must do to preserve and expand its vital national interests. At the present moment, the larger relationships in the Third World economy benefit the United States, and it is this type of structure America is struggling to preserve. Moreover, the United States requires the option to expand to regions it has not yet penetrated, a fact which not only brings it into conflict with Third World revolutions but also with an increasingly powerful European capitalism. Where neocolonial economic penetration via loans, aid, or attacks on balanced economic development or diversification in the Third World are not sufficient to maintain stability, direct interventions to save local *compradors* and oligarchies often follow. Frequently such encroachments succeed, as in Greece and the Dominican Republic, but at times, such as Vietnam, it is the very process of intervention itself that creates its own defeat by deranging an already moribund society, polarizing options, and compelling men to choose—and to resist. Even the returns to the United States on partial successes have warranted the entire undertaking in the form not just of high profit ratios and exports, but in the existence of a vast world economic sector which supplies the disproportionately important materials without which American prosperity within its present social framework would eventually dry up.

The existing global political and economic structure, with all its stagnation and misery, has not only brought the United States billions but has made possible, above all, a vast power that requires total world economic integration not on the basis of equality but of domination. And to preserve this form of world is vital to the men who run the American economy and politics at the highest levels. If some of them now reluctantly believe that Vietnam was not the place to make the final defense against tides of unpredictable revolutionary change, they all concede that they must do it somewhere, and the logic of their larger view makes their shift on Vietnam a matter of expediency or tactics rather than of principle. All the various American leaders believe in global stability which they are committed to defend against revolution that may threaten the existing distribution of economic power in the world. . . .

The intervention of the United States in Vietnam is the most important single embodiment of the power and purposes of American foreign policy since the Second World War, and no other crisis reveals so much of the basic motivating forces and objectives—and weaknesses—of American global politics. A theory of the origins and meaning of the war also discloses the origins of an American malaise that is global in its reaches, impinging on this nation's conduct everywhere. To understand Vietnam is also to comprehend not just the present purposes of American action but also to anticipate its thrust and direction in the future.

Vietnam illustrates, as well, the nature of the American internal political process and decision-making structure when it exceeds the views of a major sector of the people, for no other event of our generation has turned such a large proportion of the nation against its government's policy or so profoundly alienated its youth. And at no time has the government conceded so little to democratic sentiment, pursuing as it has a policy of escalation that reveals that its policy is formulated not with an eye to democratic sanctions and compromises but rather the attainment of specific interests and goals scarcely shared by the vast majority of the nation.

The inability of the United States to apply its vast material and economic power to compensate for the ideological and human superiority of revolutionary and guerrilla movements throughout the world has been the core of its frustration in Vietnam. From a purely economic viewpoint, the United States cannot maintain its existing vital dominating relationship to much of the Third World unless it can keep the poor nations from moving too far toward the Left and the Cuban or Vietnamese path. A widespread leftward movement would critically affect its supply of raw materials and have profound long-term repercussions. It is the American view of the need for relative internal stability within the poorer nations that has resulted in a long list of United States interventions since 1946 into the affairs of numerous nations, from Greece to Guatemala, of which Vietnam is only the consummate example—but in principle no different than numerous others. The accuracy of the "domino" theory, with its projection of the eventual loss of whole regions to American direction and access, explains the direct continuity between the larger United States global strategy and Vietnam.

Yet, ironically, while the United States struggles in Vietnam and the Third World to retain its own mastery, or to continue that once held by the former colonial powers, it simultaneously weakens itself in its deepening economic conflict with Europe, revealing the limits of America's power to attain its ambition to define the preconditions and direction of global economic and political developments. Vietnam is essentially an American intervention against a nationalist, revolutionary agrarian movement which embodies social elements in incipient and similar forms of development in numerous other Third World nations. It is in no sense a civil war, with the United States supporting one local faction against another, but an effort to preserve a mode of traditional colonialism via a minute, historically opportunistic *comprador* class in Saigon. For the United States to fail in Vietnam would be to make the point that even the massive intervention of the most powerful nation in the history of the world was insufficient to stem profoundly popular social and national revolutions throughout the world. Such a revelation of American weaknesses would be tantamount to a demotion of the United States from its present role as the world's dominant superpower.

FURTHER READING

Richard J. Barnet, *Intervention and Revolution* (1972)
Joseph Buttinger, *Vietnam: A Political History* (1970)
Chester Cooper, *The Lost Crusade* (1970)
Bernard Fall, *The Two Vietnams* (1967)
Bernard Fall, *Vietnam Witness, 1953–1966* (1966)
Frances FitzGerald, *Fire in the Lake* (1972)
Philip Geyelin, *Lyndon B. Johnson and the World* (1966)
David Halberstam, *The Best and the Brightest* (1972)
Roger Hilsman, *To Move a Nation* (1967)
Townsend Hoopes, *The Limits of Intervention* (1969)
George M. Kahin and J. W. Lewis, *The United States in Vietnam* (1969)
Douglas Kinnard, *The War Managers* (1977)
Anthony Lake, ed., *The Vietnam Legacy* (1976)
Peter Poole, *The United States and Indochina from FDR to Nixon* (1973)
Marcus G. Raskin and Bernard B. Fall, eds., *The Viet-Nam Reader* (1967)
Robert Shaplen, *Time Out of Hand* (1970)
Sheldon S. Wolin, "The Meaning of Vietnam," *New York Review of Books,* 22
 (1975), 23–33

14

Henry A. Kissinger, Richard M. Nixon, and Détente

Most observers agree that Henry A. Kissinger was a central figure in the history of the 1970s. First as an influential adviser to President Richard M. Nixon on national security affairs (1969–1973) and then as a highly visible and active Secretary of State (1973–1977), Kissinger offered advice and made decisions that reverberated across the globe. In his quest for international stability based on big-power arrangements, Kissinger practiced a personalized diplomacy that made this witty, intelligent man the most travelled Secretary of State in American history. The Nixon-Kissinger policy of détente with both China and Russia suggested that the Cold War was being shelved. Kissinger's secret negotiations permitted American withdrawal from Vietnam. His "shuttle diplomacy" in the Middle East helped to cool Arab-Israeli hostility.

But Kissinger's legacy was mixed, as the following selections indicate. Interventions and crises in Vietnam, Chile, Cyprus, Bangladesh, Angola, and elsewhere tarnished his record and raised questions about his sense of morality and judgment. His conduct of diplomacy in an administration noted for secrecy, the violation of constitutional rights, and political corruption has raised controversial questions about the Secretary of State's own participation in the "Watergate crisis."

DOCUMENTS

In February 1972, after secret negotiations conducted by national security adviser Henry A. Kissinger, President Richard M. Nixon surprised many when he journeyed to China and opened ties with that Communist government, ending over two decades of severed relations between Washington and Peking. On February 28, 1972, he reported to Congress on the meaning of his trip. Détente with the Soviet Union was another Nixon-Kissinger policy. In a September 19, 1974, appearance before the Senate Committee on Foreign Relations, Kissinger, then Secretary of State, defined détente and outlined its accomplishments.

During the 1976 presidential campaign between Democrat Jimmy Carter and Republican Gerald Ford, Kissinger's foreign policy and America's post-Vietnam international standing became the subjects of political controversy. In the October 7, 1976, televised presidential debate between the two candidates, Carter strongly criticized the Nixon-Ford-Kissinger record. The final document is a January 13, 1977, editorial by Anthony Lewis of the *New York Times* sharply indicting Kissinger's performance as Secretary of State.

Richard M. Nixon on His Trip to China, 1972

When I announced this trip last July, I described it as a journey for peace. In the last 30 years, Americans have in three different wars gone off by the hundreds of thousands to fight, and some to die, in Asia and in the Pacific. One of the central motives behind my journey to China was to prevent that from happening a fourth time to another generation of Americans.

As I have often said, peace means more than the mere absence of war. In a technical sense, we were at peace with the People's Republic of China before this trip, but a gulf of almost 12,000 miles and 22 years of noncommunication and hostility separated the United States of America from the 750 million people who live in the People's Republic of China, and that is one-fourth of all the people in the world.

As a result of this trip, we have started the long process of building a bridge across that gulf, and even now we have something better than the mere absence of war. Not only have we completed a week of intensive talks at the highest levels, we have set up a procedure whereby we can continue to have discussions in the future. We have demonstrated that nations with very deep and fundamental differences can learn to discuss those differences calmly, rationally, and frankly, without compromising their principles. This is the basis of a structure for peace, where we can talk about differences rather than fight about them.

The primary goal of this trip was to reestablish communication with the People's Republic of China after a generation of hostility. We achieved that goal. Let me turn now to our joint communique.

We did not bring back any written or unwritten agreements that will guarantee peace in our time. We did not bring home any magic formula which will make unnecessary the efforts of the American people to continue to maintain the strength so that we can continue to be free.

We made some necessary and important beginnings, however, in several areas. We entered into agreements to expand cultural, educational, and journalistic contacts between the Chinese and the American people. We agreed to work to begin and broaden trade between our two countries. We have agreed that the communications that have now been established between our governments will be strengthened and expanded.

Most important, we have agreed on some rules of international conduct which will reduce the risk of confrontation and war in Asia and in the Pacific.

We agreed that we are opposed to domination of the Pacific area by any one power. We agreed that international disputes should be settled without the use of the threat of force and we agreed that we are prepared to apply this principle to our mutual relations.

With respect to Taiwan, we stated our established policy that our forces overseas will be reduced gradually as tensions ease, and that our ultimate objective is to withdraw our forces as a peaceful settlement is achieved.

We have agreed that we will not negotiate the fate of other nations behind their backs, and we did not do so at Peking. There were no secret deals of any kind. We have done all this without giving up any United States commitment to any other country.

In our talks, the talks that I had with the leaders of the People's Republic and that the Secretary of State had with the office of the Government of the People's Republic in the foreign affairs area, we both realized that a bridge of understanding that spans almost 12,000 miles and 22 years of hostility can't be built in 1 week of discussions. But we have agreed to begin to build that bridge, recognizing that our work will require years of patient effort. We made no attempt to pretend that major differences did not exist between our two governments, because they do exist.

This communique was unique in honestly setting forth differences rather than trying to cover them up with diplomatic doubletalk.

One of the gifts that we left behind in Hangchow was a planted sapling of the American redwood tree. As all Californians know, and as most Americans know, redwoods grow from saplings into the giants of the forest. But the process is not one of days or even years; it is a process of centuries.

Just as we hope that those saplings, those tiny saplings that we left in China, will grow one day into mighty redwoods, so we hope, too, that the seeds planted on this journey for peace will grow and prosper into a more enduring structure for peace and security in the Western Pacific.

But peace is too urgent to wait for centuries. We must seize the moment to move toward that goal now, and this is what we have done on this journey.

Henry A. Kissinger on Détente, 1974

Since the dawn of the nuclear age the world's fears of holocaust and its hopes for peace have turned on the relationship between the United States and the Soviet Union.

Throughout history men have sought peace but suffered war; all too often deliberate decisions or miscalculations have brought violence and destruction to a world yearning for tranquility. Tragic as the consequences of violence may have been in the past, the issue of peace and war takes on unprecedented urgency when, for the first time in history, two nations have the capacity to destroy mankind.

The destructiveness of modern weapons defines the necessity of the task; deep differences in philosophy and interests between the United States and the Soviet Union point up its difficulty.

Paradox confuses our perception of the problem of peaceful coexistence: If peace is pursued to the exclusion of any other goal, other values will be compromised and perhaps lost; but if unconstrained rivalry leads to nuclear conflict, these values, along with everything else, will be destroyed in the resulting holocaust.

There can be no peaceful international order without a constructive relationship between the United States and the Soviet Union. There will be no international stability unless both the Soviet Union and the United States conduct themselves with restraint and unless they use their enormous power for the benefit of mankind.

Thus, we must be clear at the outset on what the term "détente" entails. It is the search for a more constructive relationship with the Soviet Union. It is a continuing process, not a final condition. And it has been pursued by successive American leaders though the means have varied as have world conditions.

Some fundamental principles guide this policy:

The United States does not base its policy solely on Moscow's good intentions. We seek, regardless of Soviet intentions, to serve peace through a systematic resistance to pressure and conciliatory responses to moderate behavior.

We must oppose aggressive actions, but we must not seek confrontations lightly.

We must maintain a strong national defense while recognizing that in the nuclear age the relationship between military strength and politically usable power is the most complex in all history.

Where the age-old antagonism between freedom and tyranny is concerned, we are not neutral. But other imperatives impose limits on our ability to produce internal changes in foreign countries. Consciousness of our limits is a recognition of the necessity of peace—not moral callousness. The preservation of human life and human society are moral values, too.

We must be mature enough to recognize that to be stable a relationship must provide advantages to both sides and that the most constructive international relationships are those in which both parties perceive an element of gain.

America's aspiration for the kind of political environment we now call détente is not new.

The effort to achieve a more constructive relationship with the Soviet Union is not made in the name of any one administration, or one party, or for any one period of time. It expresses the continuing desire of the vast majority of the American people for an easing of international tensions, and their expectation that any responsible government will strive for peace. No aspect of our policies, domestic or foreign, enjoys more consistent bipartisan support. No aspect is more in the interest of mankind.

In the postwar period repeated efforts were made to improve our relationship with Moscow. The spirits of Geneva, Camp David, and Glassboro were evanescent moments in a quarter century otherwise marked by tensions and by sporadic confrontation. What is new in the current period of relaxation of tensions is its duration, the scope of the relationship which has evolved and the continuity and intensity of contact and consultation which it has produced.

We sought to explore every avenue toward an honorable and just accommodation while remaining determined not to settle for mere atmospherics. We relied on a balance of mutual interests rather than Soviet intentions.

Our approach proceeds from the conviction that in moving forward across a wide spectrum of negotiations, progress in one area adds momentum to progress in other areas. We did not invent the interrelationship; it was a reality because of the range of problems and areas in which the interests of the United States and the Soviet Union impinge on each other. By acquiring a stake in this network of relationships with the West the Soviet Union may become more conscious of what it would lose by a return to confrontation. Indeed, it is our expectation that it will develop a self-interest in fostering the entire process of relaxation of tensions.

Cooperative relations, in our view, must be more than a series of isolated agreements. They must reflect an acceptance of mutual obligations and of the need for accommodation and restraints.

To set forth principles of behavior in formal documents is hardly to guarantee their observance. But they are reference points against which to judge actions and set goals.

The first of the series of documents is the Statement of Principles signed in Moscow in 1972. It affirms: (1) the necessity of avoiding confrontation; (2) the imperative of mutual restraint; (3) the rejection of attempts to exploit tensions to gain unilateral advantages; (4) the renunciation of claims of special influence in the world; and (5) the willingness, on this new basis, to coexist peacefully and build a firm long-term relationship.

An Agreement on the Prevention of Nuclear War based on these principles was signed in 1973. But it emphasizes that this objective presuppose the renunciation of any war or threat of war not only by the two nuclear superpowers against each other, but also against allies or third countries. In other words, the principle of restraint is not confined to relations between the United States and the U.S.S.R. It is explicitly extended to include all countries.

These statements of principles are not an American concession; indeed, we have been affirming them unilaterally for two decades. Nor are they a legal contract; rather, they are an aspiration and a yardstick by which we assess Soviet behavior. We have never intended to rely on Soviet compliance with every principle; we do seek to elaborate standards of conduct which the Soviet Union would violate only to its cost. And if over the long term the more durable relationship takes hold, the basic principles will give it definition, structure, and hope.

One of the features of the current phase of United States-Soviet relations is the unprecedented consultation between leaders either face to face or through diplomatic channels.

It was difficult in the past to speak of a United States-Soviet bilateral relationship in any normal sense of the phrase. Trade was negligible. Contacts between various institutions and between the peoples of the two countries were at best sporadic. Today, by joining our efforts even in such seemingly apolitical fields as medical research or environmental protection, we and the Soviets can benefit not only our two peoples, but all mankind.

Since 1972 we have concluded agreements on a common effort against cancer, on research to protect the environment, on studying the use of the ocean's resources, on the use of atomic energy for peaceful purposes, on studying methods for conserving energy, on examining construction techniques for regions subject to earthquakes, and on devising new transportation methods.

Each project must be judged by the concrete benefits it brings. But in their sum—in their exchange of information and people as well as in their establishment of joint mechanisms—they also constitute a commitment in both countries to work together across a broad spectrum.

During the period of the cold war economic contact between ourselves and the U.S.S.R. was virtually nonexistent.

The period of confrontation should have left little doubt, however, that economic boycott would not transform the Soviet system or impose upon it a conciliatory foreign policy. Throughout this period the U.S.S.R. was quite prepared to maintain heavy military outlays and to concentrate on capital growth by using the resources of the Communist world alone.

The question then became how trade and economic contact—in which the Soviet Union is obviously interested—could serve the purposes of peace.

We have approached the question of economic relations with deliberation and circumspection and as an act of policy not primarily of commercial opportunity. As political relations have improved on a broad basis, economic issues have been dealt with on a comparably broad front. A series of interlocking economic agreements with the U.S.S.R. has been negotiated, side by side with the political progress already noted. The 25-year-old lend-lease debt was settled; the reciprocal extension of the most-favored-nation treatment was negotiated, together with safeguards against the possible disruption of our markets and a series of practical arrangements to facilitate the conduct of business; our Government credit facilities were made available for trade with the U.S.S.R.; and a maritime agreement regulating the carriage of goods has been signed.

This approach commanded widespread domestic approval. It was considered a natural outgrowth of political progress. At no time were issues regarding Soviet domestic political practices raised. Indeed, not until after the 1972 agreements was the Soviet domestic order invoked as a reason for arresting or reversing the progress so painstakingly achieved.

This sudden, ex post facto form of linkage raises serious questions.

The significance of trade, originally envisaged as only one ingredient of a complex and evolving relationship, is inflated out of all proportion;

The hoped-for results of policy become transformed into preconditions for any policy at all.

We recognize the depth and validity of the moral concerns expressed by those who oppose—or put conditions on—expanded trade with the U.S.S.R.

But a sense of proportion must be maintained about the leverage our economic relations give us.

Denial of economic relations cannot by itself achieve what it failed to do when it was part of a determined policy of political and military confrontation.

The economic bargaining ability of most-favored-nation status is marginal. MFN grants no special privilege; it is a misnomer, since we have such agreements with over 100 countries. To continue to deny it is more a political than an economic act.

The actual and potential flow of credits from the United States represents a tiny fraction of the capital available to the U.S.S.R. domestically and elsewhere, including Western Europe and Japan.

Over time, trade, and investment may leaven the autarkic tendencies of the Soviet system, invite gradual association of the Soviet economy with the world economy, and foster a degree of interdependence that adds an element of stability to the political relationship.

We cannot expect to relax international tensions or achieve a more stable international system should the two strongest nuclear powers conduct an unrestrained strategic arms race. Thus, perhaps the single most important component of our policy toward the Soviet Union is the effort to limit strategic weapons competition.

The competition in which we now find ourselves is historically unique:

Each side has the capacity to destroy civilization as we know it.

Failure to maintain equivalence could jeopardize not only our freedom but our very survival.

The lead time for technological innovation is so long, yet the pace of change so relentless that the arms race and strategic policy itself are in danger of being driven by technological necessity.

When nuclear arsenals reach levels involving thousands of launchers and over 10,000 warheads, and when the characteristics of the weapons of the two sides are so incommensurable, it becomes difficult to determine what combination of numbers of strategic weapons and performance capabilities would give one side a military and political superiority. At a minimum clear changes in the strategic balance can be achieved only by efforts so enormous and by increments so large that the very attempt is highly destabilizing.

The prospect of a decisive military advantage, even if theoretically possible, is politically intolerable; neither side will passively permit a massive shift in the nuclear balance. Therefore, the probable outcome of each succeeding round of competition is the restoration of a strategic equilibrium, but at increasingly higher and more complex levels of forces.

The arms race is driven by political as well as military factors. While a decisive advantage is hard to calculate, the appearance of inferiority—whatever its actual significance—can have serious political consequences. Thus, each side has a high incentive to achieve not only the reality but the appearance of equality. In a very real sense each side shapes the military establishment of the other.

If we are driven to it, the United States will sustain an arms race. But the political or military benefit which would flow from such a situation would remain elusive. Indeed, after such an evolution it might well be that both sides would be worse off than before the race began.

The Soviet Union must realize that the overall relationship with the United States will be less stable if strategic balance is sought through unrestrained competitive programs. Sustaining the buildup requires exhortations by both sides that in time may prove incompatible with restrained international conduct. The very fact of a strategic arms race has a high potential for feeding attitudes of hostility and suspicion on both sides, transforming the fears of those who demand more weapons into self-fulfilling prophecies.

The American people can be asked to bear the cost and political instability of a race which is doomed to stalemate only if it is clear that every effort has been made to prevent it. That is why every President since Eisenhower has pursued negotiations for the limitation of strategic arms while maintaining the military programs essential to strategic balance.

SALT has become one means by which we and the Soviet Union could enhance stability by setting mutual constraints on our respective forces and by gradually reaching an understanding of the doctrinal considerations that underlie the deployment of nuclear weapons. SALT, in the American conception, is a means to achieve strategic stability by methods other than the arms race.

When the first agreements in 1972 were signed, the future strategic picture was not bright.

The agreements signed in May 1972 which limited antiballistic missile defenses and froze the level of ballistic missile forces on both sides represented the essential first step towards a less volatile strategic environment.

By limiting antiballistic missiles [ABM's] to very low levels of deployment, the United States and the Soviet Union removed a potential source of instability.

Some have alleged that the interim agreement, which expires in October 1977, penalizes the United States by permitting the Soviet Union to deploy more strategic missile launchers than the United States. Such a view is misleading. When the agreement was signed in May 1972, the Soviet Union already possessed more land-based Inter-Continental Ballistic Missiles [ICBM's] than the United States and, given the pace of its submarine construction program, it could have built virtually twice as many nuclear ballistic missile submarines.

The interim agreement confined an existing Soviet ICBM program to the then existing level; it put a ceiling on the heaviest Soviet ICBM's and it set an upper limit on the Soviet Submarine-Launched Ballistic Missile [SLBM] program.

In sum, we believed when we signed these agreements—and we believe now—that they had reduced the danger of nuclear war, that both sides had acquired some greater interest in restraint, and that the basis had been created for the present effort to reach a broader agreement.

The goal of the current negotiations is an agreement for a 10-year period. We shifted to the 10-year approach because the period is long enough to cover all current and planned forces but not so long as to invite hedges that would defeat the purpose of an arms control agreement.

Détente is admittedly far from a modern equivalent to the kind of stable peace that characterized most of the 19th century.

Where has the process of détente taken us so far? What are the principles that must continue to guide our course?

We and our allies are launched on negotiations with the Warsaw Pact and other countries in the European Conference on Security and Cooperation.

At the same time, NATO and the Warsaw Pact are negotiating the reduction of their forces in Central Europe.

America's principal alliances have proved their durability in a new era. Many feared that détente would undermine them. Instead, détente has helped to place our alliance ties on a more enduring basis by removing the fear that friendship with the United States involved the risk of unnecessary confrontation with the U.S.S.R.

The world has been freer of East-West tensions and conflict than in the fifties and sixties.

A series of bilateral cooperative relations have turned the United States-Soviet relationship in a far more positive direction.

We have achieved unprecedented agreements in arms limitation and measures to avoid accidental war.

New possibilities for positive United States-Soviet cooperation have emerged on issues in which the globe is interdependent—science and technology, environment, energy.

It is too early to judge conclusively whether this change should be ascribed to tactical considerations. But in a sense, that is immaterial. For whether the change is temporary and tactical, or lasting and basic, our task is essentially the same; to transform that change into a permanent condition devoted to the purpose of a secure peace and mankind's aspiration for a better life. A tactical change sufficiently prolonged becomes a lasting transformation.

But the whole process can be jeopardized if it is taken for granted. As the cold war recedes in memory, détente can come to seem so natural that it appears safe to levy progressively greater demands on it. The temptation to combine détente with increasing pressure on the Soviet Union will grow. Such an attitude would be disastrous. We would not accept it from Moscow; Moscow will not accept it from us.

To be sure, the process of détente raises serious issues for many people. We will be guided by these principles.

First, if détente is to endure, both sides must benefit.

Second, building a new relationship with the Soviet Union does not entail any devaluation of traditional alliance relations.

Third, the emergence of more normal relations with the Soviet Union must not undermine our resolve to maintain our national defense.

Fourth, we must know what can and cannot be achieved in changing human conditions in the East.

We shall insist on responsible international behavior by the Soviet Union. Beyond this, we will use our influence to the maximum to alleviate suffering and to respond to humane appeals. We know what we stand for, and we shall leave no doubt about it.

We have made the attitude of the American people clear on countless occasions, in ways that have produced results. I believe that both the executive and the Congress, each playing its proper role, have been effective. With respect to the specific issue of Jewish emigration—

> The education exit tax of 1971 is no longer being collected; we have been assured that it will not be reapplied;
>
> Hardship cases submitted to the Soviet Government have been given increased attention, and remedies have been forthcoming in many well-known instances;
>
> The volume of Jewish emigration has increased from a trickle to tens of thousands; and
>
> We are now moving toward an understanding that should significantly diminish the obstacles to emigration and ease the hardship of prospective emigrants.

We have accomplished much. But we cannot demand that the Soviet Union, in effect, suddenly reverse five decades of Soviet, and centuries of Russian, history. Such an attempt would be futile and at the same time hazard all that has already been achieved. Changes in Soviet society have already occurred, and more will come. But they are most likely to develop through an evolution that can best go forward in an environment of decreasing international tensions. A renewal of the cold war will hardly encourage the Soviet Union to change its emigration policies or adopt a more benevolent attitude toward dissent.

Jimmy Carter on the Failures of Nixon-Ford-Kissinger Foreign Policy, 1976

Our country is not strong anymore; we're not respected anymore. We can only be strong overseas if we're strong at home, and when I become President we will not only be strong in those areas but also in defense—a defense capability second to none.

We've lost in our foreign policy the character of the American people. We've ignored or excluded the American people and the Congress from participation in the shaping of our foreign policy. It's been one of secrecy and exclusion. In addition to that we've had a chance to become now—contrary to our long-standing beliefs and principles—the arms merchant of the whole world. We've tried to buy success from our enemies, and at the same time we've excluded from the process the normal friendship of our allies.

In addition to that we've become fearful to compete with the Soviet Union on an equal basis. We talk about détente. The Soviet Union knows what they want in détente, and they've been getting it. We have not known what we wanted, and we've been outtraded in almost every instance.

The other point I want to make is about our defense. We've got to be a nation blessed with a defense capability that is efficient, tough, capable, well organized, narrowly focused—fighting capability—the ability to fight, if necessary, is the best way to avoid a chance for or the requirement to fight.

And the last point I want to make is this: Mr. Ford, Mr. Kissinger have continued on with the policies and pledges of Richard Nixon. Even the Republican platform has criticized the lack of leadership in Mr. Ford and they've criticized the foreign policy of this Administration. This is one instance where I agree with the Republican platform.

I might say this in closing, and that is that as far as foreign policy goes, Mr. Kissinger has been the President of this country. Mr. Ford has shown an absence of leadership, and an absence of a grasp of what this country is and what it ought to be. That's got to be changed. And that's one of the major issues in this campaign of 1976. . . .

What we were formerly so proud of—the strength of our country, its moral integrity, the representation in foreign affairs of what our people or what our Constitution stands for—has been gone. And in the secrecy that has surrounded our foreign policy in the last few years, the American [people] and the Congress have been excluded. . . .

Every time we've made a serious mistake in foreign affairs, it's been because the American people have been excluded from the process.

If we can just tap the intelligence and ability, the sound common sense and the good judgment of the American people, we can once again have a foreign policy that will make us proud instead of ashamed.

And I'm not going to exclude the American people from that process in the future, as Mr. Ford and Kissinger have done. . . .

Recently Ian Smith, the President of Rhodesia, announced that he had unequivocal commitments from Mr. Kissinger that he could not reveal. The American people don't know what those commitments are.

We've seen in the past the destruction of elected Governments, like in Chile, and the strong support of military dictatorship there. These kind of things have hurt us very much. . . .

I notice that Mr. Ford didn't comment on the prisons in Chile. This is a typical example, maybe of many others, that this Administration overthrew an elected government and helped to establish a military dictatorship.

This has not been an ancient history story. Last year under Mr. Ford, of all the Food for Peace that went to South America, 85 percent went to the military dictatorship in Chile.

Another point I want to make is this. He said we have to move from one area of the world to another. That's one of the problems with this Administration's so-called shuttle diplomacy. While the Secretary of State's in one country, there are almost 150 others that are wondering what we're going to do next, what will be the next secret agreement. We don't have a comprehensive understandable foreign policy that deals with world problems or even regional problems. . . .

This election will also determine what kind of world we leave our children. Will it be a nightmare world threatened with the proliferation of atomic bombs, not just in five major countries but dozens of smaller countries that have been permitted to develop atomic weapons because of a failure of our top leadership to stop proliferation?

Will we have a world of hunger and hatred and will we be living in an arms camp stripped of our friendship and allies, hiding behind a tight defense that's been drawn around us because we are fearful of the outside world?

Will we have a government of secrecy that excludes the American people from participation in making basic decisions and therefore covers up mistakes and makes it possible for our government—our government—to depart from the principles of our Constitution and Bill of Rights?

Or will we have a world of peace with the threat of atomic weapons eliminated, with full trade, with our people at work, inflation controlled, openness in government, our people proud once again, Congress, citizens, President, Secretary of State working in harmony and unity toward a common future? Or will our people have enough to eat and a world where we care about those who don't? Can we become breadbasket of the world instead of the arms merchant of the world?

I believe we can and we ought to.

And we've been hurt in recent years in this country, in the aftermath of Vietnam, Cambodia, Chile, Pakistan, Angola, Watergate, C.I.A. We've been hurt. Our people feel that we've lost something precious. That's not necessary.

I want to see our nation return to a posture and an image and a standard to make us proud once again. I remember the world of NATO and the world of Point Four and the world of the Marshall Plan and the world of the Peace Corps. Why can't we have that once again? We ought to be a beacon for nations who search for peace and who search for freedom, who search for individual liberty, who search for basic human rights. We haven't been lately. We can be once again.

We'll never have that world leadership until we are strong at home, and we can have that strength if we return to the basic principles.

It ought not to be a strength of bombast and threats. It ought to be a quiet strength based on the integrity of our people, the vision of the Constitution and in a strong will and purpose that God's given us in the greatest nation on earth—the United States.

Journalist Anthony Lewis on Kissinger's Secretaryship, 1977

Henry Kissinger is leaving office in a blaze of adulation. The National Press Club produces a belly dancer for him and gives standing applause to his views on world peace. The Harlem Globetrotters make him an honorary member. Senators pay tribute to his wisdom.

Historians of the next generation will find it all very puzzling. Because they will not have seen Mr. Kissinger perform, they will have to rely on the record. And the record of his eight years in Washington is likely to seem thin in diplomatic achievement and shameful in human terms.

Anthony Lewis, "This Way to the Egress," *New York Times,* January 13, 1977, p. 37, © 1976/77 by The New York Times Company. Reprinted by permission.

The one outstanding accomplishment is Mr. Kissinger's Middle East diplomacy. He restored United States relations with the Arab world, and he set in motion the beginnings of an Arab-Israeli dialogue. Of course, the work is incomplete. But to start something after so many years of total failure was a great breakthrough and it was essentially the work of one man: Henry Kissinger.

The other undoubtedly positive entry on the record is the opening to China, but that was in good part Richard Nixon's doing. Also, the beginnings of a relationship with the People's Republic were not followed up as they might have been, and the failure may prove damaging.

With the Soviet Union, Mr. Kissinger took the familiar idea of easing tensions and glamorized it as détente. The glamor was dangerous. It fostered the illusion that détente could prevent conflict all over the world, and many Americans turned sour on the whole idea when it did not. At times Mr. Kissinger himself seemed to believe the illusion—and became apoplectic when it failed as in Angola. Détente's real achievements are scant; not much more than a halting step toward nuclear arms control.

Ignorance and ineptitude marked his policy in much of the rest of the world. In Cyprus, his blundering led to human tragedy and left America's reputation damaged in both Greece and Turkey. His insensitivity to Japanese feelings had traumatic effects on a most important ally.

In dealing with Portugal and its African territories Mr. Kissinger decided in succession that (1) the Portuguese were in Africa to stay, (2) the U.S. should help Portugal's dictatorship, (3) after the dictatorship's fall the Communists were bound to prevail in Portugal and (4) the U.S. could decide the outcome in Angola by covert aid. That parade of folly was matched in his African policy generally: years of malign neglect, then last-minute intervention for majority rule in Rhodesia.

He often talked about freedom, but his acts shows a pre-eminent interest in order. Millions lost their freedom during the Kissinger years, many to dictatorships that had crucial support from his policies, as in Chile and the Philippines. He expressed little open concern for the victims of Soviet tyranny, and he did little to enforce the human rights clauses of the Helsinki Agreement.

The American constitutional system of checks and balances he treated as an irritating obstacle to power. In his valedictory to the Press Club his only reference to Watergate was an expression of regret at "the disintegration of Executive authority that resulted."

Secrecy and deceit were levers of his power; he had no patience for the democratic virtues of openness and consultation. By keeping all the facts to himself and a few intimates, he centralized control. He practiced deceit with a kind of gusto, from petty personal matters to "peace is at hand."

His conduct in the wiretapping of his own staff gave ugly insight into his character. He provided names for investigation—and then, when the story came out, wriggled and deceived in order to minimize his role. He never expressed regret, even to those who had been closest to him, for the fact that their family conversations had been overheard for months. But when someone ransacked his garbage, he said his wife had suffered "grave anguish."

History will remember him most of all for his policy in Indochina. In the teeth of evidence well known by 1969, this supposed realist pressed obsessively for indefinite maintenance of the status quo. To that end, in his time, 20,492 more Americans died in Vietnam and hundreds of thousands of Vietnamese. The war was expanded into Cambodia, destroying that peaceable land. And all for nothing.

With such a record, how is it that people vie to place laurels on the head of the departing Secretary of State? The answer became clear the other night during an extraordinarily thoughtful Public Broadcasting television program on Mr. Kissinger's career: He has discovered that in our age publicity is power, and he has played the press as Dr. Miracle played his violin. He is intelligent and hard-working and ruthless, but those qualities are common enough. His secret is showmanship.

Henry Kissinger is our P. T. Barnum—a Barnum who plays in a vastly larger tent and whose jokes have about them the air of the grave. That we honor a person who has done such things in our name is a comment on us.

ESSAYS

John G. Stoessinger, a political scientist and friend of Kissinger, has written a sympathetic study of the Secretary of State, subtitled *The Anguish of Power*. He commends Kissinger's search for and partial success in achieving a stable world order. In the second essay, *New York Times* correspondent Leslie H. Gelb, although noting the positive aspects of Kissinger's legacy and his brilliance as a tactician, faults him as a strategist and cites some conspicuous failures and shortcomings.

Kissinger and a Safer World

JOHN G. STOESSINGER

"I know I have a first-rate mind," Henry Kissinger once told me many years ago, "but that's no source of pride to me. Intelligent people are a dime a dozen. But I am proud of having character."

Henry Kissinger never had much patience with mediocrities or fools. But when, in the rolling cadences of his Bavarian accent, he would describe some luckless academic as a "characterless bastard," he meant to convey a bottomless contempt. Kissinger reserved this ultimate epithet for those unfortunates who did not have the courage to *act* on their convictions. A man who said one thing but did another was even more certain to incur his wrath than someone

Reprinted from *Henry Kissinger: The Anguish of Power* by John G. Stoessinger, pp. 207–227. By permission of W. W. Norton & Company, Inc. Copyright © 1976 by W. W. Norton & Company, Inc.

who had no convictions whatsoever. The move to Washington did little to change Kissinger's opinion. "The worst kinds of bastards in this town," he declared three years after he had come to power, "are those who hold high positions and then go out and say they really didn't believe in Administration policies. If anyone would ever say I didn't believe in what Nixon is doing, I would publicly dispute him. I like the President. I agree with him. We've gone through all this for three years, like two men in a foxhole. . . ."

"Character" to Kissinger, had little to do with intelligence. What he admired was a man's capacity to stand up for his convictions in the world of action, alone if necessary. When, in a rare unguarded moment, Kissinger had said, "I have always acted alone," he had revealed a deep emotional conviction. Even though his intellect reminded him that "a policy that was conceived in the mind of one, but resided in the hearts of none," was doomed to failure, this *emotional* preference for solitude remained. It is for this reason that Kissinger preferred Castlereagh to Metternich. Castlereagh had a grand design and, even though it had "outdistanced the experience of his people," he had found the moral courage to remain loyal to his vision. Metternich, on the other hand, despite his brilliance and his cunning, had never found the courage to "contemplate an abyss as a challenge to overcome or to perish in the process." Thus, he had ultimately doomed himself to sterility, and with him, Imperial Austria.

Among contemporary statesmen, Kissinger most admired those who had not only conceived a vision, but had found the courage to translate it into action, even in the face of anguish and adversity. The fact that most of the men who shared these qualities happened to be adversaries, did not deter him in the least. When as a scholar at Harvard, he was preoccupied with Europe, he had often expressed considerable admiration for the strength and steadfastness of Charles de Gaulle, the *bête noire* of the North Atlantic Treaty. After he had come to power, he spoke with genuine respect of Mao Tse-tung and Chou En-lai and of their courage in adversity. Among his fellow intellectuals, he was most drawn to Hans Morgenthau, even though the older scholar had often attacked his policies on Indochina and the Middle East. But he admired Morgenthau's vision in having been the first to oppose Indochina policy under Kennedy and Johnson and his courage in making that early opposition known despite official ridicule and even harassment.

In Kissinger's hierarchy of values, courage and decisiveness came first. Loyalty, too, was prized by him. Intelligence, even brilliance, he considered fairly commonplace. If they were coupled with indecisiveness and weakness in a man, that combination was sure to arouse Kissinger's contempt. Whether one chose to describe Kissinger's ideal in the romantic terms of Hegel's *Zeitgeist,* or in the more rustic image of an embattled cowboy in a Western town, its essence was the same: a man must know how to think and act *alone.*

A great deal has been written about Henry Kissinger's personal diplomacy. His insistence on conducting important negotiations personally and his habit of establishing close relationships with adversary leaders are well known characteristics of his statecraft. His low opinion of the bureaucracy has also been widely commented upon. This penchant for the solo performance has been variously attributed to Kissinger's "enormous ego," his "obsessive secrecy" or to his "elemental need for power and for glory."

I should like to submit another interpretation. I believe that, in order for Kissinger to succeed in his most historic diplomatic initiatives, he *had to* establish personal dominance over the bureaucracy. To establish such control moreover, he had to act decisively, often secretly, and, at times, alone.

Kissinger had never had much patience with bureaucracy. When a professor at Harvard, he had reserved his most acid comments for university administrators. His tolerance for bureaucracy in government was not much greater. After having studied the American "foreign policy-making apparatus" he had come to the conclusion that it was a kind of feudal network of competing agencies and interests, in which there was a "powerful tendency to think that a compromise among administrative proposals (was) the same thing as a policy." The bureaucratic model for making a decision, in Kissinger's opinion, was a policy proposal with three choices: the present policy bracketed by two absurd alternatives.

Kissinger had been a consultant to both the Kennedy and Johnson administrations. While he never said so publicly, he had been deeply disappointed. So much had been promised; so much less had been attempted and, in his judgment, so little had been done. He had had the opportunity to observe government decision-making from a fairly close perspective. What impressed him most was that the foreign policy bureaucracy had a way of smothering initiative by advocating a path of least resistance. The lawyers, businessmen, and former academics who ran the hierarchy generally seemed to place a premium on safety and acceptance rather than on creativity and vision. The result was that any innovative statesmanship tended to expire in the feudal fiefs of the bureaucracy or come to grief on the rocks of organizational inertia.

There was ample basis for Kissinger's impatience. SALT might have been initiated at the Glassboro summit in 1967, between Lyndon Johnson and the Soviet leaders, but there had been no decisive leadership. Nor had there been a clear-cut stand on the possible limitation of strategic arms. Instead, there were endless arguments among the Joint Chiefs of Staff, the Pentagon, the State Department, and academic experts in the field of arms control. Similarly, the Arab-Israeli war of 1967 had presented opportunities for American diplomacy and mediation, but there had been no one with a plan, let alone the courage to place himself between competing claims. Instead, there emerged from the bowels of the bureaucracy countless position papers by learned academic experts. There was no agreement on an overall strategy for mediation in the Middle East, only an almost fatalistic sense of hopelessness and drift.

This was the reason why Kissinger decided, immediately after January 20, 1969, to establish personal control over the bureaucracy. Those whom he could not dominate, he would manipulate. And those whom he could not manipulate, he would try to bypass. He embarked on this course of action as a result of a rational decision. He simply feared that *unless* he dominated, bypassed, or manipulated, nothing would get done. He, too, would ultimately be submerged in a long twilight struggle of modern feudal baronies. This he was simply not prepared to accept.

In his position as Assistant for National Security Affairs, Kissinger came to dominate the bureaucracy as no other figure before him had done, and as no other is likely to do for a very long time to come. He promptly established his control through the establishment of a few small committees each of which he personally chaired. These were a number of interdepartmental groups: a Review Group, a Verification Panel for SALT, a Vietnam Special Studies Group, the Washington Special Actions Group for Crisis Control, and the Forty Committee which dealt with covert intelligence operations.

It was out of these committees that Kissinger forged the great initiatives that have assured his place in history: SALT I in 1969, the opening to China after his secret trip to Peking in 1971, and the diplomatic mediation in the Middle East after the October war in 1973. It is true, of course, that some of the more dubious decisions also had their genesis in this small elitist structure, particularly in the Forty Committee. The "destabilization" of the Allende government in Chile in 1971, alleged payments to Italian neo-fascists in 1972, and the denouement in Indochina are some of the more disturbing examples. Only history can provide the necessary distance for a balanced assessment of these various initiatives. But what can already be asserted with a fair amount of certainty is that Kissinger was right in his assumption that, in order to put into effect a coherent global policy, he would have to concentrate as much power in his hands as possible.

Kissinger's pursuit of power had a very clear-cut purpose. During two decades of reflection he had evolved a theory of global order which, in his judgment, would bring the world a few steps closer to stability and peace. Nothing was more important to him in 1969 than the chance to test that theory. He believed with the most absolute conviction that he was the one best qualified. On one occasion, in 1968, when Rockefeller's speech writers had made some changes in a Kissinger position paper, the author exclaimed furiously: "If Rockefeller buys a Picasso, he doesn't hire four housepainters to improve on it." In Kissinger's own view, this was not an arrogant statement. It was merely the reflection of an enormous, though quite genuine, intellectual self-confidence. He believed, quite matter-of-factly, that he was the Picasso of modern American foreign policy.

Henry Kissinger believed that, in creating a design for world order, realism was more compassionate than romanticism. The great American moralists, in his judgment, had been failures. In the end, Woodrow Wilson had proved ineffectual and John Foster Dulles had turned foreign policy into a crusade that had led straight into the Indochina quagmire. Kissinger did not make peace or justice the objective of his policy nor was he particularly interested in "making the world safe for democracy." He merely wished to make the world safer and more stable. This was a lesser goal, one that offered no illusions, but also brought fewer disappointments. It was also not quite in the mainstream of American history. But then, Kissinger was a European in America, his thought rooted firmly in the European philosophical tradition.

There has been a great deal of confusion about Kissinger's intellectual debt to Metternich for his vision of stability. Kissinger himself has made it abundantly clear that he never looked to Metternich for guidance on *substantive problems* of statecraft: "Most people associate me with Metternich. And that is childish . . . there can be nothing in common between me and Metternich. He was chancellor and foreign minister at a time when it took three weeks to travel from Central Europe to the ends of the Continent, when wars were conducted by professional soldiers and diplomacy was in the hands of the aristocracy. . . ." What Kissinger admired in Metternich was the Austrian diplomat's *conceptual insight* in having recognized the revolutionary character of the Napoleonic challenge, the need to neutralize that challenge without humiliating retribution, and, having achieved that end, his commitment to stability and balance which ushered in a century without a global war.

If Castlereagh taught Kissinger that a statesman must create a vision and remain faithful to it even in adversity, Metternich taught him how to adjust that vision to reality. If Castlereagh taught him about courage and a grand design, Metternich taught him about cunning and manipulation. But when all was said and done, the lessons Kissinger could learn from these two nineteenth century aristocrats were limited. In the end, Kissinger, too, had to stand alone.

Henry Kissinger once told me that a statesman, to be successful, had to have some luck. He knew well that he was no exception to this rule. His appearance on the world stage coincided most fortuitously with a new nadir in the relations between China and the Soviet Union. By 1969, Mao Tse-tung and Brezhnev feared each other more than they feared America, and thus had become more concerned with moderating their relations with the United States than with the pursuit of revolutionary goals of conquest vis-à-vis the West. Thus, the timing of Kissinger's arrival as a world statesman could not have been more fortunate for the particular objective that he had in mind: a new stability in the relations among the world's three great powers.

The drawing up of any balance sheet on the centerpiece of Kissinger's foreign policy—détente with the Soviet Union—must remain a highly personal business on which thoughtful people may have widely differing opinions. Any such analysis must enter in the realm of competing values, since in creating that centerpiece, choices had to be made and a price had to be paid. Hence, it is only fair that, as we enter this discussion, I reveal the basis of my judgment and share my values and prejudices with the reader.

I believe that Henry Kissinger was right when he declared that the overriding reason for détente with Russia was the avoidance of a nuclear catastrophe. I believe that if such a world cataclysm has become less likely, this is in no small measure to be credited to Kissinger. I am fully aware that the American relationship with Russia leaves a great deal to be desired. But there is no question in my mind that the danger of nuclear war has substantially receded. It no longer intrudes into our daily lives the way it did when Kissinger and I were students. Mothers worried about radioactive waste and strontium-90 in their children's milk; and a decade later, John F. Kennedy almost went to nuclear war with Khrushchev over missiles in Cuba. Today, we argue with the Soviet Union about strategic arms control, trade, and human rights, but we no longer live in daily terror of a nuclear exchange. The fearful scenarios that were conjured up in Herman Kahn's *Thinking About the Unthinkable* today read almost like horrible anachronisms. In addition to the elements of luck and timing, it was also Kissinger's design and courage that made détente possible at all.

I know the price that Kissinger has paid on behalf of the United States has been enormous. But, to be fair, we must ask ourselves in each case whether the alternatives would have yielded better results. In strategic arms control, Kissinger's accusers have blamed him for his acceptance in SALT I of Soviet superiority in missile numbers. They have also been suspicious of his lack of interest in alleged evidence that the Soviet Union had violated the spirit and perhaps even the letter of SALT I. Critics have also taken umbrage at his reported willingness—during the SALT II negotiations—to exclude the Soviet Backfire bomber from an overall ceiling while including the American cruise missile.

But the critics, in my judgment, have never given a convincing answer to Kissinger's own question: "What in God's name," he asked in 1974, "is strategic superiority? What is the significance of it, politically, militarily, operationally, at these levels of numbers? What do you do with it?" Kissinger simply did not believe that a marginal "overkill" capacity on either side could be translated into a meaningful strategic or political advantage. To my mind, there is no conclusive evidence that such a translation can in fact be made.

The "great grain robbery" of 1972 was not one of Kissinger's proudest moments. The Russian harvest was so poor that the Soviet leadership probably would have paid a better price. As it turned out, however, the American taxpayer helped to underwrite the Soviet purchases and got in return only a few ephemeral benefits: a little Soviet help in Hanoi and Brezhnev's decision to meet with Nixon at the Moscow summit despite the President's decision to place mines in Haiphong harbor.

Kissinger was right, however, in my judgment, in his dispute with Senator Henry Jackson over the linking of most-favored-nations status for the Soviet Union with emigration of Soviet Jews to Israel. It was unreasonable for Jackson to couple an international agreement with Russia to a demand for internal changes within the Soviet state. How would Jackson have responded if the Soviet leadership had linked the conclusion of SALT I to a demand for a lifting of all American immigration quotas? The point I am making is not that the demand was ethically unjustified, but that it was asymmetrical. A *quid pro quo* of Soviet cooperation in the Middle East would have been more sensible and would not have brought up the delicate issue of Soviet internal politics. To those who argued that he was insensitive to the human rights of Jews wishing to emigrate to Israel, Kissinger could point to his record with not inconsiderable pride. Before the Soviets cancelled the 1972 trade agreement in their anger over the Jackson amendment, the annual figure of Jewish emigrants from Russia reached 35,000. After Jackson made his public demands, this figure was cut by more than half. In this instance, without a doubt, private diplomacy tactfully conducted had yielded better results that open covenants stridently demanded.

The great paradox of Kissinger's conception of détente is in his relative tolerance vis-à-vis the Soviet Union, still the fountainhead of communism, and his combativeness toward local Communist movements in peripheral areas. How can Kissinger proclaim détente with the Soviet Union, the supporter of Communist causes everywhere, and yet fight communism to the death in Indochina, warn Western European heads of state against coalition governments with Communists, and demand action against the Communists in Angola?

The key to this riddle is to be found in Kissinger's primary commitment to stability. In the central relationship between the superpowers, there can be no decisive change in the power balance, short of nuclear war. The balance could be changed dramatically, however, if a minor nation shifted its allegiance from one side to the other and thus added appreciably to the strength of one of the two main contenders. The direct jockeying for mutual advantage between Russia and the United States was not likely to affect the global balance. But Communist advances elsewhere could, at least cumulatively, affect the balance of power in the world. Hence, Kissinger's concern with stemming Communist advances in peripheral areas.

This logic, however, runs into serious difficulties. It may stand up in an area such as Angola where thousands of Cuban troops were imported to do battle for the Communist cause. In such a case, there was at least good circumstantial evidence for direct Soviet-sponsored intervention. But there was little, if any evidence that the Soviet Union was very active in helping the Communists in Portugal, Italy, or France. The growth of the Italian Communist movement in Italy under Enrico Berlinguer might be attributable more to that Italian's "historic compromise" with democratic socialism than to subversion by the Soviet Union. Yet, Kissinger accused the Portuguese Foreign Minister of being a "Kerensky," quarantined Portugal from NATO, and had secret payments made to a neo-fascist Italian general. In such cases, a good argument can be made that, by his indiscriminate opposition to all local forms of communism, Kissinger might force breakaway groups back into Moscow's arms and thus bring about the very developments he was so eager to prevent.

On a deeper level, Hans Morgenthau has made the most telling criticism:

> Since the causes and effects of instability persist, a policy committed to stability and identifying instability with communism is compelled by the logic of its interpretation of reality to suppress in the name of anticommunism all manifestations of popular discontent and stifle the aspirations for reform. Thus, in an essentially unstable world, tyranny becomes the last resort of a policy committed to stability as its ultimate standard.

This is how, in Morgenthau's opinion, Kissinger, despite his extraordinary brilliance, often failed. He tended to place his great gifts at the service of lost causes, and thus, in the name of preserving stability and order, aligned the United States on the wrong side of the great historic issues.

Morgenthau may be a little harsh in such a judgment. What if the Italian Communists renounced their "historic compromise", made common cause with Moscow, and other European countries followed suit? The result could well be a catastrophe for the United States. Morgenthau, as critic, does not have to make that awesome choice. But can a statesman dare to take such risks at a moment when he must base his decisions on conjecture rather than on facts? Here the scholar, in my judgment, owes the statesman a measure of empathy and tolerance.

In this entire realm of argument, Kissinger is most vulnerable, in my view, on his Indochina policy. No one, of course, can blame him for the escalation which he regarded as a national disaster. But I have always differed with his judgment that the presence of 500,000 Americans had settled the importance of Vietnam since credibility was now at stake. Rather, it was my impression that American credibility rose rather than fell when that suicidal commitment finally came to an end. I have also never understood Kissinger's answer to the argument that a negotiated settlement could have been attained in 1969 on terms at least as favorable as those that he finally negotiated in 1973. His explanation that, for three years the North Vietnamese had refused to accept his "double track" plan of separating military from political matters always struck me as rather unconvincing. Finally, the Cambodian invasion that dragged a neutral nation into a war that it might have been able to avoid, struck me as the greatest, and possibly most tragic, blunder. And, in the end, when Saigon fell in April 1975, Kissinger looked like all the other Americans who had come to Indochina to lose their reputation to Ho Chi Minh and the Vietcong.

There may be a psychological interpretation of Kissinger's paradoxical approach to Communism. It may be found in his profound suspicion of the revolutionary as the greatest threat to a stable world order. In theory, as Kissinger had made clear in an essay on Bismarck, it made little difference to him whether a revolutionary was "red" or "white". But in practice, he always feared the "red" revolutionary infinitely more. It is not that he approved of a Greek or Chilean junta, but he simply did not believe that it posed the kind of threat to international stability as that presented by a Cunhal, an Allende, a Castro, or a Ho Chi Minh. These were the types of leaders, rather than a Brezhnev or a Mao Tse-tung, who were most likely to upset the global balance. They still retained that messianic revolutionary quality that had a vast potential for dislocation and contagion. In relation to the Soviet Union and China, one could afford to take some chances without risk to equilibrium. But when it came to the smaller revolutionaries, Kissinger believed that the war-maker still made the most effective peacemaker.

The opening to China was probably Kissinger's most uncontaminated triumph in his tenure as a statesman. It was also his greatest diplomatic adventure. Once he perceived the depth of the rift between China and the Soviet Union, he became convinced that rapprochement with China might make the Soviet Union more receptive to a genuine détente. In short, China, in his view, had become the key to Russia. In addition to establishing this triangular linkage, Kissinger's secret trip to Peking in 1971, had made him the first messenger of reconciliation. Furthermore to discover that beyond the Himalayas, there were men who elicited his admiration and respect only added to his elation. One of the few times that I heard Kissinger happily admit that he had been wrong was an occasion when he discussed his change of heart about Mao Tse-tung and Chou En-lai. In 1966, during the "Cultural Revolution", he had perceived the Chinese leaders as the two most dangerous men on earth. Five years later, he had come to regard them as rational statesmen who pursued China's national interest in a manner not altogether inconsistent with the rules of international stability. But then it was Henry Kissinger who had once said about himself that while he had a first-rate mind, he had a third-rate intuition about people. In the case of China, fortunately, the reality turned out to be more pleasant than the fantasy.

As for the charge that Kissinger's relationships with adversaries were often better than his relationships with friends, I would hardly cloak this statement in a mantle of universal application. There is, however, ample evidence for it if one contemplates Kissinger's policies toward the continent where he was born. Europe brought out the darker side of his personal diplomacy and his reluctance to delegate responsibility. His declaration of a "Year of Europe" in 1973 had come almost as an afterthought in response to complaints by Western European statesmen that their capitals had become little more than refueling stops for Kissinger on his way to or back from Moscow. It reminded one European diplomat of an unfaithful husband's decision to declare a "year of the wife." Kissinger's outbursts of exasperation in moments of frustration did little to improve relations. When he exclaimed in a moment of anger that he "didn't care what happened to NATO," this momentary lapse was taken seriously by his NATO partners. And his lectures to the Portuguese aroused their anger and resentment. In many of these instances, Kissinger followed his own judgment and generally ignored the advice of experienced foreign service officers.

The case that combined all the weaknesses of personal diplomacy, of course, was Cyprus. Kissinger made policy decisions with regard to Cyprus almost absentmindedly. Distracted by the final act of Watergate, he paid only the most cursory attention to events on that tormented island. His dislike for Archbishop Makarios prompted him to lean toward the Greek extremist, Nikos Sampson, of whose reputation he knew little. When the Turks, predictably enough, responded by mounting an invasion, Kissinger did little to deter them even though a democratic government in the meantime had assumed control in Athens. Thus, Kissinger managed to alienate *both* Greece and Turkey in an amazingly short period of time. Perhaps even more serious, the failure of his Cyprus policy led directly to the first of many strictures to be imposed upon him by an increasingly suspicious and hostile Congress.

Since Kissinger's main objective has always been the pursuit of international stability, his attention had been focussed on the world's major power wielders. The pawns on the global chessboard seemed quite expendable to him, until quite suddenly and without warning, some of them decided to improve their lowly status. The Arab oil embargo and the demands for a "new international economic order" that swept through the Third World like a hurricane, convinced Kissinger that he finally would have to pay attention to the smaller nations of Africa, Latin America, and Asia. He quickly realized that his vision of stability would have to become bifocal. Unless he did so, his policies might prevent World War III, but they were certain to prepare the ground for World War IV.

When, in the spring of 1976, Kissinger declared his clear support for black majority rule in southern Africa, he reversed a long tradition of American equivocation. While this reversal was triggered primarily by the Soviet victory in Angola, it was also motivated by Kissinger's desire to build détente between the races and the rich and poor. And when he pledged a dedicated effort to "roll back the desert" in famine-stricken African lands, his promise had the ring of truth. This compassion for the world's dispossessed came late, but when it came, it was sincere.

For almost thirty years, the United Nations had existed in the suburbs of Henry Kissinger's consciousness. Its lack of authority and power had convinced him that he could ignore it with impunity. The increase of Third World bloc voting, however, and the rise of a "tyranny of the majority," made him pay attention. When this majority, having driven the United States into the role of opposition, finally passed an Orwellian resolution that equated Zionism with racism, Kissinger's antennae, always sensitive to power, registered an ominous alert.

Somber warnings that the United Nations might become an empty shell, coupled with Ambassador Moynihan's blunt rhetoric, placed the Third World nations on guard that they were not immune to Kissinger's favorite mixture of diplomacy and force. When Moynihan, however, engaged in so much bluntness that it began to resemble "overkill," Kissinger became alarmed. The differences between the two men finally led to the ambassador's resignation. Even a Kissinger weakened by mounting criticism and congressional opposition was still a formidable adversary.

We cannot say with certitude whether the critics of the step-by-step approach to peace in the Middle East were justified in their assertions that Kissinger avoided the heart of the conflict by refusing to address himself to the Palestinian problem. What the record does indicate, however, is that Kissinger has managed to narrow the differences between Israel and the Arabs more successfully than any other mediator in the long history of that tragic conflict.

The essence of Kissinger's Middle East diplomacy has been the avoidance of the appearance of victory. Convinced that only a stalemate could contain the seeds of peace, he steered the October war to an inconclusive end. In doing so, he resisted enormous pressure from each side hungering for military victory. It was in the aftermath of this military stalemate that he succeeded in negotiating the two disengagement accords, first between Israel and Egypt and then, between Israel and Syria. The two agreements were achieved in no small measure because of Kissinger's personal tenacity. The Sinai agreement which followed in September 1975, was the first accord reached by Israel and an Arab state that was not an armistice to end a war. It was a voluntary agreement reached in times of peace. Even when shortly afterward Syria temporarily linked its future to the PLO, Kissinger's approach of "peace by pieces" had already achieved remarkable results.

It is in the Middle East that Kissinger's intellectual courage had to undergo its acid test. It was not easy always to negotiate between a hammer and an anvil. His striving for balance and equilibrium was never popular with either side. As a Jew, he did not find it easy to deny victory to the state of Israel. Personally, he endured considerable suffering. Yet, he remained faithful to his intellectual conviction that a victor's peace would plant the seeds of yet another war. He might be mistaken in this belief though history provides considerable evidence to back him up. But while his judgment may be open to debate, his sincerity is not. Nowhere in his statesmanship has Henry Kissinger shown greater courage than in his quest for a Middle Eastern peace.

If there is any iron law of history, Kissinger once said, it is that no longing is ever completely fulfilled. His own pursuit of a stable world order is no exception to this general rule.

After Nixon's resignation Kissinger remained the only major figure in the government who had been closely associated with the former president. He now had to pay the price exacted by a resurgent Congress in the post-imperial presidency.

Kissinger's autocratic temperament, highly personal style, and persistent secrecy, now made him a natural target. What had been admired in him earlier now was questioned and condemned. Within one year, between 1974 and 1975, the Congress placed severe restrictions on his freedom to maneuver in virtually every single area of foreign policy, from Turkey to Angola. The man who could do nothing wrong now suddenly could do nothing right. As Kissinger himself observed, "I have been praised excessively, so now I am being blamed excessively." Seldom has a man been more exposed to the fickleness of popular acclaim.

While Kissinger was still widely perceived as an asset to the United States as a *nation* in its relationships abroad, many Americans, by 1976, were deeply ambivalent about his impact on America as a *people* at home. Kissinger himself has been consistent. He has never wavered in his striving for a stable world order. But he was fated to experience in practice what he had learned in theory a quarter of a century before: that a statesman who removes himself too much from the experience of his people may doom himself to disappointment and despair. In February 1976, he stated that America was more endangered by her "domestic divisions than by her overseas adversaries." "A great nation that does not shape history," he continued, "eventually becomes its victim." In his frustration with a Congress that had persistently disavowed his policies and had simply refused to heed his counsel on Angola, he sounded a bleak and somber warning:

> Unless the country ends its divisions, our only option is to retreat—to become an isolated fortress in a hostile and turbulent global sea, awaiting the ultimate

confrontation with the only response we will not have denied ourselves—massive retaliation.

Once again, Kissinger walked as a loner, with the ghost of Oswald Spengler by his side. His career showed clearly that vision and courage may not be enough to ensure success. As he himself had written, popular support was essential as well. Luck and timing also played a crucial role. Thucydides had realized this long ago in ancient Athens when he had elevated fortune to the rank of goddess.

Perhaps the most haunting questions about Henry Kissinger's foreign policy are of a philosophical nature. What is the role of ethics in Kissinger's world of stability and power? What is the relationship between personal and political morality? What room does Kissinger's pursuit of a stable world order leave for justice? What should be our criterion for success—his intentions or the consequences of his actions? In short, what must concern us, in conclusion, is the problem of statesmanship and moral choice.

There is little doubt that Kissinger, when facing Goethe's dilemma—the choice "between justice and disorder, on the one hand, and injustice and order, on the other," has tended to prefer the latter. In Kantian terms Kissinger made the pursuit of a stable world order the categorical imperative of his foreign policy. If, in the process, the human element had to be sacrificed at times on the altar of stability or of a larger strategic vision, so be it, because without stability, peace could not be born at all and justice, too, would be extinguished. He felt that, in a tragic world, a statesman was not able to choose between good and evil, but only among different forms of evil. Indeed, whatever decision he would make, *some* evil consequences were bound to flow from it. All that a realistic statesman could do in such a world was to choose the lesser evil.

The competing claims of stability and justice permeate the world of Henry Kissinger. A few examples from the record will suffice to demonstrate the pervasiveness of this terrible dilemma.

In the Indochina war, the problem presented itself in its starkest form in the Nixon decision to mine the ports of North Vietnam and to order all-out bombing attacks on Hanoi and Haiphong in 1972. These actions, which were publicly supported by Kissinger, tested the determination of the Soviet Union and China to stand by their North Vietnamese ally. When no action was forthcoming either from Moscow or Peking, Nixon and Kissinger realized that they had managed to isolate North Vietnam. The war was therefore brought to an end for American combat soldiers, but at a price that aroused the moral indignation of many nations and that of many Americans as well. The question that remains is whether this brutal means was justified to attain the desired objective of a "peace with honor," a peace which, in the end, proved to be ephemeral. Could not another, less dreadful, way have been found?

In his relations with the Soviet Union, Kissinger has also been accused of indifference to the human element. As Richard Falk has observed in a thoughtful essay, "Kissinger's effectiveness in dealing with foreign governments arose from his capacity to avoid unpleasant criticisms about their domestic indecencies." Since most powerful states have skeletons hidden in their closets, most statesmen, Falk observed, "found Kissinger's Machiavellian posture a welcome relief." If, in short, a choice had to be made between détente and human rights within the borders of the Soviet Union, there was little doubt how Kissinger would choose.

When India went to war with Pakistan in 1971, Kissinger "tilted" toward Yahya Khan. Not only had the Pakistani president helped in the preparations for the secret trip to China, but an Indian alliance with the Soviet Union threatened to dismember a weakened Pakistan. When Yahya Khan turned on his Bengali fellow-Moslems in a ferocious civil war, and drove ten million of them into exile, Kissinger remained silent. The imperatives of the strategic balance, once again, had overshadowed the human tragedy.

Until the nations of the Third World gained a measure of power through the oil embargo and bloc alignments in the United Nations, Kissinger had little time for the problems of the small and poor. Until famines in the Third World reached catastrophic dimensions, they remained on the periphery of his political awareness. Falk observed of Kissinger's early attitude that "it was inconceivable that afflictions of this magnitude in the Northern Hemisphere would not have been perceived as a catastrophe of historic significance." "Kissinger's outlook," Falk continued, "presupposed that it (was) possible to manage international relations mainly by moderating conflictual relations among governments in the Northern Hemisphere." Once more, Kissinger stood accused of ignoring humanity in the name of order.

It would not be fair to Kissinger to let these judgments stand without giving him a hearing. On Indochina, the question he might ask is this: What is more merciful and more compassionate, an end with horror or a horror without end? On the problem of ignoring human rights in Russia, he might well respond by asking whether the avoidance of an atomic holocaust was not itself the highest moral imperative of our age. On India and Pakistan, he might query his accuser as to whether Soviet domination of the Indian sub-continent might not have been the greater evil. And on the matter of the world's poor and dispossessed, Kissinger could now respond that his numerous proposals to build bridges between the world's rich and poor more than compensated for his earlier indifference.

When Henry Kissinger entered Harvard as an undergraduate in 1946, another Jewish refugee, almost a generation older, had just published his first book in the United States. Hans Morgenthau's *Scientific Man versus Power Politics* contained a paragraph that foreshadowed Kissinger's dilemma in all its awesome starkness:

> We have no choice between power and the common good. To act successfully, that is, according to the rules of the political art, is political wisdom. To know with despair that the political act is inevitably evil, and to act nevertheless, is moral courage. To choose among several expedient actions the least evil one is moral judgment. In the combination of political wisdom, moral courage and moral judgment, man reconciles his political nature with his moral destiny. That this conciliation is nothing more than a *modus vivendi*, uneasy, precarious,

and even paradoxical, can disappoint only those who prefer to gloss over and to distort the tragic contradictions of human existence with the soothing logic of a specious concord.

In such a world, is it not easier to abstain from any decision altogether? Kissinger has never thought so. He knew that abstention from evil did not affect the existence of evil in the world, but only destroyed the faculty of choice. As Albert Camus had said, not to choose, too, was a choice.

When history would make its judgment on the foreign policy of Henry Kissinger, the chronicle would not pay much attention to his personal anguish when forced to choose between competing claims. Its iron pen would merely register the objective consequences of his acts. Nor would history reveal its alternatives had he acted otherwise. He would never know where the road *not* taken might have led. The unending quest for meaningful choices in a tragic world in which the only certainty was risk simply was a statesman's lot. It was, therefore, in action in the present that courage and humanity were born.

When a quarter of a century ago, on that October day in 1950, I first met Henry Kissinger, I had a premonition that one day he might enter history. I think the world is a safer place today because of his courage and his vision. It might even be a little better. No mortal man could ask for more.

Kissinger as Flawed Strategist, Brilliant Tactician

LESLIE H. GELB

Henry A. Kissinger will go down in history as a great statesman, but not for the reasons he would relish and not without some black marks against him. He would like to be remembered as a Bismarck or a Castlereagh who shaped a new international order, more stable and just than the one he inherited. He is more likely to be thought of as the Don Juan of international diplomacy, romancing and blundering his way through perilous affairs, to win out in the end. From the present vantage point, Kissinger seems a flawed strategist but a brilliant tactician, capable of changing and recouping when all appears lost.

Kissinger would prefer that history skim over his role in Vietnam, Cambodia and Chile, or, if that cannot be, that his actions there will come to be seen as necessary. Neither wish seems likely to be granted. The situations in all three countries were difficult enough, to be sure, by the time he came on the scene, but the traumas that developed under his stewardship were not unavoidable. What exactly, then, is the Kissinger legacy? What has he done that is irreversible and lasting? Has he been a force for change, or has he simply been ingenious at preserving the status quo? . . .

Kissinger's policies can be traced through three distinct phases. In the first,

Leslie H. Gelb, "The Kissinger Legacy," *New York Times Magazine,* October 31, 1976, pp. 13–14, 72, 76, 78–79, 82, 83, 84–85, © 1976/77 by The New York Times Company. Reprinted by permission.

which ran from 1969 to the Yom Kippur war of 1973, Kissinger held the title of Assistant to the President for National Security Affairs but functioned, for all intents and purposes, as Secretary of State, purloining the essence of that office from its formal but ineffectual holder, William P. Rogers. Kissinger's reputation skyrocketed as President Nixon revealed the former Harvard professor's secret negotiations with Moscow, which led to agreements on nuclear arms; his secret journey to Peking, which produced the opening to China, and his secret meetings with Le Duc Tho, which resulted in the Paris ceasefire accords for Vietnam.

In the second phase, Nixon was consumed by Watergate and Kissinger emerged as a virtual President for Foreign Affairs—incidentally adding unto himself the title of Secretary of State. He reached the heights of his power with his Middle East shuttle diplomacy and the first Arab-Israeli troop disengagement agreements. But in his successes were sown the seeds of his discomfiture. Charging that Russia had instigated the war and that Kissinger had robbed Israel of victory, the political right and many Jewish leaders banded together to attack détente with Moscow. And this was accompanied by two stinging setbacks.

In the fall of 1974, Congress repudiated his Cyprus policy. At a briefing, Senators asked him why he had ignored the counsel of his own State Department legal advisers—that the United States cut off military aid to Turkey for making illegal use of American arms in Cyprus. Kissinger answered, "There are times when the national interest is more important than the law," and the briefing dissolved in angry shouting, as Kissinger tried to explain.

Cyprus showed that Kissinger could fail, and he failed again later that year, when, against his opposition and much to his dismay, Senator Henry M. Jackson pushed through legislation tying normal trading status for Russia to freer emigration of Soviet Jews. In November 1975, almost as though in response to Kissinger's sagging fortunes, Ford stripped him of his second hat as the President's chief adviser on national security.

Shorn of much of his power, Kissinger in his final phase became more pragmatic, less ebullient about détente, more attentive to the country's traditional allies. He adopted the liberals' rhetoric and concerns about nuclear proliferation and relations with developing nations—and, to some extent, their proposals as well. The old Kissinger was to be seen only in his unsuccessful efforts to prevent Congress from cutting off military aid to the Saigon regime in 1975 and from stopping covert operations in Angola in 1976. But the gravest blow was still to come. In midcampaign, under pressure from the right, Ford banished the word "détente" from the Administration's vocabulary.

Détente was what Kissinger and Nixon had cared most about. It was their grand design, their ticket to history. It was not their discovery, of course; its roots went back to Dwight Eisenhower and John Kennedy, and Lyndon Johnson had agreed with Leonid Brezhnev in 1968 to start negotiations on placing limits on strategic arms. But Johnson delayed when Soviet troops marched into Czechoslovakia, and this use of force against a fraternal "Socialist" state persuaded China to make overtures to Washington. All this was in motion before Nixon was inaugurated; his contribution—and Kissinger's—was to make the growing trend for East-West accommodation into the centerpiece of American policy. They had two purposes in mind. One was to use détente as a lever to make Moscow restrain Hanoi's ambitions in South Vietnam, and thus to make it possible for the United States to withdraw its troops from Indochina. The second was to establish a new balance of power. It was their conviction that Soviet military power and influence were on the rise, while America's will to resist was on the decline because of the Vietnam experience. Their strategy was to evolve détente into a new form of containment of the Soviet Union—or, better still, self-containment on the part of the Russians.

Their first step was to break down the ideological barriers to negotiation that confronted them at home. While it is never agreeable to bargain with the Devil, it is usually permissible to negotiate with an adversary, and Nixon soon told the world that the "isms" of the cold war had no place in his diplomacy. The next step was to provide important groups in the Soviet Union with a stake in détente. In Kissinger's estimation, the "peaceful-coexistence" approach of past Administrations was too passive, taking no account of Moscow's interest in trade and access to Western credits, grain and technology, and doing nothing to cater to the Soviet quest for status—for recognition as a superpower equal to the United States. Nixon and Kissinger sought to embody these interests in formal agreements and thereby draw the Russians into a web of incentives and penalties. The common interest in avoiding nuclear war was pursued through the SALT talks. The presumption was that Moscow would not risk jeopardizing this new relationship by adventures in peripheral areas like the Middle East and Vietnam. In May 1972, this theory was committed to paper—a declaration of principles in which both Governments promised to prevent "the development of situations capable of causing a dangerous exacerbation of their relations," to eschew "unilateral advantage" and "to do everything in their power so that conflicts or situations will not arise which would serve to increase international tensions."

As a plan of action, it was all quite plausible. As a grand design, or as strategy, it was flawed both in conception and implementation.

The concept of giving Moscow tangible advantages in return for vague promises of good behavior was highly questionable. Many of these arrangements—hundreds of millions of dollars in subsidized export credits and grain sales, removal of the ban on sale of high-technology items such as computers, space spectaculars letting the Russians be seen locking spaceships with the Americans in great-power harmony—gave undeniable benefit to American businessmen and American programs, but, taken as a whole, they constituted risky politics and hazardous diplomacy. Instead of being justified on its own merits, each transaction was made to appear as an inducement or bribe. Kissinger thus conveyed the impression that he was seeking agreement for the sake of agreement, and at any price.

Anyhow, it was not reasonable to expect Russian good behavior in return. There was little basis for believing that the Soviet Union was prepared to abandon its ambitions in peripheral areas—if for no other reason than that

Moscow was not likely to abandon its gut conflict with Peking in those regions of the world. Nor, apart from mutual fear of nuclear war, was it easy to find common ground between an expansionist state like Russia and one committed to stability, like the United States.

On another plane, Kissinger seemed to have exaggerated his ability to extract advantages from the Sino-Soviet split. That schism undoubtedly disposed both Moscow and Peking to seek better relations with Washington, each hoping to improve its standing against the other, but there is less evidence that Kissinger was able to pry any extra concessions from either of them by pursuing his "triangular diplomacy." In the end, there was little to show for all his labors in that field.

The strategy contained an even grosser distortion of reality—that the Russians were 10 feet tall. When Nixon and Kissinger looked at Moscow, they saw only advancing Soviet military might and ambition. They overlooked or underestimated the evidence that, in many ways, Russia was still a developing country; that its Eastern European satellites were undependable allies; that Western Communist parties were becoming more independent of Moscow; that the Soviet economy and political system were not appealing models for the developing world, and that these nations hardly perceived Russia as a desirable or useful economic partner.

Considering the importance he placed not just on the substance but on the perception of things—and on what view of itself the United States conveyed to the rest of the world—it was odd that Kissinger should have continued for some time to portray the Soviet Union as an ascendant power with "global reach" and the United States as a declining one. He denies doing this, but most people who talked to him over the years came away with that impression. His battles with Congress over covert aid to Angola and overt aid to the Saigon regime were an outgrowth of what he saw as the need to stem the loss of American credibility and the tide of Soviet advances.

That the Vietnam War diminished the American will to play a positive role in the world is a judgment history is likely to prove wrong. If "will" were defined as unwillingness to become involved in local and regional conflicts like Vietnam, Kissinger had a point. But others would consider this wisdom. The overwhelming majority of Kissinger's liberal critics never questioned the American commitment to Western Europe and Japan—they simply refused, rightly or wrongly, to concede that the world revolved around the Soviet-American power struggle. To them, the main sources of tension and conflict were economic—among the industrialized nations, and between them and the developing nations.

The Nixon-Kissinger strategy, however, subordinated everything to the relationship between the United States and the Soviet Union. This often produced overreaction to events in other countries—or else lack of attention. Vietnam and Angola were exalted into major tests of American credibility. Nuclear proliferation, North-South economic relations, Africa as a whole, and relations with traditional allies were often ignored until they developed a "Soviet dimension," whether imagined or real.

To make things worse, the way in which the détente strategy was carried out was self-defeating domestically. Secret negotiations followed by public theatricals generated a sense of unease, fanning suspicions that Kissinger was using headlines to cover up his private give-aways. The suspicions were fueled by his constantly changing rhetoric. At first, he and Nixon described détente as a "structure of peace," picturing it as something almost already in place. After the 1973 Mideast war, Kissinger adopted the Russian view of détente and began referring to it as a "process." When the Angolan crisis flared, and when the Russians seemed to be meddling in Portugal, he was reduced to arguing that "there is no alternative to détente in the nuclear age," without trying to define it.

What got him into trouble as much as anything else—and perhaps least deservedly—were the Helsinki accords of 1975. In these accords, the United States joined the countries of Europe in agreeing to the "inviolability" of all European borders (meaning the sanctity of Russian-controlled East European borders) and to the freer movements of people and ideas (meaning the Russians would have to relax their controls). Kissinger did not want to get involved in these negotiations to begin with, but the Russians and most Western European leaders insisted, and Kissinger went along, trying to play down the import of the talks. Nevertheless, Helsinki became a symbol of Kissinger's supposed indifference to the fate of "enslaved Eastern Europeans and Russians"— especially when coupled with his advice to President Ford not to receive Aleksandr Solzhenitsyn in the White House.

When détente emerged as a political issue in 1976, he fought desperately to hold the line. To calm his critics on the right, he warned Moscow that its actions in the Middle East, Portugal and Angola "must inevitably threaten other relationships." The message was clear: Stop it, or you will jeopardize your relationship with the United States. Moscow did not desist, and Kissinger did nothing about it. He reasoned that he could not cut off grain shipments to Russia without alienating American farmers, and that the SALT talks were of such overriding importance they should not be imperiled for the sake of an Angola; but, however right he may have been in such judgments, his failure to back up his threats led to further erosion of public support for détente. When Ford consigned the word to graffiti on State Department walls, Kissinger confined himself to private headshaking and grumbling about "politics."

Whether for political reasons or because they thought Americans would not buy détente unless it was wrapped up as the millennium, Nixon and Kissinger had oversold détente and had set impossible standards for it. Perhaps they did not understand what Eisenhower, Kennedy and Johnson had learned— that Americans, by and large, were naturally and profoundly in favor of anything that gave reasonable promise of improving prospects of staying at peace with Russia. They would have saved their détente strategy much grief if they had been moderate about it from the beginning.

Yet Kissinger, as strategist, had a saving grace. He was a conceptualizer, a man who thought in terms of an overall framework, but he was not an ideologue. He would try, often mercilessly, to fit events into his grand design, but if they did not fit, he would adjust. He could change course and succeed. There lay his strength as tactician.

Earlier this year, for example, he advised the Russians privately that failure to move the new SALT talks off dead center and reach a new strategic-arms pact would increase Ronald Reagan's prospects of capturing the Republican nomination—and thus the chances of a huge leap in American military spending. At the same time, he told the Joint Chiefs of Staff that without a new pact incorporating their new strategic-weapons programs, those programs would almost certainly be eliminated by a Democratic Administration or a Democratic-controlled Congress in 1977. This particular attempt to play both ends against the middle didn't break the SALT negotiating logjam, but it is rather typical of his methods—and, more often than not, they have worked.

He has altered directions so many times that it has become fashionable to depict him as, essentially, an opportunist. Virtually everyone who has worked with him in government rejects this view, and the evidence bears them out. On some of the most critical issues like Vietnam, Angola, Cyprus and nuclear arms, Kissinger has never really changed his principles; at most, he modified his rhetoric. On almost all other issues, he changed course only in response to enormous pressure, and then only late in the game, when failure loomed as a certainty.

What was most impressive about him was his ability, at that hopelessly late stage, to turn the situation around. Not so long ago, it looked as though the Western European allies would never trust the man who seemed to be seeking a condominium with Moscow and ignoring them; as though the Japanese would never recover from the famous shocks to their pride and economy. Relations with these countries are now better than they have been in many years. After standing by while Secretary of the Treasury John Connally waged economic warfare on America's allies, Kissinger finally stepped in and reversed the protectionist trend. After paying no attention to economic relations with developing countries for five years, he successfully fended off the "strictly-business" crowd in the Treasury Department and put the United States in a tenable position—even a position of leadership—in the North-South economic negotiations. After years of mocking the significance of the black African countries and siding with racist South Africa, and then alienating most of black Africa with his covert military operations in Angola, he took the lead in seeking negotiated settlements in southern Africa—and the black African leaders accepted him. The list of such accomplishments is a long one. Nor can it be dismissed on the grounds that he did these things only because he discerned a link between them and the Soviet-American balance of power. The point is that he did them, and did them well.

Kissinger has been able to snatch success from the jaws of defeat because he has been a master of maneuver, timing and drama in Washington and abroad. He has also been better—and more unscrupulous—at gamesmanship than anyone within memory.

He started by trying to neutralize or eliminate rivals. A note to Nixon showing that Secretary of State Rogers had not hewed to the White House line in talks with African leaders over Rhodesia. Keeping Defense Secretary Melvin R. Laird out of the flow of information about matters like China. Playing on Nixon's distrust of anyone in the bureaucracy—even to the extent of involving himself in the wiretapping of his own subordinates and of newsmen. Then the courtship of the press and Congress. Kissinger exceeded all of his predecessors in imparting information and providing explanations of policy to these institutions. He told them more and misled them more. His briefing of newsmen on the Paris cease-fire accords was a model of extensiveness and lucidity, but he said no secret agreements or understandings had been reached—and Nixon, it was later revealed, had made a number of secret commitments to Hanoi about postwar aid and the withdrawal of American civilian advisers, and to Saigon about the resumption of American bombing of North Vietnam in the event of violations. His 1975 testimony before Congress on the Sinai disengagement agreement between Israel and Egypt was a marvelous exposition of the intricacies of American diplomacy in the Middle East, but he played games here, too. Several months earlier, when it had seemed there would be no pact at all, Kissinger had agreed with the Israelis not to blame anyone for the breakdown of his latest round of shuttle diplomacy. No sooner did he get on his aircraft to return home than he started blaming the Israelis. His public position was that neither was at fault; privately, he told another tale—the one he believed.

Only rarely was Kissinger so blatant. Most of the time his technique was to let his listeners draw whatever conclusions they liked from what he was saying. Thus, while the White House regarded him as a wholehearted supporter of the Christmas bombing of North Vietnam, he led reporters and legislators—by nods and grimaces, by innuendo against Nixon, and by stressing the human catastrophe of the decision—to believe that he was opposed to it, a secret dove.

The newsmen and the legislators knew, of course, that he kept some things back. But they also knew that he could pull a rabbit out of the hat, or prove them wrong, so they feared to go against him. He had a hammerlock on the most priceless commodity in Washington—information. Under the Kissinger regime, fewer people had access to sensitive information than at any time in the previous 25 years.

He was charming and witty in a self-deprecating fashion, especially when it came to his political difficulties. Under attack during the Presidential primaries, he was asked at a news conference if he wanted to be Secretary of State forever. "Well," he said, "for the morale of my staff, I have to indicate a terminal point to my services." Around the country, however, his popularity has always remained high. In 1974, he was the clear-cut choice of the beauties at the Miss Universe contest as "the greatest person in the world today."

This superstar quality has helped him enormously in his diplomacy. Foreign leaders delighted in sharing the stage with him. And he emanates sincerity—to such an extent that King Faisal of Saudi Arabia let himself be photographed kissing this Jewish refugee from Nazi Germany on both cheeks. Faisal, and others, sensed in him one who could empathize with them and identify with their problems. They gave him their trust.

Kissinger knows how to take advantage of such trust—how to seize an opportunity and move boldly. He stayed out of Middle Eastern affairs until the Yom Kippur war—then charged in with his shuttle diplomacy, a novel way to sustain diplomatic pressure on all parties. He ignored energy problems and North-South economic issues until the Arab oil embargo of 1973—then assumed leadership on these matters by establishing new, ad hoc institutions as forums for negotiations.

His record as negotiator is a controversial one. A number of legislators argue that some of his more notable diplomatic achievements consist of little more than giving money and selling arms in return for good will. They cite, in particular, his willingness to sell the most sophisticated armaments to Saudi Arabia and Iran in exchange for their promises to hold down oil price increases. Prices went up anyway. (But Kissinger and his critics disagree as to whether the increase would have been even bigger in the absence of his efforts.)

In the conservative camp, critics charge that Kissinger was so anxious to produce agreements every time he took off across the world that he was careless when it came to writing details. They particularly have in mind the first SALT agreement, placing numerical limitations on offensive nuclear missiles, in which they say he left a number of dangerous ambiguities and loopholes. Kissinger replies that these were very minor matters (which seems to be true), and that he took care of them in side understandings at the time (which seems to be false).

But the most heated opinions center on the role he played in the second Israeli-Egyptian troop withdrawal agreement of September 1975 and in the Paris cease-fire accords on Vietnam. On the first, the point of contention is whether Kissinger was right in going for this limited accord or whether he should have sought an overall peace package. Critics charge that he not only squandered American leverage on Israel over a matter of a few miles of desert but also managed to isolate President Sadat from the other Arab states and undermine his moderate position. Kissinger's retort is that the Israelis were not ready for an overall settlement, and that small steps were necessary to sustain the momentum of efforts for peace. It is difficult to say who is right.

On Kissinger's Vietnam settlement, however, the historical verdict is likely to be harsh. Under this deal, signed in January 1974, Hanoi obtained a withdrawal of all American troops; an American promise to hold down on military aid to the Saigon regime; an equal role for the Vietcong on the National Council of Reconciliation and Concord; an American commitment to billions of dollars in postwar reconstruction aid, and, above all, the right to keep North Vietnamese forces in South Vietnam. The United States got back its prisoners of war. It is virtually inconceivable that Hanoi would have rejected this deal in 1969, or in 1971—yet it wasn't offered until late 1973, lengthening the death and destruction by as long as four years.

Kissinger contends that until late 1973, Hanoi was insisting on formally sharing governmental power in Saigon and on deposing President Thieu. That Hanoi had made this an absolute condition is arguable, to say the least. Like their predecessors, Nixon and Kissinger continued the war to forestall what they saw as an inevitable nationalist-Communist victory, and they offered negotiable terms only after they felt the Saigon regime had gained enough in military proficiency to have a "reasonable chance" to survive.

True to form, Kissinger has been able to turn aside questions of his negotiating skill with a joke. "I recall meeting with a group of Greek-American leaders, and I was, I thought, extremely persuasive and asked one of them to sum up what we had discussed. He said, 'Kill the Turks.' " Jokes aside, Kissinger's record as negotiator will compare favorably with his predecessors'. Others might have gotten similar results in China, Russia and the Middle East. He *got* the results—and with skill, style, incredible persistence and timing, and a capacity to project the power and influence of the United States through his own person.

Future historians will have an unusually difficult task assessing the Kissinger years, for several reasons. He always insisted on getting the credit for anything good that happened, and he inevitably was blamed when things went wrong. He had unprecedented power for a Secretary of State, yet he was far from a free agent. He had an unparalleled appreciation of the nuances, complexities and meaning of international politics, yet his strategy was full of holes. His rhetoric was a marvel of moderation and vision, laden with respect for morality and human values, but his actions often seemed far removed from these concerns....

Withal, Kissinger's legacy is a rich one. In the Middle East, his achievement is not the troop-separation agreements—that was achieved twice before, in 1948 and 1956, and troops must be disentangled after every war—but the restoration of the United States as the dominant force in the area. Globally, he has left the next Administration in a good position to move on the new issues. The economic conferences among the industrialized states he helped promote have made a start toward harmonizing domestic economic policies and tamping down pressures for each nation to pass inflationary and unemployment problems on to the others. He has established sound policies for the North-South economic dialogue and the United Nations Conference on the Law of the Sea. He has made considerable strides toward controlling pressures for the proliferation of nuclear weapons, by getting nuclear supplier nations to exercise more caution in their sales.

Paradoxically, and contrary to his wishes, his actions also caused Congress to re-emerge as a vital part of the foreign-policy making process. There are pros and cons about this trend, but it does encourage more openness and accountability, and that is to the good.

Kissinger also leaves behind him heightened public distrust of foreign-policy makers. He extended the melancholy record, begun before his time, of official dissembling and half-truths. He contributed to the growing public feeling that foreign-policy leaders did not share the country's democratic values—and he thus contributed to the loss of public confidence in Washington.

Kissinger's bequest on the newly popular issue of morality and human rights in foreign policy is also controversial. His notion of morality was a very practical one—preserving peace and stability and basing relations with other countries on how they treat the United States, not on how they treat their own people. Using this approach, he succeeded in getting the Russians to allow an unprecedented number of Jews to emigrate—until the Jackson amendment passed and Moscow cut way back. Others, on the right and left, found this approach too sanguine. They did not feel it wise for Kissinger to embrace the Soviet dictators, or dictators in South Korea, Chile and elsewhere. They wanted the United States to stand unequivocally for "what is right." Which approach will prevail after Kissinger is far from clear.

What Kissinger most wanted to leave his successors—détente with the Soviet Union—is most in doubt. In some ways, he has made concrete progress. Thus, he took much of the ideological fervor out of Soviet-American rivalry, and that seems likely to hold. He negotiated a treaty limiting antiballistic missile systems, thereby stabilizing the strategic nuclear balance. He made episodic efforts to educate the American people on what could and could not legitimately be blamed on the Soviet Union. For example, he said at a news conference that the upheaval in Portugal "was not caused by the Soviets" but "by the internal dynamics of Portugal itself." Yet the core of his doctrine—that Washington should be prepared to deal with Moscow in a businesslike fashion and on a basis of equality—has been damaged by his own hand. By leading the public to expect more, he undermined the centrist constituency for détente and made the whole concept politically vulnerable. This is not to say that Kissinger's successors will be inclined or compelled to return to the rigidity of the cold war. But what could happen in the coming years might not be much better than that.

In some respects, in fact, Kissinger is likely to be evaluated much as he has evaluated his two 19th-century models. Like Bismarck's, his policies were so personalized they could not be institutionalized; like the Iron Chancellor, he carried the intricacies of his policy around in his head, not on pieces of paper that could be understood and followed by bureaucracies. Like Castlereagh, he ended up being repudiated at home even as his reputation soared abroad. Castlereagh wanted England to remain active in maintaining the post-Napoleonic balance of power in Europe; his nation wanted insularity. Kissinger wanted the United States to play a cold, calculating game of power politics; his nation wanted something more.

Perhaps Kissinger's greatest achievement is that he kept a discernible foreign policy together when chaos impended. He provided some coherence at a time when the nation was still coming to grips with the Vietnam experience, still trying to find a new role in the world. He held the nation together politically behind his foreign policy during Nixon's decline and Ford's interregnum, and he left the United States in a reasonably solid position in the world.

Kissinger recently said, "What will probably give me satisfaction in the longer term are structural achievements: the attempt to create a foreign policy based on permanent values and interests." The word "permanent" is striking. For Henry Kissinger never really sought to reassess American interests; these were, after all, "permanent." His was a virtuoso effort at devising new means to the old ends of containment, orderly change and stability.

What was unique was Kissinger himself. He will be remembered more for his mind than for his achievements, more for his dazzling performances than for his script for world order. And whether he continues as Secretary of State or becomes a private citizen, he will remain a major force in American foreign policy. Whatever he chooses to say will still be news, and his successors will be looking over their shoulders, hoping for his support, fearing his criticism and knowing they are being compared.

FURTHER READING

Henry Brandon, *The Retreat of American Power* (1973)
Edward Friedland et al., *The Great Détente Disaster* (1975)
Lloyd C. Gardner, ed., *The Great Nixon Turnaround* (1973)
Charles Gati and Toby Trister Gati, *The Debate over Détente* (1977)
Stephen Graubard, *Kissinger: Portrait of a Mind* (1973)
Gene T. Hsiao, ed., *Sino-American Détente and Its Policy Implications* (1974)
Alan M. Jones, Jr., *U.S. Foreign Policy in a Changing World* (1973)
Bernard Kalb and Marvin Kalb, *Kissinger* (1974)
David Landau, *Kissinger: Uses of Power* (1972)
John Lehman, *The Executive, Congress, and Foreign Policy* (1976)
Roger Morris, *Uncertain Greatness: Henry Kissinger and American Foreign Policy* (1977)
Thomas G. Paterson, "After Peking, Moscow: New Levers of Containment," *The Nation*, 214 (1972), 531–532
William L. Safire, *Before the Fall* (1975)
Edward R. F. Sheehan, *The Arabs, Israelis, and Kissinger* (1976)
Tad Szulc, "How Kissinger Did It: Behind the Vietnam Cease-Fire Agreement," *Foreign Policy, no.* 15 (1974), pp. 21–61
Garry Wills, *Nixon Agonistes* (1970)

1   2   3   4   5   6   7   8   9   0